Millions

5
10
20
40
80
120
160

ARPANET goes online — 69 — 4
Cross-country link MIT↔Utah — 70
e-mail program invented — 71 — 23
First e-mail on ARPANET — 72
@ character used
First international connections — 73
to ARPANET (Norway and UK)
— 74
Satellite link: Hawaii↔UK — 75
Queen of England sends — 76
trans-Atlantic e-mail
Apple II desktop computer — 77
TCP/IP formalized — 78
— 79
First major virus brings — 80
ARPANET to its knees
IBM PC — 81 — 200
Norway leaves ARPANET — 82
Connects via TCP/IP
Domain names invented — 83
Domain Name Service introduced — 84 — 1,000
First .com and .edu domains — 85
registered
NSFNET goes online — 86
NSFNET managed in part by — 87 — 10,000
commercial organization
— 88
First commercial e-mail — 89 — 100,000
Government restrictions lifted — 90
World Wide Web invented
ARPANET decommissioned — 91
First commercial service provider
Government releases Internet — 92 — 1 million
control to non-profit ISOC
Mosaic Web browser — 93 — 2 million
First major e-mail spam — 94
Commercial backbones take over — 95 — 5 million
NSFNET back to gov't control
Netscape 2 and 3, Explorer 3 — 96 — 10 million
Netscape 4, Explorer 4 — 97 — 20 million
W3C standards for Web — 98 — 40 million
business.com domain sells — 99
for 7.5 million
Napster peer-to-peer — 00 — 80 million
application explodes
Napster killed — 01 — 120 million
Taliban ban Internet
New domains (.name, etc.) — 02 — 160 million
begin to resolve

The
Web
as
you
know
it

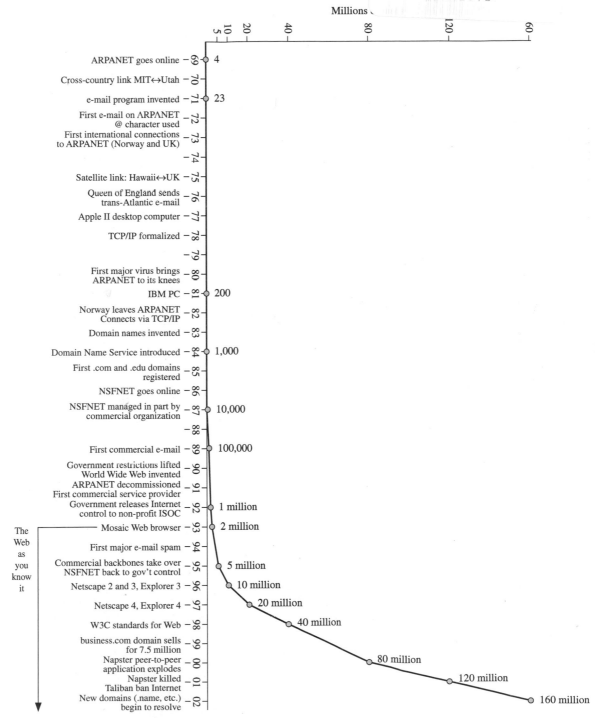

WEB APPLICATIONS
Concepts & Real World Design

CRAIG D. KNUCKLES

Lake Forest College

DAVID S. YUEN

Lake Forest College

WILEY

JOHN WILEY & SONS, INC.

To Hope, Katy, Jesse, and my parents, Rossie and Otis
Craig D. Knuckles

To Aaron and my parents, YukLam and ShuiFong
David S. Yuen

Acquisitions Editor   *Paul Crockett*
Marketing Manager   *Jennifer Powers*
Senior Production Editor   *Valerie A. Vargas*
Senior Designer   *Harry Nolan*
Production Services   *Publication Services, Inc.*
Cover Design   *Howard Grossman*
Cover Image: *© Digital Vision Limited; artist: The Vapor?*

This book was set in 10/12 Times Roman by Publication Services, Inc. and printed and bound by Malloy Incorporated. The cover was printed by Lehigh Press, Inc.

This book is printed on acid free paper. ∞

Library of Congress Cataloging in Publication Data:

Knuckles, Craig D.
    Web applications: concepts & real world design / Craig D. Knuckles, David S. Yuen.
        p. cm.
    ISBN 0-471-20458-7 (pbk)
        1. Web sites—Design. 2. Web site development. 3. Perl (Computer program language)
I. Yuen, David (David S.) II. Title.
TK5105.888K.59 2004
005.2'762—dc22
ISBN: 0-471-42929-5 (WIE)   2003063357

Printed in the United States of America

10 9 8 7 6 5 4 3 2 1

PREFACE

Many existing Web programming texts merely provide surveys of different Web programming languages and environments. This text isolates the core theoretical concepts central to Web applications. The theory-based approach fosters understanding of how HTML, Java-Script, a server-side programming language, database, and XML work together to enable three-tier Web applications and, in the process, demonstrates that the core concepts do not depend upon a particular platform or programming language.

As is true in most settings, a solid foundation in the core fundamentals leaves one armed to apply that knowledge easily in diverse environments. That is, the central concepts are more important than the particular language implementation. When one is properly armed with the fundamentals of Web applications, environments like PHP and ASP become transparent. Teaching someone *how to use a tool* only makes the person adept with that tool. Teaching someone a *craft* means that the person can adeptly apply whatever tools are available.

The choice of Perl for the server-side language was natural because of its portability, its highly developed code libraries (modules), and its widespread use in the development of Web applications around the world. Moreover, the use of Perl enabled us to expose the central concepts, that are sometimes obscured by environments, proprietary or otherwise, that were created solely as tools for Web programming. An added benefit is learning a powerful text manipulation language that is also very useful for UNIX/Linux system administration.

During the development of this text, Perl's portability was both apparent and convenient. One author developed content using the free Active Perl for Windows and the other author used the MacPerl distribution, which is also free. All the Web applications were tested both on Microsoft's IIS and PWS Web servers (running Active Perl) and on the Apache Web server in the UNIX/Linux environment. Again, the goal of this text was to isolate and expose the core fundamentals in a way not fettered by platform or proprietary constraints.

The original draft of this text was based upon the insights gained from three years of teaching client-server Web programming. It was class tested during the spring semesters of 2002 and 2003 as an upper-level elective in the Computer Science department at Lake Forest College. Based upon that experience and numerous reviews from other educators, the first draft was substantially revised into its current form. Most notably, much more emphasis was placed upon database-driven applications and the data tier in general.

Web Extended

In addition to the core theory in Chapters 1 through 13, reviewers indicated it would be helpful to have coverage of certain advanced or related topics. There were many excellent suggestions for what should be included, so we have provided supplementary chapters and appendices on the book's Web site, referred to as the **Web Extension**. As indicated in the

Contents, Chapters 14 through 19 are available on the book's Web site (www.wiley.com/college/knuckles). In these chapters you will find coverage of alternative Web programming environments, specifically PHP and ASP; XML; and client-side Web programming topics, including DHTML.

The Web Extension material makes a course based upon this text fully customizable and offers additional value to someone studying the book independently, outside of a classroom. Offered as easily printable Adobe PDF files, the Web Extensions are professionally edited and typeset in a format similar to the bound chapters. Moreover, being vital to the flexibility and scope of this text, they are summarized in the Contents along with the 13 chapters containing the core theoretical coverage of Web applications. We are certain you will find the Web Extensions a valuable resource to augment this text. Moreover, we applaud our publisher's effort to keep the size of this text manageable, and hence its price reasonable, while not sacrificing its quality or breadth.

Prerequisites

We assume the that reader is familiar with a high-level programming language such as C++, Java, or JavaScript. We don't cover the fundamental theory of variables, conditionals, arrays, functions, loops, and objects. Some HTML background would be a plus, but Appendix A covers HTML from the ground up to serve those without such a background. We assume no prior knowledge of Perl, JavaScript, SQL/database, or XML. If you do have some background in one or more of those areas, you still will find that there is much to learn in this text.

Chapter Dependencies

Figure 0 shows the major dependencies among the chapters in this book. There are very minor exceptions, for which you can easily compensate.

Content Overview

Chapter 1 introduces the five layers of the Internet, the protocols that operate at each level, and the concepts of how the protocols work. It then introduces the World Wide Web and how it operates in the Internet's application layer. It then discusses how HTTP clients and servers provide a platform for Web applications, and it gives the conceptual anatomy of a Web application.

Chapter 2 introduces the concept of markup languages, progressing from propriety markup used by word processors, to HTML, to separation of content and style using Cascading Style Sheets (CSS), and finally to style-devoid markup with XML. It then covers eXtensible HTML (XHTML) syntax issues and provides detailed coverage of lists and tables—two structures used often in subsequent chapters. It then discusses Web development in general and the role of CSS. Finally, it provides a detailed introduction to CSS.

Chapter 3 provides an overview of HTML forms and a concise language overview of JavaScript. It then explores Browser Objects and their manipulation using JavaScript. This background is applied to client-side processing of data in HTML forms in Web pages. Focus is placed in particular on client-side validation of form data for Web applications.

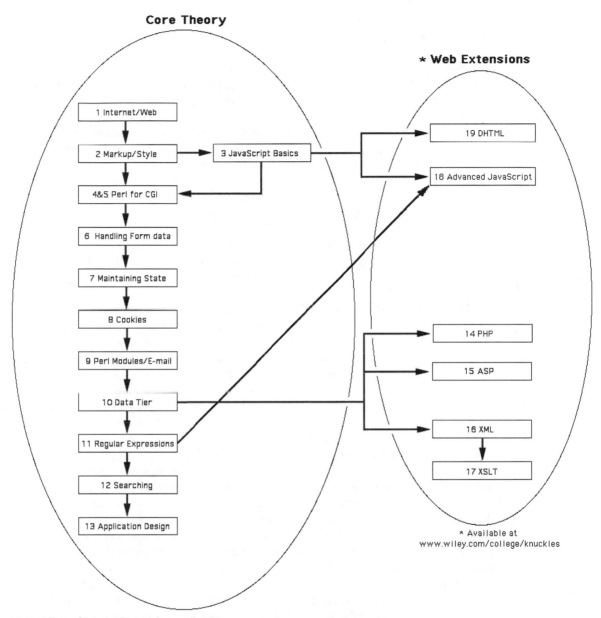

FIGURE 0 Chapter Dependency diagram.

Chapters 4 and 5 introduce the Perl language. The examples are geared toward using Perl programs to generate HTML output dynamically. Issues surrounding calling Perl CGI programs with remote URL requests are explored. These two chapters serve both as an introduction to Perl's language structures and later as a Perl language reference source.

Chapter 6 features a complete coverage of CGI programming. This includes Web server environment variables, receiving and decoding both GET and POST form data, and understanding how error channels work in the client-server environment. Examples are given for processing each of the main types of form elements (text, checkboxes, radio buttons, and menus). The coverage focuses on generating HTML forms dynamically from server-side data sources (arrays and hashes) and dealing with the hash structure of the returned data with respect to the different types of form elements. In the interest of exposing the underlying client-server interaction, we have used our own decoding routine rather than a preprogrammed Perl module.

Chapter 7 features a theoretical and detailed exposition of preserving state in Web applications among multiple HTTP transactions. It also introduces transaction diagrams and application logic (app logic) for multitransaction Web applications. The coverage progresses from using hidden form elements to propagate session state to using state files identified by long session IDs. Issues about security and the caching of state files are covered in detail. Password protection and logged-on state security issues are covered conceptually and in detail. Other state-related issues, such as session timeouts and user/administration access levels, are explored. In the interest of covering security issues and core concepts, we have provided our own "toolkit functions" to handle tasks such as session creation and propagation, automated policing of the cache of state files, logon, and session timeouts.

Chapter 8 explores both session cookies and persistent cookies and how to set them in HTTP headers. It compares and contrasts the use of cookies to propagate sessions with the use of hidden form elements and links. An example of a Web application that features long-term user preferences is provided. In particular, the effects this has on the transaction diagram and app logic are emphasized. The chapter concludes with a conceptual discussion of third-party cookies, ad servers, Web beacons, and user tracking/profiling.

Chapter 9 introduces Perl's object-oriented syntax in conjunction with external code libraries (called modules in Perl documentation). The CGI module is introduced and compared/contrasted with our toolkit functions. In particular, its limitations are discussed. The chapter then covers sending e-mail messages from within Web applications using the Mail::Sendmail module. The main example features automated user account signup for Web applications via e-mail and temporary passwords. Security issues are emphasized.

Chapter 10 introduces relational data and discusses sequential access files versus direct access files. Next, relational databases and the three-tier model for Web applications are introduced. The chapter then provides a brief primer for SQL and an overview of Perl's DataBase Interface (DBI) module. The main examples feature using state tables to implement session state for Web applications and using a database to generate pages dynamically. This chapter uses the free MySQL database system, which runs on Windows and UNIX/Linux. The chapter concludes with two optional sections discussing Perl drivers for other database systems, including a Perl database emulator that uses sequential-access files.

Chapter 11 covers regular expressions, pattern matching, and substitution. The main examples feature parsing a real Web server log file and partial content rendering. The latter example explores line processing versus batch processing of sequential access files. URL-encoding and URL-decoding are then explained in detail, along with some security remarks.

Chapter 12 puts regular expressions and SQL to use constructing search utilities for Web applications. The use of regular expressions in conjunction with SQL queries to refine searches is explored. The chapter then explores limiting the number of search results and how temporarily caching search results can increase application performance.

The chapter then turns to Web sites consisting of static HTML files. Directory scanning and file testing are used to traverse a Web site recursively, which is useful for whole-site searches and constructing dynamic site maps.

Chapter 13 puts it all together by developing an online store from the ground up, starting with an elaborate transaction diagram from which the application logic is deduced. Next, the data tier for the application is designed. The store is then built, starting from the top of the transaction diagram. The store application features dynamically generated HTML forms, session state (logged-on state, a fully functional shopping cart, and cached search results), and a searchable inventory stored in a relational database. This brings together all of the central concepts introduced in previous chapters. An elaborate transaction diagram is provided for the inventory administration Web application, but coding that is left as a group exercise. The chapter concludes with a summary of security issues for Web applications.

Web Extension

(* The following Web Extensions are available at www.wiley.com/college/knuckles.)

* Chapter 14 (roughly parallel with Chapter 15) covers the Hypertext PreProcessor (PHP) on a level that assumes that you understand the fundamentals of Web applications. The PHP scripting language is briefly overviewed, and PHP's built-in functions for Web-related tasks are covered: environment variables and form data, sending e-mail, session tools, cookies, and database interface. The chapter concludes with a reworking of a database-driven example from Chapter 10. With the core fundamentals in place, you can learn a new Web programming environment in around 40 pages!

* Chapter 15 (roughly parallel with Chapter 14) covers Active Server Pages (ASP) on a level that assumes that you understand the fundamentals of Web applications. The VBScript language is briefly overviewed, and ASP's built-in functions for Web-related tasks are covered: environment variables and form data, sending e-mail, session tools, cookies, and database interface. The chapter concludes with a reworking of a database-driven example from Chapter 10. With the fundamentals in place, you can learn a new Web programming environment in around 40 pages! The chapter concludes with an overview of ASP.NET.

* Chapter 16 is an introduction to XML. Coverage includes language rules for well-formed documents, the concept of schemas (DTDs and XML Schemas) and valid documents, namespaces and qualified elements, and the Document Object Model (DOM) levels 1 and 2. The examples use the DOM both to extract data from an XML file in Web browsers using JavaScript and to generate XML documents from raw data sources on the server using Perl's `XML::DOM` module.

* Chapter 17 first discusses XML's use in Web applications in general. A very brief overview of formatting XML using CSS is provided. The main discussion is about the eXtensible Stylesheet Language for Transformations (XSLT). Enough of the XML Path Language (XPath) is covered to enable XSLT coverage. Then XSLT is used to transform XML files into XHTML files in Web browsers. An example application is provided that sends an XML file to a browser together with an XSLT style sheet. The resulting XHTML page has data which is sortable by column. To perform sorts, the application generates XSLT style sheets dynamically and sends those to the browser so that all the data sorting is done on the client. The style sheets are stored in a self-policing cache on the server. Finally, this chapter conceptually introduces Web services and the role of XML in remote procedure calls.

* **Chapter 18** covers some advanced JavaScript topics. Mostly these topics are relevant only after one understands server-side Web programming and Web applications in general. The topics include regular expressions in JavaScript, targeting form submissions to new/secondary browser windows, managing window collections, and generating JavaScript dynamically on the server.

* **Chapter 19** provides a brief history of Browser Objects and the DOM, and then a short, but quite complete, overview of DHTML that includes dynamically changing style classes, the z-index and visibility, and moving layers on the screen.

Project Thread

There are over 150 stand-alone exercises to complement the chapters. There is also a Project Thread that runs throughout the book. Superficially, the project involves constructing a Web site where a description of, and link to, all applications created are collectively added to a homework page. That leaves a concise and organized legacy of all work done.

More substantively, the project involves creation of a fairly sophisticated Web application that keeps "growing" as the chapters progress. In addition, a "toolkit" of functions is developed in a code library. We supply some of these functions, and the project directs others to be created. The end result is a library of CGI toolkit functions that rivals the built-in functions of the CGI Perl module, PHP, and ASP.

The thread begins with some research questions in Chapter 1, for which the research is to be made into a CSS-formatted Web page in Chapter 2. This serves to provide you with an interesting topic to research and a refresher/introduction to XHTML/CSS in Chapter 2.

Chapter 3 features creation of HTML forms with client-side JavaScript validation. Chapter 4 features inclusion of these JavaScript-enabled forms into different CGI programs, which can call each other to create a crude Web application. Chapter 5 focuses on learning Perl language features and generating HTML in Perl programs. Several toolkit functions are developed to automate the process of printing HTML form elements.

Chapter 6 adds a back-end data source for the application and combines the three programs from Chapter 4 into one Web application. Chapter 7 significantly augments the application by creating logon for both users and administrators. The application now features secure logged-on session state and session timeouts.

Chapter 8 adds a "cookie sniff" using JavaScript. If a given browser has cookies disabled, the application resorts to using hidden form elements instead of cookies to propagate session IDs. Chapter 9 adds automated e-mail capability to the application and features a stand-alone exercise using Perl's CGI module. You will see that your toolkit function library is better in some respects than that preprogrammed module.

Chapter 10 converts the back-end data source of the application over to database. That includes using state tables to maintain intertransaction state data. Chapter 11 features stand-alone exercises to help you understand the complicated, but very powerful, regular expressions.

Chapter 12 adds a search capability to the application. The search form includes several refinement options. Chapter 13 culminates development of this large application. There, search results are cached to increase performance, and a fairly sophisticated administration capability is added. The administrative capability allows the back-end database to be edited and updated remotely over the Web.

The project thread in the Web Extensions (Chapters 14 through 19) recommends interesting stand-alone exercises. A link pointing to each completed exercise is added to the homework page.

Supplements

■ The Web Extensions, which provide additional topics to augment the 13 chapters containing the core theory, are available for download at

```
http://www.wiley.com/college/knuckles
```

The Web Extensions are professionally edited and typeset in Adobe's PDF format. Like all chapters, they contain chapter summaries and exercise sets.

■ The book's companion Web site is located at

```
http://www.cknuckles.com
```

The site contains links to compressed archives containing the source code for all example programs and applications in the text. Also, links are provided to working versions of all the example applications so that they can be accessed by URL calls over the Web.

There are many references within the book to items on the Web site. These items include links to complementary Web sites and general resources to enhance understanding of the material. The Web site is organized in a chapter-by-chapter format so that you can easily find supplements for a given chapter.

■ PowerPoint presentations giving detailed overviews of each chapter are available for download at either of the Web Sites listed just above. The PowerPoint presentations primarily were created as a teaching tool for instructors. But we concluded they will also prove useful to anyone reading this book, so we decided to make them readily available.

■ PowerPoint lecture notes for each chapter are provided as extra support for instructors. These can be obtained by contacting your regional Wiley representative. If you are unsure of your representative, visit Wiley's "Who's my Rep?" page at

```
http://jws-edcv.wiley.com/college/findarep
```

Acknowledgments

We would like to thank our editor, Paul Crockett, and the production crews at Wiley and Publication Services, Inc. for putting this book into polished form. Thanks also go to our students, who were helpful when we class-tested the original drafts.

We thank those professional colleagues who reviewed the manuscript at its various stages of development. A special thanks goes to Alex Ceponkus for his detailed review of the XML chapters and for allowing us to use and distribute the DOMifier utility he created.

Dr. Yuen: I would like to thank my parents for their hard work, love, and support in raising me. And Grandma too. I would also like to thank my brother Ken and my sister Lisa for their love and support, especially during my school years. I thank my life partner Aaron Parks for love and support throughout my career. Finally, I thank all the wonderful teachers whom I have encountered during my education, from elementary and high school through college and graduate school.

Dr. Knuckles: I would like to thank both Steve Galovich and the Academic Innovation Group at Lake Forest College for granting an extra course release. That was a huge help. Profound thanks go to my wife for keeping me afloat while writing this. Finally, I would like to thank my best buds, Bryan Moore and Steve Grodrian, for their long-term fortitude in friendship. One of the few things you can count on in life is a true friend. Open palm on top of closed fist.

CONTENTS

THE WEB EXTENSIONS ARE LISTED BELOW

## CHAPTER 1

INTRODUCTION TO WEB APPLICATIONS

This chapter explores the nature of World Wide Web applications and how they relate to the Internet. One usually thinks of an application as a piece of software that sits on a personal computer and accomplishes some task for the user. Some common applications are simple text editors such as NotePad and SimpleText, elaborate word processors such as Microsoft (MS) Word, spreadsheets such as MS Excel, and graphics editors such as Adobe Photoshop.

Web applications are vastly different from those, which basically perform a service for you and then save a file to your hard drive. You are no doubt familiar with the "front end" of a Web application. That is, you have cranked up your Web browser and pulled up a Web page that requested some information from you. This information likely included your e-mail address, your name, and probably your credit card number. With the information entered, you then clicked a submit button of some sort and waited a few seconds, and then a new Web page appeared in the browser that said something like "Thanks for ordering four wildebeest from bestbeest.com." The Web application has done its job, and it's all over except for finding a grazing pasture.

Just what is going on behind that pesky browser? This chapter answers that question, starting from the ground up. As we delve into the hidden world behind the Web browser, you will see how the Internet, World Wide Web, and Web applications relate to one another in the big picture. In the process, you will learn concepts and terminology that are indispensable to any programmer in the information age.

1.1 BRIEF HISTORY AND OVERVIEW OF THE INTERNET

In 1969, the *Advanced Research Projects Agency (ARPA)*, funded by the U.S. Department of Defense, created the first version of what we now term the Internet. Deriving its name from the creating organization, it was aptly called ARPANET. The first version linked four computers located in the western United States at UCLA, the University of California at Santa Barbara, the University of Utah, and the Stanford Research Institute. Original plans called for ARPANET eventually to link 128 host computers. It is widely rumored that the Department of Defense developed ARPANET with the desired end that key government agencies could maintain communication in the event of a nuclear war. But, whatever the Defense Department's end goal, the funding that kindled the ARPA scientist's creativity was certainly a direct result of the Cold War.

In brief, ARPANET worked well, new uses for it (especially e-mail) became apparent, and computers became smaller and more commonplace. By 1984, ARPANET linked

1

around 1000 hosts, but its use still required sponsorship from the U.S. government. Permission was typically limited to the military, some universities, and a few large companies. In 1986, through funding from the *National Science Foundation (NSF)*, a new "internet" called NSFnet was created with the goal of connecting all computer and engineering researchers via computer. Throughout the late 1980s, ARPANET and NSFnet coexisted as two functioning "internet" backbones. By 1987, these "internets" linked over 10,000 computers. With better funding from NSF (tons of government money), NSFnet proliferated much more rapidly than ARPANET. Attesting to the rapid expansion of NSFnet, there were around 100,000 hosts by 1989. In fact, in 1990 NSFNET took over center stage, becoming the main "internet" backbone. Also, 1990 marked the first year that access could be obtained without formal sponsorship from a government agency.

In short order, virtually every college and university was hooked up to what was then being termed the *Internet*. Many businesses now owned computers and found the Internet useful for coordinating national or global efforts. By 1992, there were over 1,000,000 host computers on the Internet. It was becoming too expensive for the government to control the burgeoning NSFnet, so, in 1992, coordination of the Internet was transferred to a nonprofit organization, whose membership includes several large corporations and scholars from several universities. This organization has evolved into a large international organization called the *Internet Society (ISOC)*, whose subcommittees set technical policy aimed toward the future health and vitality of the Internet. To get a feel for what they do, visit www.isoc.org.

As we all know, the Internet grew rapidly throughout the remainder of the 1990s and into the new millennium. Estimates now put the number of Internet hosts at over 100 million, and the number of Internet users certainly tallies in the hundreds of millions.

NOTE

The preceding paragraph draws a distinction between Internet *hosts* and *users*. Definitions of the term *host* are varied. The most clear-cut definition is that of a host *computer*—a computer with a fixed Internet address (specifically IP address, but more on that later). With a fixed Internet address, a computer can host a Web site, for example. Many computers with Internet access don't have fixed addresses. For example, a computer using a dial-up phone modem for Internet access is assigned a temporary Internet address for a given online session. Next time the computer dials up a connection, it is likely to be assigned a different Internet address. Such a computer can't effectively host a Web site, because there is no way to find it predictably on the Internet through a fixed address. For the record, cable modem and DSL connections may or may not fix your Internet address. Some of these services assign addresses dynamically as dial-up accounts do but can fix your Internet address (and raise your monthly fee) if you wish to run a Web site from home.

So you see, simply counting host computers would shortchange statistics on Internet usage. For that reason, a host is usually defined as an Internet address that is used. (Not all addresses that have been given out are actually used.) Using this definition, a host might be an Internet address shared by several people using the same dialup service. The above estimate uses that definition.

An Internet user is simply someone who accesses the Internet at home, school, work, or even the public library. Current estimates indicate that there are about 3.5 Internet users per host in the world. For the United States, most estimates give about 2.5 users per host, whereas countries such as China, with strict governmental Internet restrictions, come in at around 100 users per host at the time this was written.

It was crucial that the nonprofit ISOC was formed to set "good for everyone" standards, because the 1990s saw rapid commercialization of the Internet. Large communications corporations developed their own backbone segments. These and other smaller companies developed regional networks to bring the Internet into homes. Colleges, universities, and corporations developed small, localized networks to distribute Internet connectivity internally. That diversification leads to our depiction of the modern Internet in Figure 1.1.

Most of the networks responsible for distributing Internet connectivity worldwide are owned and operated by communications corporations. Such a corporation is termed an *Internet Service Provider (ISP)*. The larger of these operate on regional, national, or even international scales, providing segments that collectively form the Internet *backbone*—the

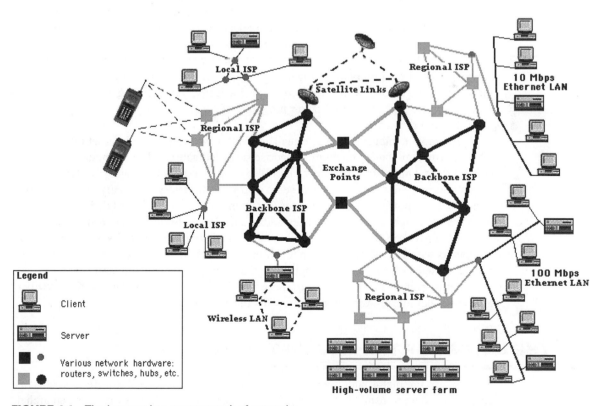

FIGURE 1.1   The Internet is a vast network of networks.

networking infrastructure that moves information around the planet virtually instantaneously. Indeed, we used the term *backbone* previously in conjunction with ARPANET and NSFnet, which provided a similar, but limited, infrastructure in the early days. Currently, backbone segments primarily use fiber optic cable, but satellite relay may play a more significant role in the future. Some links that pull up pictures of real backbone segments are provided on the Web site.

Many smaller ISPs exist on the periphery of the backbone. Some provide regional and local Internet access in the form of dial-up telephone connections, dedicated telephone Digital Subscriber Lines (DSL), and connections through cable television lines. Other ISPs provide wireless connectivity for those using digital telephones or hand-held computers. Almost any organization (such as a college, university, or corporation) must also buy access from a local or regional provider. Smaller organizations may purchase a business-grade DSL or cable service. Larger organizations often purchase a direct or semidirect backbone link in the form of a high-bandwidth dedicated telephone line (T1 line) or even a fiber optic link. Such organizations distribute the connectivity internally over a *local area network (LAN)*. The most common LAN architecture is *Ethernet*, which comes in a few different flavors. It is the prevailing LAN technology, with a typical Ethernet comprising all the computers in a room, small building, or on a given floor of a larger building, for example. The LAN for a large organization is usually several of these building- or floor-sized Ethernets networked together. A LAN can function as an isolated internal network or, with connectivity to the backbone, as one of the networks that constitute the vast Internet. Even a LAN using one of the newer wireless technologies can function as one of the Internet's constituent networks. It is truly amazing how many disparate networking technologies build up the Internet in a piecemeal fashion.

Before moving on to see how all the disparate networks form a seamless Internet, we offer some final observations regarding Figure 1.1. In the early days, all computers on the Internet were hosts with fixed addresses. Basically, you had scientists logging on to each other's computers to run bizarre programs of some sort. There was really no notion of clients and servers.

As implementations such as e-mail and Web pages turned the Internet into an accessible information-sharing medium, it made sense to dedicate certain computers as *servers*—computers that make information (such as Web pages or e-mail messages) available to users on the Internet. These computers can serve up information very efficiently because most of their processor power is dedicated to serving up information. But even a dedicated server is not always enough to meet today's demands. Large Web sites use *server farms*—groups of servers that work in concert—to distribute the load from millions of hits. In contrast, most computers with Internet access simply consume information from the servers. Such a computer is called a *client,* usually thought of as the average personal computer. Thus, we have the *client-server model* of computing specialization. We will significantly refine the client and server definitions as we explore how the Internet works.

1.2 THE LAYERS OF THE INTERNET

The modern Internet is built upon a five-layer model. At each level there are protocols that standardize data transmission. *Webster's Second Unabridged Dictionary* gives an archaic

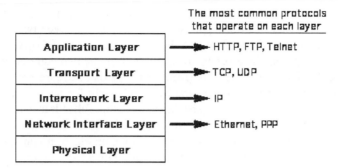

FIGURE 1.2 The Internet protocol stack and some protocol examples.

definition of a *protocol* as "a signed document containing points on which agreement has been reached by negotiating parties." As protocols pertain to the Internet, some definitions say that an *internet protocol* is a formal description of message formats and the rules two or more computers must follow to exchange those messages. Simply put, a protocol is a universally agreed-upon way for computers to transmit and receive data. With all of the different operating systems (UNIX, Linux, Microsoft, Macintosh, and so forth) and software the Internet brings together, protocols provide the standards upon which they all agree for Internet transactions.

Figure 1.2 depicts the layer structure of the modern Internet. Although the layers work together to accomplish Internet transactions, they carry out their individual tasks in a relatively independent fashion. With that in mind, we discuss the layers independently, starting from the ground up.

The Physical Layer

Physical-layer protocols define rules for movement of the actual bits across a shared medium between two pieces of hardware. The way bits are moved is dependent upon the physical medium. Thus, different hardware interfaces and drivers exist for getting bits from a computer to another through copper cable, fiber optic cable, satellites, and the new wireless LAN transmitters. Energy is transmitted through copper cable using electron streams, and through the latter three physical media using various frequencies of electromagnetic radiation (visible light, microwaves, radio). In short, the physical-layer protocols are concerned with getting electrons and photons to carry digital information from one computer to another.

Because physical-layer protocols regulate the physics of energy transmission (voltage, amperage, wavelength, amplitude, and so forth), it is impractical to discuss them here at that level. It is best to look at this layer simply as the different physical media themselves, rather than the protocols for energy transmission through them. For example, some bits on the backbone are traveling through a fiber optic cable. They may then leave the fiber optic cable and travel over a T1 telephone line. Then, depending upon a destination computer's type of network interface, they may travel over an Ethernet cable, a residential telephone line, or a cable television line. Ultimately, they end up at the network card (or serial interface for phone modems) that interfaces with the destination computer's motherboard. In a sense, a computer's network card is the end (and beginning) of the physical layer from the user's perspective. We can view the physical internet layer between two computers as their network cards at each end, together with the various hardware and drivers in between that transport the energy, and therefore the bits, to and from the two computers.

It's pretty cool to realize that a given Web page can be represented by electrons for part of its journey to your computer and by visible light for another part of its journey. Everyone should take a physics course to appreciate that fully! It is certainly worth noting that delivery of bits is uncertain at the physical level. There are many ways for energy to dissipate over various physical media. For example, an electron can slam into a copper atom's nucleus, and light can escape its fiber optic filament.

The Network Interface Layer

Although the physical layer provides a physical bit stream between two computers, it does not link them in a functional way. In other words, a group of bit stream-linked computers does not constitute a viable network. The protocols at the Network Interface level are largely implemented by software and, in essence, turn the physically linked computers into a network. There are numerous networking technologies employed at this level, but we will use Ethernet to exemplify their nature. Also keep in mind that there are several types of Ethernet: 10 Mbps, 100 Mbps, and 1 gigabit per second now becoming feasible—and that's smokin' fast.

For starters, a unique address has to be associated with each piece of hardware on an Ethernet. At the factory, each network card is given a six-byte *hardware address*. By convention, each byte is written as a two-digit hexadecimal number, 00-0A-27-7F-91-BB for example. Manufactures of network cards must coordinate with an international registry so that all addresses remain unique.

As a major step up from physical-layer bit streams, protocols are implemented to pass data around in *packets*. Think of a packet as a box where the data is stuffed inside and addressing information is stamped on the outside in the form of a header.

```
┌─────────────────────┐
│    Packet header     │
├─────────────────────┤
│                     │
│    Packet data      │
│                     │
└─────────────────────┘
```

Packets are typically 0.5K to 1.5K bytes in size. To gain some perspective, consider a 10-page term paper stored in a MS Word file. If you e-mail this to your professor, it will likely be chopped into over 50 packets for its Ethernet excursion. At first this seems odd, but think of how a large shipment of books would be handled in the real world. They would be segmented into boxes, and the boxes would be stamped with addresses. The box sizes would be chosen appropriate to the processing needs of the delivery network. Similarly, packet sizes are regulated to meet the bandwidth and processing capabilities of a particular Ethernet.

We now see the beginnings of a network where computers are uniquely identifiable and the data is segmented appropriately for ease of delivery. But more protocols are implemented to coordinate the network transactions. We provide a few examples. Data transmission is controlled so that fast computers can't overwhelm slower computers. Contingencies are in place to deal with simultaneous transfers. Computers exchange positive and negative acknowledgments to determine whether packets were damaged in transit. Damaged packets can be retransmitted (which is very important because the physical layer does not guarantee delivery). Here, the wisdom of segmenting data into packets becomes more apparent. It is far more efficient for a network to retransmit a couple of damaged packets instead of the whole file. Simply put, the physical layer provides the muscle and the network interface layer provides the brains behind LANs.

It is important that we reemphasize that Ethernet is just one implementation at this level. For contrast, suppose your computer is connected to a local ISP via a conventional phone modem. In this case, the *Point-to-Point Protocol (PPP)* is often used to link your computer to the one on ISP's end. PPP is not as rich as Ethernet, because it is not concerned with a whole network, but it does provide much of the same functionality in the context of linking two computers (hence its name). PPP provides a meaningful data-sharing link between two computers on top of the physical layer. You can see from this example why the network interface layer is sometimes called the *data link layer* or simply the *link layer*.

The Internetwork Layer

Here is where the **Internetworking Protocol (IP)** lives and dominates on the internet. The most recognizable feature of IP is the *IP address,* which is a four-byte number that uniquely identifies each computer using the Internet. Each byte in an IP address is conventionally written using a base-10 number in the range 0 through 255. For example, 164.68.21.170 is a typical IP address. Again, these are governed by an international registry and are given out so that computers can have an "identity" on the Internet. Whereas hardware addresses give computers identity on a LAN, IP addresses give computers worldwide Internet identity. You will see later how IP addresses provide such a larger scope.

Each packet destined for Internet travel is "stamped," in the packet header, with the IP addresses of the sending and receiving computers. IP is concerned solely with getting the packets through *routers* on their way from the sending address to the receiving address. Routers are simply specialized computers with IP routing software. There is no set path from the sender to the destination. In fact, given several packets from the same transaction, they might not even travel the same route across the backbone to their destination. For example, you might make a request from Chicago for a Web page in Los Angeles. Some of the packets from the chopped-up Web page might go through Dallas, while others went through St. Louis, and never came near Dallas. This feature stems from the earliest designs of ARPANET. If a router is too busy or completely goes down, packets are simply routed through another router.

To keep track of all of this, IP implements *flow control*. Basically, each router can detect what its neighbors are doing. In some sense, IP does attempt to pick an optimal path for packets to travel, but if a "best-choice" router is experiencing heavy traffic (so that its buffers are full), the sending router might choose a less busy router. However, if no desirable jump is found at the moment, the sending router might simply discard the packet with no notification to the sender or receiver. What? It's true. IP does not guarantee delivery of packets at all.

To further illustrate that IP does not guarantee delivery, every IP packet is also stamped with a *Time To Live (TTL)* in its header. The TTL is an integer that specifies the maximum number of router jumps that a packet is allowed to make. Every time a router handles a packet, the TTL integer of the packet is decremented. If the TTL hits zero at a given router, the packet is discarded. Again, no notification is given to the source or destination computer. This IP feature prevents packets from accidentally running in circles indefinitely. With multiple discard possibilities for packets, one has to wonder how likely one is to make it to its destination. IP typically delivers packets over backbone segments with less than a 1 percent loss rate, and over smaller peripheral networks with less than 3 percent loss.

It is certainly worthwhile to understand how the internetwork layer interacts with the network interface layer below it. Let's examine the path of an IP packet as it passes through two routers-Router 1 and Router 2. The situation is depicted in Figure 1.3. The packet comes through Network Link 1. The network header is then stripped from the packet, and it is passed up to IP for routing. Assuming that IP does not discard the packet, it determines the next jump and then passes the packet back down to the network interface layer. A new network header is added to the packet for its travel on Network Link 2. This header obscures the IP header, because that information is not needed for the packet to traverse the underlying network. The new header contains addressing information as needed for the particular network (hardware addresses, for example). Think back to the box analogy. The data stuffed inside the network box (packet) can actually be an entire IP packet.

After the packet traverses Network Link 2, the network header is stripped from the packet, and the rest of the packet is passed back up to IP on Router 2. IP then reads the exposed IP header, determines the next jump, and passes the packet back to the network interface software on Router 2. The packet is then given a new header so that it can navigate Network Link 3 at the network level. This process continues until the packet reaches its destination or is discarded. Not wishing to turn this into a networking text, we used simplified depictions of packets in Figure 1.3. The curious reader is invited to pull up this figure on the Web site and click on the packets at the IP and network levels to see more details.

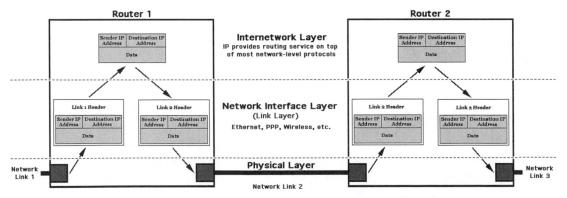

FIGURE 1.3 An IP packet, swimming in a sea of networks, pops its head above water to see where it's going.

The previous paragraphs show us that the Internet really functions as a network of disparate networks. Figure 1.1 showed that it is a vast conglomeration of network types. IP is like a blanket covering all of these networks. As a packet travels, it is passed up to this IP blanket at routing junctures and then sent back to the specific network for delivery. A given packet may go across numerous network types in its travels, but IP does not really care how the packet gets from point A to point B. It simply says "go to point B" and trusts the underlying network to do it. Without this blanketing effect of IP, we would not see an Internet where someone at home can send through a phone cable data that then hits an Ethernet, then a fiber optic backbone segment, and finally a wireless network ending in a cell phone. Aptly, IP is the *inter-net*work layer. Hence, we have the term *Internet*. Pretty cool huh?

Also from this, one can see the wisdom in making IP an unreliable delivery service. Certainly the constituent networks are not all created equal. A backbone segment is robust (perhaps millions of bits per second), whereas a dial-up phone connection is a weakling (thousands of bits per second). The ability of IP to discard packets is one way to help keep weaker networks from getting flooded. From the IP perspective, it is better to lose data than to bring a link or network down.

NOTE

With six-byte hardware addresses, LAN addressing has the benefit of nearly 300 trillion (256^6) addresses. Those are simply not going to run out. However, the four-byte IP address scheme tops out at around 4 billion (256^4) addresses. Well over half of them have already been given out. Clearly not all of those are in use. (Consider again the Internet hosts estimate and definition given in Section 1.1.) To get a head start on the potential shortage, the *Internet Assigned Numbers Authority (IANA)*, the organization that oversees distribution of IP addresses, has approved expanding the IP address to 16 bytes. This expression enables 340 undecillion addresses, probably somewhere between the number of stars in the universe and a googol.

Actually, not all of the bytes will be used strictly for addressing; that would be overkill. For example, one byte will carry an address type, so that varied address categories can be supported. The new addresses are part of IPv6 (IP version 6) which will slowly supplant the current IP version. In addition to expanded addressing, IPv6 includes provisions so that it can run on top of new networking technologies while still being efficient over traditional ones.

The Transport Layer

It is at the transport layer that we leave the domain of networks and routers and enter the realm of client-server interaction. Specifically, we will consider a file that is being sent from a server to a client. The type of file is immaterial at this layer, but it's easiest just to think of a Web page. The protocol used for sending it is the *Transmission Control Protocol (TCP)*. TCP is usually referred to in conjunction with IP as the *TCP/IP protocol suite*. Every modern operating system has a TCP/IP module built in. Thus, the type of computer involved is also immaterial.

TCP's name indicates its function: It controls the transmission of the file between the two hosts. Let us begin on the client. TCP sends a message to the server requesting a connection. If the server responds affirmatively, a connection, called a *socket,*[1] between the two computers is established. TCP then begins its work on the server in earnest. It segments the file into packets and stamps each packet with a sequence number. It also stamps each packet with a *checksum* that it calculates. A checksum is basically a count of the bits comprised in the packet. TCP then delivers the packets to IP for internetwork routing. As discussed above, the packets then bounce up and down the lower protocol levels as they traverse the internet on their way to the client.

As IP receives packets on the client, it passes them up to TCP. Each time TCP receives a packet, it recalculates the checksum for that packet. If the checksum does not match, the packet is discarded. Either way, the client then sends acknowledgment back to the server as to the sequence number and the result. Depending on the outcome, TCP on the server then retransmits the packet or notes that it has arrived intact. (Also, if no acknowledgment for a packet is received from the client within a certain period of time, TCP resends it, assuming that IP has killed it.) When TCP on the server has determined that all packets have arrived intact, it tells the client it is done transmitting, at which time the socket is closed and the transaction is complete. Using the sequence numbers, TCP then reorders the packets into the original file.

In this way, TCP provides the delivery guarantee that IP does not. This makes perfect sense if we stop to think about it. It's like a division of labor. IP decides where packets need to go and tries to optimize packet flow along the way. No way can IP attempt to monitor the state of conversations between myriad pairs of computers; it has enough to worry about seeing packets around the world. Only the client and server should worry about completing the transaction at hand. TCP is an end-to-end service that uses sockets to keep track of the states of transactions and sees them through to completion. The lower Internet layers deal with everything in between.

NOTE

User Datagram Protocol (UDP) is another protocol that is used on the Internet at the transport level. *Datagram* is no more than another name for a packet. The difference here is that UDP provides a more streamlined service. UDP is stateless, meaning that it does not maintain a socket connection. It just sends its packets out and forgets about them. Thus, there is no guarantee of delivery. UDP basically says to its packets, "Bye-bye, hope you make it."

While a service like UDP has the advantage of less overhead, potential packet loss seems to offset that advantage. However, this is acceptable in some situations. For example, in a live Internet broadcast of a huge audio or video file intended for multiple

---

[1]Technically, the term *socket* comes from the UNIX/Linux implementation for client-server transport connections. However, other operating systems implement connections in much the same way. The term *socket* is sufficiently general to illustrate the transport layer concepts used in this lesson.

users simultaneously, maintaining sockets for all of the clients could easily overwhelm the server and slow down the broadcast. Besides, the loss of a few packets out of millions would be almost imperceptible to the user. A contrasting example is when the amount of data is small, perhaps only one packet, and it makes sense for the application sending the data to handle its own error recovery above the transport layer. We will see a concrete example of this in Section 1.4.

The Application Layer

Many stand-alone applications (such as text editors, graphic editors, and spreadsheets) are installed on a personal computer. Such applications make files and save them on the hard drive for later use. In contrast, a *network application* shares files with other network applications over a network. While network applications certainly exist within the scope of LANs, our focus is on network applications that communicate over the Internet—*Internet applications,* if you will.

Of course, when people talk to each other, one usually initiates the conversation and then the other acknowledges and starts the dialog. A network application that initiates communication is called a *client,* and one that responds is called a *server.* More precisely, *client software* requests services or files from a remote server computer, and *server software* on that computer makes the services or files available. These notions significantly refine the client and server definitions used in Section 1.1. Referring to a computer as a "server" really means that the computer has special software that handles remote requests. Similarly, referring to a "client computer" really means that the computer has some sort of client software installed.

The name of the top Internet layer refers to such client-server network applications. It should come as no surprise at this point that protocols have been developed to standardize how network applications communicate. We offer some common examples.

Telnet: A telnet client allows a user to log onto a remote computer with a command-line interface. The telnet server software on the remote computer allows the user to execute system commands and run programs from afar.

FTP (File Transfer Protocol): An FTP client allows a user to log onto a remote computer for purposes of transferring files. The FTP server software on the remote computer gives the user access to directories and files from afar. The client can make requests to the server to allow both upload and download of files.

SMTP (Simple Mail Transfer Protocol): E-mail is moved around the Internet using specialized network applications. SMTP is the fundamental protocol that coordinates this. Although mail is delivered among mail servers on the Internet using SMTP, other protocols govern how you access your e-mail on the mail server on which you have an account. To access the mail account, one may use some sort of client software (e-mail client). Common examples are MS Outlook Express and Netscape Mail. The *Post Office Protocol (POP)* copies the messages from the mail server onto the client so that the user ends up with the inbox stored locally on his or her personal computer. In contrast, the *Internet Mail Access Protocol (IMAP)* copies only the message headers onto the client. When the user selects a message in the mail client window, IMAP temporarily grabs it from the inbox, which is maintained on the server.

An alternative to specialized mail clients, *Web-based e-mail* brings messages to your Web browser embedded in Web pages. Web based e-mail is similar to IMAP in that the inbox is stored on the server. The messages are temporarily sent to the browser, which functions as the mail client.

HTTP (HyperText Transfer Protocol): It was a long battle, but we have finally made it to the **World Wide Web**. You may not have noticed, but we have been talking exclusively about the Internet. The World Wide Web came into being as client software (Web browsers) and server software (Web servers) that share data over the Internet using HTTP. We defer discussion about the application-layer implementation we know as the World Wide Web to the next few sections, where we discuss it in detail.

We have just scratched the surface of the application layer in terms of the variety of protocols and network applications that use them. More examples include chat applications, newsgroup clients and servers, and networked video games. Even music-sharing utilities such as Napster and Morpheus[2] are little more than networked applications that implement some contrived application-layer protocol. In fact, given a programmer with some agenda, clients and servers can be constructed to share data using an application-layer protocol invented to implement the agenda. Students often make very simple clients and servers that utilize an invented protocol in courses that cover development of network applications.

We conclude our discussion of the Internet's entrails with an overview of how network applications interact with the lower Internet layers. Figure 1.4 provides illustration for the short discourse that follows. (Again, you can get a glimpse real of a real TCP packet by clicking the packets in the image of this figure on the Web site.)

To set the stage, suppose a client has requested some data from a server, the request has been accepted, and a socket has been established. For simplicity, you may think of a Web client (browser) and Web server, where the application data is a Web page. The server software passes its data down to TCP, which completely handles transportation of the data. As just outlined, the TCP software forms a sequence of packets and starts giving them to IP for delivery. As the packets move toward their destination, they bounce up and down the lower layers, as depicted in Figure 1.3, perhaps traversing several different network types and physical media along the way. You can see in Figure 1.4 how IP uniformly "blankets" the networks. When the IP software on the client gets a packet, it sends it up to TCP. When all packets have been delivered, and the server-side TCP software terminates the connection, the client software that made the request receives the data and formats it for the user.

It is amazing to see the complete picture of the Internet broken up into layers. The TCP/IP protocol suite is the glue that holds it all together. IP glues all of the disparate networks together into an internetwork. TCP provides the end-to-end transport services for the myriad network applications that share data over the Internet. It is interesting to note that only the net-

---

[2]A good bit different from client-server applications, Napster (rest in peace) and Morpheus are (were) peer-to-peer network applications, which implement their own application-layer protocols and utilize the transport services of both UDP and TCP.

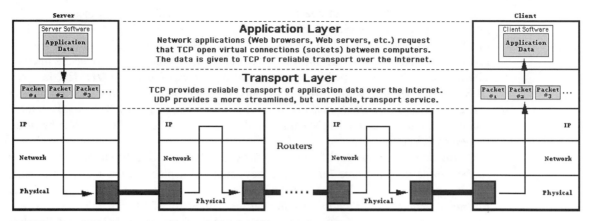

FIGURE 1.4   TCP provides "end-to-end" services for a network application.

work applications look at the actual data. There is a diagram on this book's Web site that illustrates the notion of data encapsulation and gives a final look at the Internet's layers.

NOTE

Because the transport layer on a given computer must provide service (whether TCP or UDP) for many different network applications, it needs some way to keep track of all those applications. For that purpose, the transport layer uses a virtual addressing scheme, where the addresses are called **ports**. Ports are two-byte integers (in the range 0 through 65535) and are a completely abstract transport layer contrivance. Each application that the transport layer services is associated with a port number. For example, if 10 different network applications are using transport services, then the transport layer keeps track of them using 10 different integers. The term *port* seems to indicate a physical presence, like an aperture into which you can plug something, but ports are a completely abstract notion. Integers are a fine choice to keep track of distinct network applications.

Whoever programs a customized network application may choose an unused port number to "bind" it to transport layer services. However, common network applications use standard recognized port numbers. For example, standard Web servers use port 80, and FTP servers use ports 20 (file download) and 21 (file upload). Network applications such as these are said to "listen on their port." Thus, standard Web servers listen on port 80. That means that an incoming request received by the transport layer must contain a port number. The transport layer then delivers that request to the application associated with that port.

1.3   THE WORLD WIDE WEB

The mastermind of the World Wide Web is Tim Berners-Lee, a computer scientist who in 1990, while working for the *European Organization for Nuclear Research* (*CERN,* from the French title, "Conseil Européen pour la recherche nucléaire"), outlined a way that physicists around the world could uniformly access research information. Berners-Lee, together with other scientists at CERN, developed a *hypertext*-based document system, together with client and server software that could share the documents over the Internet. The language they developed is called *HyperText Markup Language (HTML)*. In 1991, CERN unleashed the world's first Web server, which served up abstracts of physics research papers as *HTML documents* (*hypertext documents* or simply *Web pages*). In conjunction with this, Berners-Lee's team gave their text-only client software (Web browser) to the physics community.

Realizing the potential of their invention, and also their inability to develop it much further because of resource limitations, they launched a plea via the Internet for other developers to join in. In 1993, Marc Andreessen, while working for the *National Center for Supercomputing Applications (NCSA)* at the University of Illinois, released free versions of a new browser, *Mosaic,* for all three major platforms: Mac, PC, and UNIX. (It is rumored that Andreessen wrote the Mosaic client for UNIX over winter break.) The Mosaic browser featured support for graphics (hence the name "Mosaic"), and a point-and-click user interface. By the end of 1993 there were around 500 known Web servers, and WWW traffic constituted around 1 percent of Internet traffic. With Mosaic, however, *anyone* with a computer and modem could use the Internet. People who were barely computer literate could surf by clicking a mouse. Well, the rest is history. As you can imagine, Web traffic now dominates the Internet.

Andreessen went on to form *Netscape Communications,* which since has released several versions of *Netscape Navigator,* each successively expanding upon the capabilities of Mosaic. Netscape, which dominated the Web for end users on the client side during the mid 1990s, began to lose market share when Microsoft released *Internet Explorer* in 1996. The ensuing years saw the "browser wars," in which the two browsers duked it out for market share. Today, Explorer has the lion's share of the browser market, but Netscape remains alive and well and is now a subsidiary of *America Online (AOL)*. Numerous other software developers have created Web browsers, with *Opera* and *Mozilla* probably the most noteworthy, but Internet Explorer and Netscape Navigator still dominate the landscape.

Events like the browser wars provoke concern that a specific proprietary development could come to dominate the Web. (Microsoft has come the closest and has been rewarded with an extended court battle.) This concern was recognized fairly early in the development of the Web. In 1994 the *World Wide Web Consortium (W3C),* a body of institutes and companies from all over the world, was formed to set standards for all to use. One of the W3C's avowed goals is that no one lock up the Web into a proprietary system. It is interesting to visit the W3C's Web site at `www.w3c.org`. Although the W3C can't directly control Web software developers, is has been effective at setting standards with which developers comply (more or less). We will refer again and again to the W3C as we explore various Web technologies throughout this book.

The Web server software employed over the years has been more diverse than the Web-browsing client software. There is a graphic on this book's Web site that depicts usage of various Web servers. Ironically, the dust has settled, leaving only two dominant Web servers. At the time this was written, the open-source (and free) *Apache* (originally developed by some graduate students and so called because it was then "a patchy" server) software serves up about 60 percent of the world's Web pages, and Microsoft's *Internet Information Server (IIS)* about 20 percent. Apache is available for all major operating systems: UNIX, Linux, Microsoft Windows, and Macintosh OS X. IIS is available only on Microsoft's Windows platform. Apache has gained in popularity, in part because of its abundant enhancements developed by the open-source community, and in part because of its availability for all platforms. It is rumored that even Microsoft uses some Apache/ UNIX servers to augment its own IIS server farms, bringing more stability to its Web services.

Defining the World Wide Web concisely is not entirely straightforward. Berners-Lee defined it simply as the global web of hypertext documents. Indeed, the Web is the largest collection of linked electronic documents on the planet. Most estimates indicate the collection is growing by over a million documents per day. A more detailed definition depicts the Web as this (ever-expanding) document collection, together with the elaborate, distributed network application that facilitates global sharing of the hypertext documents. This network application is distributed among millions of client and server computers worldwide. Certainly Web servers and browsers play the largest role, with e-mail servers and clients coming in second. But even that definition is problematic. As you progress through this book, you will see that much of the information available on the Web is stored not simply in hypertext documents (Web pages), but in data-bases and XML files. Such information is extracted as necessary, configured into Web pages "on the fly," and sent to your browser for viewing. Although it is not often defined in this way, we prefer to view the World Wide Web as a massive, distributed information reservoir, together with an elaborate delivery system that lives in the Internet's application layer.

It will be interesting to see how future definitions regard the Web. In a practical sense, its scope is moving beyond simply sharing textual information and graphical images. The Internet infrastructure is becoming so fast that audio and video transactions are becoming practical. Basically, this boils down to redefining the information types that the web mobilizes. Whatever the case, we will say the Web mobilizes *resources*. We will, however, focus primarily on textual information in this book.

1.4 THE DOMAIN NAME SERVICE

The Domain Name Service (DNS) is an application-layer service that enables us to use recognizable names to locate servers rather than having to rely solely on IP addresses. For example, consider www.uweb.edu, a *named address* for a fictitious university, Web University. The advantage of remembering this over some meaningless IP address is obvious. Such an address is often called a *domain name,* but technically the domain name is uweb.edu. Any number of named addresses can be assigned as subdomains. For example, www.uweb.edu is given to the main university site, and departmental sites on campus can be assigned as math.uweb.edu, english.uweb.edu, and so forth.

The network software that provides the service resides on a computer called a DNS server or *domain name server* (frequently labeled with the acronym DNS as well). If you have a residential service, your ISP maintains a DNS server. Similarly,

UWEB's network administrator maintains a DNS server to provide the service for clients on UWEB's Ethernet LAN. Figure 1.5 provides illustration for the discussion that follows.

Suppose your browser wishes to request UWEB's homepage at www.uweb.edu. The browser first has to make a request to a DNS server to *resolve* the named address into the associated IP address. If the browser request comes from within UWEB's LAN, UWEB's DNS will resolve the named address. However, if the browser request comes from your house, your ISP's DNS will likely not be able to resolve the .edu address. In that case the ISP's DNS will ask other DNS servers, perhaps even UWEB's, until it is successful. Think of how many domain names there are. (Almost every word in the dictionary has been taken as a dot com. . . try one!) It is simply not possible for every DNS to know them all. UWEB's DNS can resolve any named address in the uweb.edu domain, for example, and your ISP's DNS specializes in dot coms.

Once the browser has the IP address of the server hosting www.uweb.edu, it can then call on TCP to open and manage a socket for the Web page transfer session. After all, Internet navigation requires IP addresses. TCP/IP does not care about domain names. During transit, the named address is buried somewhere below the TCP and IP packet headers. It is the Web server's job to deal with the named address back up at the application level on the server.

The service performed by the Web server is called *virtual hosting*. For example, in Figure 1.5, all four named addresses you see on the server get resolved to the same IP address: that of UWEB's server. It is up to the server administrator to tell the server software to expect requests for the four different named addresses. Each named address has its own directory (folder) on the server. So, ultimately, each named address request ends up at a directory on the server containing Web pages for that Web site. As you see, .com and .edu sites even can be virtually hosted on the same server.

Site portability is a major benefit that comes from virtual hosting. For example, it would be relatively easy to move our cknuckles.com domain to a different server. We would give the IP address of the new server to the administrator of the DNS that holds our primary record, and we would ask the webmaster of the new server to map www.cknuckles.com onto a directory on that computer. Then we would use an FTP client to transfer the files from the old server to our new directory.

To pull things together, we informally restate the foregoing paragraphs. The browser requests from DNS the IP address of the server that hosts the named address. The browser then tells TCP to initiate a socket with the server at that IP address. When the Web server software ascertains the named address, it grabs the Web page from the folder it has assigned to that named address. When the browser has all of the Web page, it's all over, and the connection is terminated.

Interestingly, transport for DNS address resolution is handled by UDP rather than TCP. UDP is ideal for this, because a single packet usually suffices and error recovery can be easily handled by the browser above the transport layer. After all, a browser can't really do anything before it finds out the IP address necessary to navigate the backbone. It may as well sit and reissue resolution requests until it succeeds or gives up. In cases like this, the extra overhead created by TCP maintaining a socket for the duration of the address resolution would be less efficient for the computer than sending out a couple of "one-shot" resolution request packets.

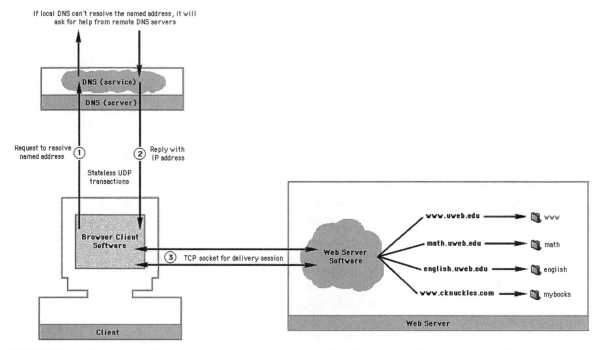

FIGURE 1.5 The Domain Name Service for requests and the virtual hosting service for named addresses on Web servers.

1.5 THE UNIFORM RESOURCE LOCATOR

Current browsers are pretty nice in that if you type www.uweb.edu into the address field, the browser will deliver UWEB's home page to you. The browser performs a courtesy by guessing your intentions and changing your request into the form http://www.uweb.edu/. Try it yourself by just typing in www.cknuckles.com. The browser changes the named address into a **Uniform Resource Locator (URL)**.

Named addresses provide addressing for the Web, but URLs provide the how, where, and what specifics of a request. Figure 1.6 shows the general form of a URL. The "how" part tells the server what type of transaction to initiate. For example, a URL such as ftp://www.uweb.edu/, specifying the File Transfer Protocol, would tell the server to transfer a file to the client's hard drive. There are several protocols that can be specified in a URL, but we will focus on HTTP URLs, which tell the server to "give me a Web page." In the next section you will learn more about the details of "how" the Hypertext Transfer Protocol works.

FIGURE 1.6 The structure of a basic URL.

We have already talked about the "where" part in detail. Each named address is no more than a directory sitting on a Web server. We call that the *root directory* of the named address. The root directory contains the *Web site* to which the named address provides reference. Basically, the URL `http://www.uweb.edu/` says, "give me a Web page in the root directory of `www.uweb.edu`." The forward slash (/) the browser has appended to the end of the URL indicates that the request is for a directory, rather than a specific file. But what file in the root directory does a URL target? That is precisely the information contained in the "what" part of a URL. Because the basic URL `http://www.uweb.edu/` specifies a directory and not a file, a *default file* (Web page) in that directory is served up. The first URL in Figure 1.7 demonstrates that. The UWEB server is set up so that the file `default.html` is automatically served up even though it has not been specifically requested.

Notice that HTML files—files that generate Web pages—have names that end with the extension `.html` to identify what type of files they are. This should come as no surprise since this is common practice: `.doc` for MS Word files, `.gif` and `.jpg` for certain image files, `.pdf` for Portable Document Format files for Adobe's Acrobat Reader, and so forth. HTML filenames sometimes end with just `.htm` because three-letter extensions are conventional (specifically, Microsoft's platforms prefer three characters).

Clearly, the default behavior just described is desirable so that our book's home page, for example, does not have to be accessed with the longer URL `http://www.cknuckles.com/default.html`, which incidentally is equivalent to `http://www.cknuckles.com/`. Crank up a browser and try both for yourself!

Let us return to the diagram in Figure 1.7. Unless a Web site has very few pages, it is going to be organized using subdirectories (subfolders). Imagine how confusing the hard drive on your personal computer would be if there were no directory structure and all the files (and other icons) were dumped together into the root directory. Figure 1.7 shows a partial directory structure for UWEB's main site, `www.uweb.edu`. Each of the other three Web site roots in Figure 1.5 would also contain its own subdirectory structure.

To target a file other than the default in the root directory, the file name is added to the URL, as the second URL in Figure 1.7 shows. The third URL specifies only a directory one below the root, so the default file in the `sports` directory would be pulled up. Of course, that would be the sports home page. (Even though there are several default files in the diagram, they are all different and apply to different directories.) Similarly, the fourth URL pulls up the volleyball home page by targeting its directory, two deep. Finally, the fifth URL would pull up the statistics page in the football directory, again two deep, bypassing the football home page. That's a long URL, but the exact file path relative to the root must be specified in the "what" part of a URL to find a particular file.

You may be wondering about a couple of things. One, why have I been surfing the Web for a long time but have not had to type in any long URLs like that? Moreover, I have no clue what a given Web site's directory structure looks like, so how could I target a specific file? The answer to both questions is that you have done so by clicking hyperlinks. The links have targeted files deep in directory structures for you, and the browser has displayed the long URL in its address field whether you were aware of it or not. Second, why do they call it a URL and not a "Uniform File Locator (ufl)"? (It's not

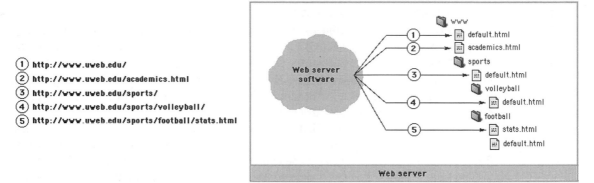

FIGURE 1.7 URLs locate specific resources on Web servers.

because they wanted to save that for the United Football League.) The Web contains a lot of resources other than HTML files (graphics, audio, video, and so forth.). Technically speaking, such resources are stored in files of various sorts. For some fun, pull up the image file in our root directory, `www.cknuckles.com/beest.jpg`. It is a stand-alone image, not even embedded in a Web page. Doesn't the Web sound more intriguing if we share resources rather than files?

NOTE

In case you have noticed that some URLs even contain more information than the "how, where, what" parts we have emphasized, we'll add one last tidbit so as not to leave you confounded. When we told the `Google.com` search engine to search for *wildebeest,* the following URL popped into the address field:

`http://www.google.com/search?q=wildebeest`

The text after the question mark is called a *query string.* That's basically extra information that a URL can carry to the server for processing. In this case, the query string is passed to a computer program on the server that executes the search. The reader is invited to do the same search at `Metacrawler.com` or some other search engine to see how much extra information gets sent back to the server.

Finally, URLs can even contain port numbers. For example, a computer science student at UWEB programs a custom web server that "listens" for requests on TCP port 81. A full URL request that sends data to the server might be as follows, with the port specified after the address:

`http://cs.uweb.edu:81/survey?response=yes`

URLs that do not specify a port number are delivered to the application listening on the standard port for a given protocol. For example, a request made by an `http:` URL that specifies no port number is automatically delivered to the application listening on port 80, usually a standard Web server.

1.6 BASIC HTTP TRANSACTIONS

We have network specific addresses, IP addresses for internetwork routing, named addresses for virtual Web addressing, and URLs to target specific Web resources. That's good! But now let's target a resource with an HTTP request and see how the transaction unfolds: the *HTTP transaction*. For convenience, we consider the specific transaction depicted in Figure 1.8. Here UWEB's music department has made a Web page for the father of heavy metal. (They have a nontraditional department.)

Whether by typing in the URL or by clicking a link, a user makes the URL request `http://music.uweb.edu/iommi.html` from a browser. HTML files are no more than text files containing ASCII characters. The contents of the file, `iommi.html`, are shown above the server in Figure 1.8. It's just plain, keyboard-generated text, and that's what is sent to the browser. But the image files have to get there also. The key is that HTTP requests have a **keep-alive** feature. That means that the socket is kept open for some time and not terminated after the HTML file has been copied into the browser's *cache* (pronounced "cash") memory.

The first order of business for the browser is to read, or *parse,* the text in the HTML file. As it does so, it encounters the references to the two image files and makes secondary requests to the Web server for those files. You can see that the source (`src`) location for each image is given as a file path, relative to where `iommi.html` sits on the server. Since the browser knows exactly where `iommi.html` is located from the original URL, it can for-

① URL request `http://music.uweb.edu/iommi.html`

② A copy of the HTML document is transferred into the browser's cache.

③ The browser starts parsing the HTML code and asks the Web server software to send the two image files. (The "kept alive" socket is still being used.)

④ The image files are transferred into the cache, completing the Web page.

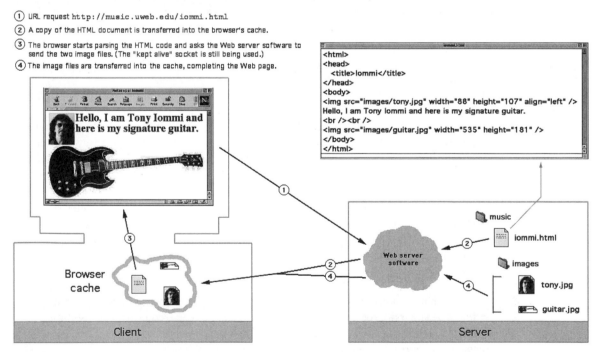

FIGURE 1.8 A basic HTTP transaction.

mulate the exact path to each image file. The images are then copied into the browser's cache over the socket, which has been "kept alive." Of course, it takes all three files to make the Web page you see in the browser window. This is the first good opportunity we have had to emphasize how vastly different a Web page is from the HTML file that tells the browser how to make it. We have abused that distinction in our language prior to now, but we hereby publicly repent.

Early HTTP transactions were not endowed with the keep-alive feature. That means TCP would have had to open and maintain a new socket for each of the two image files. When embedding objects, such as images, into Web pages became the vogue, HTTP was augmented with the keep-alive feature. As it is now, one socket maintains a connection for the multiple-file transaction necessary to get all components of a Web page. When we recently checked `Amazon.com`'s front end, they had 37 graphics. Without the keep-alive feature, such artistry would have turned the Web into a quagmire of TCP socket management.

Before we move on, a little more information on caching is in order. A browser cache is hard-drive space that the browser allocates for storing recently used files. Typically 5 to 10 megabytes by default, its size can be adjusted by changing a browser's preferences. If you have noticed that a Web page usually loads more quickly if you pull it up a second time during a surfing session, it's because the browser grabs the associated files from the cache rather than over the Internet. Of course, the browser can check with the server to see which of the files have been updated. Otherwise, you could pull up yesterday's sports news out of the cache. Hey, the Cubs won again, and by the same score! Cached files have a preset life span, but are more often forced out by files retrieved more recently. When the cache is full, older files are deleted as new ones arrive.

NOTE

HTTP is officially categorized as a **stateless** protocol. It is completely stateless in the sense of a *Web session*. A Web session entails surfing to different pages. For cxamplc, if you visit `Amazon.com`, you might visit several pages, add an item or two to the shopping cart, and submit the order. Each time you pull up a new page, the Web server software forgets about the previous HTTP transaction. The server keeps a socket alive to complete the current transaction, but the previous transaction never happened as far as the server software is concerned. This point might seem trivial to you, but not to Amazon. They need to track your Web session. For example, your shopping cart contents must be preserved as you surf among multiple pages. The browser and HTTP Web server software will not do that for them. The necessity and means for maintaining state in Web sessions will be a frequent topic in this text.

It is possible to turn off caching in most browsers. Moreover, not all documents are cached, even if caching is not disabled. For example, if the browser can't detect a last-modified property of a file, it simply won't cache it, because if the file were to be requested again, the browser would have no way to check it against the original copy on the server to see whether it had been updated. Thus, the browser would have to request it from the server anyway, and caching would be pointless.

Even if a browser doesn't cache a file, it still has to have a local copy on hand to parse and render. Typically, a noncached file survives on the client only during the HTTP transaction in which it is requested. When the browser initiates a new HTTP request, the browser flushes its memory buffer to make room for the incoming files. We will abuse terminology a bit throughout the rest of this book and avoid this distinction. We will uniformly say "a file is transferred to the browser's cache." In a worst-case scenario, the file is "cached" only during the particular HTTP transaction, and the cache would refer to the browser's input buffer. This abuse of terminology will have no impact on our discussions.

It is interesting to note that a given DNS also caches information in this way. If an address is not part of its permanent responsibility (such as UWEB's DNS being responsible for all subdomains of uweb.edu), the DNS will cache it after acquiring the resolution from some other DNS. It will cache not only the most recently used addresses, but also the ones that are requested the most often. Thus, its cache is optimized so that it need not seek outside help for addresses that were resolved yesterday or ones that have been resolved many times over the last few months. Caching is not formally part of the HTTP or DNS protocols, but is a clever implementation used by clients and servers in order to expedite their services to the user.

1.7 OVERVIEW OF WEB APPLICATIONS

Let's examine where we are. We have seen how the remarkable internetwork works. We have explored how the equally remarkable Web operates in the Internet's uppermost layer. Believe it or not, Web applications operate one level above all that. In fact, we could go back and add a sixth layer for Web applications on top of the stack in Figure 1.2. A "sixth-layer" Web application leans heavily on the services of the application layer immediately below it. In this case, the services are provided by Web browsers and Web server software.

In a standard HTTP transaction, where an HTML file is sitting on the server and a browser requests it, the browser and server are more than adequately equipped to deal with the situation. However, when an HTML form like the following,

Name:	
E-mail:	
Zip Code:	
Age:	
Submit	

appears in the Web page, the browser and server alone aren't prepared to process the data entered by the user. Depending on the nature of the requested data, a customized computer program must be in place to deal with it. How can the browsers and servers be ready to process, on their own, some bizarre type of data that someone might put a form in a Web page to collect?

For another example, we have mentioned that many Web pages are created "on the fly," customized for the moment. Consider an online stockbroker. When two different people log into their accounts, they see the same page template, but the stock information is customized for the individual accounts. They have not pulled up a Web page made from a pre-existing HTML file but have called a computer program on the server that generates different but similar HTML files, pulling from some data source to customize for the different stock accounts.

Enter the Web programmer. Conventional programmers likely using C++ make stand-alone applications that sit on your personal computer. A newer breed of network programmers have made the browsers and servers from languages such Java. Our goal is to teach you to become a Web programmer—to build Web applications. If you are reading this book, you likely know some programming fundamentals. Figure 1.9 depicts a simple Web application and shows the environment in which you will apply those programming fundamentals. This Web application produces an online survey.

We begin with the URL request for the HTML document survey.html, which produces the Web page shown in the browser. This initiates a standard HTTP transaction, copying the HTML file from the server to the browser's cache. (We have omitted graphics in this example for simplicity.) This time, however, there is *JavaScript* code in the page along with the HTML. JavaScript is a programming language with syntax very similar to that of Java and C++; you'll learn more on that in Chapter 3. Not only does the browser parse the HTML; it has a separate

(1) The front end of the Web application is passed to the client as an HTML file that contains some JavaScript code. The JavaScript validates the form data on the client.

(2) The user submits the form to a program named processsurvey.cgi on the Web server. Fundamentally, this is an HTTP transaction between the browser and the server software, but the URL points to an executable gateway program.

(3) The server software executes the gateway program and passes it the form data. This is the first part of the gateway interface.

(4) The gateway program processes the form data and interacts with a back-end data source.

(5) The gateway program passes its output back to the Web server software formatted as an HTML document. This completes the gateway interface.

(6) The server software passes the HTML document to the client, thereby completing the HTTP transaction.

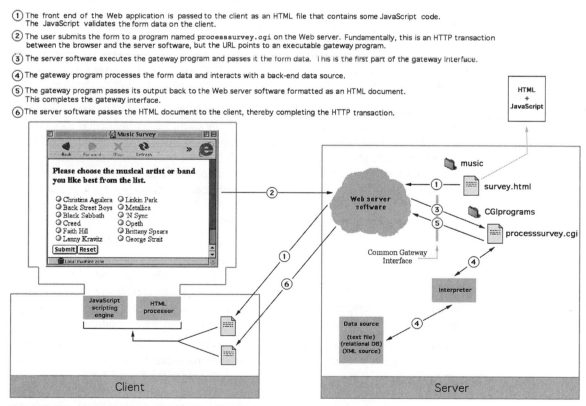

FIGURE 1.9 The anatomy of a Web application.

"brain" that reads and interprets the JavaScript instructions. The HTML markup presentation, together with JavaScript's programming ability, constitute the *front end* of the Web application. Below is a list of some of the things for which JavaScript is used on the front end.

- *Browser sniffing:* JavaScript code "sniffs" out the browser type and version before the page loads. Then, vendor- and platform-specific HTML/CSS content can be delivered. In other words, browser sniffing makes sure that the page works in the given browser. This is an artifact from the browser wars, during which Netscape and Explorer introduced somewhat different HTML and JavaScript implementations. The JavaScript coverage in this book is browser (and platform) independent, so this will not be much of a factor for us. However, Chapter 16 does use a simple browser sniff that enables us to parse XML using JavaScript in both Explorer and Netscape.

- *Dynamic HTML (DHTML):* DHTML refers to the many effects that can be created by using JavaScript to change the state of a Web page after it has been fully rendered by a browser. Typically, DHTML effects are triggered by a user event such as passing the mouse over certain regions of a Web page. The effects, determined by JavaScript functions that handle the events, involve things like causing hidden layers to appear, moving objects on the screen, and changing text and background colors of certain objects to create rollover animations. Because of browser nuances in implementing DHTML, browser sniffing is sometimes required to ensure that a given DHTML effect works in all relatively current Web browsers.

  DHTML is mainly used for aesthetics on the front ends of Web applications. Since our objective is to cover core issues, most of which involve programming on the Web server, we don't have the latitude to cover DHTML in great detail in this text. Indeed, entire books have been written on fancy visual effects enabled by DHTML. Chapter 19 does provide a brief introduction to how JavaScript is used to create DHTML.

- *Client-side form validation:* Web applications often collect user data via HTML forms. It is desirable to validate that data on the client before the data is submitted to the Web server. Data validation includes things like ensuring that required text fields have been filled out, the data in those fields is of the proper format, and that a selection from a group of option buttons has been made. If data is validated on the client using JavaScript, the user can be alerted to re-enter certain data without causing an extra transaction with the Web server. The JavaScript coverage in Chapter 3 introduces JavaScript and shows how to use it for validating data on the front end.

  So that you can see this in action now, we provide two versions of the form of Figure 1.9 on the Web site. Both versions require that one of the options is selected when the form is submitted. The reader should submit both versions without making a selection. The first version produces an instantaneous alert using JavaScript executed on your computer. The second version requires a transaction with the Web server just to see the same page returned to the browser with an admonishment.

- *Client-side utilities:* JavaScript also provides the processing capabilities necessary to create complete client-side utilities. For examples, check out the utilities provided on the Web site. These work instantaneously, because the browser executes the JavaScript code, meaning no new network connections are required. The JavaScript coverage in this book provides the background necessary to create such utilities.

So you see, the front end of this Web application is responsible for giving the user the options for the survey and verifying that the user has selected one. In general, the front end of a Web application can involve a wide variety of HTML and JavaScript implementations. As we noted just above, some are geared for aesthetics, and others for functionality.

Now we move on to the *back end* of the application. When you make a selection and hit the Submit button, the form data is submitted to the server. For evidence, you can see your selection reflected in the query string appended to the URL in the browser window. A key point is that this URL points to an executable program on the server, not an HTML file. The Web server software passes your selection to the program and causes it to execute. (Your selection simply ends up stored in a variable within the program.) The program's agenda is very simple. It reads the previous survey results from a data file, updates the previous results to reflect your selection, and overwrites the data file with the updated survey results. The program then formats the updated survey results into HTML and sends that as its output to the Web server software. The Web server software then sends the HTML file (which the program created "on the fly") to the client for markup.

If you have not yet done so, you should submit the survey to see the query string and the returned results. Here is what's interesting. The only copy of that Web page that will ever exist is the one in your browser cache. The HTML that generated the page was the output of a computer program that was directed toward your computer. When someone else submits the survey, a page will be generated on the fly for that person to reflect the newest survey results. Your page is then obsolete and, once it is flushed from your cache, it simply does not exist on our planet. Such is the nature of a dynamic Web application.

Although HTML and JavaScript are the languages of choice on the client, there are a wide variety of server-side languages and implementations. The program used in the foregoing example is written in Perl, but virtually any language could be used, including C++, Java, and Visual Basic. Irrespective of the language used, the executable program is termed a *gateway program*. Such a program serves as a gateway between Web server software and back-end data sources by handling data processing needs for the Web application, and giving output to the server software in the form of HTML documents. The specification (protocol) that standardizes how gateway programs "communicate with" Web server software is called the **Common Gateway Interface (CGI)**. Most often, gateway programs are called *CGI programs*.

1.8 GET AND POST TRANSACTIONS

The most fundamental type of HTTP transaction is a **GET transaction**—that is, basically a transaction to "get" a Web page. Indeed, any time you click a link to pull up an HTML file you are enacting a GET transaction. The basic HTTP transaction depicted in Figure 1.8 is a standard GET HTTP transaction.

GET transactions also allow a query string to be attached to the URL so that data can be sent to the Web server. In that case, the URL calls a CGI program rather than a pre-existing HTML file, and the data sent in the query string is passed to the program for processing. We didn't use the terminology at the time, but the example used in Section 1.7 to show the nature of Web applications featured a typical GET transaction. The data was sent to the server as a query string. Figure 1.10 depicts in a more general setting how a CGI program obtains data from a GET transaction. It also depicts a general POST transaction, which we discuss shortly.

GET Transaction

① The query string is sent to the Web server in the application-layer header.

② The Web server places the query string in one of its environment variables.

③ The CGI program accesses the environment variables and stores the query string into a variable within the program.

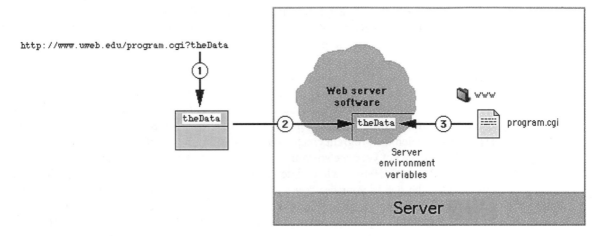

POST Transaction

① The data is included in the bodies of the application-layer packets and sent to the Web server.

② The Web server passes the data to the CGI program as the program's standard input stream.

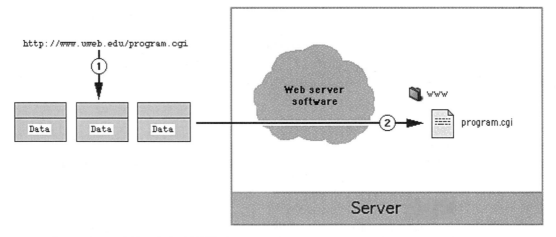

FIGURE 1.10 Comparison of GET and POST HTTP transactions.

Buried below the IP and TCP packet headers is the actual application data. In our case, the application data consists of an HTTP request from a Web browser. Even application data that is being exchanged contains both header information and actual content. The query string is included in the header information of a browser request to a Web server. In a GET transaction, the query string is placed into one of the Web server software's *environment variables.* Those are simply variables in which a Web server stores details about the current transaction. Remember, HTTP is stateless, so the environment variables' contents are unique to a given transaction.

So that you can get a feel for the types of information that a Web server puts in these variables, there is a simple CGI program named `get.cgi` on the book's Web site. You can type the following URL into the address field of your browser to initiate a GET transaction that sends some data. You can put in whatever you like for the query string. (It is possible that some browsers will truncate the query string after a space in the data. You can experiment to see whether that happens.)

```
http://www.cknuckles.com/cgi/get.cgi?put your data here
```

The CGI program does no more than retrieve the contents of the server's environment variables and return them to the Web browser. You can see that the `QUERY_STRING` variable contains the string you entered after the ? symbol in the URL.

A **POST transaction** does not use a query string to pass data to the Web server. The data is not sent in the header of the browser request but as the actual data content of the request. When the Web server receives the data from the packets, it transfers the data to the CGI program as a standard input stream. The data does not get stored in an environment variable; it is passed straight to the program.

Because data from a POST transaction is not included in a URL, you can't initiate a POST transaction by typing in a URL or by clicking a link. An HTML form is required to initiate the transaction, and the data is POSTed to the Web server as application data. So that you can contrast the two transaction types, we have prepared a simple form that can be found at

```
http://www.cknuckles.com/cgi/post.html
```

You can enter some data into the form, and submit it to the Web server. The data is sent to a program named `post.cgi`, which does no more than return the data that the form POSTed to the program, followed by the contents of the environment variables. You will notice that no query string is appended to the URL when the form calls the CGI program, and that the `QUERY_STRING` environment variable is empty when their contents are returned to the browser.

A third type of HTTP transaction is a *HEAD* request. Such requests return only information found in the head section of an HTML document: information about the Web page (meta-information) rather than the actual content of the Web page. Such requests are not useful to Web browsers, which are geared to display Web pages. HEAD requests are often used by specialized network applications that collect information about Web sites. The most common examples are Web crawlers, which are automated programs that "crawl" the Web collecting meta-information. Web crawlers populate databases used by search engines with topical information about Web sites.

1.9 SECURE TRANSACTIONS

Security at the level of Web applications is a frequently covered topic in this text. Protocol-level security issues on the Web are outside our objectives. However, this section does offer a brief look at *Secure HTTP (HTTPS)*. The concept is simple and demonstrates another "lower-layer" service that Web applications can utilize. The *Secure Sockets Layer (SSL)* is a protocol invented by Netscape that operates in conjunction with TCP/IP at both the transport and internetwork layers. SSL is now universally supported by modern browsers and TCP/IP implementations.

At the internetwork layer, SSL prevents *IP spoofing*. That means a hacker can't discard your packets somewhere along their journey and substitute some bogus ones. At the transport layer, SSL performs a service more indicative of its name. Rather than using conventional sockets, clients and servers exchange data over secure sockets. That means that the application data is encrypted in such a way that only the client and server have the necessary "key" with which to encrypt and then decrypt packet data. Each secure socket uses a different encryption key, and the keys are never reused.

Web browsers come automatically equipped to make HTTPS requests, and most Web servers can receive HTTPS requests provided that a preference is set so that the server software expects such requests. Aside from that, all that is required is the use of an HTTPS URL, which is identical to an HTTP URL except that it begins with `https://`. Next time you buy something online with a credit card or submit a sensitive password, you will likely see an HTTPS URL. Typically, only servers that deal with sensitive information are enabled to accept HTTPS requests and call for secure sockets. Since managing secure sockets incurs considerably more overhead for the server's operating system, they are used only if necessary. For example, Hotmail, the most prevalent free Web-based e-mail service, uses HTTPS to transmit passwords for login, but regular HTTP for transmitting e-mail messages. Unnecessary HTTPS would overburden its already heavily taxed servers.

1.10 SERVER-SIDE TECHNOLOGIES FOR WEB APPLICATIONS

We have seen that HTML and JavaScript are the main languages used on the client. However, there are several technologies that can be used on the server. Primarily because of its text-parsing capabilities, Perl is a very common programming language used to create CGI programs. Indeed, we will use Perl to explore the concepts fundamental to Web applications.

When a Perl CGI program is called, a new process on the server computer is spun off, independent of the Web server software. This is indicated by the (Perl) Interpreter in Figure 1.9. A distinct advantage of this approach is that you can run Perl-driven CGI Web applications on any server on which you can install a Perl interpreter. This includes Apache on virtually any platform (UNIX, Linux, Macintosh, or Windows), and IIS on Microsoft boxes. Another advantage is that if your program runs amuck, it will crash its process but likely won't crash the Web server software. That outcome results in only a Web application gone bad for a user, and not a Web server temporarily lost to the rest of the world. (Need we say that's a good thing for one just learning to make Web applications?)

Newer approaches involve modules that are either compiled directly into Web server software or dynamically linked to the server software. Either way, the processing for the Web application is handled by the same process that the Web server uses to handle

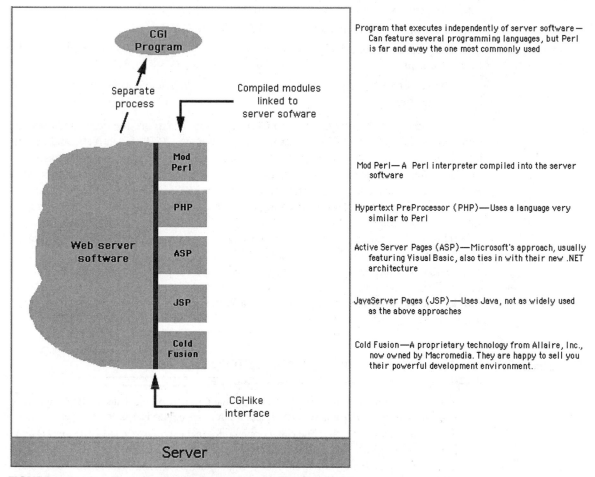

FIGURE 1.11   Common server-side technologies for Web applications.

the browser request. Figure 1.11 shows some of the most common server-side technologies used to create Web applications. You have likely heard of some of them.

An advantage of the compiled-modules approach is that the direct link to the server software creates less overhead for the server computer because only a single process is used. For the same reason, the response of the Web application is often quicker. A disadvantage is that the technologies are often proprietary. For example, Microsoft's Active Server Pages (ASP) is not ideally suited for use with an Apache/UNIX server, and Macromedia's Cold Fusion requires the purchase of an elaborate development environment.

The reader should not be daunted by the number of technologies (and acronyms) we have mentioned that can be used to build the back ends of Web applications. They all essentially work the same way. You make the front end and a computer program to run the back end, put them on a server, and beg for hits. Then, roughly six things happen.

1. The user interacts with the front end on the client.
2. The browser passes data to the server.

3. The server software passes the data to the program.

4. The program interacts with back-end data sources.

5. The program sends its output back to server software in the form of an HTML-formatted document.

6. The server software passes the newly created HTML document to the Web browser on the client.

This text uses the ubiquitous Perl/CGI approach to explore the core fundamentals. With that in place, Chapters 14 and 15 introduce PHP and ASP, respectively, and demonstrate that the same concepts apply within each development environment. Mastery of core fundamentals enables one to adapt to almost any specific technology that implements those fundamentals. The technologies shown in Figure 1.11 basically all accomplish the same things. Of course, certain technologies are better at certain things than others, but that is to be expected.

This text features JavaScript at key junctures, but our primary focus is on the server side of Web applications. You can imagine that the bulk of the processing occurs there, because that's where the bulk of the data must be stored. You certainly can't maintain data on client machines scattered around the world. Although a human is generally not amused when said to have a large back end, a Web application would take that as a huge compliment!

SUMMARY OF KEY TERMS AND CONCEPTS

Five-layer Internet model: The five layers of the Internet "protocol stack." Each layer functions independently using its own protocols but relies on services of lower layers.

Protocols: Message formats and conversation rules that are used to standardize the way computers talk to each other (that is, exchange data).

Physical Layer: The lowest layer of the protocol stack. Responsible for moving bits through circuits, wires, and cables. Protocols at this level govern things like voltage and wavelength. Data delivery is unreliable.

Network interface layer: The layer of the protocol stack that connects computers together into functioning networks. Common protocols are Ethernet and PPP. Data is divided into small packets, packet flow is regulated among computers, and data delivery and integrity (error recovery) are guaranteed.

Internetwork layer: The layer of the protocol stack that binds various network types into an internet. *The Internet* refers to the globally internetworked collection of networks, and it features the *Internetworking Protocol (IP)*, which uses IP addresses and routing. Delivery of data is not guaranteed because packets may be discarded to protect the integrity of the IP routers and underlying networks .

Transport layer: The "end-to-end" layer that forms packets on one computer, delivers packets to the interwork layer for delivery over the internet, and reassembles the packets into usable data on the destination computer. The *Transmission Control Protocol (TCP)* guarantees data delivery at this level. The *User Datagram Protocol (UDP)* does not guarantee delivery at this level. This layer and all layers below it are built into the operating systems (or hardware) of computers.

Application layer: The top layer in the protocol stack, features customized *network applications* that use the internet's infrastructure as the delivery vehicle. The protocols that operate here are created to standardize the ways various types of network applications communicate. The most common examples are *File Transfer Protocol (FTP), HyperText Transfer Protocol (HTTP), Simple Mail Transfer Protocol (SMTP),* and the *telnet protocol.* Network applications may rely on the reliable services of TCP for guaranteed delivery. Other network applications may use the unreliable services of UDP, in which case either the application doesn't care whether all the data arrives intact, or it handles data loss on its own by resending a message if a receipt acknowledgement is not received in a certain amount of time.

Socket: A connection between two computers, maintained by the transport layer for the duration of a message exchange session between two network applications. A network application can read from and write to a socket connection until it tells the transport layer to close the socket.

Ports: Virtual addresses (integers) used by the transport layer to keep track of all the network applications for which it provides service.

World Wide Web: A collection of network applications (mostly Web browsers and servers) that communicate primarily using HTTP. The WWW is implemented in the application layer. The fundamental format for the application-layer data is HTML. However, HTTP coordinates transport of other formats of application-layer data (such as graphics) necessary to create Web pages. The Internet, and network applications such as FTP and Telnet that utilize the Internet, predate the Web by some 20 years.

Web browser: A network application that calls on TCP sockets to request a server through HTTP to transfer an HTML file, and all of its embedded objects, to a client computer. Because of the keep-alive extension to HTTP, a single socket is used to transfer an HTML file and other files that are necessary to create a Web page. Web browsers also call upon UDP to make (perhaps repeated) requests for the resolution of a domain name.

Web server: A network application that listens for HTTP requests. The server software completes an HTTP request by sending all the files necessary to create a Web page to the requesting software, usually a Web browser on a remote client. Standard Web servers listen for HTTP requests on the transport layer's port 80.

Uniform Resource Locator (URL): A string that represents a client request for a resource on a server. A URL contains the application layer protocol (usually HTTP or FTP), the domain name of the server (or the IP address), and the directory path to the desired resource on the server. Additionally, a URL can contain a port number, to request a resource from a server listening on a nonstandard port, and a query string, which carries additional data from the client to the server.

Domain Name Service (DNS): An application-layer service that maps domain names (named addresses) onto IP addresses. Typically, Web browsers make UDP requests to software that resides on specialized DNS servers dedicated to resolving named addresses into IP addresses. The acronym DNS is also used loosely for "domain name servers," which can mean the computer dedicated to performing the service or even the software on that computer that performs the service.

Keep-alive: An HTTP extension feature that keeps a socket open long enough to transfer all the files necessary (HTML source, images, and so forth) to create a Web page. Thus, the HTTP keep-alive involves a transfer session at the transport layer that is responsible for completing *one* HTTP transaction.

Stateless: Not maintaining data from one event (such as an HTTP transaction) to a later event. HTTP does not coordinate multiple HTTP transactions; that is, Web browsers and standard Web server software do not pass data associated with one HTTP transaction to the next. It is the responsibility of a Web application to keep track of session data among multiple HTTP transactions if that application is to support a "surfing session."

Web application: A collection of programs and other files that uses the Web infrastructure (and thus the internet architecture indirectly) to collect data from a client, process the data on the client, server, or both; and return customized data to the client. The Web is a distributed network application that uses HTTP. A Web application is created by programming on top of the Web. JavaScript is used to program Web browsers on the front end of a Web application, which the client sees. One of several languages (Perl/CGI, ModPerl, ASP, PHP, or JSP) is used to program behind the Web server software on the back end. Without Web applications, the Web simply mobilizes and displays static information.

Common Gateway Interface (CGI): The standard way in which Web server software interacts with a program that executes on the server. Thus, a program on the back end of a Web application is often called a *gateway program,* or simply a *CGI program.* The term "gateway" refers to the way the server software passes data to the program and receives output from the program. Technically, CGI programs execute independently of the server software, but back-end technologies such as PHP and ASP, which are actually compiled into the Web server software, still feature stand-alone programs that interact with the server software through a CGI-like interface. Regardless of the technology employed on the back end of a Web application, the term *CGI programming* is sufficiently general to impart the notion of writing back-end programs for Web applications.

HTTP GET: A type of transaction primarily concerned with "getting" a resource from a Web server. A relatively small amount of data can be passed from the client to the server as a query string attached to the URL. Query string data is passed to the server in the packet header(s). A CGI program retrieves the data from the environment variables, which are global variables into which the server software temporarily stores data about a particular HTTP transaction.

HTTP POST: A type of transaction intended to transmit large amounts of data from the client to the server. In a POST transaction, the data is transported as packet payloads and is passed to a CGI program through its standard input stream.

EXERCISES

The exercises for this chapter feature research topics that expand on the concepts introduced. If the topic is partially covered in the text, don't include that information in the report. Assume that whoever reads your research would already know that information.

The amount of research should be sufficient to result in a Web page, 2 to 5 screens in length. (The length depends upon the number of supporting graphics you find on the Web.) You should document 3 to 5 Web sites upon which you base your research. Do not copy content, but make a summary based upon what you learn. If noncopyrighted supporting images or tables are found on a Web site, it is permissible to download them for use in the research report, provided that the source is well documented.

1. Research and discuss Ethernet networks: how they work, different speeds of Ethernet, and so forth. Briefly compare an Ethernet to a token ring network.
2. Research and discuss ATM wireless networks: how they work, whether there are different types, and so on.
3. Compare/contrast IP version 6 with version 4.

4. Research and discuss how secure sockets work in contrast to normal ones. What encryption/security features are in place? How does this prevent IP "spoofing"?

5. Research and discuss Simple Mail Transfer Protocol (SMTP). Include a typical SMTP header, together with an overview.

6. Compare and contrast the IMAP and POP mail client access protocols.

7. Explain hierarchical resolution with respect to domain names and routing. Provide a look at how this applies to the whole world as well as the local setting.

8. Research and discuss the protocols used in DNS resolution. Include the steps of the transaction and example headers.

9. Research and discuss the traditional seven-layer ISO networking model. Contrast with the five-layer Internet model.

10. Research and discuss the birth of NSFnet and the downfall of ARPANET.

11. Research and discuss the telnet protocol. Include the steps of a transaction and example header(s).

12. Research and discuss the FTP protocol. Include the steps of a transaction and example header(s).

13. Research and discuss the HTTP protocol. Include the steps of a transaction and show and compare headers from GET and POST HTTP transactions.

14. Contrast HEAD type HTTP transactions with GET and POST. Include the steps of HEAD transaction and example packet header(s). What kinds of network applications regularly use HEAD requests?

15. Research and discuss various phone modem speeds. How do these compare to DSL modems, cable modems, ISDN, T1, T2, and T3 connections? What are T2 and T3 lines? How fast are faster optic cables? How fast are bit rates for wireless LAN networks and satellite transmissions?

16. Research and discuss statistics on the sizes of packets that travel the backbone. What determines packet size? How do Ethernet packets compare to IP packets in size?

17. Each search engine indexes only a relatively small percentage of the Web sites on the Internet. Find statistics indicating which search engines are best and statistics giving the approximate percentages for several leading search engines. Find out what a meta-search engine is and give two examples. For each example, list the subsidiary search engines.

18. Research and discuss the transport layer's use of ports in more detail.

19. Research and discuss the history and capabilities of the Apache Web server.

20. Research and discuss the history and capabilities of the IIS web server.

PROJECT THREAD

Do at least one of the research questions above. The research will be used to construct a Web page using HTML/CSS as outlined in the project thread for Chapter 2. Carefully read the research guidelines at the beginning of the Exercises section.

CHAPTER *2*

MARKUP ON THE FRONT END

We anticipate some variance in HTML experience among readers of this book. For those who know little or nothing about HTML, Appendix A provides a thorough introduction to HTML, from the ground up. This can also serve as a refresher for those who just need to brush up on HTML a bit. For those who already have a decent understanding of HTML, the diagram of HTML element names printed inside the cover will serve as a valuable reference source when writing code.

This chapter and the rest of this text assumes familiarity with the following:

- Basic HTML syntax (tags, elements, attributes) and document structure
- Viewing local HTML files as opposed to uploading them to a server and retrieving them over the Internet
- The nature of *inline* and *block* elements
- Markup of links and images
- Deprecated HTML elements and attributes

Other topics, such as frames and logical elements, are included for completeness in the HTML introduction in Appendix A but are not used elsewhere in this book.

This chapter begins with a conceptual overview of markup languages, meant to provide perspective on XHTML and how it relates to HTML and XML. Then HTML lists and tables, which will be utilized heavily as we explore Web applications, are covered in detail using XHTML syntax. Next is a section that provides perspective on the state of HTML Web development, especially in light of the deprecated HTML elements. Finally, the essential basics of Cascading Style Sheets (CSS) are covered in detail, because use of CSS is becoming equally important as that of HTML.

2.1 WHAT IS MARKUP?

Historically, the word *markup* described annotations within a handwritten document meant to instruct a typist or compositor how the document should appear in print—how it should be *rendered*. For example, an author writing a manuscript might use a wavy underline to mark words that should be printed in boldface and might scribble font sizes and faces in the margin. The modus operandi changed with the advent of computers. Now, documents were represented electronically and rendered by computer programs. Markup instructions needed to be annotated within the electronic document.

Word processors make a fine example. Figure 2.1 shows some text written and formatted by a word processor. This particular word processor has a feature that gives you a

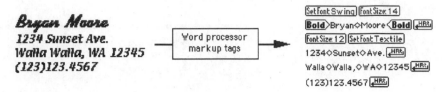

FIGURE 2.1   Typical word processor formatting.

graphical depiction of its markup tags: Font sizes and faces are specified, the name is marked for boldface, a hard return (HR) is noted each time Enter is hit on the keyboard, and spaces are marked with small diamonds. Whether you are aware of it or not, all word processors use such markup annotations behind the scenes. This particular one has a nice feature to give you a visual representation of the tags, but ultimately the word processor makes these annotations in the binary file that produces the document.

The problem with word processors is that they all use different markup schemes. If you have ever tried to transport a file between different word processors, you have seen the evidence. You may lose the integrity of formatting information (markup instructions) if you move a document even to the same word processor on a different operating system. The files created by word processors are sometimes called "binary blobs" whose structure is application- and platform-specific. There is simply no standard for what bytes represent in binary files created by word processors. Sure, each one comes with translators (a dozen or more perhaps) that might be able to transform a given blob from some other processor into one using its own markup scheme, but some formatting information is almost always lost. For the casual user who just makes a few documents, this is not really a big deal. (As long as it looks nice, give it to the boss.) Word processors are a type of "What You See Is What You Get" (WYSIWYG) editor. Indeed, for many purposes, people care what they see, not how blobbish or proprietary the underlying binary file might be.

During the 1970s and 1980s, scientists at IBM gradually developed *Standard Generalized Markup Language (SGML),* with which markup instructions are stored with the text to which they apply in plain text files (ASCII files[1]). That way, anyone with an ordinary text editor could encode an electronic document with markup instructions. Because ASCII is a common denominator for passing data among computers, any computer application (on any platform) programmed to understand SGML could render the document. Because of SGML's versatility and portability, many huge document collections based on this language have been developed. Consider the documentation a company like Boeing must keep in order to provide maintenance support for the thousands of airplanes it has built over the years, or the archived log files of a nuclear power plant that has been operating for 25 years. Some of these SGML "legacy systems" contain several million documents.

Tim Berners-Lee realized that the World Wide Web he was creating needed electronic files that were portable across all platforms and applications, so he created HTML

---

[1]Unicode, which is still evolving, is the ISO (International Organization for Standardization) standardization for digital character storage formats. UTF- 8 (Unicode Transformation Format-8) is an eight-bit Unicode standard that is backward compatible with ASCII (American Standard Code for Information Interchange). Technically, the new Web protocols specify UTF-8, whereas older protocols use ASCII encoding.

```
<FONT SIZE=14 FACE=Swing>
<B>Bryan Moore</B><BR>
</FONT>
<FONT SIZE=12 FACE=Textile>
1234 Sunset Ave.<BR>
Walla Walla, WA 12345<BR>
(123)123.4567<BR>
</FONT>
```

FIGURE 2.2 HTML code to produce the same rendition as in Figure 2.1.

using a very simplified subset of SGML. Consider the HTML markup code in Figure 2.2, which produces the same effect as that of the word processor in Figure 2.1. This code contains basically the same markup tags as the word processor version (FONT to control font size and face, B for bold, and BR for line breaks). However, this code is representable in an electronic file in which each byte is an ASCII character. The file containing the markup instructions is no longer a platform- or application-specific binary blob.

With portable files, all that you need is server software to send them around the world and client software to render the documents. Having the Web servers and browsers at its disposal, the world started churning out HTML files. HTML is a quite simple language and contains a relatively small number of markup tags. Virtually anyone who was computer literate could learn a few markup instructions and whip up some HTML files. The legacy of Berners-Lee's simplification of SGML is a Web of billions of pages—that's staggering.

Of course, not everyone wants to sit and type large volumes of HTML code. Although HTML is easy to understand and create in small volumes, hand-coding large amounts of HTML is cumbersome, to say the least. Many WYSIWYG HTML editors have been developed over the years. The most popular commercial-grade editors are currently Microsoft's FrontPage and Macromedia's Dreamweaver, but there are numerous freeware and shareware editors. WYSIWYG HTML editors are little more than word processors that spit out HTML files rather than binary blobs. They have enabled office assistants and hobbyists, with little or no knowledge of HTML, to churn out Web pages in huge volume. These editors are a major contributor to the size of the Web. However, this expansion has come at a price, as we shall see.

A shortcoming of HTML is that it specifies how to render a document, but it does not specify what is in the document. To understand what that means, you need to understand how a Web browser sees a document. For example, the browser does not see the block of HTML code in Figure 2.2 as you would in the HTML file. Instead, it parses the code into a *tree* so that its rendering algorithms have a data structure to work with. Figure 2.3 shows a *parse tree* for the block of HTML code shown in Figure 2.2. As you can see, it contains only markup instructions and some strings of text.

Suppose you have an HTML document that contains an address listing consisting of several hundred of these address blocks. The parse tree is then a huge structure composed of FONT, B, and BR instructions with text strings mixed in. The meaningfulness of the content is obscured. That is just fine if all you wish to do with the address listing is to put it on a Web server so that people can pull it up and look at it in their browsers. Indeed, HTML is the perfect solution for a Web where the only objective is to produce information for people to see.

To emphasize how meaningless the data is, suppose you wish to extract a master list of names and phone numbers from the file. Short of doing it by hand, you would write a computer program to read through the file, grabbing the text string from the first FONT

```
┌─ FONT [SIZE=14 FACE=Swing ]
│   ├─ B
│   │   └─ text string
│   └─ BR
│
└─ FONT [SIZE=12 FACE=Textile ]
    ├─ text string
    ├─ BR
    ├─ text string
    ├─ BR
    ├─ text string
    └─ BR
```

FIGURE 2.3 A parse tree for the HTML code in Figure 2.2

block and the text string following the second BR in the second FONT block. Suppose there are other similar FONT declarations in the document—headings to separate the address into categories, for example. You would then have to be careful to avoid those declarations by treating the addresses as FONT pairs and so forth. When you have to talk about data in those terms, it is not structured in a useful way. HTML creates a Web of markup instructions, meaningful only to Web browsers, in which some text is scattered.

The first thing the WWW Consortium (W3C) did to address HTML's limitations was to recommend an HTML model in which content and style are separated to some extent; that is, what's in the document is kept separate from instructions on how to render it. To store the rendering instructions, *style sheets* were introduced as part of the **Cascading Style Sheet (CSS)** recommendation. So that you can get a feeling for how CSS works, Figure 2.4 shows the HTML-coded address of Figure 2.2 redone using style definitions.

One advantage of using separate style rules is flexibility. Again, suppose you have several hundred addresses in a file. Suppose you wish to change all the names to a different font face, Verdana for example. In the straight HTML example, you have to change all instances of the font face declaration. Using CSS, you would only have to change the one style declaration for the name class. That one change handles the switch for the hundreds of names in the file in one fell swoop. Keeping style separate from content gives you flexibility and pinpoint control.

Another advantage is that a style sheet can be kept in a separate file called an *external style sheet*. You can make a text file containing the style declarations that you use frequently.

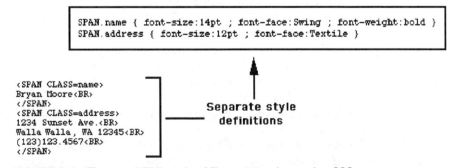

FIGURE 2.4 The pure HTML code of Figure 2.2 redone using CSS.

You can then reference that style file from any number of HTML files, effectively importing one set of style definitions into multiple documents. In that way, one set of style declarations can be used for a whole collection of Web pages. You then have a method to provide uniformity among large document collections.

One disadvantage to the CSS/HTML model is that it increases the complexity of creating Web pages. Now a Web site builder has to understand HTML syntax, CSS syntax, and how the two interact. Remember, the explosion of the Web was in large part due to the simplicity of HTML. Web programmers (that's you) will not be overly taxed by the increased demands, but WYISWYG editors will simplify large-scale document production for the masses. Most newer editors have CSS capabilities. With these, you can point and click your way to define a few style classes. Then you simply highlight a block of text and choose from the menu of styles you have created. Change a style class definition, and you update all instances of the class in the document. Again, the flexibility of keeping style separate from content is manifested.

With WYSIWYG editors and programmers on the scene, what we termed a disadvantage of CSS is little more than a trade-off—a little more complexity for a lot more flexibility. However, the HTML/CSS model still has the same shortcoming as straight HTML: The data is not really meaningful. You can see in Figure 2.5 that the parse tree for the HTML/CSS version is more concise than that for the pure HTML version. The missing complexity has been absorbed by the style rules. Through the use of descriptive style class names, the CSS version looks a little better as a data structure. For example, you could easily write a computer program to read through a file containing lots of these and extract all of the names for a master list. But the components of the address are still ambiguous. Referencing the phone number still involves talking about "the text string after the second BR in the address block." You could name a style class for each address component, but that would be redundant, since each component is to receive the same formatting. Besides, that would abuse the purpose of the CSS/HTML model. Style sheets do keep style somewhat separate from content, but they are not the solution for giving meaningfulness to information that you pass around the Web.

Drawing more upon the capabilities and power of SGML, the W3C issued standards for the **eXtensible Markup Language (XML)**, which is used to represent data rather than to specify how data should be displayed. The language is called *extensible* because you can make up your own tags, thereby *extending* the language to suit any data representation need. We coded the address example in pure XML in Figure 2.6, using tags that we completely made up for our purpose. In both preceding versions of the address, all of the

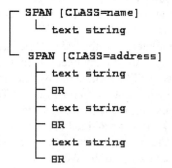

```
┌─ SPAN [CLASS=name]
│    └ text string
│
└─ SPAN [CLASS=address]
     ├ text string
     ├ BR
     ├ text string
     ├ BR
     ├ text string
     └ BR
```

FIGURE 2.5 A parse tree for the CSS-formatted address of Figure 2.4.

```
<address id="101">
  <name>Bryan Moore</name>
  <street>1234 Sunset Ave.</street>
  <city>Walla Walla</city>
  <state>WA</state>
  <zip>12345</zip>
  <phone>(123)123.4567</phone>
</address>
```

```
address [id="101"]
  ├── name
  │     └── text string
  ├── street
  │     └── text string
  ├── city
  │     └── text string
  ├── state
  │     └── text string
  ├── zip
  │     └── text string
  └── phone
        └── text string
```

FIGURE 2.6 The address coded in pure XML and the corresponding parse tree.

markup instructions were part of the HTML/CSS language specifications, but we *invented* the XML tags in Figure 2.6. XML is basically a language that specifies how you can create your own markup language!

CSS provides for a partial separation of content and style geared toward flexibility, but XML features a complete separation. Do you see any formatting markup instructions in the XML code in Figure 2.6? In order to make the address look fancy in a Web browser, you would use CSS or other mechanisms that we will introduce later in this book. Since those formatting mechanisms are a bit more complicated in this case, we have not provided any style rules for the XML-coded address. You now understand the basic principle of separate styles, and that's all we need to emphasize here. You can define some styles that a browser can apply when it marks up the address components.

The new concept here is that the address and its parts are now meaningful data for the Web. Simply put, XML is needed because the Web needs to be infused with meaningful information. The Web is no longer a place for hobbyists to post home pages. It's a global business platform—*e-business* or *e-commerce*, as the new terms go. You can imagine the variety of software currently used by businesses and organizations. There is the back-end database software, data entry software, software to automate billing and yet more software to automate shipping and tracking. Did we mention accounting and human resources? All of this software needs to mark up information for the employees and customers to see, but the different programs also need to share information. At some point one of the applications spits out a binary blob that another application can't use, and someone has to reenter data by hand.

The XML solution lets styles be created to suit specific applications (such as browsers) while data structures are provided in completely portable ASCII files. XML's extensibility ensures that data structures can be developed to suit any needs. Consider the parse tree for the XML version of the address. Without the XML context of this discussion, a programmer might say "cool, an object! . . . What do you want me to do with it?" That's getting ahead of ourselves, but you can certainly imagine writing a program to iterate over the addresses to extract the names and phone numbers. XML has provided the well-defined data structures that can easily be manipulated by software or programming languages. Figure 2.7 shows some of the versatility that meaningful data gives to the Web.

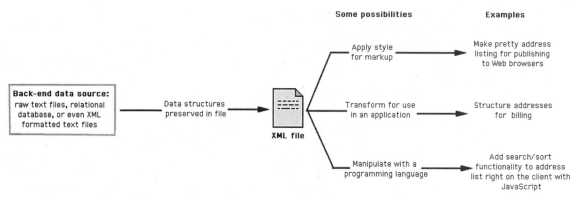

FIGURE 2.7   The versatility that meaningful data brings to the Web.

As more applications move to XML for document content, we will see a Web where information is exchanged seamlessly between computer programs without human involvement. Software can pass it around because it's ASCII; software can apply styles to it for presentation; software can transform it into other logical formats because it's structured data; and humans can easily manipulate it by writing a computer program. Perhaps Charles Goldfarb, the primary inventor of SGML, said it best (if Berners-Lee is the father of the Web, Goldfarb is its grandfather).

> *The accounting system must be integrated with inventory. Inventory must be integrated with delivery systems. Deliveries must be integrated with billing, which is part of accounting and so forth. The thigh bone's connected to the leg bone, the leg bone's connected to the ankle bone . . . XML is today's choice for the cartilage between the bones in your organizational skeleton.*

Goldfarb was commenting on the potential of XML to glue the disparate software applications of an individual organization together into a functioning skeleton—something that binary blobs or HTML can't do. But the same holds true for information interchange between e-businesses on the Web.

XML is definitely not for the hobbyist. You're not going to see people posting XML documents on the Web so that their grandmother can transform the data for her needs. Even people who design pretty front ends for Web sites (or Web applications) will stick to HTML/CSS. XML is for you, the aspiring Web programmer. But let's not get ahead of ourselves. There is a lot to learn before you get that far. The introduction to markup languages in this section provides a valuable frame of reference for the discussion of XHTML and CSS that is to follow.

2.2   XHTML AND THE SAGA OF HTML

In 1995 the Web was starting to explode. That year Berners-Lee drafted the HTML 2.0 standard, while other W3C colleagues simultaneously drafted the HTML 3.0 specification, hoping to expand the capabilities of the language significantly. Neither language specification had much impact since Netscape Navigator dominated the Web. If it worked in Netscape, it was good HTML.

Early in 1997 the W3C drafted the HTML 3.2 standard, incorporating many of Netscape's additions. This was a boon for Microsoft's Internet Explorer (remember, it didn't come out until 1996), because it could claim to be "HTML 3.2 compliant" rather than "Netscape Navigator compliant." The Web was moving fast. Later in 1997, the W3C released the HTML 4.0 specification. Although a few minor changes have been made (that is, version 4.01) HTML 4 is what we know of as HTML today. It still contains some of the useful HTML language features developed for use in Netscape by Andreessen and company. Also, HTML 4 standardizes support for CSS.

In 1998 the W3C released the XML 1.0 specification. (As explained in Section 2.1, the Web needs meaningful information.) XML 1.0 has since undergone a couple of revisions (without version change, at least at the time of this writing), and the standard is fairly well entrenched. Although Netscape 6 and Internet Explorer 5 incorporate XML processors, they are a long way off from being able to create the same type of user interface that the HTML processor can. For example, XML processors in browsers currently don't deal with form elements or even images. Older browsers don't even deal with XML at all. Nonetheless, XML is the solution for ubiquitous[2] data on the Web.

XML will not evolve to replace HTML—that is not the purpose of XML—but the two need to coexist. The solution is the eXtensible HyperText Markup Language (XHTML). The XHTML 1.0 specification was released by the W3C in 2000 and was upgraded to XHTML 1.1 in 2001. XHTML is HTML, but with more rigorous syntax rules. Figure 2.8 lists the six key XHTML syntax rules.

- XHTML inherits all of the elements and attributes from HTML. Moreover, an XHTML document must posses the same basic structure as an HTML document. (See Figure 1 in Appendix A.) In particular, exactly one `title` element must appear in the `head` element.
- If an element does not have a closing tag, it must be marked as an empty element `<elementname />`. Of course, attributes can be added after the element name. A space should be left before the `/`. Note that `<elementname />` is equivalent to `<elementname></elementname>` when an element has no content.
- There are no optional end tags. That is, if the element is not empty, it *has* to have a closing tag. Pure HTML allows things like a stand-alone `<p>` tag with no closing `</p>` tag. (Browsers just interpret that as two line breaks.) That is an XHTML no-no.
- All XHTML elements and attribute names must be in lowercase. No exceptions.
- All attribute values must be contained within single or double quotation marks:

  `attribute="value" or attribute='value'.`

- Every attribute must have a value. For example, HTML allows things like

  `<hr noshade>`

  which produces a horizontal rule whose pixels are not shaded. In XHTML, the attribute must be given a value

  `<hr noshade="noshade">`

  even though the value seems unnecessary.

FIGURE 2.8 XHTML syntax rules.

---

[2]In standard definitions, ubiquitous means "omnipresent—everywhere at once," but in computer parlance, *ubiquitous* means "usable by any platform or application."

You have no doubt violated some of the XHTML syntax rules in the past, whether you have hard-coded HTML or generated it with a WYSIWYG editor. Refer back to the pure HTML and the HTML/CSS code snippets in Figures 2.2 and 2.4, respectively. There you see capitalized tag and attribute names, attribute values without quotation marks, and empty b r elements not marked as such. However, you should note that the XML code in Figure 2.6 is XHTML compliant. Well, it had better be! *Specifically, XHTML is HTML that has been made to be syntactically XML compliant.* Here are the reasons why that compliance is important.

- XHTML can be sent to a Web browser just like ordinary HTML.

- Being syntactically XML compliant, XHTML documents can be validated and processed by the powerful software that has been developed for XML data manipulation and exchange.

- A future objective of XHTML is to become extensible, meaning that it will be able to contain portions of meaningful XML data. Internet Explorer has already introduced its proprietary answer to that in the form of XML "data islands" that can be embedded into XHTML documents.

Again, raw XML is not intended as a replacement for HTML on the Web. XHTML is to let Web programmers (that's your aspiration) use some of the power of XML, while leaving them with all the fancy stuff HTML can do on the front end of a Web application. You will see evidence of that power in Chapter 17.

NOTE

Other than the examples in Section 2.1 meant for contrast, we exclusively feature XHTML code in this book. It's not as if you will have to "switch over to" XHTML at this point. Just write HTML as you are accustomed, but adhering to the XHTML syntax requirements. As you progress through this book, that will become a reflex that doesn't require extra thought. In fact, we will refer to the code simply as HTML, which it is. Rarely will we have to make a distinction between HTML and XHTML. When you progress to the XML portion of this book, the distinction will become much more important.

2.3   HTML LISTS

There are three kinds of HTML list structures: *ordered, unordered,* and *description* lists. We begin with ordered and unordered lists. Table 2.1 shows summaries of the o l (ordered list), u l (unordered list), and l i (list item) elements. These elements enable information to be marked up in a structured way.

Figure 2.9 provides an example using ordered lists. The o l element defines the list, and each item in the list is defined with an l i element. You can see that the main list starts out numbering the list items sequentially with the default of integers starting with 1. If you don't nest lists, you get a structure resembling the first three list items. To nest a list (create a sublist), you simply put another list inside a list item. The first sublist uses the t y p e

TABLE 2.1   HTML Elements for Ordered and Unordered Lists

`<ol >...</ol>` Ordered list (block element)

ATTRIBUTE	POSSIBLE VALUES	DEFAULT
`start`	integer	1
`type`	`1, A, a, I, i`	1

`<ul >...</ul>` Ordered list (block element)

ATTRIBUTE	POSSIBLE VALUES	DEFAULT
`type`	`disc, circle, square`	`disc`

`<li >...</li>` List Item (block element)

ATTRIBUTE	POSSIBLE VALUES	DEFAULT
`type`	`1, A, a, I, i` (in `ol`)	Inherited from `ol`
	`disc, circle, square` (in `ul`)	Inherited from `ul`

* Used only inside `ol` or `ul`

attribute to override the default of numbering with integers. In this case, we specified lowercase Roman numerals, but we could have set `type="I"` to specify uppercase ones.

The second nested list specifies sequencing using uppercase letters and instructs the sequencing to `start` with the seventh letter. The `start` attribute can override the default and cause any of the sequencing options (integers, upper/lowercase Roman numerals, upper/lowercase letters) to begin numbering at a desired location. Finally, as shown in the second nested list, you can change the sequencing characters at a specific location in a list by changing the `type` inside a `li` tag. The characters change, but the sequence numbering is unaffected.

Figure 2.10 provides an example using unordered lists. These are *bullet lists,* and you can see from the main list that the default bullet is `type="disc"`. Again, you nest lists by placing a new list inside a list item. In this example, we have triple-nested the lists.

```
<ol>                                    1. list item
   <li>list item</li>                   2. list item
   <li>list item</li>                   3. list item
   <li>list item                             i. sublist item
                                             ii. sublist item
    <ol type="i">                       4. list item
       <li>sublist item</li>                G. sublist item
       <li>sublist item</li>                H. sublist item
    </ol>                                    i. sublist item
                                             j. sublist item
   </li>
   <li> list item

    <ol type="A" start="7">
       <li>sublist item</li>
       <li>sublist item</li>
       <li type="a">sublist item</li>
       <li>sublist item</li>
    </ol>

   </li>
</ol>
```

FIGURE 2.9   Ordered list example.

```
 ┌ <ul>                                 • list item
 │    <li>list item</li>                • list item
 │    <li>list item</li>                • list item
 │    <li>list item                          ○ sublist item
 │    ┌ <ul>                                 ○ sublist item
 │    │    <li>sublist item</li>                   ■ subsublist item
 │    │    <li>sublist item                        ■ subsublist item
 │    │    ┌ <ul>                             ○ sublist item
 │    │    │    <li>subsublist item</li>
 │    │    │    <li>subsublist item</li>
 │    │    └ </ul>
 │    │
 │    │    </li>
 │    │    <li>sublist item</li>
 │    └ </ul>
 │
 │    </li>
 └ </ul>
```

FIGURE 2.10   Unordered list example.

Browsers typically change the bullet `type` automatically at each nesting level to provide contrast. You can override the default at any level by specifying a different bullet `type` attribute for the whole list in the `ol` start tag. You can also change the bullet type of individual list items by using the `type` attribute in the `li` start tag. We chose to stick with the defaults to show what browsers do automatically. Note that different browsers may render bullets slightly differently.

We now turn to description lists. The `dl` (description list), `dt` (description title), and `dd` (description data) elements are summarized in Table 2.2.

Figure 2.11 gives examples of compact and noncompact description lists. The first one overrides the default and produces a compact list, where the description data is rendered on the same lines as the titles. Note that in both examples the titles will be rendered on the left margin of the Web page. The second list does not specify `compact`. In that case, descriptions are moved to a new line. Logically, the `dt` and `dd` elements are meant to come in pairs, but, as you can see in the second example, that is not required. Description lists are handy when you want to indent some lines of text but don't want the monospace font that the `pre` element gives. In that case, you wouldn't use any `title` elements. Also, description lists can be nested to create all kinds of different levels of indentation.

TABLE 2.2   HTML Elements for Ordered and Unordered Lists

`<dl >…</dl>`   Description list (block element)

ATTRIBUTE	POSSIBLE VALUES	DEFAULT
compact	compact="compact"	Not compact

ELEMENT	DESCRIPTION
<dt>...</dt>	Title for description, rendered on left margin
<dd>...</dd>	Data for description, typically rendered on a new line and indented (typically rendered on same line in a `compact` list)

* The `dt` and `dd` elements are used **only** inside the `dl` element.

```
<dl compact="compact">
  <dt>title</dt>
  <dd>description</dd>
  <dt>title</dt>
  <dd>description</dd>
  <dt>title</dt>
  <dd>description</dd>
</dl>
```

title   description
title   description
title   description

```
<dl>
  <dt>title</dt>
  <dd>description</dd>
  <dt>title</dt>
  <dd>description</dd>
  <dd>more description</dd>
</dl>
```

title

description

title

description
more description

FIGURE 2.11 Description lists.

Here are some things to note about HTML lists in general.

- The three list types can be mixed together in a nesting scheme. For example, your main list can be ordered, while its sublists are unordered.

- In order to produce a compact effect in an ordered or unordered list, simply set the font size for all the text in the list to be smaller. You can do this using the deprecated font element or by using CSS as seen in Section 2.6. We will discuss those possibilities below.

- We have been using both ordered and unordered lists regularly in the print of this book. Indeed, this note is the third list item in a bullet list. There is no telling how our word processor annotates the lists in the binary blobs it creates. But in HTML you can see the importance of the nested element structure, and how that carries over into the rendition of the list in the browser. Even though the information is nicely organized in the Web page, the browser's parse tree is a big mess of markup instructions and some text. Here is a parse tree for the HTML code of Figure 2.10.

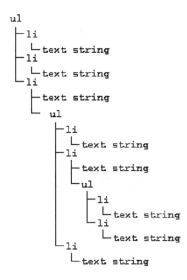

It is important that we reemphasize that proper nesting containment makes the parse tree well defined and also that HTML has the shortcoming of not representing data in a meaningful way. HTML is meaningful only for the rendering algorithms of an HTML processor.

2.4 HTML TABLES

HTML tables provide much greater flexibility for information formatting than do HTML lists. Summaries of the elements used to build tables are provided in Table 2.3. The primary elements are `table`, `tr` (table row), and `td` (table data).

We begin by showing how all these elements work together to build a table. Figure 2.12 shows a simple table. Within the `table` element, each `tr` defines a row of the table. There is no corresponding tag for columns. Rather, each column is created by a `td` element whose content is the data for that *table cell*. As you can see, the browser has rendered the table in such a fashion as to make the table cells the minimum size necessary to accommodate the data.

By default, the width of a "column" is set by the widest cell in that column and the height of a row by the tallest cell in that row. In the lower right cell, you can observe that the default for alignment of data within table cells is `align="left"` and `valign="middle"`. We did not specify any alignment in that table, so the defaults are evident. If we had not specified a two-pixel table border in Figure 2.12, the default of a borderless table would have produced the following.

```
table cell... table cell
table cell    table cell.......
table
cell          table cell
```

Figure 2.13 explores several of the other attributes. First, `width` and `height` have been set in the `table` element to override the "minimal dimensions" default. The first table further specifies `width` and `height` in the `td` elements to resize individual cells. Again, you can see that rows and columns are sized according to the largest cell in the row or column. The cells in the second table are equally sized since no specific sizes have been imposed at the `td` level.

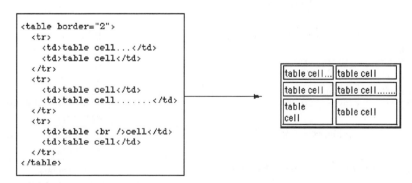

FIGURE 2.12 Basic table structure

TABLE 2.3   HTML Elements for Tables

`<table >…</table>`   Table definition (block element)

ATTRIBUTE	POSSIBLE VALUES	DEFAULT
`align`	`left`, `center`, `right`	Left with text not flowing around table. Use of this attribute causes text to flow around table.
`background` (background image)	`URL` (relative or absolute)	
`bgcolor` (background color)	*#hexcolor*, named color	Inherited from `bgcolor` of underlying Web page
`border`	Pixels	0
`cellpadding`	Pixels	Browser-dependent (about 1)
`cellspacing`	Pixels	Browser-dependent (about 2)
`height`	Pixels, percent	Minimum to accommodate table contents
`width`	Pixels, percent	Minimum to accommodate table contents

`<tr >…</tr>`   Table row (used only in `table` element)

ATTRIBUTE	POSSIBLE VALUES	DEFAULT
Uses the `align`, `valign`, and `bgcolor` attributes in the same capactiy as the `td` element does. When used in `tr`, they set properties of all cells in the row. We will set cell properties at the `td` (cell) level in this book.		

`<td >…</td>`   Table data cell (used only in inside `tr` element)*

ATTRIBUTE	POSSIBLE VALUES	DEFAULT
`align` (horizontal alignment of cell contents	`left`, `center`, `right`	`left`
`valign` (vertical alignment of cell contents)	`top`, `middle`, `bottom`	`middle`
`background` (background image)	`URL` (relative or absolute)	
`bgcolor` (background color)	*#hexcolor*, named color	Inherited from `bgcolor` of table containing the cell
`colspan`	Pixels	0
`rowspan`	Pixels	0
`height`	Pixels, percent	Minimum to accommodate cell contents
`width`	Pixels, percent	Minimum to accommodate cell contents

* `<th >...</th>` (table heading cell) element takes the exact same attributes as `td`. In heading cells, text is centered and boldface by default.

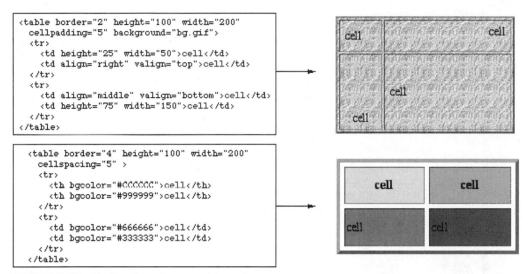

```
<table border="2" height="100" width="200"
   cellpadding="5" background="bg.gif">
   <tr>
      <td height="25" width="50">cell</td>
      <td align="right" valign="top">cell</td>
   </tr>
   <tr>
      <td align="middle" valign="bottom">cell</td>
      <td height="75" width="150">cell</td>
   </tr>
</table>
```

```
<table border="4" height="100" width="200"
   cellspacing="5" >
   <tr>
      <th bgcolor="#CCCCCC">cell</th>
      <th bgcolor="#999999">cell</th>
   </tr>
   <tr>
      <td bgcolor="#666666">cell</td>
      <td bgcolor="#333333">cell</td>
   </tr>
</table>
```

FIGURE 2.13   Exploration of some table attributes.

The two tables in Figure 2.13 contrast cellpadding and cellspacing. The padding in the first table has created a five-pixel cushion on the interiors of the cell walls. The spacing in the second table has created a five-pixel space between cells. In general, cellpadding is the more useful of the two, because it keeps the cell contents from being rendered right up against the cell walls, whereas space between cells tends to break up the table. The first table specifies a background image for the whole table, and the second specifies a different bgcolor for each table cell.

The second table uses th (heading cells) for its first row. The heading cells work just like ordinary td cells, but they automatically center cell contents and render any text in the cell in boldface. In some of the regular td cells in the first table, we used align and valign to move the cell contents around manually. Finally, we got slightly different effects when we changd border sizes.

As the Web has grown, the utility of tables has far outstripped the original intentions. Nearly every commercial Web site uses tables to set the layout of whole pages. This effect is accomplished by creating a borderless table that fills up the whole page. The entire informational content of the Web page is then placed inside the cells of the table. In other words, there is nothing in the Web page that is not inside the page-filling borderless table that creates the layout for the page, Figure 2.14 contains the source code for a simple example of such a page, and Figure 2.15 shows its rendition.

There are a few things to note about Figures 2.14 and 2.15. The main borderless table that lays out the page has only one row (one tr) and two columns (two td). The table has been set to cover 100% of the browser window. Its first cell is colored and contains a list of links. Such a cell is commonly called a *navigation bar*. The second cell contains the rest of the body of the Web page.

It is important that valign="top" has been set in both of the cells of the main table so that the links and page body appear at the top of the respective cells, hence at the top of the Web page. Also, cellpadding has been set to 10 for the whole table. Otherwise, the links would be right up against the left of the browser window and the text in the second cell would be right up against the navigation bar. The second cell contains another table, nested inside the primary table, as well as the rest of the main content of the Web page. This small table has been set to align="right" to cause the text to flow around it.

The only attributes listed in the element summaries in Table 2.3 that we have not used are colspan and rowspan. These attributes are used in the td element to cause cells to span

```
                              📄 moesplace.html
<html>
  <head>
    <title>Moe's Homepage</title>
  </head>
  <body link="#FFFFFF" vlink="#FFFF99">
    <table border="0" cellspacing="0" cellpadding="10" width="100%" height="100%">
      <tr>
        <td valign="top" width="125" bgcolor="#666666">
          <a href="http://krusty.com">KrustyLand</a>
          <br />
          <a href="http://itchscratch.com">The Itchy and Scratchy Zone</a>
          <br />
          <a href="http://bob.com">Sideshow Bob's Basement</a>
          <br />
          <a href="http://willie.com">Groundskeeper Willie's Workshop</a>
          <br />
        </td>
        <td valign="top" bgcolor="#FFFFFF">

          <table border="1" bgcolor="#999999" cellpadding="2" align="right">
            <tr>
              <td height="37"width="37" bgcolor="#FFFFFF">
                <img src="world.gif" width="33" height="33"  />
              </td>
              <td>
                Welcome to <br /> Moe's World!
              </td>
            </tr>
          </table>

          Feel free to click on one of my favorite links to the left or stick around
          and see what I have to say.
          <p>Blagh</p><p>Blagh</p><p>Blagh</p><p>Blagh</p><p>Blagh</p><p>Blagh</p>
        </td>
      </tr>
    </table>
  </body>
</html>
```

FIGURE 2.14 Source file for a table layout that formats a whole page.

other cells. (If you have ever used spreadsheet software, this is similar to merging cells.) Figure 2.16 provides a simple illustration. To construct that table, we started with a four-row, three-column table. We then imposed the following spanning (or merging) actions on the table.

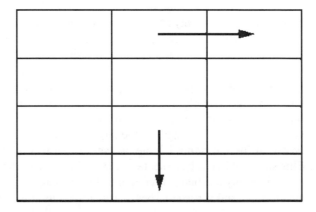

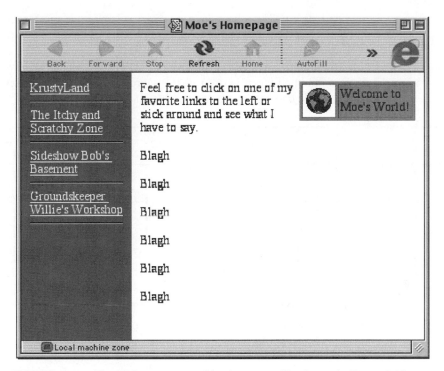

FIGURE 2.15 The Web page created by the source file shown in Figure 2.14.

```
<table border="2">
  <tr>
    <td></td>
    <td colspan="2"></td>
  </tr>
  <tr>
    <td></td>
    <td></td>
    <td></td>
  </tr>
  <tr>
    <td></td>
    <td rowspan="2"></td>
    <td></td>
  </tr>
  <tr>
    <td></td>
    <td></td>
  </tr>
</table>
```

FIGURE 2.16 Spanning table rows and columns.

Spanning in tables is always applied to the right and down. With `colspan="2"` in the second cell in the first row, that cell merges with the cell to its right. Thus, there is no `td` element in Figure 2.16 for the third cell of the first row. The second row is normal with three cells. The second cell in the third row specifies `rowspan="2"`, which merges that cell with the one below it. Thus there are only two td elements in the fourth row. The middle one has been "absorbed" by the spanning action of the cell above it.

The final example of this section puts spanning to use to create a structured border-less table layout for a whole page, somewhat more elaborate than we have yet seen. Figure 2.17 gives a slimmed-down version of the source code, and Figure 2.18 shows the full Web page. Here is how the layout was produced:

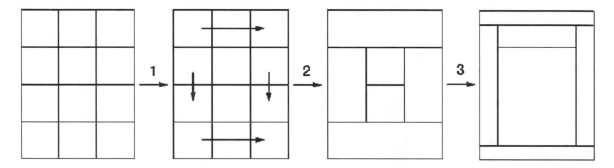

0. Start with 4-by-3 table.

1. Figure out what spanning is necessary to create the desired effect.

2. Insert the colspan and rowspan attributes, deleting the td elements (table cells) that are absorbed.

3. Resize the table cells using height and width in the td elements.

The rows in Figure 2.17 have been marked for your benefit. You can notice that the first row has only one td element, because that cell spans all three columns. The second row has three td elements. The fourth row has only one, its first and third td elements were absorbed by the rowspan of the first and third cells in the second row. Finally, the fourth row only has one td element because that cell again spans all three columns.

Here are some things to note about using tables in Web pages:

■ The align attribute is used in two different contexts. When used in the table element, it aligns the whole table and causes text to flow around the table. When used in the td element, it controls the horizontal alignment of the stuff within that cell. The valign attribute handles vertical alignment within cells.

■ Some browsers will not render a table cell that has no content. This is a factor when you are designing and testing a table layout and you have not yet added content to some cells or if you are using an empty, colored table cell to create a stripe in a page. To ensure that empty table cells are rendered, place the character code   in the table cell. That is an escape code for a blank space. A list of all HTML character codes is supplied on the Web site.

■ Browsers are somewhat less than reliable about sizing table cells properly. Especially when a table is used for page layout, it helps to specify the exact dimensions of each cell. You can see that in Figure 2.17. Note that the sum of the widths of the cells in each row is equal to the width of the entire table as specified in the table element.

```
                        ═══════ 📄 sports.html ═══════

<html>
  <head>
    <title>SPORTS</title>
  </head>
  <body link="#000066" vlink="#660066">
    <table border="0" cellspacing="0" cellpadding="5" width="600">
    ┌─<tr>
    │     <td colspan="3" width="600" height="40" bgcolor="#333333" align="center">
    │     KNUCKLES' SPORTS WORLD
    │     </td>
    └─</tr>

    ┌─<tr>
    │     <td rowspan="2" width="100" bgcolor="#999999" valign="top">
    │       Available Pages
    │     </td>

    │     <td width="400" height="40" bgcolor="#666666">
    │       Pro Football
    │     </td>

    │     <td rowspan="2" width="100" bgcolor="#999999" valign="top">
    │       This Week
    │     </td>
    └─</tr>

    ┌─<tr>
    │     <td width="400" bgcolor="#FFFFFF" valign="top">
    │       Game of the Week
    │     </td>
    └─</tr>

    ┌─<tr>
    │     <td colspan="3" width="600" height="75" bgcolor="#333333">
    │       Weekly Trivia Question
    │     </td>
    └─</tr>
    </table>
  </body>
</html>
```

FIGURE 2.17   Partial source file for a borderless table page layout.

▦ If you pull up the source code for Moe's Place (Figure 2.14) or Knuckles' Sports World (Figure 2.18) on the Web site, you will notice that the tables are not flush against the top and right margins of the browser windows as they are shown in the figures. Netscape and Internet Explorer have different ways to make that happen. For Internet Explorer put `leftmargin="0"` and `topmargin="0"` in the `body` element. For Netscape put `marginheight="0"` and `marginwidth="0"` in the `body` element. It's a bummer when you have to make special proprietary considerations, but at least this is not as much hassle as full-blown browser sniffing!

NOTE

Figure 2.14 uses a table whose width is 100 percent of the browser window width. Figure 2.18 uses a table whose width is fixed at 600 pixels. You can pull up the source files for each on the Web site and see for yourself by resizing the windows a few times. Most major Web sites use fixed-width pages in the neighborhood of 600 pixels wide. One reason for that involves the resolution of computer monitors. There is a link on the Web site that discusses that issue in some detail. Another reason involves printing. If you keep the content of your pages at around 600 pixels in width, they will not be too wide to print nicely on standard 8.5 by 11 paper.

2.5 THE STATE OF THE WEB ADDRESS

In this section we will focus on how things are done on the Web, what language features are used, and what that likely means for the future. We turn first to "how things are done," by which we mean how is it that there are billions of Web pages, with millions added daily. We break Web development into four categories: casual Web publishing, advanced Web design, beginning Web programming, and advanced Web programming.

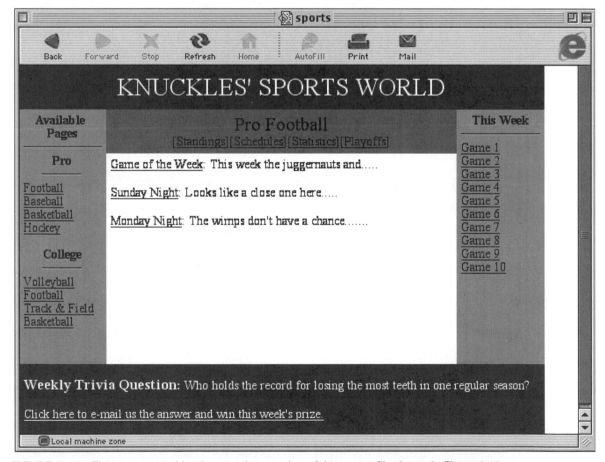

FIGURE 2.18   The page created by the complete version of the source file shown in Figure 2.17.

- *Casual Web publishing* involves putting a few Web pages onto the Web in the form of a small personal site, a site for a small business, or a project on cell mitosis for a biology professor. Typically such Web pages are generated with whatever WYSIWYG HTML editor is available. This is little more than word processing for the Web.

- *Advanced Web design* involves making high-quality Web sites for businesses or organizations. The first thing that needs to be done is to design an aesthetically pleasing front end. Often, this is done by a professional graphic artist, who makes a digital picture of the page, leaving open areas where the content is to go. The graphic artist gives the digital picture to an experienced Web designer, who chops the graphic into small GIFs and assembles an HTML version of the page, usually with a WYSIWYG HTML editor. The Web designer probably knows enough HTML to tweak the source code when the WYSIWYG steps on his or her foot. Also, the Web designer has probably learned enough about the WYSIWYG to have it generate some JavaScript code to provide some fancy DHTML effects, for example.

  The HTML template for the front end is then given to the Web programmers who supply the back-end functionality. This involves writing programs that pull from back-end data sources to provide customized content for the page or that process information that HTML forms in the page might collect. The Web programmer might also add some JavaScript for form validation on the front end, for example.

  There is certainly some overlap in the skill base. Some graphic artists are skilled with Web design, some Web designers have learned to do some programming, and some Web programmers have learned to make a few graphics (the authors, for example . . . but it was painfully time consuming). Nonetheless, this model provides a reasonable stratification of the process of serious Web design.

- *Beginning Web programming:* needs a solid HTML foundation, because the computer programs that make up the Web site's back end generate HTML documents as output. Moreover, HTML forms are used to collect data on the front end. Mastery of Web design is not required because more effort has to be placed on creating functioning Web applications than on front-end design issues. Through repetitive use of HTML, the beginning Web programmer may pick up on Web design and make some fancier pages for the front end. If some design experience is already in place, the more the better.

  A functional knowledge of JavaScript will definitely be a benefit, and not just for fancy DHTML effects. Data is collected on the front end, so it is certainly handy to learn how to do some processing of it there. Of course, mastery of programming the back end is the primary goal. Especially now, the beginning Web programmer has to understand some XML fundamentals and how XHTML helps to bridge the gap between XML and HTML.

  The beginning Web programmer will likely learn (or will have learned) how to use a WYSIWYG HTML editor to help generate some of the HTML code, and how to integrate that code into his or her Web applications. Here, the solid knowledge of HTML will help the programmer recognize the limitations of such editors, especially in light of the XHTML syntax requirements. Certainly, the beginning Web programmer needs to learn the fundamentals of CSS and its role in the scheme of things. Again, if the Web programmer is forced more into the role of Web designer, the CSS fundamentals will be of immeasurable help in trying to figure out how to get a WYSIWYG editor to generate large amounts of well-formed styles.

■ *Advanced Web programming* is done by programmers who have learned the roles of HTML, XHTML, CSS, and XML for markup purposes. They have a proficiency with client-side JavaScript programming and are adept with one or more of the server-side programming approaches. In industry, they typically rely heavily on the services of professional Web designers for front-end services. However, some will have been pressed into design themselves. They have learned to use a wide variety of software applications that produce XHTML and XML. They use other software to aid in processing XML. They write their own programming code for specialized things that need to be done on the client or server. They have transformed the Web from a collection of home pages (and scientific abstracts) into a dynamic, worldwide information delivery system. With some hard work and practice, you can become an advanced Web programmer too.

So what's the moral of all that? Well, for starters, the vast majority of Web design is going to be done with software packages. People are simply not going to hard-code a million pages per day. Casual designers won't care what a WYSIWYG spits out as long as it looks nice in a browser. Professional Web designers will care to the extent that it looks nice in several browser types and versions. Web programmers will have to be cognizant of XHTML syntax and hard-code a good bit of it, but they will use the HTML-creating software when convenient, especially for large projects.

So what's the state of the Web? There are over a billion Web pages and Web applications that spit out Web pages dynamically. A very high percentage (probably over 95 percent) contain deprecated tags and attributes. (Deprecated elemants are discussed in the HTML introduction in Appendix A.) At the time this book was written, all of the ten most visited sites in the world had `font` tags on the front page. HTML WYSIWYG editors still spit out deprecated tags. They will for some time to come.

For this reason, browsers will not drop support of deprecated tags in the foreseeable future. Few would use a particular browser if much of the Web didn't render correctly in it. The intentions of the standard makers to clean up HTML are noble, but the Web is driven by hundreds of millions of people who want to see Web pages, and the software vendors who want their browsers to be what the people use to see the pages. The elements have been deprecated for several years now, but it's likely that they will not be dropped from the specifications soon. Even if the W3C were to formally drop them in the next XHTML draft specification, it would have little impact on the Web over the next several years.

The same applies to the XHTML syntax issues. The Web is full of HTML code that is not syntactically up to XHTML (hence XML) standards. Many WYSIWG HTML editors will continue to generate sloppy HTML for some time, although the newer ones are getting pretty good about XHTML. Browsers will tolerate sloppy HTML for many years to come. Again, browser vendors want you to be able to see all of the Web in their browsers. The HTML processors in browsers that we know and love will continue in much their same form.

So how does CSS fit into all of this? Again, most of the Web is straight HTML with no CSS, but a significant portion now uses it. CSS certainly has its advantages in terms of flexibility and versatility, and its use on the Web will steadily increase, especially for the formatting of text. The newer CSS specifications provide for the ability to make elaborate page layouts. (We presented some basic tabular layouts in Section 2.4.) Virtually every fancy page currently out there on the Web uses complex table structures for page layout. Over time, more pages will be laid out entirely with CSS.

But once again, the advance of CSS will largely be up to the software. People will hard-code some simple CSS. (We present some of the basics in the next section.) People will not hard-code volumes of complex CSS any more than they will hard-code complex HTML—large, nested table structures for example. Many of the newer WYSIWYG editors are pretty good at CSS, but it takes a little more know-how than standard formatting. Without styles, to format a word you highlight the word, click a couple of buttons, and the editor slaps a `font` tag with some attributes around the word—basically the same way word processors do it.

Even word processors have their own version of style capabilities, but often even people who use them frequently don't know how to use those style capabilities. It's much easier to click a font button. The same will likely hold true for HTML software. The serious Web designers will exploit CSS in much the same way as professional office assistants get the last drop out of their word processors. But how about everyone else? Remember, the Web was built on simplicity.

So what are the implications of all that? For most people there are no implications— if it works on the Web, do it. For you, the aspiring Web programmer, we offer the following notes.

- Make well-formed XHTML documents that adhere strictly to the syntax rules. Athough that won't be necessary for years to come on the Web, the practice will reap benefits when you start working with XML.

- As long as the document is well-formed XHTML, we leave the choice of HTML implementation up to you. The Web won't care for many years. If your conscience (or professor) bothers you, use CSS in place of deprecated elements and attributes. Either way, style issues will take a back seat as we program Web applications. The most important things are a solid understanding of HTML and perhaps a working knowledge of the CSS concept.

- Use of WYSIWYG editors is also at your discretion. They will be of little help when you are writing programs. WYSIWYG editors can be of some help to Web programmers when creating forms for data collection on the front end, for example. But with the XHTML syntax issues, you'd better look out. For simple HTML purposes, one of the "smart," syntax-highlighting plain text editors listed on the Web site might be your best bet.

2.6   CASCADING STYLE SHEETS

This section explores the basics of **Cascading Style Sheets (CSS)**. A complete coverage of the CSS necessary to replace the deprecated HTML attributes used to format images, lists, and tables would require at least a complete new chapter in this book, and that is well beyond our objectives. However, the CSS features presented here are sufficient to replace the deprecated `font` and `center` elements and to provide a great deal more formatting control besides. In particular, controlling text properties, text spans, and block divisions in Web pages using CSS provides a good introduction to most of the CSS you will currently find on the Web. Moreover, should you dabble with DHTML at some point in the future, this background will prove invaluable.

NOTE

In order to realize the full formatting capabilities of CSS, you should use one of the following browser versions (or a later version): Internet Explorer 5, Netscape 6, Opera 4, Mozilla 1. Only some of the styles will render correctly in Internet Explorer 4 and Netscape 4.

To include styles in a document, you use the `style` element, typically placed in the `head` section of the document. It is a good idea to include HTML comments,

```
<style>
<!--
    style rules go here
-->
</style>
```

to "hide" the style rules from the HTML processor. The styles are processed separately by a CSS style engine.

Text Styles

We begin with text-level styles. There is a generic `span` element that does nothing by itself. For example,

```
<span>some text</span>
```

causes absolutely no formatting to be applied to the text by the HTML processor. This element was created as a generic container so that styles could be applied to "spans" of text. It is an *inline* element.

Table 2.4 shows the text-level styles we present. These style properties, together with the generic inline `span` container, provide for more control over text than the deprecated `font` element.

TABLE 2.4   Some Text-Level Styles.*

PROPERTY	VALUES	NOTES
`font-family`	Named font	Use quotations for multiple-word font names: `"Courier New"`
`font-size`	Percent	Percent relative to font size in parent element
`font-style`	`normal, italic, oblique`	
`font-weight`	`bold, bolder, lighter, normal`	`bolder` is generally equivalent to what `<b>...</b>` creates.
`color`	Named color, #hexcolor	
`background-color`	Named color, #hexcolor	Makes solid colored block around text

* These can be applied to HTML inline elements to control specific chunks of text or applied to block-level HTML elements to control all text within the block.

```
                        span.html

<html>
  <head>
    <title>Style Definitions</title>
    <style>
    <!--

      /* global rule */
      span { font-size:150%; font-family:Verdana; color:red; }

      /* class rule */
      span.small { font-size:60%; }

      /*  another class rule */
      span.other { font-style:italic; font-weight:bolder; background-color:black; }

    -->
    </style>
  </head>

  <body>
    This is normal text using the browser defaults.
     <br /><br />
    <span>This text uses the global style rule for the span element.</span>
     <br /><br />
    <span class="small">This text uses the small class rule.</span>
     <br /><br />
    <span>
        Here the small style class
        <span class="small">is used inside</span>
        the global style rule. Note that the other styles are still inherited from the global rule.
    </span>
     <br /><br />
    <span class="other">This text demonstrates some of the other properties that control text
        appearance. To do this with HTML, you would have to use the font and i
        elements. But there is no way to produce the background effect.</span>
     <br /><br />
    <span class="small">
        Here the "other" style class
        <span class="other">is used inside</span>
        the small style class.
    </span>
  </body>
</html>
```

FIGURE 2.19 Defining styles for the span element.

Figure 2.19 shown the source code for a Web page that assigns some of the styles in Table 2.4 to the span container. Figure 2.20 shows the Web page rendition. We have used the CSS comment symbols

/* *stuff in here ignored by the style engine* */

to mark the *global definition,* which applies the style to all instances of span, and the *class definitions,* which apply the styles to different *style classes* defined on the span element. The first use of span in the Web page reflects the styles defined in the global rule. The second use of span calls for the small class by using the special class attribute, whose only purpose is to assign style classes to HTML elements.

The third use first sets the text using the global rule for span. Then, nested inside, the small class is applied to a few words. Those words inherit styles from the global rule, but the

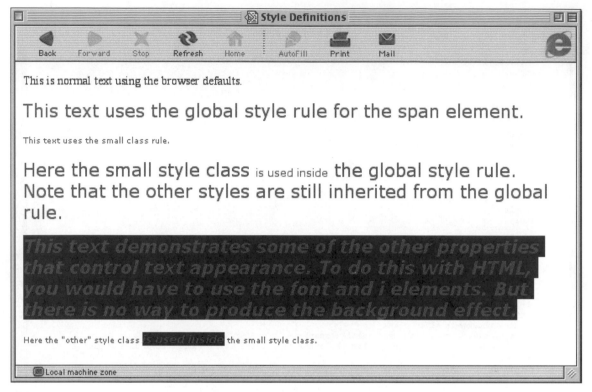

FIGURE 2.20 A browser rendition of the document of Figure 2.19.

`small` class overrides the `font-size` setting. This is the first example that shows why the styles are called *cascading*. If a style property that is used by the parent element is also used inside a nested element, the style given in the nested element overrides the one from the parent.

The fourth use of `span` calls the `other` class, which sets some text properties that are not available if you use only the `font` element to control text markup. Finally, the last use shows that calls to two different style classes can be nested. The first nesting example used a `span` style class inside a `span` that also used a global style rule.

Types of Style Classes

In general, we have the following characterizations for defining style rules. The global rule

element { *property1*: *value*; *property2*: *value*; . . . }

causes the styles specified by the property values to be applied to any instances of the *element* in the Web page.

In contrast, the styles from a class rule

element.classname { *property1*: *value*; *property2*: *value*; . . . }

are applied to the element in the Web page only if a call to the class,

```
<element class=" classname">. . .</element>
```

is made. In either type of rule definition, the style properties and their values are separated by colons, and the property: value pairs are terminated by semicolons. We have supplied extra spaces in the style definitions only for readability. They are not required.

Styles can be applied to any element, not just the generic span container. For example, the global rule

```
b { font-size:125%; }
```

is applied to all occurrences of the bold element

```
<b>bigger bold</b>
```

causing its contents to be rendered somewhat larger than the surrounding text. If you don't want all of your boldface text to be larger, you would define

```
b.big { font-size:125%; }
```

and call the *big* class,

```
<b class="big">bigger bold</b>
```

only when you want your boldface text to be larger. You can even define something like

```
i { font-weight:bolder; }
```

in which case

```
<i>bold italic</i>
```

carries the global style rule and is equivalent to the pure HTML use of

```
<i><b>bold italic</b></i>
```

when no styles are defined.

Finally, generic style classes, which can be invoked on any element, can be defined. For example,

```
.redmonospace { color:red; font-family:Courier; }
```

can be used with the bold element

```
<b class="redmonospace">bold red Courier text</b>
```

or the small element

```
<small class="redmonospace">small red Courier text</small>
```

or any other text-level element.

Block Styles

We now turn to styles at the block level. Again, there is a generic container, the `div` element, whose only purpose is for applying styles at the block level. For example, the only formatting carried out by the HTML processor on

```
<div>block content</div>
```

is line breaks before and after the block content. Thus, `div` is precisely a generic block element. Its name comes from the notion of a block as a division within the page. Table 2.5 shows the block formatting styles we present.

Figure 2.21 shows the source code for a page that assigns some of the styles from Table 2.5 to the `div` element. Figure 2.22 shows the browser rendition.

First, a global style rule for the `div` element is defined to provide a default style for paragraphs. Note that the `text-indent` property indents only the first line. Using pure

TABLE 2.5   Block Formatting Style Properties.*

PROPERTY	VALUES	NOTES
`background-image`	URL (relative, absolute)	The URL value is given in CSS as `URL(img.gif)`

`margin-right`
`-left`
`-top`
`-bottom`
	Percent, pixels†	Padding on outside of block, margin set relative to parent element

`margin`	Percent, pixels	Set all margin properties at once

`padding-right`
`-left`
`-top`
`-bottom`
	Percent, pixels	Padding on inside of block

`padding`	Percent, pixels	Set all padding properties at once
`border`	Percent, pixels	Border around block (can append with `-right`, `-top`, etc., for more control)
`text-align`	`left, right, center, justify`	Alignment of text within block
`text-indent`	Percent, pixels	Applied only to first line within block
`position`	`absolute, relative`	Position of block within parent element (`relative` is the default)
`top`	Pixels	Position of block from top of parent element
`left`	Pixels	Position of block from left of parent element
`width`	Pixels	Width of block
`height`	Pixels	Height of block

* Also use text-level style properties to control text for whole blocks.
† Pixel values for CSS properties are given as `50px`

```
                               div.html
<html>
  <head>
    <title>Block Style Definitions</title>
    <style>
    <!--

      div { font-size:110%; font-family:Geneva; text-indent:15px; text-align:justify; }

      div.note { font-size:95%; font-family:"Times New Roman"; text-indent:0px;
               margin-left:25px; margin-right:25px; padding:5px; background-color:#CCCCCC; }

      span.noteheading { font-size:125%; font-weight:bolder; color:#FFFFFF;
                  background-color:#333333; }

      -->
    </style>
  </head>

  <body>
    This is normal text using the browser defaults.
    <br /><br />

    <div>
      This block uses the global style rule for the div element. Such a global style might
      be set so that normal paragraphs can be formatted nicely using one style rule. Note
      that CSS does a nice job of fully justifying the text on both margins. Using
      attribute based formatting with HTML to the same thing (align="justify") is far more
      unreliable.
    </div>

    <div>
      This is another paragraph which gets the global div styles. You can see that the div
      element has caused a line break, which is the only formatting the HTML processor
      applies to div blocks. The style engine does all the rest.
    </div>

    <br />

    <div class="note">
      <span class="noteheading">Note:</span>
      A note class can be defined to emphasize special notes, much like the ones we use in
      this book.  The note class overrides the font-size, font-family, and text-indent
      properties set by the global rule for the div element. Also, a note block is given a
      background-color, some padding between the text and block "walls," and indentations
      on either side.
    </div>
  </body>
</html>
```

FIGURE 2.21   A document using styles for the div element.

HTML, you would have to "rig" such an indentation (using a transparent "spacer image," for example.) The rest of the global styles are self-explanatory. The first two paragraphs you see in Figure 2.22 use the global div rule.

Next, a div.note class defines the special colored block you can see at the bottom of Figure 2.22. The note rule first overrides the global font-size, font-family, and text-indent settings for how the text should be rendered. The note rule does not override the text-align setting for full justification. Next, the note rule sets the left and right margins of the box in a few pixels, supplies some padding within the box, and gives it some background-color. Note that the padding property is analogous to cellpadding used in table cells.

We have also used some text-level styles in the form of a noteheading class on the span element. That class, illustrated by the first word in the note block, and features bold

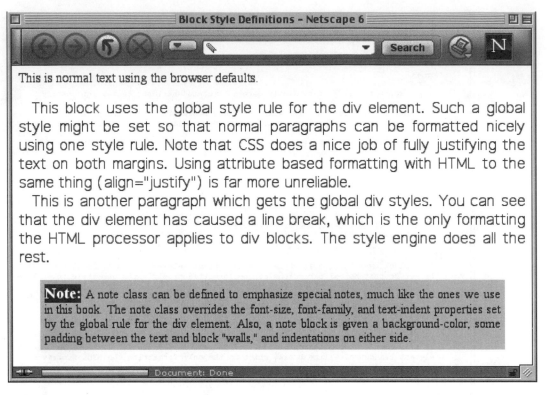

FIGURE 2.22   The document of Figure 2.21 in a browser.

white text on a darker background. These text-level styles override those from the parent `div` element. Here you see three levels of cascade: a global `div` rule, which is overridden by the `div.note` class, which in turn is overridden by the `span.noteheading` class. In particular, the `font-size` property was reset on each level.

Like text-level styles, block styles can be applied to block elements besides the generic `div` container. Of course, `body` is the mother (father?) of all block elements, and block properties can be set for the whole body of the Web page. The following global rule for `body` defines some text formatting styles and sets the width of the page.

```
body { font-family:Geneva; text-align:justify;
   background-color:red; width:600px;}
```

Because there is only one instance of the `body` element in a Web page, it does not make sense to define style classes for the `body` element. Simply use a global rule to specify some default properties you desire the whole page to have.

If a style property is set that corresponds to an HTML attribute (`background-color:red` instead of `bgcolor="red"`, for example), the style setting wins out.

Figure 2.21 used `div` elements to apply all styles. Suppose we want paragraph breaks (line break + blank line) instead of the single line breaks caused by the `div` element. We easily could have defined the styles on the paragraph element.

```
p { font-size:110%; font-family:Geneva; . . . }
p.note { font-size:95%; font-family:"Times New Roman"; . . . }
```

Another option is to define a generic class,

```
.solidblock { margin-left:25px; margin-right:25px; padding:5px;
              background-color:#CCCCCC; }
```

which can be applied to either the p or div element to provide a solid note with or without the paragraph break. Notice in Figures 2.21 and 2.22 that we had to use an extra <br /> to get the paragraph break before the solid note.

A final example using basic block formatting creates paragraphs and section headings (using <h2> . . . </h2>) that are slightly indented on the left, and chapter headings (using <h1> . . . </h1>) that are negatively indented.

```
h1 { margin-left:-5px; background-color:#999999; }
h2 { margin-left:10px; }
p { margin-left:10px; text-indent:5px; }
```

Here is a depiction of how this might look in a Web page. Just keep in mind that negative margins can cause block elements to be rendered partially off the page. If we had specified the h1 to have a negative 50-pixel indentation, part of the Chapter 1 heading would not be visible on the page.

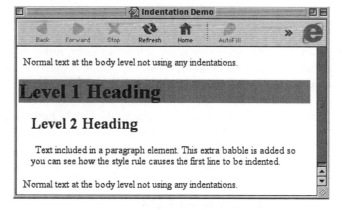

In some cases block styles can be applied to inline elements. You saw in Figure 2.20 that inline elements are basically just inline "blocks" of text. For example, padding can be added to the inside of a text block. However, not all styles are viable for inline elements.

NOTE

Word processor styles, as in MS Word, behave in the same way as CSS styles do in HTML. You can set global styles that pertain to the whole document and local ones that you name. The word processor even cascades styles, meaning the style rules for an element (such as this note) override the global rules for the document. For local styles, you simply create a style by giving it a name and setting its properties by clicking some buttons. You then highlight the text to which you want to apply the style, choose the name of the style you just created from a pull-down menu, and WYSIWYG. There are paragraph styles, which correspond to block styles in CSS, and character styles, correspnding to CSS inline styles. In concept, that is no different at all from using CSS with HTML. You have global styles and local style classes, and you code your own styles, apply them to the HTML elements, and test them in a browser. Indeed, WYSIWYG HTML editors that handle styles work nearly exactly like word processors. They just spit out CSS style rules and HTML elements that use them, rather than binary blobs.

Pseudo-classes

CSS *pseudo-classes* are related to attributes of the `body` element that control link properties. Typically, setting a pseudo-class property is just like setting the corresponding HTML attribute. For example, consider the following style settings for the `body` element.

```
body { font-family:Georgia; text-align:justify; }
:link { color:blue; }
:visited { color:purple; }
:active { color:red; }
:hover { color:orange; }
```

As you can see, pseudo-classes are marked syntactically with a leading colon. The preceding declaration starts by defining a couple of global styles for the page body. Then colors are set for unvisited, visited, and active links, respectively. This has little advantage over setting the corresponding HTML attributes in the `body` element. Indeed, we were tempted to forgo mention of pseudo-classes in this text were it not for `hover`, the last one listed.

The `hover` class has built-in behavior. Given the style rules in this example, putting the mouse pointer over a link causes the link to turn orange, and the link turns back to its original color (blue or purple) when the mouse pointer moves off the link. You have, no doubt, seen such links in Web pages. Once you learn some JavaScript, you will see that a hover link automatically "listens" for the `onmouseover` and `onmouseout` events.

Page Layout with CSS

The CSS example in this section puts much of what we have learned together in one Web page. The source file shown in Figure 2.23 produces a Web page nearly identical to the Knuckles' Sports World page of Figure 2.18 in Section 2.4. That version used tables to lay out the page and used HTML attributes to supply all of the formatting. This time we have exclusively used styles to lay out the page. You can begin by pulling up the source of Figure 2.23 from off of the Web site and observing what the `hover` pseudo-class accomplishes when you pass your mouse over the links. It's pretty cool, creating an effect much like that accomplished by roll-over images. But that's just a novelty and outside of the main objective of this example. (Depending upon which browser and platform you use to view the page, it may look slightly different from its rendition in Figure 2.24, especially if you are using an older browser.)

```
                          ▒ sports(slim).html ▒
<html>
  <head>
    <title>Sports</title>
    <style>
    <!--
      body { text-align:left; color:#000000; background-color:#FFFFFF; }
        :link { color:#000066; }
        :vlink { color:#660066; }
        :hover { color:#FF6633; }

      div { position:absolute; padding:5px; }

      div.top{ text-align:center; font-size:200%; font-face:"BernhardMod BT Bold Italic";
           background:#333333; color:#FFFFFF;
           top:0px;
           left:0px;
           width:600px;
           height:40px; }

      div.leftnav { background:#999999;
           top:40px;
           left:0px;
           width:100px;
           height:300px; }

      div.bodytop { text-align:center; background:#666666;
           top:40px;
           left:100px;
           width:400px;
           height:50px; }

      div.rightnav { text-align:left; background:#999999;
           top:40px;
           left:500px;
           width:100px;
           height:300px; }

      div.body { background-image:URL(gifs/football.gif);
           top:90px;
           left:100px;
           width:400px;
           height:250px; }

      div.bottom { background:#333333; color:#FFFFFF;
           top:340;
           left:0px;
           width:600px;
           height:70px; }

      div.boldcenter { font-weight:bolder; text-align:center; padding:0px; position:relative; }
      div.bigcenter { font-size:150%; text-align:center; padding:0px; position:relative; }
      span.bigbold { font-size:125%; }
      hr.half { width:50%; font-weight:bolder; }
      a.white { color:#FFFFFF; }
    -->
    </style>
  </head>
```

FIGURE 2.23(a)   The `head` section for a Web page using a complete CSS layout.

The first thing we have to address is how all of those colored `div` blocks are positioned on the page. They are all *absolutely* positioned in the page using the `top`, `left`, `width`, and `height` properties. The diagram in Figure 2.25 shows how that works. The `top` and `left` properties give the coordinates of the upper left corner of the block, with the origin at the upper left corner of the browser window. (Down and right are positive values.) The `height` and `width` properties give the actual size of the block. We put those properties for each block on separate lines in the style rules in Figure 2.23(a) so that

```
<body>

    <div class="top">
    KNUCKLES' SPORTS WORLD
    </div>

    <div class="leftnav">
      <div class="boldcenter">
        Available Pages <hr />
        Pro <hr class="half" />
      </div>

      <a href="x">Football</a><br /> . . .
    </div>

    <div class="bodytop">
      <div class="bigcenter">Pro Football</div>
      [<a href="x">Standings</a>][<a href="x">Schedules</a>] . . .
    </div>

    <div class="body">
      <a href="x">Game of the Week</a>: This week the juggernauts and.....
    </div>

    <div class="rightnav">
      <div class="boldcenter">
        This Week <hr />
      </div>

      <a href="x">Game 1</a><br /> . . .
    </div>

    <div class="bottom">
      <span class="bigbold">Weekly Trivia Question: </span>
      Who holds the record . . .<br /><br />
      <a class="white" href="x"> Click here . . .</a>
    </div>

</body>
</html>
```

FIGURE 2.23(b)   The body section for a Web page using a complete CSS layout.

they are easy to see. You should take a minute to become comfortable with how the absolute positioning has been set so that there is no space between the blocks and that they don't overlap.

Now, let's discuss how the style definitions cascade starting with the body element, the parent block. Because most of the text in the page is to be black and left-aligned within each block, we specify so in the body style rule. The div blocks, being children of the body block, will inherit those styles. We also set some colors and the cool hover effect for all the links in the page.

Now for the div blocks. First, we make a global rule, because each block is to be positioned absolutely on the page with an inner padding of five pixels. We could have specified that in each div block, but we would then have had to include those properties in each specific div class rule. As you progress through the rules for the different div classes, you will see that all but the rule for div.body has overridden the white background color. The top and bodytop classes are the only ones in which all their text is to be centered, so text-align has been specified accordingly in those. We have set a background image in div.body to emphasize that URLs are given with unusual syntax in CSS. (When you look at the rendition of the page, you will see that we didn't do it for aesthetics!)

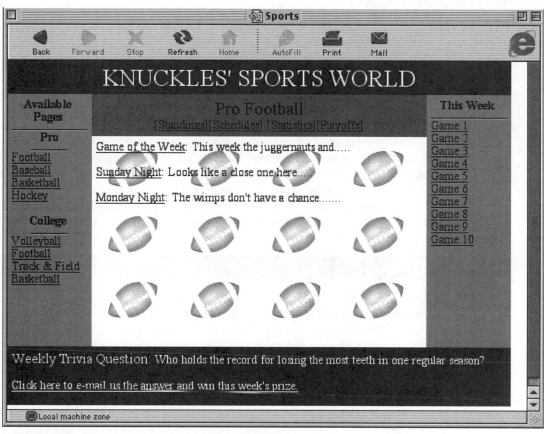

FIGURE 2.24   A rendition of the document of Figure 2.23.

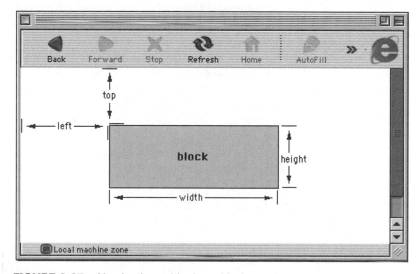

FIGURE 2.25   Absolutely positioning a block.

The only things left to figure out were some of the positioning issues within the blocks. We needed some boldface centered text for the headings in the navigation bars and some larger boldface text for the "Pro Football" heading. That's what the `boldcenter` and `bigbold` `div` classes are for. (We were tempted to use `span` but alignment is logically a property of blocks, not a text formatting issue.) It was important to set `padding` to zero pixels in those blocks. Otherwise they would have inherited five pixels of padding from the global rule. In that case, there would have been 5 pixels on the inside of the main `div` blocks and five more on the inside of the nested `div` blocks.

Finally, some other minor formatting details had to be ironed out in the last three style rules. Some of the horizontal rules needed to be half as wide, and we needed some different font characteristics for the weekly trivia question and the link below it. In particular, the link at the bottom needed to be white, so we made a `white` class anchor to override the anchor pseudo-class settings made in the `body` element. We say "needed" because we were trying to duplicate the tabular layout version of Section 2.4. It took a good bit of trial and error.

NOTE

All of the main layout blocks in Knuckles' Sports World are positioned absolutely on the page. However, the `boldcenter` and `bigcenter` `div` classes are formatting blocks of text within the layout blocks. Those are relatively aligned. That means that they are aligned relative to the page layout flow, just like regular paragraphs, for example. That is in fact the default positioning for `div` blocks.

Page Layout Flow

In HTML in general, the flow of page layout is relative, which is also the default for `div` blocks. Absolute positioning of blocks creates layers in the page indexed by the *z-index*. When straight HTML is used or when no absolutely positioned CSS blocks are present, everything on the page has a z-index of 0. Absolutely positioned blocks are assigned z-indices starting with 1, in the order in which they are defined within the document.

Figure 2.26 illustrates that and the flow of page layout in general. We don't show the actual HTML/CSS code that creates the page, because the large volume of code would obscure the main concept here. Indeed, creating all the margin space around the blocks, the padding within the blocks, the borders, and the text alignment requires a good number of style rules.

Here is skeletal code to aid with the discussion.

```
<div class="black">relatively positioned block</div>
<span class="ltgray">inline element</span>
<span class="ltgray">inline element</span>
<div class="black">
 <span class="ltgray">inline element</span>
 <span class="ltgray">inline element</span>
 <br />
 <span class="ltgray">inline element</span>
 <br />
 relatively positioned block
</div>
```

```
<div class="grayAbsolute">
<span class="ltgray">Inline Element</span>
<span class="ltgray">Inline Element</span>
<br />
absolutely positioned block
</div>
<div class="blackAbsolute">absolutely positioned block</div>
```

We have used `div` and `span` containers to illustrate the page layout flow, but the same concepts apply to other HTML block and inline elements as well.

Starting from the top, a relatively positioned block automatically reserves all horizontal space in the page, hence there are automatic line breaks before and after block elements. Next in the flow are two inline elements that are rendered inline with the page flow, so only as much space as necessary is allocated for the element.

Next comes another relatively positioned block, which again reserves all horizontal space across the page. Within that block are three more inline elements. Again, those

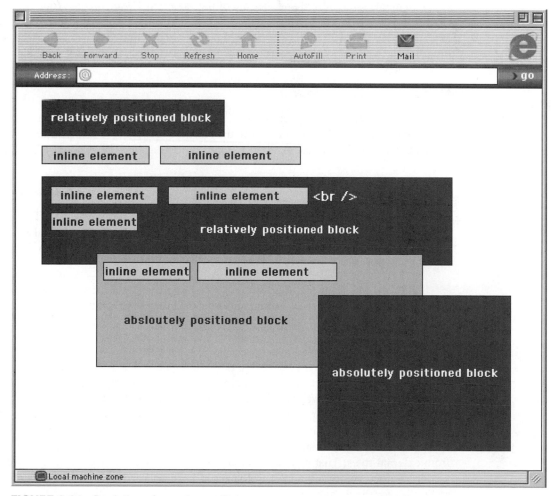

FIGURE 2.26 Depiction of page layout flow.

assume only the required space, and an HTML `br` element was required to move the third element to the next line (barring automatic wraparound if there were enough inline elements to reach the right side of the block). So far this is all *relative* layout flow in the z-index 0 layer, just as in ordinary HTML.

The final two blocks are absolutely positioned. The gray block is defined first in the HTML code, so it is rendered in z-index 1. It is placed so that its layer is apparent by partially obscuring the relatively positioned block. There are some inline elements inside it. The layout flow within the gray block is relative to the constraints of the inside of the block.

Finally, the last block is absolutely positioned and gets z-index 2, because it is defined in the HTML code after the gray block. It is positioned so that its layer is apparent relative to the others.

So, basically, absolutely positioning "rises above" the relative layout flow of the main page. But within a block, layout flow is relative to that block.

We have provided this example so that you can better understand how inline and block elements are rendered and the role of the `span` and `div` elements. You will not need to deal directly with the z-index unless you program some DHTML effects, as discussed in Chapter 19. When absolutely positioned blocks are positioned so as not to overlap, as in Figure 2.24, you cannot even perceive that there are multiple layers in the page.

Cascading Overview

We now tie together our discussion of CSS by presenting the full cascading model for CSS. An *external style sheet* is no more than a text file that contains style rules. The `link` element is used to import the externally stored style rules into one or more HTML files:

```
<link rel="stylesheet" href="path/to/mystyles.css">
```

Here, the `rel` attribute specifies the *rel*ationship of the imported file to the HTML file that is importing it. The `href` attribute simply provides the URL of the external style sheet, which typically has the .css file extension. Keep in mind the following two things when importing style sheets:

- Put the `link` element in the `head` section. Put it by itself, *not* within `<style>` . . . `</style>` tags. The `rel` attribute informs the browser that it is getting style rules.

- For the same reason, do *not* put `<style>` . . .`</style>` tags in the external file—just raw style rules.

External styles are useful if you want to reuse the same styles in several HTML files without cluttering up the files with redundant style rules. That way, you can update the one style file, and all of the Web pages that use the styles are updated.

It is interesting that external style sheets bring yet another level of cascade into the picture. A style rule defined in an external style sheet is the most general. Styles rules defined in a document inside the `<style>` . . . `</style>` element can override and inherit from external rules. That way, an external style sheet can specify general styles for a collection of documents, and a `style` element in each document can contain more specific style rules for the document.

MORE GENERAL

> **EXTERNAL** -- Applies to a collection of documents.
> ```
> <link rel="stylesheet" href="path/to/mystyles.css">
> ```
>
> **GLOBAL RULE** – Applies to any occurrence of element in document.
> ```
> P { font-size:90% }
> <p>...</p>
> ```
>
> **CLASS RULES** – Applies when called by the class attribute.
> **GENERIC CLASS** – Used by any element.
> ```
> .bold { font-weight:bolder }
> <p class="bold">...</p>
> <i class="bold">...</i>
> ```
>
> **SPECIFIC CLASS** -- Used by one element.
> ```
> p.smaller { font-size:85% }
> <p class="smaller">...</p>
> ```
>
> **ELEMENT LEVEL** – Apply the style attribute to any element.
> ```
> <p style="font-size:80% ; color:#330033">...</p>
> ```

MORE SPECIFIC

FIGURE 2.27 The levels of inheritance in CSS.

There is yet another level of cascading in CSS that is applied at the level of the HTML elements themselves. The `style` attribute can be used inside any HTML element to apply styles only to that instance of the element. For example,

```
<p style="font-size:80% ; color:#330033">some text</p>
```

applies two style rules to only one instance of the p element. When styles are applied at the element level, the style rules are given as a semicolon-delimited list as the value of the `style` attribute. This is the most specific level at which styles can be applied.

Figure 2.27 demonstrates the levels of cascading in CSS, progressing from the most general down to the most specific. Here we see the full picture of the levels of style inheritance. (The term *inheritance* can be used loosely here in the same sense in which it is used in talking about inheritance of classes of objects.) Any style rule defined on a more general level is inherited at the more specific level. Moreover, any style property that is defined at a more specific level overrides any occurrence of the *same* property that may have been defined at a more general level.

We conclude our presentation of CSS with some notes.

- The boxed note on window width at the end of Section 2.4 also applies to page layout with CSS. In particular, it's best to use around a 600-pixel-wide presentation if you lay out a Web page with CSS blocks. However, most commercial pages use tabular layouts, leaving styles for formatting text and DHTML.

- We reiterate that the common browsers that are fully CSS-capable are Netscape 6, Internet Explorer 5, Opera 3.6, and Mozilla 1. Of course, subsequent versions should be CSS-savvy also. Netscape 4 and Internet Explorer 4 basically deal with only simple text-level formatting with CSS.

- If you contrast the tabular version in Section 2.4 and the CSS version of Knuckles' Sports World, you see a drastic difference. The contrast is especially striking if you pull up and view the complete source code for the tabular version on the Web site. It's replete with `font` tags and the like. The tabular version exhibits complete *attribute-based formatting*, while the CSS version is virtually devoid of HTML attributes except for calling style classes. The W3C hopes for a decline of attribute-based formatting in favor of CSS. Certainly, there will be a gradual decline, but, once again, the software that people use to generate HTML will play a key role.

SUMMARY OF KEY TERMS AND CONCEPTS

HyperText Markup Language (HTML): A language that provides instructions for how data should be rendered in a Web browser or similar software. The markup instructions are similar in concept to those used by word processors to annotate data for presentation, but HTML annotations are created using ASCII text characters rather than the proprietary binary annotations used by word processors.

eXtensible Markup Language (XML): A language that uses annotations to describe data, rather than specifying how the data should be rendered by an application. XML is actually a language that provides syntax rules that govern how new "languages" can be invented to describe specific collections of data.

eXtensible HTML (XHTML): HTML with the more strict syntax rules of XML.

Cascading Style Sheets (CSS): A language that can be used to define style properties for HTML elements. CSS provides for reusable styles and provides much more control over Web page rendition than pure HTML does. CSS also serves to help keep content separate from style.

Deprecated HTML elements: Elements and attributes that are earmarked to be dropped from the HTML/XHTML standard at some point in the future. Most deprecated elements and attributes are on such status in favor of using CSS to accomplish the same things.

Sloppy code: HTML code that is not up to XHTML standards or to future HTML standards. The Web is littered with sloppy HTML code, much of which has been generated with WYSIWYG (What You See Is What You Get) HTML-generating software. For this reason, Web browsers will tolerate sloppy code, including deprecated HTML elements and attributes, for many years to come.

Inline HTML elements: Elements that, by default, take up the minimum amount of space necessary for rendition and do not cause a break (with the exception of `br`) in the flow of page layout. The `span` element is the generic inline container used to apply styles.

Block HTML elements: Elements that cause a break in the flow of page layout. By default, a block element uses (or restricts from other use) all of its surrounding horizontal space. The `div` element is the generic block container used to apply styles.

Cascading Styles: The principle that lower levels of style application inherit from higher levels and that style properties set at lower levels override corresponding properties set at higher levels. From highest to lowest, the levels of cascade are:

- External style sheet
- Global style rule for an element
- Generic style class, which can be applied to any (appropriate) element.
- Style class, which is defined on a single element
- Style applied to a specific instance of an element using the HTML `style` attribute

Absolutely positioned blocks: Block elements rendered at specific coordinates on the Web page. Overlapping absolutely positioned blocks are treated as layers with distinct z-index values.

Relatively positioned blocks: Blocks that are not absolutely positioned. This is the default behavior of blocks. A relatively positioned block is rendered as a standard HTML block element according to the layout flow of the Web page.

Inline styles: CSS styles that specify properties for specific text within an inline element or all text within a block element.

Block styles: CSS styles that specify formatting styles for blocks. These can also be applied to inline elements in some cases.

EXERCISES

Use XHTML syntax for all exercises in this section (and throughout this book).

1. On the Web site, under Exercise 1 chapter 2, you will find a picture of a personal résumé template. Construct a personal résumé using the general idea of that template. You may embellish the résumé, but use the same general structure in terms of the lists and borderless tables used to create columns. Use CSS (*not* the deprecated `font` element) to format the text (face, size, color), applying at least three different style classes.

2. On the Web site, under Exercise 2 Chapter 2, you will find a picture of a personal résumé template. Construct a personal résumé using the general idea of that template. Use the same general structure in terms of the lists and borderless tables used to create columns. As in the template, use the side-by-side lists in the computer skills section. Use CSS (*not* the deprecated `font` element) to format the text (face, size, color), applying at least three different style classes. Note that the colored stripes can be accomplished using either colored table cells or `div` blocks formatted using CSS.

3. On the Web site, under Exercise 3 Chapter 2, you will find a picture of a personal résumé template. Construct a personal résumé using the general idea of that template. Use the same general structure in terms of the lists and borderless tables used to create columns. Use CSS (*not* the deprecated `font` element) to format the text (face, size, color), applying at least three different style classes. You may use some `div` blocks formatted using CSS to "spice up" the résumé (see Exercise 2), but don't overdo it and make the résumé too busy.

4. Peruse the résumé templates given on the Web site for Exercises 1, 2, and 3. Use a combination of those layout ideas to create a personal résumé. Make heavy use of borderless tables for page layout and lists to organize information. Use CSS (*not* the deprecated `font` element) to format the text (face, size, color), applying at least three different style classes. Use some careful planning on scratch paper and some imagination to construct a superior résumé!

5. On the Web site, under Exercise 5 Chapter 2, you will find a picture of a Web page and all images necessary to create the page. Depending upon your objectives (or directions from your instructor), the page layout can be constructed using borderless tables or CSS formatted blocks. Use CSS (*not* the deprecated `font` element) to format the text (face, size, color), applying at least three different style classes.

6. On the Web site, under Exercise 6 Chapter 2, you will find a picture of a Web page and all images necessary to create the page. Depending upon your objectives (or directions from your instructor), the page layout can be constructed using borderless tables or CSS formatted blocks.

7. On the Web site, under Exercise 7 Chapter 2, you will find a picture of a Web page and all images necessary to create the page. Depending upon your objectives (or directions from your instructor), the page layout can be constructed using borderless tables or CSS formatted blocks.

PROJECT THREAD

Use XHTML syntax for all pages created here (and throughout this book).

A. Create a simple Web page that is to be your homework page. This page will be used to provide links to all of your completed exercises. The main feature of the page is a table, each row of which provides a description of the exercise and a link that can be used to access it. An example table is shown below. Add each new assignment to the top of the table.

A simple Perl CGI program that generates a web page as output.	Exercise 4.20
An HTML quiz form with JavaScript support that won't allow the form to be submitted without until the proper data is entered.	Chapter 3 project thread
A web page featuring research from a Chapter 1 exercise.	Internet research (Chapter 2 project thread)

B. Organize your research from Chapter 1 into a Web page (or series of pages) three to five screens in length. Use a borderless table layout to provide some structure to the page(s). Make the display width of the page 700 pixels. Use at least one HTML list in the page. All text formatting should be done using at least three CSS style classes (*not* the deprecated font element). Make sure that your research sources are well documented in the page(s).

C. Add a brief description of and link to your research to the table in your homework page. If you are assigned any other exercises from this chapter, add a description(s) and link(s) to the homework page as well.

D. Upload the homework page and all other files to a Web server. Type its URL into a browser and pull up the homework page. Thoroughly test all the links.

## CHAPTER 3

PROCESSING ON THE FRONT END

As you can imagine, using HTML forms to collect user data is an integral part of almost any Web application. This chapter first explores the HTML elements and attributes responsible for creating HTML form elements. Located conveniently at the beginning of this chapter (sounds like a sales pitch), Section 3.1 will prove valuable in a reference capacity as you construct HTML forms throughout the rest of this text. The remainder of this chapter is dedicated to an exploration of the JavaScript programming language. JavaScript can accomplish many things on the front end of Web applications, but we focus on using it to manipulate user data entered into HTML forms. We explore both creating client-side processing utilities and validating user data before it is submitted to a CGI program on the Web server.

3.1 HTML FORMS

We title this section "HTML Forms," but we continue to adhere to XHTML syntax rules. The `form` element is merely a container that holds the *form elements*.

```
<form> form elements go here </form>
```

From a pure markup perspective, it behaves just like the paragraph block element. For example,

```
In terms of <form>pure markup</form> I am a paragraph block element.
```

only causes paragraph breaks before and after its contents:

```
In terms of

pure markup

I am a paragraph block element.
```

The `form` element is summarized in Table 3.1. Primarily, its attributes are responsible for where and how the actual data carried by the form elements is submitted for processing.

Control Buttons

There are a variety of form elements that go inside a form. Many carry data for the form, while others provide controls that trigger the processing of the data. We first discuss the form control elements, which are just buttons that are clicked to cause something to happen.

TABLE 3.1 The `form` HTML Element

`<form >. . .</form>` Block element

ATTRIBUTE	POSSIBLE VALUES	DEFAULT	DESCRIPTION
`action`	`URL` (relative or absolute)		Specifies the URL of the server-side program that is to receive data from the form's elements
`method`	`get, post`	`get`	Specifies one of the two ways that the form's data can be sent to a server-side program (recall the discussion about `GET` and `POST` HTML transactions in Section 1.8)
`name`	Any text string		A variable name, given to the form, that is used to refer to the form as a JavaScript object

Command Button

```
<input type="button" value="Click Me" />
```

A command button (or *generic button*) is used to call a programmer-defined mechanism that initiates processing of the form's data. Command buttons are used on the Web almost exclusively to call JavaScript functions. The `value` attribute specifies the text that appears on the button.

Submit Button

```
<input type="submit" value="Submit Form" />
```

A submit button initiates server-side processing of a form's data. They cause the data contained in a form's elements to be submitted to a CGI program located by the URL specified in the `action` attribute of the `form` container. The `value` attribute specifies the text that appears on the button.

Image Submit Button

```
<input type="image" src="images/clickme.gif" />
```

An image submit button is no more than a submit button that lets you choose your own graphic to represent the button rather than having the browser draw the button for you. A graphic command button can take any of the attributes of the `img` element (`align`, `alt`, `hspace`, etc.) to help position it within the form block. As with other images, is a good idea to specify `height` and `width` attributes, although, to simplify the definition, we have not done so here.

Reset Button

```
<input type="reset" value="Reset Form" />
```

[Reset Form]

When clicked, a reset button automatically resets a form's elements to their original state. By "original state" we mean how the HTML attributes instructed the form elements to be rendered. User changes to the form are wiped out. The value attribute specifies the text that appears on the button.

Text Elements

The remainder of the form elements are responsible for carrying data. These can be grouped into two categories: elements that only carry text strings and those that provide choices for the user. We begin with the four that only carry text.

Text Field

```
<input type="text" value="Initial Contents" size="13" maxlength="20" />
```

| Initial Conter |

This is a single-line text entry field. The `value` attribute specifies any initial contents the field is to have. The `size` attribute specifies the width in characters of the field. The default is about 20 characters. The `maxlength` attribute specifies the maximum number of characters that the field will accept. If `maxlength` exceeds `size`, you can see that some characters are not visible in the field.

Password Text Field

```
<input type="password" value="obscured text" size="15" maxlength="15" />
```

| ████████████ |

A password text field is no more than a text field, where the characters are all rendered as asterisks or bullets. Appropriately named, it is usually used to obtain passwords. That way, someone looking over your shoulder will not see on the screen what you typed. It uses the same attributes as a standard text field.

Hidden Field

```
<input type="hidden" value="hidden data" />
```

This is a text-carrying form element where absolutely nothing is rendered in the Web page. The `value` attribute carries hidden data. There are several uses for hidden information, as we shall see.

Text Area

```
<textarea cols="25" rows="3">initial contents</textarea>
```

A text area is a multiple-line text entry or display area. In contrast to a text field, where the initial contents come from the value attribute, a text area gets any initial content from the contents of the `textarea` element. Text is automatically wrapped around in the text area, and scroll bars are provided so that content can exceed the height of the area.

Option-Creating Elements

The remainder of the form elements provide choices for the user. The choices can be simple "on/off" (Boolean in nature), or choices that allow the user to choose from a list.

Checkbox

```
<input type="checkbox" />
<input type="checkbox" checked="checked" />
```

☐ ☑

A checkbox provides an on/off choice. If two or more checkboxes are provided, the user can choose any number of them. That is, the user can "check" none, one, two, . . . ; or all of the checkboxes. By default, a checkbox is "unchecked" when it is marked up. The `checked` attribute causes a checkbox to be initially checked when it is rendered. (Before XHTML, `checked` was included as a stand-alone attribute without a value.)

Radio Button

```
<input type="radio" name="group1" />
<input type="radio" name="group1" checked="checked"/>
```

Radio buttons are similar to checkboxes in that they can be either checked or unchecked. However, if a group of them share the same name, only one in that group can be selected. This is the *unique-selection* property. Using the two shown here for example, if we were to select the first one, the second one would automatically uncheck. The two radio buttons share the same name, so they form a *unique-selection* group. Multiple unique-selection groups can be formed by choosing different names, each one common only to all radio buttons in a given group.

Radio buttons should not be used like checkboxes. If you click on a checked checkbox, it becomes unchecked. However, you can't unselect a radio button by clicking on it. If a radio button is part of a unique-selection group, clicking another in the group will uncheck it. The only other way to unselect one is if the form is provided with a reset button (which also clears the rest of the form). In a sense, each radio button does have an on/off functionality, but they really work together to form lists of options, where only one in a given list can be selected. (They get their name from the old car radios, where you selected among preset stations by pushing a button. When you did, the button that had previously been selected popped out automatically. You show your age if you admit to remembering those radios!)

Pop-up Menu (Pull-down Menu)

```
<select>
  <option>item 1</option>
  <option>item 2</option>
  <option>item 3</option>
  <option>item 4</option>
</select>
```

```
<select multiple="multiple">
  <option>item 1</option>
  <option>item 2</option>
  <option>item 3</option>
  <option>item 4</option>
</select>
```

```
  item 1
  item 2
✓ item 3  ↕
  item 4
```

```
item 1
item 2   ▲
item 3
item 4   ▼
```

A pop-up menu, sometimes called a *pull-down menu*, organizes a list of items from which the user can make a selection. The menu on the left, the default variety, allows the user to make only one selection. It is a *single-selection menu*. A single-selection menu basically functions like a unique-selection group of radio buttons, but in a single-selection menu the choices are hidden and only pop up when the menu is clicked by the user. This is advantageous when the list of choices is long and would otherwise clutter up the Web page if a group of radio buttons were used.

The menu on the right uses the `multiple="multiple"` attribute, which allows the user to make more than one choice. (Again, before XHTML the attribute was included as `multiple` without a value.) This type of menu does not pop up on the screen but forms a visible *multiple-selection menu*. The `multiple` attribute gives the list a functionality similar to that of a group of checkboxes, but with a selection list there is a `size` attribute that limits the number of options that are displayed on the screen at a given time. Again, a multiple-selection list is used when the amount of options would clutter the Web page if checkboxes were used. Physically, multiple selections are made by using the ctrl (or command) key in concert with the mouse.

Attribute Summaries

Text fields, hidden fields, text areas, checkboxes, radio buttons, and pop-up menus are all of the form elements (or form components) we will use for collecting and displaying data. You may have noticed that most of them are `input` HTML elements, where the `type` attribute determines which element is created. Only two are created with different tags: the `textarea` element and the `select` element.

In the preceding descriptions the attributes specific to each `type` of `input` element were given. It's a strange HTML feature that one element, the `input` element, uses different attributes depending upon which `type` has been set for the element. Thus, the `input` element summary in Table 3.2 lists only those attributes used by all types. Summaries for the two form elements that use their own tags follow in Tables 3.3 and 3.4.

TABLE 3.2   HTML Elements for Input

`<input />`   Inline element

ATTRIBUTE		POSSIBLE VALUES	DEFAULT
type	Control buttons	`button, submit, image, reset`	`text`
	Data-carrying elements	`text, password, hidden, checkbox, radio`	
name		Any text string	
value		Any text string	

*Other attributes may be used depending upon the type of input element.

TABLE 3.3   The `textarea` HTML Element

`<textarea >. . .</textarea>`   Inline element

ATTRIBUTE	POSSIBLE VALUES	DEFAULT
cols	Integer*	Browser-specific
rows	Integer*	Browser-specific
name	text string	

*Integer values for columns and rows represents text characters, not pixels.

TABLE 3.4   HTML Elements for Pop-up Menus

`<select >. . .</select>` Inline Element

ATTRIBUTE	POSSIBLE VALUES	DEFAULT	DESCRIPTION
`multiple`	`multiple="multiple"`	Single-selection menu	Allows the user to make multiple selections from the menu. If `multiple` is set to `"multiple"`, the menu is displayed as a selection list rather then a pop-up menu.
`size`	Integer	1	Specifies the number of items to be displayed. If set to a number greater than 1, the menu is displaycd as a selection list, rather then a pop-up menu. It is commonly used to limit the number of visible options in a selection list (multiple-selection menu).
`name`	Any text string		

`<option >. . .</option>`* Used only inside the `select` element

ATTRIBUTE	POSSIBLE VALUES	DEFAULT	DESCRIPTION
`selected`	`selected="selected"`	No items are selected	Causes an option to be initally selected. If `multiple` is enabled in the `select` element, more that one option can be initially selected.
`value`	Any text string	1	

*This is not a form element per se, but an element used to create a list of options within the `select` form element.

NOTE

You may have noticed that all form elements have a `name` attribute. The `name` attribute is used to identify a form element. In contrast, the `value` attributes of form elements carry the actual data. The "`name` for identification, `value` for data" principle is used for two different purposes.

First, form data is organized into *name-value pairs* before it is submitted to a Web server. For example, when the text field

`<input type="text" name="address" value="" />`

is submitted to the server, its data is summarized with the name-value pair

`address="1234 Maple Ave."`

where the text string carrying the actual address is what the user enters into the field. The name provides identification back on the server as to what piece of data has been submitted.

The second use is for form processing on the client, where names and values are treated differently. The `name` attribute is used to provide reference to a particular `value` attribute. In other words, the form's data is contained in a bunch of attributes, all called value, and you need to reference a particular one. The name attribute gives you that specific reference. For example, for the text field in this example, address.value is a JavaScript variable containing whatever text string the user enters into the text field.

A Form Submission Example

We conclude this section with an example that uses many of the form elements we have introduced. The example serves two purposes. It shows you the form elements put together into a large form, and it shows how name-value pairs are submitted to the server. Figure 3.1 shows an HTML form that simulates an online survey that UWEB's computer science department might use to collect information from transfer students.

The first thing to note is that the value of the action attribute of the form element specifies the URL of a server-side CGI program to which the form's data is to be submitted. The program, echo.cgi, is a special program we have prepared that does nothing more than send the data submitted by the form back to the browser in a Web page.

The second thing to note, besides the syntax of the form elements themselves, is the names and values given to the form elements. Neither the text fields nor the text area, however, were assigned a value in the HTML code. Those values are supplied by the user. The option-giving elements (checkboxes, radio buttons, and menu) have each been given value attributes. The user can't supply a value, since those elements carry no mechanism to collect text from the user. Effectively, those values are hidden data corresponding to the choices given to the user.

You can assume that the hidden field at the bottom of the form definition is used to carry additional information for some administrative purpose. In the source code for Figure 3.1 we have omitted the rest of the HTML document (head, body, and so forth) to save some space. In the full document, the form is contained inside the body element.

Let's suppose that the form has been filled out as shown in Figure 3.1 and Frodo hits the submit button. The output returned by the echo program is shown in Figure 3.2. Notice that the data is organized into name=value pairs, where the names are those given to the form elements in the HTML code. For the text-carrying elements, the values are the user's text entries. For the option-creating elements, the values are the "hidden values" corresponding to the user's choice.

There are two reasons why you should go to the Web site and submit the form for yourself a couple of times using your own values. The first is so that you can see firsthand how the submitted data relates to the names and values hard-coded into the HTML form and to the data you enter. The second reason is so that you see how the data gets to the server. Notice that the form's method attribute specifies get. That means that the data is appended onto the URL that calls the CGI program as a query string. When you try it, you will see a query string like

```
http://www.cknuckles.com/cgi/echo.cgi?name=Frodo+Baggins&email=ring-
bearer@shire.com&language=java&language=javascript&addi-
tional=XHTML&year=sophomore&country=0&admin=hidden+data
```

As you see, the name=value pairs are concatenated into one long string using ampersands, which are boldfaced here for emphasis, as the delimiting character. Web browsers do the concatenation automatically as part of HTTP. So basically all the echo program does on the server is split the individual pairs back out and return them in a Web page.

```
<form action="http://www.cknuckles.com/cgi/echo.cgi" method="get">

    <b>UWEB Computer Science Department Survey</b><hr />
    Name:
<input type="text" name="name" /><br />
    E-mail
<input type="text" name="email" /><br />
    <b>Check any programming languages you know.</b><br />
<input type="checkbox" name="language" value="cplusplus" /> C++<br />
<input type="checkbox" name="language" value="java" /> Java<br />
<input type="checkbox" name="language" value="javascript" /> JavaScript<br />
<input type="checkbox" name="language" value="perl" /> Perl<br />
    <b>List any additional programming experience.</b><br />
<textarea name="additional" rows="3" cols="35" value=""></textarea><br />
    <b>What year have you completed in college?</b><br />
<input type="radio" name="year" value="none" /> None<br />
<input type="radio" name="year" value="freshman" /> Freshman<br />
<input type="radio" name="year" value="sophomore" /> Sophomore<br />
<input type="radio" name="year" value="junior" /> Junior<br />
<input type="radio" name="year" value="senior" /> Senior<br />
    <br />
<input type="submit" value="Submit The Form" /><br />
<input type="reset"  value="Reset The Form" /><br />
    <br />
    <b>In what country were you born?</b><br />
<select name="country">
  <option value="0">Middle Earth</option>
  <option value="1">Afghanistan</option>
  <option value="2">Albania</option>
  <option value="236">Zambia</option>
  <option value="237">Zimbabwe</option>
</select>

<input type="hidden" name="admin" value="hidden data" /><br />
</form>
```

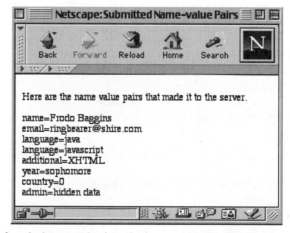

FIGURE 3.1   A typical HTML form.

FIGURE 3.2   The form's data sent back to the browser by the server-side echo program.

You will soon see that the names of form elements take on a distinctly different role when HTML forms are processed using JavaScript on the client. In that case, the names are used as variable names in object references. The names reference the form elements in JavaScript statements, but the values still carry the form's data. That being said, let's learn some JavaScript!

> **NOTE**
>
> Although we won't formally deal with submitted form data in CGI programs until Chapter 6, the echo program will be helpful in the mean time. Any time you build an HTML form, simply submit it to the following URL.
>
> ```
> http://www.cknuckles.com/cgi/echo.cgi
> ```
>
> That program accepts both the GET and POST methods of form submission. The echo program will prove particularly handy later in this chapter, when you will validate that the user has entered proper information into a form before submitting it to the server.

3.2 THE JAVASCRIPT LANGUAGE

JavaScript was developed by Netscape Communications to provide client-side programming support for its browser. It reared its head onto the Web in late 1995. The language is syntactically based on Java, but is very different from Java in its functionality. (People often lump the two together. They shouldn't.) With JavaScript gaining in popularity, Microsoft soon introduced its version, called Jscript, in 1996 for use in Internet Explorer 3. But JavaScript was too well entrenched for Microsoft to bully it off the Web. What is used on the Web today is a common subset of JavaScript and Jscript that is platform- and browser-independent. It is simply called JavaScript[1].

We won't be able to deal with form data on the back end until we learn some CGI programming with Perl. However, JavaScript provides for a rich processing tool for the data right on the client. There are several useful chores that JavaScript can tackle on the front end of a Web application. Before we get to that, we look at JavaScript as a traditional programming language. If you are familiar with C++ or Java, you will find that the programming concepts you have learned are no different here. Even the syntax is similar. The transition should be seamless.

The HTML `script` element is a container whose only purpose is to contain client-side scripting instructions, JavaScript in our case. In fact, if

```
I am <script>thinking that you are</script> uncool.
```

is included in an HTML document, it will render as

```
I am uncool.
```

---

[1]Similar to what the W3C has done for HTML, an international standards organization (ECMA International, `http://www.ecma-international.org`) has issued a core standardization for JavaScript. Technically, the current cross-platform JavaScript version is ECMA-262, or simply ECMAScript.

(That's enough incentive to use it only as a script container.) When the HTML processor encounters the `script` element, it ignores it. The element's contents are processed by a browser's scripting engine, in our case the JavaScript interpreter. It is best to include Java-Script in an HTML file as follows.

```
<script language="javascript">
<!--

JavaScript statements

//-->
</script>
```

The HTML comment markers hide the JavaScript statements from older browsers that don't know to ignore the `script` element, and the two forward slashes are a JavaScript comment marker to hide the closing HTML comment marker. Since JavaScript has become ubiquitous, most browsers will still execute the statements assuming they are JavaScript even if `language="javascript"` is not included.

NOTE

Your best bet is simply to make a new skeleton document containing the above construct. That way, each time you make a new Web page that uses JavaScript, you can copy the skeleton file. Theoretically, only once is it necessa.ry to type the `script` element construct with the comment symbols.

To show you how simple the language is, we start with an example that any programmer can understand, even if she has never seen JavaScript. Figure 3.3 shows a very basic JavaScript program, together with its rendition. The first thing to note is that you just load the HTML file into a browser, and the JavaScript interpreter handles the code. JavaScript is an interpreted language, meaning that JavaScript programs (*scripts*[2]) are never compiled into a platform-specific executable. The same script you see in Figure 3.3 can be passed to browsers around the world to be interpreted time and time again, and on any operating system that supports a JavaScript-capable browser.

When JavaScript is used like a traditional language, many of the same principles apply: Get input from the user, store the input in variables, process the input with control structures (`if . . . else`, loops, arrays, and so forth), and then give output. In Figure 3.3 the output is simply written to the HTML document using `document.write()` statements. You can see from the HTML code produced by the statements that the quoted text strings have been written to the document "as is," and the variables were replaced by their

---

[2]By definition, *programs* give instructions to the operating system, whereas *scripts* give instructions to other programs (such as a browser application). We may abuse the terminology from time to time.

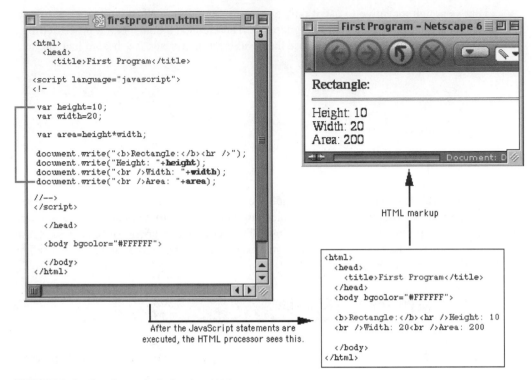

FIGURE 3.3 Our first calculation in a Web page.

contents. We will forgo crude methods for acquiring user input in favor of waiting until we learn enough to process input from HTML forms.

Don't worry if you don't fully understand the example in Figure 3.3. As we summarize language features in the course of this lesson, the details of that script will become clear. If you know some C++ or Java (or even Pascal or some other language), we think you will be surprised to find out that you are already familiar with the majority of the language. The power to use standard programming constructs to give processing capability to a Web page is the new concept here. Alone, HTML can't even perform the simple multiplication calculation accomplished in Figure 3.3.

Statements

A JavaScript statement is terminated with a semicolon. It is customary to put statements on separate lines for readability. *Important:* If a JavaScript statement gets so long as to wrap around in the window that you are using to edit the script, let it. Do not hit Enter on the keyboard in the middle of a statement. In some cases, that confuses the interpreter into thinking the statement is terminated.

Variables

In JavaScript, variables, are **loosely typed**. (That does not mean you should stretch out before typing in variable declarations.) It means any of the primary literal types—

numeric, string, or Boolean—can be assigned to a variable with no formal type declaration. The following three statements declare a variable initializing it with a numeric literal, reassigning it a string literal, and then reassigning it a Boolean literal.

```
var x=3.14;
x="a string";
x=true;
```

No harm, no foul. That's a huge difference from *strongly typed* languages such as C++ and Java, where each variable's type must be strictly defined. Also, there is no type for single characters. Characters are simply one-character strings.

A variable should be declared using `var`. You can see in the first statement in the preceeding example that a variable can be declared and initialized in one statement. After that, it can be reassigned values of the three primary types at will. Assignment of numbers and strings is straightforward, but note that strings can also be assigned using single quotes:

```
x = 'a string';
```

However, the convention is to use double quotes.

A Boolean literal is not a string. For example,

```
x = "false";
```

merely stores a five-character string into `x`. JavaScript reserves `true` and `false` as special unquoted Boolean literal values. Storing other nonreserved unquoted values into a variable results in an error.

```
x = oops;   //bad statement (unless oops is a variable)
```

JavaScript has the same rules for variable names as almost any other language. They must start with an alphabetic character, they can contain numeric characters (not as the first character, of course), and the only allowed special character is the underscore (_). The names `num`, `num2`, and `num_2` are legal, but `2num`, `_num`, and `num-2` are not legal. You should also avoid the JavaScript reserved words listed in Appendix B. As in most languages, variable names are case sensitive.

NOTE

In addition to the standard literal types (number, string, and Boolean), JavaScript has special literal types that it uses when calculations go bad. For example, a statement like

```
var y=2*"oops";
```

causes `y` to contain the literal value `NaN` (Not a Number). If a variable has been declared but not initialized,

```
var z;
```

it is assigned the literal value `undefined`. Even division by zero,

```
var a = 2/0;
```

results in the special literal value `Infinity`.

Remember, JavaScript code is completely portable, being embedded in Web pages flying around to client browsers all over the planet. Moreover, one of its main uses is processing user data while it is still on the client. Inherently, user data is unreliable in that you don't know in advance what you are going to get. Thus, it is desirable for JavaScript to generate special literals upon encountering bad calculations rather than crashing the browser, for example. When you see special literals (`NaN`, `undefined`, `Infinity`), you can assume that a calculation has gone bad in your script or that a variable has been left uninitialized.

Operations

Operations in JavaScript are standard. For numeric quantities there are the *arithmetic operations* listed in Table 3.5, which return numbers. There are *comparison operations,* listed in Table 3.6, which return Boolean values. For example, `x=(4!=4);` causes x to contain `false`, and `x=(4==4);` causes x to contain `true`. We have to take this opportunity to make the important note that `=` *is for variable assignment, and* `==` *is for equality comparison.*

Also, comparison of strings is standard, with characters inheriting a sequential ordering from their ASCII numbers. For our purposes, it is sufficient to note that string equality implies that the strings match character for character. So the expressions `"abC"=="abc"` and `"bac"=="abc"` both evaluate to `false`.

Finally, there are the *logical operations*, listed in Table 3.7, which compare Boolean expressions and return Boolean values. For example, the expression `(2==3)||("abc"=="abc")` evaluates to `true` since the second operand is `true`, but `(2==3)&&("abc"=="abc")` evaluates to `false` since the first operand is `false`. It never hurts to emphasize that and and or are radically different. To throw in a negation, `(!(2==3))&&("abc"=="abc")` evaluates to `true`.

TABLE 3.5 JavaScript Arithmetic Operations

OPERATION	MEANING
+	Addition
–	Subtraction
*	Multiplication
/	Division
%	Modulus*

*Modulus is the remainder when one integer is divided into another. For example, `x=11%3;` causes x to contain the number 2.

TABLE 3.6   JavaScript Comparison Operations

OPERATION	MEANING
==	Equal to
!=	Not equal to
>	Greater than
>=	Greater than or equal to
<	Less than
<=	Less than or equal to

TABLE 3.7   JavaScript Logical Operations

OPERATION	MEANING
&&	And: `true` only if both operands are `true`
||	Or: `false` only if both operands are `false`
!	Not: Negates its operand

> **NOTE**
>
> Rather than memorizing rules for associativity that govern the order of evaluation in expressions that mix the operator types, it's best simply to use parentheses liberally to force the expression to evaluate properly.

Shortcut Assignment Operators

JavaScript uses the same shortcut assignments (++, +=, and so forth) as C++ and Java. The only one we will use in this text is

```
x++;
```

which has the same effect as

```
x=x+1;
```

which increments a numeric variable x by one.

Concatenation (Duality of +)

The + operator has a *duality* in JavaScript (that is, it's overloaded). Used strictly with numbers, it adds numbers. Used with strings, it *concatenates* (joins together). For example,

```
x=3;
y=4;
z=x+y;
```

causes z to contain the number 7 as you would expect, but

```
x="3";
y="4";
z=x+y;
a=y+x;
```

causes z to contain the string "34" and a to contain the string "43".

If types are mismatched in an expression, strings win out. For example,

```
x=3;
y="4";
z=x+y;
```

causes z to contain the string "34". This duality can cause problems in dealing with data from HTML forms. All form data (that is not Boolean) is stored as strings. An HTML form doesn't care whether the user enters numeric or alphabetic quantities; it just wants ASCII characters from the keyboard. If we want to add two pieces of form data, we will use the parseFloat() function to parse the strings into (floating-point decimal) numbers. For example,

```
x="3";
y="4";
z= parseFloat(x)+parseFloat(y);
```

causes z to contain the number 7. If a string is intrinsically a number, the parseFloat() function returns the numeric equivalent. In contrast, parseFloat("abc") returns the special value NaN.

For a practical example, we could have put the concatenation operator to good use in the script of Figure 3.3. We can simply concatenate all of the arguments of the document.write() statements together into one long string. The following statement produces the exact same result. We have applied boldface to the variables so that you can easily see where the strings begin and end.

```
document.write("<b>The following summarizes the rectangle </b><hr/>Height:
"+height+"<br />Width: "+width+"<br />Area: "+area);
```

Also, we re-emphasize that in a long statement like the foregoing, we let it wrap around according to the margin. Hitting Enter in the middle of a statement is often problematic.

NOTE

JavaScript chooses the most basic way to represent a numeric quantity. For example, if you assign 4.0 to a variable, you will get the integer 4 when you write the variable's contents. So even though the parseFloat() function purports to return floating-point decimal numbers, you will get an integer if no decimal points are required to represent the number. For that reason, we generally stick to parseFloat(), but there also is a parseInt() function.

Conditionals

Conditional structures provide for decision making capabilities. In JavaScript their general forms are given as in the following display.

```
if (Boolean expression) {

   block of statements;

}
```

```
if (Boolean expression) {

   block of statements;

}
else {

   block of statements;

}
```

```
if (Boolean expression) {

   block of statements;

}
else if (Boolean expression) {

   block of statements;

}
    .
    .
    .
else if (Boolean expression) {

   block of statements;

}
else {

   block of statements;

}
```

Some simple examples will help to acclimate you further to the language. We directly assign the values to the variables, but in practice they can come from user input. The following code simulates user input that is stored in the bid variable.

```
var bid="35";
if(bid <= 50) {
   document.write(bid+" does not meet the minimum bid.<br />");
}
else {
   document.write("Your bid of "+bid+" will be considered.<br />");
}
```

The code would result in

```
35 does not meet the minimum bid.<br />
```

being written to the body of the HTML document. The following code simulates validating user input. Assume the user input is stored in the quantity variable. The example uses the isNaN() function, which returns true if its argument is intrinsically not a numeric quantity (that is, if the quantity evaluates to the special variable type NaN). If the quantity is numeric, the isNaN function returns false.

```
var quantity="4x";
var price=19.99;
var discount=0;
var total=0;
if(isNaN(quantity)) {
   document.write("Error : non-numeric quantity");
```

```
}
else {
  if((quantity > 10) && (quantity <100)) {
    discount=.1;
  }
  if((quantity > 100) {
    discount=.25;
  }

  total=price*quantity*(1-discount);
  document.write("Order Total: "+total);
}
```

The code would result in the error message being written to the body of the HTML document.

NOTE

In both of the foregoing examples we stored the simulated user input as string data. Again, that's how any piece of data is stored in an HTML form `value`. You can see here how flexible JavaScript is. The comparison (`bid <= 50`) reduces to (`"35" <= 50`), which is a problem in a strongly typed language. However, JavaScript converts the comparison into a numeric context on the fly. The duality of `+` is the only thing to watch out for. The expression (`"35"+50`) converts to string context and concatenates the strings into `"3550"`.

When dealing with HTML forms, we will often use conditionals in the manner shown in the following pseudocode. We use pseudocode to get the logic of a programming implementation across to the reader, without having to use full syntax. The logic behind this idea is very simple.

```
if (user enters bad input into form) {
    give an alert—don't process the form data
}
else {
    process the form data
}
```

Loops

The JavaScript `for` and `while` loops are standard. In the following figure you see a `for` loop whose counter runs from 1 to 100, and the general form of a `while` loop.

```
for (var x=1 ; x<=100 ; x=x+1) {

    block of statements;

}
```

```
while (Boolean expression) {

    block of statements;

}
```

Since most of the looping we need for form processing in this text involves a predetermined number of executions, we use the `for` loop in the following examples. This example writes the even numbers from 2 to 2000, each on a separate line in the Web page.

```
for (var x=2 ; x<=2000 ; x=x+2) {
   document.write(x+"<br />");
}
```

The following loop is equivalent to the previous one. It uses the shortcut assignment x++ (which is the same as x=x+1), and demonstrates that the loop counter can be altered inside the body of a loop.

```
for (var x=1 ; x<2000 ; x++) {
   x++;
   document.write(x+"<br />");
}
```

A more interesting example prints out a table with r rows and two columns. Each table cell contains the HTML escape sequence for a space ( ). (If you recall, some browsers don't like to render empty table cells.)

```
document.write("<table border='1'>");
var r=45;
for (var x=1 ; x<=r ; x++) {
   document.write("<tr><td> </td><td> </td></tr>");
}
document.write("</table>");
```

That's a big HTML table for just a few lines of JavaScript code! Here you start to see the power that a programming language can bring to a Web page. To create a table with a variable number of rows and columns, you need to nest two loops. We leave that as an exercise.

NOTE

Be careful if you write HTML attributes to the document using the document.write() function. In the preceeding loop that prints out the table, we used single quotes to delimit the value of the border attribute. Using regular quotes in that case would cause a syntax error. The JavaScript interpreter would treat "<table border=" as the argument of the document.write() statement.

For the last loop example, we turn to more pseudocode to emphasize the logic of how we can apply loops to HTML form processing. Suppose a form has a bunch of checkboxes for selecting products in an online store. The price of each product is stored in the value property of the corresponding checkbox. Remember how checkboxes work—any number of them can be selected. One way to add up the prices is to use if statements.

```
if (first checkbox selected) {
   add its price to total
}
```

```
if (second checkbox selected) {
    add its price to total
}
    .
    .
    .
```

But if there are 50 checkboxes, that would require 50 if statements. Of course, the way to deal with the need for repetition is to loop over the checkboxes:

```
var num=the number of checkboxes;
for (var x=1 ; x<=num ; x++) {
    if (checkbox x is selected) {
      add its price to total
      }
}
```

In JavaScript the scope of the loop counter of a for loop is not limited to the execution of the loop. For example, in the preceding loop that prints out the table, the variable x still exists and contains the value 46 after the loop has terminated. The foregoing examples all used x as the loop counter. If we were to put all those loops into the same script, that would cause no problem. Although a variable declared as a for loop counter is effectively a global variable, it is allowed to be redeclared repetitively in the for loop context.

Functions

The following figure shows the general form of a JavaScript function. A function can be defined anywhere in a script, but it is customary to define one before you need to use it. When the JavaScript interpreter reads a script, it merely makes note of any functions it may encounter. No functions are executed until they are called.

```
function function_name(parameter1, parameter2, . . . ) {

    block of statements;

}
```

Following the function keyword, the name of the function must adhere to the same rules that govern variable names. Literals are passed to the parameters by value rather than by reference. Thus, when literal values are passed to function parameters, the parameters behave like local variables within the function. However, JavaScript does pass objects to functions by reference.

The first example creates and calls a *void function*—one that affects the global environment and does not return a value.

```
function customrule(width,char) {
  for (var x=1 ; x<=width ; x++) {
    document.write(char);
    }
    document.write("<br />");
}
```

When the function is called, it must be sent two values, one for each parameter. For example, the call

```
customrule(25,"#");
```

copies the two literals into the function parameters. The function then writes a customized horizontal rule to the document. For the call just shown, it would look like

```
#########################
```

Note that the function writes a line break only after the loop has written the 25 characters.

The second example creates and calls a *return function*—one that returns a value when called and does not affect the global environment.

```
function times10(num) {
  num=num*10;
  return num;
}
```

It's pretty obvious what the function does. The thing to note is that a return function can't be called as a stand-alone statement. A call to a return function is replaced with the returned value. For example, the statement

```
times10(2);
```

looks like

```
20;
```

after the value is returned. That is not a viable statement. Rather we assign the returned value to a variable:

```
var num=times10(4);
```

which causes the variable num to contain 40. If decisions need to be made in a return function, multiple return statements can be included. The function simply terminates and returns the value specified by the first return statement it encounters in the flow of execution.

The scope of function parameters and any local variables defined within a function is limited to that function. For example, consider the following block of code.

```
function scopedemo(x) {
  var y=10;

  x++;
  y=x+y;
  z++;
}

var x=2;
```

```
var y=3;
var z=4;

scopedemo(z);
```

In the flow of execution, nothing happens until the three variable declarations below the function are encountered. They are initialized with the numbers 2, 3, and 4. Next, the function is called, copying the contents of z into the parameter x. The parameter x, which contains 4, is distinct from the global variable x, which contains 2. Next, the local function variable y is created and assigned 10. Again, the local variable is distinct from the global y which contains 3. The next two assignments involve only the x and y local to the function. The global x and y are neither altered nor accessed. Next, since there is no local variable z in the function, the z++ assignment acts on the global level. The legacy of this block of code is that the global variables x, y, and z contain the values 2, 3, and 5, respectively. The two local variables x and y simply no longer exist in the computer's memory. They were erased as soon as the function ceased execution.

Below is a pseudocode example to show how we will employ functions for HTML form processing. Again, the logic is very simple. We revisit the earlier pseudocode example, in which we wished to validate a form's contents before processing it. Suppose the form has a button that calls the following JavaScript function:

```
function validateform() {
    if (user enters bad input into form) {
        give an alert
        return false;  (don't process the form data)
    }
    else {
        return true;  (OK to process the form data)
    }
}
```

As we shall see, a form's data is carried in global variables. We simply access the global variables from within a function. No parameters are required. If no parameters are used in a function, the parentheses () must still be provided in both the function definition and the function call. Note that this function both performs a procedure by alerting the user and returns a value.

Objects

JavaScript supports programmer-defined objects, but it lacks the inheritance mechanism of fully object-oriented languages such as C++ and Java. Programmer-defined objects are not often used in JavaScript, because you mainly instantiate built-in objects or simply use the ones a Web browser creates for you. For that reason, JavaScript is sometimes called an *object-based* language, rather than object oriented. We will see ample evidence of this characteristic beginning in Section 3.3. (Note that future versions of JavaScript are slated to be fully object-oriented, with classes and inheritance.)

Reading and Writing to Files

JavaScript is client-side code, meaning that the code someone else writes is transported to your computer and executed there. Feeling uneasy? You needn't. The only file on your computer that JavaScript can read from and write to is the cookie file, which is used to store user information (unreliably) on the client between Web transactions.

JavaScript would have been a disaster if it had access to other files on you computer. Oops, there go all your documents. We think you get the idea. JavaScript is not often used to manipulate the cookie file, in favor of dealing with cookies on the server or not using them at all. We will discuss that later in this text.

Arrays

JavaScript fully supports programmer-defined arrays, which technically are objects. A constructor is called to instantiate an array.

```
var list=new Array();
```

The list[] array, then contains an arbitrary number of indices, each vacuously containing the undefined literal. For example,

```
document.write(list[100]);
```

would write undefined to the HTML document (literally!). With no predefined size or index range, indices can be added on the fly.

```
list[0]="hello";
list[1]=3.14;
list[1000]=true;
```

You can see that literal types can be mixed and matched in an array.

Every array object has a length property that gives the range of the indices that have been assigned. For example, after only the three preceding assignments, list.length is a variable that contains 1001. For that reason, it is best to stick with standard indexing—start at 0 and progress sequentially through the positive integers. That way, you can predictable loop over the array indices.

```
for(var x=0 ; x < list.length ; x++) {
   alter or access list[x]
}
```

In JavaScript, programmer-defined arrays are useful for storing lists of images for use in rollover displays, for example. In traditional languages, arrays are often used to store lists of data read in from files. In JavaScript that's not a factor.

Most of your use of arrays will involve those that a browser automatically creates. For example, a browser automatically creates an elements[] array so that you can sequentially access a form's elements. Then, elements[0] references the first of a form's elements, elements[1] references the second, and so forth.

JavaScript supports multidimensional arrays. In JavaScript, a multidimensional array is technically an array of objects, where the objects are other arrays. Since there is no application for these in this book, that is all we will say here.

We offer one more example to re-emphasize that objects are passed to functions by reference. Suppose you have an array

```
var a = new Array();
a[0] = 23;
a[1] = 44;
a[2] = 67;
```

which, for simplicity, holds only three values. Now suppose you define and call a function intended to swap two values in the array.

```
function swap(j,k) {
   var temp = j;
   j = k;
   k = temp;
}

swap(a[0],a[2]);
```

Here the `swap` function does not affect the global array `a[]` in the least, because the two literals are passed to it by value, as all literals are. A solution that actually works is to pass a reference to the array to the function, along with the two indices that are to be swapped:

```
function swap(anArray,j,k) {
   var temp = anArray[j];
   anArray[j] = anArray[k];
   anArray[k] = temp;
}

swap(a,0,2);
```

The function call passes reference to the global array into the parameter `anArray`. Of course, the indices are passed by value because they are literal values. In other languages, one can designate whether values are passed by value or reference. In JavaScript, when an object name is passed to a function, it is always passed by reference. Literals are always passed by value.

Another solution is to pass only the indices to the function and alter the array as a global variable inside the function.

```
function swap(j,k) {
   var temp = a[j];
   a[j] = a[k];
   a[k] = temp;
}

swap(0,2);
```

It is often considered bad practice, however, to alter global variables inside a function without formally passing reference to the global variable to the function. Such an alteration is sometimes called a *side effect* of a function. In JavaScript code used to process form data, global variables are often altered inside functions without references being passed. Those global variables, however, are properties of the Browser Object (discussed in Section 3.3), rather than being programmer-defined objects.

Comments

Single-line comments in JavaScript are of the form

```
//  text ignored by JavaScript interpreter
```

and multiple-line comments are of the form

```
/*  text ignored by
JavaScript interpreter  */
```

We do not use comments in the examples in this chapter because the scripts are fairly short, and we don't want to create extra clutter.

Scripts in General

All of the JavaScript code in a given HTML file collectively forms the *script* for that file. Script snippets can be mixed in with the HTML at various locations. Of course, JavaScript code has to be contained in the HTML `script` element. Figure 3.4 shows the source code and rendering of a Web page that features three different JavaScript code blocks.

There are variations among the ways browsers handle scripts when a document is first loaded, but basically, the JavaScript interpreter goes first, then the HTML parse tree is constructed. The different script sections don't really make any difference to the JavaScript interpreter. It simply starts executing statements from the top down. It does, however, preserve the ordering within the HTML to the extent that a `document.write()` statement writes its argument at the location the statement appears.

You can also see from this example that the scope of a global variable is that of the whole document. The `astring` variable in Figure 3.4 is declared and initialized in the head section, but its contents are not retrieved until much later in the document. There is no such thing as variable scope within a `script` element. To the JavaScript interpreter it's just one script.

Debugging Scripts

For the first five years or so of its existence, JavaScript lacked the robust syntax-debugging support that compiled languages enjoy. Java and C++ development environments usually have elaborate debuggers built in. Moreover, if one of those programs has syntax errors, it simply won't compile. However, if you load a broken script into a browser, any number of things can happen. You might get a blank Web page if the interpreter is completely confounded. (In some cases broken JavaScript will even crash a Web browser.) If the browser can make some sense out of the code, you might just get some partial results. Or the script might work except for a small glitch.

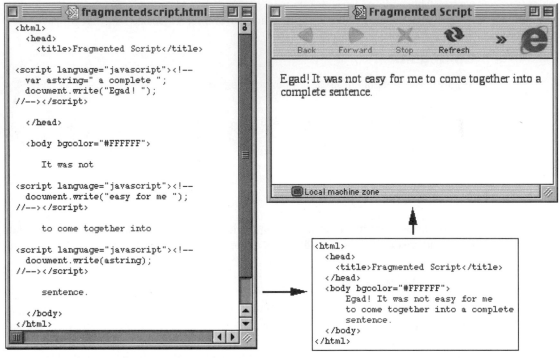

FIGURE 3.4 A script is a global entity for the document.

The easiest strategy for JavaScript is to load the document into a browser and see what you get (jokingly, WYCIWYG—"what you code is what you get"). Often you can figure out what has gone wrong by observing the Web page that results. Another good method is to put in a `document.write("hello")` statement (or a call to the `alert()` function which you will see shortly) at various locations in the script to see how far the JavaScript interpreter made it through the code. If `"hello"` shows up when the statement is at one location in the code but not another, you can figure (most of the time) that the error is in between.

Fortunately, browsers have error-reporting consoles for JavaScript. We highly recommend that you make regular use of one of them. The ones we know of are shown in the following list. Even if a new browser comes out that we like better than the current ones ("Internet Pillager" would be a cool name for a browser), if it doesn't have a JavaScript error console, we will certainly still keep one of these browsers around just to help debug scripts.

For Windows

Internet Explorer 5 and 6: After executing broken JavaScript code, this browser displays a small exclamation-point icon in the lower left corner of the window, in the status bar. Clicking that icon will report syntax errors.

Netscape 4.7: After the browser executes broken JavaScript code, you simply type **javascript:** (that's lowercase *javascript* followed by a colon) into the address field of the browser and hit Enter. You get a JavaScript error console.

Netscape 6: After the browser executes broken JavaScript code, go to the **Tasks** menu, select **Tools**, and then JavaScript Console.

For Mac OS

Netscape 4.7: This has the same error console as Netscape 4.7 for Windows.

Netscape 6: This has the same error console as Netscape 6 for Windows.

NOTE

To our delight, Mozilla released a full-featured JavaScript debugger shortly before this book went off to production, so we were just able to slip this note in. The debugger, which has the powerful features you know and love from IDE-based debuggers, works in conjunction with any browser built on the Mozilla code base. That includes both Netscape 6 and the new Mozilla browser, on any popular platform. If you end up working with JavaScript a lot (or get a seriously confounding JavaScript error while progressing through this book), it will be worth your while to download Mozilla and learn to use it. You will find a link to it on the book's Web site.

Final Language Notes

We have tried to be succinct. The goal here is to learn enough about JavaScript so that you can process HTML form data on the client. If there is some language detail left out, about which you are wondering, it probably works the same way in JavaScript as it does in C++ or Java.

Certainly, fancy things that JavaScript can do on the front end (swapping images in and out, moving CSS blocks around, and so forth) are beyond the scope of our objectives. Our first book, *Introduction to Interactive Programming on the Internet* (John Wiley & Sons,) covers JavaScript from a more basic perspective and in more detail, including some of its "fancy" implementations. Chapter 19 of this book does survey DHTML

From the perspective of raw programming, you have seen enough to create really powerful (and portable!) programs. For example, with just the features we have described, a mathematician could write an elaborate 10-page JavaScript program that uses numerical analysis to approximate solutions to a differential equation; the language features are all there. JavaScript should not be dismissed as a trivial "scripting" language. Lack of support for reading data in from files might seem a limitation, but JavaScript has direct access to user data collected in HTML forms and even XML-formatted data when it is passed to a browser.

3.3   THE BROWSER OBJECT

Recall Section 2.1, where we represented two blocks of HTML code in terms of parse trees. We wanted you to think of a data structure that an HTML document represents based upon the containment relationships (nesting) of the HTML elements. Those were small trees, but if we consider the Web page as a whole, we get a potentially large tree. The parse tree is what the HTML processor uses to render a document. In addition to the

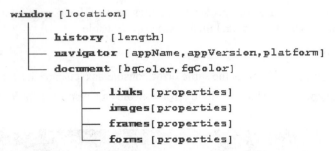

FIGURE 3.5 A depiction of the Browser Object.

parse tree, however, a browser also creates an object based upon the browser window and the HTML document it contains: the **Browser Object**, shown in Figure 3.5. It is often, and somewhat incorrectly, called the *Document Object Model (DOM)*.[3]

On one level, the Browser Object is a data structure that holds "state" information for the open window that contains the Web page and, more importantly, for the objects inside the Web page itself. The primitive variables[4] that hold the state information are listed in brackets after the boldfaced object names. Object properties can be other objects, but eventually there are primitive variables at the ends of the branches that carry the literal values.

On another level, the Browser Object has built-in methods that can be called to change its state. After all, objects by definition have both state and behavior. We discuss the properties of the Browser Object in this section and its methods in the next section.

NOTE

The main purpose of the Browser Object is to provide an *application programming interface (API)* between the Web browser software and the JavaScript language. JavaScript statements can directly access and update properties of the Browser Object and can call its methods.

The parent is the `window` object. The `window.location` variable contains the URL of the Web page (or other resource) currently displayed in the browser window. You can use JavaScript to change the state of the `window` object by assigning a new value to its `location` property,

```
window.location="http://www.cknuckles.com";
```

---

[3]The DOM is a very general application programming interface used to expose XML documents to various programming languages in various settings. HTML DOM, the full object exposed to JavaScript in Web browsers, is a "subset" of the DOM. DOM Level 0, which we call the Browser Object, is a "subset" of the HTML DOM. See Chapter 19 for more details and some history.

[4]Primitives are standard variables that contain literal values, primarily strings, numbers, and Boolean. Objects are not primitives but bind primitives together in a structured way.

which instantly loads the page that the URL points to. (Try it yourself; it's just a one-line script!) Changing that property with JavaScript is commonly used to transfer to a new page after a few seconds (as when a site has moved) or to load new pages when form buttons are clicked.

One level down in the hierarchy, the `window.history` object contains the list of URLs that have been stored in `window.location` since the window has been open. There is a history button/or menu, when a browser window is open, which lists titles of the last few pages to which you have surfed. Maybe you have used it to go back a few pages in your surfing history. The `window.history` array is parallel to that array (menus are just arrays) and contains the URLs of the pages whose titles you see when you click the history button or menu on your browser. The primitive variable `window.history.length` contains the length of the array (number of items in the surfing history).

The `window.navigator` object, whose name comes from Netscape's original Browser Object, has primitive properties that contain information about the browser type, browser version, and platform on which the browser is running. They are used for browser sniffing so that customized content can be delivered. The properties of this object are summarized in Appendix B, and an elementary browser sniff is given as an exercise.

The `window.document` object refers to the actual Web page. Its primitive properties and the rest of the objects you see nested below it in Figure 3.5 contain state information for the Web page. Two primitive properties whose values can be set using JavaScript are listed in Figure 3.5. Setting the two properties

```
window.document.bgColor="#000000";
window.document.fgColor="#FFFFFF";
```

in a script causes the background and foreground (text) colors to be instantly changed in the Web page to black and white, respectively. Including those statements in the Web page is equivalent to setting the values using HTML attributes. Either way, the colors are set as the Web page loads.[5]

The `window.document.images` object is an array that indexes all of the graphics that have been marked up in the Web page. Rollover graphics are created by using JavaScript to swap images in and out of that array. OK, we're starting to stray off the path. In fact, we're not going to talk about the `window.document.links` or `window.document.frames` arrays, which index those components of Web pages. The point here is that there is a big object that contains information about the current state of the Web page. JavaScript has access to many of the state variables and can assign values to them to affect the state of the Web page.

> **NOTE**
>
> Figure 3.5 does not show the complete Browser Object. Different browsers make somewhat different Browser Objects. Even if we were to stick to an object hierarchy common to all newer browsers, it's much too large for our purposes here. The `window.document.form` object is our primary agenda. To comprehend that object fully, it helps to know its place in the scheme of things.

---

[5]Setting colors in the `body` section of the document will override the corresponding HTML attributes set in the `body` element. However, the HTML color attributes in the HTML `body` tag may override color settings made by JavaScript in the head section. (There are browser-dependent nuances that determine this.)

3.4 METHODS FOR THE BROWSER OBJECT

We have seen a few instances of how JavaScript statements can be used to influence the state of the Browser Object and hence the Web page. Now we discuss some of its ***methods***—the built-in functions that can be called on the Browser Object to change its state. Of course, the methods will be called using JavaScript statements.

We will spend most of the rest of our time in this chapter manipulating the Browser Object with programmer-defined JavaScript functions, but some of the built-in methods are quite useful. We discuss a few of those here and explore some others in Chapter 18, which discusses some more advanced JavaScript topics. We provide a rather complete reference to the methods of the Browser Object in Appendix B.

At the `window` level, there is the `window.alert()` method. It takes one argument, a string, and causes a small window to pop up containing the string. Figure 3.6 shows a one-line script and the result. (We still haven't figured out what the guy in the MacOS alert window is saying.)

Other than the message, all the alert does is to halt the flow of execution of the script. For example, if the line of code in Figure 3.6 appeared in a longer script, the script would stop indefinitely at the alert call. The user would have to hit the OK button before the window would go away; only then would the JavaScript interpreter pass to the next statement in the script.

Another window method, of which you have seen evidence time and time again, is `window.open()`. A call to this method creates one of those pesky pop-up windows that typically contain an advertisement. Chapter 18 explains how to use the `window.open()` method to redirect the output from CGI programs to a new window.

Another method that you have called time and time again is `window.history.go()`. It takes one parameter, an integer, that moves you to a different index in the `window.history` array. The current page in the window is at index 0. So, for example, the call

```
window.history.go(-1);
```

is equivalent to hitting the "back" button on your browser. Incidentally, `window.history.go(-1)` is equivalent to `window.history.back()`.

We have been using a method of `window.document` for much of this chapter. The method does no more than write strings of text into the HTML document. It is `window.document.write()`.

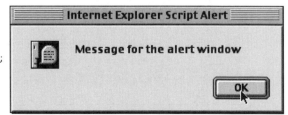

```
window.alert("Message for the alert window");
```

FIGURE 3.6 The `alert` method of the `window` object.

> **NOTE**
>
> There are two items of importance here. First, why have we been calling the method `document.write()` without using the full reference to the `window` object? Well, you don't have to. Because `window` is the parent object, you lose no specificity if you simply don't reference it. In fact, we could have accessed all of the object properties and methods in this section, and the last, without referencing the `window` object. We will still use the `window` reference for things like `window.alert()` and `window.history`, even though they are equivalent simply to `alert()` and `history`, in order to emphasize their place in the Browser Object. However, we will forgo reference to `window` at the `document` level and below.
>
> Second, all of the object, property, and method names we have used are case sensitive. So, for example, `document.bgcolor` would *not* be a recognized property in the Browser Object.

3.5 EVENTS

Interactive programming involves dealing with a ***user event***—when the user clicks a link or a form button, for example. An **event handler** is a special property of the Browser Object that can detect user events. The easiest way to handle a user event is to place an HTML attribute corresponding to the event handler inside an HTML tag.

For example, `onload` and `onunload` are two event handlers of the `window` object that are triggered when the Web page in the browser window loads and unloads, respectively. Formally, the event handlers are special properties of the `window` object:

```
window.onload
window.onunload
```

These handlers, however, are commonly put into action by placing corresponding event-handling attributes in the HTML `body` element. For example, the document shown in Figure 3.7 reacts to both the user loading the page and the user leaving the page.

When this Web page first loads into the browser, the `onload` event handler is triggered, and it executes its value as a JavaScript statement. In this case, the statement is a call to the `window.alert()` method. Similarly, the `onunload` event handler calls the `window.alert()` method, sending it a different message. You should go to this book's Web site and load the

```
<html>
  <head><title>Event Handlers</title></head>
  <body onload="alert('Hello!')" onunload="alert('Bye!')">
  Event Handler Demo.
  </body>
</html>
```

FIGURE 3.7 Reacting to `onload` and `onunload` events

page. The `onunload` event handler is triggered when you cause the browser to load another page, even if you reload the same page. So hitting the Refresh button on the browser triggers `onunload` and then `onload` again as the page reloads.

When an event handler is placed as an HTML attribute, the value of the handler can be any JavaScript statement (or sequence of statements separated with semicolons). For example, you could change the background and text colors of the Web page when it loads (although a reason to do so is hard to imagine).

```
<body onload="document.bgColor='red'; document.fgColor='blue';">
```

Note in the boldfaced JavaScript statements here and in Figure 3.7 that single quotes are used on the inside so that the event handler is well defined as an HTML attribute. Using double quotes on the inside will prematurely terminate the value of the HTML attribute.

In practice, the JavaScript statement called by an event handler is usually a function call, as in Figure 3.7, rather than an assignment statement. In Figure 3.7 we called a built-in function, but an event handler can call a programmer-defined function created to handle the event in a specialized way.

One thing a Web programmer needs to understand is the built-in event handler used by the `link` object to handle link click events. It is triggered using the `href` attribute. Consider the following two anchor elements.

```
<a href="http://www.cknuckles.com">go</a>

<a href="javascript:window.location='http://www.cknuckles.com';">go</a>
```

If you put these links in a Web page, they both accomplish the exact same thing. What we have done in the second one is override the built-in event handler. Rather than specifying a URL, as is normal, the `javascript:` directive in the value of the `href` attribute causes the rest of the value (shown in boldface) to be executed as a JavaScript statement. That causes the browser to load our home page, just like the ordinary link.

Pretty tricky—we have programmed our own link. But, as we have said, event handlers are usually used to call functions. If multiple JavaScript statements are required to handle the event, it's best simply to call a programmer-defined function and deal with the event elsewhere. That's precisely what we do in the HTML file in Figure 3.8.

When the user causes the `click` event on the link, control is given to the JavaScript interpreter. The JavaScript statement is a call to the programmer-defined `handle_event()` function. That function changes the text and background colors of the Web page, calls the `alert()` method, and then transfers the browser one back in the surfing history (hits the back button). Try it! As always, the source code is on this book's Web site.

Although it's cool to make a link do whatever you want it to, the script shown in Figure 3.8 is not practical. However, custom event handlers for links are often used to open a new Web page in a pop-up window, for example. The important concept for us here is this: The user causes an event, a JavaScript function is called, and that function does something to the Browser Object to change its state.

Since the primary focus of this chapter is on manipulating the `form` object, we will primarily use event handlers associated with that object. Typical form events are clicking a

```
┌─────────────────────────────────────────────────────────┐
│ □        📄 linkevent.html              □ ▤ │
├─────────────────────────────────────────────────────────┤
│ <html>                                                    ⌐ │
│   <head><title>Custom Link Event</title>                  │
│ <script language="JavaScript"><!--                        │
│                                                           │
│ function handle_event(){                                  │
│   document.bgColor="#000000";                             │
│   document.fgColor="#FFFFFF";                             │
│   window.alert("Hit OK for another surprise");            │
│   window.history.go(-1);                                ▤ │
│ }                                                         │
│                                                           │
│ //--></script>                                            │
│   </head>                                                 │
│   <body>                                                  │
│     <a href="javascript:handle_event();">change</a>       │
│     <br />some text                                      ▲ │
│   </body>                                                ▼ │
│ </html>                                                   │
├─────────────────────────────────────────────────────────┤
│ ▥        ◀ ▶ ◢ │
└─────────────────────────────────────────────────────────┘
```

FIGURE 3.8 A custom event handler for a link.

command or submit button. We shall shortly learn how to handle those events, but it still boils down to calling functions. With that in mind, there is a subtlety that must be addressed. The subtlety pertains to all event handlers, so `window.onload` is sufficiently general to make the point.

Technically, the JavaScript code executed by an event handler should return a Boolean value to the event handler. For example,

```
<body onload="document.bgColor='red'; return true;">
```

purports to inform the event handler that the event was handled successfully. When a function is used to handle the event, the function should return a Boolean value.

```
<body onload="somefunction()">

<script language="JavaScript"><!--
function somefunction() {
     handle event
     return true or false depending upon success or failure
}
//--></script>

</body>
```

Returning success or failure status to event handlers is a common error control practice (and not just in JavaScript). However, when the HTML attribute form of the event handler is used, the function is "loosely bound" to the event handler. That means that the returned value does not actually reach the event handler. This is just the way the Browser Object works. For that reason, there is no need to return Boolean values when the HTML attribute form of the event handler is used.

We defined user events as special properties of the Browser Object. Indeed, the actual event handler is

```
window.onload
```

The rigorous way to bind a JavaScript function to an event handler is to assign the function formally to the event handler:

```
<body>

<script language="JavaScript"><!-
window.onload = somefunction;

function somefunction() {
    handle event
    return true or false depending upon success or failure
}
//--></script>

<body>
```

Here the function is assigned[6] without using parentheses (). Formally assigning the function to the event handler ensures that the returned Boolean value reaches the event handler. If the event handler has a contingency in place to deal with a potential failure message, it will do so.

However, very few event handlers of the Browser Object actually care about returned Boolean values. In fact, the `onload` event handler will simply ignore a returned value. That is why the HTML attribute form of almost any event handler is used. In general, it is a moot point as to whether an event handler in the Browser Object receives a returned value or not, so you might as well use the HTML attribute form and not worry about returned values.

But there is one case of importance to us where an event handler needs to receive a returned success/failure message. As we shall soon see, that event handler has to do with the user event of submitting the data from an HTML form to the client. In that case, we will formally assign a function to the event handler as just demonstrated.

In the next few sections we will fully explore the `form` object's event handlers. However, there are a host of other event handlers in the Browser Object, used for various purposes. We don't have space to cover them all in this text, but you have unwittingly triggered many of them while surfing. The most common are `onmouseover` and `onmouseout`, which are commonly used to call functions when the mouse passes onto and off of an image, respectively. These handlers create the rollover effect you get when your mouse passes over certain images that are active as links: `onmouseover` calls a function that swaps in a new image, and `onmouseout` calls a function that swaps the original image back in. The swaps are accomplished by updating the `document.images[]` array in the Browser Object. (These event handlers don't care about returned values, so they are called as HTML attributes.)

---

[6]Although there is no need to do so in this text, self-defined JavaScript objects can be created. In that case, assigning a function to an object in this fashion establishes the function as a method of the object.

NOTE

There is a stark contrast between how JavaScript was used in this section compared to the previous ones. Before we covered user events, the JavaScript statements were executed when the page first loaded. The first examples used `document.write()` to include the content of a variable (containing the result of a calculation, for example) in the Web page. The next examples in Sections 3.3 and 3.4 used JavaScript to set properties of the Browser Object as the page was first loading.

With user events, the JavaScript statements are in functions that are bound (loosely or formally) to the event handler and not executed as the page loads. Only when the user event occurs do the statements in the functions get executed. That means we are updating the state of the Browser Object after the page is fully loaded. Not all properties of the Browser object can be changed after the page is fully rendered. For example, calling `document.write()` can't update the state of the `document` object once a page is rendered. At that time, the text of the page is fixed in place. However, properties such as the background color can be updated via the Browser Object long after the page is fully rendered, because that doesn't require updating the layout of the Web page. In general, the following notes hold true about what can happen as the result of a user event once a Web page is fully rendered by the browser.

- The state of the `window` object can be updated after the page is fully rendered. That includes changing properties such as `window.location` and changing properties of the `window.history` object. Also, methods such as `window.alert()` can be called at any time.

- Many properties of the state of the `document.form` object can be updated after the page is fully rendered. That includes the strings contained in text fields and text areas, whether checkboxes and radio buttons are checked or not, and the currently selected item in a pop-up menu.

- As we have mentioned, objects such as images can be swapped in and out after the page is fully loaded to create rollovers. As long as two images are the same size, they can be swapped in and out of the Browser Object without affecting the layout of the Web page.

- Image rollovers are, historically, the most common Dynamic HTML (DHTML) effect. Other fancy DHTML effects, such as moving blocks around and working with layers can't be accomplished by manipulating the Browser Object. That requires use of CSS and exposure of the style properties to JavaScript through the full HTML DOM. We do discuss the relationship of the Browser Object to the DOM in Chapter 19.

3.6   THE FORM OBJECT

We saw in Figure 3.5 that an HTML form is an object that is a property of the `document` object. Most properties of the form object can be both accessed and changed after the Web page containing the form has been loaded. Figure 3.9 shows an HTML form and its structure

```
<form name="formName">
  <input type="text" name="fieldName" value="some data" />

  <input type="checkbox" name="checkboxName" value="some data" />

  <input type="radio" name="radioName" value="some data" />

  <select name="menuName">
    <option value="data1">description1</option>
    <option value="data2">description2</option>
  </select>

  <input type="reset" value="Reset Form" />

  <input type="button" value="Process Form" onclick="someFunction()" />

  <textarea name="areaName" rows="4" cols="15">some data</textarea>
</form>
```

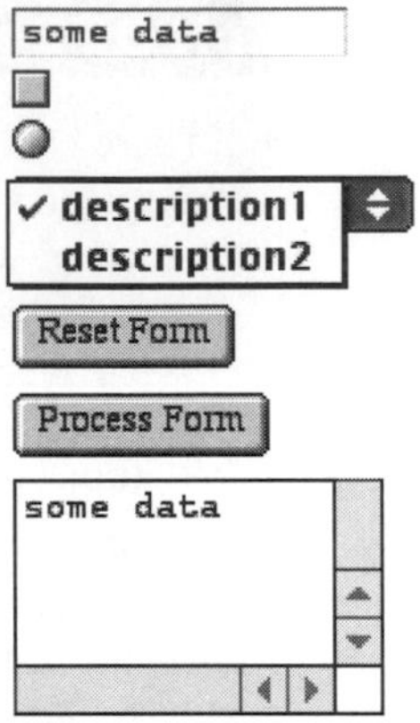

```
document
  └── formName
          ├── fieldName [value]
          ├── checkboxName [value,checked]
          ├── radioName [value,checked]
          ├── menuName [selectedIndex]
          │       ├── options[0] [value]
          │       └── options[1] [value]
          └── areaName [value]
```

FIGURE 3.9 The Browser Object contains an object to represent the HTML form.

as an object. Only the data-carrying elements are represented in the depiction of the form object `document.formName`. The only purpose of form buttons is to trigger event handlers.

The name of the form and the names of the form elements, set by the `name` attributes in the HTML code, give reference to the particular form elements in the object. The primitive data-carrying variables for each element are given in brackets at the ends of the branches. For example, the text field contents are in

```
document.formName.fieldName.value
```

which is a primitive variable containing the string literal "some data".

The checkbox and radio button each have two primitive properties. The variables

```
document.formName.checkboxName.checked
```

and

```
document.formName.radioName.checked
```

are Boolean. Since neither of them is checked in Figure 3.9, both of the Boolean variables currently contain the literal `false`.

The menu is somewhat more complicated. The menu itself has a `selectedIndex` (note the capital I) property, which contains an integer corresponding to which menu option is currently chosen. The first option is selected in Figure 3.9, so the primitive

```
document.formName.menuName.selectedIndex
```

currently contains the integer 0. That might seem strange, but as you can see, the menu's options are represented by the `options[]` array. Using standard array indexing,

```
document.formName.menuName.options[0]
```

refers to the first option in the menu. But to get at the data carried by that particular option, you have to reference the primitive variable

```
document.formName.menuName.options[0].value
```

which contains the string `"data1"`. Now, that's a long object reference, but you can easily trace the reference path by looking at the depiction of the object in Figure 3.9.

Finally, the string data carried by the text area is contained in

```
document.formName.areaName.value
```

as you would expect.

The control buttons are not given in the object depiction because we do not need to access any of their properties. The buttons are simply there to cause something to happen to the form. The Reset button has a built-in event handler, which calls a built-in `reset()` method that returns the form object to its original state. The command button simply calls a programmer-defined function using the `onclick` event handler. You can see the call to `someFunction()` in Figure 3.9.

Earlier, we discussed what the various properties of the form object contain, based on the current state of the form as you see it in Figure 3.9. Those contents can be changed simply by assigning new values to the form's properties in `someFunction()`. For example, in the source code on this book's Web site, the function is defined as follows

```
function someFunction() {
  document.formName.fieldName.value="What's ";
  document.formName.radioName.checked=true;
  document.formName.menuName.selectedIndex=1;
  document.formName.areaName.value="up!";
}
```

When the user event of clicking the command button calls this function, the state of the form is instantaneously updated. The text display elements are changed to contain new strings, the radio button is "turned on," and the current menu selection is changed to the second item. Try it for yourself on the Web site.

There is a limitation to using the names of the form elements to provide reference to them in the Browser Object: It is difficult to iterate over names. Suppose there are 50 checkboxes whose value properties carry prices for items that can be chosen. If you recall the pseudocode example for loops in Section 3.2, one solution is to include 50 "if" statements. We can now replace the pseudocode with real code:

```
var total=0;
if (document.formName.checkbox1.checked) {
    total=total+parseFloat(document.formName.checkbox1.value);
}
if (document.formName.checkbox2.checked) {
    total=total+parseFloat(document.formName.checkbox2.value);
}
.
.
.
```

Each of the 50 "if" statements sees whether a checkbox is checked. If it is, its value is added onto a running total. Remember, *all* form values are strings, so in this case the values have to be parsed into numbers, or else + will concatenate them.

Clearly it would be better to iterate over the checkboxes with a loop and do away with the 50 conditionals. The solution is to use an alternate representation of the form object that does not use names to reference the form elements. The elements[] array automatically gives an indexed referencing scheme for them. To show that, we offer a second version of the object for the form of Figure 3.9.

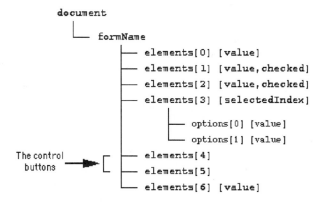

In this version, reference to a specific form element is given by its position in the elements[] array, rather than by its name. The elements[] array uses standard indexing, so the first form element is referenced by elements[0]. Accessing or changing an element's property is no different from before. For example,

```
document.formName.elements[2].checked
```

references the radio button's Boolean property. Similarly,

```
document.formName.elements[3].options[0].value
```

references the data carried by the pop-up menu's first option.

Indexing a form's elements does add one factor that has to be taken into account. The `elements[]` array indexes all of a form's elements, not just the data-carrying ones. Thus, to reference the text area you have to be careful to skip over the index positions occupied by the form's two control buttons. The button positions are emphasized in the depiction of the indexed version of the form object. Skipping over those, `elements[6]` references the text area. With names, you simply don't name the control buttons and don't reference them.

If we go back to the case of the 50 checkboxes, we can now iterate over them. Assuming they are the first 50 elements defined in the form, they occupy positions 0 through 49 in the `elements[]` array, so each execution of the loop

```
var total=0;
for (var x=0 ; x<=49 ; x++) {
 if (document.formName.elements[x].checked) {
   total=total+parseFloat(document.formName.elements[x].value);
 }
}
```

tests whether `elements[x]` has been checked and if so, adds its value onto the running total. As x runs from 0 to 49, all of the 50 checkboxes are tested.

If that doesn't convince you of the utility of the `elements[]` array, recall that the radio buttons in a unique-selection group all share the same name. That's no problem if the form is being submitted to the server, because only the selected button is submitted. For processing on the client, however, there is no way to reference radio buttons in a unique-selection group individually by name. You have to use the `elements[]` array in that case.

In practice, you will probably want to use a mixture of naming and using the `elements[]` array. When you are writing a function to process a form, it's easy to remember which element to reference if you have given them descriptive names. Sometimes, though, you will need to iterate over form elements or refer to specific radio buttons in a unique-selection group. In those cases, names won't help you in an object reference capacity.

In like manner, there is a `forms[]` array that indexes all of the different forms in an HTML document. That means you don't even have to name the form. Using both of these built-in arrays, all of the forms and their elements in a page have the following concise object representation:

```
document
  └─ forms[ ]
        └─ elements[ ]
```

For example, assuming that the form in Figure 3.9 is the only form in the Web page, we can reference the data carried by the second of the pop-up menu's items with

```
document.forms[0].elements[3].options[1].value
```

and that's a big, ugly object reference. In a case like that it is better just to reference the form and menu with their names. That way, you can tell at a glance what you are dealing with.

NOTE

If you are processing form data on the client, it really doesn't matter whether you name a form and its elements. If you can keep up with all of the array indices, you are good to go using the built-in arrays. However, you should get in the habit of naming *all* of your data-carrying form elements. When a form is submitted to the server, an element with no name is not submitted, even if it has a value. There is no way for the browser to construct the name= value pair.

In contrast, you usually don't want to name submit, reset, or generic buttons in a form. That will trick the browser into sending a name= value pair for the button. You usually don't want something like `buttonName="Click Me"` being submitted. However, naming submit buttons can be useful when a form has more than one submit button used to trigger different types of processing on the server. The CGI program on the server side can then determine which type of processing to enact, based on the name of the particular submit button that is clicked.

The preceding discussion covers how the data from the current state of a form is exposed to JavaScript via the Browser Object. But, of course, the `form` object also has methods and event handlers. We now give an overview of the most commonly used ones. Full reference to the properties, methods, and event handlers can be found in Appendix B.

The common form-level methods are `reset()` and `submit()`. You can call these methods directly to return the form to its original state as it was when the page loaded or to submit the form to the Web server, respectively:

```
document.formName.reset();
document.formName.submit();
```

You would scarcely have cause to do so, however. The reset and submit form buttons have built-in event handlers that call these two methods.

The methods we feature that apply to specific form elements are `focus()` and `select()`. These are most often used on text fields. By default, none of a form's elements is in focus.[7] This method call

```
document.formName.textFieldName.focus();
```

focuses a text field, which puts the cursor in the field. Such a call might be made from the `onload` event handler to bring the text field for a search engine into focus when the page loads. Otherwise, the user first has to click the mouse on the text field before typing in a query. (There is a `blur()` method that accomplishes the opposite of `focus()`, but is rarely needed.)

---

[7]Load the form of Figure 3.9 into your browser. Then hit the Tab key a few times and you will see the focus move sequentially among the form elements.

Another use is to put focus in a particular text field after a form is validated. If there are several text fields, this lets users know the one into which they entered faulty data. In that case, it is common to call, additionally,

```
document.formName.textFieldName.select();
```

which selects all of the text in the field. Selecting the text means that it becomes highlighted, as when you highlight some text to copy and paste it.

The event handlers we present for form elements are `onclick`, `onchange`, and `onsubmit`. We saw `onclick` used in the command button in Figure 3.9. That is the only element in which we will use `onclick`. Its purpose is to call a JavaScript function that performs client-side processing of the form's data. This event handler does not require a return value, so we simply supply it as an HTML attribute.

The `onchange` event handler is available for most form elements. Its two main uses are in text fields and pop-up menus. It does not require a return value, so its attribute form is used. When included in a pop-up menu, it is used to call a function each time the user selects a new menu item. Triggering `onchange` from a text field requires adding or deleting a character from the field and then removing focus from the field (by clicking on a different form element with your mouse, for example). The act of typing in a text field technically changes it, but the change is not registered in the Browser Object until focus is removed. That is when the Browser Object knows you are done typing.

The `onsubmit` event handler is built in to the submit button. Clicking a submit button automatically triggers this handler, which then calls the `submit()` method on the form. Of all the event handlers discussed in this book, this is the only one that benefits from receiving a Boolean return value. In Section 3.9 we will see how to override its default behavior of calling the `submit()` method, and assign it a programmer-defined function that returns a Boolean value that depends upon whether or not the form's data passes client-side validation.

3.7 PROCESSING FORM ELEMENTS

Now that you know the basics of the form object, we offer some examples so that you can get a feel for client-side processing of the various types of form elements. The examples of this section are basically client-side utilities that do not feature submission of data to the Web server.

Most any strictly client-side form-data-processing utility utilizes the strategy depicted in Figure 3.10. A control button is supplied with the `onclick` event handler. The page loads into the browser, and the event handler just sits and waits for the click event. When the event happens, a programmer-defined JavaScript function is called do handle the data processing. For convenience, we placed the function in the head section, although it could go in the body section as well.

Processing Text

The first example is a simple calculator. Figure 3.11 shows the HTML form used in the example. The form elements have been formatted with a borderless table, but only the

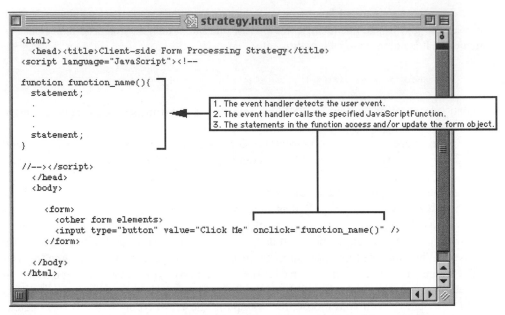

```
strategy.html
<html>
  <head><title>Client-side Form Processing Strategy</title>
<script language="JavaScript"><!--

function function_name(){
  statement;
  .
  .
  .
  statement;
}

//--></script>
  </head>
  <body>

    <form>
      <other form elements>
      <input type="button" value="Click Me" onclick="function_name()" />
    </form>

  </body>
</html>
```

1. The event handler detects the user event.
2. The event handler calls the specified JavaScriptFunction.
3. The statements in the function access and/or update the form object.

FIGURE 3.10   Using button events to initiate client-side processing of form data.

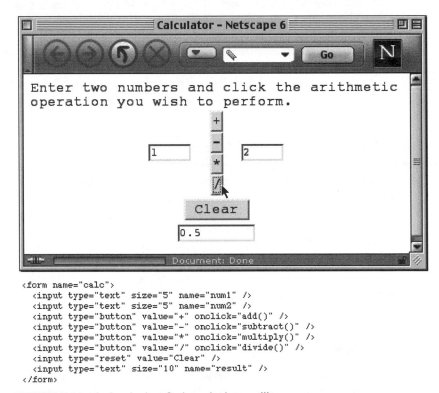

```
<form name="calc">
  <input type="text" size="5" name="num1" />
  <input type="text" size="5" name="num2" />
  <input type="button" value="+" onclick="add()" />
  <input type="button" value="-" onclick="subtract()" />
  <input type="button" value="*" onclick="multiply()" />
  <input type="button" value="/" onclick="divide()" />
  <input type="reset" value="Clear" />
  <input type="text" size="10" name="result" />
</form>
```

FIGURE 3.11   A simple JavaScript calculator utility.

```
document                          <script language="javascript">
                                  <!--
    └── calc                      function add(){
                                    var num1=parseFloat(document.calc.num1.value);
         ├── num1 [value]          var num2=parseFloat(document.calc.num2.value);
                                    document.calc.result.value=num1+num2;
         ├── num2 [value]          }
         ┊                        function subtract(){
         ┊                          var num1=document.calc.num1.value;
         └── result [value]         var num2=document.calc.num2.value;
                                    document.calc.result.value=num1-num2;
                                  }
                                  function multiply(){
                                    var num1=document.calc.num1.value;
                                    var num2=document.calc.num2.value;
                                    document.calc.result.value=num1*num2;
                                  }
                                  function divide(){
                                      var num1=document.calc.num1.value;
                                      var num2=document.calc.num2.value;
                                    if (num2==0) {
                                      window.alert("Egad man! You can't divide by 0.");
                                      document.calc.num2.value="";
                                    }
                                    else {
                                      document.calc.result.value=num1/num2;
                                    }
                                  }
                                  //-->
                                  </script>
```

FIGURE 3.12 An object model and the JavaScript to support the form of Figure 3.11.

HTML code for the form has been provided. The full source code can be observed by pulling up the source file on this book's Web site.

The user enters the two operands for the arithmetic calculation into text fields, and the calculated result appears in the bottom text field. Those elements have been named so that their contents can easily be accessed or updated in the form object. Each of the four buttons that is to initiate an arithmetic operation has an onclick event handler. Each event handler calls a different JavaScript function, named appropriately for the operation. An object model for this form and the JavaScript functions that manipulate it are given in Figure 3.12. In the full source document, the JavaScript code is located in the head section, although that's not a must.

We begin with the add() function. First, the numbers entered by the user are to be added, so they are parsed into numbers. (Otherwise, they would be concatenated as strings.) The numbers returned by the parseFloat() function are stored into local variables inside the function. Then the sum of those two numbers is assigned to be the value of the result text field. That's all there is to it.

The subtract() and multiply() functions are nearly identical to the one that adds, except that the user input is not parsed into numbers. This is a reminder of the flexibility of JavaScript. With no string context for the - and * operators, the strings are automatically converted into numbers at the time of the calculations.

The divide() function is a bit different. The form values are still "dumped" into local variables. Then the function features a bit of validation: To avoid possible division by 0, the function employs the logic given in the following pseudocode.

```
if(second operand is 0) {
  alert the user
  clear the second operand
}
else {
  complete the calculation
}
```

The pseudocode should be compared with the actual code in Figure 3.12.

It is not necessary to store the form data into local variables in the latter three functions, but that is a technique we will continue to employ. That way you can do calculations using short variable names rather than the long object references. In the add() function, however, there is no alternative. Again, the value primitives are among the few JavaScript variables that are not loosely typed—they are always strings. So the following assignment,

```
document.calc.num1.value=parseFloat(document.calc.num1.value);
```

accomplishes absolutely *nothing*. The parseFloat() function returns a numeric literal as usual, but assigning it to the form value converts it right back into a string. Assigning the returned value into a local variable, however, preserves the numeric format returned by the parsing function.

One important concept in this example is that different command buttons can call different functions. However, we could have constructed the example so that only one function is called by all four of the buttons. That function would have to take a parameter so that different calls to it could tell it which operation should be performed. Also, other validations of the input could be performed. For example, the calculator might also give an alert if one of the operands is left blank or some joker enters alphabetic characters rather than numbers. Those modifications are left as an exercise.

NOTE

We don't wish to keep referring the reader to this book's Web site to check out these examples firsthand. With interactive examples a much better feel can be obtained by playing with them. In particular, one needs to test the form validation mechanisms firsthand.

Processing Options

The second example of this section focuses on processing radio buttons and checkboxes. Figure 3.13 gives a form that simulates a simple client-side shopping cart. Like the previous example, this form is also formatted with a borderless table. There is less code for the table this time, though, so the whole contents of the HTML body element are listed.

The functionality of the form is straightforward. The user can select any or all of the checkbox items. Although the prices are in the Web page for the user to see, they are also stored in the checkbox value properties as hidden data. The checkboxes have also been given names, although the names are not used in this example. (Recall the note at the end

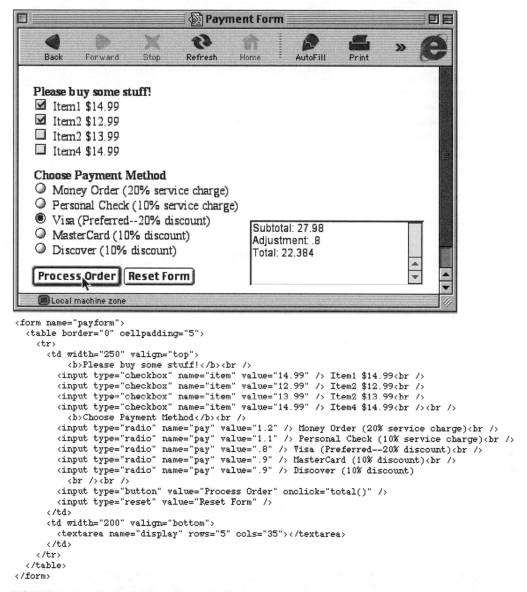

```
<form name="payform">
  <table border="0" cellpadding="5">
    <tr>
      <td width="250" valign="top">
          <b>Please buy some stuff!</b><br />
        <input type="checkbox" name="item" value="14.99" /> Item1 $14.99<br />
        <input type="checkbox" name="item" value="12.99" /> Item2 $12.99<br />
        <input type="checkbox" name="item" value="13.99" /> Item2 $13.99<br />
        <input type="checkbox" name="item" value="14.99" /> Item4 $14.99<br /><br />
          <b>Choose Payment Method</b><br />
        <input type="radio" name="pay" value="1.2" /> Money Order (20% service charge)<br />
        <input type="radio" name="pay" value="1.1" /> Personal Check (10% service charge)<br />
        <input type="radio" name="pay" value=".8" /> Visa (Preferred--20% discount)<br />
        <input type="radio" name="pay" value=".9" /> MasterCard (10% discount)<br />
        <input type="radio" name="pay" value=".9" /> Discover (10% discount)
          <br /><br />
        <input type="button" value="Process Order" onclick="total()" />
        <input type="reset" value="Reset Form" />
      </td>
      <td width="200" valign="bottom">
        <textarea name="display" rows="5" cols="35"></textarea>
      </td>
    </tr>
  </table>
</form>
```

FIGURE 3.13 The form for a client-side shopping cart.

of Section 3.6.) In contrast, the names of the radio buttons are necessary for this example because they form a unique-selection group. The radio button values store information that is used to adjust the order total based on payment type. (If any of our students pay with a money order, they lose a letter grade!) Aside from the command button, which calls a total() function to process the form, the only other point of interest is the text area, which is to serve as the display for the shopping cart.

We now explain the JavaScript support for this example, which is shown in Figure 3.14 together with an object model for the form. Since we will be iterating over the checkboxes

```
document
    └── payform
         ├── elements[0] [checked,value]
         :           (checkboxes)
         ├── elements[3] [checked,value]
         ├── elements[4] [checked,value]
         :           (radio buttons)
         ├── elements[8] [checked,value]
         └── display [value]
```

```
<script language="javascript">
<!--

function total() {
  var subtotal=0;
  var total=0;
  var adjustment=1;
  payment=false;

  var elmnts=document.payform.elements;

  for(var x=0 ; x<=3 ; x++) {
    if (elmnts[x].checked) {
      subtotal=subtotal+parseFloat(elmnts[x].value);
    }
  }

  for(var x=4 ; x<= 8 ; x++) {
    if (elmnts[x].checked) {
      adjustment=elmnts[x].value;
      payment=true;
    }
  }

  if(payment) {
    total=subtotal*adjustment;
    document.payform.display.value="Subtotal: "+subtotal
                           +"\rAdjustment: "+adjustment
                           +"\rTotal: "+total;
  }
  else {
    window.alert("Please choose payment type.");
  }
}

//-->
</script>
```

FIGURE 3.14 An object model and JavaScript support for the form of Figure 3.13.

and radio buttons, we have shown the `elements[]` array. Besides, we don't have unique names with which to work anyway. We do refer to the display area using the name we have given it. That way we don't have to worry about its index position in the `elements[]` array.

The first four local variables are to help with the calculations and validation. We will see what those do as we talk through the function. The first main feature is the statement

```
var elmnts=document.payform.elements;
```

This statement creates the local variable `elmnts` and assigns it the form's `elements[]` array.

> **NOTE**
>
> Here you see just how loose JavaScript's typing of variables is. Not only can any literal type be assigned, but here we have assigned an array object to the variable. Objects are assigned by reference in JavaScript, rather than by value. (We saw this in Section 3.2 when we passed an array to a function.) So the local variable `elmnts` is merely a reference (or pointer) to the actual `elements[]` array of the form. Thus `elmnts[0].checked` accesses the Boolean state of the first checkbox in the form, for example.

We made that assignment in order to have a concise reference to the forms data, dispensing with repetitive long object references. But contrast the assignment here with the ones in Figure 3.12. Those assign the actual primitive data values of the form to local variables. Those primitive assignments transfer the literals by value rather than by reference.

The first loop tests all the checkboxes, adding the parsed price of any selected ones onto the local `subtotal` variable. The second loop tests all of the radio buttons, storing the chosen payment adjustment into the local `adjustment` variable. We also see the form's validation feature in that loop. The local `payment` variable was initialized to `false` when it was declared. Only if one of the payment options is found to be checked is payment set to `true`.

The remainder of the function is straightforward. We illustrate the logic of the conditional with pseudocode.

```
if(user has selected a payment option) {
   calculate the total
   update the display
}
else {
   give an alert
}
```

If no payment option is chosen, the display is left blank in favor of the alert. There is one last detail to be explained. Test areas display plain text, not HTML. Thus, if you want a line return in a text area, `<br />` will be of no help. In Figure 3.14, you can see that line breaks were forced inside the long string using the carriage *r*eturn escape character `\r`. Note that the *n*ew line character `\n` may also be used, but we have found that less reliable among all the browser versions than the carriage return. Go figure.

The last example of this section demonstrates how to deal with pop-up menus on the client. Figure 3.15 shows both the source code and the rendering of a Web page that features a simple utility with two pop-up menus. Some HTML formatting detail has been removed from the source code to keep it as uncluttered as possible. However, the essential code for the form and the JavaScript code are all there. You can see in the code for the form that we have named all of the form elements. The form is pretty simple, so we do not supply an object diagram.

In contrast to the previous examples, this one does not use a command button to trigger the processing of the form. Rather, each menu is endowed with the `onchange` event handler. As soon as a new choice is made in either menu, the `calc()` function is called. That function computes the sales tax on the dollar amount given as the current choice in the first menu, based on the tax rate that is given as the current choice in the second menu.

Aside from two local variables used to store results from the computations, the first noteworthy lines of JavaScript code store indices of the currently chosen menu options into the local variables `i` and `j`. Next, the `values` for the selected menu options are stored into the local variables `price` and `taxrate`. We hate to be anticlimactic, but there is little else to it besides a couple of calculations and updating the display area.

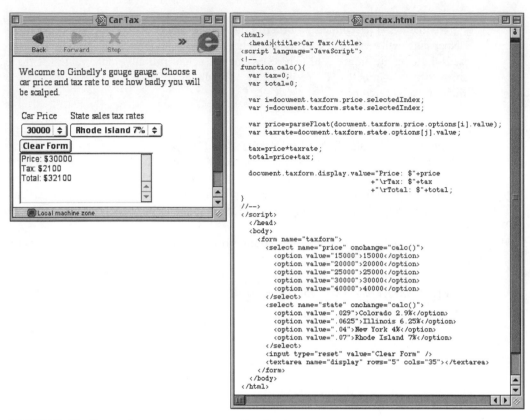

FIGURE 3.15 Processing pop-up menus on the client.

Although a pop-up menu is similar in functionality to a unique-selection group of radio buttons, it is much easier to extract the value of the selected menu option in a client-side script. You have to loop over the radio buttons until the selected one is found, but the `selectedIndex` property of a menu essentially does that for you. The general strategy is as follows. The object references are ugly, but the concept is simple. The variable i is the selected index, so grab the value of the ith `option`.

```
i=document.formName.menuName.selectedIndex;
thevalue=document.formName.menuName.options[i].value;
```

There was no compelling reason to use the `onchange` event handler instead of a command button other than for a change of pace (`onchange` does work with checkboxes and radio buttons as well, and one can sometimes find good uses for it). Certainly, a command button would have worked nicely, perhaps even better. For example, in the `onchange` version, you can't do the calculation for the two menu options that appear when the page first loads without making a change to a menu, and then making a change back to the original option. One could add

```
<body onload="calc()">
```

to alleviate that shortcoming.

> **NOTE**
>
> If you played with the examples of this section, you may have noticed that the results from some of the calculations were not rounded off very well. Occasionally, 16 decimal places result, and other times there are three decimal places for a dollar amount where it would be customary to include only two. There is a stand-alone `Math` object whose methods can be called to round numbers or to help with calculations in other ways. Its methods can be found in Appendix B. The `Math.round()` method rounds to the nearest integer. So to round to two decimal places, multiply by 100, `round`, and then divide by 100. For example, the following code results in the variable `num` containing 3.15.
>
> ```
> var num = 3.141592654;
> num = Math.round(100*num)/100;
> ```

3.8   FORM VALIDATION BEFORE SUBMISSION

The calculator example of Figure 3.11 validated the value entered into a text field to prevent division by 0. The shopping cart simulation in Figure 3.13 validated a group of radio buttons to ensure that a payment method was chosen. But the real flavor of client-side validation of form data for Web applications involves testing the data (under various constraints) before submitting it to a program on a Web server. In that case, we no longer use a command button but rather a submit button.

The Strategy for Validation Before Submission

The general strategy for client-side validation before submission involves the `onsubmit` event handler of the `form` object.

```
document.formName.onsubmit
```

This event handler expects a Boolean return value. So we must formally assign it the function we create to handle the event of the user clicking the submit button.

```
document.formName.onsubmit=validate;

function validate() {
    statements to test the form data for validity
    return false if the data fails, true if it passes
}
```

If the programmer-defined validation function returns `true`, the event handler automatically calls the form's submit method. If it returns `false`, the event handler simply does not submit the form. In that case, the function would alert the user that the entered data is faulty. Note that this event handler can be called as an HTML attribute of the submit button (`onsubmit="validate()"`), but that renders its return value ineffective, as discussed in Section 3.5.

This strategy is contingent on assigning the function to the event handler in the HTML document **after** the form that is to be submitted is defined. The browser must read the HTML code for the form and create the corresponding form object before its `onsubmit` event handler is available to be assigned a value. Hence, you will no longer be able to place the validation scripts in the `head` section of the document, as will be apparent in the examples that follow. Also, the examples of this section and the next are submitted the same `echo.cgi` program to which we alluded in the note at the end of Section 3.1. It simply echoes the submitted name=value pairs back to the Web browser in a Web page. (It won't be long before we learn how to do meaningful calculations with the data on the back end!)

NOTE

We have introduced formal binding of functions to event handlers by assignment because that works in all cases. There is also one "shortcut" way to ensure that the `onsubmit` event handler, placed as an HTML attribute, receives a value returned from a function. Simply place the `return` command before the function call.

```
<input type="submit" onsubmit="return validate();"
value="Submit Form" />
```

We mention this because you will see this "shortcut" employed if you look at much JavaScript code on the Web.

Menu Validation

We first turn to pop-up menus, because validation for those is relatively simple. If no special provisions are provided in a menu, no validation is required. Consider again the sales tax menu used in Figure 3.15.

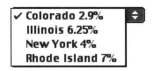

There is nothing to verify. When the page first loads, Colorado is the visible and chosen option, being the first one defined in the menu. If the user makes no change to the menu, Colorado remains chosen. Thus, the first option defined in a menu is the default selection for submission. (Recall that the `selected` attribute can also be placed in a menu option to make it the default selection.)

Suppose that the menu is supplied in a form used for online purchases so that the user can choose the appropriate state tax rate used to assess the sales tax. In such a case, it is not desirable for the menu to have a default selection. For example, if someone from Rhode Island forgets to choose a state, the default, Colorado, would be used. A better solu-

tion is to force the user to make a selection. The strategy for that is to make the menu's
first option a "dummy" option. That way, the user gets

when the page first loads. Then supply JavaScript validation so that the form is not submitted if the user forgets to make a selection. That is, give an alert if the user clicks the
submit button when the `selectedIndex` of the menu still contains 0.

Figure 3.16 uses that strategy in a second version of the car tax form of Figure 3.15.
This version does not do any calculations with the data and has no text area. Rather, it
verifies that the user has made a selection from both of the menus. If the form fails the

FIGURE 3.16   Client-side validation for pop-up menus.

validation, the user is alerted. If the form passes the validation, the form's data is submitted to the echo program on the server.

First note that the form has been supplied with the `action` attribute whose value gives the URL of the CGI program to which the form's data is submitted. Also, `method="GET"` specifies that the name value pairs be sent to the server as a query string appended to the URL.

The first statement in the script assigns the `validate` function to the `onsubmit` event handler. Again, we stress that it is important that the assignment occur after the form has been defined. (The actual function could be placed in the head section.) The validation function first extracts the indices of the selected menu options. If either index is still 0, a `false` value is returned to the event handler, causing the submit action to be aborted. Otherwise, a `true` value is returned to the event handler, causing the form to be submitted to the echo program on the server for this book's Web site.

NOTE

Validation of multiple-selection menus is problematic. Because multiple options can be selected, the `selectedIndex` property does not apply. Rather, the `selected` property is used with multiple-selection menus.

```
document.formName.menuName.selected
```

The property is Boolean, containing `true` if the user has made at least one selection in the menu, and `false` otherwise. Thus, client-side validation for multiple selection menus can ascertain whether at least one option has been selected, but not whether, for example, exactly two options have been selected.

A Larger Validation Example

We now apply the validation-before-submission strategy to a second version of the client-side shopping cart of Figure 3.13. The HTML portion of the new payment form is shown in Figure 3.17. The new version replaces the text area with three text fields to collect shipping information from the user. The following three things are validated on the client before the form is allowed to be submitted.

1. The user must choose (at least) one item.
2. The user must choose a payment type.
3. The user must not leave any of the text fields blank.

The JavaScript function that implements the validation is supplied in Figure 3.18 along with an object diagram for the form. We have not shown the whole document this time, but the script in Figure 3.18 appears in the document after the definition of the HTML form.

The general strategy is the same: Formally assign the validation function to the `onsubmit` event handler of the form. That is the first line of the script. Following that is the validation function. Its first line assigns the reference to the form's `elements[]` array to the local variable `elmnts`.

Next we loop through the checkboxes, setting the `buy` variable to `true` if one of them is found to be checked. If none of them is found to be checked, the user is alerted and

```
<form action="http://www.cknuckles.com/cgi/echo.cgi" method="GET" name="payform">
  <table border="0" cellpadding="5" width="600">
    <tr>
      <td width="250" valign="top">
        <b>Please buy some stuff!</b><br />
        <input type="checkbox" name="item1" value="14.99" /> Item1 $14.99<br />
        <input type="checkbox" name="item2" value="12.99" /> Item2 $12.99<br />
        <input type="checkbox" name="item3" value="13.99" /> Item2 $13.99<br />
        <input type="checkbox" name="item4" value="14.99" /> Item4 $14.99<br /><br />
        <b>Choose Payment Method</b><br />
        <input type="radio" name="pay" value="1.2" /> Money Order (20% service charge)<br />
        <input type="radio" name="pay" value="1.1" /> Personal Check (10% service charge)<br />
        <input type="radio" name="pay" value=".8" /> Visa (Preferred--20% discount)<br />
        <input type="radio" name="pay" value=".9" /> MasterCard (10% discount)<br />
        <input type="radio" name="pay" value=".9" /> Discover (10% discount)
        <br /><br />
        <input type="submit" value="Submit Order" />
        <input type="reset" value="Reset Form" />
      </td>
      <td valign="bottom">
        Name:<br />
        <input type="text" name="name" size="25" /><br />
        Address:<br />
        <input type="text" name="address" size="40" /><br />
        E-mail:<br />
        <input type="text" name="email" size="25" /><br />
      </td>
    </tr>
  </table>
</form>
```

FIGURE 3.17 A payment form that submits the data to a Web server only if it passes some client-side validation.

the function returns `false` to the `onsubmit` event handler. Ensuring that one of the radio buttons is checked is handled similarly.

Next we loop through the text fields. If one of them is found to be empty, the user is alerted, that particular text field is brought into focus and selected, and the function returns `false`. (Recall the form object methods near the end of Section 3.6.) If all of the text fields pass the test, the function finally progresses to the statement that returns `true`, allowing the form to be submitted.

```
document

    └── payform
         ├── elements[0] [checked,value]
         │        ⋮        (checkboxes)
         ├── elements[3] [checked,value]
         ├── elements[4] [checked,value]
         │        ⋮        (radio buttons)
         ├── elements[8] [checked,value]
         ├── elements[11] [value]
         │        ⋮          (text fields)
         └── elements[13] [value]
```

```
<script language="javascript">
<!--
document.payform.onsubmit=validate;

function validate() {
    var elmnts=document.payform.elements;

    var buy=false;
    for(var x=0 ; x<=3 ; x++) {
        if (elmnts[x].checked) {
            buy=true;
        }
    }
    if(!buy) {
        alert("You must buy something.");
        return false;
    }

    var pay=false;
    for(var x=4 ; x<= 8 ; x++) {
        if (elmnts[x].checked) {
            pay=true;
        }
    }
    if(!pay) {
        alert("You must choose a payment method.");
        return false;
    }

    for(var x=11 ; x<= 13 ; x++) {
        if (elmnts[x].value == "") {
            alert("Required field.");
            elmnts[x].focus();
            elmnts[x].select();
            return false;
        }
    }
    return true;
}

//-->
</script>
```

FIGURE 3.18 The JavaScript support for the form of Figure 3.16.

NOTE

There are two things to note here. First is the technique used in the validation function. The same technique was used in Figure 3.16, although there was only one validation performed. Test each form element (or group of elements) separately. If the test fails, return `false`. There is no need to test any further form elements in that case. Only when all tests pass can the function reach the line that returns `true`.

Second, testing for the empty string is a pretty lame validation test. For example, if some joker enters a single white space into one of the text fields, that field will not cause the alert to be triggered. Also, in this case the `select()` method will have no effect. The only time that method is called is when a text field is empty. But in that case, the browser will not highlight the field, because there is no text in it. However, browsers will bring focus to an empty text field. The next section explores better verification techniques for text fields. In the mean time, focusing and selecting the erroneous field is a good habit to get into.

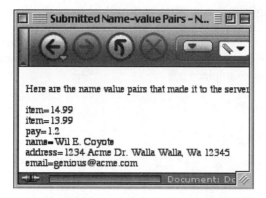

FIGURE 3.19 The data returned by the server-side echo program from the form submission pictured in Figure 3.17.

Just in case you don't have a computer handy to submit the working version at this book's Web site, Figure 3.19 shows the data returned by the echo program when the form is filled out as shown in Figure 3.17 and submitted.

3.9 TEXT VALIDATION WITH THE String OBJECT

We conclude this chapter by using the String object to provide somewhat more rigorous validation of text input. While we have spoken often of string literals, strings also have an object context. A string not explicitly assigned to a variable is a string literal. In the statement

```
document.write("Scooby Doo");
```

the string "Scooby Doo" is not an object. Once assigned to a variable, however,

```
var str="Scooby Doo";
```

it is an object. Any string stored in a variable may use the length property or any of the methods of the String object. We mention only one property because there is only one. Using the preceding declaration, the assignment

```
var x=str.length;
```

causes the variable x to contain the integer 10.

There are several methods that can be called on strings, but we discuss only those used in the following validation example. The rest are listed in Appendix B. It should be no problem to figure out how to use those if the need arises. First, the charAt() method takes an integer parameter and returns the character at that position in the string. A string is an array of characters that uses standard array indexing. So the first character in a string has index 0. The assignment

```
x=str.charAt(1);
```

causes x to contain the string "c" and

```
x=str.charAt(6);
```

causes x to contain the string " " consisting of one white space. There is no character type in JavaScript. Characters are simply one-character strings.

The indexOf() method takes a one-character string as its argument and returns the *first* index at which the character is found. If the character is not found in the string, indexOf() returns −1. For example,

```
x=str.indexOf("o");
```

causes x to contain the integer 2, and

```
x=str.indexOf("O");
```

causes x to contain the integer −1. In contrast, the lastIndexOf() method takes a one-character string, and returns the *last* index at which the character is found in the string. It also returns −1 if the character is not found in the string.

Following is a function we have defined that counts the number of occurrences of a given character in a string. We will make heavy use of it in the main example of this section. The function takes two parameters: the string to be tested and a one-character string corresponding to the character to count. It returns the number of occurrences of the character in the string.

```
function countchar(thestring,thechar) {
  var count=0;
  for(var x=0 ; x<thestring.length ; x++) {
   if(thestring.charAt(x)==thechar) {
    count++;
   }
  }
  return count;
}
```

The countchar() function loops through thestring one character index at a time (that is, from character 0 to character thestring.length-1). If the character at the current index matches thechar, the counter is incremented. After the loop has run its course, the counter value is returned.

Figure 3.20 shows the form for which we will employ the character-counting function. The form is rather simple, and we have provided only an object diagram so that you

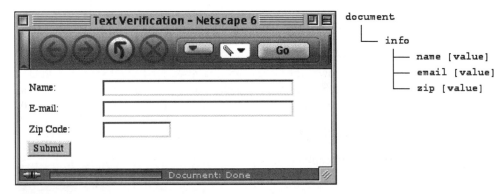

FIGURE 3.20 An information collection form.

can easily follow the object references that are to follow in the validation code. The form is to have the following client-side validation features.

1. The name must be at least four characters long, must contain at least one blank space, and must neither begin nor end with a space.

2. The e-mail address must be at least five characters long, must contain no blank spaces, must contain exactly one @ character, and must contain at least one period.

3. The ZIP code must be numeric and exactly five characters long.

```
<script language="JavaScript">
<!--
document.infoform.onsubmit=validate;

function countchar(thestring,thechar) {
 var count=0;
    for(var x=0 ; x<thestring.length ; x++) {
       if(thestring.charAt(x)==thechar) {
        count++;
      }
    }
     return count;
}

function validate(){

 var name=document.infoform.thename.value;
 if(   (name.length<4) ||
        (countchar(name," ")==0) ||
        (name.indexOf(" ")==0) ||
        (name.lastIndexOf(" ")==(name.length-1)) ) {

  alert("Invalid name format.");
  document.infoform.thename.focus();
  document.infoform.thename.select();
  return false;
}

 var email=document.infoform.email.value;
 if( (email.length<5) ||
        (countchar(email," ")>0) ||
        (countchar(email,"@")!=1) ||
        (countchar(email,".")==0) ) {

    alert("Invalid email format.");
    document.infoform.email.focus();
    document.infoform.email.select();
  return false;
}

 var zip=document.infoform.zip.value;
 if( isNaN(zip) || (zip.length!=5) ) {

  alert("Invalid zip format.");
  document.infoform.zip.focus();
  document.infoform.zip.select();
  return false;
}

 return true;
}
//-->
</script>
```

FIGURE 3.21   The JavaScript support for the form of Figure 3.20.

These restrictions allow for a minimal full name like `"Ty X"`, an e-mail address basically of the form `"x@y.z"`, and a standard ZIP code. Note that the e-mail validation does not rule out something like `"@x.y.z"`. Some more stringent validations are left as exercises. Also, note that a name with at least one blank space rules out a numeric value, because `isNaN("1 23")` returns `true`, for example. For the same reason, a ZIP code that must be numeric rules out a five-character erroneous ZIP such as `"123 5"`.

Figure 3.21 displays the complete JavaScript validation support that implements the list of constraints. Again, because of the formal assignment of the validation function to the form's `onsubmit` event handler, the script follows the definition of the HTML form in the complete document.

We have already discussed the `countchar()` function. Following that is the validation function. The first block of code stores the `name` field of the form into a local variable and then performs the specified validation tests. If any of the tests fail, the user is alerted, the text field is focused, any text in the fields is selected, and the function returns `false` to the event handler. The next two blocks of code perform the specified tests on the `email` and `zip` fields, respectively. The validation function returns `true`, causing the form to be submitted, only if each of the three fields passes its test.

SUMMARY OF KEY TERMS AND CONCEPTS

Form control buttons: Buttons on an HTML form that cause some action. **Submit** and **reset buttons** have built-in event handlers that submit a form to the server and return the form to its state when the page first loaded, respectively. **Command** (generic) **buttons** must be supplied with the `onclick` event handler, which calls a programmer-defined JavaScript function to handle the event in a customized way.

Form text elements: HTML form elements that allow the user to enter and modify text. **Text fields** (single-line) and **text areas** (multiple-line) are text entry boxes. Defaults for their values, which appear in the boxes, can be hard-coded into their HTML `value` attributes. When the user enters text into a box, that text becomes the current `value` of the form element.

Form option buttons: HTML form elements that allow a user to select fixed options. A group of checkboxes forms an option list, from which any number of options can be chosen. A single **radio button,** once checked by the user, can't be manually unchecked by the user. A group of radio buttons, each given the same name, form a *unique-selection group*, in which only one button can be selected at a given time. The `value` property of a checkbox or radio button holds hidden data that relates to that option.

Form menus: HTML form elements that allow the user to select options from a pop-up or scolling list. A **single-selection menu** functions like a unique-selection group of radio buttons. A **multiple-selection menu** functions like a group of checkboxes. The `value` property of an option of either menu type holds hidden data that relates to that option.

Names and values: Information associated with all HTML form elements. The names of form elements are used both for object reference in JavaScript and to form name=value pairs for submission to the Web server. Whether on the client or on the server, the values carry the data for the form elements.

The Browser Object: Formally termed the *Document Object Model Level 0*, a Web browser's in-memory (RAM) representation of a rendered Web page and the window that contains it. When a Web page first loads, the properties of the Browser Object are initialized according to the HTML markup instructions. After the page is fully loaded, JavaScript can be used to change the state of the Browser Object, thereby changing the rendered state of the Web page. In particular, the data contained in an HTML form is accessible to JavaScript through the Browser Object.

JavaScript: A programming language, syntactically similar to C++ and Java, that is used primarily to script Web browsers. The typical use is to place JavaScript statements in functions, which are called when a user event occurs and which typically manipulate the Browser Object in some way (by changing its properties or calling its methods). For that reason, JavaScript is sometimes called an *object-based* language. JavaScript (at the present) lacks the formal object classes and inheritance of fully object-oriented languages.

Loosely typed: Able to contain data of different kinds, such as strings, integers, floating-point numbers, or Boolean values, interchangeably. JavaScript's variables are loosely typed. Type conversions are handled "on the fly" by the JavaScript interpreter as necessary when evaluating expressions. JavaScript has special literals (`NaN`, `Infinity`, `undefined`, `null`) that are stored into variables when an unresolvable type mismatch makes storing a valid piece of data impossible. The built-in primitive variables bound to the Browser Object, however, are of fixed types. The most noteworthy example is the `value` property of a form element, which is always a string, even if a number is entered into the element.

Function parameters: Information passed to a function. JavaScript always passes primitive variables to function parameters by value, and objects by reference.

Event: A Web browser's recognition that the user has done something to the Web page. Events are caused by a wide range of user actions, such as clicking a form control button (`onclick`), changing a form element in some way (`onchange`), or submitting a form (`onsubmit`).

Event handler: A property of the Browser Object that "listens" for events. Some form elements (submit and reset buttons) have built-in event-handling capability, whereas others require programmer-defined JavaScript functions to be assigned to the event handler.

Assignment of a function to an event handler: A JavaScript statement such as `document.myForm.elements[3].onclick=dosomething;` formally assigns an event handler property in the Browser Object to a function. In that case, the event handler receives any return values from the function. By contrast, when a function is associated with an event handler by treating the event handler as an HTML attribute (such as `onclick="dosomething()"`), the event handler does not receive return values from the function. That suffices in most cases because most event handlers in the Browser Object don't care about returned values.

Client-side form validation: The process of verifying that a user has entered proper data into an HTML form before it is submitted to the Web server. Client-side validation is much faster than server-side data validation, because no network transaction is required. The strategy is to bind a programmer-defined function to the `onsubmit` event handler of a submit button. If the function returns `true`, the form is automatically submitted. If the function returns `false`, the form submission is automatically aborted. In the latter case, it is customary to alert the user in some informative way.

Client-side utility: A combination of JavaScript and HTML forms that can perform a certain many type of computation. A client-side utility is a portable program that many different people can load into Web browsers over the Internet. Common examples are portable interest and mortgage calculators, annuity calculators, forms that give unit conversions (such as between Fahrenheit and degrees Celsius or between gallons and liters), and self-grading (insecure) quizzes.

EXERCISES

Dynamic Content

1. Create a JavaScript array that contains 10 dot-com Web site names (such as `amazon`). As the page is first loading, use that array to print out an HTML unordered list of links pointing to the Web sites. Use the names in the array as the underlined text that appears on the links and to construct the URLs to which the links point. (Contrast with Exercise 3.)

2. Work Exercise 1, except generate a list with n list items, where n is a randomly chosen integer in the range from 5 to 10. The n links that appear in the list should also be chosen randomly, with no duplicate links appearing in the list.

3. Work Exercise 1, but the array should contain the full domain names of the Web sites (such as `www.amazon.com`). Use the domain names to construct the URLs for the links. However, only the Web site name (`amazon`) should appear as the underlined text of the link. Use the string object to extract the site names from the domain names.

4. Create a Web page that uses JavaScript to generate a multiplication table as the page is first loading.

1	2	3	4	5	6	7	8	9
2	4	6	8	10	12	14	16	18
3	6	9	12	15	18	21	24	27
4	8	12	16	20	24	28	32	36
5	10	15	20	25	30	35	40	45
6	12	18	24	30	36	42	48	54
7	14	21	28	35	42	49	56	63
8	16	24	32	40	48	56	64	72
9	18	27	36	45	54	63	72	81

(a) Generate a $9 \cdot 9$ multiplication table.

(b) Generate an $n \cdot n$ multiplication table where n is a randomly generated integer in the range from 5 to 25.

5. Do Exercise 4, but with the following additions:

(a) The rows are given alternating background colors, and the numbers in the first row and first column are rendered in boldface.

(b) The numbers in the first row and first column are rendered as boldfaced white text in table cells with a black background. Within the rest of the table, the rows should alternate background colors between white and light gray.

Client-Side Utilities

6. Make a conversion calculator that can perform the following conversions:

Fahrenheit $<->$ Celsius : $F = (9/5 \times C) + 32$

Gallons $<->$ liters : 1 gallon = 3.77 liters

Miles $<->$ kilometers : 1 mile = 1.61 kilometers

The calculator should be able to make the conversions in both directions. Use only two text fields: one for the input and one for the converted value. You will then need one command button for each of the conversions. If a nonnumeric value or a negative number is entered by the user, the user should be alerted and the calculation aborted. Round all answers to two decimal places.

7. Make a calculator similar to the following.

> Amount you wish to borrow (principal): `0`
> Interest rate as a **yearly** percentage: (Example: 7.25) `0`
> Loan term in **months:** `0`
>
> [CALCULATE] [CLEAR]
>
> Monthly payments: [ ]
> The sum of all the payments: [ ]
> The total interest paid: [ ]

This calculates the monthly payment for a loan, based on monthly compounding of interest, as well as the sum of payments and total interest. The formula is as follows:

$$R = P \cdot \frac{r}{1 - \dfrac{1}{(1+r)^n}}$$

```
P = loan amount (Principal)
r = monthly interest rate (yearly rate divided by 12)
n = number of months
R = monthly payment (called Rent)
```

If any nonnumeric values or negative numbers are entered by the user, the user should be alerted and the calculation aborted. As an added precaution, round the number of months entered by the user to the nearest integer. Round all answers to two decimal places.

8. Make a calculator similar to the following.

> Savings each month: `0`
> Interest rate as a **yearly** percentage rate (**APR**): (Example: 7.25) `0`
> Length of savings program in **months:** `0`
>
> [CALCULATE] [CLEAR]
>
> Your money has grown to: [ ]
> Total amount of your payments: [ ]
> Total interest earned: [ ]

This calculates the effect of saving a fixed amount of money each month over a period of time (that is, an annuity). The savings accrue interest based upon monthly compounding of interest. The formula is as follows:

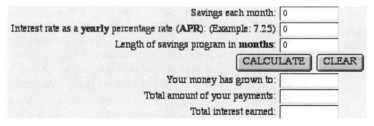

$$F = R \cdot \frac{(1+r)^n - 1}{r}$$

```
r = monthly interest rate (yearly rate divided by 12)
n = number of months
R = monthly payment (called Rent)
F = accumulated amount (Future value)
```

If any nonnumeric values or negative numbers are entered by the user, the user should be alerted and the calculation aborted. As an added precaution, round the number of months entered by the user to the nearest integer. Round all answers to two decimal places.

9. Construct a self-grading quiz that consists of

   (i) A multiple-choice question where only one answer can be selected. Use radio buttons.

   (ii) A multiple-choice question where multiple answers can be correct. Use checkboxes.

     (iii) A multiple-choice question where only one answer can be selected. Use a single selection menu.

     (iv) A short-answer question where the answer is only one word entered into a text field.

     If the user fails to supply an answer for each question, the user is alerted and the quiz is not graded. Otherwise, the correct answers appear in a text area along with the number of correct responses. Use a method of the `String` object (see Appendix B) to ensure that the user does not get the short-answer question wrong because of the case (upper vs. lower) of the letters in the word. Note that this quiz is insecure, because the answers are stored in JavaScript variables on the client.

10. Make the following lottery number generator. A unique-selection group of radio buttons gives options so that the user can choose to generate three, four, five, or six lottery numbers. A single-selection menu allows the user to choose the maximum size (25–60) of the numbers generated. For example, if the user chooses to generate five numbers of maximum size 50, then five lottery numbers, each in the range from 1 to 50, are generated. The form should have six text fields into which the generated numbers appear when a command button is clicked. (If the user chooses to generate fewer than six numbers, not all of the text fields are filled.) Generate the random numbers in such a way that they are all distinct. That is, the same number should not appear twice.

11. Construct a Web page that contains 25 text fields. (The text fields can be generated as the page first loads by using a JavaScript loop to write 25 text fields to the Web page.) One command button causes the text fields to be filled with 25 randomly generated integers in the range from 1 to 1000. Another command button causes the numbers to be sorted using a bubble sort. (The bubble sort algorithm can be found in almost any introductory C++ or Java text, or online after a quick search.)

Form Submission and Validation

12. Make a page with a form that includes the radio buttons and checkboxes from Figure 3.13 and the tax menu from Figure 3.16. The form should have two control buttons (besides the reset button). The first button is to "preview order" and the second is to "submit order." The preview button causes the order summary to be displayed in a text area. The submit button causes the form to be submitted to the echo program on this book's Web site. Both buttons should enact the same validation: At least one item is selected for purchase, a payment method is chosen, and a tax state is chosen. If the validation fails, the user is alerted and the order is either not summarized or submitted, as the case may be. Note that the discount for payment type should be applied after tax is applied to the purchase.

13. Construct the self-grading quiz of Exercise 9, but using both a command button and a submit button. When the command button is clicked, the quiz is graded if the validation constraints are met. When the submit button is clicked, the quiz is submitted to the echo program on the server if the validation constraints are met. Otherwise the user is alerted and the form is not submitted.

14. Construct a form for an online quiz with the following form elements and validation constraints. Submit the form to the echo program on the server if the validation constraints are met. Otherwise, alert the user.

     (i) A text field for a first name; it must be filled out and contain at least two characters.

     (ii) A unique-selection group of radio buttons for a multiple-choice question; an answer must be made.

     (iii) A group of checkboxes for a multiple-choice question that can have more than one right answer (such as "Which of the following apply?"). At least one checkbox must be chosen.

     (iv) A single-selection menu that provides choices for a multiple-choice question. The menu must be moved from the first index, which is a "dummy" choice.

     (v) A multiple-selection menu for a multiple-choice question that can have more than one right answer (that is "Which of the following apply?"). At least one option must be chosen.

15. Construct a form with two text fields: one for a user name and one for a password. When a submit button is clicked, the form is submitted to the echo program if validation is successful. Otherwise, the user is alerted and the form is not submitted. The validation is as follows:

    ▦ Both the user name and password must be from four to eight characters in length.

    ▦ The user name must be composed only of alphanumeric characters (a–z, A–Z, 0–9). The user name must begin with an alphabetic character.

    ▦ The password must adhere to the same constraints as the user name with the exception that it may also contain the underscore (_) or hyphen (-), but not as the first character.

    Hint: The allowed characters can be stored as one long string. You can then test each character in the user name and password against characters in that string.

16. Construct a form that collects information for a demographics survey, as shown in the figure. When a submit button is clicked, the form is submitted to the echo program if validation is successful. Otherwise, the user is alerted and the form is not submitted.

    The validation is as follows:

    Name fields:

    ▦ The first and last names must each be more than two characters, but no more than 20 characters. They must not contain any nonalphabetic characters.

    ▦ The middle-initial field may be left blank, but if it is filled in, it must be exactly one alphabetic character.

    Phone number fields:

    ▦ The first two fields must be exactly three characters, and the third field must be exactly four characters. All fields must contain integers.

    ZIP code fields:

    ▦ The first field must contain exactly five characters and must be an integer.

    ▦ The second field may be left blank, but if it's filled in, it must contain exactly four characters and must be an integer.

    Hint: Read the hint at the end of Exercise 15.

17. Make a form with one text field for an e-mail address. When a submit button is clicked, the form is submitted to the echo program if validation is successful. Otherwise, the user is alerted and the form is not submitted. The following are the constraints on the e-mail address.

    ▦ It must have one @ character.

    ▦ The @ character must not be the first or last character of the address.

    ▦ It must have at least one period (.), and if it has more than one, no two periods can be consecutive (..). It can have no more than three periods. (We wish to allow x@y.a.b.c, but not x@a..b).

    ▦ The address can have no period (.) before the @.

    ▦ A period (.) must not be the first or last character of the address.

PROJECT THREAD

Here you construct two forms with client-side validation. The forms will also be used for the project thread in subsequent chapters as part of a larger Web application.

A. Work Exercise 14.

B. Work Exercise 15.

C. Add a brief description of and link to each assignment to the table in your homework page. Note that each assignment should be in a separate Web page, and separate links should be added in the Homework page. If you are assigned any other exercises from this chapter, add a description(s) and link(s) to the homework page as well.

D. Upload the updated homework page and all other files to the Web server.

## CHAPTER 4

INTRODUCTION TO PERL AND CGI PROGRAMMING

In Section 1.7, we briefly discussed the theory of Common Gateway Interface (CGI) programming. Perl is the language of choice for many CGI programmers for several reasons: it is free, it is platform-independent for the most part, it has powerful text-processing capabilities, and it can process huge amounts of data with ease.

The name **Perl** is an acronym for **Practical Extraction and Report Language**. Perl was invented in the late 1980s by Larry Wall as a language specializing in parsing text files. When the Web was born, Perl became the choice for programming on the back end of Web applications because of the ease and power with which it deals with text files, and plain text files are the easiest means to store data on a Web server. With Perl it is possible to develop powerful Web applications quite quickly.

But with Perl's power comes some language features that are not standard in languages like C++ and Java. In this chapter, we learn some basics of programming using the Perl programming language. Those basics are then applied to create simple server-side CGI programs.

4.1 EXECUTING A PERL PROGRAM LOCALLY

Since HTML and JavaScript are used for the front end of a Web application, testing that code is quite simple: Just load it into a browser, and the code is interpreted. Because everyone has a Web browser, the development strategy is straightforward: Keep testing the source file in a browser locally until you get it right, then transfer it to the Web server. However, a Perl CGI program executes on the back end, and testing it locally in a browser is not an option, because browsers don't deal with Perl. But it is still desirable to test CGI programs locally before putting them on the server. You certainly don't want to publish broken Perl code to a Web server.

Perl is an interpreted language. This means that in order to execute a Perl program, you run a Perl interpreter on the source file, rather than compiling it into a separate executable program. See Appendix D on setting up your system to run a Perl interpreter. We now focus on simple Perl programs that generate standard output locally. Once that is mastered, it is a simple matter to construct them so that they are viable on a Web server.

The two steps in executing a Perl program are the following:

Step 1: Create a source file. This source file is what we would refer to as your Perl program. Like HTML files, the source should be created with a plain text editor and not a word processor. Many people find it helpful to use an "intelligent" text editor, such as those referenced on the Web site.

141

Step 2: Execute the program by running a Perl interpreter on the source file. Depending on the operating system of your local computer, you may want to execute the program from a command-line. However, if you have an available IDE,[1] that may be the way to go. We briefly discuss both command-line execution and execution within an IDE here. Suppose a Perl program is stored in a source file named `prog.pl`.

Executing the program via a command line:

In UNIX or Linux, at a command prompt, you would type the command

```
> perl prog.pl
```

Here the `>` stands for a command prompt, so you would not type it in. The actual prompt you see depends upon the particular Unix shell. Note that MacOS X also offers a UNIX command prompt.

In Windows, at an MS-DOS prompt, you can type the command

```
> perl prog.pl
```

Again, the `>` stands for a command prompt. As you see in Figure 4.1, the directory (in this case, `C:\`) is part of the prompt. However, we will continue simply to use `>` to represent the variety of command line prompts that are possible. It is *important* to note that you must first navigate to the directory containing the program before attempting to run it from the command line. (An alternative is to give the full path to the program after the `perl` directive.)

Executing the program from an IDE:

In MacOS 9, you can run MacPerl, choose **Run Script** from the **Script** menu, and navigate to the file `prog.pl`. MacPerl may also be used as the text editor for Step 1, in which case one of the menu items is **Run prog.pl**, as shown in Figure 4.2.

In Windows, using an IDE (either a free one, or one of the many you can purchase), you would select Run from a menu, in a way similar to the description just given for MacPerl. Some Perl IDEs for Windows are referenced on the Web site.

Figure 4.3 shows our first Perl program. It is a one-line program whose purpose is to print out the sentence, "Hello World!" Notice that this is a complete program. There is no extra baggage. Type this into a file named `hello.pl` using your favorite text editor. Then execute the program using a Perl interpreter invoked by one of the methods just described.

Using a command prompt in Windows, UNIX, or Linux, you will see something similar to what is shown in Figure 4.4. The output is printed on subsequent lines after the command line. In an IDE we would choose **Run** (or similar command) from a menu and would see something similar to what is shown in Figure 4.5. In an IDE, the printed output is in a separate window.

---

[1] An Integrated Development Environment (IDE) is a programming environment that is integrated with a particular operating system. Examples include the environment in which you may have learned C++ or Java. Among other things, an IDE usually supplies an intelligent text editor, a compiler/interpreter, and a syntax debugger.

FIGURE 4.1 Running a Perl program from the command line in ActivePerl.

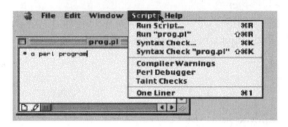

FIGURE 4.2 A Perl IDE.

FIGURE 4.3 A simple Perl program.

FIGURE 4.4 The "Hello World!" program run from a command line.

From now on, we will just speak of the output of a program, no longer referring to the execution method and platform-dependent differences that come from executing the Perl program from a command line (as in UNIX, MS-DOS, or MacOS X UNIX) or from within an IDE.

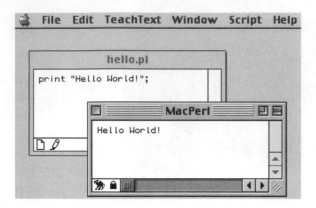

FIGURE 4.5 Running the "Hello World!" program in an IDE.

For the rest of this section, we discuss some fundamental Perl syntax issues related to output. First of all, Perl statements are terminated by semicolons. The `print` command has the syntax

```
print "some string";
```

where a string literal follows the `print` keyword.

A second `print` statement does not print on a new line; rather, the printing is continued where the previous printing left off. For example, the following produces the exact same output as the `hello.pl` program just shown:

```
print "Hello ";
print "World!";
```

To print the second word on a new line, a newline character must be printed after the first word.

```
print "Hello\n";
print "World!";
```

The escape sequence `\n` causes subsequent text to begin on a new line. Such escape sequences will be explained further in the next section.

Single-line comments, which are ignored by the Perl interpreter, are entered by using the special character `#`. Any characters following a `#` on the same line are ignored. Figure 4.6 shows two programs that output a poem from J.R.R. Tolkien's *The Hobbit*. The two programs produce the exact same output. You can see from the second version of the program that a more general syntax for the `print` statement is

```
print "a string","another string","yet another string";
```

where a comma-delimited list of strings is supplied. Note that the commas merely delimit the strings and do not cause new lines. The second version of the program also illustrates that a single Perl command may span multiple program lines. (But, as in JavaScript, don't press Enter in the middle of a string.)

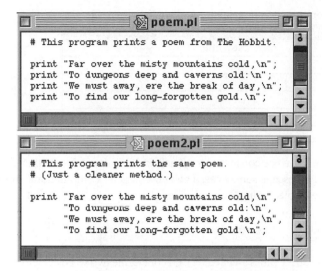

```
# This program prints a poem from The Hobbit.

print "Far over the misty mountains cold,\n";
print "To dungeons deep and caverns old:\n";
print "We must away, ere the break of day,\n";
print "To find our long-forgotten gold.\n";
```

```
# This program prints the same poem.
# (Just a cleaner method.)

print "Far over the misty mountains cold,\n",
      "To dungeons deep and caverns old:\n",
      "We must away, ere the break of day,\n",
      "To find our long-forgotten gold.\n";
```

FIGURE 4.6 Two programs that produce the same output.

NOTE

As with nearly any programming language, everything in Perl is case-sensitive. For example,

```
Print "Hello World\N";
```

would cause two errors because of the capital P and N.

It is certainly advantageous to enable warnings to help find potential syntactical and logical errors. To turn warnings on, do one of the following:

■ From a command line in both UNIX/Linux and Windows, use the switch `-w`:

```
> perl -w program.pl
```

■ In an IDE, find the menu item for warnings and turn it on.

4.2 STRINGS AND ESCAPE CHARACTERS

A string is a sequence of characters that includes any combination of letters, numbers, symbols, newlines, tabs, and all other ASCII characters. In Perl, there are two ways to delimit a string: using single quotes or double quotes. For example, both

```
"Scooby Doo"
'Scooby Doo'
```

denote 10-character strings. The main difference is that there are two features for double-quoted strings: You may use escape sequences, and variables are interpolated.

TABLE 4.1 Common Escape Sequences Used in Perl

ESCAPE SEQUENCE	INTERPRETATION
\n	Newline
\t	Tab
\"	"
\\	\
\$	$
\@	@

An escape sequence consists of a \ (backslash) followed by another character. Table 4.1 lists some common escape sequences. The two-character combination is treated as one character in a double-quoted string. For example,

```
"Scooby\nDoo\n"
```

is an 11-character string (not 13-character). Of course, the two words would be on different lines, with any subsequent text also on a new line if this string printed as output. For another example,

```
print "scoob\@afraid.com\n";
```

directs a 17-character string (not 19-character) to output, yielding

```
scoob@afraid.com
```

again causing subsequent text to begin on a new line. For reasons that will become apparent, it is a good habit to terminate printed lines of output with a newline character \n.

We can see from the two preceding examples that the escape sequence \n has a special meaning, whereas \@ stands for the actual symbol. In the latter case, the character is *escaped*, so that any special meaning it might have otherwise is obscured. That is important since the characters $ and @, as well as several others, have special meaning for Perl variables, which are **interpolated** (to be explained soon) when placed inside double-quoted strings. As a general rule of thumb, escape sequences using alphanumeric characters (such as \n and \t) have a special meaning, and ones using nonletter, nondigit keyboard characters (like \" and \$) are for escaping the characters to obscure other meanings they might have in Perl.

Whereas double quotes specify that escape sequences will be interpreted, single quotes enclose a string without interpreting any escape sequences except for the two cases shown in Table 4.2. Remembering just those two exceptions, it is easy to understand what single quotes do. For example,

```
'Scooby\nDoo\n'
```

is a 13-character string that yields

```
Scooby\nDoo\n
```

TABLE 4.2   The Only Escape Sequences Interpreted in Single-Quoted Perl Strings

ESCAPE SEQUENCE	INTERPRETATION
\'	'
\\	\

with no line breaks when printed as output. For another example,

```
print 'scoob@afraid.com';
```

prints the e-mail address without need of escape characters. However, there is no way to include a newline character using a single-quoted string. A new line after the e-mail address can be produced by the following.

```
print 'scoob@afraid.com',"\n";
```

A big advantage of single-quoted strings is that double quotes need not be escaped inside them. Remember, our Perl CGI programs will output HTML code, which uses many of Perl's reserved characters. In particular, XHTML attribute values must be delimited with quotes. For example, the following `print` statement

```
print "<a href=\"mailto:scoob\@afraid.com\">email Scoob</a>\n";
```

produces

```
<a href="mailto:scoob@afraid.com">email Scoob</a>
```

where any subsequent output would begin on a new line. It was necessary to escape the quotes for the value of the `href` attribute and the special @ symbol (which otherwise signifies a Perl array). Using single quotes, an equivalent `print` command is

```
print '<a href="mailto:scoob@afraid.com">email Scoob</a>',"\n";
```

which is cleaner without the escaped characters. But we did have to double-quote the newline character at the end so that it would be interpreted.

NOTE

Recall that we use a # symbol for Perl comments. A # symbol that occurs inside quotes is not considered a comment character. That will be a factor when you output HTML code. For example,

```
print '<body bgcolor="#336699">' , "\n";
```

results in

```
<body bgcolor="#336699">
```

where subsequent output would begin on a new line.

For further contrast, the following example prints the sentence

```
The Perl string for $2.95 is "\$2.95".
```

using double quotes,

```
print "The Perl string for \$2.95 is \"\\\$2.95\".\n";
```

and using single quotes,

```
print 'The Perl string for $2.95 is "\\$2.95".', "\n";
```

A bareword results if you forget to put any quotes around a string literal and the word happens not to have any other meaning (such as a reserved word or Perl function). Being somewhat friendly, Perl will interpret a bareword as a string literal if the context calls for a string. For example,

```
print "Bareword: ", spoon, "\n";
```

will output

```
Bareword: spoon
```

although a warning will be generated, if warning are enabled. On the other hand,

```
print "Bareword: ", fork, "\n";
```

would generate an outright error, because `fork` happens to be a Perl function, and it is used incorrectly here.

The bottom line is *never use barewords for string literals*. Indeed, the following,

```
print spoon, "\n";
```

would also generate an error because the `print` statement can also be used to print to a file, as you will learn in Chapter 5. In such a case, the `print` command would interpret the bareword `spoon` as a file handle, causing an error (unless `spoon` happens to *be* a file handle!).

4.3 SCALAR VARIABLES

Perl has three fundamental variable types: scalars, arrays, and hashes. In stark contrast to other programming languages you may have seen, the type of a Perl variable is indicated by special symbols. Names of **scalar variables** begin with a $ symbol, those of arrays begin with a @ symbol, and hashes begin with a % symbol. We discuss scalars in this section, leaving arrays and hashes for Chapter 5.

The name of every scalar variable must begin with a $ symbol. Aside from that, standard naming conventions apply. Variable names can contain only alphabetic characters, digits, and the underscore symbol. As always, good programming practice is to use mostly lowercase letters and short descriptive names. For example, the following are good variable names.

```
$count
$grand_total
$num2
```

Another difference from other languages is that Perl variable names can begin with digits or an underscore. However, variable names like $_ and $2 are reserved in Perl with special meanings and restrictions, so you should use only variable names that begin with a letter (after the initial $) as we showed.

Variable assignment in Perl has the syntax

```
$variableName = value;
```

where value could be a scalar literal or the result of some complex expression involving operations and functions. There is no formal type declaration, but the $ indicates that $*variableName* is of scalar type. There is no formal declaration of variables in Perl. So an assignment such as this one both declares and initializes the variable. It is possible for a variable to exist but not be initialized. In that case, the uninitialized scalar variable is undefined, and it evaluates to the empty string if used in an expression. That generates a warning if warnings are enabled.

The primitive data types that can be stored in a scalar variable are strings and numbers. String literals are stored as sequences of bytes, and numeric literals as either integers or double-precision floating-point numbers. The following assignments illustrate the basic storage options.

```
$x="hello";
$x=2;
$x=3.14;
```

Perl (like JavaScript) converts between strings and numbers as necessary. We don't really need to concern ourselves with the technical storage issue, since Perl handles conversions seamlessly. However, in the next section we do elaborate on how Perl handles type conversions in different contexts.

The contents of scalar variables can be included in `print` statements. The following

```
$x = "blah";
print "You say ", $x, $x, $x, ".\n";
```

gives the output

```
You say blahblahblah.
```

An easier way to output the contents of scalar variables is simply to include them within double-quoted strings so that they are interpolated—replaced by their values. For example, the following would result in the same output as the preceding.

```
$x = "blah";
print "You say $x$x$x.\n";
```

That's pretty handy! To include the contents of a variable in output, just slap the variable into a double-quoted string. Having read the previous section, one would be tempted always to use just single-quoted strings because special symbols don't have to be escaped, making the code cleaner. However, in many instances we will need to include contents of variables within our output, and single quotes are not up to the task.

We now provide two examples where scalar variables are interpolated in `print` commands. The first program features three variables that are interpolated. The program and its output are shown in Figure 4.7. Note especially that the $ had to be escaped in order to get it to appear in the output. Otherwise, the Perl interpreter would think it signified a scalar variable.

The next program, shown in Figure 4.8, is a slight modification of the one in Figure 4.7. Again, the output is shown below the program. Notice that in the last line, we could not do

```
print "we are out of $products.\n";
```

because in that case `$products` would be the scalar variable that would be interpolated, and in this program it would interpolate to the empty string, because no `$products` variable had been initialized. Interpolating an uninitialized variable generates a warning if warnings are enabled.

The previous example shows that mixing variables in with text can create problems if you are not careful. When an unescaped $ symbol is encountered within double quotes, the longest legal variable name starting with the $ will be interpolated. For example, the string

```
"a$x2:$yz"
```

will have the scalar variables `$x2` and `$yz` interpolated. A common mistake is typing something like that (maybe less ugly) when you had intended `$x` to be the variable to be interpolated. Because variables do not have to be declared, such a mistake would not register an error. If warnings are turned on, however, the uninitialized `$x2` would generate an uninitialized-variable warning (unless you are *un*lucky enough that `$x2` happens to be an existing variable also). If you want `$x` and `$y` to be the interpolated variables in this output, then you can write

```
print "a$x","2:$y","z";
```

which is a similar tactic to how we dealt with the `$product` variable in the previous program.

```
[interpolate1.pl]

$name = 'Mary';
$product = "encyclopedia";
$cost = 34.99;

print "Dear $name:\n";
print "Thank you for your purchase of: $product.\n";
print "You will be billed for \$$cost.\n";
print "Thank you.\n";
```

```
Dear Mary:
Thank you for your purchase of: encyclopedia.
You will be billed for $34.99.
Thank you.
```

FIGURE 4.7 Interpolating Perl variables in printed output.

```
[interpolate2.pl]

$name = 'Mary';
$product = "encyclopedia";
$cost = 34.99;

print "Dear $name:\n";
print "We are sorry to inform you that ";
print "we are out of $product", "s.\n";
```

```
Dear Mary:
We are sorry to inform you that we are out of encyclopedias.
```

FIGURE 4.8 Avoiding a potential pitfall when interpolating variables.

NOTE

Now that you are familiar with including variables in output, you can better contrast the utilities of single- and double-quoted strings in print statements. Because the two string formats are quite different in their functionality, here is a concise summary of the utility of each.

- Double-quoted strings allow escape sequences to be interpreted and scalar variables to be interpolated. In fact, the main utility of double-quoted strings in print statements is to be allow the contents of variables to be mixed in with the output. It is important that escape sequences are interpreted so that special symbols can be included in the output. Good examples are \$, so that the $ is not mistaken for the start of a variable name, and \", so that the presence of an extra " doesn't prematurely terminate the string.

- Single-quoted strings don't feature interpolation of variables or escaped characters (other than the two listed in Table 4.2). That might seem a limitation, but you will use Perl to output HTML code, which is replete with special symbols, especially ", which is required for attribute values in XHTML. Thus, single-quoted output is ideal for HTML output, because we don't have to worry about escaping special characters. Many of the single-quoted examples in Section 4.2 attest to that.

4.4 BASIC OPERATIONS; NUMERIC AND STRING CONTEXTS

We have seen that scalar variables can contain either numbers or strings. Perl does differentiate between integers and floating-point numbers. Numbers are represented in the most simple format possible. Consider the following assignments.

```
$x = 1000;
$x = 1000.0;
$x = 1E3;    #scientific notation
```

In each case, the statement `print "$x";` gives the integer 1000 as output. Since all three numbers are inherently integers, Perl stores them as such. Of course,

```
$x=3.14;
```

causes $x to contain a floating-point number. In contrast, the assignments

```
$x = '100.0';
$x = "1E2";
```

cause $x to contain a five-character string in the first case, and a three-character string in the second case.

Perl's arithmetic operations are standard and are listed in Table 4.3. For a quick refresher, the modulus is the remainder when the first operand is divided by the second. So, `9%4` evaluates to 1. (Romulus, on the other hand, is a planet from *Star Trek*.)

In an arithmetic operation like

```
expression1 + expression2
```

both expressions are placed into numeric context. For example, the following

```
$x="11";
$y="3";
$z=$x+$y;
```

causes $z to contain 14. The operands were converted into numbers during the calculation. During calculations, all numbers in Perl are represented as double-precision floating-point

TABLE 4.3 Perl Arithmetic Operators

OPERATION	MEANING
+	Addition
-	Subtraction
*	Multiplication
/	Division
%	Modulus

numbers. However, when the assignment to $z was made, Perl chose the most simple representation—integer.

In string `concatenation`,

```
expression1 . expression2
```

both expressions are placed into string context regardless of whether or not the expressions are inherently numeric. For example,

```
$x="base";
$y="ball";
$z=$x.$y;
```

causes $z to contain `"baseball"`, as you would expect. But,

```
$x=21;
$y=12;
$z=$x.$y;
```

causes the $z to contain `"2112"`. Even though the expressions were inherently numeric, they were placed into string context for concatenation. Moreover, the concatenation operator returned the value as a string.

NOTE

Unlike C++, Java, and JavaScript, the + operator has no duality in Perl. It means numeric addition only, whereas a period (.) is used for string concatenation. If you are accustomed to one of the other languages, you will have to get used to concatenation in Perl.

Perl has a string replication operator, which repeats a string. The syntax is

```
string x number
```

which results in the *string* concatenated onto itself *number* of times. For example

```
"blah" x "3"
```

evaluates to `"blahblahblah"`. More interestingly,

```
$x=2;
$y="5";
$z=$x x $y;
```

causes $z to contain `"22222"`. The interesting point is that the first operand is placed into string context, and the second operand is placed into numeric context. (Kind of like the ol' double switch in baseball!)

The main concept to take from the last few examples is that of context. The interpreter attempts to be smart enough to know when to interpret a string as a number in certain contexts and as a string in other contexts. Conversely, numbers need to be represented as strings in other contexts. This simplifies matters for the programmer, because variables' types don't have to be formally declared, but it may also cause confusion in some cases.

If a string is placed into numeric context, it will be represented as a number as well as possible. If the string is not a well-formatted number ("23x"), then a number will be read as much as possible (23) from the string. If no number can be read ("xx"), the string will be given a value of 0 if placed into numeric context. (Often, unnatural contextual conversions cause a warning if warnings are enabled.) An understanding of the important concept of context will save many headaches later on.

Table 4.4 gives examples of various context scenarios. The examples clarify some of the oddities that can arise. They will be particularly useful for reference when you (inevitably) get unpredictable results from a calculation, and you become confounded. The context of an expression is determined by how the value of the expression will be used. That is, the actual value of an expression may vary depending on its context.

If you need to use multiple operations in an expression, parentheses should be used for grouping. As always, it is best to apply parentheses liberally to force the order of operations that you intend. For example

```
$s = ($a . $b) x $c;
```

is unambiguous, but

```
$s = $a . $b x $c;
```

TABLE 4.4 Examples of Context in Perl

The following examples assume that $x = "a"; has been executed.

STATEMENT	OUTPUT	EXPLANATION
print "7.000";	7.000	String literal
print "7.000" + 0;	7	Calculation placed into numeric context
print 7 + 5;	12	Numeric context
print "7" + "5";	12	Calculation placed into numeric context
print "7+5";	7+5	String literal; operations not evaluated inside double quotes
print "x7" + "x5";	0	Malformed numbers treated as 0
print "7x" + "5x";	12	Malformed numbers read as far as possible
print 7.5;	7.5	Just a number
print 7 . 5;	75	String concatenation
print 7 . $x;	7a	String concatenation
print 7.$x;	Error	Looks like a number (7.) next to a variable $x; code does not parse
print "7".$x;	7a	Now code parses correctly; string concatenation

leaves you at the mercy of operator precedence. Forcing grouping with parentheses is far better than memorizing precedence tables for operators, especially for Web programmers who code in several languages.

> **NOTE**
>
> In our discussion of operators, we have largely ignored operators for variable assignment. We have seen that = is for standard assignment. Perl does have the common shortcut assignment operators such as ++ , -- , and += . Use of these is at your discretion.

4.5 SOME USEFUL BUILT-IN FUNCTIONS

There are two viable formats for calling a built-in Perl function. You can use

```
functionname argument
```

or

```
functionname (argument)
```

The parentheses are optional.[2] Perl programmers have grown accustomed to using parentheses for certain functions and not using them for others. The reasons are mostly for esthetics and readability. However, parentheses are sometimes necessary to force precedence when several operations are involved.

One usually uses parentheses with functions where it would otherwise look a bit strange. The following common math-related functions are one such case.

```
sqrt
abs
sin
cos
int
```

They take numeric arguments; that is, their arguments are in numeric context. They return numeric values. The int function truncates the decimal part of a number. The rest are self-explanatory. An example stores a root of a quadratic equation in the variable $x.

```
$x= (-$b + sqrt($b*$b - 4*$a*$c))/(2*$a);
```

The sqrt function is used to implement the quadratic formula.

---

[2]Technically, Perl's built-in functions are considered operators, and operators do not require parentheses. For example, we have been using Perl's built-in print function without parentheses.

Some basic Perl string functions are quite useful. Here is a quick example using each of them. Suppose the variable `$str` is initialized as.

```
$str= "Hello\n\n";
```

The `chop` function

```
$x= chop $str;
```

alters `$str` by "chopping" off the last character and then returns the chopped character. Thus, `$str` contains `"hello\n"` and `$x` contains `"\n"`. We reset

```
$str= "Hello\n\n";
```

to its original state and apply the `chomp` function

```
$x= chomp $str;
```

which alters `$str` by chopping off *all* newline characters at the end of `$str`, and then returns the number of characters chopped. Thus, `$str` contains `"hello"`, and `$x` contains `"2"`. Note that `chop` removes the last character, even if it is not a newline. However, `chomp` will leave the string unharmed if there are no newline characters at the end of the string.

The length function

```
length $str;
```

returns the number of characters in `$str`. For example,

```
print "The string \"$str\" has ", length $str, " characters.\n";
```

gives the output

```
The string "hello" has 5 characters.
```

Functions such as `chomp` and `chop` alter the original variable, but functions such as `length` leave the original variable alone. (Food processors have a button for "chop," there are no built-in Perl functions corresponding to "mince" or "liquefy.")

NOTE

Variables are interpolated within double quotes. However, operations and functions are not evaluated within double quotes. The above example did not attempt to call the `length` function within the double quotes.

4.6   STANDARD INPUT

In this section, you will learn how to read keyboard input. Learning the Perl constructs in this simple setting will be of great help when we get to more complicated CGI programs. To read from the standard input, which is the keyboard when you run the program locally, the operator <> returns one line of characters, including the newline character entered when you press Enter.

Consider the program shown in Figure 4.9, which gives the user a personalized greeting. Because the input string contains a newline character, we often want to `chop` it off. However, it is preferable to use `chomp`, so that in some situations we don't have to worry about altering a string if it has no newline characters. You should try the program in Figure 4.9 for yourself. Especially, try it without the `chomp` statement so that you see that the string input into `$name` does indeed contain a newline character.

For another example, consider the program in Figure 4.10, which requests two numbers and prints their quotient. An example run of this program is also shown in Figure 4.10. The boldfaced characters indicate user keyboard input.

The program shown in Figure 4.11 is similar to the previous one in terms of programming tactics. An example run of this program is provided. Again, user input is in boldface. Especially notice that without all the "chomping," the newline characters from the user input would cause the sentence generated by the last `print` statement to be fragmented into four different lines in the output. Try it for yourself!

4.7   FORMATTING NUMERIC OUTPUT

You already know how to print output. However, some situations call for precise formatting of numbers. For example, consider the output from the quotient program of the previous section. In many situations it is desirable to limit the number of decimal places in the output by rounding. Certainly if that were a dollar amount, you would want only two decimal places. Also, situations involving the need for well-formatted times and dates require precise formatting.

You will be outputting HTML documents, where spacing is generally ignored, so you have no need to generate output like

```
$4.99
$39.99
```

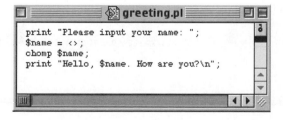

```
                    greeting.pl
print "Please input your name: ";
$name = <>;
chomp $name;
print "Hello, $name. How are you?\n";
```

FIGURE 4.9   Using the standard input operator

```
quotient.pl

print "Please enter a number: ";
$x = <>; chomp $x;
print "Please enter another number: ";
$y = <>; chomp $y;
print "The quotient of your two numbers is ";
print "$x / $y = ", $x/$y, "\n";
```

```
Please enter a number: 2
Please enter another number: 3
The quotient of your two numbers is 2 / 3 = 0.666666666666667
```

FIGURE 4.10 Obtaining two lines of standard input.

```
nouns.pl

print "Please enter any noun: ";
$noun = <>; chomp $noun;
print "Please enter another noun: ";
$noun2 = <>; chomp $noun2;
print "Please enter any verb: ";
$verb = <>; chomp $verb;
print "\nDid you know that when you $verb a $noun, the $noun becomes a $noun2?\n";
```

```
Please enter any noun: cat
Please enter another noun: dog
Please enter any verb: paint

Did you know that when you paint a cat, the cat becomes a dog?
```

FIGURE 4.11 The importance of chomping lines of input.

where both quantities are right-aligned in print field of width 15. That type of formatting can be handled with HTML tables, for example. Thus, print field widths are unimportant compared to numerical formatting such as precision of floating-point numbers and whether integers should be preceded by zeros. With that in mind, we won't go into the long, sordid details of all possible formatting options, but we offer a brief overview of those that will be relevant for CGI programs.

The printf statement (similar to the same statement in C) is used to force formatting in output. The general syntax is

```
printf formatstring , list;
```

It is best to proceed with a simple example. The following statement,

```
printf "round to two decimals: %.2f and to no decimals: %.0f" , 1.6667,2.6667;
```

produces

```
round to two decimals: 1.67 and to no decimals: 3
```

The % symbol indicates that a formatting instruction (technically a *field specifier*) is to follow. In this case, %.2f specifies to round to two places after the decimal, and %.0f specifies no decimals. Here f signifies a floating-point decimal number. Going back to the general syntax, the *formatstring* is the string that is to be printed, and the field specifiers are placeholders within that string. The field specifiers are replaced, in order, by the numbers supplied in the *list* with the specified formatting applied. So, in this example, 1.6667 takes the place of %.2f, inheriting the specified formatting, and 2.6667 takes the place of %.0f, inheriting the specified formatting.

The only other field specifier we present is for integers. The specifier %d calls for formatting as an integer. (Why d? Just think of integers as *d*igits.) For example,

```
$x=4.99;
$y=7;
printf "integer: %d   funky integer: %03d", $x,$y;
```

prints

```
integer: 4   funky integer: 007
```

The integer specifier %d simply truncates the decimal in 4.99. However, the second field specifier requires more explanation. The specifier %03d says to put the integer in a field of size 3, and the 0 indicates that leading zeros should be inserted to fill up the size-3 print field. Similarly, %05d would produce 00007 in this example. You can also specify a print field width for floating-point numbers. For example, %12.2f specifies that the number should be printed in a field of width 12 (right-aligned by default) rounded to two decimals. But since output to a Web browser as an HTML file would render the extra spaces useless, there is no point expending further thought on that. However, there are applications to specifying print field widths for integers where extra spaces are filled with zeros.

The example in Figure 4.12 shows applications to two numeric quantities commonly used in Web applications—time and money. The output is shown below the program.

NOTE

The example in Figure 4.12 demonstrates that escape characters can be used inside a printf statement (using double quotes, of course). However a % symbol can't be escaped in printf, because it signifies a field specifier. The solution is to use the special construct %%, which "escapes" to a single percent sign in a printf statement. For example,

```
$change="14.333333333";
printf "Your account has changed by %.1f%%.\n", $change;
```

prints as

```
Your account has changed by 14.3%.
```

```
                              format.pl
$balance=1005.2;
$hour=5;
$minute=1;

printf "The value of your stock account at %d:%02d pm is \$%.2f.", $hour,$minute,$balance;
```

```
The value of your stock account at 5:01 pm is $1005.20.
```

FIGURE 4.12 Formatting time and monetary values.

There will be occasions when we wish to format a number and save it into a variable without printing. This is accomplished by the sprintf function, whose syntax is exactly the same as that of printf:

```
sprintf formatstring , list;
```

This function returns the string that would have been printed by printf but does not print it. Here are two typical examples using sprintf.

```
$cost="19.3333333";
$formattedCost = sprintf "\$%.2f" , $cost;

$hours=4.05;
$minutes=3;
$time = sprintf "%d:%02d" , $hours , $minutes;
```

These lines of code result in $formattedCost containing the string "$19.33" and $time containing the string "4:03". The sprintf function is especially useful when a formatted string needs to be printed several times. In that case you have to specify the formatting instructions only once.

4.8 GENERATING HTML DOCUMENTS WITH PERL

We are now ready to write our first Perl CGI program. Figure 4.13 provides illustration for the discussion. It would be useful to recall Figure 1.9 in Section 1.7. The current situation is a simplified case of the general principle presented there. The CGI program is named firstpage.cgi and is stored in UWEBs root directory in a folder named cgi. You can see that this location is reflected in the URL that calls the program.

In the program itself, the first line simply gives the location of the Perl interpreter on the server (more on that in a bit). Now comes the printed output. In CGI programming, the first two lines of printed output must be a line containing the Content-type of the data followed by a blank line. The Content-type line becomes part of the header for the application-layer data. The Web server software and browser use the Content-type (and other heading information that applications need during HTTP transactions) to coordinate the

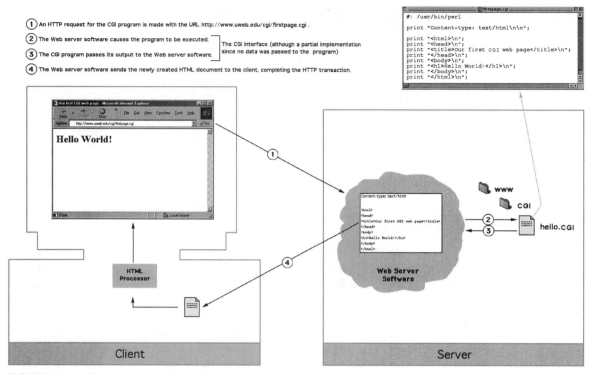

FIGURE 4.13 Executing a simple CGI program.

type of information being exchanged. Even though the line is printed in the output of the program, it doesn't appear in the resulting Web page.

To understand the significance of that line, consider what occurs if it is omitted. The server software is unable to complete the HTTP transaction, because application-layer headers are insufficient. (It is possible that some servers will attempt to complete the transaction, in which case the browser may give an error saying it was not given a complete set of header information.) Whatever the case, the program simply will not work. For contrast, suppose we use

```
print "Content-type: text/plain\n\n";
```

which can cause the HTML to be rendered as plain text, as shown in Figure 4.14. However, a modern browser is pretty clever about not displaying HTML as plain text, even if you try to trick it into doing so by specifying that the transaction is for plain text.

NOTE

As we have recommended for HTML and JavaScript, you should just make a template called something like `skeleton.cgi` that contains the first two lines, *exactly* as you see them in `firstpage.cgi`. Each time you make a new CGI program, simply copy the skeleton file and rename it. Theoretically, it is only necessary to type those two lines once.

```
<html>
<head>
<title>Our first CGI web page</title>
</head>
<body>
<h1>Hello World!</h1>
</body>
</html>
```

FIGURE 4.14 A Web browser is tricked into thinking it's getting plain text.

The rest of the program is easy to understand. The `print` statements simply generate a complete HTML file for the output of the program. In Figure 4.13 you see the program's output inside the server software. As indicated, the program doesn't pass the output directly to the client. Rather, the program completes the CGI interface by passing the output to the server software. That is much different from executing the program locally from a command line or IDE, where the output is directed back to the command window or to a new window, respectively.

We have been putting newline command characters at the end of `print` statements for much of this chapter, even if they were not required. Now you can see why. Without them, the entire HTML file you see inside the server software would be on one line.

```
<html><head><title>Our first CGI web page</title></head><body><h1>Hello
World!</h1></body></html>
```

The Web browser does not care, since it constructs the parse tree based upon the containment relationships of the HTML elements. But remember that CGI programs should be developed and tested locally, before they are transferred to the Web server. It is much easier to determine what the program is spitting out if the output is formatted as a human-friendly HTML file.

Once it is determined that the CGI program is working properly and you have put it on the server, you can then type in the URL pointing to the program and test it from a remote browser request. In fact, a prudent move for you would be to get `firstpage.cgi` running in your local environment and then test it on a Web server (see the following bulleted notes first). That way you can get the feel for how a Perl program on a server spits out a complete HTML file to be read by an application on the client. That's pretty cool if you stop to think about it.

There are some subtleties that need to be covered. We provide those in the following bulleted notes.

■ This one is *very important* if you have an account on a UNIX or Linux server. When you transfer a CGI program to a UNIX/Linux server, you must enable read and execution permissions for the CGI program. An HTML file is automatically transferred with the correct remote access privileges; CGI programs are not. Unlike HTML files, which are merely read, CGI programs are read and then executed. The default for new files is that they are not executable (by anyone). You do not have to do anything extra after transferring an HTML file (because UNIX/Linux accounts are usually set up so that new files have read permissions by everyone), but you must give your CGI program execute permissions. Failing to do so will cause the server software to send an error massage back to the browser when the CGI program is requested via a URL.

In UNIX/Linux, you can telnet to the server and run the following command for any CGI program that is to be viable for remote requests:

```
chmod +rx programName.cgi
```

The command name `chmod` stands for *ch*ange *mod*e, and this command gives read/execute privileges for `programName.cgi` to anonymous remote users (and that includes you if you make a remote browser request for a program, even if it is in your account on the server). In case you are not familiar with UNIX/Linux, note that you have to supply the full path to the program from the root, or navigate to the directory containing the program, before executing the command. For example,

```
chmod +rx  /usr/students/jones/public/cgi/programName.cgi
```

shows a typical full path from the root. Alternately, you can change your current directory to the `cgi` directory and set the permissions without supplying the full path to the Perl program. Keep in mind that when you log on to the server, you will be in your account directory, so you have only to navigate to the program's directory from there. So type

```
cd public/cgi/
```

(where the `cd` command name stands for *c*hange *d*irectory.) Once there, you simply run the `chmod` command using only the file name,

```
chmod +rx programName.cgi
```

See Appendix C for even more details on permissions.

■ This one is also *very important* if you have an account on a UNIX or Linux server. The location of the Perl interpreter can vary from system to system. This information is very important, because the location must be given in the first line of the program. On most systems, the interpreter is either `/usr/bin/perl` or `/usr/local/bin/perl`. If you don't know, telnet to the server and type

```
> which perl
```

at the command line. That will tell you where Perl is located.

■ Microsoft's IIS server, in conjunction with ActivePerl, does not require the path to Perl. Such information resides with the IIS server and is entered as part of the Perl installation process. Thus, you need not worry about it.

■ It is possible on Linux/UNIX machines to execute a CGI program from the command line rather than by using a URL call from a browser. The only advantage to that is that you can enable warnings to be generated by the server's Perl interpreter. Although you will use warnings generated by your local interpreter to help you test programs locally, two types of errors cannot be tested locally: Perl path errors (first line of program) and permissions errors (forgetting to `chmod`). If you simply can't get your program running, it could be one of those problems, so try this. Alter the first line of the program to be as follows:

```
#!/usr/bin/perl -w
```

adding the option `-w` to turn warnings on. You can then execute a program if you telnet to the server and type

```
> ./programName.cgi
```

at the command line while inside the directory containing the source file. The `./` is necessary if the enclosing directory (or the general `./`) is not already part of your command path. In ActivePerl on Windows, you cannot run a program in that manner from the command line. (Here, we are not referring to running a Perl program with the `perl` command method of Section 4.1. You can always do that.)

■ This one is *very important* if you have an account on a server running IIS in on a Microsoft platform. Make sure the file has read permissions for everyone. See Appendix C for more information.

■ This one is also *very important* if you use ActivePerl for your local environment or an IIS server. A Perl program must have the `.pl` file extension. This is the default configuration when ActivePerl is installed. See Appendix D for more information. (UNIX/Linux Perl interpreters accept either `.pl` or `.cgi` for CGI programs, depending upon the configuration of the Web server software.)

4.9 DYNAMIC OUTPUT

The example in the previous section showed that Perl programs can generate entire HTML files, but the true spirit of CGI programming is to generate Web pages dynamically—that is, to let the contents of Perl variables determine what gets produced in the generated HTML file. Change the contents of the variables, and you get a different Web page.

Before we get to such an example, we offer a new Perl output construct that is very useful for printing HTML code. A **print block** has the syntax

```
print <<SOMELABEL;
text to be printed
SOMELABEL
```

Here *SOMELABEL* can be any legal variable name, but good programming practice is to use all capital letters with some meaning. The effect of this statement is that all text between the first and last lines is printed literally. Note that there is no space between << and *SOMELABEL*. Also, the terminating *SOMELABEL* marker is on a line by itself with no extra spaces in front and no semicolon at the end. A common mistake is indenting the terminating label just because the beginning `print` statement is indented for some reason.

Not only is this `print` construct ideal for printing large amounts of text, but it enjoys the best features from printing with double-quoted strings or single-quoted strings, as follows:

- Variables are interpolated and escape sequences are interpreted. In that respect, the print block is very similar to double-quoting a string literal.

- A big advantage is that " does not have to be escaped. In that respect, the print block is similar to single-quoting a string literal. So, for example, it is easy to output HTML code containing lots of attributes.

```
$value="1234 Maple Ave.";
print <<AFORM;
<form action="http/www.uweb.edu/cgi/program.cgi" method="GET">
 <input type="text" name="address" value="$value" size="10">
 </form>
AFORM
```

That is much easier to produce without all the escapes \", yet variables are interpolated.

- Although quotes don't need to be escaped, other special characters do. For example, you have to escape $ symbols. Since variables are interpolated, an unescaped $ symbol is assumed to be the beginning of a variable.

- Expressions and function calls are not evaluated inside a print block. (The same is true inside single- or double-quoted string literals.)

We now use a print block in an example that generates a dynamic page, albeit a very simple one. Many commercial sites display advertising graphics to help generate revenue. In this example, three advertising agencies have each paid the same amount for their ads to be displayed. However, this Web site will display only one ad at a time (they have some principles!). So this CGI program randomly chooses from among the three images to see which one gets embedded in the Web page. The program and typical output are shown in Figure 4.15. To get a feel for the "randomness" of the image display, you will need to go to the Web site and execute the program a few times.

We now explain the program. First, a randomly generated number in the interval [0,3), obtained using the functions listed in Table 4.5, is stored onto $which. Then the number is truncated using the `int` function, giving each of the integers 0, 1, 2 an equal chance of being stored in $which. The three advertising images are stored in files named `ad0.gif`, `ad1.gif`, and `ad2.gif`. In our case, the images are in the same directory as the CGI program `randomimage.cgi`. So an HTML `img` element like

```
<img src="ad0.gif" />
```

TABLE 4.5 Perl Functions Used in Generating Random Integers

FUNCTION	DESCRIPTION
rand *argument*	The rand function returns a floating-point number between 0 (inclusive) and *argument* (exclusive)—that is, a real number in the interval [0, *argument*). If *argument* is omitted, its default is to return a real number in the interval [0,1). The rand function is pseudo-randomly seeded, which is adequate for most purposes.
int *argument*	The int function returns a truncated (decimal places chopped off) version of its numeric *argument*.

FIGURE 4.15 A CGI program that dynamically generates a Web page.

is sufficient to embed an ad in the outputted Web page. But the catch is that the name of the ad must be chosen randomly. That is accomplished by interpolating the variable `$which` inside the `print` block that generates the HTML code. For example, if `$which` contains 1, then the quantity

```
src="ad$which.gif"
```

becomes

```
src="ad1.gif"
```

when printed.

That's really all there is to this program. Random number generation is a common programming concept. But generating the name of the source file for the image dynamically is new in concept. That tactic is very common in CGI programming. For a last tidbit, when you call the program from off the Web site, select **View Source** from one of the browser's menus and notice that all of the text formatting (spaces and newline characters included) within the `print` block is preserved. The body of the `print` block is just a big, multiline string literal. Of course, you can also grab the source file from the Web site and run it locally to see how the program's output is formatted.

NOTE

It is time to emphasize the different types of errors and how to deal with them. The first kind is a Perl syntax error. If the syntax is bad, your local environment will give you diagnostic error messages. The Perl Interpreter will attempt to tell you what the problem is. However, if an erroneous program on a server is executed by a remote browser call, the program will just cause an internal server error message to be returned to the browser. Remember, the server software is concerned with completing the current HTTP transaction. If a CGI program fails to pass output to the server software, the server's only recourse is to send its own error message to the browser to complete the HTTP transaction. That really emphasizes the necessity for making a program that is interpretable in the local development before you put it on a server.

Even if a Perl program runs, its programmer may have made logical errors. Examples include bad calculations and variables with undefined values. It's these types of errors that enabling warnings in your local environment helps you to catch. We have mentioned warnings repetitively throughout the foregoing Perl sections. With no syntax errors, the program will still run on the server, but the output will not be as intended. Again, warnings in your local environment will help you catch a few logical errors.

But there is another level of potential errors to which a programmer generally is not accustomed. Normally, if a program runs (or compiles in other languages) and the output makes logical sense, you are good to go. But with CGI programs, the output has to be used by another application—a Web browser. Thus, there are potential HTML syntax errors with which to contend as well. For example, it may be that your program runs as intended, the output is returned to the browser, but there is an error in the returned HTML code that causes the Web page not to render properly.

You basically have two options to explore *after* you have dealt with the Perl syntax issues and made the program run. Copy the output from your local execution of the program, paste it into a text file, and load it into a browser to see what it looks like. Fix it and then try again. Or load the program onto the Web server and call it with a URL to see a rendition of the output. Fix it, upload the updated program to the server, and execute it again from a remote browser request. The first method involves some cutting and pasting, while the second involves transferring the file to the server over and over until you have tweaked the HTML output just right.

SUMMARY OF KEY TERMS AND CONCEPTS

Practical Extraction and Report Language. (Perl): A platform-independent language widely used in CGI programming. We have discussed how to run Perl programs from a command line, in an IDE, and by Web Server software through CGI.

Scalar variables: In Perl, scalar variables must begin with the $ character, and then standard naming conventions should be used. Like JavaScript variables, Perl variables are loosely typed. There are only two basic literal types that can be stored into a scalar variable: number and string.

Context: The principle in Perl of evaluating variable contents as strings or numbers based upon how the variable is being used in an assignment or calculation. In interpreting the type of a variable based on context, Perl is somewhat more adaptive in its type conversions than JavaScript is.

Interpolate: To insert the contents of a Perl variable in place of the variable name where it occurs in a double-quoted string or print block.

Single-quoted strings: A Perl string enclosed within single quotes ' . Variables are not interpolated inside single-quoted strings. However, special characters need not be escaped inside single quoted strings (with the exception of ' and \). Thus, they are useful for printing HTML code, which contains lots of " characters.

Double-quoted strings: A Perl string enclosed in double quotation marks " . Scalar variables are interpolated inside double-quoted strings. However, special characters such as $ and " must be escaped inside double-quoted strings in order to be taken at face value.

Concatenation: The action of putting the contents of one string immediately after the contents of another. Unlike many languages, Perl uses the period (.) as the concatenation operator.

Standard input: The default source of data to a Perl program, chosen by the operating system when the program is invoked. In the examples in this lesson, standard input was the keyboard. The Perl operator <> returns one line of text from standard input. It is important to remember that, since we will later use the same operator to return one line from a text file. In both cases, the operator returns the newline character at the end of the line, so it is important to chomp each line of input if you do not want to pass the newline along to output.

Formatted Output: Output in which the number of digits, number of decimal places, and other aspects of the appearance of a number can be precisely determined using symbols called *field specifiers*. In Perl, printf (*print f*ormatted) works just like a normal print statement except that the output is formatted according to the field specifiers. sprintf (*s*tore *print f*ormatted) is used to store formatted strings into variables.

Perl CGI program: A Perl program on the server side of a Web application that communicates with the Web server software. Although we have not seen how to pass data from the client to a CGI program, we have seen how a CGI program passes data back to the browser in the form of a complete HTML page. In particular, the program must first print the last line (`Content-type` line) of the application-layer HTTP header. A blank line must be printed after the last line of the HTTP header and before the HTML page. Note that the rest of the HTTP header is added automatically be the Web server software. (A typical HTTP header generated by the Apache server can be observed at the beginning of Section 8.2.)

Permissions: On UNIX/Linux systems, bits indicating whether and by whom a file may be read, written, or executed. When you ftp a file into your account directory (or subdirectory therein), *you* have `rwx` (read-write-execute) permissions to the file, but *anonymous* users have only `r` (read) privileges, by default, so you can telnet to the server and run (execute) the program from the command line, for example. However, anyone (including you) attempting to call the program using a URL over the Internet is considered an anonymous user. Thus, no one (including you) can execute your CGI program from a remote Web browser unless you first telnet to the server and change the file's permissions to `rx` (read-execute) for anonymous users. (Some FTP programs will let you change the permissions as well.) Failure to do so will result in an HTTP 403 error code, which is the code for a forbidden HTTP access attempt.

Warnings: Informative alerts issued by the Perl intrepreter when it encounters strange things, such as unnatural type conversions in expressions or empty variables. The interpreter does not issue warnings unless explicitly told to. Perl programs with outright syntax errors simply will not run, but, sometimes Perl programs run but give output other than what is intended, because of logic errors. Turning on Perl warnings in your execution environment helps to detect these problems.

Print blocks: Perl code that prints a series of lines between a `print<<` *LABEL* and the line consisting only of *LABEL*. Print blocks are ideal for printing large amounts of HTML code. Morover, they behave like double-quoted strings in that variables are inperpolated.

EXERCISES

Non-CGI Programs

1. Which of the following are legal scalar variables? Which ones are legal, but you should avoid using them? Why?

    (a) `$four`

    (b) `$4`

    (c) `$for`

    (d) `$blah-blah`

    (e) `$blah_blah`

2. Assuming that the two statements `$x="7.0"; $y="yyy";` have been excecuted, what are the values of the following expressions? Which cause warnings (if warnings are enabled)?

    (a) `$x+$x`

    (b) `$x . $x`

    (c) `"$x+$y"`

    (d) `'$x+$y'`

    (e) `$x+$y`

3. Write a Perl program that prints each of the strings in parts (a) through (e) using

   (i)   Single quotes
   (ii) Double quotes
   (iii) A print block

   For (i) and (ii), the string in part (e) should be printed as it appears, but the addition operation that produces the 5 should be done in the `print` statement (it is not possible in a print block).

   (a) `$14.95`
   (b) `This " is a double quote.`
   (c) `I don't care.`
   (d) `\/\/`
   (e) `3+2=5`

4. Write a Perl program that prints out the poem in Figure A.6 in Appendix A. Just print the actual poem part. The indentations can be achieved using blank spaces. (See Exercise 8.)

5. Write a program that prompts the user to input two nouns, two adjectives, and two verbs. Then use these to print out a story.

6. Write a Perl program that requests the user's name and prices corresponding to two products via standard input from the keyboard. The program should add the prices and compute a 7.5 percent sales tax on the total. The output should be formatted with the numeric values right-aligned as shown.

```
Ozzy Ozbourne
Item1           4.99
Item2          14.88
-----------------
Subtotal:      19.87
Tax:            1.49
-----------------
Total:         21.36
```

7. Do Exercise 6, but format the output as shown.

```
Ozzy Ozbourne
Item1          $4.99
Item2         $14.88
-----------------
Subtotal:     $19.87
Tax:           $1.49
-----------------
Total:        $21.36
```

   Hint: In order to achieve this exact formatting, which includes the $ character, you will likely need to use the field specifier for formatting strings. Not mentioned before in this chapter, it is simply `s`, and it can be used to add leading blank spaces onto strings in a way similar to how `d` is used to add leading zeros onto integers.

CGI Programs

8. Write a CGI program that returns the whole Web page in Figure A.6 in Appendix A. (See Exercise 4.)

9. Write a CGI program that outputs the following Web page.

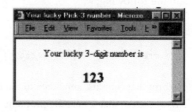

The number should be randomly generated, and the format of the the page should be produced using a borderless HTML table.

10. Write a CGI program that returns a Web page containing three HTML horizontal rules. The thickness in pixels of each horizontal rule should be a random integer in the range from 2 through 10, and the width of each should be a randomly generated percentage in the range from 25 percent to 75 percent. Different randomly generated numbers should be generated for each horizontal rule. Moreover, a sentence that reports the thickness and width should appear under each horizontal rule.

11. Write a CGI program that returns the order summary of Exercise 7. The order summary should be produced using a borderless HTML table. Construct an HTML file containing a form with three text fields: one for the name and one for each of the two prices. The form should be submitted to the CGI program you create. Provided that your form submits only three `name=value` pairs and uses the GET method of submission, the following code will recover the user's name and the two prices in your CGI program:

```
($name,$price1,$price2) = split(/&/,$ENV{"QUERY_STRING"},3);
($junk,$name) = split(/=/,$name,2);
($junk,$price1) = split(/=/,$price1,2);
($junk,$price2) = split(/=/,$price2,2);
```

Here, the `$junk` variable contains the names you have given to the text fields. You do not need to use that variable in your program, because only the values entered into the text fields are important. (See the note at the end of the exercises.)

12. Write a CGI program similar to the "echo" program used in Chapter 3. This version accepts only GET requests. First, print the entire query string as output. Simply print the contents of

```
$ENV{"QUERY_STRING"}
```

which is a special scalar variable that contains the query string. Then, beginning on a new line, print the `name=value` pairs, each on a new line with each pair boldfaced. The following line of code recovers the `name=value` pairs from the query string.

```
($pair1,$pair2,$pair3,$pair4,$pair5) = split(/&/,$ENV{"QUERY_STRING"});
```

This works only for a maximum number of five `name=value` pairs. Each pair is stored in one of the "pair" variables. If fewer than five pairs are submitted, then the extra "pair" variables will simply contain empty strings. Thus, you can interpolate all five of the "pair" variables, and any empty ones will simply not show up in the HTML output.

Construct an HTML page to call and test the CGI program. The HTML test page should contain the following:

(i) A link that calls your echo program and manually sends it a query string:

```
<a href="http://?.?.?/myecho.cgi?name1=value1&name2=value2…">test link</a>
```

(ii) A form that submits some data to the echo program.

Also, use the link to test the program, sending it more than five `name=value` pairs. Add a final statement to your CGI echo program that includes an explanation of what happens in that case and why you think that happens. (See the note at the end of the exercises.)

Note for Exercises 11 and 12: These exercises feature submission of form data to a CGI program. The code given in these exercises is a crude way to decode a query string. Thus, any blank spaces or special characters that you may include in the data you submit may wind up encoded as hexadecimal character codes in your CGI programs. Either don't use any spaces or weird characters in the data you submit to the programs, or ignore the hex encodings in the output of the programs. However, letters and numbers will be transferred to your program at face value, receiving no special endoding.

PROJECT THREAD

This project stage features creating two CGI programs whose output generates the two HTML/JavaScript pages you created for Chapter 3. Note that the Perl programs pass the HTML and JavaScript code to the Web server software as application-layer data, which is then passed to the requesting Web browser. The HTML and JavaScript code is not "executed" on the server side. It's just raw character data as far as the server is concerned.

A. The first CGI program should generate as output the password page you created for Part A in Chapter 3. When this program is called by a URL in a browser, it simply returns that page to the browser. Note that you can copy and paste the HTML/JavaScript code into a Perl print block. The returned form is to be submitted to the CGI program for Part B. Note that the password data submitted with that form basically goes nowhere, because the Perl program for Part B merely generates the quiz page. Moreover, the only validation of the user name and password is handled on the client with JavaScript and entails only proper format, not whether the user actually exists or whether the password is the correct one. Future project threads will test the user name and password against a master list stored in a text file on the server.

B. The second CGI program should generate the HTML/JavaScript quiz page as output. The quiz form should be set to be submitted to the "echo" program.

C. Thoroughly test your CGI programs. The result should be a sequence of three HTTP transactions as follows: A browser URL request for the first program loads the password page. Submission of that form calls the second program, pulling up the quiz page. Submission of the quiz form calls the "echo" program, which simply returns the quiz data to the browser.

D. Add a description and link to your homework table. The link merely needs to point to the CGI program of Part A.

E. If you are assigned any other exercises from this Chapter, add another row to your homework table for each exercise. Note that for any non-CGI Perl program (not executable over the Internet), just post a link that pulls up the text file containing the program.

## CHAPTER 5

GENERATING HTML DYNAMICALLY

In Chapter 4 you learned the basics of Perl and how Perl programs can generate HTML documents as output. Moreover, you learned how to set the permissions necessary so that anonymous surfers can execute a Perl CGI program remotely using a URL. In that case, the Web server software returns the generated Web page to the requesting browser. When the contents of Perl variables are interpolated into the generated Web page, its contents are generated dynamically according to the contents of the variables. That was your first endeavor in creating dynamic Web applications.

In this chapter we explore Perl's more powerful features, including arrays, hashes, and file operations. Using such language features, Web page content can be generated in a much more dynamic fashion. You are already familiar with many of the programming concepts, so the examples focus on generating Web pages dynamically rather than on pure programming theory. Of course, there are some Perl details that must be ironed out along the way.

5.1 CONDITIONAL STATEMENTS

In this section, you'll learn the syntax for if ... else statements and Boolean comparison operators in Perl. These control structures are syntactically similar to those in other languages, so there is not too much new to learn in that respect. However, there are a few Perl peculiarities that have to be mentioned. Moreover, applying the control structures in a CGI environment brings some new ideas.

Perl's comparison operators are shown in Table 5.1. The result of a comparison operation is either true or false, and such comparisons are used in the same way as in any standard programming language. Such comparisons are examples of Boolean expressions.

TABLE 5.1 Perl Comparison Operators

FOR NUMERIC COMPARISON		FOR STRING COMPARISON	
OPERATOR	MEANING	OPERATOR	MEANING
==	Equal to	eq	Equals
!=	Not equal to	ne	Not equals
>	Greater than	gt	Greater than
>=	Greater than or equal to	ge	Greater than or equal to
<	Less than	lt	Less than
<=	Less than or equal to	le	Less than or equal to

For example,

```
if($x < $y) {
    print "$x is less than $y.\n";
}
```

The operators for numeric comparison are standard. The comparisons do look a bit different because of the pesky $ symbols for Perl scalar variables. The numeric comparison operators place their operands into numeric context. As an example, in

```
$x="2.0";
$y="2";
if($x == $y) {
    print "The two numbers are equal.\n";
}
```

the comparison is made according to numeric ordering even though the scalars are stored as strings. So the comparison would yield a true value, and the `print` command is executed.

The operators for string comparison are not standard in many languages, although they are easy to understand. The string comparison operators place their operands into string context. In that case, string comparison is done as usual using ASCII codes to order the characters. As an example, in

```
$x="2.0";
$y="2";
if($x eq $y) {
    print "The two strings are equal.\n";
}
```

are compared as strings, resulting in the comparison being false, so the `print` statement is not executed. As another example,

```
("a." gt "a")
```

is true. Of course, string comparison is case sensitive because the ASCII codes for letters of different cases are different; the ASCII number for "A" is less than that for "a", for example.

NOTE

In other languages, such as C++, Java, and JavaScript, the operators (==, !=, ...) are also used for string comparison, with the effect being the same as the operators (eq, ne, ...) here in Perl. The reason Perl does not use the same operators (==, !=, ...) for both numbers and strings has to do with the way Perl handles type conversions "on the fly" in its loosely typed variables. By contrast, JavaScript is also loosely typed but uses the standard comparison operators for both strings and numbers. The moral here is that you have to be careful to remember not to do something like `"a"` `==` `"b"` when you mean to compare strings. Believe it or not, that expression doesn't give an error in Perl because if an inherently nonnumeric string is placed into numeric context, it evaluates to 0, and that expression becomes $(0==0)$, which is true. Even though an error is not caused, a misuse like that gives logic errors that are hard to diagnose. That's another incentive to test locally and turn warnings on, because you should get one in that case.

Case-insensitive comparison is a common need in CGI programming—for example, so that we don't have to worry about whether someone enters "Jones" or "jones" into an HTML form for a user name. The *lowercase function* `lc` can be applied. For example, the comparison

```
(lc $username eq "jones")
```

would be true whether `$username` is `"Jones"` or `"jones"` (or even `"JoNeS"`), because the `lc` function would return a lowercase version of any of these.

Perl also has the standard logical operators, which operate on Boolean expressions. These are listed in Table 5.2. For example, the expression `(2==3)||("abc" eq "abc")` is true because the second operand is true, but `(2==3)&&("abc" eq "abc")` is false because the first operand is false.[1] It never hurts to emphasize that `and` and `or` are radically different. To throw in a negation, `(!(2==3))&&("abc" eq "abc")` evaluates to true.

The results of Boolean expressions may also be saved in scalar variables. For example, we can do the following.

```
$match = (lc $username eq "jones");
```

Then subsequently, we may use this saved result to perform tests such as

```
if($match) {
   print "User name matches!\n";
}
```

TABLE 5.2 Perl Logical Operators

OPERATOR	MEANING
`&&, and`	True only if both operands are true
`||, or`	False only if both operands are false
`!, not`	Negates its operand

---

[1]One can also use the words `and`, `or`, and `not`. These are basically equivalent to `&&`, `||`, and `!`, respectively, but there are some precedence differences. As long as you use parentheses liberally for grouping, you really needn't worry about the differences.

and

```
if(!$match){
  print "User name fails to match!\n";
}
```

Both of these expressions have the result you expect.

Now we discuss some details of how Boolean values are saved into scalar variables. Although this knowledge is not necessary for general programming, we give the details here because such issues will arise when you try to find bugs in your programs. For example, we may wish to trace the execution of a program by printing out certain variables that happen to contain results of Boolean expressions.

When the result of a comparison is stored into a scalar variable, the result is 1 if true and is 0 if false. That is very similar to the usage in C and C++. To appreciate this fully, we need to discuss the third possible context for scalar expressions: Boolean context. That is, if we put an expression that evaluates to a scalar into a conditional such as

```
if( "hello"."there" ){. . .}
```

or

```
if( 3*2 ){. . .}
```

the scalar expression is in Boolean context. In this case, the rules are simple. The empty string is false, and any other string is true. The number 0 is false, and any other number is true. So the arguments of the above two bizarre `if` statements both evaluate to true in Boolean context. In fact, many built-in Perl Boolean constructs will return 1 if true and return either 0 or the empty string if false.

Because any expression can be used as a Boolean expression, a use like

```
if ($x = 3){. . .)  #variable assignment instead of comparison (==)
                    #also a common C, C++, Java mistake
```

does not cause an outright error as it does in many other languages. When $x is assigned the value 3, the whole expression gets the value of 3, which in Boolean context is true. It is because of strange cases such as this that we have discussed the Boolean issue at length.

NOTE

The bottom line is that Boolean expressions work as you would expect in normal situations, and you can save Boolean results in scalar variables. Perl has no explicit Boolean type with `true`/`false` values as JavaScript does, for example. Simply use `0` and `1` as if they were `false` and `true` Boolean literal values, respectively.

The foregoing discussion shows that the if statement works as you would expect, aside from the lack of a formal Boolean type. Here are the formats in general for the conditionals in Perl.

```
if (Boolean expression) {

   block of statements;

}
```

```
if (Boolean expression) {

   block of statements;

}
else {

   block of statements;

}
```

```
if (Boolean expression) {

   block of statements;

}
elsif (Boolean expression) {

   block of statements;

}
   .
   .
   .
elsif (Boolean expression) { {

   block of statements;

}
else {

   block of statements;

}
```

These are the same as used in Java, C++, and JavaScript, except for two very important exceptions.

- The braces { } are mandatory, even if only one statement is included in the body of the conditional.
- Perl requires elsif (rather than else if). A common error for those who code in other languages is to write else if.

We offer one quick example here to reinforce some of what we have been discussing, and then we will move on to loops. In practice, conditionals work as you would expect if you remember the two important exceptions just noted above and the lack of a formal Boolean type.

```perl
$password="Wildebeast";
if(lc $password ne "wildebeest");) {
  print "Please re-enter your password. $password does not match.";
}
else {
  print 'Thanks for logging on!';
}
```

For this data, the if rather than the else executes, because the expression evaluates to 0, a false value.

5.2 LOOPS AND ITERATIVE HTML GENERATION

In this section we introduce Perl's two standard types of loops. The loops are exactly the same as in other standard languages, so we spare you a lengthy discussion. Instead, we provide two example CGI programs that use loops to generate HTML iteratively.

The syntax for the **while loop** is

```
while ( Boolean expression ) {
    block of statements
}
```

where the *block of statements* in the body of the loop continues to be executed as long as the Boolean expression remains true. Note that the braces { } are required even if there is only one statement in the body of the loop.

Rather than giving a general definition, we show a specific example of the **for loop**. It executes the statements in its body 100 times.

```
for ($i=1 ; $i<=100 ; $i++ ) {
    block of statements
}
```

The first expression initializes the loop counter. The body of the loop is executed as long as the second expression is true. The third expression, which augments the loop counter by 1 in this case, is executed at the end of each pass of the loop. Again, note that the braces { } are required even if there is only one statement in the body of the loop.

We conclude this section by providing two examples that make use of the two types of loops in ways common in CGI programming. The first program and its output are shown in Figure 5.1. Figure 5.2 shows the result of an HTTP transaction that calls the program on a Web server.

Two print blocks have been employed, one for the top part of the HTML output and one for the bottom part. Between the two print blocks, the while loop prints out the links. That is absolutely necessary, because Perl control structures can't be executed inside a print block. (That should not come as a surprise, because expressions and functions can't be used either.) Rather, a conventional print statement is used to print out the list items on the inside of the loop.

Each chapter of the book is stored in an HTML file contained in the directory http://www.uweb.edu/book/. You can see that the URL is stored into a variable near the top of the program. Also, $number is initialized to control how many list items are to be printed. It was necessary to define $number near the top, because that variable is interpolated in the first print block. Besides, collecting variable declarations at the top of a program is good practice.

The loop executes five times, once for each list item. Each pass of the loop prints an li (list item) HTML element that contains a link. We have used the trick introduced in Section 4.9 to generate names for the different HTML files dynamically. As the loop counter progresses, the file names are generated with

```
chapter$i.html
```

which has to be double-quoted so that the variable is interpreted. Using the previously stored URL, the complete URL of each file is given by

```
$directory, "chapter$i.html"
```

```
whileloop.cgi

#! /usr/bin/perl

print "Content-type: text/html\n\n";

$number= 5;
$directory= "http://www.uweb.edu/book/";

print <<TOP;
<html>
<head>
<title>While Loop Demo</title>
</head>
<body>
<h1>List of links to Chapters 1 through $number.</h1>
<ul>
TOP

$i = 1;
while($i <= $number) {
    print '<li><a href="', $directory , "chapter$i.html\">" , "Chapter $i</a></li>\n";
    $i++;
}

print <<BOTTOM;
</ul>
</body>
</html>
BOTTOM
```

The List

```
Content-type: text/html

<html>
<head>
<title>While Loop Demo</title>
</head>
<body>
<h1>List of links to Chapters 1 through 5.</h1>
<ul>
<li><a href="http://www.uweb.edu/book/chapter1.html">Chapter 1</a></li>
<li><a href="http://www.uweb.edu/book/chapter2.html">Chapter 2</a></li>
<li><a href="http://www.uweb.edu/book/chapter3.html">Chapter 3</a></li>
<li><a href="http://www.uweb.edu/book/chapter4.html">Chapter 4</a></li>
<li><a href="http://www.uweb.edu/book/chapter5.html">Chapter 5</a></li>
</ul>
</body>
</html>
```

FIGURE 5.1   A CGI program that creates a list of links.

The print statement is fairly ugly with all of the symbols. We were tempted to use one long double-quoted string so that the variables would be interpolated. We simply would have escaped out all of the " symbols needed for the HTML attributes. But there was one problem. That would have resulted in

```
href=\"$directorychapter$i.html\"
```

which produces the uninitialized (and unintended) variable $directorychapter. You can carefully examine the print statement to see how we got around that problem. Understanding exactly how that statement produces the output you see at the bottom of Figure 5.1 will save you headaches in the future.

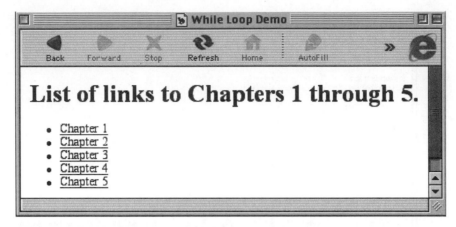

FIGURE 5.2   The result of an HTTP request for the `whileloop.cgi` program of Figure 5.1.

The next example employs nested `for` loops to create a table in which each row corresponds to a chapter of a book and the second cell in each row contains links to the figures for that chapter. The CGI program and an abbreviated version of the output are given in Figure 5.3. Figure 5.4 shows the result of an HTTP transaction that calls the program on a Web server.

We only offer a brief explanation for this program. It's quite similar to the previous one in that print blocks generate as much HTML as possible, but once again we have to use conventional `print` statements inside the loops that create the table. The outer loop starts a row, prints the first cell of that row, and starts the second cell of the row. The middle loop then runs through all of the links for the examples that are content of the second cell. Finally, before the outer loop takes another pass, the second cell (and the whole row) is closed.

There are a lot of newline characters mixed in with the `print` statements, because we wanted the HTML output formatted nicely. However, in practice that many might not be necessary so long as the output is formatted well enough that you could detect HTML syntax errors. Again, understanding exactly how the `print` statements produce the output will help you in the long run.

5.3   ARRAYS

Arrays in Perl are similar in concept to arrays in other languages: They store lists of values. However, Perl is more flexible in the way arrays can be assigned values than other languages are. In particular, there is a special type of literal that can be used to assign values to an array.

A `list` is an ordered sequence of scalar values. A `list literal` may be entered as comma-delimited scalar values enclosed within parentheses. For example,

```
("a", 'b', 3+4, $x, sqrt(2))
```

is a list of five items. Note that each item in the list is a scalar, with the fourth item being whatever scalar the variable `$x` holds and the fifth being the value returned by the `sqrt`

```
forloops.cgi
#! /usr/bin/perl

print "Content-type: text/html\n\n";

$chapters = 5;   # The number of chapters
$examples = 3;   # The number of examples in each chapter.
$directory = "http://www.uweb.edu/book/";

print <<TOP;
<html>
<head>
<title>List of all examples</title>
</head>
<body>
<h1>List of all examples.</h1>
<table border="2">
TOP

for($i = 1; $i <= $chapters; $i++) {

  print "<tr>\n<td>Chapter $i</td>\n<td>\n";

  for($k = 1; $k <= $examples; $k++) {

    print '<a href = "', $directory, "example$i-$k.html\">","Example $i-$k</a><br />\n";
  }

  print "</td>\n</tr>\n";
}

print <<BOTTOM;
</table>
</body>
</html>
BOTTOM
```

```
Content-type: text/html

<html>
<head>
<title>For Loop Demo</title>
</head>
<body>
<h1>Table of Examples</h1>
<table border="2">
<tr>
<td>Chapter 1</td>
<td>
<a href = "http://www.uweb.edu/book/example1-1.html">Example 1-1</a><br />
<a href = "http://www.uweb.edu/book/example1-2.html">Example 1-2</a><br />
<a href = "http://www.uweb.edu/book/example1-3.html">Example 1-3</a><br />
</td>
</tr>

<tr>
<td>Chapter 5</td>
<td>
<a href = "http://www.uweb.edu/book/example5-1.html">Example 5-1</a><br />
<a href = "http://www.uweb.edu/book/example5-2.html">Example 5-2</a><br />
<a href = "http://www.uweb.edu/book/example5-3.html">Example 5-3</a><br />
</td>
</tr>
</table>
</body>
</html>
```

Middle three rows removed to save space in Figure →

FIGURE 5.3 A CGI program that uses nested loops to create an HTML table

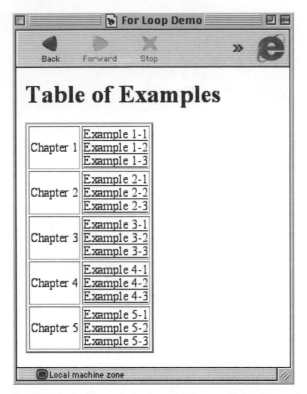

FIGURE 5.4 The result of an HTTP request for the `forloops.cgi` program of Figure 5.3.

function. Lists are always automatically **flattened** in the sense that if a list occurs inside a list, the inner parentheses are removed. Thus,

```
("a", ('b', 3+4), $x, sqrt(2))
```

is the same as the preceding list.

Interestingly, you can perform multiple variable assignments using list notation. For example,

```
($x, $y) = ($y, $x);
```

has the effect of swapping the values of $x and $y. That works because the right-hand side is evaluated first, and the scalar literals that result are simply assigned (in order) into the variables on the left-hand side. This makes multiple variable assignments considerably more efficient. That's pretty slick if you consider that a third temporary variable is needed to swap the values of two variables in many languages.

An **array** is a variable that stores a list literal. Thus, because lists can contain only scalars, an array is a list of scalars. An array variable is specified by having a first character of @, followed by a name governed by the naming conventions used for Perl scalar variables. The following are typical names for array variables:

```
@list
@list1
@first_names
```

You can directly assign a list literal to an array variable, as in

```
@example=("a", 'b', 3+4, $x, sqrt(2));
```

Like scalar variables, an array does not have to be declared formally. Simply assigning it a list both creates and initializes the array.

The items of an array are indexed using the standard array indexing familiar to users of C, C++, Java, or Java Script, with the first item being in index position 0. Elements of an array are accessed using square-bracket syntax again familiar from other languages. For example,

```
print $example[2], "\n";
```

accesses the third item in the @example array just defined, so the printed output would be 7, and subsequent output would be on a new line.

You may think that the $ symbol is a typo in that print statement, but it's not. Remember that arrays hold lists of scalars. So $example[2] refers to a scalar literal stored in the array. In Perl you can always tell the type of a variable from the symbol that precedes the variable's name. Something like @list always refers to a whole list, whereas $list[0] refers to the first scalar in the list. That is the main thing you will have to get used to when working with arrays in Perl.

You can also assign values to an array using the index notation. For example

```
$example[4]="hello";
```

assigns the string to the last index of @example, replacing the square root of 2. Arrays can also be created by direct assignment. We could have created @example by assigning $example[0]="a", $example[1]='b', and so forth, but creating it by assigning a list literal is notationally cleaner than five separate scalar context assignments.

Suppose an array is named @list. The special scalar variable $#list contains the largest index position of @list. Of course, because array indexes begin with 0, $#list is one less than the number of elements in the list. Again using the array @example,

```
for($i=0 ; $i <= $#example ; $i++) {
  print $example[$i], "\n";
}
```

prints all five scalars stored in @example on consecutive lines of output. Such a loop is a standard technique for iterating over an entire array in almost any language, although Perl's special symbols make the for loop look a bit different.

In addition, Perl has a special loop made for arrays. The **foreach loop** has the general form

```
foreach $item (@list) {
  block of statements
}
```

The parentheses around the array and the braces around the statements are mandatory. A foreach loop executes the block of statements one time for each item in @list. That's automatic. You don't have to tell it how many times to execute. If @list has 10 items, the loop executes 10 times. During each pass of the loop, the scalar variable $item is a reference for the item in @list corresponding to the index for that particular pass of the loop. For example, on the first pass $item references $list[0]. On the second pass, $item references $list[1], and so forth. On a given pass, you can both access and change the contents of the current @list item by accessing or changing $item.

So that you can get a feel for how nice a loop the foreach loop is, consider a for loop you would write in hope of accomplishing the same thing.

```
for($i=0 ; $i <= $#list ; $i++) {
  $item = $list[$i];
  block of statements
}
```

There are two differences between the for version and the foreach version. Understanding the differences helps you understand better how the foreach loop works. First, in the for loop version, you have access to the particular array index corresponding to the particular pass of the loop. For example, on the third pass of the for loop, $i contains 2. Second, changing the contents of $item in the for loop has no effect on whichever $list[$i] has been stored into it. A scalar value has merely been assigned to $item. In the foreach version, however, $item is not passed a value, but rather references the actual array item. That is, $item acts like a concise name for the actual array element. One often sees more foreach statements in a typical Perl program because of the simplicity with which it handles arrays. Regular for loops are more suited for parallel arrays.

Figure 5.5 shows a CGI program that uses a foreach loop to generate a Web page containing an unordered list of links to Web sites. Notice that the array values are interpolated twice in the print statement. Figure 5.5 also shows the HTML code generated by the program and an execution of the program by a URL request to a Web server.

NOTE

Note: Some technical details about Perl arrays are worth noting. The value of an uninitialized array is the empty list (). The $# (size) of an empty array is −1. If an element of an array is not yet defined, such as an element requested beyond the last index of the array, then using the element in an expression yields an undefined value, which evaluates to an empty string (just as in the case of an uninitialized scalar variable), along with a warning if warnings are enabled. Using a *negative* index returns a value counting backward from the end of the array. This feature differs from most languages. For example, $array[-1] is the last element of an @array.

We have written in detail about context within the scope of scalar variables. The contents of a scalar variable are put into different contexts automatically if the variable is

```
 links.cgi

#! /usr/bin/perl
print "Content-type: text/html\n\n";

@websites=('amazon' , 'ebay' , 'cknuckles' , 'etrade');

print <<TOP;
<html>
<head>
<title>Foreach Loop Demo</title>
</head>
<body>
<h1>Happy Surfing!</h1>
<ul>
TOP

foreach $name (@websites) {
    print "<li><a href=\"http://www.$name.com\">go to $name</a></li>\n";
}

print <<BOTTOM;
</ul>
</body>
</html>
BOTTOM
```

```
Content-type: text/html

<html>
<head>
<title>Foreach Loop Demo</title>
</head>
<body>
<h1>Happy Surfing!</h1>
<ul>
<li><a href="http://www.amazon.com">go to amazon</a></li>
<li><a href="http://www.ebay.com">go to ebay</a></li>
<li><a href="http://www.cknuckles.com">go to cknuckles</a></li>
<li><a href="http://www.etrade.com">go to etrade</a></li>
</ul>
</body>
</html>
```

FIGURE 5.5 A CGI program that generates a list of links from array values.

TABLE 5.3 The Perl `print` Function

FUNCTION	DESCRIPTION
`print @`*list*	Prints items in list concatenated together

an operand in an arithmetic operation or in concatenation, for example. Arrays, however, bring about a new context that we must consider. List literals are stored into array variables, and list context is different from numeric or string context.

To see that, let's revisit some familiar functions that take list literals for arguments, beginning with `print` (Table 5.3). Remember, Perl functions can be used with or without parentheses. So `print "a", "b";` and `print ("a", "b");` are equivalent. In other words, you have been sending lists to the `print` function all along. The statement

```
print 'h','e','l','l','o';
```

is equivalent to

```
@x=('h','e','l','l','o');
print @x;
```

both printing the string `'hello'`.

Two functions that you have seen before also take lists as arguments: `chomp` and `chop` (Table 5.4). You have been sending scalars to these functions, as in `chomp $input`. In that case, however, the scalar is actually put into list context as a one-element list. So the function effectively sees `chomp ($input)`. We have said that these functions take lists as arguments. A more accurate description is that their arguments *must* be lists. If a scalar is sent to one of those functions, it is simply put into list context as a one-element list. The same is true for the `print` function.

In general, when an expression that normally evaluates to a single scalar value is put into list context, the value of the expression is interpreted as a list containing just that one single scalar value. Actually, that's a pretty handy feature. You can send scalars to `chomp` to have newline characters removed without worrying about using notation to indicate that the scalar is a one-element list. Just as Perl handles numeric-to-string conversion automatically in different contexts, it handles scalar-to-list conversion automatically.

Not using list notation for function arguments can cause problems if you are not careful, however. For example,

```
print "a", somefunction "b", "c";
```

will often be interpreted as

```
print "a", somefunction ("b", "c");
```

TABLE 5.4 The Perl `chop` and `chomp` Functions

FUNCTION	DESCRIPTION
`chomp @`*list*	Removes all terminating newline characters from each item in the *list* and returns the total number of characters chomped
`chop @`*list*	Chops off last character of each item in the *list*, and returns the last chopped character

even if you mean

```
print "a", somefunction ("b"), "c";
```

because most functions look for lists, rather than scalars, as their arguments.

We have seen that putting scalars into list context is handled seamlessly. Putting lists into scalar context, on the other hand, is not entirely straightforward. There are two possibilities. An array variable put in scalar context evaluates to the size of the array. Thus,

```
@a = (14, 15, 16);
$x = @a;
```

assigns the number 3 to $x. In contrast, putting a list literal into scalar context evaluates to the last element in the list. Thus,

```
$x = (14, 15, 16);
```

assigns the number 16 to $x. You would not consciously make such assignments, but things like that can happen inadvertently. For example, if you are storing into a scalar whatever some function returns, and the function actually returns a list, you have a situation like those we have shown here. Remembering the scalar versus list context rules can help you to catch errors that are otherwise difficult to diagnose unless you have gotten into the habit of using warnings in your local environment, but even that is not always foolproof.

Some Perl functions return something entirely differently depending on whether they are called in scalar or list context. Consider the reverse function (Table 5.5). For example,

```
@x = reverse (14, 15, 16);
```

assigns (16, 15, 14) to @x, but

```
$x = reverse (14, 15, 16);
```

assigns "615141" to $x. For another example,

```
print reverse (14, 15, 16);
```

gives 161514 as output, because the print function takes a list argument.

TABLE 5.5 The Perl reverse Function

FUNCTION	DESCRIPTION
reverse @list	In list context, returns a list with order reversed; in scalar context, concatenates the list and returns the string reversed.

TABLE 5.6 Perl Array Functions

FUNCTION	DESCRIPTION
push @*array*, *list*	Pushes the *list* onto the back of the *array*, returns new length
unshift @*array*, *list*	Pushes the *list* onto the front of the *array*, returns new length
pop @*array*	Deletes last element of *array*, returns the element
shift @*array*	Deletes first element of *array*, returns the element
join *expr*, *list*	Returns a string that is the concatenation of all the elements in the *list*, with *expr* in between each two array elements
sort *list*	Returns the *list* sorted by string comparison
sort <=> *list*	Returns the *list* sorted numerically
splice @*array*, $*index*, $*number*	Deletes $*number* of elements of *array* starting at index number $*index*, returns the list of deleted elements (if a list is supplied as a fourth argument, the list is "spliced" into the array replacing the deleted elements; hence the name of the function)

We conclude this section by listing some other functions that are useful when manipulating arrays. Rather than giving examples showing the use of the functions here, we will refer back to the definitions in Table 5.6 when we need the functions later in this text.

The last function we introduce is the split function. We provide an example for this function, because we will use it so frequently. The split function is used to take apart a string that contains a delimited list of smaller strings. For example,

```
$str="colon:delimited:list:of:strings";
@thelist=split(/:/ , $str , 3);
```

causes @thelist to contain the list

```
("colon" , "delimited" , "list")
```

The split function has split $str into a list of the first three colon-delimited items. The function can be used without the third parameter, which specifies how many of the delimited items to return. For example,

```
@thelist=split(/:/ , $str);
```

returns all five of the delimited items into @thelist. Of course, the choice of the delimiting character(s) supplied inside the // symbols is up to you.

5.4 HASHES

A *hash* is similar to an array in that a hash stores a collection of scalar values, but in a hash the values are indexed by strings rather than by numbers. The indexing strings are called *keys*. With each key is associated one scalar value. Often a hash is called an *associative array* because each key is associated with a value. A hash variable name begins with a % symbol. A hash can be initialized as follows:

```
%hash = (key, value, key, value, . . .);
```

where the associated *key-value* pairs are entered consecutively. For example, we may build a hash in which the keys are names of colors and the values are corresponding hexadecimal RGB colors:

```
%hexColor = ("red", "#ff0000", "green", "#00ff00", "blue", "#0000ff");
```

An alternate way of entering a hash is to use the following, more readable syntax:

```
%hexColor = ( "red"=>"#ff0000",
              "green"=>"#00ff00",
              "blue"=>"#0000ff" );
```

which more clearly identifies the key-value pairs.

We access a hash value associated with a given key using the syntax

```
$hash{ key }
```

The hash name begins with a $ symbol when referring to a specific hash value, and curly braces surround the key. Going back to the %hexColor hash, the statement

```
print "$hexColor{'green'}";
```

causes the string "#00ff00" to be printed. %hexcolor refers to the hash as a whole, $hexColor{"green"} refers to a scalar. Recall that the type issue is similar to that encountered in referring to an array value rather than the whole array. Also note that hash keys and values can be delimited with single-quoted strings when convenient. One example is found in the print statement just above. Giving the key as a double quoted string would foul up the print statement.

Hash values not only are accessed as scalar values, but they can be individually assigned scalar values as well. The %hexColor hash could have initialized as follows.

```
$hexColor{"red"}="#ff0000";
$hexColor{"green"}="#00ff00";
$hexColor{"blue"}="#0000ff";
```

Regardless of how the key-value pairs are assigned, hashes are a common way to store collected data (as from HTML forms). In many cases, named hash keys are preferential to the numeric indexes of arrays.

Two functions that are very useful when dealing with hashes are given in Table 5.7. These functions can be used to extract the arrays of keys and values from the hash. For example, the assignments

```
@k = keys %hexColor;
@v = values %hexColor;
```

TABLE 5.7   Perl Hash Functions

FUNCTION	DESCRIPTION
`keys %hash`	returns the list of keys from %hash
`values %hash`	returns the list of values from %hash

create two arrays. However, it is important to note that the two arrays `@k` and `@v` are not necessarily parallel in the sense of preserving the key-value relationships from the hash. For example, `@k` is a three-element list with `"red"`, `"green"`, and `"blue"`, indexed in some unpredictable order. In other words, these two functions return arrays indexed in ways completely unrelated to the order in which the hash was initialized. Effectively, keys and values share a parallel relationship while stored in a hash, but when extracted as individual arrays, the keys and values lose the parallel relationship.

Because the keys come out in an unpredictable way when using the `keys` function, it is useful to sort the keys using the array function `sort`. For example, the expression

```
sort keys %hexColor
```

returns the list (`"blue"`, `"green"`, `"red"`) with the keys sorted according to their ASCII numbers, alphabetically in this case.

A common way to iterate over all the entries in a hash is to extract and sort the keys and then iterate over them in an array context. For example the loop

```
foreach $key (sort keys %hexColor) {
    print "$key : $hexColor{$key}\n";
}
```

prints

```
blue : #0000ff
green : #00ff00
red : #ff0000
```

The loop causes `$key` to pass over the list of sorted hash keys, and `$hexColor{$key}` accesses the associated hash value on each pass.

Recall the example in the previous section where we used an array of Web site names to create an HTML list of links to those sites. The following example creates a similar list of links to Web sites, but this time, information about the Web sites is stored in a hash.

```
%websites=( 'perl' => 'www.perl.org',
            'princeton' => 'www.princeton.edu',
            'amazon' => 'www.amazon.com',
            'ebay' => 'www.ebay.com' );
```

Given the multiple domain suffixes, the list of names (keys) is no longer sufficient to generate the domain names. The hash gives more flexibility and enables the names to be associated with the corresponding domain names.

The code below creates an unordered list of links based upon the information in the hash. Again, the interpolated scalar variables have been emphasized for clarity.

```
print "<ul>\n";
foreach $name (keys %websites) {
  print "<li><a href=\"http:// $websites{$name}\">$name</a></li>\n";
}
print "</ul>\n";
```

The HTML output of the code is

```
<ul>
<li><a href="http://www.ebay.com">ebay</a></li>
<li><a href="http://www.princeton.edu">princeton</a></li>
<li><a href="http://www.perl.org">perl</a></li>
<li><a href="http://www.amazon.com">amazon</a></li>
</ul>
```

Note that for emphasis we did not apply the sort function to the list of keys returned from the hash. Thus the key list was returned in the unpredictable order ('ebay', 'princeton', 'perl', 'amazon'), and that order is reflected in the iteration order of the foreach loop. Interestingly, different Perl interpreters may return the list of keys in different orders.

Attempting to access a value for a key that does not exist returns an undefined value, which evaluates to the empty string (just as in the case of an uninitialized scalar variable). Although that generally does not cause a syntax error, it can cause a program to go awry in a way that is hard to detect. Fortunately, that error will generate a warning if you have enabled them.

Table 5.8 shows two functions that deal with existence of hash keys. Note, however, that the expression

```
exists $somehash{ "somekey" }
```

is still true as long as somekey exists in the hash, even if its associated value is the empty string.

The final example of this section puts the exists function to practical use. Figure 5.6 shows a CGI program that uses an array and a hash to store information about links that are to be printed. The figure also shows the HTML code generated by the program and the screen resulting when the program is executed by a URL request to a Web server.

The @topics array is a list of potential topics for links, and the %domains hash contains Web addresses for those topics for which Web sites are available. The main idea is that not every item in the @topics array has a corresponding entry in the %domains hash. The program generates an HTML list of topics and provide links wherever a domain name exists in the hash for that topic.

TABLE 5.8 Perl Hash Key Existence Functions

FUNCTION	DESCRIPTION
exists $somehash{ "somekey" }	Returns true if somekey exists in %hash
delete $somehash{ "somekey" }	Deletes the entry for somekey from %hash

```
topics.cgi

#! /usr/bin/perl
print "Content-type: text/html\n\n";

@topics = ("apples", "bananas", "durians", "kiwis", "oranges");
%domains= ( "apples"  => "www.apples.com",
            "durians" => "www.durian.net",
            "oranges" => "www.oranges.com" );

print <<TOP;
<html>
<head>
<title>Arrays and Hashes</title>
</head>
<body>
<h1>Happy Surfing!</h1>
<ul>
TOP

foreach $topic (@topics) {
    if(exists $domains{$topic} ) {
        print "<li><a href=\"http://$domains{$topic}\">$topic</a></li>\n";
    }
    else {
        print "<li>$topic</li>\n";
    }
}

print <<BOTTOM;
</ul>
</body>
</html>
BOTTOM
```

```
Content-type: text/html

<html>
<head>
<title>Arrays and Hashes</title>
</head>
<body>
<h1>Happy Surfing!</h1>
<ul>
<li><a href="http://www.apples.com">apples</a></li>
<li>bananas</li>
<li><a href="http://www.durian.net">durians</a></li>
<li>kiwis</li>
<li><a href="http://www.oranges.com">oranges</a></li>
</ul>
</body>
</html>
```

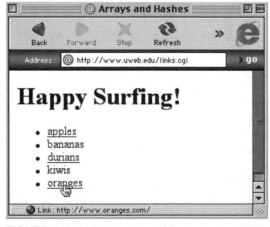

FIGURE 5.6 Using arrays and hashes to generate a list of links.

5.5 VARIABLE CONTEXTS AND NAME SPACES

Now that we have explored the three main variable types—scalars, arrays, and hashes—it is important to consider all three in the big picture. A scalar variable begins with a $ and can contain a numeric or string literal. An array variable begins with a @ and contains a list literal. A hash variable begins with a % and contains a hash literal. The first symbol ($, @, %) of a variable always signals the type that is returned by the variable expression. For example, you have seen that %hash and @array both refer to the entire entity, whereas $hash{"key"} and $array[index] refer to particular scalar values. The biggest hurdle for beginning Perl programmers is to become used to the special symbols that indicate variable types and to understand the context issues.

Sometimes variables are accidentally used in the wrong context. For example, you might accidentally send an array to the keys function or assign a hash to an array variable. Fortunately the results are predictable, and such errors can be detected. A hash in list context evaluates to a list with the key-value pairs becoming flattened into a list in some order. When a list is put into hash context, keys and values are constructed in alternating fashion. For example, the assignment %hash=@array; results in $array[0] and $array[1] becoming a key-value pair of %hash, and so forth. If the size of the array ($#array) is an odd number, assigning the array to a hash or referencing it in hash context causes a syntax error, because there is no value left for the last key.

You have also seen that a list in scalar context evaluates to the size of the array. That is, $x=@array; causes $x to contain the size of @array. (that is, the same as $x=($#array+1)). A hash in scalar context, however, is not so straightforward. For those readers who may have studied data structures in some detail, a hash in scalar context evaluates (in Perl 5) to a string consisting of the number of buckets used in the hash table, followed by a slash, followed by the total number of buckets in the hash table. In Perl 6, on the other hand, a hash in scalar context evaluates to the number of keys in the hash.

Scalars, arrays, and hashes have different *name spaces* for their variables. That is, you can use $x, @x, %x in the same program, and there is no confusion. Also note that the following variables are all scalars, but they have different origins and are unrelated to each other.

$x	Basic scalar variable
$x[*expr*]	An element of an array @x, no relation to $x whatsoever
$x{ *expr* }	A value from a hash %x, no relation to $x whatsoever

5.6 FUNCTIONS

In this section we explore user-defined functions in Perl. To complement our Web programming agenda, we give examples that are useful in the CGI setting. To that end, we first present a built-in function that is very useful to Web programmers. The localtime function is often used to grab details about the current time as reported by the computer running the Perl program. It is often used in CGI programs to get time and date information from

TABLE 5.9 Components Returned for the Perl time Function

COMPONENT	MEANING
$sec	Number of seconds elapsed in the current minute
$min	Number of minutes elapsed in the current hour
$hour	Hour in the current day (given in military time in the range from 0 to 23)
$mday	Day in current month (in the range from 1 to 31)
$mon	Month in current year (January is 0, so the range is from 0 to 11)
$year	Number of years elapsed since 1900 (102 indicates 2002, for example)
$wday	Current weekday (Sunday is 0, so the range is from 0 to 6)
$yday	Day in current year (January 1st is 0, so the range is from 0 to 364)
$isdst	Is daylight savings time currently in effect? (0 for no, 1 for yes)

the Web server during an HTTP transaction. That way, time- and date-specific content can be returned in the output Web page.

The localtime function in list context returns a list of nine time components:

```
($sec,$min,$hour,$mday,$mon,$year,$wday,$yday,$isdst)=localtime;
```

The returned time components are summarized in Table 5.9. That's a lot of returned time components. A more concise way to store the returned list is to store it into an array variable.

```
@timeParts=localtime;
```

That way, if you need only the current hour, for example, you can refer to

```
$timeParts[2]
```

Using the full list-notation version of returned time components, you can easily deduce which time component is in a particular index of the @timeParts array. The localtime function can also take a parameter and is often used in the following way:

```
localtime(time + $seconds_offset_from_current_time)
```

where time is a function that returns an integer representing the number of seconds since January 1, 1970. The bottom line is that this function call has the effect of returning the date and time offset from the current time given the number of desired offset seconds.

In scalar context, the localtime function returns a string giving date and time information in the following format.

```
Wed Feb 5 18:11:05 2003
```

However, if the particular format is important, then we must construct the date or time string ourselves.

We now turn to the syntax for declaring programmer-defined functions in Perl. Perl functions are often called *subroutines* (a term from earlier days in computer science), so they are declared with the keyword sub. We will simply refer to them as *functions*. This is the general form of a function declaration:

```
sub functionName {
    statements executed by the subroutine
}
```

Although a function definition can appear in the file either before or after it is called, it is customary to organize all the function definitions at the end of a Perl program. That is a practice to which we will adhere throughout the rest of the book.

We call the programmer-defined function using the syntax:

```
&functionName
```

In contrast to many languages, use of parentheses following a function name &*functionName*() is optional in Perl when there are no parameters. That feature is often disconcerting to programmers new to Perl. However, the presence of the & (ampersand) serves to remind the programmer that a function is being called. The & is actually optional in some cases, but we will always use it when calling programmer-defined functions so that no confusion arises.

For a simple example, consider the following function, which could be used to print a footer for any CGI-generated Web pages produced by a certain programmer.

```
sub printWebPageFooter {
    print "This Web page was designed by " ,
        '<a href="mailto:me@myaddress.com">send me mail</a>', "\n";
}
```

The call to the function

```
&printWebPageFooter;
```

could then be placed in a Perl CGI program at the proper location to create the footer.

Functions can also return a value. As in many other programming languages, a return statement returns its argument and terminates execution of the function. The following function makes use of the localtime function and returns the current date in the standard format of *month/day/year*.

```
sub currentDate {
    my @timeParts=localtime;
    my ($day, $month, $year) = ($timeParts[3],$timeParts[4],$timeParts[5]);
    return ($month+1)."/".$day."/".($year+1900);
}
```

The keyword my makes the array @timeParts and the scalar variables $day, $month, and $year local to the function. We used the multiple-assignments technique to store the desired time components into the local variables in a concise fashion. Note that to return the date in standard format, we had to add 1 to $month because localtime months count starting at 0. Also, $year is adjusted because 1900 is year 0 according to localtime. Here is an example use of the currentDate function, as part of the header for an online broker.

```
print "<title>Stock Quotes for ", &currentDate , "</title>\n";
```

Recall that functions are not interpolated inside double quotes, whereas variables are. Here is an example of the HTML output:

```
<title>Stock Quotes for 11/1/2001</title>
```

As in many other languages, multiple return statements can be used in a function. As soon as one is encountered in the flow of execution, its value is returned, and no further statements in the function are executed. The following function returns the current season (roughly) based upon the month returned by localtime.

```
sub season {
    my @timeParts=localtime;
    my $month = $timeParts[4];

    if($month < 2){return "winter";}
    if($month < 5){return "spring";}
    if($month < 8){return "summer";}
    if($month < 11){return "fall";}
    return "winter"; #December
}
```

A sample use of this function prints a link whose text automatically reflects the current season based upon the time returned by the server when the CGI is called by a browser request:

```
print '<a href="saleitems.html">special ' , &season , " sale items</a>\n";
```

Again note that we did not attempt to interpolate the function call inside double quotes. Here is an example of the HTML output:

```
<a href="saleitems.html">special fall sale items</a>
```

In the foregoing example we have the keyword my to designate a variable as *local* in a function. Local variables declared that way in Perl have the scope we are accustomed to in other programming languages such as C++, Java, and JavaScript. That is, changing the local variable $x inside a function

```
$x=1;
&noChange;
print "$x";

sub noChange {
    my $x=2;
}
```

leaves the global $x unchanged. So the print statement writes 1 as output. However, if $x had not been declared to be local inside the function using my, the print statement would have written 2 as output. The keyword my is unusual for this purpose, but speaking from the function's perspective, one could say, "It's my variable." Since variables are not formally declared in Perl, some mechanism must be in place to designate variables that are local to functions.

Over time, it is possible that you will run across Perl programs that declare local variables using the local keyword, as in local $x; There are subtle differences, but my local variables are scoped like those with which we are accustomed in other languages. We will use my throughout this book. The curious reader can go to this book's Web site and examine the scoping example that explains the difference between local and my.

Parameters are passed to programmer-defined Perl functions in a novel way. For example, consider the call to a function (which we will define shortly).

```
$domain="www.cknuckles.com";
$text="Web applications site";
&makeLink($domain,$text);
```

So that you can understand the purpose of the function, this call prints the line

```
<a href="http://www.cknuckles.com">Web applications site</a>
```

The interesting feature is that the parameters are passed to the function into the array @_ (the **arguments array**). In this case, there are two parameters, so there are two elements in the arguments array, namely $_[0] and $_[1]. With that in mind, we next define the makeLink function, with the parameter variables highlighted for emphasis.

```
sub makeLink{
    print "<a href=\"http://$_[0]\">$_[1]</a>";
}
```

Formal parameters are not given in the function definition, in contrast to the syntax

```
sub makeLink($d,$t){function body}  OOPS!
```

common in other languages. That is not necessary (and not legal) in Perl, because the actual parameters are passed into the arguments array, @_ .

Perl always passes parameters to programmer-defined functions by reference rather than by value. For example, the code

```
$x=1;
&change($x);

sub change {
    $_[0] = 2;
}
```

causes the global variable $x to contain 2. Because $_[0] is a reference for $x, changing its value changes the value of $x. Passing a scalar literal to the change function,

```
&change("1");
```

is a syntax error, and the error message says that an attempt was made to change a read-only value. In that case, $_[0] references a literal value, so it can't be changed. You can, however, pass literal values to a function so long as no attempt is made to change those elements of @_. For example, the following call to the makeLink function is perfectly fine and produces the exact output as the very first call we made to it previously.

```
&makeLink("www.cknuckles.com" , "Web applications site");
```

One alternative to alleviate that potential problem is simply to transfer the elements of @_ into local variables. The following version of makeLink is equivalent to the first version:

```
sub makeLink{
    my ($domain, $text) = @_;
    print "<a href=\"http://$domain\">$text</a>";
}
```

That basically has the effect of passing the function parameters into $domain and $text by value. The local function variables can be altered (if desired) inside the function without changing their global counterparts or causing an error, as the case may be.

For those used to other languages, where scalar variables (and especially literal values) are passed to functions by value, understanding the previous examples is important. But even if no potential problems could arise in a given situation, it is often desirable to transfer the elements of @_ into local variables anyway. The second version of makeLink is perhaps more readable than the first version. It is especially desirable when several parameters are sent to a function. In that case, assigning the values to named local variables may be better than having to keep track of all the different elements of @_ by their index positions $_[0], $_[1], $_[2], and so forth, especially if you want to modify the function later. Also, immediately storing the arguments into local variables has the added bonus of documenting how the function should be used, in terms of what arguments are expected.

However, there are times when simply using the arguments array is advantageous. In particular, it allows a given function to accept different numbers of parameters during different calls to the function. Consider the following function, which prints an unordered HTML list consisting of an item for each element of @_.

```
sub makeList {
    print "<ul>\n";
    foreach $item (@_) {
        print "<li>$item</li>\n";
    }
    print "</ul>\n";
}
```

One call to makeList,

```
&makeList("apples" , "oranges");
```

generates

```
<ul>
<li>apples</li>
<li>oranges</li>
</ul>
```

Another call, sending more parameters,

```
&makeList("apples" , "oranges" , "bananas");
```

generates

```
<ul>
<li>apples</li>
<li>oranges</li>
<li>bananas</li>
</ul>
```

As you can see, passing all parameters into @_ enables one not only to send differing numbers of parameters to the same function, but also to iterate over all the parameters quite easily.

NOTE

When several functions are used in a given program, a different copy of @_ is created for each function call. In other words, each instance of @_ is limited in scope to a particular function call. You needn't worry about the potential reuse of the arguments array among several functions.

The previous calls to makeList sent list literals to the function. An array variable can also be sent to a function. Consider the following call to makeList:

```
@fruits=("apples" , "oranges");
&makeList(@fruits);
```

You might think that this call sends only one parameter to the function, which might result in $_[0] being a reference to the array @fruits. However, recall that @_ is an array, and that an array is a list of *scalars* only. So what actually happens is that the list ("apples", "oranges") is passed into @_. That is equivalent to simply passing two arguments to the function, as we did in the first example call to makeList.

Similarly, the call

```
&makeList(@fruits , "bananas");
```

is equivalent to passing a three-element list ("apples", "oranges", "bananas") to the function. The two-element array parameter and the scalar parameter are flattened into one three-element list. As a result, it would be difficult to pass two different arrays to a function. The two arrays would get flattened into one list, and their individuality would be lost to some extent. The same inherent difficulty also arises, because of the "flattening effect," when arrays are returned from functions.

One solution to that problem is to also pass the sizes of the arrays to a function as extra parameters. That way, those sizes can be used to recover the original arrays that were flattened into @_. Another solution is to use references or *typeglobs*, which are discussed in the optional Section 5.9.

5.7 FILE OPERATIONS

In this section, we explore reading, writing, and appending text files. For the main examples we focus on generating dynamic output for CGI programs based on data stored in files.

In Perl, access to files is managed through the use of file handles. A *file handle* is an identifier such as

```
DATAFILE
INFILE
OUTFILE
```

with no special symbols preceding the name, as is the case with variables. It is customary to use all capital letters for file handles (in contrast to variables, where we discouraged the use of all capitals).

A file handle is associated with a certain file by using the built-in open function:

```
open (FILEHANDLE, filename_with_qualifier_for_access_mode)
```

Table 5.10 shows the most common access modes. The first entry in the table uses no access mode qualifier, meaning that reading is the default mode when a file is opened with no specified access qualification. Note how the angle brackets used as the access mode qualifier symbols suggest the flow of data out of or into the file. That is an easy way to remember them.

Logically, file operations work in Perl just as in other languages. For example,

```
open (FILEHANDLE , "<data.txt");
    read data from the file
close (FILEHANDLE);
```

would leave the file in a closed state after whatever data was read from the file. A file should be closed as soon as it is no longer needed.

TABLE 5.10 Common Access Modes for Perl File Operations

ACCESS MODE	QUALIFIER
Read	open (FILEHANDLE, *filename*)
Read	open (FILEHANDLE, "<*filename*")
Write (overwrite)	open (FILEHANDLE, ">*filename*")
Append	open (FILEHANDLE, ">>*filename*")

> **NOTE**
>
> Since CGI programs are ultimately executed by URL requests over the Web, who-ever executes the program is an anonymous user. Most Web servers actually execute anonymous URL requests under a generic `anybody` or `nobody` user account. That means that a data file may not have the necessary access permissions. For example, when you transfer a text file that is to support a CGI program to your account on a Web server, you automatically have read/write privileges to the file from your account. However, anonymous Web surfers (including you) may not.
>
> For a CGI program executed by an anonymous user to be able to open a file suc-cessfully, you may have to set its permissions manually so that it is accessible by everyone through the CGI program. That means that you not only have to FTP the data file to the server, but also may have to Telnet to the server to relax the file's access permissions. Appendix C discusses setting file permissions for common Web servers. Keep in mind that, as we discussed in Chapter 4, the CGI programs them-selves may require a change in access privileges before they are viable for anony-mous requests.

The syntax for reading from a file is very similar to that of reading from a keyboard, in that angle brackets are used to read a line of input. The following scalar-context assign-ment returns the next line from the associated text file (if there is one), and stores it into $line as a string.

```
$line = <FILEHANDLE>;
```

The lines from a text file could be read in manually,

```
$line1 = <FILEHANDLE>;
$line2 = <FILEHANDLE>;
.
.
.
```

but usually a loop is used to iterate over the lines of the file.

The string returned for a given line contains the terminating newline character. If there is no next line, the empty string is returned. Thus, a common way to read a file to its end is

```
while ($line = <FILEHANDLE>) {
    do something with each $line
}
```

On each pass of the loop, $line contains the current line that was read in from the file. Even seemingly blank lines are read. As long as the end of the file is not yet reached, the variable $line will always contain at least one character, because blank lines contain a newline character (the only character in a blank line):

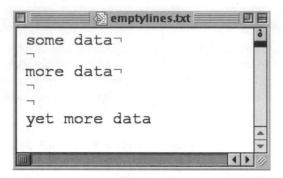

As we stated earlier, an assignment, used as an expression, evaluates to the value assigned, and a nonempty string is true in Boolean context. So, even when a "blank" line is read into $line, the loop condition is true in Boolean context, making the loop continue. The loop terminates when the end of the file is reached, because that's when $line will be given the empty string value, which is false in Boolean context.

In list context, reading from the file handle returns the rest of the lines in the text file and stores them into an array. Thus,

```
@all_lines = <FILEHANDLE>;
```

returns the rest of the lines (including all the newline characters on given lines) in the file, and stores them as distinct elements of @all_lines. Storing the whole file into an array is useful when the file is not too large. It is also good if what we have to do to each line of the file takes some time, and we do not wish to hog up access to the file. On the other hand, if the file is large, then use of a loop is recommended so that we do not overburden the heap memory with a huge array.

NOTE

Depending on the configuration of the Web server, the default directory while a CGI program is executing may or may not be the same directory where the CGI program resides. For example, if

```
open (DATAFILE, "data.txt")
```

appears in a program that is being executed by a URL call, through the Web, the file named "data.txt" may be looked for in some default directory. This default directory may *not* be the same as the directory in which the CGI program resides. Of course, there is no such concern when the program is executed offline (the file will be looked for in the current directory) but remote CGI execution through the Web is handled differently in terms of which is the "current directory."

On some Web servers the data file is looked for in the same directory as the Perl program. On other Web servers, the data file is looked for in some other default directory, such as the cgi-bin directory or the Web server root directory. However, we can be sure that the correct file is accessed by specifying the complete path of the file. For example, the following might be used on UNIX/Linux, Windows, and Macintosh, respectively.

```
open(DATAFILE, "/home/users/me/public/data/data.txt");
open(DATAFILE, "C:/Inetpub/wwwroot/data/data.txt");
open(DATAFILE, "HD:Documents:Public:Data:data.txt");
```

Note that a forward slash / is used as the directory delimiter, even for ActivePerl running on a Windows machine. (The Windows operating system normally uses a backslash \ as the directory delimiter.)

The best programming practice is to set a global scalar variable to store the directory in which you will keep your data files, perhaps something like

```
$dataDir = "/home/users/me/data/";           #UNIX
$dataDir = "C:/Inetpub/wwwroot/data/";        #Windows
$dataDir = "HD:Documents:Public:Data:";       #Macintosh
```

Then a complete file path can be created by concatenating the name of the file onto the end of the $dataDir. Note the trailing delimiter in these directory variables, so the necessary concatenation is simply

```
"$dataDir"."filename"
```

So, for example, when we wish to open a file in the data directory called "datafile.txt" for writing, we simply use

```
open(DATAFILE, ">$dataDir"."datafile.txt");
```

Note that $dataDir=""; can be used in those situations where relative file names are allowed and the program resides in the same directory as the data file. Of course, some nontrivial relative path can also be used to locate a data file relatively, when that is allowed.

There are several advantages to store directory information in this fashion using scalar variables.

- Much less repetitive typing is needed when full file path names are required; hence there are fewer chances of typographical errors.

- It is easy to move entire directories of data without having to change several instances of a directory path in a program.

- It is easy to move the program to different machines (either between a server and a local machine, or on different servers). In that case, the data directories will often be different, so you simply can change the data directory variable. The program and its data are then readily portable.

We now offer an example where data is read into a CGI program from a text file. Consider again the hash we used in Section 5.4 to generate an unordered HTML list of links dynamically.

```
%websites=( 'Perl' => 'www.perl.org',
            'Princeton' => 'www.princeton.edu',
            'Amazon' => 'www.amazon.com',
            'Ebay' => 'www.ebay.com' );
```

In the current example, instead of manually initializing this hash, we will set up the hash by reading the information from a text file. That way, if we ever wish to modify our data-

FIGURE 5.7 A typical text file containing structured data.

base of Web sites, we would not have to modify the CGI program—only the data file. Moreover, the program could be used to generate lists of links from other text files, with only a very slight modification. The many advantages to using data files over manually initialized variables should be clear to most any programmer.

The Web site's information is stored in the file websites.txt shown in Figure 5.7. Note that the entry for each Web site is on a separate line. We have decided to use an equals sign to delimit the names and Web addresses, but any character can be used as the delimiter as long as the character does not otherwise appear in the actual data. Remember that this file must be uploaded to the server in the appropriate directory, and the permissions on this file may have to be relaxed (depending upon your server) to allow it to be readable by everyone.

We would then use code similar to the following to read the data into a CGI program.

```
$dataDir = "directory/path/";      # to the directory
                                   # containing websites.txt

%websites=();
open(INFILE, "$dataDir"."websites.txt");
while($line = <INFILE>) {
   chomp $line;
   ($name, $address) = split(/=/, $line);
   $websites{$name} = $address;
}
close(INFILE);
```

Rather than processing the data line by line as we read it in, we have chosen to read the data into a hash. In fact, the %websites hash created from the data file is identical to the manually initialized version previously shown. Note that it was important to chomp each $line so that the newline characters in the file don't become part of the data in the hash. The split function, discussed at the end of Section 5.3, is used to split each $line of data at the = symbol. The %websites hash can now be used to generate a list of links, as in Section 5.4, or for some other purpose.

Whenever an attempt is made to access a file, there is always a chance that for some reason the access attempt is unsuccessful. This could be due to an error in programming (such as misspelling the file name), or an error in set up (such as wrong file permissions), or even some unforeseen circumstances on the server (file is busy, or server is overloaded). The first two of these problems would require fixing by the Web programmer (that's you), whereas the third problem would likely fix itself if the user tried again.

If a file cannot be opened by a Perl CGI program for some reason, you usually just wind up with no data. For example, if your program failed to open the websites.txt file, you would simply end up with an empty %websites hash. If that hash were used in a CGI program to generate a list of links, that list would be absent (no list items) in the Web page returned to the browser. It is usually desirable to have a mechanism in place so that an error page is returned to the browser, rather than a broken Web page caused by a failed file access.

To accomplish that goal, we exploit the fact that the `open` function not only performs its obvious task but also returns a `1` or `0` value (true or false) depending upon whether the file was successfully opened. So it can be used in a conditional,

```
if(open (FILEHANDLE, "$dataDir"."file.txt")) {
    proceed with program . . .
}
else {
    print error page . . .
}
```

to both open the file and test whether the operation was successful. Better yet,

```
if(!open (FILEHANDLE, "$dataDir"."file.txt")) {
    print error page . . .
    exit;
}
proceed with program  . . .
```

opens the file if possible, otherwise it prints a suitable error page and then exits the program. Notice that we negated the value returned by the `open` function. This is just a more concise way to accomplish the same thing as the `if . . . else` version.

Even better yet, the following

```
open (FILEHANDLE, "$dataDir"."file.txt") or &errorPage;
```

either opens the file successfully *or* calls an `errorPage` function, which we will have to write. The reason this `or` construct works is fully explained in the last note at the end of this section.

Figure 5.8 contains a complete program that reads the `websites.txt` file (shown in Figure 5.7) and outputs a Web page with a list of links to the Web sites. If the file cannot be opened, the `errorPage` function returns an error message to the user as a Web page. Figure 5.9 shows the result of calling `links2.cgi` when the program has failed to open the data file. The logic of the program is very simple:

- Make sure you have the correct path to the file and open the file for reading. If the file cannot be opened, a function prints an error page and exits the program.
- Read the data line by line into a hash.
- Print the list of links just as in the first version of this program in Section 5.4.

It is important to return meaningful error message pages when file operations fail. Indeed, this is imperative for commercial Web sites. It usually takes only a small fraction of a second to open a file, do something, and then close the file, but with many users hitting a page, a file is sometimes "busy" when a CGI program tries to open it. The surfer should see an intelligible message as opposed to a "broken" Web page. A retry is usually successful. If you stop and think about it, this situation has likely happened to you when surfing in the past. This `errorPage` function will be used frenquently in subsequent chapters. It takes an optional message parameter, which we have not used here. You will later see why that is desirable.

```
                          ▒ links2.cgi ▒

#!/usr/bin/perl
print "Content-type:text/html\n\n";

$dataDir = "/some/directory/path/";  # to directory containing websites.txt

open (INFILE, "$dataDir"."websites.txt") or &errorPage;

%websites=();
while($line = <INFILE>) {
  chomp $line;
  ($name, $url) = split(/=/, $line);
  $websites{$name} = $url;
}
close(INFILE);

print <<TOP;
<html><head><title>A list of websites</title></head><body>
  <h1>Happy Surfing!</h1>
  <ul>
TOP

foreach $name (keys %websites) {
  print "<li><a href=\"http://$websites{$name}\n\">$name</a></li>\n";
}

print<<BOTTOM;
  </ul>
  </body></html>
BOTTOM

##############################################################################
sub errorPage {
 my $message = $_[0];  # optional message parameter

 print<<ALL;
 <html><head><title>Server Error</title></head><body>
  <h2>Server Error Encountered</h2> $message
   The server was unable to open a data file. Please try again. If the problem
 persists, please notify the <a href="mailto:admin\@uweb.edu">webmaster</a>.
 </body></html>
ALL

exit;  # terminate program since failure to open data file
}
```

FIGURE 5.8 A program that returns an error page if the open file operation is not successful.

NOTE

In public directories on most Web servers, new text files are automatically given read permissions (for everyone) because those are precisely the permissions that HTML files need to be publicly accessible. In fact, we had to tighten permissions on the text file manually to get the error message in Figure 5.9. However, new files are rarely given write permissions. If that's the case on your particular Web server, you must not forget to give text files write permissions (for everyone) before attempting write operations from a CGI program.

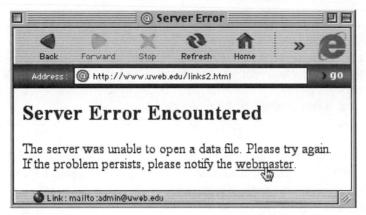

FIGURE 5.9   Result of executing the program of Figure 5.8 by a remote URL request when the data file cannot be opened; in this case the data file does not have adequate permissions.

Writing (either overwriting or appending) to a file is conceptually similar to reading from a file:

```
$writableDataDir = "directory_path";
open (FILEHANDLE , ">>$writableDataDir"."data.txt") or &errorPage;
    append more data onto the file
close (FILEHANDLE);
```

Notice that the append qualifier is added onto the front of the directory path. It is important to use one of the mode qualifiers when opening files for writing. Otherwise, the file is opened with only the default of reading. In general, such qualifiers go on the front, as in `>path/to/file.txt`.

When a file is open for writing, using the FILEHANDLE in a print statement

```
print FILEHANDLE list_of_strings;
```

directs the printing to the file as opposed to standard output. Notice that there is *no* comma between the FILEHANDLE and the list of strings. Aside from the destination of the strings to be printed, this print statement works just like the regular print statement. For example,

```
printf FILEHANDLE format_string, list_of_strings;
```

can do formatted printing (Section 4.7) in a text file. If more than one file is open at a given time, print statements using different file handles can direct output toward the different files.

NOTE

As we have stressed, appropriate permissions may have to be set in order to be able to write to a file from a CGI program. If the file already exists, just set its permissions as outlined in Appendix C. If open for writing is called for a file that does not exist, then

a new file is automatically created. For that action to be possible, the enclosing directory may need to have write permissions by everyone. (In some cases, *all* enclosing
directories in the directory tree may need write permissions by everyone.) For security purposes, it is sometimes advantageous to keep writable data files in their own
directory, especially if you want the directory to be writable (so that new files can be
created in that directory by a CGI program).

We now provide an example that uses a file to record a hit counter. Figure 5.10
shows the CGI program that implements the counter. The actual Web page generated by
the program is rather generic. The main idea is that a similar counter could be provided for
any page generated by a Perl CGI program.

Before the Web page is printed, the addHit function is called to return the newly
updated number of hits. (Function calls are not interpolated inside print blocks.) Then the
page is printed with a sentence at the bottom informing the surfer how popular (or unpop-
ular) the page is. The main work is done by the function. The text file is very simple: Just
one line, containing a single number that reflects the hits total.

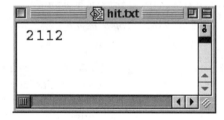

The outline of the function is as follows.

- Open the file, store the previous hit total into a local variable, and close the file. If that
  file operation is unsuccessful, the function returns an error message ("This page has
  been accessed (Error accessing counter) times.") instead of the hit count.
- Remove the newline character and add 1 to the variable to reflect the current hit.
- Open the file for overwrite, write the updated hits total, and close the file. If that file
  operation is unsuccessful, return the updated hit total. (The user will never know
  that his or her hit was not actually recorded into the file.)
- Otherwise, all operations were successful, and the updated hits total is returned.

Of course, we would first need to create the file hit.txt ourselves and transfer it to the
server (with correct write permissions, of course).

Our one example on writing to a file in this section uses the overwrite mode. The
syntax and procedure for using append mode is pretty much the same. The difference in
syntax is that in append mode there are two angle brackets, >>, as opposed to one > for
overwrite mode. The difference in outcome is that when opened for overwriting (often just
called writing in books) a file is first erased. When opened for appending, the original file
is left intact, and any printing to the file merely adds data.

```
┌─────────────────────────────── hit.cgi ───────────────────────────┐
│ #! /usr/bin/perl                                                   │
│ print "Content-type: text/html\n\n";                               │
│                                                                    │
│ $hits = &addHit;                                                   │
│                                                                    │
│ print <<PAGE;                                                      │
│ <html><head><title>Some Web page</title></head>                   │
│  <body>                                                            │
│   Blagh....Blagh....Blagh...<br/>                                  │
│   This page has been accessed $hits times.                         │
│  </body>                                                           │
│ </html>                                                            │
│ PAGE                                                               │
│                                                                    │
│ ############################################################       │
│ sub addHit {                                                       │
│   $writableDataDir= "/www/book/wdata/"; #the writable data directory│
│                                                                    │
│   open(INFILE, "$writableDataDir"."hit.txt") or return "(Error accessing counter)";│
│   my $hits = <INFILE>;                                             │
│   close(INFILE);                                                   │
│                                                                    │
│   chomp $hits;                                                     │
│   $hits++;                                                         │
│                                                                    │
│   open(OUTFILE, ">$writableDataDir"."hit.txt") or return $hits;    │
│   print OUTFILE $hits;                                             │
│   close(OUTFILE);                                                  │
│                                                                    │
│   return $hits;                                                    │
│ }                                                                  │
└────────────────────────────────────────────────────────────────────┘
```

FIGURE 5.10 A typical hit counter.

Although we don't supply an example of its use, we mention a Perl function that is useful in some situations. When multiple print statements are used to write data to a file, the select function

```
select (FILEHANDLE);
```

enables the print function to write to FILEHANDLE without having to refer to FILEHANDLE by name. It selects the specified file handle as the default for printing. That is, any subsequent

```
print list_of_strings;
```

statements are equivalent to

```
print FILEHANDLE list_of_strings;
```

Once printing to FILEHANDLE is completed, the printing default can be changed back to standard output by using the following statement.

```
select (STDOUT);
```

The built-in file handle for standard output is `STDOUT`. That is always the default for `print` if no `select` statement intervenes. As a side note, the built-in file handle for standard run-time errors (where error messages are directed) is `STDERR`.

NOTE

You might be wondering why you can always use relative path names in links that point to files (HTML pages and CGI programs) requested by URLs, but you may not be able to use relative path names for accessing files for reading and writing from within a CGI program. That is particularly an issue on UNIX machines (Solaris UNIX, BSD UNIX, and so forth). The reason is that a URL request is processed by the Web server software, which knows the base URL of the Web page in which a link appears. The server software resolves the URL request by "adding" the relative directory path information onto the base URL.

However, on some systems when a file operation is attempted by a CGI program called through the Web, the server software passes the file operation to the operating system. It is the responsibility of the operating system to handle formal file operations, and the "working directory" as known to the operating system may not be the directory of the CGI program as known to the server software from the base URL. On UNIX systems, this is related to the issue that a CGI program is running as a "nobody" user. The directory (in the Web programmer's user account) into which the CGI program was uploaded is different from the root directory of the anonymous "nobody" user.

NOTE

We end this section with comments on the fact that many top-notch Perl programmers handle error messages using the `die` function rather than printing an error page. However, that option is not desirable when using Perl to develop Web applications. We make these comments because if you continue as a Web programmer, you will no doubt encounter Perl code written by others that uses the `die` function. This is an artifact carried over from classic, non-CGI Perl programming.

The `die` function has the form

```
die "some error message"
```

which prints `"some error message"` to the standard error channel, `STDERR`, and then exits the entire program. It is sometimes used to handle errors from file operations in a manner similar to what we have done in this section.

```
open(FILEHANDLE, "somefile.txt") or die "failed file access";
```

If the Perl program is executed offline, the standard error channel is simply the screen or output window. In that case, `die` works just fine for diagnostic purposes. However, if the Perl program is executed as a CGI program over the Web, then the standard error channel goes into an error log file. In that case the server software will return a blank or broken Web page to the browser when a CGI program "dies" prematurely. Typically, only the server administrator has access to the server's error log, so die error messages are of no use to you in the development process or to a surfer. As we mentioned above, it is desirable to send the user an error page instead because the file access error will likely correct itself. Big-time, commercial Web applications may actually send professional-quality (in terms of design) error pages.

We conclude with an explanation of why the open or &errorPage and open or die statements are viable syntactically. As in many languages, the Boolean operator or (also ||) "short-circuits" meaning that if the left-hand value is true, the right-hand value is not evaluated, because it does not need to be: The total value in that case would be true regardless of the right-hand value. This feature is often called *lazy evaluation*. So a statement such as

statement1 or *statement2*;

has the effect that *statement2* is executed only if *statement1* is false. Thus, in the open or &errorPage statement, the errorPage function is called only if the open statement returns a false value, meaning that the file operation has failed.

5.8 EXTERNAL SOURCE FILES

Perl code stored in separate, auxiliary files can be imported into a given program using the require function.

    require *filename*;

The file name is subject to the same considerations as in performing file operations. That is, on some systems, the full directory path is required. On others, a relative path suffices.

If the file is not readable (either because it does not exist or because of permissions), then an attempt to require it crashes the program. This behavior is different from when a standard file operation fails.

For a practical example, we put the errorPage function from the previous section into an auxiliary file named aux.pl.[2] Since that function (or a similar one) is very useful any time file operations are needed in a CGI program, we can simply require the file in programs rather than copying and pasting the whole function. Figure 5.11 shows the auxiliary file. Figure 5.12 shows a simple program that "imports" this file. You will note that the only purpose of the program is to require the auxiliary file and to print the error page.

---

[2]External source files that contain function definitions are sometimes called *libraries* and are given .lib extensions.

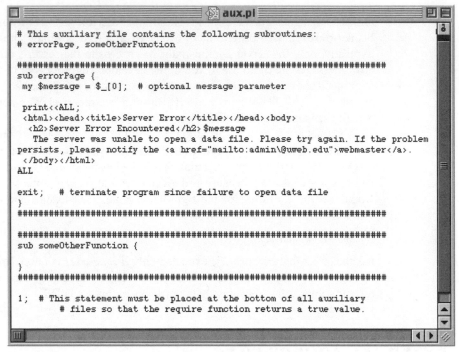

```
# This auxiliary file contains the following subroutines:
# errorPage, someOtherFunction

#######################################################################
sub errorPage {
 my $message = $_[0];  # optional message parameter

 print<<ALL;
 <html><head><title>Server Error</title></head><body>
  <h2>Server Error Encountered</h2> $message
    The server was unable to open a data file. Please try again. If the problem
persists, please notify the <a href="mailto:admin\@uweb.edu">webmaster</a>.
 </body></html>
ALL

exit;  # terminate program since failure to open data file
}
#######################################################################

#######################################################################
sub someOtherFunction {

}
#######################################################################

1;  # This statement must be placed at the bottom of all auxiliary
        # files so that the require function returns a true value.
```

FIGURE 5.11   A typical auxiliary file containing some functions.

```
#! /usr/bin/perl
print "Content-type: text/html\n\n";

$auxDir = "directory_path";      # to the directory
                                 # containing aux.pl
require "$auxDir"."aux.pl";

$dataDir = "directory_path";     # to the directory
                                 # containing data files

open (FILEHANDLE, "$dataDir"."nonExistentFile.txt")  or  &errorPage;
close (FILEHANDLE);

# This program prints the error page from the auxiliary file
# because it tries to open a file for reading that does not exist
```

FIGURE 5.12   A program that imports aux.pl shown in Figure 5.11.

NOTE

It is very important that the statement 1; appear in the last line of the auxiliary file. The content of the file is evaluated with a return value, usually just the last expression evaluated. The return value is interpreted in Boolean context, indicating success or failure. If the return value is false (as would happen if the file could not be read or contained a syntax error), the whole Perl program quits. To mark success in processing the entire auxiliary file, a true value is returned on the last line. If you forget that, requiring an external file will likely crash your program.

Auxiliary files commonly are used to perform initialization tasks, such as initialization of data arrays and hashes, or to parse data strings. It is usually considered poor programming style, though, to move a series of statements from the main program's sequence of execution into a separate file. It is better to collect tasks into functions in a separate file and then call them in the main program file. That way, you can follow what the program is doing by reading the main program file.

In summary, auxiliary files can be used to organize common subroutines for a large project that involves several Perl CGI programs. However, our examples are small, so we won't have many occasions to utilize auxiliary files. Furthermore, overuse of auxiliary files brings extra hazards to the beginning Web programmer. Certainly, more errors can arise, especially because Web programmers have to upload all files for a given Web application to a server. For relatively small projects it is usually not worth the trouble.

5.9* ADVANCED PERL TOPICS

In this section we provide a brief introduction to references, multidimensional arrays, function prototypes, and typeglobs. The motivation for including this section comes from the difficulties surrounding sending multiple arrays to a function as parameters. Recall the "flattening" effect discussed in Section 5.3. Also, *typeglob* is a cool word (but not as cool as *wildebeest*).

References to Variables

A **reference** in Perl is like a pointer in other languages. References are inherently scalar values, meaning that they are stored in scalar variables. The reference can "point to" another scalar, an array, a hash, or even a function. We discuss only references to variables here.

To make a reference to an existing variable, simply put a backslash (\) in front of the variable name. Consider the following references to various variable types.

```
$ref1 = \$sca;      # $ref1 is a reference to scalar $sca
$ref2 = \@arr;      # $ref2 is a reference to array @arr
$ref3 = \%has;      # $ref3 is a reference to hash %has
```

In this way, we can even reference a scalar stored in an array.

```
$ref4 = \$arr[3];   # $ref4 is a reference to fourth element of $arr
```

A reference to a literal can be created as well. Technically, the reference is made to an anonymous variable, with the literal as its value. Following are two examples. The difference between these reference declarations and standard variable assignments is the choice of brackets. For normal array and hash assignments, parentheses are used.

```
$ref5 = ["a", 2, "xy"];          # $ref5 is a reference to an array
                                 # that has 3 elements.
$ref6 = {"red"=>"#ff0000",
         "blue"=>"#0000ff"};     # $ref6 is a reference to a hash
                                 # that has 2 keyvalue pairs
```

To access a referenced variable, a syntax is used that is best remembered as treating the reference variable as the string part of the name of a variable. We call this process *dereferencing*. We'll dereference the references created in the preceding examples. For the reference $ref1,

```
$$ref1
```

accesses the value stored in $sca. For example, if $sca holds a string, then

```
($$ref1 eq $sca)
```

is true. For the reference $ref2,

```
@$ref2
```

accesses the array stored in $arr. For example,

```
foreach $element (@$ref2){}
```

is equivalent to

```
foreach $element (@arr){}
```

For the reference $ref3,

```
%$ref3
```

accesses the hash stored in $has. For example,

```
foreach $key (keys %$ref3){}
```

is equivalent to

```
foreach $key (keys %has){}
```

For the reference $ref4,

```
$$ref4[3]
```

accesses the value in the fourth index position of $arr. So, if $arr[3] holds a string, then ($$ref4[3] eq $arr[3]) is true.

There is a potential for ambiguity in interpreting such complicated expressions. Suppose we have an array containing a reference to a scalar variable:

```
@arr = ("a", \$sca);
```

Now suppose we wish to access the variable $sca through this array. For such situations, we use curly braces { } to group the symbols. So

```
${$arr[1]}
```

gives the desired result of first getting the index 1 element of @arr and then dereferencing it to the scalar variable $sca.

One would have been tempted to think that $$arr[1] would be the appropriate dereference in that case, since $arr[1] is a reference to $sca. However, as the example using $ref4 shows, $$arr[1] treats $arr as a reference to an array element, and $$arr[1] would attempt to dereference to that array element. Instead, when the array element is itself a reference, the curly braces are required. As a side note, this grouping capability can also give alternative solutions to situations from Chapter 4 where we had to print something like

```
print "we are out of $product", "s.\n";
```

to avoid trying to interpolate a non-existent variable $products. A cleaner solution is

```
print "we are out of ${product}s.\n";
```

which has the same effect.

We apply these ideas by writing a function that takes two arrays as parameters. First we show an example call to the function, sending it references to two arrays @arr0 and @arr1. Following that is the function definition.

```
&somefunction(\@arr0, \@arr1);

sub somefunction {
    my @a = @{$_[0]};
    my @b = @{$_[1]};
    Do something with the two arrays @a and @b.
    Alterations to the original arrays can be made by modifying @{$_[0]} and @{$_[1]}.
}
```

When the function call is made, $_[0] and $_[1] are passed the references to @arr0 and @arr1. Those are then dereferenced (using curly braces) and passed by value into @a and @b. The result is that @a and @b contain only copies of @arr0 and @arr1, respectively. If the contents of @{$_[0]} are altered, however, then @arr0 would be altered.

We now offer a more substantive example. Suppose we wish to write a function that takes an array of Web site names and a hash of Web site URLs, where the keys are the Web site names. The array and hash are the same as those used in Figure 5.6 to print out an HTML list of links.

```
@topics = ("apples", "bananas", "durians", "kiwis", "oranges");
%domains= ("apples" => "www.apples.com",
           "durians" => "www.durian.net",
           "oranges" => "www.oranges.com" );
```

The following function call sends references to the two variables to the function.

```
&makeListOfURLs(\@topics, \%domains);
```

The definition of this function follows. The array and hash that are passed to the function are dereferenced and passed by value into local variables. Otherwise, the rest of the function is straightforward.

```
sub makeListOfURLs {
    my @names = @{$_[0]};
    my %urls = %{$_[1]};
    print "<ul>\n";

    foreach $name (@names) {
        if(exists $urls{$name}) {
            print "<li><a href=\"$urls{$name}\">$name</a></li>\n";
        }
        else {
            print "<li>$name</li>\n";
        }
    }
    print "</ul>\n";
}
```

Multidimensional Arrays

The concept of multidimensional arrays is basically the same as in other languages, but the syntax uses references and is nonstandard. For illustrative purposes, we consider two-dimensional arrays. Recall that we can't define a two-dimensional array as

```
@arr = ( (1, 2), ("a", "b", "c") );
```

because that gets flattened into (1,2,"a","b","c").

In Perl, a two-dimensional array is actually an array of references to arrays. Consider the array

```
@arr = ( [1, 2], ["a", "b", "c"] );
```

Note that this array is not "rectangular," nor do they have to be in general. Alternatively, we can define @arr as follows:

```
@a1 = (1, 2);
@a2 = ("a", "b", "c");
@arr=(\@a1,\@a2);
```

The individual entries can be accessed using the dereferencing rules. For example,

```
${$arr[1]}[0]
```

contains "a", because $arr[1] is the reference to ["a", "b", "c"] and so @{$arr[1]} is
the array ("a","b","c").

Fortunately, Perl allows a shortcut that looks like two-dimensional arrays from other
languages. The following standard notation,

```
$arr[1][0]
```

is the same as

```
${$arr[1]}[0]
```

Prototyping Functions

References are one solution to the "flattening" problem associated with passing individual
arrays and hashes to functions, but it can also be solved through the use of a predeclared
function *prototype*. For example,

```
sub arraysFunction (\@\@);
```

predeclares a function named arraysFunction that is to accept two individual arrays as
parameters. Subsequent to the prototype declaration, the function can be formally defined.

```
sub arraysFunction (\@\@) {
    my @a = @{$_[0]};
    my @b = @{$_[1]};
    Do something with the two arrays @a and @b.
    Alterations to the original arrays can be made by modifying @{$_[0]} and @{$_[1]}.
}
```

Two arrays, @arr0 and @arr1, can be sent to the function by making the call

```
arraysFunction (@arr0, @arr1);
```

The arrays, @arr0 and @arr1, are passed into the arguments array @_. Notice that a & character is not used in front of the function as with normal, nonprototyped functions. Moreover, references to the two arrays are not created before passing them into the function.
Predeclaring a function with a prototype turns the function into an operator, like the built-
in Perl functions, allowing it to take variables other than scalars as arguments.

However, strangely enough the call

```
&arraysFunction (\@arr0, \@arr1);
```

still works, because putting the & character in front takes away the power of treating
arraysFunction as an operator. So you are passing references, which are scalars, as the
function expects in that case. Thus

```
&arraysfunction (@arr0, @arr1);   #does NOT work
```

causes a run-time error in the body of the function, because &arraysfunction expects scalars because of the & symbol. A bad call to a predeclared function does not even generate any kind of error or warning! These types of subtle errors are particularly insidious.

A prototype must be declared *before* calling the function. However, the actual calls to the function can still precede the function's definition, as with ordinary Perl functions.

```
sub arraysfunction (\@\@);   # prototype declaration

arraysfunction( @array0, @array1 ); # call the function

sub arraysfunction (\@\@) { # the actual declaration.
    my @a = @{$_[0]};
    my @b = @{$_[1]};
    Do something with the two arrays @a and @b.
    Alterations to the original arrays can be made by modifying @{$_[0]} and @{$_[1]}.
}
```

Functions that take distinct hashes and scalars as parameters can also be prototyped as in

```
sub someFunction (\%\@\$);      # prototype declaration
```

which expects a hash, an array, and a scalar in that order. Here you would have to be careful to dereference the elements of the arguments array, @_, accordingly.

Typeglobs

Yet another solution to the "flattening" problem when passing two arrays to a function is to use *typeglobs*. A *typeglob* is a symbol for a name that enables you to refer to different variable types (scalars, arrays, hashes), each having the same name. The syntax for a typeglob is a star (*) followed by a symbolic name. For example,

```
*name
```

refers to $name, @name, and %name simultaneously. Hence the term "typeglob." You can think of * as a wildcard.

Suppose we have two arrays, @name1 and @name2. Then, the following mechanism for passing parameters does the trick for the two arrays.

```
&someFunction(*name1, *name2);

sub someFunction {
    local (*a1 , *a2) = @_;
    Now manipulation of @a1 and @a2 serves to manipulate @name1 and @name2.
}
```

In effect, @a1 and @a2 are local to the function, but they reference the global @name1 and @name2 that were sent to the function. This is because in essence the names a1 and a2 symbolically stand for the names name1 and name2, respectively. For that reason, changing $a1 in the function would actually change a global scalar $name1 if it existed. Similarly, changing %a1 in the function would change a global hash %name1, if it existed.

We conclude with an important note. When passing globbed types to a function in this manner, local function variables must be declared as local instead of my. The reason is kind of a long story. To make it short, the scope of a my variable does not permit it to be in a symbol table. If you mistakenly use my with typeglobs, you will get an error.

SUMMARY OF KEY TERMS AND CONCEPTS

Comparison operators: Perl uses standard comparison operators for numeric comparison. However, Perl uses special operators (eq, ne, gt, ge, lt, le) for string comparison.

No explicit Boolean type: Perl has no explicit true/false Boolean literals, so 0 and 1 suffice. Actually, both strings and numbers are interpreted as Boolean when placed into Boolean context. For numbers, 0 gives false, and any other number is true. For strings, the empty string "" gives false and any other string is true.

Conditionals: Perl uses elsif rather than else if in conditionals. Grouping brackets {} are required in conditionals (and other structures) even for a code block containing only one statement.

Loops: The for and while loops are standard in Perl. Perl has a very handy **foreach** loop, which automatically iterates over each element of an array.

Arrays: Perl array variables must begin with a @ character (@array). However, array elements are scalar variables, which are referred to as such ($array[0]). An array placed into scalar context ($scalar=@array;) evaluates to the number of elements in the array. The special scalar variable $#array contains the highest filled index of the array. (Section 2.9: A multidimensional array's elements are references, which are scalars, to other arrays.)

Flattening: When an array variable or list literal is "nested inside" a larger list, its elements and all those of the larger list are "flattened" into one list. We primarily have to worry about this when passing an array to a function, in which case the array is "flattened" into one list together with any other scalars or arrays that may be passed to the function. Thus, the passed array "loses its identity." The easiest solution is to pass the array as the last parameter to the function so that it can easily be recovered from the function's arguments array. (Section 2.9: Passing references to an array to a function, and then dereferencing the arrays inside the function, is one way to alleviate that problem.)

Hash: A data structure comprising *keys* and their associated *values*, enabling a value to be accessed using the associated key. Hashes are often called associative arrays because the values are associated with keys, rather than with numeric indexes as in arrays. Hash variables must begin with a % character (%hash). However, hash keys and values are scalar variables, which are referred to as such ($hash{"somekey"}). There is no order assigned to the hash keys, and hence when the keys are extracted from the hash into an array for the purpose of iterating over the hash, the order of the extracted keys is unpredictable. (Section 2.9: If a hash is passed to a function, it is put into list context, which suppresses its hash structure. The solution is to pass reference to a hash and then dereference the hash inside the function.)

The arguments array `@_`: All parameters passed to a function are flattened into one array of scalars, which is automatically stored into the built-in arguments array. All variables are passed to functions by reference. Thus, `$_[0]` is a reference to the first argument passed to the function, and so forth. Any array or hash variables passed to a function are "flattened" into their constituent scalars, which become elements of `@_`.

Functions: Programmer-defined functions are called using an ampersand character `&` followed by the name of the function. The built-in arguments array `@_` receives all parameters, which are scalar variables. Since parameters are passed by reference, altering `$_[0]` alters the first scalar variable sent to the function, for example. To avoid that, and for clarity, incoming parameters are often transferred from the arguments array into local variables, declared using `my`. Local variables are scoped as you would expect. Receiving parameters through the arguments array allows a Perl function to receive any number of parameters, the number not being predefined.

File operations: Perl provides standard (`read`, `write`, `append`) file operations. Because CGI programs are executed by anonymous users over the Internet, files to which CGI programs write must be given write permissions (`rw`) for everyone by their owner (that's you) ahead of time. Read permissions for everyone is the default, so you simply are adding write permissions. Moreover, calling a write on a file that doesn't exist creates the file. For that to happen, the directory into which the file is to be placed must be given write permissions for everyone ahead of time. A file created in this manner by an anonymous user is actually owned by all anonymous users. Thus, any other Web surfer has full (`rwx`) privileges to the file.

The `errorPage` function: This might seem like a trivial matter, but is of huge importance. Any time a file operation is conducted by a CGI program, `errorPage` or a similar function should be called if it fails. A failed file operation causes the CGI program to die, sending its error message to the standard error channel, which goes to the Web server software. The server software then dumps that message into an `errorlog` file. But the Web server's job is to complete the current HTTP transaction, so it sends a Web page containing a generic error report (HTTP error 500, internal server error) to the requesting Web browser. Generic error pages returned by Web servers do not include details about why the Perl program died. When you develop Web applications that use many file (or database) operations, it is very difficult to debug failed file operations using HTTP error reports. The optional message parameter we have provided in the `errorPage` function will be used to report exactly which File (or database) operation has failed.

External source files: An external file containing Perl functions is imported in a program using the `require` statement. Once an external source file is required, the functions it contains can be called in the main program. It is imperative to include the statement `1;` at the end of an external source file. That statement returns true to the main program, indicating success in parsing the external Perl code.

EXERCISES

1. Write a CGI-program that generates a multiplication table as follows

1	2	3	4	5	6	7	8	9
2	4	6	8	10	12	14	16	18
3	6	9	12	15	18	21	24	27
4	8	12	16	20	24	28	32	36
5	10	15	20	25	30	35	40	45
6	12	18	24	30	36	42	48	54
7	14	21	28	35	42	49	56	63
8	16	24	32	40	48	56	64	72
9	18	27	36	45	54	63	72	81

(a) Generate a 9×9 multiplication table.

(b) Generate a $n \times n$ multiplication table where n is a randomly generated integer in the range from 5 to 25, inclusive.

2. Do Exercise 1, but with the following additions:

(a) The rows have alternating background colors

(b) The numbers in the first row and first column are rendered as boldfaced white text in table cells with a black background.

(c) Other than the cells in the first row and first column, the rows should alternate background colors between white and light gray.

3. Write a CGI program that randomly picks an advertisement, as in Figure 4.15, but this time the images are links to the corresponding ad site. The ad images can be obtained from the Web site, and you can link to unrelated Web sites. Make two versions of the program:

(a) Use parallel arrays to store the images and corresponding URLs.

(b) Use a hash that stores the image numbers as keys and the corresponding URLs as values.

4. Write two Perl functions, `head`, and `foot`, that print the top and bottom of an HTML page, respectively.

(a) The `head` function takes a string parameter and returns a string containing the top portion of an HTML page (`<html>` tag down to and including opening `<body>` tag). The string sent to the function should appear as the title of the Web page.

(b) The `foot` function simply returns the string `"</body></html>"`.

Write a CGI program to test the functions. Just make up some sentence to use as the body of the Web page. (Note to instructors: Use other exercises as the body of the generated page.)

5. Write a function `randomColor()` that returns a string containing a randomly generated hexadecimal color, such as `"#4e71a0"`. Make two versions of the function:

(a) Use the Perl function `hex()`, which takes a base-10 number and returns the hexadecimal equivalent.

(b) Do this without using the `hex()` function.

6. Using the `randomColor()` function(s) from Exercise 5, write a CGI program that returns a Web page containing:

(a) A random background color

(b) A 3 × 3 HTML table where the background colors of each of the nine table cells are chosen randomly. Each table cell should have dimensions 50 × 50 pixels. Moreover, the hex color value should be printed in each table cell using black text. (Note that there is a risk that the black text may not show up, depending upon the color of the table cells. Don't worry about that.)

7. Do Exercise 6, but ensure that the generated table cell colors are toward the dark end of the color spectrum. Moreover, the hex color values printed in each table cell should be rendered with a randomly generated text color. For contrast, ensure that the generated text colors are toward the light end of the color spectrum. You must use CSS to generate the font colors (not the deprecated font element).

8. Do Exercise 4, but put the functions into an external library code file. Also write one or more of the functions outlined in Section 5.12 and add those to the function library. Make a CGI program that imports the function library and utilizes all of functions to print a Web page. The content of the Web page can be simply the form elements produced by the functions from Section 5.12. Include a submit button in the form, which submits the form to the echo program introduced in Chapter 3.

9. This is a user verification exercise. Create an HTML page that contains a form with two text fields: one for a user name and one for a password. The form should be submitted to a CGI program that you create. Store five user names and passwords in a text file. If the submitted user name and password match (test using case-*in*sensitive string equality) a pair found in your file, return a page to the browser that states "logon successful." Otherwise, return a page to the browser that contains one of the two messages: "User not found" or "User valid, but password does not match." If you use the GET method of form submission, the following lines of code will recover the user name and password submitted to the program from the form.

```
($user,$pass) = split(/&/ , $ENV{"QUERY_STRING"} , 2);
($junk,$user) = split(/=/ , $user , 2);
($junk,$pass) = split(/=/ , $pass , 2);
```

The $user and $pass variables will contain the entered data. The $junk variable will contain the name you give to the password element, which is not needed in the program. (*See the note at end of this section.)

10. This is a user signup exercise. Create an HTML page that contains a form with two text fields: one for a user name and one for a password. The form should be submitted to a CGI program that you create. Store five user names and passwords in a text file on the server. If either the submitted user name or password match (test using case-*in*sensitive string equality) ones found in your file, return a page to the browser that states which is the case. Otherwise, append the new user name and password to your file and return a page to the browser that informs the user that they have been signed up successfully. If you use the GET method of form submission, the following lines of code will recover the user name and password submitted to the program from the form.

```
($user,$pass) = split(/&/ , $ENV{"QUERY_STRING"} , 2);
($junk,$user) = split(/=/ , $user , 2);
($junk,$pass) = split(/=/ , $pass , 2);
```

The $user and $pass variables will contain the entered data. The $junk variable will contain the name you give to the password element, which is not needed in the program. (*See the note at end of this section.)

11. Work Exercises 9 and 10. Construct an HTML "welcome page" with two links: one to log on and one to sign up. The logon link calls the CGI program from Exercise 9. Successful logon returns a Web page that says "members only". Failed logon returns a copy of the welcome page with a message indicating why the logon attempt failed. The signup link calls the CGI program from Exercise 10. Successful signup returns a copy of the welcome page with a message indicating successful signup and to please logon. Failed signup should return a copy of the welcome page with a diagnostic failure message.

12. (*Advanced*) Exercise 11 involves printing the same code for the welcome page over and over. That screams "use a function" to an experienced programmer. Write a function that takes one parameter and prints the welcome page. The parameter is used to send messages, which appear at the top of the welcome page, to the function. Store the function in an external library code file. The first welcome page received by the user is then generated by a third, but trivial, CGI program that merely calls the welcome page function with no message. The other two CGI programs can then call the function with a message whenever they need to return the welcome page. (Better yet, the three programs can condensed into one CGI program that runs the whole application. However, that would take some cleverness—reading ahead in the text!)

Note for Exercises 8 and 9: It is important that you do not use any weird characters in your user names and passwords. Just use letters and numbers. This is a rather crude way to decode the query string. If you enter weird characters into the user or password field in the form, the Web browser will likely encode them with hexadecimal character codes. That will cause problems when testing them against the original user names and passwords in your text file.

PROJECT THREAD

This step features the development of a function library, which will be augmented throughout subsequent chapters. Most of the functions added after this chapter will be toolkit functions, such as `errorPage`, which we will provide. The library will be used in nearly every project thread you do in the next several chapters. Its culmination will be a library that, although not as extensive, has much of the functionality of the `CGI.pm` Perl module discussed in Chapter 9. Indeed, constructing this library will enable you to appreciate fully the benefits (and shortcomings) of `CGI.pm`. Moreover, constructing this library will enable you to understand and appreciate fully features built in to other Web programming languages such as PHP and ASP, which are covered in Chapters 14 and 15, respectively.

A. Construct the six functions as shown in Figure 5.13. It will be helpful to use a simple driver program to develop and test them. Note that there are primarily only three functions to create: `&text`, `&check`, and `&menu`. The other three are basically modifications of those three. Use the following notes and guidelines:

(i) Each function should return a string containing the HTML output.

(ii) The last character in each returned string should be a newline character. Moreover, include newline characters in the returned strings for the menus so that the HTML code is printed on separate lines. (Tab characters may also be included in the strings so that the menu options are indented.)

(iii) The last parameter of each of the functions is optional. If a function is called and the last parameter is not included, the resulting HTML code simply doesn't contain the attribute corresponding to the missing parameter. (Note that is not sufficient to print something like `maxlength=""` if an optional parameter is not sent in a function call. Rather, the attribute should be completely absent.) Each function expects all but the last parameter to be sent on each function call.

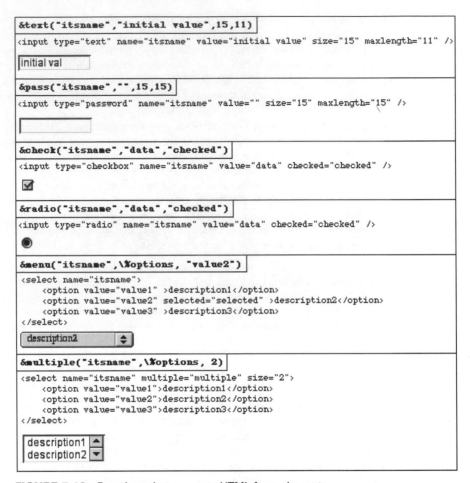

FIGURE 5.13   Functions that generate HTML form elements.

(iv) The menu functions take a hash that carries the data for the menu options. The example output in Figure 5.13 was generated by sending the following hash to the functions.

```
%options = ("value1" => "description1",
            "value2" => "description2",
            "value3" => "description3" );
```

The hash keys become the "hidden" values behind the options, and the hash values become the text descriptions displayed in the menu.

(v) To avoid the hash being placed into list context and then "flattened" in with the rest of the function parameters, references to the hashes are sent to the functions. Thus, each menu function takes two scalar parameters, three if the optional one is sent. In each case, the reference to the hash will become the second element of the function's arguments array ($_[1]). To recover the hash inside the function, simply dereference the reference into a local hash variable. One way to do that is as follows:

```
$hashreference = $_[1];
my %hash = %$hashreference;
```

Then %hash contains a copy of the original one sent to the function. (This was covered in the optional Section 5.9.)

(vi) *Hint regarding the optional parameters:* If the arguments array is transferred into local function variables,

```
my ($a, $b, $c) = @_;
```

for example, but only two parameters are sent to the function, the $c variable will contain the empty string. In that case, $c evaluates to false when put into Boolean context. Any other content of $c (except 0) evaluates to true in Boolean context. If this hint is appreciated to the fullest, then one could send *any* nontrivial string to an optional parameter of the radio function, for example, and the checked attribute would be generated.

B. Collect all the functions into an external code file named cgi.lib. (Make sure the required statement is at the bottom of the file.) Also, put the errorPage function, which you can get from the source files on this book's Web site, into your function library.

C. Make a CGI program that calls each of the functions you have created. The result should be Web page with a form containing each of the six types of form elements. Create your own hashes to send to the menu functions. Include a submit button in the form to submit it to the echo program. The submit button should be printed manually, because you have not created a function for that.

D. Add a new row for the CGI program to the table in your homework page. If you are assigned any other exercises from this chapter, add another row to your homework table for each exercise.

E. Optional: Do Exercise 4. Also, make functions that return the HTML code for submit and reset buttons. Make a function that generates the HTML code for a hidden form element. Add all of these functions to your function library.

CHAPTER 6

PROCESSING FORMS

In Chapter 5 you learned how to generate dynamic page content based on data stored in hashes and arrays, but a dynamic Web application takes user input, not just information we manually set into Perl variables. The returned Web page is based on the user's input. In this chapter, we focus on sending user data, collected in HTML forms on the client, to a server-side Perl CGI program for processing. In many cases, the HTML forms themselves are dynamically generated from a server-side data source.

As a primer for some of the topics presented in this chapter, we recommend that you reacquaint yourself with some of the fundamentals pertaining to HTTP transactions and the nature of Web applications in general that were presented in Sections 1.6, 1.7, and 1.8. Also, Section 3.1 provides the necessary background on HTML forms. We will also allude to these sections when they become relevant at specific junctures in this chapter.

6.1 CGI ENVIRONMENT VARIABLES

Web server software packages such as Apache and IIS need to keep track of certain pieces of information about the state of the software and about HTTP transactions with which they may be involved at a given time. The software stores the information in its **environment variables.** Table 6.1 shows a small sample of the environment variables and the nature of the values they hold.

The environment variables store information about both the client and the server during a given HTTP transaction. It is worth noting that the server software gets part of the information it stores into the environment variables from the application layer HTTP headers it receives from the browser request. The server software gets other information about the current transaction through its interaction with the server computer's TCP layer, which coordinates the actual transfer of data.

When Web server software accepts an HTTP request, its primary job is to complete the HTTP transaction by returning the resource requested by the URL. If the URL requests an HTML file, GIF image, or some other type of nonexecutable resource, the server simply returns it to the browser. (Recall Figure 1.8 and the surrounding discussion.) However, a

TABLE 6.1 Some Environment Variables

NAME	VALUE
HTTP_HOST	Web server's domain name
QUERY_STRING	Data appended onto the end of the URL
REMOTE_ADDR	IP address of client
REQUEST_METHOD	GET or POST

URL request for an executable CGI program causes the server software to establish a CGI interface with the requested program. (Recall Figure 1.9 and the surrounding discussion.)

An integral part of the CGI interface involves the server software passing the information stored in its environment variables to the CGI program. A CGI program often can make good use of details about the current transaction. For example, the HTML document generated by the CGI program can be customized based upon those details.

If you look at the names and values of the environment variables in Table 6.1 as key-value pairs, the concept of a hash comes to mind. Indeed, the server software passes the environment variables to a Perl CGI program into the

```
%ENV
```

hash. That is, when a CGI program executes, the `%ENV` hash automatically becomes a global variable within the program. Its keys are the names of all the environment variables, and its values are the contents of the respective environment variables. Figure 6.1 shows a program named `env.cgi` that returns an HTML table to the browser listing all of the keys of `%ENV` and their values.

Following the hash examples from Chapter 4, the keys are extracted with the `keys` function and then sorted. The loop passes over each `$key` and prints a table row where the first column contains the key and the second column contains the associated value from `%ENV`. You should note that the HTML table is started and ended before and after the loop, respectively.

Figure 6.2 shows the result of a URL call to `env.cgi` from one author's PC. For that figure, the program was executed on a Linux server running Apache. Figure 6.3 shows the result of a URL call to `env.cgi` from the other author's Macintosh. For that figure, the program was executed on a Windows NT machine running the IIS server. This illustrates that the CGI protocol transcends the platform issue.

As you can see from Figures 6.2 and 6.3, the `%ENV` hash contains many details about the HTTP transaction, and the two different Web servers pass somewhat different information to the CGI program. The majority of the environment variables are not overly important in CGI programming, but some are very useful. For example, the value associated

```
env.cgi

#! /usr/bin/perl
print "Content-type:text/html\n\n";

print "<html><head><title>ENVIRONMENT VARIABLES</title></head><body>";
print "<table border=1>";
print "<tr><th>Environment Variable</th><th>Value</th></tr>";

foreach $key( keys %ENV){
  print "<tr><td>$key</td><td>$ENV{$key}</td></tr>";
}

print "</table></body></html>";
```

FIGURE 6.1 A program that prints all keys and values of the `%ENV` hash.

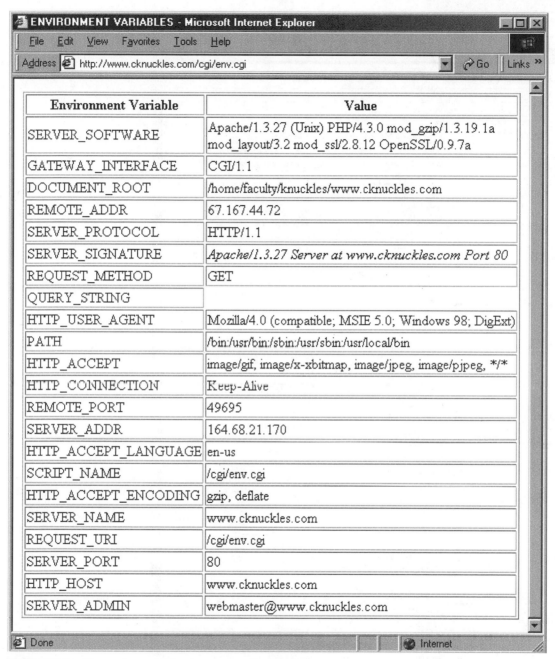

Environment Variable	Value
SERVER_SOFTWARE	Apache/1.3.27 (Unix) PHP/4.3.0 mod_gzip/1.3.19.1a mod_layout/3.2 mod_ssl/2.8.12 OpenSSL/0.9.7a
GATEWAY_INTERFACE	CGI/1.1
DOCUMENT_ROOT	/home/faculty/knuckles/www.cknuckles.com
REMOTE_ADDR	67.167.44.72
SERVER_PROTOCOL	HTTP/1.1
SERVER_SIGNATURE	*Apache/1.3.27 Server at www.cknuckles.com Port 80*
REQUEST_METHOD	GET
QUERY_STRING	
HTTP_USER_AGENT	Mozilla/4.0 (compatible; MSIE 5.0; Windows 98; DigExt)
PATH	/bin:/usr/bin:/sbin:/usr/sbin:/usr/local/bin
HTTP_ACCEPT	image/gif, image/x-xbitmap, image/jpeg, image/pjpeg, */*
HTTP_CONNECTION	Keep-Alive
REMOTE_PORT	49695
SERVER_ADDR	164.68.21.170
HTTP_ACCEPT_LANGUAGE	en-us
SCRIPT_NAME	/cgi/env.cgi
HTTP_ACCEPT_ENCODING	gzip, deflate
SERVER_NAME	www.cknuckles.com
REQUEST_URI	/cgi/env.cgi
SERVER_PORT	80
HTTP_HOST	www.cknuckles.com
SERVER_ADMIN	webmaster@www.cknuckles.com

FIGURE 6.2   The environment hash generated by Apache.

Environment Variable	Value
INSTANCE_ID	1
SERVER_PORT_SECURE	0
HTTP_ACCEPT_LANGUAGE	en
PROCESSOR_IDENTIFIER	x86 Family 6 Model 8 Stepping 3, GenuineIntel
HTTP_USER_AGENT	Mozilla/4.7C-CCK-MCD {C-UDP; EBM-APPLE} (Macintosh; I; PPC)
HTTP_ACCEPT	image/gif, image/x-xbitmap, image/jpeg, image/pjpeg, image/png, */*
REMOTE_HOST	164.68.21.48
HTTP_HOST	164.68.70.131
GATEWAY_INTERFACE	CGI/1.1
TMP	C:\WINNT\TEMP
OS2LIBPATH	C:\WINNT\system32\os2\dll;
SCRIPT_NAME	/knuckles/env.pl
TEMP	C:\WINNT\TEMP
USERPROFILE	C:\Documents and Settings\Default User
SERVER_NAME	164.68.70.131
HTTP_ACCEPT_ENCODING	gzip
OS	Windows_NT
HTTP_ACCEPT_CHARSET	iso-8859-1,*,utf-8
CONTENT_LENGTH	0
PATH	C:\WINNT\system32;C:\WINNT;C:\WINNT\System32\Wbem;C:\Program Files\Support Tools\;C:\Program Files\Resource Kit\;C:\Program Files\Microsoft SQL Server\80\Tools\BINN
PATHEXT	.COM;.EXE;.BAT;.CMD;.VBS;.VBE;.JS;.JSE;.WSF;.WSH
COMPUTERNAME	1132996H
COMMONPROGRAMFILES	C:\Program Files\Common Files
PROGRAMFILES	C:\Program Files
SYSTEMROOT	C:\WINNT
LOCAL_ADDR	164.68.70.131
PROCESSOR_ARCHITECTURE	x86
PROCESSOR_REVISION	0803
ALLUSERSPROFILE	C:\Documents and Settings\All Users
SERVER_PROTOCOL	HTTP/1.0
HTTP_CONNECTION	Keep-Alive
SYSTEMDRIVE	C:
COMSPEC	C:\WINNT\system32\cmd.exe
PATH_TRANSLATED	C:\Inetpub\ftproot\WWW\knuckles\env.pl
WINDIR	C:\WINNT
SERVER_SOFTWARE	Microsoft-IIS/5.0
PATH_INFO	/knuckles/env.pl
REMOTE_ADDR	164.68.21.48
PROCESSOR_LEVEL	6
NUMBER_OF_PROCESSORS	1
HTTPS	off
REQUEST_METHOD	GET
SERVER_PORT	80

FIGURE 6.3 The environment hash generated by IIS.

with `HTTP_USER_AGENT` identifies the client's browser and operating system. One can use the information from this value to tailor the returned Web page according to whether the user is running Windows, Macintosh, UNIX, or some other OS, or according to the user's browser type or vendor. This is basically platform and browser sniffing done on the server. (If you recall, browser sniffing can also be implemented on the client with JavaScript.)

The reader is invited to call the `env.cgi` program by typing the URL

```
http://www.cknuckles.com/cgi/env.cgi
```

into the address field of a browser (or by visiting the book's Web site). That way, you can see the information that is recorded in a transaction between the server that is hosting `www.cknuckles.com` and whatever computer you may be using.

The final example of this section accesses a particular environment variable rather than processing the whole hash. The value of `REMOTE_ADDRESS` is used to indentify the IP address from which the user is surfing. The program and a sample URL request for the program are shown in Figure 6.4. As always, you are encouraged to visit this book's Web site and call the example program from your browser.

NOTE

Web server software has uses for the environment variables other than merely passing them to a CGI program. One such use involves log files on the server, which keep records of past HTTP transactions. Recall that HTTP is a stateless protocol, meaning that once the Web server software completes a given HTTP transaction, it forgets about it. That means the transaction-specific details stored in the server's environment variables are wiped out by the server software when it completes an HTTP transaction. For that reason, much of that information is written to various log files (usually just text files) on the server before it is lost. As the HTTP transactions come and go, the transaction-specific environment information is recorded in the log files. Thus, the log files contain historical records of the past HTTP transactions completed by the server. As we shall see later in this text, those historical records are used for things like counting the number of visits to a given Web site and compiling demographic information (such as browser and platform information) about a site's visitors.

6.2 QUERY STRINGS

The notion of passing user data from Web browsers to Web servers is so central to Web applications that we already have shown you query strings on several occasions (as in Sections 1.5, 1.7, 1.8, and 3.1). A query string is appended to the end of a URL, following a question mark, and so transmitted to the server. The general syntax is as follows:

```
http://webaddress?querystring
```

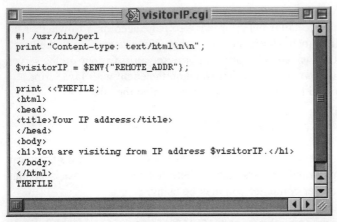

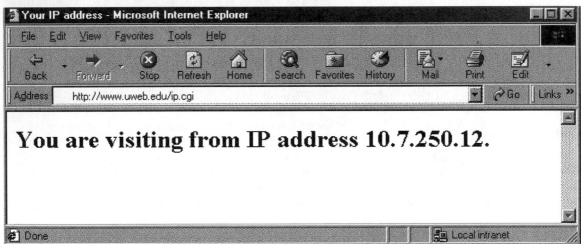

FIGURE 6.4 A CGI program that returns a specific environment variable.

A query string is no more than a string of ASCII characters. The ? character is not part of the query string but signifies that a query string is to follow. For a simple example, the URL

```
http://www.cknuckles.com/cgi/env.cgi?hello there
```

sends the query string `"hello there"` to the server. Note that quotes are not used to delimit the query string in a URL. For that reason, spaces in a query string are problematic in some cases. Newer browsers will substitute the ASCII number for a space (that is, represent the space as a % followed by the ASCII number in hexadecimal form), as in

```
hello%20there
```

to eliminate explicit spaces in a query string. This substitution is one instance of *URL encoding*. However, some older browsers will send an explicit space (not URL-encoded) in a query string to the Web server. Some Web servers will then truncate the query string at the space, chopping off the rest of the data.

Notice in Figure 6.2 that the QUERY_STRING environment variable is empty (actually the empty string) because we called env.cgi using no query string. The reader is invited to call that CGI program again, but using a query string. You can then observe that your data made it to the Web server. You should experiment by putting some spaces and other weird symbols (*&^%$) into the query string and observing what happens. Newer browsers will automatically URL-encode the spaces, and perhaps some other symbols depending upon your browser.

When a URL request is made from a Web browser, the query string is passed into the server's QUERY_STRING environment variable and hence into the %ENV hash created within the program when it is executed. Within the environment hash, QUERY_STRING is the key used to access the actual query string. Thus, the query string can be easily retrieved by

```
$ENV{"QUERY_STRING"}
```

For example, using

```
print "Your query string is $ENV{"QUERY_STRING"}.\n";
```

in a CGI program similar to the one of Figure 6.4 would return just the query string to the browser.

We now provide an example that uses a query string to determine the output of a CGI program. The query string consists of a single positive integer. The program generates that many links, where the links are chosen randomly. The program is shown in Figure 6.5. Three example URL calls to the program are shown in Figure 6.6. Following is a top-down explanation of the program:

- The Web sites to which the links are to point are stored into a hash.
- The array of keys is extracted from the hash. Then the number of keys is stored in $maxnumber. We need that number, because we don't wish to allow a request for more Web sites than we have available.
- Print the top of the HTML page.
- If the query string is empty, print a short message and the rest of the page. Exit the program. (The QUERY_STRING variable contains the empty string if no data is sent to the program.)
- If we make it this far, the query string is not empty, and we store it into $number.
- If $number is not in the proper range, print a message and the rest of the page. Exit the program.
- If we make it here, $number is in the range from 1 to the number of Web sites in our hash. In other words, we have valid input for the program. So start an ordered HTML list for the links.
- Loop from 1 to the number of links we are to print.
  - Get the number of keys that are left.
  - Generate a random number from 0 to the number of keys left minus one. Extract the key with that index in the @keys array.
  - Print a list item containing a link using that key and its associated Web address.

```
#! /usr/bin/perl
print "Content-type: text/html\n\n";

%websites = (
    "amazon" => "www.amazon.com",
    "ebay" => "www.ebay.com",
    "etrade" => "www.etrade.com",
    "perl" => "www.perl.org",
    "apples" => "www.apples.com",
    "durians" => "www.durian.net",
    "oranges" => "www.oranges.com" );

@keys = keys %websites;        # extract array of keys for the web sites
$maxnumber = @keys;            # number of keys in the hash--same as ($#keys+1)
                               # also the largest number accepted in query string
print <<TOP;
<html>
<head>
<title>List of random Web sites</title>
</head>
<body>
TOP

if($ENV{"QUERY_STRING"} eq "") {
    print "<h1>Try attaching a positive integer as a query string.</h1>\n",
          "</body></html>\n";
    exit;
}

$number = $ENV{"QUERY_STRING"};
if(($number <1) || ($number > $maxnumber)) {
    print "<h1>Please use a number between 1 and $maxnumber.</h1>\n",
          "</body></html>\n";
    exit;
}

print "<h1>Here is a list of $number websites.</h1>\n";
print "<ol>\n";

for($i=1; $i<=$number; $i++) {
    $range = @keys;
    $randomIndex = int rand $range;
    $randomKey = $keys[$randomIndex];
    print "<li><a href=\"http://$websites{$randomKey}\">$randomKey</a></li>\n";

    splice @keys, $randomIndex, 1;      #remove used key from @keys array
}
print "</ol>\n";

print <<BOTTOM;
</body>
</html>
BOTTOM
```

FIGURE 6.5 A program whose output is determined by the value of the query string.

- Remove the key we just used from the @keys array. (Recall the splice function from Section 5.3.) So, next time through the loop, there is one less key available. Accordingly, the random number generated in the next pass of the loop selects an index position in the newly shortened @keys array. Note that removing a key from the @keys array has no effect on the %websites hash. It simply shortens the list of keys that are still available.
- Close the HTML list and print the rest of the page.

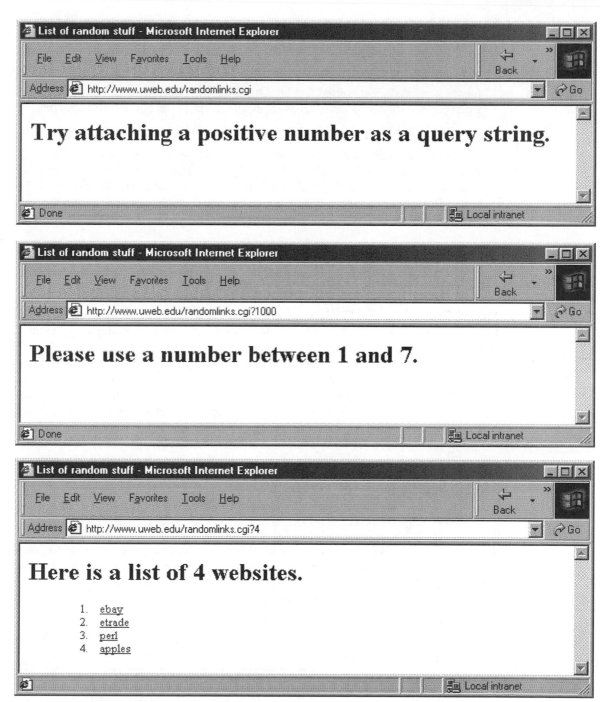

FIGURE 6.6 URL calls to the program of Figure 6.5 that send different query strings.

NOTE

Typing a URL with a query string into the address field of a browser is one example of manually sending data to a Web server. If you went to the Web site to execute this program (as we suggested), you noticed that links using different query strings were provided. Links provide another means to send data manually. Here is an example of such a link.

```
<a href="http://www.uweb.edu/randomlinks.cgi?5">give me five links</a>
```

In either case, manually sending data to the Web server means that the query string does not result from submission of an HTML form but is physically typed onto the end of a URL. As we shall see shortly, submission of an HTML form automatically constructs a query string for you so that you do not have to type it manually.

6.3 THE GET METHOD OF FORM SUBMISSION: DECODING THE QUERY STRING

We are now ready to use HTML forms to submit data to CGI programs on the server. In this section we consider only the text field and submit button form elements. A quick refresher on those form elements can be found in Section 3.1.

Consider the HTML form shown in Figure 6.7. Only the HTML tags responsible for defining the form and its elements are shown. You can assume that the form is part of a normal HTML file. Other HTML formatting tags (such as line breaks to put the form elements on separate lines) are also omitted. This is a practice we adopt so as not to clutter up the examples with HTML code. Only the form itself is necessary to understand the examples in most cases.

For this example, the form is to be submitted to someCGIprogram.cgi, which is fictitious. The submit method is specified as GET, so the data from the form will be sent to the program as a query string. The following query string is automatically created by the browser when the submit button is clicked.

```
name=Frodo+Baggins&email=frodo@shire.com
```

The data from the HTML form is formatted into name=value pairs, one pair for each named text field. The values are the data entered into the respective text fields by the user. If the user were to submit the form leaving both text fields blank (their initial state when this form is rendered), the following query string results.

```
name=&email=
```

```
Frodo Baggins              <form action="someCGIprogram.cgi" method="GET">
frodo@shire.com                <input type="text" name="name" value="" />
 Submit                        <input type="text" name="email" value="" />
                               <input type="submit" value="Submit" />
                           </form>
```

FIGURE 6.7   A form with two text fields and a submit button.

In both of the preceding cases, you can see that the name=value pairs are separated by an & character. In general, an encoded query string consists of a name=value pair for each named form element, and there could be many of them.

```
name1=value1&name2=value2&name3=value3 . . .
```

It is crucial that any form elements that are to be submitted have names. Otherwise, no name=value pair is submitted for the form element. Notice in Figure 6.7 that the submit button is not named. If it had been, a third (and useless in this case) name=value pair would have been part of the query string.

When a submit button is clicked, it calls a built-in method of the Browser Object that handles the form submission process. That method performs the encoding of the query string, but there is more to it than just forming the string of name=value pairs delimited with & characters. Additionally, space characters in the data are replaced with + characters. Recall the problem we discussed in Section 6.2 about spaces in query strings. When browsers construct query strings from form data, they replace blank spaces with + characters rather than the ASCII number for a space, as is the case with manually submitted query strings. (The ASCII number would work just as well, however.)

But how will the special characters used to structure the query string (=, &, +) be transmitted? For example, suppose that "frodo@barnes&noble.com" had been entered into the second text field of Figure 6.7. The name=value pairs would then not be well defined in the query string because of the presence of the extra delimiting character & in the user's data. The solution is that browsers URL-encode the special formatting characters that occur within the user data, but not the special symbols used to structure the query string.

For example, a query string such as

```
name=C%2B%2B+Programmer&email=frodo%40barnes%26noble.com
```

results from "C++ Programmer" and "frodo@barnes&noble.com" being submitted from the two text fields of Figure 6.7. Notice that the & character separating the name=value pairs was not URL-encoded, but the & character in the actual form data was encoded. Moreover, the two + characters in the data were URL-encoded, and the space was converted into a + character. That is absolutely necessary if special query string formatting symbols are to be differentiated from those that may appear in the actual data. Also note that the @ character is encoded in the query string just shown but not in the query shown for the data submitted in Figure 6.7. Such weird characters are encoded by some browsers and not by others. As a general rule, browsers ASCII-encode weird characters more often than not, but never the ones (&, =, +) needed to extract the name=value pairs once the data reaches the server.

As you have just seen, query strings full of ASCII numbers marked with % characters can get pretty ugly. The good news is that there is no need for you to memorize the ASCII codes for characters. It is important only that you are aware of the encoding and the steps necessary to decode the query string once you get hold of it in a CGI program. Even though it may be long and ugly, it is still stored as one string in the environment hash. Notationally, it is best to transfer it into a variable

```
$querystring = $ENV{"QUERY_STRING"};
```

```
$querystring = $ENV{"QUERY_STRING"};#first get it from the %ENV hash

@nameValuePairs = split(/&/, $querystring);                    #step 1

foreach $pair (@nameValuePairs) {
  ($name, $value) = split(/=/, $pair);                         #step 2

  $name =~tr/+/ /;                                             #step 3
  $name =~s/%([\da-fA-F]{2})/pack("C",hex($1))/eg;             #step 3
  $value =~tr/+/ /;                                            #step 3
  $value =~s/%([\da-fA-F]{2})/pack("C",hex($1))/eg;            #step 3

  $formHash{$name}=$value;                                     #step 4
}
```

FIGURE 6.8 The steps to decode a query string.

so that it can be manipulated easily. Now we need to break it apart, decode it, and store the parts somewhere. The natural solution is to form a hash from the name=value pairs, preserving the name=value relationships as the key-value pairs of the hash. We choose to name the hash will construct as %formHash.

The Perl code shown in Figure 6.8 constructs %formHash from the query string. Do not attempt to understand the code at this point; You will learn fully how it works in Chapter 11. In the meantime, consider what the code accomplishes in terms of decoding the query string. To that end, we give an explanation of the steps involved, rather than an explanation of the code itself.

Step 1: Split $querystring into an array at the & delimiters.

Step 2: For each name=value pair, split it at the = into the name part and the value part.

Step 3: For each $name and $value, convert the + symbols back into spaces and convert the ASCII numbers back into the characters they represent.

Step 4: Store the decoded $value into the hash with the decoded $name as the key.

For a concrete example, suppose a Web browser submits the following query string from a client:

```
$querystring = "address=123+Maple+Ave.&language=C%2B%2B";
```

The code in Figure 6.8 results in %formHash having a value of

```
("address"=> "123 Maple Ave.",
 "language"=> "C++")
```

where the address and language keys are the names of the text fields that were submitted, and their values contain the user's data.

NOTE

The code in Figure 6.8 looks daunting, but the steps are understandable. Until the code is explained in detail in Chapter 11, it is necessary only to copy the code verbatim into the top of any CGI program that gets its data through a GET transaction. A text file containing the code is available on this book's Web site so that you don't have to reproduce it by hand. Just keep in mind that decoding is not necessary if you construct query strings manually as we did in Section 6.2. It is the browser's form submit method that URL-encodes query strings as it assembles data from an HTML form for delivery to the server.

We conclude this section with a complete example that returns to the user a Web page that is customized based upon the user's input into an HTML form. The form shown in Figure 6.9 requests the user's name. The CGI program to which the form is submitted simply returns a personalized message.

Notice that the form is to be submitted to the program `personalMessage.cgi`. That would require the CGI program to be in the same directory as the HTML page, `nameForm.html`, that calls the CGI program. On many systems, CGI programs are required to be in a particular directory. In that case you will need the full (or relative) URL to the CGI program, in the same manner in which you would link to regular HTML pages. Figure 6.10 shows the `personalMessage.cgi` program.

Aside from the routine that decodes the query string, the program is very simple. It recovers the data entered into the text field by the user by using the proper key in `%formHash`. Of course, the name given to the text field in the HTML file is that key. Even though only one name=value pair is submitted to the program in this case, you can see that you will have to keep track of the names you give to HTML form elements so that you can access the data those elements pass to the server.

Figure 6.11 shows a sample submission of the form and the page returned by the `personalMessage.cgi` program. Especially notice the URLs shown in the browser windows. There are three files associated with this transaction: the HTML file containing the form, the CGI program, and the page returned to the browser window. The first two are sitting in the same directory—Uweb's root directory, in this example. The page that

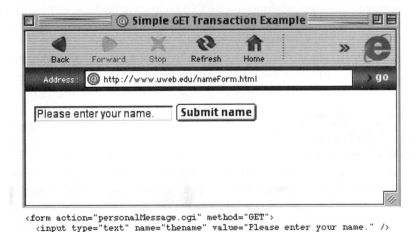

```
<form action="personalMessage.cgi" method="GET">
   <input type="text" name="thename" value="Please enter your name." />
   <input type="submit" value="Submit name" />
</form>
```

FIGURE 6.9   A form that requests the user's name.

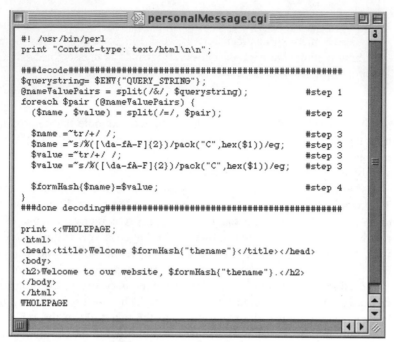

```
                         personalMessage.cgi

#! /usr/bin/perl
print "Content-type: text/html\n\n";

###decode###############################################
$querystring= $ENV{"QUERY_STRING"};
@nameValuePairs = split(/&/, $querystring);         #step 1
foreach $pair (@nameValuePairs) {
  ($name, $value) = split(/=/, $pair);              #step 2

  $name =~tr/+/ /;                                   #step 3
  $name =~s/%([\da-fA-F]{2})/pack("C",hex($1))/eg;   #step 3
  $value =~tr/+/ /;                                  #step 3
  $value =~s/%([\da-fA-F]{2})/pack("C",hex($1))/eg;  #step 3

  $formHash{$name}=$value;                           #step 4
}
###done decoding########################################

print <<WHOLEPAGE;
<html>
<head><title>Welcome $formHash{"thename"}</title></head>
<body>
<h2>Welcome to our website, $formHash{"thename"}.</h2>
</body>
</html>
WHOLEPAGE
```

FIGURE 6.10   The CGI program to which the form of Figure 6.9 submits its data.

was generated by the program "on the fly" and returned to the browser exists only in the browser's cache. The URL in the front window in Figure 6.11 points to the CGI program and contains the data necessary to cause the program to regenerate the same page as output.

You could in fact bookmark that URL (add it to your Favorites). Requesting that URL again a few seconds later or on another day would not pull up the same Web page, but a duplicate copy generated by the CGI program at the time of the URL request. In fact, you could manually change the value of the query string in the browser's address field and cause the CGI program to generate a new page based upon your manual input. In other words, once you have the URL with the query string, you can make a similar URL request, bypassing the form that made the initial request.

6.4 THE POST METHOD OF FORM SUBMISSION

The POST method of form data submission was explored in generality in Section 1.8. In this section we implement the POST method. As far as the HTML form goes, the submit method simply is changed from GET to POST:

```
<form action="someCGIprogram.cgi" method="POST" > . . . </form>
```

When a form is submitted to the server via POST, the form's data is not appended onto the URL in the packet header information as it is in a GET submission. Instead, the form's

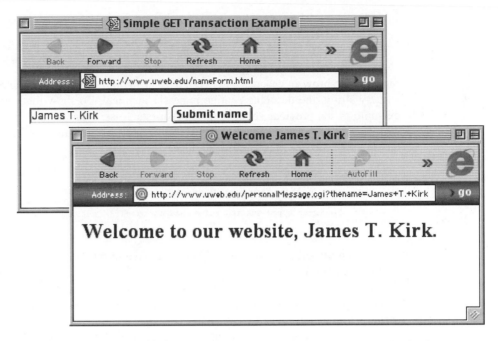

FIGURE 6.11   Before and after pictures when the form of Figure 6.9 is submitted.

data is part of the packet data. Thus, the form's data is not placed into one of the server's environment variables and, hence, not into the %ENV hash. Rather, it is delivered straight to the CGI program as standard input.

In Perl, standard input can be read with the `read` function as follows:

```
read(STDIN, $datastring, number of bytes to read);
```

This command's three arguments say to read a certain number of bytes from STDIN (standard input) and store it in the $*datastring* variable. Of course, the choice of the name of that variable is up to the programmer.

Even though the data comes through the program's standard input stream, it is still data from an HTML form. A Web browser's form submit method for POST is somewhat different from that for GET, but the form's data is still encoded into a string using =, &, and +. After all, the relationships of the names of the form's elements and their values must be preserved so that the information can be extracted on the server. In the context of a POST transaction, we call this the *data string*.

In most cases there is no way to know in advance how much data a user might enter into a form. The `read` function, however, needs to know the number of bytes it is to read from STDIN. Fortunately, this information is stored in the environment hash under the key CONTENT_LENGTH. The POSTed data is not sent in the packet headers, but the packet headers do have fields that say how much data the packets are carrying. So the length of the data string is recorded in the CONTENT_LENGTH environment variable and, hence, in the %ENV hash under that key. (In case you are wondering why the CONTENT_LENGTH environment variable did not appear in Section 6.1, where we listed "all" of the environment variables, CONTENT_LENGTH exists only during POST transactions.)

So, in a CGI program the data string is read from POSTed forms as follows:

```
read(STDIN, $datastring, $ENV{"CONTENT_LENGTH"});
```

Since a Web browser encodes a POSTed data string into exactly the same format as it does a query string, the decoding routine is nearly identical. To show that, we redo the main example of the previous section, which requests a user's name, and returns a Web page with a personalized greeting. The HTML form is nearly identical except for the changes rendered in boldface in the following display.

```
<form action="personalMessage2.cgi" method="POST">
    <input type="text" name="thename" value="Please enter your name." />
    <input type="submit" value="Submit name" />
</form>
```

Since the submission is now POST, we have to modify the CGI program that is to receive the data. We call the new program personalMessage2.cgi. The modified program is shown in Figure 6.12. Only the modified parts are rendered in boldface. Notice that the two changes are the method in which the program receives the data, and the name of the variable into which we store that data.

Figure 6.13 shows an example submission of the new form and the page that is returned. Of course, since we changed only the submission method, the appearance of the form and the page generated as output are identical to the ones shown in Figure 6.11. The

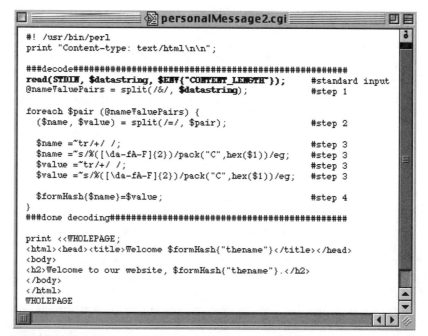

```
#! /usr/bin/perl
print "Content-type: text/html\n\n";

###decode#############################################
read(STDIN, $datastring, $ENV{"CONTENT_LENGTH"});      #standard input
@nameValuePairs = split(/&/, $datastring);             #step 1

foreach $pair (@nameValuePairs) {
  ($name, $value) = split(/=/, $pair);                 #step 2

  $name =~tr/+/ /;                                      #step 3
  $name =~s/%([\da-fA-F]{2})/pack("C",hex($1))/eg;      #step 3
  $value =~tr/+/ /;                                     #step 3
  $value =~s/%([\da-fA-F]{2})/pack("C",hex($1))/eg;     #step 3

  $formHash{$name}=$value;                              #step 4
}
###done decoding######################################

print <<WHOLEPAGE;
<html><head><title>Welcome $formHash{"thename"}</title></head>
<body>
<h2>Welcome to our website, $formHash{"thename"}.</h2>
</body>
</html>
WHOLEPAGE
```

FIGURE 6.12 The personal message program modified to accept data via the POST method.

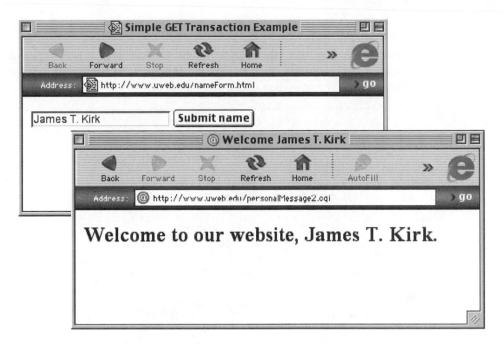

FIGURE 6.13 Before and after pictures when the form submitted using the POST method.

one visible difference is that the URL for the resulting page does not contain a query string. It would be impossible to cause the CGI program to regenerate the same Web page without resubmitting the form. In particular, there is no way to bookmark the data that was sent to the program or to send the data manually as a query string.

6.5 GET VS. POST

A natural question is how the method, GET or POST, should be chosen for submitting data from HTML forms. There is no concise answer to that question. Certain situations benefit more from one method than the other, but sometimes either suffices. Table 6.1 lists the common advantages and disadvantages of the two methods.

A Web programmer should choose the submission method based on the considerations set forth in Table 6.1. Because it is easier to debug using the GET method while a CGI program is in development, however, developers often use the GET method in development and then switch to POST once the final CGI product is finished. Thus, it is desirable to develop CGI programs that are capable of receiving data from both the GET and POST methods.

Furthermore, there will be many times when we encounter a programming error that is difficult to find. In these cases, an excellent technique is to run the Perl program offline, because the error messages are much more useful in that case, especially when warnings are enabled. But for that to be effective, we need an efficient way of setting test values for the input to the program to help narrow down the error. A nice solution is to have our Perl program automatically detect whether it is being run offline. If so, the program will prompt the user for keyboard data.

A solution that meets all three needs is to test whether GET or POST is being used. If neither is being used, the program defaults to accepting keyboard input in the local setting. We can ascertain the submission method simply by checking the environment hash value corresponding to the REQUEST_METHOD environment variable. Figure 6.14 shows the top of a CGI program that implements these ideas.

```perl
#! /usr/bin/perl
print "Content-type: text/html\n\n";

if ($ENV{"REQUEST_METHOD"} eq "POST") {
  read(STDIN, $datastring, $ENV{"CONTENT_LENGTH"});
}
elsif (exists $ENV{"REQUEST_METHOD"}) {
  $datastring = $ENV{"QUERY_STRING"};
}
else {
  print "Offline execution detected\n";
  print "Please enter some data.\n";
  $datastring = <>;
  chomp $datastring;
  print "== data accepted == HTML output follows ==\n\n";
}

###decode#########################################################
@nameValuePairs = split(/&/, $datastring);              #step 1
foreach $pair (@nameValuePairs) {
  ($name, $value) = split(/=/, $pair);                  #step 2
  $name =~tr/+/ /;                                       #step 3
  $name =~s/%([\da-fA-F]{2})/pack("C",hex($1))/eg;       #step 3
  $value =~tr/+/ /;                                      #step 3
  $value =~s/%([\da-fA-F]{2})/pack("C",hex($1))/eg;      #step 3
  $formHash{$name}=$value;                               #step 4
}
###done decoding##################################################

#################################################################
# %formHash is at your disposal for the rest of                 #
# the program regardless of the input method                    #
#################################################################
```

FIGURE 6.14 The steps to decode a query string.

TABLE 6.1 Comparison of GET and POST Methods

GET	POST
The query string is part of the URL so the resulting Web page, whose content depends upon that information, can be bookmarked. For the same reason, you can make links in a Web page that manually send data to a CGI program using a query string.	The data is not sent as part of the URL, so the resulting page can't be bookmarked. It is also more difficult to send data to a CGI program using a link. (You need JavaScript support for that.)
The query string is visible. That's not good when sending sensitive data, such as passwords. Visited URLs are usually saved in the browser's history list.	The path to the CGI program is saved in the browser's history list, but the data is not. That's obviously good when sending sensitive data.
Visible data in the query string is good for debugging purposes. You can readily see what is being passed to the server-side program.	It can be hard to debug a CGI program when you can't see what is being sent to it.
There is usually a limit to the length of a query string, imposed by the limit on the total length of a URL.	With no limitations imposed by the length of a URL, large amounts of data can be submitted to the server.

If a CGI program is on a Web server and is being executed by a browser request, GET or POST are the only possibilities. In that case, the first two expressions in the conditional will store either the POSTed data or the query string into the `$datastring` variable. Otherwise, the program is being executed offline. In that case, no `%ENV` hash is passed to the program and the first two expressions in the conditional are inherently false—requests for the nonexistent hash values evaluate to the empty string. The program then requests standard keyboard input. (Recall Section 4.6.) Finally, the program decodes the string stored in `$datastring`, as we are accustomed.

NOTE

You might wonder why, in Figure 6.14, we did not just do

```
elsif ($ENV{"REQUEST_METHOD"} eq "GET") {
```

instead of testing for the existence of the request method. The reason is that we wish our code to be as flexible as possible. Recall from the last paragraph of Section 1.8 that special network applications, such as Web crawlers, use a third type of HTTP request, namely HEAD, to index the Web. If we were to include the above code for the second clause in the conditional, a Web crawler that stumbled upon the program would cause the `else` clause to execute, leaving the program waiting for keyboard input. Eventually, the operating system would likely kill the process, but this is certainly not desirable behavior. In the solution we presented in Figure 6.14, a HEAD request would be treated as a GET request, resulting in an empty query string and a useless Web page returned to the Web crawler.

Many CGI programs obtain data from online submission of HTML forms. (There are uses for CGI programs that accept manually constructed query strings. One such use is given as an exercise.) Unless you tamper with it using JavaScript, HTML form data is always encoded into name=value pairs just like a query string. Even though no query string is used in a POST transaction, the data is still encoded as if it were a query string. That's why the one decoding routine works for both GET and POST. Just keep in mind that if you choose to run a program offline for debugging purposes using the code of Figure 6.14, you will need to simulate the standard query string encoding in your test data. It is usually not necessary to URL-encode characters in that case.

NOTE

The code in Figure 6.14 is so ubiquitous that you should make a skeleton file, with a name such as `skeleton.pl`, with this code at its top. The code is available on this book's Web site. It is not advisable to type this code in by hand, because a small error will give you headaches. Just copy and paste from (or copy) the skeleton file whenever you write a new program. You could keep one skeleton around for GET and one for POST, but one that covers all cases is advantageous. For the remainder of our examples we will omit this code and just indicate its place in the program.

6.6 DYNAMIC WEB APPLICATIONS

In this section we first present an example Web application that is inherently nondynamic. (Sounds like a cop-out, huh?) Then we rework the example so that the application becomes dynamically generated from data on the back end. Figure 6.15 shows a Web page containing an HTML form for taking an online food order. (Admittedly, we should sell less perishable items over the Internet.) The user can enter the quantity of each food item desired. Only the HTML code for the form is provided.

The form is to be submitted to the CGI program `food.cgi`. Figure 6.16 shows a sample submission of the form, and Figure 6.17 shows the CGI program. All the CGI program does is to summarize the order, giving a total for each item and a grand total. The basic outline for the program is as follows:

- The quantity of each item is multiplied by its price. Remember, the name of a text field is used to reference its submitted value. For example, `%formHash{"cheeseburger"}` contains the value 2.
- The `sprintf` function (recall Section 4.7) is used, so the item totals are stored formatted for two decimal places. This is just a cosmetic enhancement for the output.
- The total for the whole order is calculated and formatted with two decimal places.
- The order is summarized in an HTML table. A table row is printed to summarize each item, and a final table row is printed for the order total.

NOTE

This example has a major limitation. The form is stored in `food.html`, an ordinary HTML file. The program that handles the submitted data is in a separate file, `food.cgi`. If we ever wanted to add or delete food items or change the price of an item, we would have to edit both the HTML file and the CGI program in several places. We would certainly have to be careful that all names and prices are updated to be consistent in both files.

The key to making this application dynamic is that the food items and prices should be stored as a single data source on the server. Both the HTML form and the summary returned to the user should be generated based upon the current items and prices in the data source. If that single data source is updated, both the HTML form and the user summary automatically adjust to the changes, because they draw from the common source. That is the main notion of this section. A dynamic Web application is one in which the front and back ends dynamically adjust according to a common data source.

Now let's move on to the improved version. We are not yet ready to discuss structured data sources on the server, which are stored in separate files or databases, so we use a hash as the data source for the food items and corresponding prices. Both the Web page containing the HTML and the Web page summarizing the user's order are generated by looping over this hash. Moreover, we generate both Web pages using only one CGI program, which we name `food2.cgi`. The data hash for the food items simply is defined within that program. If we were to use two programs, the data hash would need to be defined in each program, and our desire for a unified data source would be defeated. With only one data source, we never have to worry about consistencies in food items or prices!

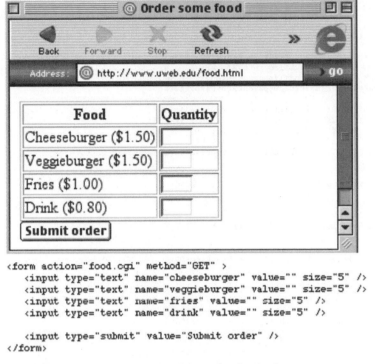

```
<form action="food.cgi" method="GET" >
    <input type="text" name="cheeseburger" value="" size="5" />
    <input type="text" name="veggieburger" value="" size="5" />
    <input type="text" name="fries" value="" size="5" />
    <input type="text" name="drink" value="" size="5" />

    <input type="submit" value="Submit order" />
</form>
```

FIGURE 6.15 A Web page containing a food order form.

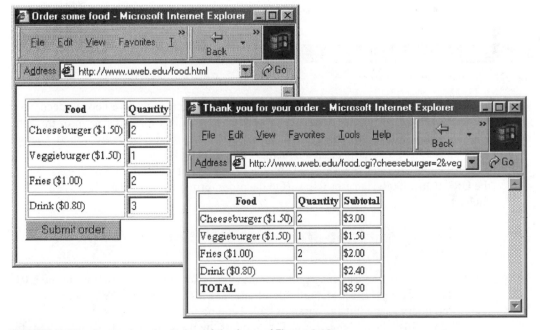

FIGURE 6.16 A sample submission of the form of Figure 6.16.

```
 food.cgi
#! /usr/bin/perl
print "Content-type: text/html\n\n";

############################################################
#    code for decoding input $datastring into %formHash    #
#        (works for GET, POST, and offline execution)       #
############################################################

$cheesetotal = sprintf "%.2f", $formHash{"cheeseburger"}*1.50;
$veggietotal = sprintf "%.2f", $formHash{"veggieburger"}*1.50;
$friestotal = sprintf "%.2f", $formHash{"fries"}*1.00;
$drinktotal = sprintf "%.2f", $formHash{"drink"}*0.80;
$totalCost = sprintf "%.2f", $cheesetotal+$veggietotal+$friestotal+$drinktotal;

print <<WHOLEPAGE;
<html><head><title>Thank you for your order</title></head>
<body>
<table border="1">
  <tr>
    <th>Food</th><th>Quantity</th><th>Subtotal</th>
  </tr>
  <tr>
    <td>Cheeseburger (\$1.50)</td><td>$formHash{"cheeseburger"}</td><td>\$$cheesetotal</td>
  </tr>
  <tr>
    <td>Veggieburger (\$1.50)</td><td>$formHash{"veggieburger"}</td><td>\$$veggietotal</td>
  </tr>
  <tr>
    <td>Fries (\$1.00)</td><td>$formHash{"fries"}</td><td>\$$friestotal</td>
  </tr>
  <tr>
    <td>Drink (\$0.80)</td><td>$formHash{"drink"}</td><td>\$$drinktotal</td>
  </tr>
  <tr>
    <td colspan="2"><b>TOTAL</b></td><td>\$$totalCost</td>
  </tr>
</table>

</body></html>
WHOLEPAGE
```

FIGURE 6.17 The source code for `food.cgi`.

Since one CGI program is used to generate both Web pages, we need a mechanism in place so that the CGI program knows whether to print out the order form or the summary. It's clear that the user's data is submitted when the food form is submitted. Using a GET transaction, that means that a nonempty query string is necessarily submitted.

In contrast, when the user pulls up the order form, there will be no query string on the URL. Most likely, the user will surf to the order form by clicking an advertisement link such as

```
<a href="http://www.uweb.edu/food2.cgi">order snacks to go from the campus
snack shop</a>
```

Alternatively, the user may pull up a previously set bookmark pointing to the URL, or maybe `food2.cgi` is the default file at `www.snacksgalore.com`. Whatever the case, there is no query string if the program is called and no form data is present.

Figure 6.18 shows `food2.cgi`. The logic of the program is quite simple. First, the data hash for the food items is defined. If the query string is empty, call a function that

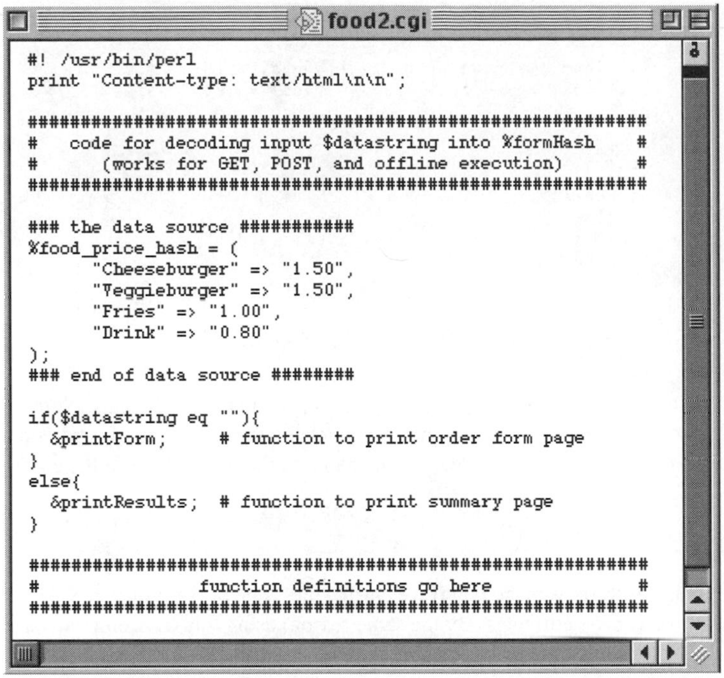

```
#! /usr/bin/perl
print "Content-type: text/html\n\n";

############################################################
#   code for decoding input $datastring into %formHash    #
#       (works for GET, POST, and offline execution)       #
############################################################

### the data source ###########
%food_price_hash = (
     "Cheeseburger" => "1.50",
     "Veggieburger" => "1.50",
     "Fries" => "1.00",
     "Drink" => "0.80"
);
### end of data source ########

if($datastring eq ""){
  &printForm;     # function to print order form page
}
else{
  &printResults;  # function to print summary page
}

############################################################
#               function definitions go here               #
############################################################
```

FIGURE 6.18 The dynamic version of the food order program.

prints out the food order form. Otherwise, call a function to print out an order summary. Recall that the $datastring variable (see Figure 6.14) contains the query string.

NOTE

The data source for this program is stored in a hash that is manually initialized within the program. For simplicity, we use manually initialized arrays and hashes for server-side data sources throughout this chapter. Another option, and better in many circumstances, is to keep the information in separate data files and read it into the programs. Many of the homework exercises for this chapter feature that approach.

Of course, the functions do most of the work for this program. We show the two functions next, with a brief outline following each function.

```
sub printForm {
  print<<TOP;
  <html><head><title>Order some food</title></head>
  <body>
    <form action="$ENV{'SCRIPT_NAME'}" method="GET"> # submit to same program!
    <table border="1">
      <tr><th>Food</th><th>Quantity</th></tr>
TOP

  foreach $food (keys %food_price_hash) {
```

```
  print<<ITEM;
  <tr>
    <td>$food (\$$food_price_hash{$food})</td>
    <td><input type="text" name="$food" value="" size="5"/></td>
  </tr>
ITEM
}

  print<<BOTTOM;
    </table>
    <input type="submit" value="Submit order"/>
    </form>
  </body>
</html>
BOTTOM
}
```

- Print the top of the page, including the form and table start tags. Note that the form gets submitted to the same program that generates the form! Instead of hard-coding the program name into the action attribute, we get the name of the program from the environment variable

```
$ENV{"SCRIPT_NAME"}
```

This has the advantage that if we change the name of the program, we do not have to change all of the action attributes. By the same reason, using this environment variable makes such code fully reusable in another program without any changes. From now on, we always use this technique when a program calls itself, either from a form or a link.

- For each $food key in the data hash

  - Print a table row. The first column contains the $food and its price, which is the corresponding value in the data hash. The second column contains a text field whose name is the $food key.

- Print the bottom of the page, including the closing table and form tags.

```
sub printResults {
  print <<TOP;
<html><head><title>Thank you for your order</title></head>
  <body>
    <table border="1">
    <tr><th>Food</th><th>Quantity</th><th>Subtotal</th></tr>
TOP

  $total=0;
  foreach $food (keys %food_price_hash) {
    $subtotal = sprintf "%.2f", $food_price_hash{$food}*$formHash{$food};
    $total = $total + $subtotal;
    print<<ITEM;
    <tr>
      <td>$food (\$$food_price_hash{$food})</td>
      <td align="right">$formHash{$food}</td><td align="right">\$$subtotal</td>
    </tr>
ITEM
  }

  $total = sprintf "%.2f", $total;
  print<<BOTTOM
    <tr>
    <td colspan="2"><b>TOTAL</td><td align="right">\$$total</td>
```

```
   </tr>
   </table>
  </body>
 </html>
BOTTOM
}
```

■ Print the top of the page, including the beginning of the table that summarizes the user's order.

■ For each `$food` key in the data hash

   ■ Store a subtotal for the `$food`. Note that the price of the `$food` is the value in the data hash, but the number of `$food` the user has ordered is the value in `%formhash`, which comes from decoding the query string. The two hashes share common keys.

   ■ Add the subtotal to the total counter.

   ■ Print a table row. The first column contains the `$food` and its price. The second column contains the (nicely formatted) subtotal for `$food`.

■ Print the bottom of the page, including the last row of the table, containing the order total and the closing table tag.

Figure 6.19 shows a typical execution of the program. The first URL, with no query string, has caused `food2.cgi` to output the order form, and the second URL, with the user's data, has caused `food2.cgi` to output the summary table. We re-emphasize the dynamic nature of this application. Any change to the data hash will change both pages next time the program is called upon. Double the number of food items in the hash, and both the order form and the summary table will be doubled in size. Now think about what you would have to do manually to double the number of food items in both files in the first, nondynamic version of this example!

NOTE

One easily could overlook the glue that holds this example together. The names given to the text fields in the HTML form are the keys of the data hash, `%food_price_hash`. When the form is submitted, those are then the names in the name=value pairs in the query string. Thus the keys of the data hash become the keys of the `%formHash` when the query string is decoded.

So the two hashes are "parallel" in a sense. For a given key, the value in the data hash, `%food_price_hash`, is the price from the server-side data source, and the value in the `%formHash` is the order quantity from the client-side data. We have created a relationship between the client-side and server-side data submitted by the user.

You can now see that the testing-the-query-string "trick" we used to consolidate the example into one program is actually less important conceptually than the technique used to generate the form dynamically, while providing a relationship between the server-side data source and the data collected on the client. In fact, several techniques could be used to separate the example into two programs: One way is to store the data hash in an auxiliary

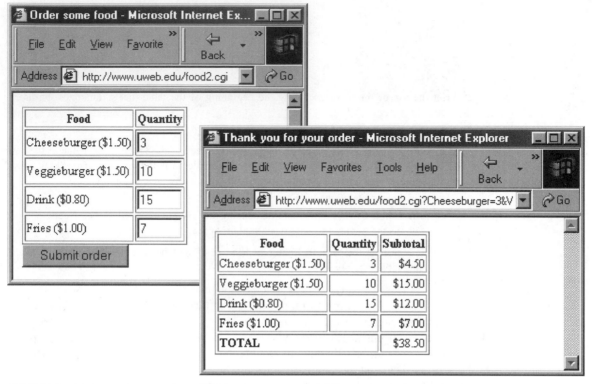

FIGURE 6.19   A sample execution of the food application of Figure 6.18.

text file and simply import the data into the top of two programs: one to dynamically generate the form and the other to summarize the order. That two-program solution would be nearly identical to our current solution, except without the query string trick.

There are advantages to consolidating into one CGI program, however. There are times when we wish to generate the form as part of the output page to let the user "go again" if desired. Also, there will be times when the form generating subroutine and the processing subroutine share common tasks. In that case, it is much more efficient to separate those common tasks into further subroutines within the same program.

We conclude this section with the observation that the food items were returned to both output pages in Figure 6.19 in a different order than we entered them into the hash. As we discussed in Lesson 4, the `keys` function applied to a hash returns the list of keys in some unpredictable order. If all we require is alphabetical order, then doing

```
foreach $food (sort keys %food_price_hash)
```

would suffice nicely each time we iterate over the food items. If we really wanted to enforce a specific ordering for the foods, it would be necessary to create another array, say

```
@sorted_foods = ("Cheeseburger", "Veggieburger", "Fries", "Drink");
```

as part of the server-side data source. Then we would simply iterate over this array,

```
foreach $food (@sorted_foods)
```

rather than the array of keys returned by the `keys` function.

> **NOTE**
>
> The method we used to test the query string to determine which page is printed works equally well for POST transactions and offline executions. The `$datastring` is used in Figure 6.14 to store input to the program, regardless of the input method. That is important if we want to switch `food2.cgi` to POST to hide the data or need to run it offline for diagnostic purposes.

6.7 UNDERSTANDING ERRORS IN THE CLIENT-SERVER ENVIRONMENT

Now that you have seen several substantive CGI programs (and are coming dangerously close to having to write one of your own), we provide some perspective into the types of errors you may encounter and how you might diagnose them. In this section we provide three diagnostic examples. We have been preaching all along about the benefits of offline execution of programs and of enabling warnings. Now it's time to back up the sermon.

Diagnostic Example 1

Suppose we purposely create a syntax error in the `food2.cgi` program of Figure 6.18 by removing the closing brace from the `if` part of the conditional.

```
if ($datastring ""){
   &printForm;          # function to print order form page
else {
   &printResults;       # function to print summary page
}
```

We name the new erroneous program as `food3.cgi`.

If we try to run this CGI program by a URL request through the Web, we would see a result similar to that shown in Figure 6.20. The actual error message varies with the Web server software being used. When a CGI program "crashes," it sends its error message to the Web server software; you never see it. The Web server still has to complete the current HTTP transaction by returning some kind of Web page to the browser. Typically, the returned Web page has a very generic and nondiagnostic error notification, to say the least.

More information can be obtained by running the program offline. If your program contains the code from Section 6.5 that handles GET, POST, and offline execution, altering the program for that purpose is not necessary. Figure 6.21 is a snapshot of a command-line execution of the program through a UNIX window.

FIGURE 6.20 A typical error message returned by a Web server when a CGI program crashes during execution.

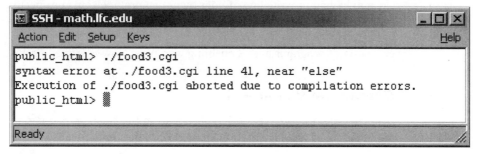

FIGURE 6.21 A typical error message when a Perl CGI program is run offline.

A very similar error message is generated if the program is run offline using MacPerl or a Windows DOS prompt. The error message suggests that we should look near the keyword `else` on line 41. And, as any experienced programmer should know, one should always look at the mentioned line and the lines above it. Following this advice, we quickly see that the line immediately above is missing a closing brace.

Diagnostic Example 2

Suppose we now go back to `food2.cgi` and create a logic error on purpose by changing the line in the `printResults` function from

```
$subtotal = sprintf "%.2f", $food_price_hash{$food}*$formHash{$food};
```

to

```
$subtotal = sprintf "%.2f", $food_price_hash{$food}/$formHash{$food};
```

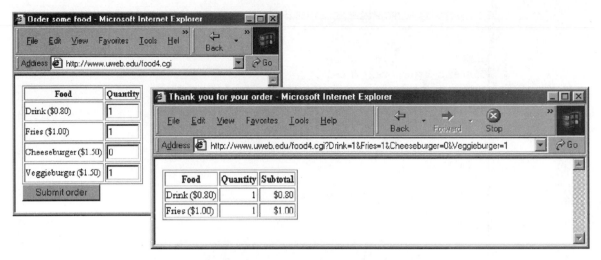

FIGURE 6.22 Partial results returned from a CGI program because of a logic error.

so that division is used instead of multiplication. We name this new program file `food4.cgi`. Logic errors are different from syntax errors, because syntax errors will almost always crash a program, whereas logic errors may or may not crash a program. Depending on the input, you may not even notice the error at first. For example, if we entered 1 for the quantity of each food item, then we would actually get the correct result using `food4.cgi`! However, if a vegetarian enters the data shown in Figure 6.22, a surprising summary page is generated.

The CGI program did not crash and cause the server to send back a generic error notification Web page. Rather, it looks like the CGI program terminated in the middle of the output of the order summary. That can be confirmed by viewing the HTML source code (using the browser's View menu) that was returned to the browser. Once again, more information can be obtained by running the program offline and the capability of our program to detect its being run offline comes in handy. Figure 6.23 shows an offline execution of `food4.cgi`.

Notice that when prompted to "Please enter a querystring.", we typed in

```
Drink=1&Fries=1&Cheeseburger=1&Veggieburger=1
```

by hand. We then realized that we could have copied the query string from the Web browser window shown in Figure 6.22 and pasted it in at the prompt. (Oh, well.) One of the advantages of using the GET method while a CGI program is in development is being able to copy and paste (or type,) the query string for offline diagnostic purposes. The resulting information, namely the part that says "Illegal division by zero at . . . ", points out the logic error. Looking at the HTML code the program spits out can help sometimes, too.

Diagnostic Example 3

For our last diagnostic example, suppose we defined the data hash for the food program incorrectly, using the scalar variable symbol $ instead of the hash symbol %.

```
$food_price_hash = (
  "Cheeseburger" => "1.50", . . .
```

```
SSH - math.lfc.edu                                    _ □ ✕
 Action  Edit  Setup  Keys                             Help

public_html> ./food4.cgi
Content-type: text/html

Offline execution detected
Please enter a querystring.
Drink=1&Fries=1&Cheeseburge=0&Veggieburger=1
== querystring accepted == HTML output follows ==
<html>
<head>
<title>Thank you for your order</title>
</head>
<body>

  <table border="1">
   <tr><th>Food</th><th>Quantity</th><th>Subtotal</th></tr>
    <tr>
    <td>Drink ($0.80)</td>
    <td align="right">1</td><td align="right">$0.80</td>
   </tr>
    <tr>
    <td>Fries ($1.00)</td>
    <td align="right">1</td><td align="right">$1.00</td>
   </tr>
Illegal division by zero at ./food4.cgi line 93, <> chunk 1.
public_html> █

 Ready
```

FIGURE 6.23 Entering a query string during an offline execution.

We name the new program file food5.cgi. This kind of error would become evident fairly early in the development stage, because we would test the printForm function first. One should always test a program at various development stages. With the printForm function completed, we do an offline run to see whether there are any syntax errors that crash the program. Figure 6.24 shows the result.

Since we were testing the function that gets called when the query string ($datastring) is empty, we simply hit Enter when prompted for data. There were no error messages from the Perl interpreter, and the HTML output was printed. The problem is that only the first row of the table was printed. No table rows for the food items are present. If we had been testing the program via the Web, we would have seen the following.

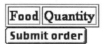

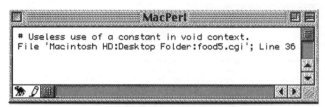

```
                        MacPerl
  Content-type: text/html

  Offline execution detected
  Please enter some data.

  == data accepted == HTML output follows ==

  <html>
   <head>
    <title>Order some food</title>
   </head>
   <body>
    <form action="test.cgi" method="GET"/>
    <table border="1">
     <tr><th>Food</th><th>Quantity</th></tr>
    </table>
    <input type="submit" value="Submit order"/>
   </form>
   </body>
  </html>
```

FIGURE 6.24   Offline execution of the erroneous `food5.cgi`

```
                        MacPerl
  # Useless use of a constant in void context.
  File 'Macintosh HD:Desktop Folder:food5.cgi'; Line 36
```

FIGURE 6.25   A warning message.

The problem seems be with the loop that prints the table rows. Apparently it didn't execute even once. So we go back and examine the loop with a fine-tooth comb. It seems fine. Hmmm.

We then remember that we forgot to enable warnings in the local environment. Even though the program didn't crash the Perl interpreter and didn't cause a syntax error, a warning message might save the day. Indeed, Figure 6.25 shows the warning message. It's not immediately clear what the warning is saying to us, but it points to a line number in the declaration of `$food_price_hash`. Seeing the mistake now, we replace the `$` character with the hash symbol `%`.

6.8 PROCESSING CHECKBOXES AND RADIO BUTTONS

In this section we explore the processing of user choices. A quick refresher on the HTML markup and basic functionality of checkboxes and radio buttons can be found in Section 3.1.

The main example of this section contrasts the functionalities of checkboxes and radio buttons and shows how to deal with the data submitted to the server by these two mechanisms for obtaining user choices. The example features a pizza order form on which the user can order a personalized pizza. To help you understand its nature, Figure 6.26 shows an example execution the of the CGI program. The program processes the user's choices and returns a Web page summarizing the pizza order. As an aid for the discussion that is to follow, the figure also shows the essential code for the dynamically generated HTML form.

```
<form action="pizza.cgi" method="GET">
  <input type="radio" name="chosen_size" value="large" /> <b>large</b> . . . <hr/>
  <input type="radio" name="chosen_size" value="medium" checked="checked" /> <b>medium</b> . . .<hr/>
  <input type="radio" name="chosen_size" value="small" /> <b>small</b> . . . <hr/>

  <input type="checkbox" name="m_pepperoni" value="yes" />Pepperoni<br/>
  <input type="checkbox" name="m_sausage" value="yes" />Italian Sausage<br/>
  <input type="checkbox" name="v_peppers" value="yes" />Green Bell Peppers<br/>
  <input type="checkbox" name="v_mushrooms" value="yes" />Mushrooms<br/>
  <input type="checkbox" name="v_onions" value="yes" />Vidallia Onions<br/>
  <input type="checkbox" name="v_olives" value="yes" />Black Olives<br/>

  <input type="submit" value="Submit order"/>
</form>
```

FIGURE 6.26 An execution of a Web application that features user choices.

A *unique-selection group* of radio buttons is used for the choice of the pizza's size. Thus, all of the three radio buttons share the same name. Note that the radio button for "medium" is set to be checked by default when the form first loads. A group of checkboxes is used to provide selections for extra ingredients. Any number of the checkboxes can be checked at a given time. That illustrates the difference between the functionality of radio buttons and that of checkboxes. The user must choose exactly one pizza size but may choose as many toppings as desired, or even none.

This application is dynamically generated, meaning that a server-side data source determines the elements that get marked up in the HTML form and the values used to process the form's submitted data. A combination of arrays and hashes is used to store the back-end data source. One CGI program generates both the form page and the order summary page. Figure 6.27 shows the outline of the pizza.cgi program.

The outline of pizza.cgi is very similar to that of the dynamically generated example of Section 6.6. The back-end data is initialized, and then two functions print either the order form page or the order summary page, depending upon whether the program is called with no input data.

As for the data, the pizza sizes are stored into an array. A default pizza size is then set into $default_size, which will be used to set which of the radio buttons is initially checked.

```perl
#! /usr/bin/perl
print "Content-type: text/html\n\n";

###############################################################
#    code for decoding input $datastring into %formHash      #
#       (works for GET, POST, and offline execution)          #
###############################################################

### the data source ##################
@sizes = ("large", "medium", "small");
$default_size="medium";

%size_prices = (
   "large"  => "8.00",
   "medium" => "6.00",
   "small"  => "4.00"
);

%topping_prices = (
   "large"  => "1.00",
   "medium" => "0.75",
   "small"  => "0.50"
);

%toppings = (
   "m_pepperoni" => "Pepperoni",
   "m_sausage" => "Italian Sausage",
   "v_peppers" => "Green Bell Peppers",
   "v_mushrooms" => "Mushrooms",
   "v_onions" => "Vidallia Onions",
   "v_olives" => "Black Olives"
);
### end of data source ###############

if($datastring eq "") {
   &printForm;     # function to print order form page
}
else {
   &processForm;   # function to print summary page
}

###############################################################
#                function definitions go here                #
###############################################################
```

FIGURE 6.27   The outline of the program that dynamically generates the pizza order application.

The keys of the next two hashes are the same as the size values of the `@sizes` array. For a given size, those hashes contain the base price of the pizza and the cost per topping for that size pizza. Finally, the `%toppings` hash keys are symbolic names for the various toppings, and the associated values are the actual topping descriptions. Note that the `%toppings` keys are named in such a way that when they are extracted into an array (in an unpredictable order) using the `keys` function, they can be sorted alphabetically and the meat toppings will be listed first. (It's conventional to list meat toppings first, especially at a carnivore convention!)

With a feel for the back-end data source in place, we turn to the function that prints the order form. It is provided below, followed by an overview. The `printForm` function generates the form exactly as you see it in Figure 6.26, minus all the table tags. Note that single-quoted strings are used when lots of HTML attributes are printed to avoid escaping all of the quotes that surround the attributes.

```perl
sub printForm {
  print<<TOP;
<html><head><title>Personalize a pizza</title></head>
<body>
  <form action="$ENV{'SCRIPT_NAME'}" method="GET" >
  <table border="1">
    <tr><th>Select size</th><th>Select ingredients</th></tr>
    <tr><td>
TOP

  foreach $size (@sizes){
    print '<input type="radio" name="chosen_size" value="', $size, '"';

    if($size eq $default_size){
      print ' checked="checked"';
    }

    print " /><b>$size</b> <br/>Base Price: \$$size_prices{$size} <br/>",
      "Each Topping: \$$topping_prices{$size}<hr/>\n";
  }
  print " </td><td>\n";

  foreach $topping (sort keys %toppings) {
    print '<input type="checkbox" name="',$topping, '" value="yes" />',
      "$toppings{$topping}<br/>\n";
  }

  print<<BOTTOM;
    </tr>
    </table>
    <input type="submit" value="Submit order"/>
    </form>
  </body>
</html>
BOTTOM
}
```

▧ Print the top of the page, including the beginning tags for the form and the table that formats the form. At the end of this print block, we start a new table row and then a table cell, to contain the radio buttons.

▧ For each `$size` in the pizza `@sizes` array

  ▧ Begin a radio button. The printed result is

```
<input type="radio" name="chosen_size" value="$size"
```

    where `$size` is determined by the particular pass of the loop. The same name is given to each button so that they have the unique-selection property.

    ▧ If the current pass of the loop corresponds to the default size that is to be checked, add `checked="checked"` to the radio button.

    ▧ Print the closing `/>` for the HTML input element and then a textual description for the price information for that `$size`.

▧ Close the table cell and start the new one for the checkboxes.

▧ For each `$topping` key in the `%toppings` hash

  ▧ Print a checkbox whose name is the `$topping` key. (The values are unimportant, so we just set them to `yes`.) The textual description of the particular `$topping` key is retrieved from the `%toppings` hash.

▧ Close the table cell, row, the whole table, and the form. Print the closing HTML tags for the page.

It is important to understand how the HTML form and submitted data relates to the server-side data source. When the form is submitted with the user choices as shown in Figure 6.26, the following query string results.

```
chosen_size=large&m_pepperoni=yes&m_sausage=yes&v_mushrooms=yes
```

This shows the four name=value pairs that are stored into `%formHash` as keys and values when the query string is decoded.

The names of the radio buttons are all the same (unique-selection property), and their value attributes have been set with the values of the `@sizes` array. So the value in

```
chosen_size=value
```

will be one of the elements of the `@sizes` array. Moreover, there will be only one such `chosen_size=`value pair submitted to the server, because of the unique-selection property. We can easily recover that single size choice,

```
%formHash{"chosen_size"}
```

from the submitted group of radio buttons.

On the other hand, the names of the checkboxes are all different, being set with the keys of the `%toppings` hash. You don't know how many of the toppings will be returned, if any. But if a topping was selected, then a name=`yes` pair for that topping is part of the query string. Thus, `%formHash` contains an entry for a given topping if and only if the topping was selected. To test which toppings the user has chosen, we loop over all the `%toppings` keys (potential submitted names in the name=`yes` pairs) seeing whether they exist in `%formhash`.

We could have omitted value attributes in the checkboxes, because we don't use them. In that case the query string would look like the following.

```
chosen_size=large&m_pepperoni=&v_sausage=&v_mushrooms=
```

Without complete name=value pairs, that looks quite funny, but it would work just fine. Our arbitrary choice of `yes` at least indicates affirmatively that a given topping was chosen.

The ideas from the foregoing above are implemented in the following `processForm` function, followed by an overview. This section then concludes with two notes that emphasize some important concepts.

```perl
sub processForm {
  print <<TOP;
  <html><head><title>Thank you for choosing your pizza</title></head>
  <body>
TOP

    $size = $formHash{"chosen_size"};
    $total=$size_prices{$size};

    print "You have selected a $size pizza "
    print "with the following extra ingredients:\n<ul>";
```

```
    foreach $topping (sort keys %toppings) {
      if(exists $formHash{$topping}) {
        $total = $total + $topping_prices{$size};
        print "<li>$toppings{$topping}</li>\n";
      }
    }
    print "</ul>\n";

    $total = sprintf "%.2f", $total;
    print "for a total of \$$total.\n";

    print<<BOTTOM
  </body>
</html>
BOTTOM
}
```

- ■ Print the top of the page.
- ■ Store the pizza $size chosen by the user. Then $size is an element of the @sizes array, and hence a key of %size_prices and %topping_prices hashes.
- ■ Add the base price from %size_prices for that $size onto the total.
- ■ Print a message and start an unordered list.
- ■ For each $topping key
  - ■ If $topping exists as a key in %formhash (that is, a checkbox name corresponding to $topping was returned), then add the price of the topping (as determined by the $size of the pizza in %topping_prices) to the total and print out a list item containing the description of the topping.
- ■ Close the unordered list, and then format and print the total for the pizza.
- ■ Print the bottom of the page.

NOTE

It is important to consider the strategy for handling checkboxes and radio buttons in a general setting. Suppose we have an @array holding server-side data. Suppose we generate a unique-selection group of radio buttons, one for each array element. Their names must all be the same, so their HTML value attributes are set by the @array values. Because of the unique-selection property, only one name=value pair is submitted for the whole group of radio buttons. The name of the pair is predetermined, and the value holds the information about which radio button was selected. That name, shared by all the radio buttons, is the key we use to access the submitted value in %formHash. The user has effectively chosen an element of the server-side data @array by selecting a radio button on the client.

Now, suppose we generate a group of checkboxes, one for each @array element. The elements of the @array are assigned to the HTML name attributes of the checkboxes. The values given to the checkboxes are immaterial, so we use yes. Only the checkboxes chosen by the user are submitted to the server in name=yes pairs. So the names of selected checkboxes become keys in %formHash. To see which checkboxes have been selected, see which `@array` elements exist as keys in `%formHash`. The user has effectively chosen a subset of the elements of the server-side data `@array` by selecting a subset of the checkboxes on the client.

Of course, not all HTML forms are dynamically generated from data on the back end. If the names and values of the form elements are hard-coded into a static HTML page, you still have to keep track of them in your CGI program. The matter is simple, with only one name, for a unique-selection group of radio buttons. For checkboxes, an array of their names is still needed in the program to test whether the submitted names exist as keys in `%formHash`. The situations are quite similar, except that updating the form elements in a static HTML page also requires updating the CGI program.

NOTE

The preceding note spoke of arrays generating form choice elements. But we used the keys of a hash to generate the checkboxes for the pizza program. Once extracted from the hash, those keys are an array. So the situation is little different.

One would be tempted just to do away with the hash in that example and just use an array of topping descriptions to generate the names of the checkboxes. However, there is a subtle issue with that approach. Remember that the names of form elements are also used on the client for JavaScript references to form elements in the Browser Object. In that case, the names of the form elements basically act like variable names. A name like "Italian Sausage" is not a viable JavaScript variable name because of the space, so it is bad practice when writing CGI programs to use it as a name for a form element.

6.9 PROCESSING MENUS

Recall the overview of pop-up (pull-down) menus and the `select` HTML element provided in Section 3.1. In default mode (single-selection menu), the `select` element appears as a pop-up choice menu and behaves exactly the same way as a unique-selection group of radio buttons. The main advantage of a single-selection menu is that many choices can be provided without cluttering up the Web page.

Submitting a single-selection menu to a Web server is handled very similarly to submitting a unique-selection group of radio buttons. Let's examine how the following menu would be submitted.

```
<select name="country">
  <option value="0">Middle Earth</option>
  <option value="1">Afghanistan</option>
  <option value="2">Albania</option>
  <option value="236">Zambia</option>
  <option value="237">Zimbabwe</option>
</select>
```

The entire menu is named `country`, and the value of each option is a country code number. Suppose the menu is submitted with the following choice having been made.

Then the name=value pair

```
country=2
```

is part of the submitted form data (query string in a GET transaction). Just as with unique-selection groups of radio buttons, one name is used for the whole group of options, and only the value changes depending on which option is selected. If the user had chosen Middle Earth, `country=0` would have been submitted. Thus, `country` is the unique key in the `%formHash` that accesses the user's choice from the single-selection menu,

```
$formHash{"country"}
```

A multiple-selection menu allows several choices to be made, so several name=value pairs may be sent to the server. In that respect, the situation is the same as with a group of checkboxes. Again, the advantage of a multiple-selection menu is that a large group of options can be provided without cluttering up the Web page. An HTML attribute can be used to set how many of the options are actually visible at a given time on the screen.

Although a multiple-selection is similar to a group of checkboxes in functionality, an inherent difficulty arises when a multiple-selection menu is submitted to a Web server. Consider the following multiple-selection menu.

```
<select name="country" multiple="multiple">
    <option value="0">Middle Earth</option>
    <option value="1">Afghanistan</option>
    <option value="2">Albania</option>
    <option value="236">Zambia</option>
    <option value="237">Zimbabwe</option>
</select>
```

Suppose we select the following options (recall that to make multiple selections the users need to hold down an extra key, such as Ctrl, Alt, or Option, depending on the operating system and browser, while clicking with the mouse.)

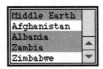

When the form is submitted, three name=value pairs are constructed, as you would expect.

```
country=0&country=2&country=236
```

The problem is that the menu provides only one name: the name given in the `select` element for the whole menu. Each of the multiple user choices is submitted using that one name. Recall that with checkboxes, we have the freedom to assign each one a different name.

When `%formHash` is constructed from these three name=value pairs by our standard decoding algorithm, we lose information, because only one key in the hash results from all three pairs. As we loop through the name=value pairs, the first pair sets the value of `$formHash{"country"}` to `"0"`, the second causes the value of `$formHash{"country"}` to be replaced by `"2"`, and the third leaves `$formHash{"country"}` containing `"236"`. All but the user's last selection in the menu are lost.

The solution is to modify the decoding routine so that no values are lost. Our modified decoding routine will result in `$formHash{"country"}` containing the value `"0;2;236"`. All three of the user's selections are present and can be accessed using the single menu name. The values are included together, delimited by some predetermined "separator," which is just a character that we know does not appear in any of the values.

You may wish to refer back to Figure 6.8 for a refresher on the steps of the decoding routine. As the loop passes over the submitted name=value pairs, each pair is transferred into `%formHash`:

```
$formHash{$name}=$value;
```

To eliminate the possibility of replacing the value of a key that was initialized on a previous pass of the loop, we test whether that key already exists in `%formHash`:

```
if(exists $formHash{$name}) {
  $formHash{$name} = $formHash{$name}.";".$value;
}
else {
  $formHash{$name} = $value;
}
```

If it does, we concatenate a semicolon and the new value onto the value previously assigned to that key. If not, a new key and value are added to `%formHash`.

Going back to the submitted country values in our example, we see that the first name=value pair would result in a new `country` key whose value is `"0"`. When the loop encounters the second pair, the `country` key already exists, so its value becomes `"0;2"`. Similarly, the third pair results in `"0;2;236"`.

When the time comes in a CGI program to ascertain which options the user has selected, we use the `split()` function to recover the multiple values. For example,

```
@countries = split(/;/, $formHash{"country"});
```

splits `"0;2;237"` at the semicolons, causing the array `@countries` to be assigned the value (`"0"`, `"2"`, `"236"`). The user's submitted values then can be processed as desired.

To apply these ideas, we redo the pizza example from Section 6.8 using menus instead of radio buttons and checkboxes. Figure 6.28 shows a sample submission of the new version and the dynamically generated HTML form. A single-selection menu is used for the pizza size, and a multiple-selection menu for the toppings. Aside from the use of menus and the resulting ramifications on handling the data submitted from the form, the `pizza2.cgi` program accomplishes the same thing as the version using radio buttons and checkboxes.

Although the toppings selection box has six options, only four are visible. Because we did not specify the size of that menu using an HTML attribute, the Web browser chose the default display size (and that varies depending on the browser). The query string that results from submitting the form as you see it in Figure 6.28 is

```
size_menu=large&toppings_menu=m_pepperoni&toppings_menu=m_sausage&toppings_men
u=v_mushrooms
```

The single-selection menu for the pizza size has returned the user's choice. In the CGI program the value `"large"` is stored in `$formHash{"size_menu"}`.

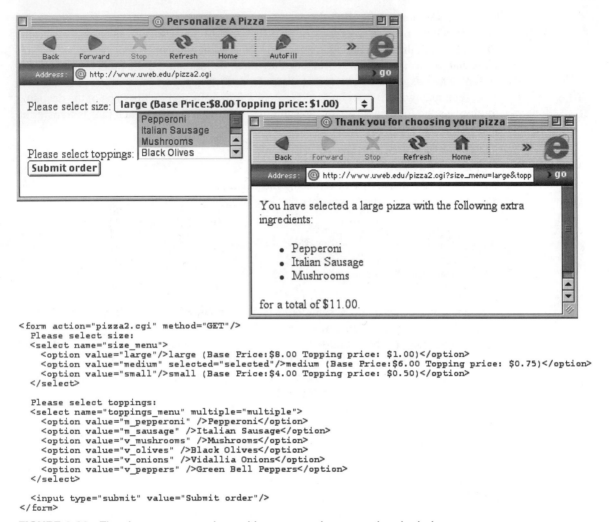

```
<form action="pizza2.cgi" method="GET"/>
  Please select size:
  <select name="size_menu">
    <option value="large"/>large (Base Price:$8.00 Topping price: $1.00)</option>
    <option value="medium" selected="selected"/>medium (Base Price:$6.00 Topping price: $0.75)</option>
    <option value="small"/>small (Base Price:$4.00 Topping price: $0.50)</option>
  </select>

  Please select toppings:
  <select name="toppings_menu" multiple="multiple">
    <option value="m_pepperoni" />Pepperoni</option>
    <option value="m_sausage" />Italian Sausage</option>
    <option value="v_mushrooms" />Mushrooms</option>
    <option value="v_olives" />Black Olives</option>
    <option value="v_onions" />Vidallia Onions</option>
    <option value="v_peppers" />Green Bell Peppers</option>
  </select>

  <input type="submit" value="Submit order"/>
</form>
```

FIGURE 6.28 The pizza program, redone with menus, and an example submission.

However, the multiple topping choices each have been returned as name=value sharing the same name. When the extra decoding step just discussed is used in the pizza2.cgi program, $formHash{"toppings_menu"} will contain the value.

```
"m_pepperoni;m_sausage;v_mushrooms"
```

We provide the main outline of pizza2.cgi in Figure 6.29, along with an overview. The printForm and processForm functions are provided after that, again followed by overviews. This section concludes with a note about the new step necessary to decode data submitted from multiple-selection menus.

```
####################### pizza2.cgi #######################

#! /usr/bin/perl
print "Content-type: text/html\n\n";

###########################################################
#code to get $datastring from GET, POST, or offline execution #
###########################################################

###decode###################################################
@nameValuePairs = split(/&/, $datastring);               #step 1
foreach $pair (@nameValuePairs) {
  ($name, $value) = split(/=/, $pair);                   #step 2

  $name =~tr/+/ /;                                        #step 3
  $name =~s/%([\da-fA-F]{2})/pack("C",hex($1))/eg;        #step 3
  $value =~tr/+/ /;                                       #step 3
  $value =~s/%([\da-fA-F]{2})/pack("C",hex($1))/eg;       #step 3

  if(exists $formHash{$name}) {                           #improved step 4,
    $formHash{$name} = $formHash{$name}.";".$value;       #now handles multiple
  }                                                       #select menus
  else {
    $formHash{$name} = $value;
  }
}
###done decoding############################################

@sizes = ("large", "medium", "small");
$default_size="medium";

%size_prices = (
  "large" => "8.00",
  "medium" => "6.00",
  "small" => "4.00"
);

%topping_prices = (
  "large" => "1.00",
  "medium" => "0.75",
  "small" => "0.50"
);

%toppings = (
  "m_pepperoni" => "Pepperoni",
  "m_sausage" => "Italian Sausage",
  "v_peppers" => "Green Bell Peppers",
  "v_mushrooms" => "Mushrooms",
  "v_onions" => "Vidallia Onions",
  "v_olives" => "Black Olives"
);

if($datastring eq "") {
  &printForm;     # function to print order form page
}
else {
  &processForm;   # function to print summary page
}

###########################################################
#             function definitions go here             #
###########################################################
```

FIGURE 6.29   The outline of the `pizza2.cgi` program.

- Add the extra provision for decoding data submitted from multiple-selection menus. That replaces step 4 from the original decoding algorithm.
- The rest of the program proceeds as before.

```
sub printForm {
  print<<TOP;
  <html><head><title>Personalize A Pizza</title></head>
    <body>
      <form action="$ENV{'SCRIPT_NAME'}" method="GET"/>
        Please select size:\n
        <select name="size_menu">
TOP

    foreach $size (@sizes) {
      print "<option value=\"$size\"";

      if($size eq $default_size) {
        print ' selected="selected"';
      }
      print "/>$size (Base Price:\$$size_prices{$size}",
            " Topping price: \$$topping_prices{$size})</option>\n";
    }
    print "</select><br/>\n";

    print "Please select toppings:\n",
          '<select name="toppings_menu" multiple="multiple">',"\n";

    foreach $topping (sort keys %toppings) {
      print "<option value=\"$topping\" />$toppings{$topping}</option>\n";
    }
    print "</select><br/>\n";
    print<<BOTTOM;
      <input type="submit" value="Submit order"/>
    </form>
  </body>
</html>
BOTTOM
}
```

■ Print the top of the page, including the beginning tags for the form and the single-selection menu.

■ For each $size in the pizza @sizes array

    ■ Begin a menu option whose value is $size. Thus far we have printed

```
<option value="$size"
```

    If the current pass of the loop corresponds to the default size that is to be checked, add selected="selected" to the menu option.

    ■ Print the closing /> for the option start tag, the text that gets marked up on the menu for that option, and then the closing </option> tag.

■ Print the closing tag for the single-selection menu and then the starting tag for the multiple-selection menu.

■ For each $topping key in the %toppings hash

    ■ Print a menu option whose value is the $topping key and whose text description is the corresponding value in the %toppings hash.

■ Close the multiple-selection menu and the form. Print the closing HTML tags for the page.

```
sub processForm {
  print <<TOP;
  <html><head><title>Thank you for choosing your pizza</title></head>
  <body>
TOP

  $size = $formHash{"size_menu"};
  $total=$size_prices{$size};

  print "You have selected a $size pizza ";
  print "with the following extra ingredients:\n<ul>";

  @chosen_toppings = split(/;/, $formHash{"toppings_menu"});

  foreach $topping (@chosen_toppings) {
    $total = $total + $topping_prices{$size};
    print "<li>$toppings{$topping}</li>\n";
  }
  print "</ul>\n";

  $total = sprintf "%.2f", $total;
  print "for a total of \$$total.\n";

  print<<BOTTOM
  </body></html>
BOTTOM
}
```

- Print the top of the page.
- Store the pizza $size chosen by the user.
- Add the base price from %size_prices for that $size onto the total.
- Print a message and start an unordered list.
- Store the user's topping choices into an array. If multiple selections have been made, $formHash{"toppings_menu"} contains a semicolon-delimited string of the selections.
- For each $topping in the user's @chosen_toppings
    - Add the price of the topping (as determined by the $size of the pizza) to the total and print out a list item containing the description of the topping.
- Print the closing tag for the unordered list, then format and print the total price for the pizza.
- Print the closing tags for the page.

NOTE

The new step 4 in the decoding routine shown in Figure 6.29 works for the other form elements we have covered as well. When a multiple-selection menu is used and duplicate names appear in the string of submitted name=value pairs, the if clause performs the concatenation trick. If no multiple-selection menus are submitted, the else clause is invoked on each pass of the loop. Thus, the new step 4 works exactly like the original step 4 when no multiple-selection menus are in play. You should update your skeleton file to contain the new step 4, because it covers all cases.

6.10 PROCESSING TEXT AREAS

A text area is similar to a text field in that both are used to acquire text from the user. Recall the textarea HTML element introduced in Section 3.1. The following two features distinguish a text area from a text field, in terms of the entered text:

- A text area can contain distinct lines of text, with line breaks in between, whereas a text field can contain only a "one-line" string.
- To accommodate multiple lines of text, a text area can be scrollable.

These features make text areas ideal for asking a user to enter a paragraph of text, or perhaps a list of things. However, there are subtleties involved with submitting text areas to the server that are not a factor with text fields. When submitted, the text in the text area is encoded as a single string, even though the text may have been entered as multiple lines.

Figure 6.30 shows an example submission of a text area and the query string that results. Note that GET or POST will result in the same format, but you won't see the submitted data string in a POST transaction. As you would expect, spaces are encoded with + characters. Also, when text wraps around automatically because of the width of the text area, no newline characters are added to the submitted data, as demonstrated by the first sentence in Figure 6.30. When the user presses Enter on the keyboard, on the other hand, that keystroke is encoded into the submitted data.

One would expect that each line break entered by the user would be encoded as the ASCII newline character, but in Figure 6.30 the browser has encoded the line breaks in the text area using two ASCII characters: %0D%0A. These two ASCII characters, a "carriage return" followed by a "line feed," are commonly used to represent line breaks. (See the historical note at the end of this section.)

Because of the carriage return–line feed encoding, a submitted line break from a text area essentially decodes into *two* newline characters back on the server. To solve that problem, we must intervene in our decoding routine in order to preserve the submitted line structure. In a CGI program, we simply substitute a Perl newline escape sequence, \n, for each six-character encoded carriage return–line feed sequence, %0D%0A, in the submitted data string. The Perl statement that accomplishes those substitutions is as follows (don't worry; substitutions will be explained fully in Chapter 11):

```
$datastring =~s/%0D%0A/\n/g;
```

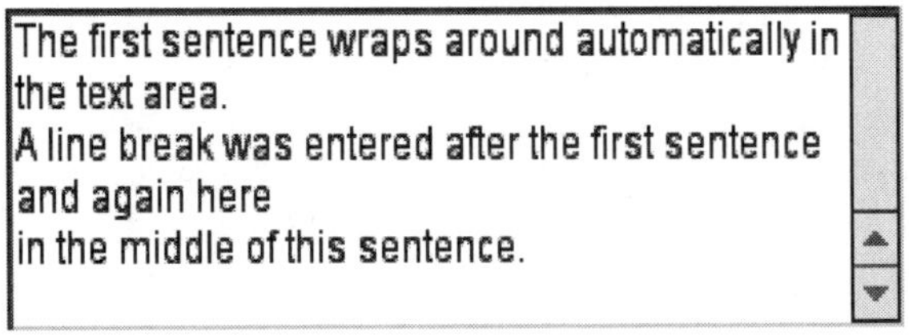

The first sentence wraps around automatically in
the text area.
A line break was entered after the first sentence
and again here
in the middle of this sentence.

```
The+first+sentence+wraps+around+automatically+in+the+text+area.%0D%0AA+line+break+was
+entered+after+the+first+sentence+and+again+here%0D%0Ain+the+middle+of+this+sentence.
```

FIGURE 6.30 Standard encoding of data submitted from a text area.

For now, we must be content with adding this step into our standard form data-decoding algorithm. We will show its place in the decoding routine in the example that follows. You can add this extra line to your skeleton file, and it will have no effect on decoding data submitted from other form elements.

The main example of this section is a simple guestbook. The static HTML page comments.html, shown in Figure 6.31, contains a form where a user can enter comments into a text area. We have shown just the HTML code for the form, rather than the code for the whole page. Note that, in contrast to some previous examples, there is really no reason to generate this page dynamically from a CGI program.

Upon submission, the program comments.cgi processes the submitted data. Rather than simply returning the user's comments to the browser, the program writes the comments to a text file on the server named comments.txt. This text file contains not only the user's current submission but also submissions made by previous users. Thus, upon a new submission, the text file is opened for appending rather than for writing, which would overwrite previous entries to the guestbook. You may wish to peruse Section 5.7 on file operations for a refresher, although the file operation in this example is very straightforward.

Of course, the HTTP transaction that submits the comments form must end with a Web page being returned to the user's browser. For this example, the returned page simply thanks the user for submitting an entry and provides a link that the user can click to see the entire guest book file. An example submission of the program is shown in Figure 6.32. Keep in mind that this is a very simplified guestbook utility compared to those you may have used on the Web.

The link in the thank-you page points to the comments.txt file, which stores the guestbook entries on the server. Because the file is an ordinary text file containing no HTML markup instructions, a URL request for it just displays the contents of the file without any HTML markup. (The .txt file extension helps the Web browser recognize that the file does not contain a formal Web page.) Notice in Figure 6.32 that a line break was

```
<form action="comments.cgi" method="GET">
  Please enter comments here.<br/>
  <textarea name="comments" rows="3" cols="40"></textarea>
  <input type="submit" value="Submit comments" />
</form>
```

FIGURE 6.31 A Web page that submits user comments to a guestbook.

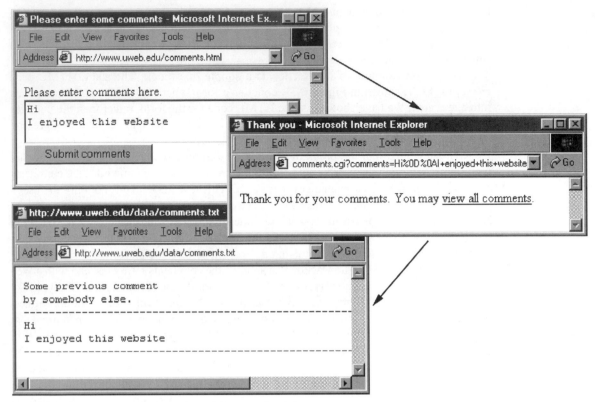

FIGURE 6.32 A sample submission of the guestbook form.

entered after "Hi" and the line break was preserved into the text file. In particular, the carriage return and line feed you see in the query string were converted into one \n in the CGI program before it was written to the text file. An outline of the CGI program is shown in Figure 6.33. A brief overview of the program follows the figure.

```perl
#! /usr/bin/perl
print "Content-type: text/html\n\n";

##################################################################
#code to get $datastring from GET, POST, or offline execution #
##################################################################

###decode##########################################################
$datastring =~s/%0D%0A/\n/g;                         #step to deal with line
                                                     #breaks in text areas
@nameValuePairs = split(/&/, $datastring);           #step 1
foreach $pair (@nameValuePairs) {
  ($name, $value) = split(/=/, $pair);               #step 2

  $name =~tr/+/ /;                                    #step 3
  $name =~s/%([\da-fA-F]{2})/pack("C",hex($1))/eg;    #step 3
  $value =~tr/+/ /;                                   #step 3
  $value =~s/%([\da-fA-F]{2})/pack("C",hex($1))/eg;   #step 3

  if(exists $formHash{$name}) {                       #improved step 4,
    $formHash{$name} = $formHash{$name}.";".$value;   #now handles multiple
  }                                                   #select menus
  else {
    $formHash{$name} = $value;
  }
}
###done decoding###################################################

$dataDir = "/www/data/"; # the directory containing the file comments.txt
$dataURL = "http://www.uweb.edu/data/"; # the corresponding URL

$comments = $formHash{"comments"};
chomp $comments;

# open for appending
open(DATA, ">>$dataDir"."comments.txt") || &errorPage;

print DATA $comments;
print DATA "\n", "-" x 70, "\n"; # a line of 70 dashes to separate comments
close(DATA);

$url = $dataURL."comments.txt";
print<<PAGE;
<html><head><title>Thank you</title></head>
 <body>
 Thank you for your comments. You may
 <a href="$url">view all comments</a>.
 </body>
</html>
PAGE

##################################################################
#              function definition for errorPage                #
##################################################################
```

FIGURE 6.33   The comments.cgi program.

- Add the extra step to deal with the double line breaks returned by Web browsers from text areas. Finish decoding as usual.
- Set the correct path and URL for the data file.
- Get the data from the text area and remove any unnecessary newline characters that may follow the data.
- Open the file and print the data. Then print 70 dashes to delimit the current entry from those that may follow. The string replication operator x is used to print the 70 dashes. That could be done by hand, however.
- Close the file.
- Print the thank-you page using the correct URL to point to the data file.

For this program to work, you must remember to create a file called `comments.txt` in the data directory, and remember to give it write permissions by everyone. It is interesting to reconsider that the entire contents of the text area are stored into one string. After the data from the example submission shown in Figure 6.33 is decoded, the text area data is stored as the following string.

```
"Hi\nI enjoyed this web site"
```

Even if a multiple-paragraph text area is submitted, it still becomes one long string. Everywhere a line break is entered into a text area, a `\n` appears in the long string at that point. Once written to the text file and viewed in a browser or text editor, the long string is distributed on multiple lines. (All text files are really stored as single strings with invisible formatting characters mixed in!)

Browsers are peculiar with the text nuance of a carriage return followed by a line feed. In fact, the `comments.cgi` program as presented might still work the same without replacing the carriage return–line feed combo with a single `\n`. When a non-HTML text file is rendered by a browser, such a combo might actually be rendered as a single line break, but that property varies among browsers and platforms. Considering the historical note below, browsers are built to exchange data from varying platforms and deal with line breaks regardless of the text's originating platform.

At first you might it is not very important to remove the pesky combo. However, many CGI programs feature reading from text files and then formatting that text into HTML pages. Typically, line breaks simply are replaced with `<br/>` tags in that case. When we write a better "guestbook-viewing" program later in this text, such a strategy will be used to preserve the format of the text into the HTML page. Without removing the carriage return–line feed combo, our guestbook-viewing utility would end up double-spacing things in Web pages because of two `<br/>` elements.

NOTE

The way line breaks are stored varies with the operating system for historical reasons that go back to electromechanical teletypewriters. On those machines, a *carriage return* moved the print head back horizontally to the beginning of the line, whereas a *line feed* scrolled the paper vertically to the next line. Both actions were usually necessary at the end of a line. Early computers transmitted both codes for compatibilty with these terminals. As a result, on DOS (Windows) systems, line breaks are stored as a two-character carriage return–line feed sequence (ASCII 0D followed by 0A). On UNIX systems (where Perl was first developed), on the other hand, line breaks are stored as line feeds alone (0A). That is why, when a DOS text file is transferred to a UNIX system, you often see extra junk in the file corresponding to all the extra 0D characters. On Macintosh systems, a line break is usually stored as 0D. (In fact, MacPerl uses ASCII code 0D for `\n`.) Fortunately, many modern word processors (and sometimes operating systems) are friendly enough that they try to recognize foreign line break encodings and deal with them.

SUMMARY OF KEY TERMS AND CONCEPTS

Environment variables: A collection of variables that the Web server software uses to maintain all sorts of information about the HTTP transaction that is under way. When an HTTP request calls a CGI program, those variables are passed to the CGI program in the **%ENV hash** as part of the CGI interface. The %ENV hash functions as a global variable during the execution of the program. Because HTTP is stateless, the sever purges these variables when a given HTTP transaction is completed. However, the server does record many of the environment variables into various *log files* on the server before purging them.

Query string: A string that carries data from a browser to a Web server in an HTTP GET transaction. The string is appended onto the end of a URL following a ? character. When a form is submitted, a Web browser automatically forms a query string, which consists of name= value pairs of submitted form elements. The pairs are delimited with & characters. To preserve the delimiters and = characters that format the string, browsers URL encode any such characters that appear in the actual data using hexadecimal character codes. Spaces in the data are encoded as + characters. Depending upon the particular browser, other nonalphanumeric characters may be hex-encoded as well. Although HTTP POST transactions don't feature a query string in the URL, a form's submitted data is encoded the same way for delivery to the server.

Receiving input: The conditional code in Figure 6.14 accepts input from HTTP POST transactions (where the data is read from the standard input stream), from HTTP GET transactions (where the data is obtained from the QUERY_STRING environment variable), and from offline, non-CGI executions of your programs (where you enter the data from the keyboard). The conditional uses the REQUEST_METHOD environment variable to make the decisions. Note that the conditional shunts HEAD requests to the GET method, so your programs won't hang if some network application stumbles onto one of them while crawling the Web (mindlessly but algorithmically).

Decoding the query string: The routine shown in Figure 6.8 takes the incoming string of delimited name= value pairs, parses it, decodes it, and stores the pairs into %formHash, where the hash keys are the names. Parsing and decoding involves splitting out the name= value pairs, splitting those pairs into the names and values, and then decoding any hex-encoded characters in the data.

Dynamically generated HTML forms: HTML forms in which both the number of form elements and the data they carry are determined by a *back-end data source*. Use of these forms has the advantage that, to update a Web application, one merely has to update the data source. We have used global arrays and hashes to carry the back-end data in this chapter. In general, that data would be stored in text files or a relational database. Later chapters explore both topics in detail. However, such data is often read into CGI programs and stored in hashes and arrays. Thus, the concepts of dynamic form generation presented here are actually very applicable in more general settings.

Submitting a form to the same program that generates it: If the query string is empty, a function in the program prints the form. Otherwise, a function in the program processes the form. Beginning students often want to construct two different programs to handle the generation and processing, but the one-program strategy has many advantages. In this chapter you saw that the two functions can share the same data source. In subsequent lessons you will see that this strategy generalizes into larger single-program applications that can both generate and process a variety of forms.

Processing text fields: Using several text fields to contain order quantities makes an ideal example to demonstrate processing dynamically generated forms. A single hash glues the whole example together. One text field is generated for each key in the hash. The keys become the names of the text fields in the HTML code. When the form is submitted, the hash keys are then the names of the name=value pairs in the query string. Thus, the keys become the keys of the %formHash created from the submitted data. The result is "parallel hashes" that share the same keys. The values of the original hash are the prices of the items for sale, and the values of %formHash are the order quantities submitted by the user. It is then very easy to process the order by iterating over the keys and extracting the relevant data from the two "parallel" hashes.

Processing radio buttons: When a unique-selection group of radio buttons is dynamically generated from a server-side hash, the hash keys are placed as the values of the radio buttons in the HTML code. That is necessary because all of the radio buttons in the group must share the same name. Because only one of the group can be checked, %formHash will contain only one entry from the group, and that key is the name common to all the radio buttons. You can then extract the associated value from %formHash, and know which radio button was selected.

Processing checkboxes: When a group of checkboxes is dynamically generated from a server-side hash, the keys are placed as the names of the checkboxes in the HTML code. (The checkbox value attributes are immaterial.) When the form is submitted to the program, %formHash will contain one entry for each checkbox chosen by the user. To deduce which were selected, iterate over the keys of the original hash, testing whether a corresponding key exists in %formHash. Those keys found to exist in %formHash are precisely the checkboxes chosen by the user.

Processing single-selection menus: When a single-selection menu is dynamically generated from a server-side hash, the keys become the values of the menu options. Processing the submission of the menu is handled identically to processing a unique-selection group of radio buttons. Only one entry for the menu will be in %formHash, under the key given by the name of the menu. We then extract the associated value from %formHash, and we know which menu option was selected.

Processing multiple-selection menus: Although it functions on the client like a group of checkboxes, a multiple-selection menu has only one name, whereas each checkbox in a group can be given a different name. Thus, multiple selections from the menu result in multiple name=value pairs, each with the same name. To counter that problem, we alter step 4 of the decoding routine as shown in Figure 6.29, so that the multiple values are concatenated into a delimited string in %formHash, where the menu name is the key. To recover the selected options, we split out those values into an array. We then know which options the user selected, because the array carries keys from the original hash corresponding to the user's selections. (Note that this alteration to step 4 will also handle multiple checkboxes sharing one name.)

Processing text areas: There is scarcely any cause to generate a group of text areas from a back-end data source. When a text area is submitted, %formHash will contain only one entry for it, the key being the name of the text area and the value being the text entered by the user. Browsers encode hard line breaks (entered by the user) in text areas as two hexadecimal character codes: an ASCII carriage return followed by an ASCII line feed. On many Web servers, that sequence will result in double-spaced text. To combat that, we add an extra line at the top of the decoding routine. That line simply substitutes one \n character for every occurrence of the carriage return–line feed combination.

Debugging hints: Remember that in the CGI environment, Perl errors go to the standard error channel, which goes to the Web server software. The server software dumps those into an *error log* file, which you typically don't see. This shows the importance of local (non-CGI) executions of programs so that you see Perl's error messages. Moreover, enabling warnings will report irregularities, even if there are no outright syntax errors in the program.

EXERCISES

1. Write a CGI program that expects a query string consisting of only one integer in the range from 1 to 5, inclusive. If the program receives anything else than such an integer, it returns a warning page to the browser. Otherwise, the program returns a Web page that displays one of five images (`0.gif, 1.gif, ..., 5.gif`). Acquire five small images from a free online icon library for use in this problem. Do not use the decoding routine for this exercise.

2. Write a CGI program that expects a query string consisting of two integers, m and n, each in the range from 2 to 25, inclusive. You will have to invent your own query string format using a delimiting symbol to separate the integers. If the program receives anything else than two such integers, it returns a warning page to the browser. Otherwise, the program returns an $n \times m$ borderless HTML table whose cells are colored like a checkerboard (alternating black and white squares). Make the table cells each 20×20 pixels. Do not use the decoding routine for this exercise.

3. It is possible to submit a form using the POST method and also to send a query string on the URL in the same transaction.

    (a) Make a form that accomplishes that. Test it by submitting it to the echo program, which will return the name=value pairs from the POSTed data as well as those from the query string you submit.

    (b) Modify our GET=POST-offline conditional so that such an extra query string will be concatenated onto the end of the POSTed data, and the extra name=value pairs will make it into `%formHash`.

    (c) Make a simple CGI program to test this using your form from part (a). The program need only iterate over `%formHash` printing out all the name=value pairs it contains to a Web page.

4. Work the following exercises from Chapter 5. Now, however, you should use the full decoding routine. In particular, weird characters may now be used in the user names and passwords.

    (a) Exercise 9

    (b) Exercise 10

    (c) (Advanced) Exercises 11 and 12

5. Write a CGI program similar to the music survey example featured in Figure 1.9 of Section 1.7. The program is explained in detail in that section. In particular, don't provide a default selected radio button, but supply JavaScript support that alerts the user and aborts the form submission if the user submits the form without making a choice.

6. The source code for the `food2.cgi` program of Figure 6.18 can be obtained from the Web site.

    (a) Redo the program so that the data source is stored in a text file. *Hint:* Choose a "hash like" format (that is, lines like `fries:1.00`) for the data source in the file and split out the values in the program, storing them into a hash.

    (b) Not only should an order summary be returned to the user, but the summary should also be appended onto a text file that keeps records of all past orders. Choose a suitable format for the summaries in the file.

    (c) Client-side validation support makes sure that nonnegative integers are entered into each text field.

    (d) Write a second CGI program that functions as an administration program. The program reads the data source file, putting the prices into text fields. The administrator can use the program to change prices for the application remotely from a browser without physically having to edit the data file.

(e) Add client-side validation support to protect the administrator from accidentally updating the data source with prices that are not positive numbers.

(f) Write a third CGI program that functions as an administration program. Calling that program reads in the cumulative orders file from part (b), creating a separate HTML table for each order.

7. The source code for the `pizza.cgi` program of Figure 6.27 can be obtained from the Web site.

(a) Redo the program so that the data source is stored in a text file(s). *Hint:* Choose a "parallel hashlike" format (that is, lines like `large:8.00:1.00`) for the prices in the file, and read the data into two hashes in the program.

(b) Also include a single-selection menu that lets the user choose thin, thick, or cheesy crust. The crust choice should affect the price of the pizza in some way. Also keep a data source for this in a text file.

(c) Not only should an order summary be returned to the user, but the summary should be appended onto a text file that keeps records of all past orders. Choose a suitable format for the summaries in the file.

(d) No default choices are provided in the form, and client-side validation support makes sure that a size and a crust type are chosen before allowing the form to be submitted.

(e) Write a second CGI program that functions as an administration program. The program reads the data source file(s), putting all the prices and toppings into text fields. The administrator can use the program to change prices and toppings for the application without physically having to edit the data file(s). *Hint:* The easiest way to do this is to keep each chunk of related data in its own text file, and read that data into a separate form in the administration page. Submitting a particular form overwrites a particular text file.

(f) Add client-side validation support to protect the administrator from accidentally updating the data source with prices that are not positive numbers.

(g) Write a third CGI program that functions as an administration program. Calling that program reads in the cumulative orders file from part (c), creating a separate HTML table for each order.

8. Make a music survey based upon the idea of the one in Exercise 5, but more elaborate. The program should return some sort of cumulative results for each survey question. Four different survey questions should be featured, using form elements of the types in (a) through (d):

(a) A unique-selection group of radio buttons

(b) A group of checkboxes

(c) A single-selection menu

(d) A multiple-selection menu

(e) Add client-side JavaScript validation support for each of (a) through (d). In this case, no default selections should be given to the user. The user is required to answer each survey question or else the form submission is aborted.

9. Redo the guestbook program of Figure 6.33 so that the "view all comments" link calls a second CGI program, which you have to create. This program returns only one previous guestbook entry at a time. For example, the first returned guestbook entry contains a *Next* link. Clicking the link then returns a page containing the second guestbook entry. That page now has *Previous* and *Next* links. The page showing the final guestbook entry should have only a *Previous* link. *Hint:* The links need to submit data to the program indicating which guestbook entry is currently on display and which is being requested. That information is then used to locate the next or previous entry, as the case may be. This is an example of a Web application that preserves state information between transactions. That is the topic of Chapter 7.

PROJECT THREAD

Here you will use the quiz you developed in Chapters 3 and 4. The quiz will be modified so that it is generated dynamically from a back-end data source, is able to grade the questions and return the results to the user, and is able to save the quiz results into a master file. You will *not* need to use the password form developed in Chapters 3 and 4. Rather, that will be integrated with the quiz in Chapter 7 to add security.

A. Decide upon a suitable format in which to store the data for the quiz questions in text file(s). You will also need to devise how to read the data into the program (that is, whether to use arrays or hashes).

B. Write the function that prints the quiz from the back-end data. Test it thoroughly.

C. Write the function that processes the quiz when it is submitted. You will have to decide upon the format and amount of detail with which you return the results to the user. This function should also append the quiz results onto the end of a text file that records all quiz results. Use some kind of separator between quiz results as in the guestbook example of Section 6.10. At the top of the quiz results page returned to the user, place a link that directly targets the quiz results text file.

D. Add a new row for the updated quiz application to the table in your homework page. Make sure you preserve the version from the previous lesson and keep the link to it active. If you are assigned any other exercises from this chapter, add another row to your homework table for each exercise.

E. (Optional) Write a separate administration CGI program that reads all the the quiz data into an HTML form and allows the administrator to update/change the quiz from a remote browser.

CHAPTER 7

MAINTAINING STATE
IN WEB APPLICATIONS

Chapter 6 demonstrated Web applications that were able both to print an HTML form and to process the user's data returned from the form. That involves two HTTP transactions: one to get the data and the other to process it and return a summary to the user. This lesson focuses on Web applications that enable a sequence of three or more HTTP transactions, where subsequent transactions have some "memory" of prior ones. The goal is to provide you with an in-depth understanding of what is involved with making a Web application "remember things." In the process, we explore password protection and maintaining logged-on state in detail.

7.1 STATE IN WEB APPLICATIONS

It is definitely not trivial to enable a Web application to remember details from previous transactions. Recall from Section 1.6 that HTTP is a stateless protocol. When a Web application makes a transaction, the only memory of the event is a Web page sitting in the browser's cache and some entries in the Web server's log files. The Web server software is oblivious about past transactions. Its main concern is listening for and answering new HTTP requests.

With respect to Web applications, **state data** refers to data collected or generated by the application during one HTTP transaction that is made available to subsequent HTTP transactions enabled by the application. Such data enables a Web application to have "memory" of a past transaction. When a Web application preserves state data among two or more HTTP transactions, we say that it *maintains state*. The act of maintaining state for a user among multiple transactions creates a *browsing session*, or simply a **session**. When you open a browser window, pull up a certain site, surf among a few of its pages, and the Web application somehow keeps track of what you are doing on the site, you are involved in a session on that Web application. The most recognizable examples are sites that first require you to log on and then remember you through the session, and sites that keep a cumulative shopping cart throughout a session.

When we say "state data," we don't mean personal account data that is obtained when you register with a site, which ends up in a permanent file with your name on it. In that case a CGI program creates a file (or database record) with your name on it and uses it to store personal information you entered into some forms. Crank up your browser several days later, enter your name and password into a form, and the CGI program opens your file and grabs the personal data. Certainly that data is preserved between multiple HTTP transactions, but such "permanent" *account data* or *customer profile data* is not what we mean by state data.

The idea of a browsing session is that of pulling up a site and visiting a few pages. When you quit the browser or go to a different site, the session is over. State data is relevant only during the session and typically exists only during the session. The most common ways to maintain state data during a session involve the use of hidden form elements, temporary files created on the server, or cookies set on the user's browser. The focus of this chapter involves the first two ways, and the concept of keeping state in general. Cookies bring up some other issues, which are covered in Chapter 8.

7.2 HIDDEN FORM ELEMENTS FOR APPLICATION LOGIC AND STATE

Recall the `pizza.cgi` program of Section 6.8. That program simply returns a summary of the user's order back to the client. Most order forms used on commercial Web sites provide an intermediary step that allows the user to confirm order details before actually submitting the order. It is customary to allow the user to confirm prices and selections before finalizing an order.

The main example of this section updates `pizza.cgi` to provide such an intermediary confirmation step. The updated version is named `pizza3.cgi`. (Recall that `pizza2.cgi`, presented in Section 6.9, merely reworked `pizza.cgi` using menus rather than checkboxes and radio buttons.) But before one begins to develop a multi-transaction Web application, some careful planning is in order.

The best way to begin is by drawing (on scratch paper or otherwise) a **transaction diagram** for the application to be created. A transaction diagram shows both an abstract overview of the Web pages the application will be capable of generating and the transactions necessary to create those pages. Figure 7.1 shows a transaction diagram for the `pizza3.cgi` application we will create.

You can see in Figure 7.1 that the concept for the application is quite straightforward: Take order, allow user to confirm order, finalize order. We also wish to keep a permanent record of the order by writing it to a file on the server. The next order of business is to figure out how the application is to handle the job of generating three different Web pages. In Chapter 6 the strategy used in CGI programs that could generate two different pages was to print the form if the query string was empty; otherwise, process the submitted form data. We now generalize that idea.

The general strategy is to write a different function to handle the generation of each of the three Web pages. Those functions correspond in a one-to-one fashion to the arrows in the transaction diagram. As you can see in Figure 7.1, we have already supplied the names of the main functions that will drive the program. The key is that each time the application is called by a URL, it needs to be told which function should be called.

That is handled by submitting "requests" of the form `request=confirm_order` to the program. Those requests will be generated by hidden form elements each time a form is submitted. In this way, a given form submits a request that calls the appropriate function to process that form's data. A conditional expression is used to call the appropriate function based upon the incoming request. We call that conditional the **application logic** of the Web application, or simply the application's *app logic* for short. The app logic can be constructed straight from the transaction diagram.

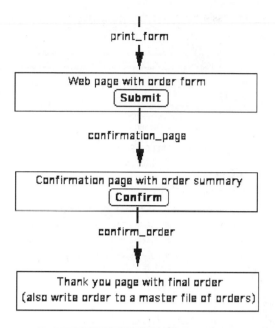

FIGURE 7.1 A transaction diagram for the new pizza program.

```
if ($formHash{"request"} eq "confirmation_page") {
   &confirmation_page;
}
elsif ($formHash{"request"} eq "confirm_order") {
   &confirm_order;
}
else {
   &print_form;
}
```

Because the incoming requests are name=value pairs, where the name is always request, the app logic conditional simply tests the corresponding value and calls the appropriate function. The only time there is no incoming request is when the application is first called. Thus, the app logic shunts all "requestless" transactions to the print_form function, which prints the application's first page—its *welcome page*.

The next order of business is to figure out exactly how all of the requests are submitted and how the data handled by the confirmation_page function is still available to the confirm_order function. Again, this is to be accomplished using hidden form elements. At this stage in application development, it is advantageous to sketch out the HTML forms that the application will use to collect and submit data. In particular, it is advantageous to determine ahead of time the nature of the data that will be concealed in hidden elements in the forms. Figure 7.2 shows our "sketch."

Of course we have the benefit of being able to take screenshots of the actual application in action, but you will find that a cruder diagram on scratch paper is a major help. The requests that drive the app logic are straightforward. The print_form function hides only an app logic request in the order form. The confirmation_page function hides both an app logic request and the data submitted from the order form. Since both that data and the new name and phone number data is submitted to the confirm_order function, it has all of the data from both forms.

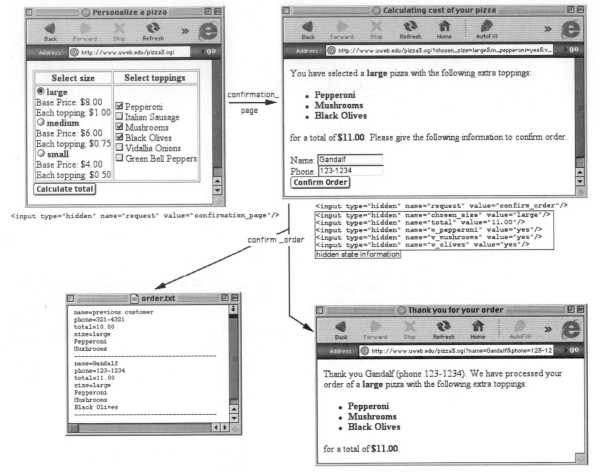

FIGURE 7.2 An example session created by `pizza3.cgi`.

Here you see a session. The third HTTP transaction (call to `confirm_order`) remembers the second HTTP transaction (call to `confirmation_page`). One would be tempted to think that the confirmation page remembers the initial order because that page displays the order details (in boldface). However, that is not usable data, merely being contained in HTML `b` (bold) and `li` (list item) elements. The hidden data is usable in the sense that it gets submitted to the server with the next transaction.

As you can see in Figure 7.2 below the confirmation page, the actual "remembered" data is contained in hidden form elements within the page. When the "Confirm Order" button is clicked, that hidden data is submitted to the server along with the name and phone number requested from the user.

Of course, there are many more HTML form elements used in `pizza3.cgi` than the ones for which we have shown HTML code in Figure 7.2. We have shown code for only the hidden ones, because those are responsible for driving the app logic and preserving state data. Figure 7.3 shows the outline of `pizza3.cgi`. The outline is very similar to that of the `pizza.cgi` program of Lesson 6. One addition is that a global `$dataDir` variable is

```
                          pizza3.cgi

#! /usr/bin/perl
print "Content-type: text/html\n\n";

##############################################################
#    code for decoding input $datastring into %formHash     #
#        (works for GET, POST, and offline execution)       #
##############################################################

$dataDir = "/www/pizza/orders/";

### the data source ########################################
@sizes = ("large", "medium", "small");
$default_size="medium";

%size_prices = (
   "large"  => "8.00",
   "medium" => "6.00",
   "small"  => "4.00"
);
%topping_prices = (
   "large"  => "1.00",
   "medium" => "0.75",
   "small"  => "0.50"
);
%toppings = (
   "m_pepperoni" => "Pepperoni",
   "m_sausage"   => "Italian Sausage",
   "v_peppers"   => "Green Bell Peppers",
   "v_mushrooms" => "Mushrooms",
   "v_onions"    => "Vidallia Onions",
   "v_olives"    => "Black Olives"
);
### end of data source ####################################

### app logic #############################################
if($formHash{"request"} eq "confirmation_page") {
   &confirmation_page;
}
elsif($formHash{"request"} eq "confirm_order") {
   &confirm_order;
}
else {
   &print_form;
}
### end app logic #########################################

##############################################################
### Definitions of app logic functions go here.            #
### Definitions for toolkit functions used:                #
#    &errorPage  (from Section 5.7)                         #
##############################################################
```

FIGURE 7.3   Outline for `pizza3.cgi`.

assigned the absolute path to the directory that contains the order log file. Then, the main data source is initialized as before. Following that is the app logic conditional. All that remains is to code the function definitions.

The `print_form` function is nearly identical to the one for `pizza.cgi` in Section 6.8, so we don't show it. The only difference is that the form contains the extra hidden element shown in Figure 7.2. The code for the `confirmation_page` and `confirm_order` functions follows. The application does call the standard `errorPage` function if the order log file fails to open.

```perl
sub confirmation_page {
  print <<TOP;
    <html><head><title>Calculating cost of your pizza</title></head><body>
TOP

  $size = $formHash{"chosen_size"};
  $total=$size_prices{$size};
  print "You have selected a <b>$size</b> pizza";
  print "with the following extra toppings: \n<ul>";

  foreach $topping (sort keys %toppings) {
    if(exists $formHash{$topping}) {
      $total = $total + $topping_prices{$size};
      print "<li><b>$toppings{$topping}</b></li>\n";
    }
  }
  print "</ul>\n";

  $total = sprintf "%.2f", $total;
  print "for a total of <b>\$$total</b>.\n";

  print<<CONFIRM;
    Please give the following information to confirm order.<br/>
    <form action="$ENV{'SCRIPT_NAME'}" method="GET">
      Name: <input type="text" name="name" value="" size="20"/><br/>
      Phone: <input type="text" name="phone" value="" size="20"/><br/>
      <input type="hidden" name="total" value="$total"/>
      <input type="hidden" name="chosen_size" value="$size"/>
      <input type="hidden" name="request" value="confirm_order"/>
CONFIRM

  foreach $topping (sort keys %toppings) {
    if($formHash{$topping} eq "yes") {
      print '<input type="hidden" name="', $topping, '" value="yes"/>', "\n";
    }
  }

  print<<BOTTOM;
      <input type="submit" value="Confirm Order"/>
    </form>
    </body></html>
BOTTOM
}
```

- Print the top of the confirmation page.

- Get the pizza size (chosen radio button) selected by the user and the base price for that size, and print a message indicating the chosen size. Note that the unordered HTML list for the toppings is started in the `print` statement.

    - For each available `$topping`

        - If the `$topping` is found in `%formHash` (the user selected that checkbox)

            - Add the price for the topping onto the total bill; print a list item containing that topping.

- Close the HTML list.

- Format the `$total` to two decimal places and then print it.

- Start printing the confirmation form: the text fields for the name and phone number, the hidden element that tells the program next to `confirm_order`, the hidden element containing the user's size choice, and the hidden element containing the order total. (It is best to preserve the order total in the hidden data. Otherwise it would have to be recalculated during the HTTP transaction that finalizes the order.)

- For each available $topping

    - If the $topping is found in %formHash (the user selected that checkbox)

        - Print a hidden form element to record that the user chose the topping.

- Print the form's submit button, the closing form tag, and the rest of the page.

```
sub confirm_order {
  open (ORDERFILE, ">>$dataDir","order.txt") or &errorPage;
  print ORDERFILE "name=$formHash{'name'}\n" , "phone=$formHash{'phone'}\n",
                  "total=$formHash{'total'}\n" , "size=$formHash{'chosen_size'}\n";

  foreach $topping (sort keys %toppings) {
    if (exists $formHash{$topping}) {
      print ORDERFILE "$toppings{$topping}\n";
    }
  }
  print ORDERFILE "----------------------------------------\n";
  close(ORDERFILE);

  print <<TOP;
    <html><head><title>Thank you for your order</title></head><body>
      Thank you $formHash{"name"} (phone $formHash{"phone"}).
      We have processed your order of a <b>$formHash{"chosen_size"}</b> pizza
      with the following extra toppings:<ul>
TOP

  foreach $topping (sort keys %toppings) {
    if(exists $formHash{$topping}) {
      print "<li><b>$toppings{$topping}</b></li>\n";
    }
  }

  print<<BOTTOM;
    </ul>
    for a total of <b>\$$formHash{"total"}</b>.
  </body></html>
BOTTOM
}
```

- Open the data file (for append) or return an error page to the user. (It could say something like "We are too busy to process the order. Try again shortly.")

- Append the order to the file. That includes the newly submitted data (name, phone) and the "remembered" data in the hidden elements. A loop is used to iterate over the available toppings and record the chosen ones into the file.

- Print a line to provide a break before the next recorded order, and close the file.

- Print the top of the returned HTML page, including a message for the user.

- Use a loop to print an HTML list of the chosen toppings.

- Print the order total and the rest of the page. (Note in Figure 7.2 that the two-decimal-place formatting is still preserved in the $total. Indeed, the sprintf command formatted the total in the processForm function before it was stored into the hidden form element!)

> **NOTE**
>
> It is important to emphasize the "glue" that holds this Web application together. Of course, the main adhesive is the hidden data that remembers the user's choices during the finalizing transaction. There is a more subtle issue, however, that enables the application to work smoothly: The order form is dynamically created from the data source. The hash data structures are "preserved" throughout all the transactions.
>
> For example, the keys of the `%toppings` hash become the names of the checkboxes in the order form as a result of the first HTTP transaction. Those names then become keys of `%formHash` during the second HTTP transaction. Those keys then become the names of the hidden elements for the toppings in the confirmation form. During the third HTTP transaction those names are then again keys of `%formHash`, which are tested for existence in the original `%toppings` hash data source. Without use of the hash keys of the data source for the names of the form elements, the logistics of this program would be considerably more cumbersome.

Of course, several improvements and enhancements could be programmed into `pizza3.cgi`. For example, you would want to obtain the address to which the pizza is to be delivered and a credit card number. (How practical an online pizzeria actually is in real life can be left to the imagination.) Also, it is customary to allow the user to confirm not just the order details, but the delivery address and billing information. One improvement that definitely would be beneficial is to include JavaScript that verifies that sufficient information is collected before the forms are submitted. Such improvements are left as exercises.

> **NOTE**
>
> An important idea, central to many Web applications, is the idea of another program that provides administrative capabilities. Such an *administrative program* is a program, hidden from the public, that the owner of the Web application (here the pizzeria) can use to update the data source and monitor data that the application collects. For example, it would be beneficial for the server-side data source for this example to be kept in a separate text file (or database). The store manager could call a Web-based administration program with which she could remotely update the pizza prices and available toppings in the file.

7.3 SESSION STATE

The pizza example from the previous section illustrates a one-step state preservation. That is, only one intermediary page contains hidden state data—a very short session. This section provides an example in which hidden form elements are used to preserve state data over a sequence of several form submissions. The example features an online trivia quiz, where several questions are sent to the user in sequence.

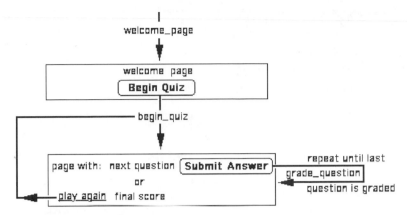

FIGURE 7.4 Transaction diagram for an online quiz.

Figure 7.4 shows the transaction diagram for the quiz we will develop. On first "hitting" the application, the user is greeted with a welcome page, which contains a form button that is used to start the quiz. The begin_quiz function prints a page containing the first question. Submitting the answer results in a page with another question. Thus, we see that the grade_question function is to be responsible for both grading a question and returning the next one until the quiz is over. The last time the grade_question function is called is when the last question is submitted, at which time it prints a page with the final score. As you see in the transaction diagram, the final page is to have a link that can be used to start the quiz again. That link merely needs to call the program with a request to call the begin_quiz function.

The app logic is similar to the previous example in that there are three functions that run the application, based upon requests. In this application, however, the grade_question function is called repetitively. As before, hidden form elements carry the app logic requests to the application when forms are submitted. As you shall see, the "play again" link submits its app logic request via a manually constructed query string. The only planning that remains before we start coding involves how the application is to keep track of the current qnumber, and the total number of correct answers at any given point. A "sketch" of the hidden form elements is shown in Figure 7.5.

There are many more HTML form elements than for which we have shown HTML code in Figure 7.5. Again, code for only the hidden ones is shown. The thing to note about the app logic requests is that the grade_question function hides requests that call itself when questions are submitted. Two other hidden form elements keep state for the application. One tracks the current qnumber, and the other tracks the number of correct answers so far. You can easily track the progress of the quiz in Figure 7.5. Effectively, those two hidden elements act like hidden counters that track the progress of the quiz session.

Figure 7.6 shows the outline for quiz1.cgi. Following the standard decoding routine, the data source for the quiz questions is initialized. The arrays @quiz_question, @quiz_choices, and @quiz_answer carry the data. The arrays are parallel so that data for a given question can be accessed from the arrays using a single array index. Next comes the app logic and definitions of those functions. There is one function, print_question, that is not part of the app logic. Both the begin_quiz and the grade_question functions must print quiz questions, so it is logical to write a helper function to handle the repetitive task.

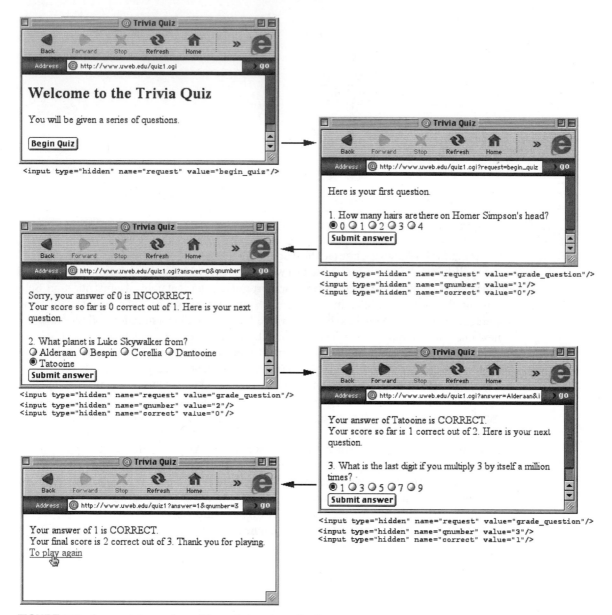

FIGURE 7.5 A complete session of the `quiz1.cgi` application.

Now let's code the functions. The `welcome_page` function does no more than print a Web page containing a form whose hidden element will trigger the `begin_quiz` function when the form is submitted. Note that we could have used a link

```
<a href="quiz1.cgi?request=begin_quiz">Begin Quiz</a>
```

manually coded with the data necessary to trigger `begin_quiz` in the app logic. Instead we chose to use a form button.

```
#! /usr/bin/perl
print "Content-type: text/html\n\n";

##############################################################
#    code for decoding input $datastring into %formHash     #
#       (works for GET, POST, and offline execution)        #
##############################################################

### the data source ##################################
@quiz_question = (
  "How many hairs are there on Homer Simpson's head?",
  "What planet is Luke Skywalker from?",
  "What is the last digit if you multiply 3 by itself a million times?"
);
@quiz_choices = (
  "0;1;2;3;4",
  "Alderaan;Bespin;Corellia;Dantooine;Tatooine",
  "1;3;5;7;9"
);
@quiz_answer = (
  "2",
  "Tatooine",
  "1"
);
### end data source ##################################

### app logic ##################################
if($formHash{"request"} eq "begin_quiz") {
  &begin_quiz;
}
elsif($formHash{"request"} eq "grade_question") {
  &grade_question;
}
else {
  &welcome_page;
}
### end app logic ##################################

##############################################################
### Definitions of app logic functions go here.            #
### Definitions for helper functions:                      #
#    &print_question                                        #
##############################################################
```

FIGURE 7.6   The outline for `quiz1.cgi`.

```
sub welcome_page {
  print <<PAGE;
  <html><head><title>Trivia Quiz</title></head><body>
    <h2>Welcome to the Trivia Quiz</h2>
    You will be given a series of questions.
    <form action="$ENV{'SCRIPT_NAME'}" method="GET">
      <input type="hidden" name="request" value="begin_quiz">
      <input type="submit" value="Begin Quiz">
    </form>
  </body></html>
PAGE
}
```

The real work of the application begins when the form in the welcome page is submitted. The `begin_quiz`, `print_question`, and `grade_question` functions follow. An outline follows each function.

```
sub begin_quiz {
  print <<TOP;
  <html><head><title>Trivia Quiz</title></head><body>
    Here is your first question.<br/>
TOP

    &print_question(1, 0);

    print <<BOTTOM;
  </body></html>
BOTTOM
}
```

■ Print the top of the page for the first question.

■ Call the `print_question` function to print the first question. Note that the `print_question` function takes two parameters, which correspond to the state data for the quiz. Here, 1 is the `qnumber` of the first question, and obviously there have been 0 correct answers.

■ Print the bottom of the page.

```
sub print_question {
  my ($qnumber, $correct) = @_;
  my $index = $qnumber-1;
  my @choices = split(/;/, $quiz_choices[$index]);

  print<<QUESTION;
  <form action = "$ENV{'SCRIPT_NAME'}" method="GET">
    $qnumber. $quiz_question[$index]
    <br/>
QUESTION

    foreach $answer (@choices) {
      print '<input type="radio" name="answer" value="', "$answer\" />$answer";
    }
  print<<FORM;
    <br/>
    <input type="hidden" name="qnumber" value="$qnumber"/>
    <input type="hidden" name="correct" value="$correct"/>
    <input type="hidden" name="request" value="grade_question"/>
    <input type="submit" value="Submit answer"/>
  </form>
FORM
}
```

■ Pass the incoming parameters into local variables. (The parameters contain the state of the quiz application.)

■ A local variable `$index` is set to the index of the current question number, which is one less than `$qnumber` because the index of an array begins at 0, whereas our question numbers begin at 1.

■ A local `@choices` array is initialized to contain the possible answers to the current question. The global `@quiz_choices` array contains possible answers for all questions, and `$quiz_choices[$index]` contains the answers for the current question. The possible answers are split into the individual `@choices` at the delimiting semicolons.

- Print the beginning form tag and then the text that asks the current question.
- For each possible $answer
    - Print a radio button whose value is the $answer. The $answer is also printed as text following the radio button so that the user can see it.
- Print the rest of the form: the hidden element indicating the qnumber, the hidden element indicating the number of correct answers, the hidden element telling the program to grade the question when the form is submitted, and the submit button.

```
sub grade_question {
  print<<TOP;
  <html><head><title>Trivia Quiz</title></head><body>
TOP

    my $qnumber = $formHash{"qnumber"};
    my $correct = $formHash{"correct"};
    my $index = $qnumber - 1;

    if($formHash{"answer"} eq $quiz_answer[$index]) {
      print "Your answer of $formHash{'answer'} is CORRECT.<br/>\n";
      $correct++;
    }
    else {
      print "Sorry, your answer of $formHash{'answer'} is INCORRECT.<br/>\n";
    }

    $qnumber++; # Either way, the question has been answered.

    if($qnumber > scalar @quiz_question) {
      print "Your final score is $correct correct out of ", $qnumber-1, ".\n",
        "Thank you for playing.<br/>\n",
        "<a href=\"$ENV{'SCRIPT_NAME'}?request=begin_quiz\">To play again</a>";
    }
    else {
      print "Your score so far is $correct correct out of ", $qnumber - 1, ".\n",
        "Here is your next question.\n";
      &print_question($qnumber, $correct);
    }
    print<<BOTTOM;
  </body></html>
BOTTOM
}
```

- Print the top of the page.
- Store the state of the quiz into two local variables. Note that the state values come from the hidden elements in the question that has just been submitted. Also, the array $index is one less than $qnumber.
- If the submitted answer matches the correct answer for the current question,
    - Inform the user the answer is correct and add one to the number of $correct answers.
- Else
    - Inform the user the answer is wrong.
- Add one to $qnumber.
- If there are no more questions,
    - Print a message containing the final state of the quiz and a link the user can use to start the quiz over. (We could have used a form button with a hidden request.)

- Else (there is another question)

  - Print a message containing the current state of the quiz.
  - Call `print_question` to print the next question. Recall that the current state of the quiz is sent to the `print_question` function. That way, it knows which question to print next and it can hide the state info in the form for that question.

- Print the rest of the page.

In practice, one builds an application like this from the ground up. First make a transaction diagram that outlines the structure of the program. Then it really helps to sketch a diagram like Figure 7.5 on scratch paper before starting to write code. That way, you can envision the steps involved in the session and devise what hidden state data needs to be passed around. Once the objectives are understood, start writing functions from the top of the transaction diagram.

For example, we first wrote and tested the `welcome_page` function. Then we wrote the `begin_quiz` function and made sure that submitting the form in the welcome page passed the right information to cause the page containing the first question to be generated properly and with the right hidden data. It was at that time that we realized that a question would also need to be printed in the `grade_question` function, so we devised the `print_question` function to handle the repetitive task. Of course, the `grade_question` function then had to be developed and tested. That function also needed to detect when the quiz was over. It is always important to remember that planning is *essential* when writing Web applications (or other applications), and that modular development and testing makes coding easier.

Again, this example could be improved by keeping the server-side data source in a separate file. Then an administrative program could be created to allow the quiz administrator to change, add, or delete questions remotely. That would make this a self-contained Web application, in which the quiz could be periodically updated remotely over the Web. Web applications become "living entities" when content can be changed without having to update code in source files on the server manually. Also, it might be desirable to record quiz results in a file so that users can see cumulative statistics after taking the quiz.

NOTE

It is certainly worth noting that this program has security weaknesses. For starters, someone could easily examine the HTML source code and query string to deduce how the hidden elements keep track of state and how the quiz answers are submitted. It would be a good idea to switch the submit method to POST for the final version so that at least the submitted data is not visible. However, in this case, that doesn't help much. The user can simply click the back button on the Web browser to reanswer a question that was answered incorrectly. Go to the book's Web site and try it for yourself by missing a question, clicking the back button, and then submitting the right answer.

The best solution to that problem is to store state data in files that are kept on the server, as we shall see in the next section. Of course, one could make a version of the quiz where all the questions are on the same page and the answers are submitted at once, but that would defeat the purpose of this section. Sequential form submission sessions are used often on the Web, especially in cases where the content of one form is dependent upon data that was submitted from a previous form.

7.4 TEMPORARY STATE FILES

The previous examples in this lesson featured state data that was hidden on the client between transactions. A **state file** is a text file on the server created by a CGI program to store state data during a session. The idea is that each time a user starts a new session of the Web application, a new state file is created to keep track of the data for that session. This notion brings up several logistical issues that must be addressed.

1. In order that different users can use the application at the same time, a different state file must be created for each user.

2. The name of the state file for a given session must be passed to the Web browser hidden in the different Web pages involved with the session, and resubmitted to the server in subsequent transactions. Otherwise, subsequent transactions of the session won't know which state file to access.

3. A suitable format for storing the state data in the files must be devised.

4. Some naming scheme must be devised for the state files so that one state file is not corrupted by being used for two different sessions simultaneously. That is, a given state file should be unique for a session.

5. As more and more users do sessions with the application, more and more state files are created on the server. There needs to be a contingency in place so that the number of state files created on the server does not grow without bound.

Item 5 in this list indicates that the state files must in some sense be temporary. That might involve deleting or reusing old state files. Hence, the title of this section indicates that we use "temporary state files." There are several possible strategies for managing the collection of state files available to a Web application. We now present a strategy that addresses all the points listed except for the last point; we will discuss the "policing" of state files in the next section.

The `quiz1.cgi` application makes a perfect example with which to illustrate the use of state files. In the process, we fix its security hole, which the note at the end of the previous section points out. The new version is named `quiz2.cgi`. Each session of the application involves a user taking the quiz. A state file is created for each quiz session. The following points outline the strategy (out of many possible) we use to accomplish this. These points illustrate a specific implementation of the general ideas given in the preceding, corresponding list.

1. Each time a user starts the quiz by clicking the submit button in the welcome page, the program generates a random 32-character string. We refer to this string as the **session ID**. Each session ID is just a string of alphanumeric characters, such as `"C9JzoLZh998LKJtyfl98GV76Y8H8kjoi"`. Each session ID is used to create a text

file with name *sessionID*.state. For example, this hypothetical session ID would result in a state file with name C9JzoLZh998LKJtyfl98GV76Y8H8kjoi.state. This choice of .state for the file extension is somewhat arbitrary; on systems that prefer three-character file extensions, one might use an extension like .stt. In fact, we could even use the session ID itself, without any extension, as the file name. For organizational and identification purposes, though, it is desirable to give files meaningful extensions.

2. The session ID is embedded in the Web pages of the session using hidden form elements. The name of the state file for a given session can easily be constructed when submitted back to the CGI program from the session ID.

3. The best format for storing state data in a file is in a hashlike format, placing each name-value pair on a separate line. We can use an equals sign (=) as the delimiter between the name and value, just as in a URL-encoded query string. We will also URL-encode the two parts, just like a URL-encoded query string. That is, the only difference between this format and a URL-encoded query string is that a query string uses ampersands (&) to separate name=value pairs, whereas here we use newlines to separate name=value pairs. For the current example, there are only two pieces of state data for the quiz application, the qnumber and the number of correct answers. So a typical state file after completion of the quiz looks like the following, if the state hash is ("qnumber"=>3, "correct"=>1). Notice the similarity to Figure 5.7.

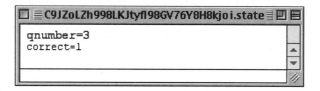

A first thought might have been just to put the state data in an array and to place each item of the array on a separate line in the file. Although the array method would have the advantage of being simpler in the short run, the **state hash** method is far superior in the long run. One clear advantage of the hash method is that we do not need to remember the predetermined order of data, as we would in the array method. Also, as experience will demonstrate, the hash method allows for much more flexibility in that it is much easier to modify a program where state data is stored in a hash format.

4. This strategy in practice assures the uniqueness of the state files. These session IDs are so large that there is effectively probability 0 that the same session ID would *ever* be used twice. With 62 possible characters, there are 62^{32} possible IDs, and the probability of generating a given session ID is $1/62^{32} = 2.3 \times 10^{-57}$. You're simply not going to generate the same ID twice randomly in your lifetime. (It's more likely to win several major lotteries in a row!) We will say more on this subject in Section 13.6 on security issues.

5. Because of the "nearly infinite" (mathematicians cringe at such wording) supply of state file names, the directory containing the state files, like the one shown here, will

gradually become more and more populated with files, growing virtually without bound if left unchecked. Again, we will address this important issue in the next section.

Before showing the entire `quiz2.cgi` program that uses these ideas, we present some toolkit functions that will help us deal with state files. With that done, the rest of the program will fall into place. The first function, named `generate_random_string`, is shown in Figure 7.7 followed by an overview. This function returns a random alphanumeric string of length specified by its one parameter.

```
sub generate_random_string {
  my $length = $_[0];
  my $result = "";
  my @chars = (0..9, 'a'..'z', 'A'..'Z');
  my $which;
  for($i = 1 ; $i <= $length ; $i++) {
    $which=int rand 62;
    $result = $result . $chars[$which];
  }
  return $result;
}
```

FIGURE 7.7 The `generate_random_string` toolkit function.

- Receive the incoming parameter, which is the length of the string that is to be generated.
- Declare some local variables, including an array containing the 62 possible characters that are used to build up the random string.
- For `$i` from 1 to the number of characters to generate
  - Randomly choose `$which` integer from the range 0 through 61.
  - Concatenate the character at that index of the `@chars` array onto the `$result`.
- Return the long string.

Using the `generate_random_string` function, we can easily generate a new 32-digit session ID when a user starts the quiz.

```
$sessionID = &generate_random_string(32);
```

Using the `$sessionID`, the name of a state file is easily constructed by concatenation.

```
$filename = $sessionID . ".state";
```

Or better yet, interpolate the $sessionID variable inside double quotes to construct the file name.

```
$filename = "$sessionID.state";
```

Of course, all the state files need to be kept somewhere, so we assign the path to an appropriate directory to a global variable.

```
$stateDir = "/home/data/stateDir/";
```

The remaining toolkit functions we develop here automate the process of reading and writing to state files. When a state file needs to be updated, we call the write_state function, which takes three pieces of information: the path to the directory containing the state files, the session ID to identify the particular file, and the hash containing the state data.

```
&write_state($stateDir, $sessionID, %stateHash);
```

When we merely need to read the current state data in a file, the read_state function is called. The only parameters it takes are the state file directory and the session ID to identify the file:

```
%stateHash = &read_state($stateDir, $sessionID);
```

It returns a hash consisting of the state data found in the file.

Both of these functions are shown in Figure 7.8. Here, $fileroot stands for the part of a file before the file extension, namely the session ID. The write_state function receives the incoming $dir, $fileroot, and hash of %states. It then constructs the full file name and opens the file for writing using the full directory path; if the state file does not already exist, opening it for writing creates it. The function then URL-encodes the names and values, writing each pair on a separate line of the file using = as the delimiter.

The read_state function receives the incoming $dir and $fileroot, constructs the full file name, opens the file for reading, and reads the whole file into @array. It then builds the %hash by chomping each $line from the file, splitting the $line into $key and $value parts, URL-decoding the $name and $value, and adding the name-value pair to the hash.

Note that we URL-encode the name-value pairs before saving them to the file. This is necessary in case either the name or value contains an equals sign or newline character, because those two characters are used as delimiters. More importantly, without such a precautionary URL-encoding, there could be a big security hole (see Section 13.6). Thus we URL-encode when saving to a state file, and we URL-decode when reading from a state file. Because this is all done in our read_state and write_state functions, once we have them programmed, the URL-encoding/decoding is done happily behind the scenes, transparent to the rest of the application. The URL-encoding/decoding functions are presented here and will be explained in Chapter 11.

```
sub write_state {
  my ($dir, $fileroot, %states) = @_;
  my $filename = "$fileroot.state";
  open(OUTFILE, ">$dir$filename") or &errorPage("Error writing to state file.");
  foreach $key (keys %states) {
    $value = &URLencode($states{$key});
    $name = &URLencode($key);
    print OUTFILE "$name=$value\n";
  }
  close(OUTFILE);
}
####################################################################
sub read_state {
  my ($dir, $fileroot) = @_;
  my $filename = "$fileroot.state";
  open(INFILE, "<$dir$filename") or &errorPage("Error reading state file.");
  my @array =<INFILE>;
  close(INFILE);
  my %hash = ();
  foreach $line (@array) {
    chomp $line;
    my ($key, $value) = split(/=/, $line, 2);
    $key = &URLdecode($key);
    $value = &URLdecode($value);
    $hash{$key} = $value;
  }
  return %hash;
}
####################################################################
sub URLencode {
  my $string = $_[0];
  $string =~ s/([^\w])/"%".sprintf("%02x", ord($1))/eg;
  return $string;
}
####################################################################
sub URLdecode {
  my $string = $_[0];
  $string =~ tr/+/ /;
  $string =~ s/%([\da-fA-F]{2})/pack("C",hex($1))/eg;
  return $string;
}
```

FIGURE 7.8 The functions that handle the state file operations for `quiz2.cgi`.

We are now ready to present the new quiz application. The same transaction diagram (Figure 7.4) applies, but now the `begin_quiz` function has more responsibilities. Figure 7.8 shows a sample session of `quiz2.cgi`. When the user clicks the button in the welcome page, three things take place: A session ID is generated, a new state file corresponding to that session ID is created on the server, and the first question is returned to the user. When the first question is submitted, three things take place: The contents of the state file are read (`read_state` function), the state file is updated (`write_state` function), and the second question is returned to the user. These events keep happening until the quiz is completed. Then the session is over, and the state file sits (uselessly) on the server until it is cleaned up by some policing action (which we discuss in the next section) or until it is coincidentally overwritten by another session (which probabilistically will never happen in our lifetime if the session IDs are truly random).

You can see that the `name="id"` hidden elements carry the session ID so that the proper state file can be identified during each transaction. The `name="request"` hidden elements make the same app logic requests as before. From the user's perspective, `quiz2.cgi` would appear to work identically to `quiz1.cgi`, unless they happen to notice

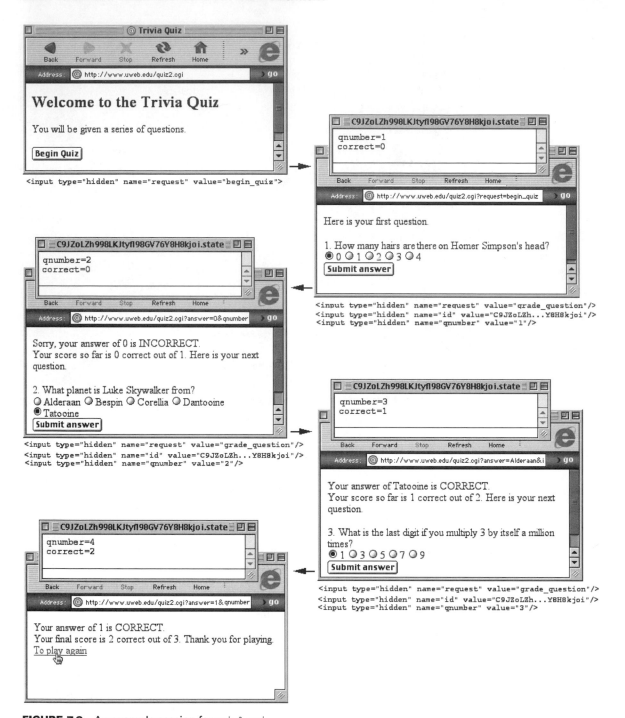

FIGURE 7.9 An example session for `quiz2.cgi`.

that different data is sent in the query string (if the application uses GET), or if they look at the HTML source code and the different hidden form elements.

The observant reader may notice that it is not necessary to carry the `name="qnumber"` hidden elements in this example, because that information is readily available in the state file on the server. That's true, but they are included so that the application can detect erroneous repeated submissions and attempted cheating. To see how that works, suppose the user gets the Homer Simpson question wrong and decides to press the back button on the browser to have another go, as we discussed in the note at the end of the previous section. That page contains the hidden `qnumber` value 1. However, the state file on the server contains the `qnumber` value of 2, because the first question has already been submitted and the user is looking at the second question when the back button is pressed. In this application, that discrepancy is detected and the question is not allowed to be resubmitted. Try it out on this book's Web site! We should mention that even without the hidden `name="qnumber"` element, the user effectively would not be able to cheat, because the state data is kept on the server. However, the inclusion of this hidden element allows the application to distinguish repeated submissions (either by cheating or by an honest error, say through clicking Refresh erroneously) from a true submission.

The outline of the program, shown in Figure 7.10, is quite similar to that of the first quiz version. The first addition is the global variable `$stateDir`, which contains the absolute path to the directory that is to contain all the state files; of course, the path may look different depending upon the operating system and setup. We also initialize a global variable `%stateHash` to hold state data. The only other changes to the application are the functions that have been updated; the added new functions that deal with the state files; and the inclusion of the standard `errorPage` function.

NOTE

On some systems, the directory for the state files *must* be preset to have full read–write–execute privileges for anonymous users. (See Appendix C.) Otherwise, the CGI program will not have proper access to the state files.

The `welcome_page` function is unchanged in this version, because all it does is print the form that, when submitted, tells the program to start the quiz. Thus, we do not show it again. The `begin_quiz`, `print_question`, and `grade-question` functions have all been updated. The new versions follow, with overviews of the modifications. Aside from initializing a state file for the new session and hiding slightly different data in the question form, the functions are very similar to the original ones.

```
sub begin_quiz {
  my $sessionID = &generate_random_string(32);
  %stateHash = ("qnumber"=>1, "correct"=>0);
  &write_state($stateDir, $sessionID, %stateHash);

  print <<TOP;
<html><head><title>Trivia Quiz</title></head><body>
  Here is your first question.<br/>
```

```
TOP

&print_question($sessionID, 1);

print <<BOTTOM;
</body></html>
BOTTOM
}
```

- Get a new $sessionID.

- Create (or overwrite) a state file corresponding to the $sessionID. The file is initialized to reflect the beginning of a session by initializing the %stateHash (0 questions answered and 0 correct).

- The rest of the function is the same, except that the print_question function now takes different parameters. Of course, it must be sent the $qnumber so that it knows what question to print. Its other job is to print the hidden form elements. So, in this example, it also needs the $sessionID. It does not need the current number of $correct answers, as in the first version, because that data is now kept in the state file instead of being hidden in form printed by print_question.

```
sub print_question {
  my ($sessionID, $qnumber) = @_;
  my $index = $qnumber - 1;
  my @choices = split(/;/, $quiz_choices[$index]);

  print<<QUESTION;
<form action = "$ENV{'SCRIPT_NAME'}" method="GET">
  $qnumber. $quiz_question[$index]
  <br/>
QUESTION

  foreach $answer (@choices) {
    print '<input type="radio" name="answer" value="', "$answer\" />$answer";
  }
  print<<FORM;
  <br/>
  <input type="hidden" name="id" value="$sessionID"/>
  <input type="hidden" name="qnumber" value="$qnumber"/>
  <input type="hidden" name="request" value="grade_question"/>
  <input type="submit" value="Submit answer"/>
  </form>
FORM
}
```

- Pass the incoming parameters into local variables. (Here, the parameters don't contain all of the state data, but just enough information to print the current question and the hidden form elements.)

- The only difference in the rest of the function is that the $sessionID is hidden in the form instead of the current number of $correct answers.

The updates to the grade_question function are more significant. In particular, this function is now responsible for reading and updating the state file. Also, the function now implements a provision that prevents cheating.

```
□ ≡≡≡≡≡≡≡≡≡≡≡≡≡≡≡≡  quiz2.cgi ≡≡≡≡≡≡≡≡≡≡≡≡≡≡≡  ▣▤

#! /usr/bin/perl
print "Content-type: text/html\n\n";

###############################################################
#   code for decoding input $datastring into %formHash      #
#       (works for GET, POST, and offline execution)        #
###############################################################

$stateDir = "/home/data/states/";
%stateHash= ();

### the data source ###########################################
@quiz_question = (
  "How many hairs are there on Homer Simpson's head?",
  "What planet is Luke Skywalker from?",
  "What is the last digit if you multiply 3 by itself a million times?"
);
@quiz_choices = (
  "0;1;2;3;4",
  "Alderaan;Bespin;Corellia;Dantooine;Tatooine",
  "1;3;5;7;9"
);
@quiz_answer = (
  "2",
  "Tatooine",
  "1"
);
### end data source ###########################################

### app logic #################################################
if($formHash{"request"} eq "begin_quiz") {
    &begin_quiz;
}
elsif($formHash{"request"} eq "grade_question") {
    &grade_question;
}
else {
    &welcome_page;
}
### end app logic #############################################

###############################################################
### Definitions of app logic functions go here.            #
### Definitions for helper functions:                      #
#     &print_question                                       #
### Definitions for toolkit functions used:                #
#     &generate_random_string    (new)                      #
#     &write_state               (new)                      #
#     &read_state                (new)                      #
#     &URLencode                 (new)                      #
#     &URLdecode                 (new)                      #
#     &errorPage                 (from Section 5.7)         #
###############################################################
```

FIGURE 7.10 The outline of `quiz2.cgi`.

```
sub grade_question {
   my $sessionID = $formHash{"id"};
   %stateHash= &read_state($stateDir, $sessionID);

   if ($stateHash{"qnumber"} > scalar @quiz_question) {
     $sentence = "Quiz is over.";
   }
   elsif($formHash{"qnumber"} < $stateHash{"qnumber"}) { # don't cheat!
     $sentence = "You have already answered that question.";
```

```
  }
  else {
    if($formHash{"answer"} eq $quiz_answer[$stateHash{"qnumber"}-1]) {
      $stateHash{"correct"}++;
      $sentence = "Your answer of $formHash{answer} is CORRECT.<br/>\n";
    }
    else {
      $sentence = "Sorry, your answer of $formHash{answer} is INCORRECT.<br/>\n";
    }
    $stateHash{"qnumber"}++;
    &write_state($stateDir, $sessionID, %stateHash);
  }

  print<<TOP;
  <html><head><title>Trivia Quiz</title></head><body>
  $sentence
TOP
  if($stateHash{"qnumber"} > scalar @quiz_question) {
    print "Your final score is $stateHash{correct} correct out of ",
      scalar @quiz_question, ".\n",
      "Thank you for playing.<br/>\n",
      "<a href=\"$ENV{'SCRIPT_NAME'}?request=begin_quiz\">To play again</a>";
  }
  else {
    print "Your score so far is $stateHash{correct} correct out of ",
      $stateHash{qnumber}-1, ".\n",
      "Here is your next question.\n";
    &print_question($sessionID, $stateHash{"qnumber"});
  }
  print<<BOTTOM;
  </body></html>
BOTTOM
}
```

- Get the `$sessionID` (which was submitted to the server as a hidden element in the question's form).
- Get the current state data from the proper file.
- If the quiz is over
  - Save a `$sentence` saying so.
- Else, if the submitted question is not the current one,
  - Save a `$sentence` saying so. This part of the conditional is activated only if the number value from the submitted question is less than the number value from the state file, as when the user tries to cheat by resubmitting a question.
- Else the question is current and the quiz is not over.
  - Grade the question.
  - Increment the question `$qnumber`. Note that this is not done in the "cheater clause."
  - Update the state file.
- Print the top of the page.
- Either terminate the quiz or print the next question. Note that if the "cheater clause" was invoked, the `$qnumber` was not updated, so the user is asked the current unanswered question again.
- Print the bottom of the page.

NOTE

A subtle issue in the `grade_question` function arises from the use of file operations. That was not an issue in the previous version. In particular, all file operations must be done before the top of the HTML page is printed. That is because a failed file operation (in the `read_state` or `write_state` function) causes the `errorPage` function to print a complete Web page for the user. Otherwise, you could end up with an error page sent to the user that contains two HEAD and TITLE HTML elements, for example.

That is why there appears to be some "redundant logic" in the function. In particular, the decision on whether to update the state file has to be made before the top of the HTML page is printed. In contrast, the decision on exactly what to print in the page must come after the top of the HTML page has been printed. One could circumvent that issue by not generating an error page if a file operation fails. However, if you recall, failed file operations cause a CGI program to crash, in which case the Web server software (typically) sends a very lame page back to the browser in an effort to complete the HTTP transaction.

7.5   STATE FILE CACHING

You might wonder "Why not just stick with hidden form elements for state data?" After all, using state files is somewhat more work. However, in general, storing data in state files on the server is the far more versatile solution. For starters, it is cumbersome to pass large amounts of data back and forth between the server and browser using hidden form elements. A shopping cart application could easily result in dozens of hidden form elements being passed around. A state file makes for a compact, self-contained, server-side depository for temporary data.

Another advantage of state files is that form submissions need not have a predetermined linear dependence. To propagate session state using only hidden form elements, each app logic function has to embed all state data collected so far in the Web page it prints. If any data is "dropped" along the transaction sequence, it simply will not be available during subsequent transactions. Thus, all data has to be passed along the transaction sequence. It is very difficult to design applications that use only hidden form elements to accomplish that. The back button of browsers is one inhibiting factor.

To see that, consider again the shopping cart concept. Hidden form elements fall short, because shopping is not necessarily a linear process. Suppose the user just selected an item to be purchased by filling out and submitting a form. Suppose the user then clicks the back button, going back to the same form to select another product. Using only hidden form elements, the original purchase selection would be lost. With a state file, purchases are accumulated in the shopping cart regardless of the sequence of form submissions.

Although shopping carts make perfect motivational examples for the need for using state files, we are not yet ready to provide such an example. There are many more crucial concepts to learn first. An elaborate Web application for an online store with a shopping cart is presented in Chapter 13.

The rest of this section is devoted to managing a collection of state files. We term a directory containing a managed collection of state files a **state file cache**. As we noted in the previous section, there are 62^{32} possible session IDs represented by our 32-character strings. Without some strategy for managing, or *policing*, the collection of state files that result from more and more sessions, the number of state files will tend to grow without bound for all practical purposes. A Web application with a load of thousands of sessions per day would generate tens of thousands of new state files each month, and millions per year.

A very naïve strategy would be to shorten the length and character pool of the session ID string, so that the number of possible state files is limited to, say 10,000 files. Then, at about 2K each, for example, the collection of all possible state files would occupy about 20 megabytes of hard drive space. Such a strategy, however, seriously compromises the uniqueness of the session IDs. For example, 10,000 possible IDs gives a probability of 10^{-4} of randomly producing a given ID. Such a probability is unacceptable, both because of the likelihood of generating the same ID twice (overwriting someone else's state file) and because of the security risk (a hacker being able to produce the string). Even a lower probability of 10^{-5} is not even close to being acceptable for security reasons, and probabilities significantly lower than that result in too many potential state files—our existing problem with the 32-character strings.

A better, but still not ideal, strategy is to write an administration program that runs periodically to delete old state files. For example, a program could be set so that it automatically runs every Sunday night at midnight (or some other off-peak server activity time), deleting any state files that have not been modified in the last day or two. Such a program would effectively police the state file cache at regular time intervals. Depending upon the average load of the application, the policing program might be run every few days, once a week, or even once a month. However, this solution leaves the server vulnerable to a *denial-of-service attack*.[1] If such an attack hits a Web application that generates state files using only a periodic policing strategy, the hard drive could fill up with state files in no time.

The preferred solution for policing a state file cache (and for many other caching needs, we might add) is to impose a limit on the number of files that are cached at any given time. We refer to that as the *cache limit*. When the number of state files reaches the cache limit, a policing program on the server is automatically triggered to go through the state directory, deleting old state files, (say, older than one or two days). The cache limit would be chosen based upon the load of the application so that the cache is always more than large enough to accommodate the application's users, but not so large as to leave the server vulnerable to a rapid growth spurt of state files from a denial-of-service attack.

When considering how to manage a collection of state files, one must first consider the expected *load* on the Web application. One could define the load on a Web application as the average number of sessions that are under way at any given time. However, that quantity is hard to measure in practice. Rather, we consider the load on a Web application to be the number of sessions that occur over a given period of time. For our purposes here, we define the load on a Web application to be the average number of sessions it services per day (or 24-hour period). Certainly, other time periods could be used to define the load.

The load easily can be determined by software packages that compile statistics based upon entries into a Web server's log files, which record details of each transaction. Such software packages can compile statistics for hits on an entire Web site (or domain) or simply for a certain Web application that is part of the site. Such commercial (or freeware) site analysis tools are usually quite elaborate in terms of the myriad of statistics that they generate, but a Web programmer could fairly easily write an administration program to determine the load on a given Web application. We will analyze a real server log file in Chapter 11.

---

[1] A denial-of-service attack occurs when a hacker's program attempts to bombard a server with more requests than it can handle. Such an attack can effectively clog up a server, denying legitimate users a chance to access it. For you Web programmers who might get bright ideas, don't try that unless you feel like spending some time in jail.

For a quick example to show how server load breaks down, consider a Web application that has an average load of 500 sessions per day. Suppose each session lasts about 20 minutes on average. That breaks down to the application managing about 7 different sessions at any given instant in time on average. For concurrent session states, 7 might seem like a small number, but a load of 500 is certainly not small in general. (Try to put a Web page or application out there and coax hits from 500 visitors a day.)

We now create a new toolkit function, named `get_long_id`, to implement cache management. On the surface, this function will simply return randomly generated 32-digit session IDs with the help of the `generate_random_string` function we already have at our disposal. Behind the scenes, the `get_long_id` function will police the state file cache if it is full, as determined by the cache limit. Thus, the act of generating a long ID for state files in our applications will automatically implement the cache policing quietly behind the scenes. So, basically, we will have cache management in our applications without having to do anything special. The algorithm the `get_long_id` function employs is as follows:

- Obtain the current number of files in the state file cache.
- If the cache limit is reached,
    - Delete any state files that have not been modified recently.
    - Again, obtain the current number of files in the state file cache.
    - If the cache limit is still reached,
        - Deny the user a session by sending an error page indicating that the site is busy. Also, notify the site administrator that that the cache still exceeds the cache limit, even after it was policed. The administrator needs to see whether a denial-of-service attack is occurring and, if not, to increase the cache limit to accommodate the load of the application.
- Return a long session ID.

We need two Perl file test operators to accomplish this algorithm. These operators are listed in Table 7.1. Such file test operators are unary, taking a single file (or directory) name as an argument. They are typically used in conditionals, as the following pseudocode examples demonstrate:

```
if (-f "/path/to/somefile.txt") {
  then somefile.txt is a file (hence exists in the directory)
}

if ((-M "/path/to/somefile.txt") > 1){
  then somefile.txt has not been modified in the last 24 hours
}
```

See Section 12.6 for more on file test operators.

The new toolkit function is shown in Figure 7.11. As you can see from the foregoing algorithm outline, if the cache limit is not exceeded, the function accomplishes no more than returning a long session ID. Otherwise it polices the cache and then returns a long ID.

TABLE 7.1   Two Perl File Test Operators

OPERATION	RESULT
-f *filename*	Returns true if *filename* is a file (as opposed to a directory or nonexistent)
-M *filename*	Returns the time (in days as a real number) since filename was last modified

There are two main things to note about the `get_long_id` function. First, it takes three parameters: the path to the directory containing the state files, the cache limit, and the life span for the files in the cache. Second, Perl's built-in `unlink` function is used to delete any state files that have exceeded their life span. The name of that function is indicative of what it accomplishes. When you delete files on a computer (as in emptying the recycle bin), they are not really wiped from the computer's memory, as you might expect. They are "unlinked" from the main directory tree. Unlinked files are effectively deleted[2] because the memory blocks they occupy are freed to be overwritten later by new data that may be added to the computer.

```perl
sub get_long_id {
  # incoming $dir must contain a trailing /
  my ($dir, $cache_limit, $file_life_span) = @_;

  opendir(DIR, $dir) or &errorPage("Error Logging On.");
  my @files = readdir(DIR);
  closedir(DIR);

  if($#files >= $cache_limit) {
    foreach $file (@files) {
      if((-f "$dir$file") && ((-M "$dir$file") > $file_life_span)) {
        unlink "$dir$file"; # delete the file
      }
    }
    opendir(DIR, $dir) or &errorPage("Error Logging On.");
    @files = readdir(DIR);
    closedir(DIR);

    if($#files >= $cache_limit) {
      # should generate e-mail message to warn administrator (see Section 9.3)
      &errorPage("Site busy. Please try again later.");
    }
  }
  return &generate_random_string(32);
}
```

FIGURE 7.11 A function that generates long session IDs and automatically polices the state file cache.

- Store the incoming parameters into local variables.
- Store the names of the directory contents into the `@files` array. (Reading directory contents is straightforward, but a detailed discussion can be found in Section 12.5.)
- If the number of `@files` has reached the `$cache_limit`
  - For each `$file` in the cache
    - If it's a file and it has exceeded its `$file_life_span` (Here we use the `-f` tester to make sure what we are deleting is actually a file; we don't want to delete any directories that might be in the cache).
      - Delete the file.
  - Store the names of the directory contents into the `@files` array.

---

[2]When computer forensics experts recover information from confiscated computers, one of the simplest tasks is to recover data unlinked from the directory tree. The owner of the computer may think it had been deleted, but unless it has been overwritten by new data, it's still there!

- ■ If the number of `@files` is still as large as the `$cache_limit`
  - ■ Send an `errorPage` to the user.
- ■ Call the helper function `generate_random_string` to generate the long string.

The quiz example, `quiz2.cgi`, of the previous section could be updated to use the `get_long_id` function. We would set a global variable `$cache_limit` to something like 300 and another `$file_life_span` to, say, 3.0/24 (3 hours). We would send those quantities to the `get_long_id` function as the "cache parameters." No other modifications would be required, and the application would have a managed cache.

Because the `get_long_id` is called any time a new session is to be created, the policing action occurs during runtime of the CGI program. If the load on the Web application is reasonably small, the overhead that causes will be imperceptible to the user. However, for a major Web application that services tens of thousands of sessions per day, the policing action could noticeably slow down the application for those users who trigger it. The ideal solution to that problem is to rework the function so that the policing action is "forked" off on a new process that runs independently of the CGI program. Since multithreading is not covered in this book, we forgo that added feature.

NOTE

You will find it interesting to compare our caching strategy with those built into languages such as PHP and ASP. Even popular Web programming tools sometimes leave things to be desired. In the long run, you will find that understanding the fundamental issues will be of great assistance when programming in different environments!

7.6 PASSWORD PROTECTION

For identification purposes, we will require that no two users share the same user name. Thus, the collection of all user names for a given application will contain no duplicates. Although it is sometimes done, we will not require passwords to be unique among users. Even with possible redundant passwords, a user-password pair is still guaranteed to be unique. We will impose other restrictions, such as length constraints, in the next section.

In our examples here, the user-password pairs are stored in a plain text file on the server. Of course, some format for storing user names and passwords in the password file must be devised. A standard format is to put each user on a different line in the file and choose a symbol to delimit the user names from the passwords. We choose to use a colon as the delimiter, but one can choose any symbol so long at it is not allowed to appear in the user name. An example password file is shown here.

It is a simple matter to retrieve the user information from the password file. When a line from the password file is read into a scalar variable, say $line, then the code

```
chomp $line;
($user, $pass) = split(/:/, $line, 2);
```

removes the pesky newline character and splits the $line at the colon. Note that the third argument of the split function causes it to split at the first colon, returning only two strings. Thus, the colon in smiley's password would cause no problems, but a colon in one of the user names would. User names and passwords are often restricted to letters, numbers, and the underscore character, so such factors are not a concern.

We now write a toolkit function that tests whether a given username:password combination is found in the password file. The function, shown in Figure 7.12, takes three arguments (name of password file, username, and password) and returns "yes" if the logon is successful. Otherwise, it returns a message indicating what aspect of the logon attempt failed. An overview of the function follows the code. We will use the function in the main example of this section and also in other Web applications that require basic logon verification.

```
sub logon {
  my($file, $alleged_user, $alleged_pass) = @_;
  my($user, $pass, $line);

  open(PASS, $file) or &errorPage("Failure to access user/pass info.");
  while($line = <PASS>) {
    chomp $line;
    if($line ne ""){ ### precaution only ###
      ($user, $pass) = split(/:/, $line, 2);
      if(lc $alleged_user eq lc $user) {
        if($alleged_pass eq $pass) {
          close(PASS);
          return "yes";
        }
        else {
          close(PASS);
          return "Invalid password.";
        }
      }
    }
  }
  close(PASS);
  return "Invalid user.";
}
```

FIGURE 7.12 A logon user and password verification function.

- Receive the incoming path to the password $file and the alleged user name and password.
- Declare some local variables to aid in parsing the password file.
- Open the $file or return an error page.
- While there are still lines in the file
  - Remove the newline character from the $line.
  - If the $line is blank, we skip it. This is only a precautionary matter, because in a perfect world, blank lines would not be in your password file. But inadvertent blank lines often sneak in when a password file is edited manually and when password file administration programs aren't programmed perfectly. Without this precautionary step, a blank line in the password file would allow someone to logon as user " " with password " "!

- ▦ Recover the $user and $password from the $line.
- ▦ If the alleged user name matches the one found on the current line of the file (note that we apply the lowercase function to the user names to take case out of consideration)
  - ▦ If the passwords also match (unlike the user names, the passwords must match case for case).
    - ▦ Close the password file and return "yes".
  - ▦ Else (the user name matches but the passwords have failed to match)
    - ▦ Close the password file and return "Invalid Password".
- ▦ If we make it here, the user name was not found in the file. So close it and return a message indicating that.

NOTE

For security, keep password files (and all sensitive data) out of the part of the directory tree that is publicly accessible. That usually means somewhere in the file system "above" the public directory. This way, someone on the Web will not be able to browse his way (inadvertently or otherwise) into your password file. For the administrator of a Web server, that is easy to do. That could be difficult to do from a user account, however, depending upon how the account is configured. If it is necessary to keep sensitive data inside a public part of the document tree, one can still provide a measure of protection. First make sure that the directory listing is obscured, either as the default of the Web server software or by including an index or default HTML file in the directory. Then, if the name of the password file is strange enough so that no one would be able to guess it and type it into a URL, the data would be relatively safe. In general, though, putting the password file out of the Web document tree is the preferable solution. In that case, setting a path to the file from the system root is usually imperative. Web servers often don't allow relative paths to "back up" out of the public tree during HTTP requests.

The main example of this section features an online guestbook in which anyone can submit an entry, but only a valid user-password combination will allow someone to view the entire guestbook. Such programs are often used to collect feedback over the Web, where the feedback comes from wide variety of sources, but only certain parties are to be privy to the submitted information.

The example extends the guestbook example of Section 6.10. One CGI program, named guestbook.cgi, runs the whole guestbook application. (The program from Section 6.10 was named comments.cgi.) A transaction diagram for the application is shown in Figure 7.13. The welcome page provides a form that enables anyone to submit a guestbook entry. Upon submission, a simple thank-you page is returned to the user by the add_comments function. Note that the welcome page is capable of initiating two different transactions: one by submitting the guestbook form and one by clicking a link.

Both the welcome page and the thank-you page contain a link that calls the logon_page function, which prints a page with the logon form. Submission of the logon

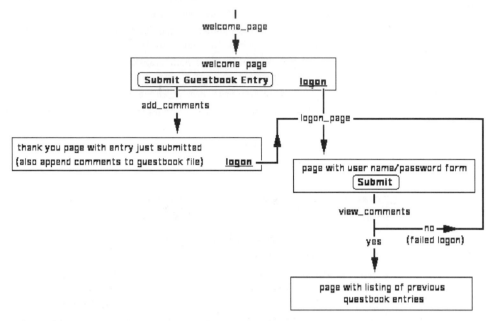

FIGURE 7.13 A transaction diagram for a password-protected guestbook.

form calls the `view_comments` function, which employs the `logon` toolkit function of Figure 7.12. If the user name and password are valid, the complete file of past guestbook entries is returned to the browser. If the logon attempt fails, the user is returned to the logon page to try again.

From the transaction diagram we see that the app logic for the guestbook contains four conditional clauses:

```
if($formHash{"request"} eq "add_comments") {
  &add_comments;
}
elsif($formHash{"request"} eq "view_comments") {
  &view_comments;
}
elsif($formHash{"request"} eq "logon_page") {
  &logon_page;
}
else {
  &welcome_page;
}
```

Figure 7.14 shows a more detailed "sketch" of the application showing the hidden elements and links that make the app logic calls. Submission of the guestbook form simply calls the `add_comments` function using a hidden form element. Note again that both logon links (welcome page and thank-you page) call the `logon_page` function using a link-submitted request. The logon page on the right shows the result of a failed logon attempt. As you can see from the transaction diagram, repeated logon failures would result in cyclic behavior.

The outline of the `guestbook.cgi` program is provided in Figure 7.15. It is important that the extra step presented in Section 6.10 for text areas be included in the decoding

```
<input type="hidden" name="request" value="add_comments"/>
```

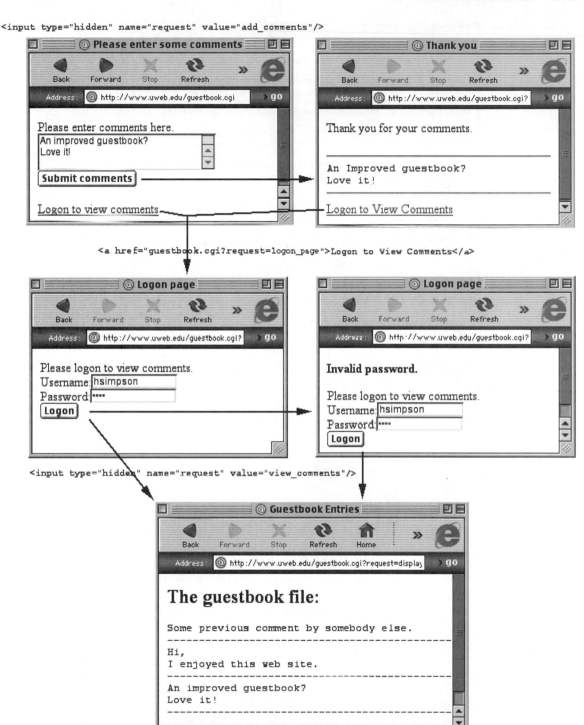

```
<a href="guestbook.cgi?request=logon_page">Logon to View Comments</a>
```

```
<input type="hidden" name="request" value="view_comments"/>
```

FIGURE 7.14   The functionality of the password-protected guestbook application.

```
#! /usr/bin/perl
print "Content-type: text/html\n\n";

############################################################
#   code for decoding input $datastring into %formHash    #
#      (works for GET, POST, and offline execution)        #
############################################################

$dataDir = "/usr/securedata/";   # secure directory above public
                                  # portion of directory tree

### app logic #############################################
if($formHash{"request"} eq "add_comments") {
    &add_comments;
}
elsif($formHash{"request"} eq "view_comments") {
    &view_comments;
}
elsif($formHash{"request"} eq "logon_page") {
    &logon_page;
}
else {
    &welcome_page;
}
### end app logic #########################################

############################################################
### Definitions of app logic functions go here.           #
### Definitions for toolkit functions used:                #
#    &logon            (new)                                #
#    &errorPage        (from Section 5.7)                   #
############################################################
```

FIGURE 7.15 The outline of guestbook.cgi.

routine. When the program is first called with no hidden requests, the welcome_page function is called. This program uses two toolkit functions.

```
sub welcome_page {
  print<<WHOLEPAGE;
  <html><head><title>Please enter some comments</title></head><body>
    <form action="$ENV{'SCRIPT_NAME'}" method="GET">
      Please enter comments here.<br/>
      <textarea name="comments" rows="3" cols="40"></textarea>
      <input type="submit" value="Submit comments"/>
      <input type="hidden" name="request" value="add_comments"/>
    </form>

    <a href="$ENV{'SCRIPT_NAME'}?request=logon_page">Logon to view comments</a>
  </body></html>
WHOLEPAGE
}
```

This function is straightforward. Just note again the boldfaced portions that enable the welcome page to initiate two different app logic transactions: one from a form submission and one from a link.

The add_comments function, called when the form button is submitted, is shown next, followed by an overview. You can see in Figure 7.14 that, after appending the new comment to the guestbook, the `add_comments` function returns only the newly submitted message to the user, rather than the whole guestbook.

```
sub add_comments {
  $comments = $formHash{"comments"};
  chomp $comments;

  open(DATA, ">>$dataDir"."comments.txt") or &errorPage("Error saving comments.");
  print DATA $comments;
  print DATA "\n", "-" x 70, "\n"; # a line of 70 hyphens to separate comments
  close(DATA);

  print<<PAGE;
  <html><head><title>Thank you</title></head><body>
  Thank you for your comments.
  <hr /><pre>
  $comments
  </pre><hr />

  <a href="$ENV{'SCRIPT_NAME'}?request=logon_page">Logon to View Comments</a>
  </body></html>
PAGE
}
```

- Get the `$comments` from the submitted text area. Of course, the name given to the text area in the HTML code for the form had to have been `comments`.
- Remove the trailing newline character to prevent an extra blank line in the text file to which the comments are written.
- Append the `$comments` to the comments file. Note that the file for the comments is also in the secure directory set by the global `$dataDir` variable.
- Print the acknowledgment page, enclosing the comment between horizontal rules and using the `pre` element to render the comment in a monospace font and preserve the line breaks. Without using the `pre` element to preserve line breaks in the text, we would have to substitute in an HTML `br` element for each line break entered by the user in order to preserve the format of the comment. (We won't get to substitutions until Chapter 11.)
- Also print the link that can be clicked to tell the CGI program to call the `logon_page` function.

Unless the user wishes to go back and submit another comment, the application provides no other options than to click a link and call the `logon_page` function. That function simply prints the logon form. When the logon form is submitted, the hidden data tells the CGI program to call the `view_comments` function. That function first uses the `logon` function of Figure 7.12 to verify the user's password data. Depending upon the result, the `view_comments` function either reloads the logon page with an error message or shows the guestbook to the user. The `logon_page` and `view_comments` functions follow each with an overview.

```
sub logon_page {
  $message = $_[0]; # an optional message
  print<<WHOLEPAGE;
  <html><head><title>Logon page</title></head><body>
    $message

    <form action="$ENV{'SCRIPT_NAME'}" method="POST">
      Please logon to view comments.<br/>
```

```
        Username:<input type="text" name="user" value="" size="20"/><br/>
        Password:<input type="password" name="pass" value="" size="20"/><br/>
        <input type="hidden" name="request" value="view_comments"/>
        <input type="submit" value="Logon"/>
      </form>
    </body></html>
WHOLEPAGE
}
```

■ Receive an incoming message parameter. When this function is called as the result of one of the links being clicked, no message is sent.

■ Print the top of the page, including the (potentially empty) message.

■ Print the form for the user's password information, including the hidden data that triggers the `show_comments` function. Note that the submission method is POST, as it should be when passwords are submitted.

■ Print the rest of the page.

```
sub view_comments {
  my $result = &logon("$dataDir"."password.txt", $formHash{"user"},
    $formHash{"pass"});
  if($result ne "yes") {
    &logon_page($result);
    exit;
  }
  open(DATA, "$dataDir"."comments.txt") or &errorPage("Error viewing comments.");
  my @guestbook = <DATA>;
  close(DATA);
  my $guestbook = join("", @guestbook);

  print<<PAGE;
    <html><head><title>Guestbook Entries</title></head><body>
    <h2>The guestbook file:</h2>
    <pre>$guestbook</pre>
    </body></html>
PAGE
}
```

■ Store the $result of the logon attempt. (Note that the full path to the password file is sent to the function. Also, the submitted user name and password are sent.)

■ If the $result is not equal to "yes"

　　■ Call the `logon_page` function, sending it the failure message. This is the first time we have manually called an app logic function. All other calls have been from browser requests to the app logic conditional. This call is what creates the cyclic behavior shown in the transaction diagram.

　　■ Exit the program. A complete page with the logon form and failure message will have been printed, and we certainly don't want to show the guestbook.

■ Otherwise the password was found in the file, so open the guestbook file and print the page that displays the guestbook. Note that we dump all the lines of the guestbook file into the `@guestbook` array and then join the array into one long string. Then we display the string using the HTML `pre` element so that all of the line breaks in the long string are obeyed. (An alternative would be to read the guestbook file line by line and print an HTML `br` element at the end of each line.)

7.7   AN EXAMPLE USING LOGGED-ON STATE

In the online quiz application in Section 7.4, the purpose of the state file was to keep track of state data between transactions. In that example, the user is anonymous and the state files simply track the session by keeping track of the current question and the number of correct responses. However, if a user logs on with a username and password, then the state file can contain more personalized information. Figure 7.16 shows a state file that records a user's **logged-on state**.

The idea of logged-on state is that after logging on to a Web application, a user stays logged on by merit of the session ID hidden in the Web pages returned to his browser. After the initial logon, subsequent requests to the Web application from his browser include the session ID. The existence of the state file on the server corresponding to the long ID verifies that the user is logged on, and the data in the state file indicates who is logged on and what access privileges he has. Thus, the session ID functions like a **validation certificate** for the user, verifying that the user did in fact supply a valid user name and password. This strategy both avoids repeated requests for logon information and circumvents the obvious problems inherent to hiding the sensitive user name, password, or both in the returned Web pages.

The example we use to illustrate this features an administration program (see note at the end of Section 7.2) that allows the owner of the guestbook application of the previous section to add more allowed users to the password file through a Web interface. That is, the owner can add new users to the password file from any Web-enabled computer in the world. Moreover, the administration program will allow the owner to maintain a logged-on state while adding multiple users.

The administration program for the guestbook is a stand-alone CGI program that we name `admin.cgi`. Typically such a program is hidden somewhere on a Web site where only the owner (administrator) can find it. For example, the owner might type the URL pointing to the program into her browser and then add it to her favorites list for easy access in the future. But even if someone else finds the administration program, it is password protected.

Since there are two levels of security (user and administrator) involved with the guestbook application, we use separate password files for users and administrators (owners). As shown in Figure 7.17, we use the same password file for guestbook access as before, and the password file for administrators is named `adminpw.txt`. There is only one administrator, who is also a user. There is one user in the password file who wasn't present in the previous section. The administration program we develop simply appends new users, much as Scooby has been appended in Figure 7.17.

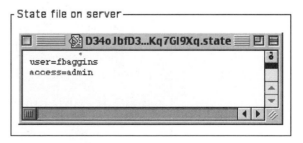

FIGURE 7.16   Long IDs for logged-on state.

FIGURE 7.17 Password files for different levels of access.

We first write a toolkit function that does the work when the password file is appended with a new user. While the `logon` function of the previous section merely tests a submitted user name and password against the file, the `logon_new` function of Figure 7.18 imposes some constraints when text fields such as those following are filled out.

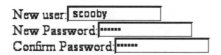

This form requires that the user enter the password twice (for typo protection), tests to see whether a submitted user name is already in use, and imposes some minor restrictions on the lengths of the user name and password. (Regular expressions, covered in Chapter 11, provide for more stringent constraints, such as not accepting blank spaces and other problematic characters.)

The `logon_new` function takes four pieces of information: the path to the password file to be appended, the proposed user name, the proposed password, and the (we hope)

```
sub logon_new {
  my($file, $new_user, $new_pass , $confirm_pass) = @_;

  if((length($new_user)<4) || (length($new_pass)<4)) {
    return "User name and password must be least 4 characters long.";
  }
  # We could impose other restrictions here as well,
  # such as no white space characters and no colons.

  if($new_pass ne $confirm_pass) {
    return "Passwords do not match.";
  }

  my($user, $pass, $line);
  open(PASS, $file) or &errorPage("Failure to create new account.");
  while($line = <PASS>) {
    chomp $line;
    ($user, $pass) = split(/:/, $line, 2);
    if(lc $new_user eq lc $user) {
      close(PASS);
      return "User name already taken.";
    }
  }
  close(PASS);
  open(PASS, ">>$file") or &errorPage("Failure to create new account.");
  print PASS "$new_user:$new_pass\n";
  close(PASS);
  return "yes";
}
```

FIGURE 7.18 The logon_new functon for adding new users to a password file.

duplicate copy. It returns `"yes"` if it succeeds in appending the new user and password onto the file. Otherwise it returns one of several error messages, depending upon what went wrong, and does nothing to the file.

- Store the incoming parameters into local variables.
- If the user name and password are not long enough, return a message. (Here the `length` function returns the number of characters stored in a scalar variable.)
- Also return an error message if the two passwords don't match.
- Declare some local variables to help parse the file and open it.
- While there are still lines in the file

  - Remove the newline character and recover the `$user` name and `$pass` from the `$line`.
  - If the proposed user name matches the current one in the file (lowercase match)
  - Close the password file, and return an error message.

- Close the password file.
- If we make it here, everything checks out. So append the new user information onto the file and return `"yes"`.

With the new toolkit function at our disposal, we now turn to writing the administration program. Figure 7.19 shows the transaction diagram. Here, the welcome page is called the logon page, which the administrator must get past before new users can be added. Failed logon

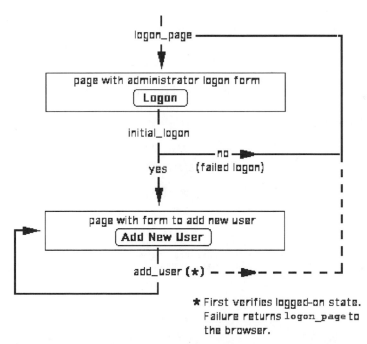

FIGURE 7.19   A transaction diagram for the password administration program.

attempts by a (would-be) administrator simply return the logon page to the browser. If the administrator does prove to be valid, a form used to add new users is returned. When that form is successfully submitted, the `add_user` function returns the same form so that another user can be added (or so the administrator can try again if the user name was already taken, for example). The crucial security feature is that the `add_user` function first verifies that whoever is calling it has the proper logged on state. If logged on state verification fails, the very first logon page is returned to the browser. That transaction is shown as a dotted line in Figure 7.19.

Figure 7.20 shows a "sketch" of the application's functionality and the specific forms used. The three browser windows on the left of the diagram show a successful sequence of submissions. Although the state file created on the server is only shown superimposed on the second window, it would persist on the server throughout all subsequent transactions (until deleted by the cache policing action, of course).

The windows (and box) on the right in Figure 7.20 show failed submissions. Failure of initial logon results in a failure message and another try. Failure to add a user results in another try and one of several messages returned by the `logon_new` helper function. At any time after the initial logon, failure to demonstrate logged on state sends you back to the very beginning. We have not shown the hidden form elements for the forms in the windows on the right in Figure 7.20, because they are exactly the same as in their counterparts on the left. In particular, after the initial logon, all Web pages would contain the long ID "validation certificate".

The outline for `admin.cgi` is shown in Figure 7.21. We reuse the `logon` function from the previous section, this time to verify the administration user name and password. The other state file-related functions are also used, in addition to the standard `errorPage` function. In addition to the app logic functions, one helper function, specific to this application, is used to print the page with the form used to add users. Note in the transaction diagram in Figure 7.19 that two different app logic functions need to print that page: the perfect situation for a helper function. The app logic functions and the helper are listed next, with overviews. Also note that the POST method is used in all of the forms, so that password information is not left behind on client machines in query strings in the history lists of browsers.

```
sub logon_page {
  $message = $_[0]; # an optional message
  print<<WHOLEPAGE;
  <html><head><title>Logon page</title></head><body>
  <b>$message</b>

  <form action="$ENV{'SCRIPT_NAME'}" method="POST">
    Verify administration privileges.<br />
    Username:<input type="text" name="user" value="" size="20"/><br/>
    Password:<input type="password" name="pass" value="" size="20"/><br/>
    <input type="hidden" name="request" value="initial_logon"/>
    <input type="submit" value="Logon"/>
  </form>
  </body>
  </html>
WHOLEPAGE
}
```

- Receive the incoming optional `$message`.
- Print the page, including the possibly empty `$message` and the logon form, which includes the app logic call.

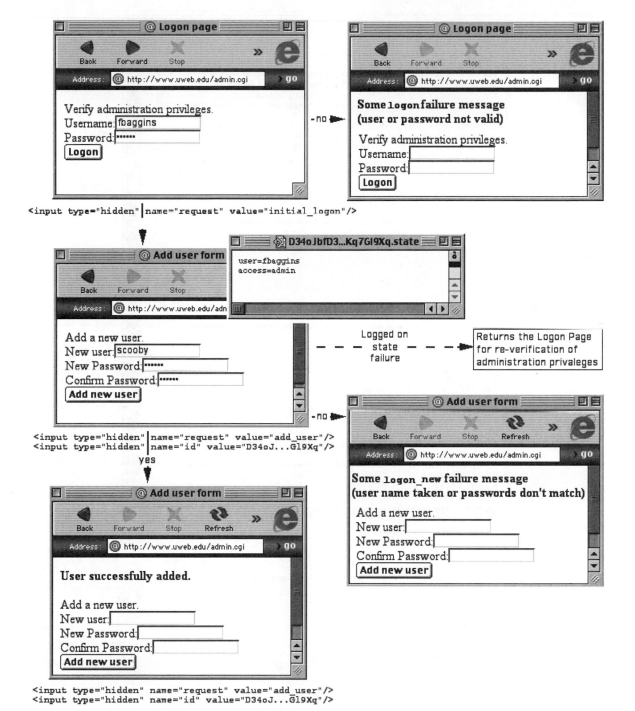

```
<input type="hidden" name="request" value="initial_logon"/>
```

```
<input type="hidden" name="request" value="add_user"/>
<input type="hidden" name="id" value="D34oJ...Gl9Xq"/>
```

```
<input type="hidden" name="request" value="add_user"/>
<input type="hidden" name="id" value="D34oJ...Gl9Xq"/>
```

FIGURE 7.20   Example executions of admin.cgi.

```
admin.cgi

#! /usr/bin/perl
print "Content-type: text/html\n\n";

############################################################
#   code for decoding input $datastring into %formHash    #
#        (works for GET, POST, and offline execution)      #
############################################################

$dataDir = "/home/securedata/";     # directory for password files
$stateDir = "/home/public/states/"; # directory for state files
$cache_limit = 100;                 # max number of files in cache
$file_life_span = 1;                # kill files older than one
day

%stateHash=();
$sessionID = $formHash{"id"};

### app logic #############################################
if($formHash{"request"} eq "initial_logon") {
  &initial_logon;
}
elsif($formHash{"request"} eq "add_user") {
  &add_user;
}
else {
  &logon_page;
}
### end app logic #########################################

############################################################
### Definitions of app logic functions go here.           #
### Definitions for helper functions:                      #
#   &add_user_page                                         #
### Definitions for toolkit functions used:                #
#   &logon_new          (new)                              #
#   &logon              (from Section 7.6)                 #
#   &get_long_id        (from Section 7.5)                 #
#   &generate_random_string    (from Section 7.4)          #
#   &write_state        (from Section 7.4)                 #
#   &read_state         (from Section 7.4)                 #
#   &URLencode          (from Section 7.4)                 #
#   &URLdecode          (from Section 7.4)                 #
#   &errorPage          (from Section 5.7)                 #
############################################################
```

FIGURE 7.21 The outline of admin.cgi.

```
sub initial_logon {
  my $result = &logon("$dataDir"."adminpw.txt", $formHash{"user"},
    $formHash{"pass"});
  if($result ne "yes") {
    &logon_page($result);
    exit;
  }
  $sessionID = &get_long_id($stateDir,$cache_limit,$file_life_span);
  %stateHash = ("user"=>$formHash{"user"}, "access"=>"admin");
  &write_state($stateDir, $sessionID, %stateHash);
  &add_user_page("You are now logged in as administrator.");
}
```

- Attempt to log on as administrator using the admin password file.
- If successful, get a new session ID, store the two pieces of state data into %stateHash, and write it to the proper state file.

■ Call the `add_user_page` function.

```
sub add_user_page {
  $message = $_[0]; # takes an optional message parameter
  print<<WHOLEPAGE;
<html><head><title>Add user form</title></head><body>
<b>$message</b>

<form action="$ENV{'SCRIPT_NAME'}" method="POST">
  Add a new user.<br />
  New user:<input type="text" name="newuser" size="20"/><br />
  New Password:<input type="password" name="newpass" size="20"/><br />
  Confirm Password:<input type="password" name="confirm" size="20"/><br /><br />

  <input type="hidden" name="id" value="$sessionID"/>
  <input type="hidden" name="pass" value="$formHash{pass}"/>
  <input type="hidden" name="request" value="add_user"/>
  <input type-"submit" value="Add new user"/>
</form>
</body></html>
WHOLEPAGE
}
```

■ Receive an incoming `$message`.

■ Print the form used to enter new user data. Include the appropriate app logic call.

```
sub add_user {
  %stateHash = &read_state("$stateDir", $sessionID);
  if($stateHash{"access"} ne "admin") {
    &logon_page("You need to first logon as administrator.");
    exit;
  }

  my $result = &logon_new("$dataDir"."password.txt" , $formHash{"newuser"},
                          $formHash{"newpass"}, $formHash{"confirm"});

  if ($result eq "yes") {
    &add_user_page("User successfully added.");
  }
  else {
    &add_user_page("User not added. $result");
  }
}
```

■ Read the state hash in from the state file. Recall that the session ID is loaded into a global variable in the main part of the program.

■ Verify the logged-on state. (Note that it would be sufficient in this program merely to verify the existence of the proper state file. We further discuss that notion in the next section.)

■ Assuming that the logged-on state is validated, attempt to add the new user data to the password file.

■ If the `$result` is positive

   ■ Return the add-new-user page to the administrator with a message of success.

■ Else (the information for the new user didn't pass the scrutiny of the `logon_new` function)

■ Return the add-new-user page to the administrator with a message of failure together with the specific failure `$result`.

In conclusion of this section, it is worth noting the importance of passing a long ID to the client rather than the actual user name and password. We could indeed have passed the user name and password to the add-user page in hidden form elements. With that information resubmitted to the application each time, the `logon` function could easily reverify the logged-on state. However, that approach is unthinkable, leaving sensitive information (the admin password!) sitting in the browser's cache of recently displayed HTML documents. (That's the client-side cache maintained by the Web browser, not to be confused with a server-side state file cache.)

You might not think that's a big deal for an administration program, because the administrator likely uses only a home or office computer to access the program. In that case, the password information is stored in a browser cache on a relatively secure client computer. But all sorts of programs feature logged-on state, and no experienced Web programmer in his or her right mind would hide password information in *any* Web pages, period.

NOTE

One might be tempted to employ a strategy to keep track of logged-on state using user names instead of long IDs. Upon a successful initial logon, a state file could be created whose name contains the user name

```
hsimpson.state
```

for example. That way, the state file is unique to a given user and can be used to monitor logged-on state. In that case, only the user name would need to be passed back and forth between the server and the clients. In fact, that approach is basically equivalent to the method of using long random strings for session IDs but for two main drawbacks.

First, someone could easily deduce that logged-on state is being achieved with the user name as the identifier and try to hack into a logged-on state using a common user name such as `"jones"`. For applications where logged-on state gives access to personal account data, that is a major security risk. A way around that problem involves storing a long ID inside the session file, but that is basically equivalent to the strategy we have used in this lesson.

Second, with a user name assigned as the name of a state file, the user would not be able to use the application from two different browser windows (or two different browsers) at the same time. In that case, each window would be using the same session identifier, the user name, and state data from the two logged-on states would be jumbled together in the same state file. Again, one could compensate by adding a long ID to the file for each window session, but that overcomplicates the situation, opening up a whole new can of worms.

Using our approach (the way it's usually done in practice), logged-on sessions by the same user from two different browser windows result in two distinct state files, named with different long IDs but containing the same user name. Each state file is free to carry data specific to what the user is doing in that specific browser window. Basically, logged-on state is unique, both up to the user and up to the browser window.

7.8   GENERAL STATE AND SECURITY ISSUES

The example of the previous section demonstrated a specific case where logged-on state can be employed, but it failed to provide a concise definition of the term. Moreover, the astute reader might ask, "Why use a state file at all? Once the administrator proves his or her identity by getting past the initial logon form, why require repeated verification each time the `add_user` function is called? Also, why put the user name in the state file, given that it was never used after the initial logon?"

This section answers those questions and more by addressing the following topics:

- Logged-on state security
- Validation certificates
- Different levels of access privileges
- Anonymous state versus logged-on state
- Setting timeouts for session state
- Limiting logon attempts

First, however, we provide a reasonably concise definition. We say that a Web application maintains a logged-on state when it provides a logon form and then verifies the logged-on status each time a subsequent request is made for a restricted or user-specific page. Basically the concept of "keeping someone logged on" is more formally stated as maintaining a logged-on state.

Security Issues

We return to the verification step at the top of the `add_user` function in the administration program of the previous section. On the surface, it seems that the only way to call that function is to submit the form to add a new user, and you have to be an administrator to get to that form in the first place. Recall again the transaction diagram in Figure 7.19. But in reality, that function can be called directly through the app logic by manually constructing and submitting a query string that contains `request=add_user` together with a properly formatted user name and password for a new user. Anyone with a suitable working knowledge of the application could then compromise the application and add new users with no need for the administration password and add-user form whatsoever!

Even if the decoding routine were modified so that the application accepts only POST transactions, a hacker could build his own form that sends the `add_user` request straight to the program using POST. But who would know enough about the program to make a special request straight for the `add_user` function, bypassing the initial logon form? The answer is that you never know.

For starters, many Web developers use code issued under public license, and many people might know its details. A hacker may recognize that a certain publicly available package is being used by a certain Web application. Second, many consulting Web programmers do similar work for several employers. Again, several people could have knowledge of internal features of a given Web application. Further, some Web developers work on projects for their employer, become disgruntled employees, quit, and . . . ? Finally, the main hobby of some people is to sit around and try to hack into things for the fun and challenge of it. We believe you get the idea why it's important to write Web applications that are as secure as possible.

NOTE

The moral of this story is that logging on once is not good enough. Even protected pages produced "after" initial logon should reverify the user. That means any function that produces protected pages that can be called directly by a URL request over the Web (that is, an app logic function) should reverify the user. Even if a would-be hacker has knowledge about how to call a sensitive function directly over the Web, that hacker would then have to know the password (for initial logon) or a long session ID (for logged-on state). Note that probabilistically it is actually much easier to guess a password than to guess a sufficiently long session ID.

There is a version of the `admin.cgi` on the Web site that does not feature the added verification step in the `add_user` function and does not feature any passwords we have used in this book. It would be instructive for you to bypass the logon page and hack the program by adding a new user. (We will be watching to see how industrious you are!) You would be surprised to know how many existing Web applications are poorly-programmed and vulnerable. Recently, one of our students was involved in a stock trading simulation, run by a Web application, in an upper-level economics class. He had realized a 1000% profit after the first few days of the simulation, and not by buying and selling stocks!

Figure 7.22 shows the secure way to maintain logged-on state in general. Although the administration program example used hidden form elements to embed the session IDs in Web pages, manually constructed query strings in links can easily be used as well. Moreover, as the next lesson demonstrates in detail, many applications use HTTP cookies for that purpose. Regardless of how the session ID is returned to the client, all app logic functions "below" the initial logon should verify the ID against the state file cache. Of course, to propagate the logon session, the session ID must be hidden in all Web pages "below" the logon page.

Validation Certificates

The logged-on state in the administration program of the previous section could have easily been accomplished using a completely empty state file. When a browser passes a session ID to the server, the ID is valid if and only if a state file with the same name exists in the server-side cache. That is, there is a one-to-one correspondence between state files and session IDs. Thus, an empty state file serves as a perfectly viable validation certificate for the corresponding session ID passed to the client.

That means that basic logged-on state as depicted in Figure 7.22 can be securely achieved without even reading a state file. Each function after the initial logon could revoke logged-on state simply by testing whether a state file named with the submitted ID exists in the state file directory.

```
if (!(-e "$stateDir$StateFileName")) {
  &logon_page; # or call some customized function
  exit;
}
```

The mere existence of the file is sufficient to verify that the ID was in fact obtained by supplying a valid user name and password at some point.

Different Levels of Access Privileges

The data in the state file shown in Figures 7.16 and 7.20 is included to demonstrate added functionality that can be used in conjunction with logged-on state. As we discussed just above in the previous subsection, an empty state file would have sufficed in that example. Here, we discuss the access level and we discuss the line with the user name in the next subsection. Clearly, many Web applications feature different levels of access. A stock trading site might have user-level access for members, administrator-level access for account managers, and some sort of super-user access for whomever manages the account managers, the webmaster, or both.

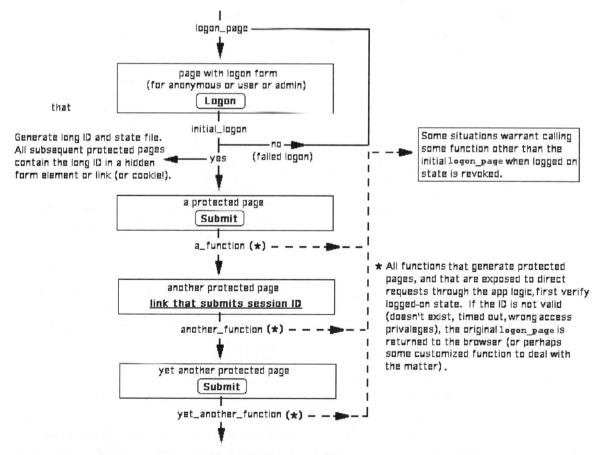

FIGURE 7.22   The general strategy for secure logged-on state.

FIGURE 7.23 Multiple state file caches for different levels of logged-on state.

In that case, there might be different logon forms for each level of access, and successful logon might open up different features of the application for different levels of access. One can picture Figure 7.22 generalized to a tree-like structure with different chains of pages progressing downward that can be accessed through different access levels of logged-on state. For example, someone with only user-level access can't get past the logged-on state verification steps in any function below the logon page for administrators.

Figure 7.23 depicts a strategy for accomplishing that where multiple state file caches differentiate from among different levels of access. When someone logs on with a certain level of access, a state file is added to the appropriate directory. Then an app logic function in the admin-only part of the application, for example, need only check for the existence of a submitted ID in the directory holding the cache for administrators. If the ID is not there, administration logged-on state is revoked. Using this strategy, the mere existence of a state file in the proper directory is sufficient.

One drawback to this approach is the way that state file caching capabilities are built into other Web programming environments such as ASP and PHP. Those languages have built-in features, similar in concept to our state-handling toolkit functions, that can be used for easy state maintenance. However, those built-in features typically use only one state file cache for an entire application. It may take a substantial workaround to create multiple caches, depending upon the development environment in which you end up working. Our toolkit functions easily handle multiple caches, but such a strategy may not be your best bet in the long run. However, the concept certainly promotes deeper understanding of Web applications.

Of course, the easiest one-cache solution is simply to place the access level in the state file when it is created. The one-cache analog to Figure 7.23 is depicted in Figure 7.24. The existence of a submitted ID in the cache indicates some level of logged-on state.

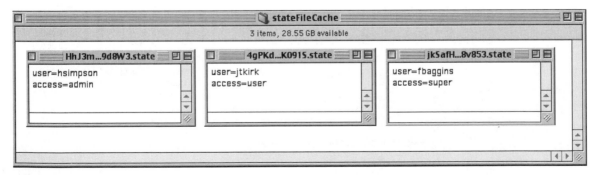

FIGURE 7.24 One state file cache where the access level is recorded in the state files.

An app logic function then determines the particular access level by reading the file. Indeed, that approach was used in the administration program of the previous section, although the mere existence of the state file would have sufficed in that example because it featured only one access level. (Note that, even though we are reading the state file in this case, we still haven't explained the utility of the line with the user name.)

We conclude this subsection with two related points whose details are left to the exercises. These points are independent of whether one or multiple cache directories are used. First, the access levels can be "cascaded," meaning that higher-level access automatically implies lower-level access. That means that someone logged on with superuser state would also have access to all app logic functions that validate logged-on state at lower levels.

Second, it may be desirable to use only one password file for everyone, regardless of access privileges. The guestbook application and its separate administration program used distinct password files, as shown in Figure 7.17. A suitable format for a one-file solution might be something like the following.

```
jtkirk:user:enterprise
fbaggins:super:hobbit
hsimpson:admin:D'oh
```

Any of several other formats would also suffice. Of course, our toolkit `logon` function is not equipped to handle such a customized password file format.

Anonymous State versus Logged-On State

Here we address why we have included the user name in state files in the logged-on state examples even though it was not used. We have used state in two distinct ways in this chapter. The first use was to keep track of state data between transactions in the online quiz application of Section 7.4. In that example, the user is anonymous and the state files simply track the session. We say that a Web application maintains **anonymous state** when it keeps session state but the user is not required to log on.

The second use of state files was in the administration program of Section 7.7. That example featured logged-on state, which we have already defined. To explain the distinction fully, we turn to Web applications that feature shopping carts. Some shopping carts feature anonymous state, some only logged-on state, and some feature both options.

Anonymous shopping carts allow you to start adding items to the cart without ever logging on. You are effectively shopping and building a cart of items to buy, but they don't yet know who you are. You are just some long session ID to their application. Of course, when it comes time to check out, the application will ask for your billing information (name, address, e-mail, credit card). That information typically goes into a permanent account file (or database record) created for you. Or, if you already have an account at the site, at checkout time the application simply asks who you are. Regardless of the case, it keeps anonymous state in the form of a shopping cart, and you remain anonymous until the end.

Sometimes you log on before you start shopping. In that case, your state file contains your user name (or customer profile identification number) in a way similar to what we have shown. You can shop all you want. When you check out, the application simply uses your session ID to read your user name from the state file. That information is then used to access your permanent account file for billing and shipping. With logged-on state, you can check out at any time and the application already knows who you are.

Many e-tailers give you the option of either shopping anonymously or logging on first. Either way, they are keeping state. It's just a matter of when they put your identity into the state file—now or later. The online music store we develop in Chapter 13 features a fully functional shopping cart that allows both anonymous and logged-on shopping.

Timeouts for Sessions

Many Web applications feature sessions that time out. For succinctness, we call this a **session timeout**. Once a session has begun, a session timeout occurs after some predetermined period of inactivity, maybe a few minutes or a whole day. That is, the session continues as long as the user keeps making transactions with the application. If the user has not made a transaction with the application recently, as determined by the timeout period, the session is killed.

A session timeout might involve killing an anonymous session. For example, it might be desirable for the quiz application of Section 7.4 to time quizzes by allowing only 2 minutes for each question. If the session times out, the quiz is invalid, and the user might not get another chance to take it.

Alternately, a session timeout might involve killing a logged-on session. For example, it might be desirable for the administration program of Section 7.7 to revoke logged-on state after 30 minutes of inactivity. That is, if no new users are added for a half-hour, an attempt to add a new user returns the administrator to the initial logon screen. Such timeouts are often used in conjunction with logged-on state in case someone logs on but then fails to close the browser window (or the whole browser application) before leaving the computer. That prevents someone else (perhaps with malicious intent) from stumbling onto the computer at some later time and resuming the session. Basically, logged-on state is propagated as long as the application perceives continuing activity within the preset timeout period.

The easiest way to monitor a session against a timeout period is to use the last-modified property of the state file. If the application detects that the state file has not been modified within the timeout period, the session is killed. (Timing a session will not be so easy when we use database "state tables" in Chapter 10). Recall that the last-modified unary operator (-M), used in Section 7.5 for the policing action of the get_long_id function, returns a real number that is the time in days since the file was last modified.

The best way to implement session timeouts is to automate the process in a toolkit function. To that end, we offer a final, updated version of the read_state function that automatically handles timeouts. The new version is shown in Figure 7.25 with the additions in boldface. The way the new version of the function is constructed, it can be called without sending it the three added parameters shown in boldface. That is, the function will work like the original version if you call it sending it only the first two parameters. Thus, to read states without using a timeout feature, just call the function as in the previous examples using only the two original parameters. The reason the function attains that level of flexibility is indicated in the overview that follows the function.

```
sub read_state {
  my ($dir, $fileroot, $time_out, $time_out_function, $time_out_message) =
@_;
  my $filename = "$fileroot.state";

  if (($time_out > 0) && (-e "$dir$filename")
                      && ((-M "$dir$filename") > $time_out) ) {
    if ($time_out_function) {
      &$time_out_function($time_out_message);
      exit;
    }
    else{
      &errorPage("Your session has timed out");
    }
  }
  my $now = time;
  utime $now, $now, "$dir$filename";
  ### updates modification time without altering file contents

  open(INFILE, "<$dir$filename") or &errorPage("Error reading state file.");
  my @array =<INFILE>;
  close(INFILE);

  my %hash = ();
  foreach $line (@array) {
    chomp $line;
    my ($key, $value) = split(/=/, $line, 2);
    $key = &URLdecode($key);
    $value = &URLdecode($value);
    $hash{$key} = $value;
  }
  return %hash;
}
```

FIGURE 7.25 The final version of the `read_state` function, which now handles session timeouts.

- Receive incoming parameters. The new parameters are optional, so this function is backwards-compatible with the original version.

- If the session is not timed out (Here we see why the `$time_out` parameter is optional. If a timeout is not passed to the function, the `$time_out` variable will contain the empty string, which evaluates to 0 in numeric context. In that case, this `if` clause is skipped, and no timeout occurs. Note also that the timeout clause is also skipped if the state file does not exist—a nonexistent state file will trigger the `errorPage` upon attempting to open the state file.

  - If the `$time_out_function` parameter, which holds the name of some function that is to deal with the timeout, is present (here we see that the fourth and fifth parameters are optional, even if the `$timeout` parameter is present).
  - Call a custom function to handle the timeout.
  - Exit the application.

- Else let the standard `errorPage` function handle the timeout. Recall that `errorPage` exits automatically.

- The next two lines "touch" the state file, updating its last-modified property without messing with its contents. The `time` function returns the current time as one integer containing all time components. (Recall that `localtime`, used in previous lessons, returns an array of time components. Or, when called in scalar context, `localtime` returns a time string in a human-readable format, which is of no use for our purposes here.) The `utime` function (update time) updates both the last-modified and last-accessed times for the file (hence its first two parameters). We aren't concerned with the last-accessed property here, but `utime` expects both parameters. Theoretically, the last-accessed property could be of use here, but it is not reliable among different platforms (see Section 12.6).

■   The rest of the function returns the state file as a hash as before.

Two points do warrant clarification. First, why the optional `$time_out_function` parameter? In most situations, it is not desirable to handle a session timeout using the standard `errorPage`. Rather, one often wants to return a logon page of some sort. Specifically, one might wish to let the user resume a logged session by reentering the user name and password. The `$time_out_function` and `$time_out_message` parameters allow any function to be called with a message.

For example, suppose we call the new `read_state` function as follows.

```
%stateHash = read_state($stateDir, $sessionID, 3/24, "revoke_session",
                    "Session timed out. Log back on to resume session");
```

The line in the `read_state` function then becomes

```
&revoke_session("Session timed out. Log back on to resume session");
```

Here `revoke_session` could be an app logic function such as an initial `logon_page` function. Initial logons create new session IDs and new state files. Other situations might warrant the current session being resumed, as demonstrated by the following pseudocode.

```
sub revoke_session {
    print incoming "please log back on" message
    supply a "log back on" form WITH the original session ID hidden inside
}
```

Unlike initial logon forms, a form that logs back on and resumes a timed-out session needs to resubmit the old session ID so that the same state file can be accessed. Since we have adopted the practice of storing the session ID into a global variable (see Figure 7.21), it is readily available to any function that needs it.

The second point involves the need for "touching"[3] the state file to update its last-modified property. By placing a call to `read_state` at the top of *all* protected app logic functions, an expired session will automatically time out. It's as simple as that: The act of reading in the `%stateHash` automatically monitors session timeouts. However, not all protected functions need to perform a write to the state file. Consider the `add_user` function from the administration example of Section 7.7. It merely needed to verify logged-on state.

It is common that some functions need only read, rather than update, state data, thereby leaving the last-modified property of the file untouched. Nonetheless, calling such a function qualifies as a transaction with the application, meaning that the state file should be touched to avoid an unwanted timeout. It is for that reason that the new `read_state` function always touches state files.

---

[3]There is a UNIX command, named `touch`, that updates the last-modified property of a file without affecting its contents. That name is rather indicative of what is accomplished. For platform portability, we have used Perl's `utime` function, which basically accomplishes the same thing.

> **NOTE**
>
> One might be tempted to think that the automatic policing action of the state file cache done by the `get_long_id` function creates session timeouts by destroying "old" state files. In some sense that is true, but it is likely that a given state file exists in the cache after it has lived longer than the `$file_life_span` imposed by the `get_long_id` function. This is because old state files are killed only when the state file cache limit is reached.
>
> Just be careful, when setting timeouts using the `read_state` function, that you set its `$time_out` to be less than the `$file_life_span` of the policing action. Otherwise, the policing action could delete state files that belong to active sessions. Also, one might be tempted to add a line to the updated `read_state` function so that timed-out sessions cause the associated state file to be deleted. But that would make it impossible for the application to allow the user to resume the same session by logging back on just as discussed.

Limiting Logon Attempts

An interesting security feature that some sites employ is to limit logon attempts from a given IP address to a certain number per time period. If that many logon failures occur, then a "dead period" is imposed, during which no more logon attempts can be made from that IP address. For example, if five failed logon attempts originate from a given IP address within 15 minutes, then no more logon attempts can be made from that IP address for, say 30 minutes.

This is to prevent hackers' programs from attempting logons systematically, in the hope of stumbling upon the correct combination. A hacker would not be able to stumble upon a long session ID in that fashion, but, as we have mentioned, stumbling upon passwords is probabilistically much more likely.

One solution is for the application to cache a file whose name is the IP address corresponding to a failed logon attempt. One record in the file is the time of the initial failure and a counter for the number of failed access attempts. Each subsequent failed access attempt augments the counter. Upon a given failed logon attempt, if the counter reaches the logon limit (5, maybe), a dead period is imposed on that IP address by adding some sort of flag to the cached file. Of course, there would need to be some policing mechanism for these cached files so that IP addresses are freed when dead periods are over or insufficient logon failures occur in the given time period. This is not trivial to implement, because there are some additional logistics to work out, and we leave this feature as an exercise. (Another solution is to use one text file, where each line records the IP address and other information necessary to monitor a failed logon. However, the cache solution is somewhat easier to implement.)

*7.9 ENCRYPTED PASSWORD FILES

The concern with the nonencrypted password files we have used in this lesson is that anyone who has access to the file is privy to everyone's passwords. Consider the scenario where a site administrator moves on to a new job. Presumably, that site administrator had access to the password file. For security, the new administrator would have to change not only the administration password but the password of every user of the site!

The idea of encrypted passwords is that instead of saving the original password to the password file, we save the result of some encryption function applied to it.

```
$encrypted_password = &encryption_function($original_password)
```

So, a given password file might end up looking like the following, depending upon what encryption function is used.

The original password is not saved *anywhere*! Thus, when somebody attempts to logon with an $alleged_password, we have to test whether

```
$encrypted_password eq &encryption_function($alleged_password)
```

Even if someone has access to an encrypted password file, it is extremely difficult for that party to recover the original passwords. (Here, "difficult" means that it might take many years of guessing or a mathematician who can find the inverse of the encryption function.) It really depends on the "strength" of the encryption function. A good encryption function is generally mathematically sophisticated, with no well-defined inverse, and results in a probability of effectively 0 that two different passwords result in the same encryption.

There are various encryption functions out there that people use. We will use Perl's built-in function, named crypt. (The publisher would not let us title this section "Tales from the Crypt.") The crypt function takes two arguments: the original password and a *salt* value:

```
crypt(password, salt)
```

The *salt* value is a two-character string that must come from the set of 64 characters comprising the 52 upper- and lowercase letters ('a'..'z' , 'A'..'Z'), the 10 digits ('0'..'9'), the period ('.'), and the forward slash ('/'). The salt string is usually generated randomly. The standard way to encrypt a password is as follows:

```
@list64=('.', '/', 0..9, 'A'..'Z', 'a'..'z'); # allowable salt characters
$salt = $list64[int rand 64].$list64[int rand 64];
$encrypted_password = crypt($original_password, $salt);
```

Each $salt value causes a different encryption. For example, the two function calls

```
crypt("scooby", "A9")
crypt("scooby", "./")
```

return the values `"A9mfz.aq1Mp5A."` and `"./F5IeTc3Avic"`, respectively. Since there are 64 allowable salt characters, there are $64^2 = 4096$ possible encryptions for a given password using `crypt`. So, when it comes time to test an alleged password against an encrypted one,

```
if ($encrypted_password eq crypt($alleged_password, ??)) {
    the alleged password matches an encrypted one
}
```

how will we know the salt string that was used to create the `$encrypted_password`? After all, it was chosen randomly. We don't want to execute the `if` statement 4096 times, with all different possible salts, just to determine that `$alleged_password` doesn't match.

The answer is that the two salt characters are saved as the first two characters of the encrypted password, as you can see in the two example encryptions of `"scooby"`. We test an `$alleged_password` against an `$encrypted_password` by making the following comparison:

```
$encrypted_password eq crypt($alleged_password, $encrypted_password)
```

Since the `$salt` parameter of the `crypt` function accepts only a two-character string, it grabs the first two characters of the `$encrypted_password`, which are the original salt string.

If no salt string were used in the `crypt` function, then an adversary could try the following scheme: Make a huge list of common passwords (maybe 50,000 dictionary words). Then apply the encryption function to each of these, making a table of possible passwords and their encrypted counterparts. The adversary could then attempt to find the original password given an encrypted password by simply writing a program to look for the encrypted password value in the table! But with the added salt string, there are 4096 possible encryptions for a given password. Suddenly, the table for the 50,000 dictionary words has grown to around 200 million encrypted passwords.

That number is certainly not unreasonable to search through, given today's computing power. That's one reason many operating systems give you a warning when you try to enter a password for a user account that is based upon a dictionary word. If you want a table to try to hack all passwords that are, say up to 7 characters in length and may include any of the (around 90) common keyboard characters, you're talking about a table of size about 10^{17} by the time the salt value is factored in.

Another interesting thing to note is that the encrypted string may contain only the same 64 allowable characters as the salt string. The encryption algorithm spits out the encrypted password as a binary string. Every group of six bits is then turned into a number from 0 to 63, corresponding to one of the 64 characters. This is *base-64* encoding, a common way of encoding binary data into printable characters.

Another usefulness of salt is that if two people by coincidence have the same password, the probability is near 1 (actually 4095/4096) that the two encrypted passwords will be different! That is desirable for a couple of reasons. First, if one of these two users ever saw the encrypted password file, he or she would not be able to deduce that someone else is using the same password. Second, a third person wouldn't be able to attempt to guess the common password based upon some personal commonality between the two users who share the same password.

NOTE

The `logon` and `logon_new` functions we developed in this lesson to verify against and append to the password file, respectively, can be upgraded to deal with encryption relatively easily. That being done, those functions could be used in the examples of this lesson with no other alterations to the examples. The only difference would be behind the scenes. In particular, administrators and Webmasters would not be able to edit encrypted password files manually, aside from simply deleting a line. In this case, it would be almost imperative that the application have an accompanying administration program that allows new encrypted entries to be created or existing ones modified. Such an implementation is left as an exercise.

SUMMARY OF KEY TERMS AND CONCEPTS

State data: In the context of Web applications, data collected or generated by the application during one HTTP transaction that is made available to subsequent HTTP transactions enabled by the application. State data may be embedded in Web pages using hidden form elements or query strings in links. Alternately, state data may be kept in a temporary file on the server. (State data may also be set in HTTP cookies on a browser, as explored in Chapter 8.)

Session: A sequence of HTTP transactions between which state data is preserved. From the surfer's perspective, a session involves surfing among a sequence of Web pages generated by the application. State data is inherently session oriented and should not be confused with permanent user profile or account data, which persists between sessions.

Transaction diagram: A diagram or sketch that depicts the different Web pages an application can generate. The HTTP transactions necessary to create those pages are depicted using arrows. The different HTTP transactions are handled by corresponding functions in the application logic.

Application logic (app logic): The conditional expression that handles the different types of URL requests that the application accepts. The requests, sent URL-encoded from links or hidden form elements, are shunted to corresponding functions by the conditional. Thus, these functions, which we call *app logic functions*, can be called by anyone (who knows where they are) directly over the Web by sending a properly encoded request to the application.

Session ID: A unique character string, by which each session is identified. Session IDs are ensured uniqueness by containing a sufficient number of characters from among a set of many possible characters. Our session IDs are built from a pool of 64 possible characters and are 32 characters long. These IDs are very similar to those generated by built-in utilities in almost any Web programming environment (PHP, ASP, JSP, CGI.pm, and so forth).

State file: A temporary server-side text file that stores state data for a session. Because each session ID is used to create a state file, whose name is the ID, session IDs and state files share a one-to-one correspondence. It is sufficient to pass only the session ID back and forth between client and server to propagate a session using state files.

State file cache: A managed directory that contains a collection of state files. Each time a new session ID is generated, we test whether the cache is full—that is, whether it has reached its preset *cache limit*. If it is full, we *police* the state cache, deleting any files that have not been modified in a time period exceeding a preset file life span.

State hash: A hash (named `%stateHash` in our programs) in which we store in-memory state data. The hash structure is preserved when state data is written to a state file. This gives maximum scalability for a Web application because state data can be added to or deleted from the state file with no concern for its storage order. Moreover, the hash structure facilitates hiding state data in Web pages as name-value pairs.

Password protection: The task of making it necessary to enter a valid user name and password in order to access protected pages generated by a Web application. The user names and passwords are kept in a text file, preferably "above" the public directory in the server's directory tree.

Logged-on State: A web application's ability to require only one successful logon in order to access a sequence of protected pages securely, informally stated as "keeping a user logged on." A session ID, generated upon initial logon, serves as the logon validation certificate. For security, it is important that *every* app logic function that produces a protected page for the session revalidate the logged-on state. Otherwise, the initial logon form can be bypassed, and protected pages accessed, with no password whatsoever.

Validation certificate: Digital proof of the validity of some claim, such as that a user has successfully logged on and has the right to access protected content. A state file serves as the "validation certificate" of a session ID by its very existence. That is, a session ID is valid if and only if a state file exists with the corresponding name. Even if no data is contained in a state file, its existence validates the authenticity of the corresponding session ID. For example, logged-on state can be propagated using empty state files. The user has successfully logged on at some point if and only if the user's browser submits a valid session ID.

Access levels: Different levels of privilege to view or keep or change protected information, such as those of anonymous users, members, and administrators. In a Web application, access levels require different levels of logged-on state. The way to accomplish this that is most compatible with various Web programming languages is to store the access level in the state file created when a logon occurs. The state file then both serves as the validation certificate and contains the privilege level.

Anonymous state: A session that does not require logon. Whereas logged-on state requires propagating sessions using session IDs (so that user names and passwords are not passed back to browsers), embedding all state data in Web pages may suffice for anonymous state. However, state files and session IDs still do provide for much more flexibility. With anonymous state, the state file still serves as a validation certificate for the session, although there may be no personalized data (such as a user name) in the state file.

Session timeouts: "Killing" a session if it becomes idle (no transactions are made) over a preset time interval. Idleness is detected by testing the last-modified property of the state file. The final version of the `read_state` toolkit function takes optional parameters that automate timeout controls. The act of reading a state file at the top of an app logic function either kills a timed-out session (by default the `errorPage` function is called) or continues the session (by "touching" the state file, ensuring that it stays current).

Password encryption: (optional section): Passwords for Web applications can be stored in password files in an encrypted format in much the same way as operating systems encrypt passwords for shell accounts. Thus, even if someone (such as another person with an account on the server) stumbles onto the password file, the passwords remain secure. Theoretically, it is possible to implement secure logged-on state by passing an encrypted password back and forth between client and server. However, in practice, the long session IDs are a more versatile solution.

EXERCISES

1. The source code for the `admin.cgi` program of Figure 7.21 can be obtained from this book's Web site. Re-work the application so that the session times out. When the session times out, the administrator is given a new page with a form that allows her to resume the same session by resupplying the user name and password. Upon successfully logging back on, the same session ID and state file are used in the resumed session. Use a 1-minute timeout interval so that you can quickly test the feature. (Note that reusing the same state file has little advantage in this exercise, but when state files keep cumulative data, such as shopping carts, resuming sessions is often preferable over killing them outright.) *Hint:* Be careful to allow only the same user to resume the logged-on state. That is, some other user can't resume the session by supplying his own valid user name and password in the form to log back on. Thus, at "log back on time," the state file must be read in order to ascertain the user name of the original user. Be careful not to touch the state file at this time and thereby refresh the session. That is, a failed re-logon attempt could inadvertently touch the state file and make the timed-out state file current again!

2. Some Web applications provide a logout option.

   (a) Write a `kill_state` function that immediately kills logged-on state. The function should be general enough that it can be used as a toolkit function in any Web application when called by a form button or link. The function should delete the state file.

   (b) Use the function by adding a kill-state form button to the add-user form in the admin example of Section 7.7. Return the initial logon page with a suitable message when a session is killed.

3. As discussed at the end of Section 7.8, implement a security feature that limits failed logon attempts. To test the feature, make a driver program with a logon form. Successful logon returns a thank-you page, and failed logon causes the logon form to reload with a failure message. *Hint:* Here is one possible solution. Save the number of attempts in a file *IPADDRESS*.`tries` in a directory. When a failed login attempt occurs, check the existence and the age of the corresponding *IPADDRESS*.`tries` file, either setting its contents to 1 or incrementing it by 1. If this number is beyond a certain number, then deny the login process for some dead period. You will find some toolkit functions, such as those for reading and writing states, to be very handy as models. However, you will have to devise your own strategy for cache policing. For easy testing, set the security feature to reject after two failures and to impose a 3-minute dead period.

4. Design an application that features "cascading" access privileges. A welcome page has three forms (or one form with three submit options) that provide logon attempts for users, administrators, and a superuser. After the welcome page, the application should have three more app logic functions: one to deliver content (some very simple protected page) specific to each of the three access levels. Of course, one way to get one of these protected pages is to log on at a certain access level.

   There should also be three links in the welcome page that call the three content-specific functions. Someone who has logged-on state at a given access level can use the link to pull up the page accessible to her access level as well as the pages for lesser access levels if any. If someone clicks a link and either has no logged-on state or is not logged on with sufficient access privileges, the welcome page is reloaded with a warning message.

5. Work Exercise 4 but using only one password file, which stores entries for all access levels.

6. Write a toolkit function that allows someone to change his own password. The function should be reusable in the sense that a link that calls the function can be placed in any page with a logon form. The function prints a form containing fields for the user name, old password, new password, and duplicate copy of the new password. If the old user name and password info are

not valid, the password is not changed. Make a driver program to test the function. *Comment:* In theory, the function may not always need the current password as a parameter (because the user could be in a logged-on state, for example), but good security mandates that one should *always* ask for the old password before changing it. In other words, don't trust logged-on state as authorization to change a password.

7. The source code for the admin.cgi program of Figure 7.21 can be obtained from this book's Web site.

   (a) Rework the application so that it allows the administrator both to delete users from the password file and to change their information from a remote Web browser. The application should verify logged-on state in any function exposed to the public in the app logic.

   (b) The logged-on state should feature a timeout. A timeout simply returns the administrator to the initial logon form. Use a 1-minute timeout interval so that you can quickly test the feature.

   (c) Do part (b), but allow the administrator to resume the same session as described in Exercise 1.

8. The source code for the pizza3.cgi program of Figure 7.3 can be obtained from this book's Web site. Add any or all of the following features to the application.

   (a) Add fields for an address and credit card number to the order confirmation page. Add a pull-down menu that allows a credit card type to be selected. Add another transaction to the application that generates a second confirmation page for all of the data collected in the order confirmation page. Submitting this second confirmation page finalizes the order. The thank-you page should summarize *all* of the data collected by the application.

   (b) Use state files rather than hidden form elements.

   (c) When the user clicks the back button to cancel either of the two confirmations, the form in the previous page should contain the data that had previously been entered into it. Thus, the user doesn't have to fill out the forms from scratch but can just make some minor changes. Note that part (b) is required to accomplish this. *Note:* Some browsers may feature some autofill capability for forms reloaded by the back button, but for ensured reliability, the function that prints a form can hard-code it with any corresponding data already in the state file.

   (d) Add client-side JavaScript validation for the forms. The radio buttons for the pizza sizes should have no default selection, and the user must select one before submitting the form. Devise some suitable constraints that must be satisfied before the billing information form in the first confirmation page can be submitted.

9. The source code for the quiz2.cgi program of Figure 7.10 can be obtained from this book's Web site. Add any or all of the following features to the application.

   (a) There is a predetermined list of people who are allowed to take the quiz, as determined by users in a password file. The welcome page requires users to log on before beginning the quiz. Then, submitting the answer to each question reverifies logged-on state.

   (b) The application creates a text file, specific to each user, in which quiz results are stored. Use the user name for the file name, as in hsimpson.quiz, and store all quiz files in a separate quiz directory. As each question is submitted, the user's answer is appended onto the quiz file for that user in some human-readable format. Thus, completion of the quiz leaves a human-gradable quiz file. This application need not grade the questions (so that users can't tell the answers to other users).

   (c) Add a provision to the initial logon that doesn't allow a user to retake the quiz. That is, if a user attempts an initial logon, but a corresponding quiz file already exists, reject the logon.

(d) Add a session timeout that allows the user only 30 seconds to complete each question. Because of part (b), if a session does time out, the user's quiz file contains only those questions answered so far. If the first question times out, an empty quiz results for that user. Thus, someone can't let the first question expire and then log back on to retake the quiz.

(e) Add JavaScript validation to ensure that a question can't be submitted with no answer chosen.

(f) Make an administration program that allows an administrator to log on. Upon successful logon, a page containing a list of links, one to pull up each quiz, is returned. The administrator can then browse one quiz at a time.

10. Do Exercise 9, but with the following alterations. The quiz grades each question as it's submitted, and it places the graded results in the quiz file for each user. It also features a log file that keeps cumulative results for the administrator. The administration program should return a page that lists final scores for each user who has taken the quiz, those users who have not taken the quiz, and cumulative statistics that include the percentage of correct answers for each question and the overall quiz average.

11. This exercise is inspired by the functionality of the `Nytimes.com` online news site (at the time this was written). The welcome page provides a list of links to news stories. However, you have to be registered at the site in order to read the stories. For this exercise, registration involves only creating a new (unused) user name and password. When one of the links for the stories in the welcome page is clicked, a page with both a logon form (for existing members) and a signup form is returned. Successfully logging on or signing up delivers the desired news story. The key is that the user then has logged-on state and can click any of the links for other stories without having to log back on. Three news stories to use can be found on the Web site under this exercise. Depending upon your solution to the problem, you may wish to reformat the files as HTML. *Hint:* The crucial app logic function, in terms of security, is the one that delivers news stories. The links for the stories can't directly point to the stories, but contain requests of the form `request=show_story&which=someStoryIdentifier`. The `show_story` function returns the story only if the user is logged on. Otherwise, it returns the logon forms.

12. (requires optional section) This example feature the creation of utilities for encrypted passwords in Web applications.

(a) Make a new version of the `logon` toolkit function that takes an additional, optional Boolean parameter that "turns on" encryption. If the optional parameter is not sent, the updated version is backwards compatible with the original.

(b) Also, update the `logon_new` toolkit function as described in part (a).

(c) Create an administration password file as shown in Figure 7.17, but with the password encrypted. *Hint:* Create the file with a very simple Perl (non-CGI) program.

(d) Get the `admin.cgi` program of Figure 7.21, whose source code can be obtained from this book's Web site, up and running where all passwords are encrypted. Create an encrypted user password file with a few entries.

(e) Augment the application so that the administrator can both change and delete entries in the user password file through a Web interface.

PROJECT THREAD

Here you augment the quiz application from the Chapter 6 project. In this version, the users are predetermined (like a class of students), and only an administrator can see the results. When someone takes a quiz, which has a time limit, it is automatically graded and then stored in a text file, to which only the administrator has access. The administrator can log on and receive a list of links that pull up the individual quiz files. The transaction diagram for the application is shown in Figure 7.26. Use the JavaScript-validated logon form you created in the Chapter 3 project thread.

A. Add all new toolkit functions to your library (they can be obtained from the Web site): `&generate_random_string`, `&get_long_id`, `&logon`, `&logon_new`, `&write_state`, `&read_state` (final version from Figure 7.25), `&URLencode`, `&URLdecode`.

B. Write the user part of the application. Start with a password file containing several users.

(i) Successful logon initiates a logged-on session and returns the quiz.

(ii) Submitting the quiz returns a thank-you page and the score on the quiz, but not the correct answers (a user might give them to someone else in the class). A quiz summary should be added to a text file named with the user name (such as `hsimpson.quiz`). This can basically be the same summary returned to the user in the previous version. Data should also be added to a separate log file that keeps cumulative statistics for all users (see part C(i)).

(iii) The user has only five (5) minutes to submit the quiz. If the quiz is submitted after 5 minutes, the session times out. In that case, the user is returned to the logon page with an appropriate message. Also, an empty quiz file should be created for the user in that case (that is, the user fails).

(iv) All of the quiz files should be kept in a separate (and secure) directory. An added security feature is that once someone has submitted the quiz (that is, a quiz file for a given user exists) the application prevents that user from submitting it again. *Hint:* Beware of the back button from the thank-you page.

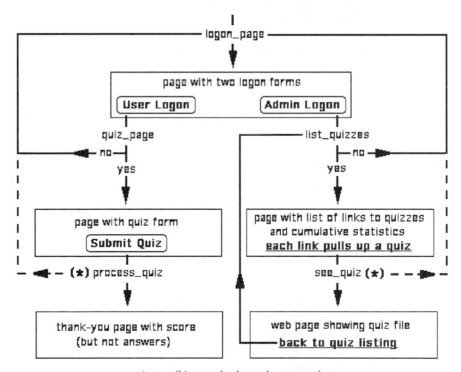

FIGURE 7.26 The transaction diagram for Chapter 7 Project Thread.

    (v) (optional) As an added twist, allow potential users to choose their user names from a pull-down menu in the initial logon page. That is, rather than using a text field to collect the user name, create a menu with one item for each user in the user password file.

C. Write the administration part of the application. Start with a password file containing at least one administrator.

    (i) Successful logon initiates a logged-on session and returns a list of links that can be used to pull up an individual quiz file. Generate the list by creating one list item for each quiz file found in the quiz directory. This page also contains cumulative statistics, calculated from the log file. The statistics can be minimal (just a cumulative average for the class), or more elaborate if you wish. *Hint:* The data submitted by each link can be something like `request=see_quiz&which=hsimpson.quiz`.

    (ii) For security, the `see_quiz` function should verify logged-on state.

    (iii) A quiz should be returned embedded in a Web page. The Web page should contain a link that returns the page with the list of links. So that the administrator does not have to log back on, the `list_quizzes` function needs to print the links page if either a valid user name and password are submitted (as from the logon form) or a valid session ID is submitted (as passed from the link). *Note:* Just returning the raw text file containing the quiz results is very insecure. It is far better to let the function first verify access privaleges and only then return the quiz. Just read the file line by line, replacing line breaks with `<br/>` elements.

D. Add a new row for the updated quiz application to the table in your homework page. Make sure you preserve the version from the previous chapter and keep the link to it active. If you are assigned any other exercises from this chapter, add another row to your homework table for each exercise.

E. (optional) Use encrypted password files (see Exercise 12(a)).

## CHAPTER 8

COOKIES

The examples in Chapter 7 featured Web applications that provide a session by hiding data within Web pages in order to maintain state between transactions. We showed that the data can be embedded in the Web pages in hidden form elements or added onto the URL behind a link. Moreover, the hidden information can be the actual data that maintains state or can be a session ID that points to a state file on the server, containing the actual state data.

An extension of HTTP enables a Web browser to store state data in cookies and automatically pass that data back to a given Web server. The new concept with cookies is that the stored data is not hidden in an HTML file sent from the server but is stored by the Web browser software on the client machine itself. This chapter explores the nature of cookies and the advantages (and disadvantages) of using cookies rather than hiding data inside Web pages.

NOTE

Before beginning this lesson, you are (strongly) encouraged to go into the preference settings of your favorite Web browser and set the browser to give you a warning before accepting cookies. The browser will then throw up a small alert window each time a cookie is set. Surf around to some major commercial Web sites and observe all the cookies that get set on the browser. That will likely be an eye-opening experience for you. Notice that many of the cookies contain data that appears to be just a ridiculously long string composed of randomly chosen characters. Does that sound familiar?

8.1 WHAT ARE COOKIES?

Netscape Communications introduced cookies with the release of Netscape Navigator version 2. Cookies soon became a universally accepted extension[1] of the protocol HTTP. A **cookie** is a small piece of data that is sent to a client from a Web server and is stored on the client machine by a Web browser. When the Web browser makes subsequent requests back to the Web server, the cookie is automatically sent back to the Web server as part of the request. The situation is depicted in Figure 8.1.

---

[1]Cookies are not actually part of the protocol standards for HTTP 1.0 or HTTP 1.1, but are defined in the separate specification RFC2109 (http://www.ietf.org/rfc/rfc2109.txt). Virtually all modern browsers and Web servers support cookies in HTTP transactions.

① A request for a CGI program that sends a cookie to the browser in the HTTP header.

② The browser stores the cookie in the cookie file or the temporary cookie cache, depending upon whether or not the cookie has an expiration date.

③ Any subsequent requests to www.uweb.edu return the cookie to the server, which stores it in the HTTP_COOKIE environment variable.

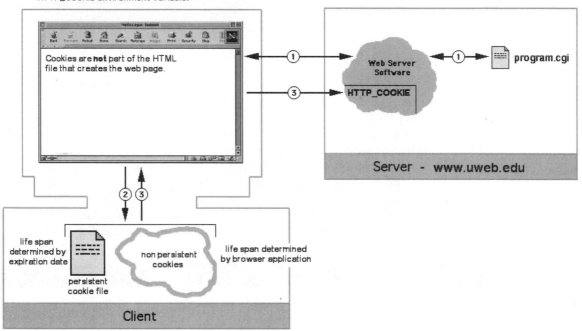

FIGURE 8.1 The general idea behind cookies.

The data stored in a cookie is simply a name=value pair. In Figure 8.1, the CGI program is responsible for "setting" a cookie. When the Web browser requests that program, it might set a cookie with data, `name1=value1`, for example. The Web browser stores that data along with the domain name of the server from which the cookie originated. So, in this case, the browser stores a cookie containing the following information. (Note that we have not shown the actual native format the browsers use to store the cookie. That is not important here.)

> `www.uweb.edu` *name1=value1*

When the Web browser makes a request back to the Web server (for `program.cgi` or some other resource) at some point in the future, the `name1=value1` data is automatically sent back to the Web server and stored into the `HTTP_COOKIE` environment variable.

Whenever a Web browser makes a request to a Web server, it scans its cookies to see whether it has any associated with the domain name it is requesting. All cookies the browser finds containing that domain name are sent to the server along with the request. If one or more CGI programs at `www.uweb.edu` had previously set several cookies, then all such cookies would be returned in future requests to that domain. But a Web browser returns cookies only to the domain name from which they originated. For example, requests to `math.uweb.edu` or `www.uweb.com` would not return the cookie `name1=value1` set from `www.uweb.edu`.

Cookies have a life span. By default, a cookie's life is determined by the Web browser. As shown in Figure 8.1, a Web browser keeps a RAM cache of **nonpersistent cookies**. The purpose of nonpersistent cookies is to live on the browser for a single session. For that reason, we will often just call them *session cookies*. Session cookies are automatically deleted by the browser application when it is quit.

N O T E

Because the browser software is responsible for storing cookies, there are platform- and vendor-specific nuances that arise. Some browsers keep a separate session cookie cache for each open window. If a session cookie is set while the user is surfing in one window, a transaction with the same domain in another window will not return the cookie. In contrast, some browser applications maintain a common session cookie cache for all open windows. In that case, any cookies set by a given domain are returned during another transaction with that domain from any open browser window. Of course, two different browser applications running on the same computer never share cookies.

The default, browser-determined life span of a cookie can be lengthened by giving it an `expires=`*date* pair. Going back to the preceding example, an expiration date could be added to the cookie from `www.uweb.edu`.

```
www.uweb.edu    name1=value1    expires=Thu, 01-Jan-2005 03:24:33 GMT
```

Cookies set with an expiration date are added as a line in the browser's cookie file, rather than merely to the browser's RAM cache of single-session cookies. The *cookie file* is merely a text file in which the browser stores *persistent cookies*. Netscape's original cookic implementation used a single file to store all cookies as shown in Figure 8.1. Some browsers still store persistent cookies that way. However, some browsers use a "cookie directory" where each cookie is stored as a separate file. Whatever the case, the general concept is the same, so we will simply refer to the cookie file.

Browser behavior is more uniform for persistent cookies. All open browser windows share the same persistent cookie file, and cookies are deleted from the file when they reach their expiration dates. The purpose of persistent cookies is to provide a mechanism for long-term storage of data on a given browser, transcending the short-term, session-oriented nature of nonpersistent cookies.

The constraints on storing cookies are browser dependent. Typical constraints are a limit of around 20 cookies from any one domain, each containing a maximum of 4KB of data. Such constraints usually apply to both the session cookie caches and the persistent-cookie file. The cookie file usually has a limit of about 300 total cookies. When the total number of cookies allowed in the file is reached, the browser starts deleting those that have not been used recently (even if they are not expired) in order to make room for new ones. Presumably, session cookie caches have a similar limit on the total number of cookies.

TABLE 8.1 Fields Used to Customize Cookies

FIELD	CONTENTS
name = *value* (mandatory)	The data for the cookie. The *name* and *value* can contain any ASCII printable character except a semicolon (;), comma (,), or white space. If a cookie is set whose name coincides with one already on the browser, the new cookie overwrites the existing one. (*Note:* Cookies with the same name are distinct if they have different `domain` or `path` restrictions (see below). In that case, two cookies with the same name can coexist.)

`expires` = *date* (optional)	Including this causes a cookie to be persistent. The maximum life span is browser dependent, usually from 1 to several years. The date is in the format
	
	`Day, dd-Mon-yyyy hh:mm:ss GMT`
	`Fri, 03-Nov-2001 15:09:33 GMT`
	
	where the `Day` and `Mon` are the first three letters (that is, `"Jan"`, `"Feb"`, `"Mar"`, and so forth) beginning with a capital. The time zone is standardized to GMT (Greenwich Mean Time) so that Web applications don't have to factor geography in. A persistent cookie can be prematurely deleted by overwriting it with one whose expiration date is already past.

`domain` = *domainname* (optional)	By default, the value of *domainname* is the full domain name of the site that sets the cookie (`www.uweb.edu`, for example). This field cannot specify that the cookie be sent to a domain other than the one that sets the cookie. It can be used to generalize the domain to which the cookie will be sent back. For example, setting `domain= .uweb.edu` will cause the cookie to be sent back to any subdomain, such as `math.uweb.edu` or `english.uweb.edu`. In contrast, the domain field can also be used to provide a more specific domain, such as `students.www.uweb.edu`, to which to return cookies, even if the cookie were set from `www.uweb.edu`. However, the generalization or specification must involve the same root domain, `uweb.edu` in our examples.
`path` = *directorypath* (optional)	This further restricts where the cookie will be sent. For example, including `path=/cgi` a cookie set from `www.uweb.edu` allows the cookie to be sent back to the server only in requests for resources at or below `www.uweb.edu/cgi/` in the public directory tree (or at or below anything beginning with `www.uweb.edu/cgi`, such as `www.uweb.edu/cgi-bin/`). This directive is useful if there are multiple scripts on your Web site that use cookies and you wish to share certain cookies among some scripts but not others. *Note:* Some Web browsers default to the root of the public domain, `path=/`, regardless of where the program that sets the cookie resides. Other browsers default to the actual directory where the program resides, `path=/cgi/somedir`, for example. In the former case, all programs in the public directory tree will share all cookies. In the latter case, only programs residing at or below `/cgi/somedir` in the public tree will be able to use cookies set from there.
`secure` (optional)	This valueless field causes the cookie to be sent back to the server only if the request is using secure shell https transactions for security. (Recall Section 1.9.)

A total of five fields are commonly used to customize cookies. The only mandatory field is the *name=value* field, which carries the actual data for the cookie. The similarity to the name and value parts of HTML form elements is intentional. The five fields are summarized in Table 8.1.

NOTE

As you shall soon see, cookies provide a novel way to preserve state data during a browsing session or to preserve a piece of persistent data. However, there is one major drawback to cookies: A user can simply go to the preferences of a browser and turn cookies off. (You may have noticed that, if you surfed for a while with cookie warnings enabled, as we suggested in the opening paragraphs of this chapter.) With cookies disabled, a browser simply won't accept any cookies, and any attempts by a given Web application to keep state data in cookies is rendered useless. But, given the volume of cookies that commercial sites set, they are counting on you not having disabled them. Indeed, if you disable cookies, some sites will even inform you that their site will not work properly, or not at all!

8.2   SETTING AND READING COOKIES

A cookie is set by a `Set-cookie` line in the HTTP response header that a Web server sends back to a Web browser when it answers a request. For example, suppose a Web browser requests a CGI program that sets three cookies. The HTTP application-layer header[2] in the Web server's response might look like the following:

```
HTTP/1.0 200 OK
Date: Fri, 30 Nov 2001 15:24:33 GMT
Server: Apache/1.3.1
Set-cookie: name1=value1
Set-cookie: name2=value2
Set-cookie: name3=value3
Content-length: 341
Content-type text/html
... blank line containing only a newline character
... data returned from the CGI program (that is, the HTML page)
```

All the lines above the blank line are what the browser reads to determine the nature of the returned data before deciding what to so with it. You can now see why we always print two newline characters in the `Content-type` line,

```
print "Content-type: text/html\n\n";
```

in our CGI programs prior to printing the HTML page. The HTTP protocol expects the extra blank line that separates the header information from the body of the message (the returned HTML page in this case).

---

[2]We have shown an HTTP version 1.0 header for simplicity. Most Web servers and browsers can also communicate using more elaborate HTTP version 1.1 headers.

This particular header tells the browser to set three session cookies. If the browser has not been set to ignore cookies, it will do so. Note that these cookies only set the required data-carrying field. The date line in the header is set automatically by the server software and really has nothing to with the cookies. In fact, the Web server software automatically prints all of the header lines except the ones containing `Set-cookie` and `Content-length`.

It is a simple matter to set cookies from a CGI program. Just include one or more statements that print a `Set-cookie` directive in the program *prior* to the print statement that generates the `Content-type` line.

```
print "Set-Cookie: name1=value1\n";
print "Set-Cookie: name2=value2\n";
print "Set-Cookie: name3=value3\n";
print "Content-type: text/html\n\n";
....now print the HTML page to be returned to the browser
```

It is important that each cookie you set be printed on a separate line in the header information and that an extra blank line be included only after the `Content-type` line. Hence, we will not be able to put one blanket statement at the top of our programs to print the `Content-type` line, as we have grown accustomed to doing. That `print` statement will have to be delayed until after any cookies are set by the program, but before printing any HTML pages.

If optional fields are used to fine-tune a cookie's behavior, they must be included in the `print` statement, delimited with semicolons. For example, the following statement sets all five of the fields we have introduced.

```
print "Set-Cookie: name=value; expires=Thu, 01-Jan-2005 03:24:33 GMT;
       domain=.uweb.edu; path=/cgi; secure\n";
```

This particular cookie is persistent (assuming the date is not past), and it sends its data back to the server upon any request for a resource in the public directory tree at or below

```
anySubDomain.uweb.edu/cgi
```

but only in an HTTPS transaction. The only nonoptional fields we use in the remainder of this lesson are the `expires` and `path` fields.

The optional cookie fields are used by the browser to determine whether it should submit a cookie during a given request. If the cookie is viable for a given request, the browser sends only the name=value part of the cookie to the server along with the request. Again, the data is sent in the HTTP header. We don't show such a request header. It is sufficient to know that only the data part of a cookie is sent back to the server. The other optional parts merely determine whether or not it should be sent. If there are multiple cookies that are viable for a browser request, the browser delimits the name=value pairs with a two-character combination of a semicolon followed by a space. For example, if the browser sends the three cookies set by the example HTTP header just shown, their data is sent back to the server formatted as follows.

```
name1=value1; name2=value2; name3=value3
```

When the Web server software receives the string of cookie data, it places it into the `HTTP_COOKIE` environment variable. Of course, that data is then accessible to a CGI program via `$ENV{"HTTP_COOKIE"}` in the `%ENV` hash, which is automatically passed to the program through the CGI interface. A convenient way to recover the name=value pairs is to create your own hash as follows:

```perl
%cookieHash = ();
@nameValuePairs = split(/; /, $ENV{"HTTP_COOKIE"});
foreach $pair (@nameValuePairs) {
  ($name, $value) = split(/=/, $pair);
  $cookieHash{$name} = $value;
}
```

First, split out the individual cookies (name=value pairs) from the HTTP_COOKIE environment variable. Note that we split around a semicolon followed by a space. Then, for each pair, split out the $name and $value parts, storing the $value into the hash with the $name as the key.

We conclude this section with a short example that uses a nonpersistent cookie to record state data during a session. The cookie simply counts how many times a given browser requests the CGI program during a given session. Each time the user calls the CGI program, he is informed how many times he has called the program during the current session.

The program, named visitcounter.cgi, is shown in Figure 8.2 followed by an overview. Note that the program uses no data submissions other than through cookies. Thus, the code for decoding form data into %formHash is omitted in favor of the code for creating the %cookieHash.

FIGURE 8.2 Maintaining session state with cookies.

- Initialize the `%cookieHash` with any incoming cookies. Note that the hash is empty if the browser does not send any cookies.
- If the browser submitted a `VISITS` cookie
  - Augment the cookie's value by one and store the updated value into the variable, `$numvisits`.
  - Set the `$welcome` message to the empty string, because the session is continuing.
- Else (first visit of session)
  - Set `$numvisits` to 1.
  - Set a `$welcome` message.
- Set a session cookie on the user's browser. On the first visit, the cookie's data will be `VISITS=1`. On subsequent visits, browser will overwrite the cookie with the new data, `VISITS=2` for example.
- Print the `Content-type` line (after the cookie, but before the HTML page).
- Print the page with the (potentially empty) `$welcome` message and the current number of visits during the session.

NOTE

Some browsers set `path=/` by default, and others set `path` to the actual directory containing the program that set the cookie. Thus, it is a good idea to get in the habit of always including the path field to factor out that inconsistency. In Figure 8.2, we set `path=/` so that the cookie would be returned to any program below the domain root, regardless of the browser vendor or version. If we had wished to restrict the cookie, we would have manually set the path, again not trusting the browser to do it by default. Keep in mind that if you have an account on a Web server, maybe `www.uweb.edu/~jones`, then your user name will be part of the path, `path=/~jones/cgi`, for example.

A natural enhancement of `visitcounter.cgi` that contrasts session and persistent cookies is to use one or more persistent cookies in conjunction with the single-session counting cookie. The persistent cookie(s) can store data necessary to inform the user how many different sessions he has done with the program and the average number of calls he makes per session. This idea, with further embellishments, is outlined as an exercise.

8.3 COOKIES VERSUS DATA EMBEDDED IN WEB PAGES

Cookies could have been used to carry the state data in *every* example of Chapter 7. That includes storing the actual state data in cookies or merely storing a session ID that identifies the state data in a file on the server. Several homework exercises involve reworking those examples using cookies. In many respects, it is easier to implement temporary state using session cookies. On the other hand, if a particular browser is set not to accept cookies, then the application simply won't work. That drawback aside, the following points compare and contrast using cookies to store state data with hiding the data in Web pages.

▩ Cookie data for a given application stored one time on a browser is automatically returned every time that browser makes a transaction with the application. Thus, propagating session state among Web pages does not require that the data be manually reembedded in each Web page that is to continue the session.

▩ The previous item has ramifications on the continuity of sessions. For example, in the `visit counter.cgi` program of the previous section, the user could surf to many other sites, then merely type the URL of the program back in to resume the session—that is, unless he had switched to a different browser window. In contrast, propagating a session using Web page-embedded data requires a "continuous" embedding of data from one page into the next. The user could not surf to other sites, type the URL in, and resume the session from the original site. Rather, he would have to go back in the browser's history list and find a page with the hidden data in order to resume the continuity of the session.

▩ For logged-on state, don't set sensitive password information in a cookie. The cookies set on a given browser can easily be located and read by anyone who has access to the browser. Again, the best solution is to store a long session ID in a cookie.

▩ Depending upon the browser, session cookies may not be shared between two windows open in the same browser. Typically you would not want two windows to share the same state data so that two different shopping carts don't get jumbled together, for example. So in this respect, session cookies bring the same functionality as Web page-embedded data.

▩ If for some reason you need multiple browser windows to share the same state data (for example, to arm a particular Web browser with long-term, multiple-session logged-on state), persistent cookies are an easy solution, because they are made available to multiple windows open at one time and to new windows created when a browser is quit and restarted.

▩ As you will see in the next section, user preferences can be stored on a given browser in persistent cookies. Each time that browser visits the site, it gets customized page content based upon the preferences. However, if those preferences need to apply regardless of the particular browser someone is using, a permanent user profile record would be kept on the server in a text file or database table.

8.4 PERSISTENT COOKIES FOR SITE PREFERENCES

The second-to-last bulleted item in the previous section mentioned that it is possible for an application to arm a browser with long-term, multiple-session logged-on state. However, that is usually not desirable. Even if the application is not sensitive in the least (in which case it probably doesn't require logon in the first place), more than one person might use the same browser. In that case, cranking up the browser and finding someone else automatically logged onto a given site would not be good. Leaving a particular browser armed with long-term logged-on state for a sensitive application such as an online banking account would be unthinkable.

However, it is a very common practice to store nonsensitive user data in persistent cookies on a particular browser. Many sites let you customize the content you see when you visit their site. For example, when you first visit a news site, you might get links to a variety of stories by default, but you can pull up a page that lets you choose which story types you would prefer to see more of (such as sports, weather, and financial) next time you visit. Setting that data in a persistent cookie enables the application to deliver customized content to the same browser for a year or more.

This is the idea of storing **user preferences** for a Web application on a given browser. If it is important that the preferences be accessible from different browsers, or if the application requires personal information, then the data should be stored in a permanent user account on the server. However for many sites the preferences are simply to make the user feel more at home when surfing from her usual browser, and persistent cookies are perfect for that.

We leave the personalized news site content concept for an exercise and present an example that simulates a Web site that requires the user to choose the language in which the site's content is delivered. The Web site is demonstrated in Figure 8.3. On the very first visit to the site, the user is given a page with which to set preferences by choosing a language from a pull-down menu and possibly clicking the flag option. Submitting the preferences form sets preference cookies on the browser. When that browser visits the site again at a later time, the cookies are detected and a customized language page is delivered. That is, the existence of the cookies enables the application to bypass the preference page on future visits from the same browser. Of course, a real site that sets a language preference would deliver a more elaborate page with specialized language content, but we did not wish to hire several translators for this example.

On the surface, the logic of the problem seems straightforward: The first visit gives the preference page, and subsequent visits bypass the preference page. However, the preferences will be stored in persistent cookies that live for a year. Moreover, subsequent visits to the customized page refresh the cookie's `expires` field. Without a further provision to allow the preferences to be reset, a given user would be forced to use the same preferences for at least a year, maybe indefinitely if she keeps visiting the site. Implementing such a provision involves a slightly convoluted transaction diagram, as shown in Figure 8.4.

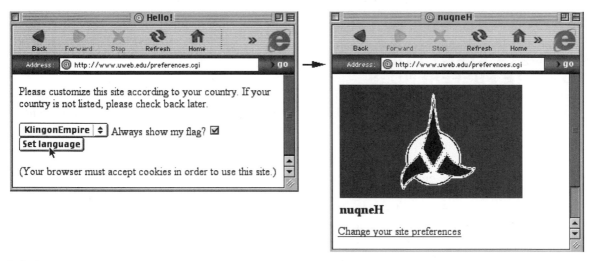

FIGURE 8.3   A Web site that requires the user to set a language preference.

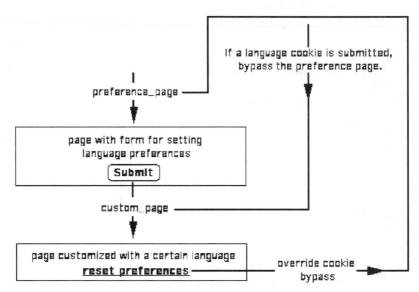

FIGURE 8.4   The transaction diagram for the long-term language preferences.

If preference cookies have been set on a browser, a request to the application from that browser is shunted straight to the function that prints the customized language page. However, the reset preferences link must override that behavior and cause the initial preferences page to be loaded. This results in precedence considerations in the app logic, as follows.

```
if($formHash{"request"} eq "reset") {
    &preference_page;
}
elsif(exists $cookieHash{"language"}) {
    &custom_page;
}
elsif($formHash{"request"} eq "custom_page") {
    &custom_page;
}
else {
    &preference_page;
}
```

A reset request takes precedence over everything and loads the preference page. The next priority is that a submitted language preference cookie causes a bypass of the preference page. Of course, submitting the preference form also loads the custom page. Finally, requestless and cookieless (for example, the initial hit on the application) default to the preference page.

It is imperative that the reset request appear in the app logic above the cookie detection. That is the only way to override the bypass of the preference page caused by the cookie! However, the order of the middle two clauses is unimportant, and they can be combined into one clause, as can be seen in Figure 8.5, which shows the outline of the actual program. In the order in which those two clauses currently appear in either version of the app logic, submitting the preferences form to reset old preferences actually triggers the custom_page function because of the old cookie rather than because of the request

```perl
#! /usr/bin/perl
# must print Content-type line after printing cookies

############################################################
#   code for decoding input $datastring into %formHash    #
#       (works for GET, POST, and offline execution)      #
############################################################

############################################################
#   code forstoring incomming cookies into %cookieHash    #
############################################################

%greetings = (
   "USA" => "Welcome",
   "UK" => "Welcome",
   "Canada" => "Welcome",
   "France" => "Bienvenue",
   "Germany" => "Wilkommen",
   "Spain" => "Bienvenidos",
   "KlingonEmpire" => "nuqneH",
   "Romulus" => "Aefvadh"
);

### app logic ############################################
if($formHash{"request"} eq "reset") {
    &preference_page;
}
elsif( (exists $cookieHash{"language"}) || ($formHash{"request"} eq "custom_page") ) {
    &custom_page;
}
else {
    &preference_page;
}
### end app logic ########################################

############################################################
### Definitions of app logic functions go here.          #
### Definitions for toolkit functions used:              #
#    &one_year_from_now      (new)                        #
############################################################
```

FIGURE 8.5 The outline of the language preferences program.

made by the preferences form. If you understand the issues in this paragraph, you have thoroughly thought through the logic of this example.

There are a few things to note about the program. First, the Content-type is not printed at the top, so cookies can be printed later. Second, this program deals with both submitted form data and submitted cookies, so the two standard decoding routines are included. (Just add the routine for %cookieHash to the standard decoding routine, and you needn't ever worry about that again.) Third, for simplicity, we use only a simple hash as the source of the customized content. Finally, we employ a new toolkit function named one_year_from_now to handle setting the expiration date, which checks the time on the Web server and returns a time and date (properly formatted for cookies) exactly one year from when it is called. We do not show the code for the function because it contains some nitpicky details to deal with leap years, but its source code is available on this book's Web site.

The initial call to the application (or a call to reset preferences) simply loads the preference page, which contains a form that submits its data to the custom_page function.

The only noteworthy issue in the `preference_page` function is that the values of the language menu are the keys of the hash.

```perl
sub preference_page {
print "Content-type: text/html\n\n";
print <<TOP;
<html><head><title>Hello!</title></head><body>
  Please customize this site according to your country.
  If your country is not listed, please check back later.
  <form action="$ENV{'SCRIPT_NAME'}" method="GET">
    <select name="language">
TOP
  foreach $key (sort keys %greetings) {
    print "<option value=\"$key\">$key</option>\n";
  }

  print <<BOTTOM;
    </select>
    Always show my flag? <input type="checkbox" name="flag" value="yes" /><br />
    <input type="hidden" name="request" value="custom_page" />
    <input type="submit" value="Set Language" />
  </form>
  (Your browser must accept cookies in oder to use this site.)
</body></html>
BOTTOM
}
```

The `custom_page` function, which we show next, does most of the work. It is followed by a detailed overview.

```perl
sub custom_page {
  my ($language, $flag);

  if(exists $formHash{"language"}) { # the preference form has been submitted
                                     # to set or reset the preferences
    $language=$formHash{"language"};
    if(exists $formHash{"flag"}) {
      $flag="yes";
    }
    else {
      $flag="no";
    }
  }
  else { # use the preferences set in cookies on the browser
    $language=$cookieHash{"language"};
    $flag=$cookieHash{"flag"};
  }

  my $expires = &one_year_from_now;
  print "Set-cookie: language=$language; path=/; expires=$expires\n";
  print "Set-cookie: flag=$flag; path=/; expires=$expires\n";

  my $greeting = $greetings{$language};

  print "Content-type: text/html\n\n";
```

```
  print <<TOP;
  <html><head><title>$greeting</title></head><body>
TOP

  if($flag eq "yes") {
    print "<img src=\"$language.gif\" />";
  }

  print <<BOTTOM;
    <h3>$greeting</h3>
    <a href="$ENV{'SCRIPT_NAME'}?request=reset">Change your site preferences</a>
  </body></html>
BOTTOM
}
```

- ▦ Define local variables in which to store the users preferences.
- ▦ If (a language preference is submitted from the preference form)
  - ▦ The flag preference should be set to `yes` only if the checkbox was checked.
- ▦ Else
  - ▦ Use the submitted preference cookies.
- ▦ Set the cookies. Note that the cookies get reset each time the customized page is generated. This keeps the expires field updated. The only way for the cookies to expire naturally is not to visit the site for a year.
- ▦ Grab the proper `$greeting` from the data hash.
- ▦ Print the page, including the flag image (possibly), the language-specific greeting, and the link that triggers the reset preferences capability. Note that the flag images are named using the hash keys for easy reference.

One additional thing to note is that this application sets two persistent cookies: one for the country and one for the flag option. The flag option, not essential to the basic language preference theme of this example, is included so that the example features two cookies.

In particular, the role of the flag cookie is Boolean in nature. One could set a cookie when the flag option is checked, and simply not set a cookie for the flag otherwise. That is, if no flag cookie is submitted to the application, it simply wouldn't show a flag image. Then, in order to "turn off" a previously set flag cookie when the reset preferences option is exercised, one would overwrite it with a persistent cookie with an expired date, thereby deleting it. But the easiest way is simply always to set a Boolean-style flag cookie with data `flag=yes` or `flag=no`.

NOTE

In general, when cookies are used to hold ordinary single-session state data or a session ID, the main logic of an application is no different than when hidden form elements or state files are used. In that case, the state-related data is merely stored in `%cookieHash` rather than `%formHash`. However, as we have just demonstrated, other uses of cookies can actually influence the application's underlying request logic.

8.5 THIRD-PARTY COOKIES

When something is used for a purpose other than for what it was intended, it's sometimes called an "abuse" and at other times a "clever adaptation". In this section we provide an overview of **third-party cookies** and how they are used. Online marketing companies and large Web site networks claim that third-party cookies are a harmless way to monitor advertising effectiveness and compile impersonal demographics about Web surfers. Others claim that they are an invasion of privacy. In fact, several new laws taking various forms have been considered by U.S. legislative brahches. One example was the Consumer Online Privacy and Disclosure Act, introduced in the House of Representatives in 2001. The bill called for Web sites to obtain a user's permission before setting third-party cookies on the user's browser. At the time this was written, no U.S. laws have been passed that impose such stringent privacy constraints regarding cookies.

We're not advocating either side. In our opinion, the issue of third-party cookies will likely boil down to requiring that Web browsers provide a preference setting that can be used to disable them. Indeed, most modern browsers already have such an option, although many people are not aware of it, and it may not be the default setting. Perhaps the third-party cookie issue will boil down simply to requiring that browsers ask people whether they want to enable third-party cookies when the browser application is installed or started for the first time.

Of course, the public needs to be aware of what third-party cookies are and how they are used in order to make an educated decision on whether or not to turn them off. To that end, this section provides a conceptual introduction to third-party cookies and their uses. You will get a good feel for how they are used, but the details of actually implementing Web applications with the capabilities illustrated by examples of this section are well beyond the scope of this text.

NOTE

If you surf to a few major sites with your browser set to alert you before accepting cookies (as we suggested in the note in the introduction to this lesson), you will see that the volume of cookies you get cannot be attributable to setting some session data or long-term user preferences on your browser. Many, perhaps the majority, of those are set by third parties.

A third-party cookie is one that is set on a browser in a transaction with one domain (such as `x.com`), but has a `domain` field that specifies a different domain (such as `y.com`). The result is that the browser can have a cookie from, say, `y.com` when, ostensibly, the browser has never visited `y.com`. On the surface, that seems to contradict the fact that the domain field that can be included when a cookie is set can specify only a value that is a subdomain of the one that sets the cookie. The key is that, during the act of loading a Web page such as from `x.com`, secondary transactions with other servers are possible. Figure 8.6 shows how a third-party cookie is set.

① The client loads a web page from x.com that contains an image which must be acquired from y.com.

② The server software at y.com is specialized so that it returns the image and a cookie.

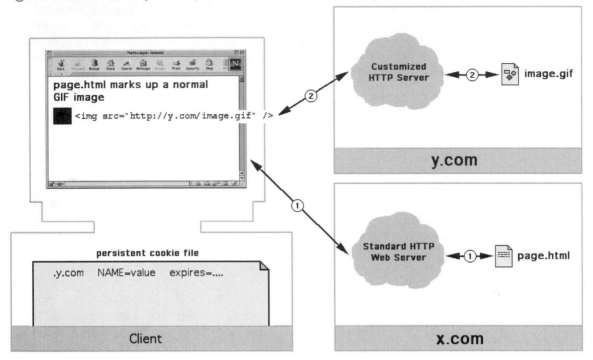

FIGURE 8.6 Setting a third-party cookie.

The client browser and x.com are the two primary parties, because the browser is loading a page from x.com. But the browser ends up with a cookie from y.com, which is a third party; hence, we have the term *third-party cookie*. Recall from Section 1.6 that a browser parses the HTML file and makes secondary requests for images as it finds the img elements. When the images come from the same source as the HTML file, the same transport-layer socket that transferred the HTML file is kept alive and used for the subsequent image transfers. When an image is requested from a third-party source, however, the Web browser opens a distinct connection to acquire the image. It is during that extra HTTP transaction that a third-party cookie can be set.

There is little use in using standard Web servers to deliver third-party images by themselves. Indeed, requiring images from multiple servers slows down the act of retrieving and rendering Web pages. Third-party images are served solely for the purpose of exchanging cookie data between the browser and third-party server. The benefits of the third-party data exchange obviously outweigh (from the point of view of the sites employing it) the overhead of the extra transaction, or else third-party cookies would not be used. Standard Web servers can easily deliver third-party images, but, as indicated in Figure 8.6, customized HTTP servers are required to deal with the extra baggage (the cookie data) delivered with the image. The rest of this section shows how "big business" on the Web makes use of the third-party data exchange enabled through third-party cookies.

1. A page from x.com contains an ad banner that must be acquired from y.com's ad server.

2. The ad server returns the image along with a cookie whose data contains their ID string for x.com.

3. If the client's browser visits y.com's main site, their CGI program receives the cookie and knows that the browser has been to x.com.

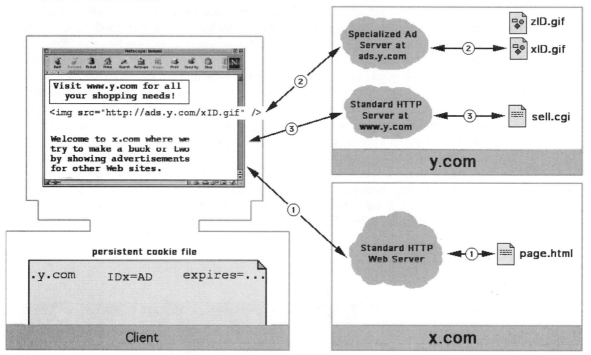

FIGURE 8.7   A third-party ad server.

Ad Servers

One of the most common uses of third-party cookies involves a specialized **ad server**, whose primary job is to hand out advertising banners to those Web pages that request them. Of course, third-party ad graphics arrive with extra baggage: third-party cookies set on unsuspecting browsers. The concept is depicted in Figure 8.7. Suppose y.com is selling stuff online and has an ad server running at its subdomain ads.y.com. It has paid x.com to display its advertising banner in Web pages. The ad banner is responsible for initiating the transaction that sets the third-party cookie from y.com.

Now, y.com advertises on sites other than x.com, so it assigns identification numbers to each site on which it advertises. We have symbolically represented the ID for x.com as xID. As you can see in the figure, the ID is the name of the ad banner. When the specialized ad server receives the request for xID.gif, it quickly parses out the ID and knows that x.com is requesting the image. When it sends the image to the browser, it also sets a cookie whose name[3] is that ID. Note that we have named the actual ad banner image file xID.gif for simplicity. More

---

[3]We use xID=AD rather than AD=xID for the cookie data so that if x.com and z.com both cause cookies to be set on a given browser, then the cookie names are distinct and one cookie doesn't overwrite the other.

likely, the ad server would use that ID to identify the banner it wants to send to x.com's Web page and sends the image under the pseudonym of xID.gif. In that way, it could deliver each of several banners in its ad campaign to x.com in a cyclic fashion.

Since the cookie has set domain=.y.com, it will be returned whenever that browser hits www.y.com or whatever full domain name from which y.com is selling stuff. Now, www.y.com is not just serving up static Web pages but using a Web application to deliver dynamic content. Of course, the application at www.y.com is looking for incoming cookies. When it finds one of the xID=AD cookies on a browser, it knows that the browser has not only loaded one of its ads at x.com, but has also subsequently visited its site. If y.com also serves ads to v.com, w.com, and z.com, it can monitor the IDs in the incoming cookies to determine which advertising campaign is the most effective. In this way, companies that advertise on the Web can cancel ad campaigns that are ineffective and reward the hosts of effective campaigns based upon commission.

Online advertising has actually developed its own terminology. In our example, y.com can easily measure *impressions* and *clickthroughs* using the third-party cookies. When its xID.gif ad is requested from its ad server, it knows someone has loaded a page from x.com containing its ad. In that case, it registers an *ad impression* from x.com—presumably, someone has seen its ad. When their Web application that does the selling receives an xID=AD cookie from a browser, it registers an *ad clickthrough* from x.com—presumably someone has clicked its ad at x.com to come to y.com. They can even determine which clickthrough hits stick around and buy something, using session state in some form.

> ## NOTE
>
> Even with ad serving, treachery is sometimes afoot. There have been cases where someone has spammed an ad server in order to rack up advertising commissions for a rival. So, of course, ad servers have security provisions in place. Some of those measures have to do with the third-party cookie data itself. If you look at some incoming third-party cookies, you will note that the matter is not quite as simple as what we have shown. In particular, you will see a lot of really long IDs in the names and values, seemingly composed of randomly chosen characters. All sorts of information can be "scrambled" into cookie data for uniqueness and authentication purposes.

Mass Marketing and Consumer Tracking on the Web

What we have shown so far is rather innocuous: a company sets cookies on your browser in order to help analyze its advertising effectiveness. But some companies have come into existence almost solely to set cookies on your browser! Most companies who market online don't have the desire (or wherewithal) to run and monitor their own third-party ad server. Mass marketing firms were common long before the Web came into existence. It should come as no surprise that mass marketing has evolved onto the Web.

Figure 8.8 depicts a mass marketing strategy where a company, a.com, runs a high-volume server farm dedicated primarily to implementing and monitoring ad campaigns for a large number of Web sites. That's how a.com makes a living. When your browser hits a

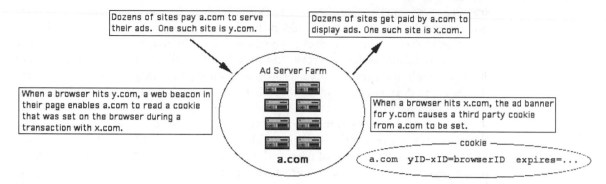

FIGURE 8.8 Mass marketing on the Web.

site like x.com, whose pages contain y.com's ads, the image is actually served from a.com. The corresponding cookie, whose return domain is a.com, is marked with identification numbers for both y.com and x.com. Thus, the request to a.com for the ad banner carries enough information so that the ad server knows that a y.com ad has made an impression in a page at x.com. In addition, the cookie contains some sort of browser ID, perhaps a randomly generated long ID, which is effectively a long-term *tracking ID* to identify your browser if it hits other sites in a.com's advertising ring.

Consumer tracking enables a.com to compile elaborate statistics for its clients. On one level, a.com's revenue flow is dependent upon its analysis of impressions and click-throughs. The more effective its marketing plan, the more money it makes for itself and its clients. On another level, the browser identification allows it to compile impersonal demographics about consumer trends. For example, browsers that visit x.com might tend to visit a certain subset of its clients often while scarcely visiting another subset. Another subset of its clients, on the other hand, might share frequent users who rarely visit x.com. Using such statistics, a.com can sniff out user trends and focus certain ad campaigns on certain subsets of its clients, generating more revenue for its clients (and itself).

Web Beacons

Before reading this subsection, do a search on your favorite search engine using the following three words: *web*, *beacon*, *privacy*. Many of the results that are returned will be privacy statements issued by major commercial Web sites concerning their use of Web beacons and cookies. Peruse a few of them. They readily admit that they are tracking you, but they assert that the information they pass around can't identify you personally.

A **Web beacon** is typically a transparent GIF image with dimensions of 1×1 pixel. Thus, it is completely imperceptible when displayed in a Web page. The sole purpose of putting a Web beacon in a page is to cause a secondary transaction with a third-party "cookie server" as the page is rendered. The transaction may set new cookies from the cookie server or return its cookies previously set on your browser. So, as a means to enable third-party data exchange, Web beacons work exactly like third-party ad graphics. It's just that you can't see them!

To show you one use of beacons, we return to the unfinished discussion surrounding a.com's ad server farm shown in Figure 8.8. We mentioned that the advertising agency can track both impressions and clickthroughs for its clients, but we only explained how it tracks impressions. Those are easy—one of y.com's ads loads into x.com's page, and since the ad comes from a.com, that secondary transaction registers an impression (ad from y.com seen at x.com). If the surfer clicks on the ad—a clickthrough—the browser makes a transaction to pull up a page at y.com. But for a.com (the advertising agency) to register the clickthrough, the page at y.com also needs a third-party image served from a.com. Because y.com does not display its own ad banners, it simply puts an a.com Web beacon in each of their pages.

Because of the use of Web beacons in conjunction with ad banners, virtually no one can hit a site in a.com's advertising ring without a.com knowing about it. Once a given browser enters the "fellowship of the ring," it is marked with a third-party cookie, replete with a browser ID, from a.com. Thus that particular browser can be tracked by a.com, the "lord of the ring," as it visits any other Web sites in the advertising ring (or perhaps in Middle-earth). If a.com is sufficiently sophisticated, it might even record in what order your browser visits pages, and for how long!

As the Web continues to evolve, more and more sites are coagulating into large online networks. The individual sites often retain their identity, but they reap the benefits of mass advertising and tracking. You would be surprised to know how many sites are affiliated (directly or indirectly) with major Web presences like MSN, AOL, and Yahoo!. Such Web conglomerates likely have their own server farms dedicated to tracking consumers. All that is required is Web beacons in the pages of all affiliate sites, a clever tracking scheme, and a program to crank out descriptive statistics based upon the results. Now you can begin to understand the reason for the five or ten cookies you may get in one transaction with a large commercial site. Throw in a few ad servers, a couple of Web beacon-tracking servers, and some session data on top of that, and there you have it.

Before you get up in arms that you may not be as anonymous as you like when you surf the Web, and rush to your browser preferences to turn off third-party cookies, it pays to remember that mass advertising on the Web generates a lot of revenue for Web sites. Many sites are able to stay accessible to the public free of charge only because of advertising revenue. Without such revenue, a lot of valuable free information could vanish from the Web. On the other hand, there are some legitimate privacy issues to consider.

SUMMARY OF KEY TERMS AND CONCEPTS

Cookie: A chunk of data stored by Web browser software on the client machine at the request of Web server software. The data is sent from a server to a browser in a `Set-cookie` line in the HTTP application-layer header. When a browser initiates a transaction with a Web server, any cookies (subject to constraint fields) that were set from the domain of the server are automatically returned to the server. The Web server puts returned cookies into the `HTTP_COOKIE` environment variable. We have provided a second decoding routine that URL-decodes incoming cookies, storing them into a global `%cookieHash`.

Cookie fields: A cookie can be set on a browser using a maximum of five fields, but only the field that carries the data is returned from the browser to the server. The other four fields, which are optional, merely impose constraints upon whether or not a browser should return a cookie's data to a given server or whether a browser should delete a cookie.

Data field (required): A name=value pair that holds a cookie's data. Setting a new cookie whose name is the same as that of a cookie already stored on a browser overwrites the original cookie.

expires field (optional): A field in a cookie that sets the date/time at which the cookie expires. Browsers will not return expired cookies. Cookies with an expiration date/time are called *persistent*. Browsers periodically police the cache of persistent cookies. A Web application can delete a persistent cookie by overwriting it with a new cookie that has the same name in its data field and is already expired.

domain field (optional): Browsers only send a cookie back to the domain from which it originated. The domain field is used to restrict (or generalize) further where the cookie will be returned within that domain.

path field (optional): A browser will return a cookie only to a program at or below the specified path in the directory tree below the public folder. This field is used to control which Web application within a site receives which cookies. If you have an account on a Web server, it is important to restrict your cookies to your account (that is, path=/~jones). Otherwise CGI programs in other accounts on the server may get your cookies.

secure field (optional): If this field is present, a browser returns a cookie only if the transaction is using a secure socket (HTTPS).

Nonpersistent cookies: Cookies without an expires field, also called *session cookies*. Depending upon the particular browser vendor and version, session cookies are deleted when a browser window is closed or when the entire browser application is quit.

Unreliability: If cookies are turned off in a Web browser's preference settings, they will not work. Many commercial Web applications will not work properly in your browser if you disable cookies. Cleverly programmed Web applications can sniff for cookies and resort to hiding data in Web pages if they are disabled.

Cookies versus Web page-embedded data: Reliability concerns aside, session cookies work just like hiding session data in Web pages when used in that capacity, except for some subtle differences. Persistent cookies are the only means with which a Web application can store data on the client between sessions.

User preferences: Persistent cookies are often used to store long-term preferences on the client. This feature can be used to deliver customized content automatically to a given Web browser on subsequent visits. Preferences set in this way are browser specific.

Third-party cookies: When a Web page contains a graphic whose source is from a different Web server from that of the Web page, a browser makes a secondary transaction to the third-party server to acquire the graphic. A cookie can be set during the secondary transaction. Specialized HTTP server software is used to set third-party cookies upon requests for such graphics.

Third-party ad servers: Specialized servers that deliver and track advertisement graphics, using third-party cookies. Ad servers may track *impressions* (when somebody sees the ad) and *clickthroughs* (when the ad actually generates a hit for a site). There are large advertising companies that deliver and track ads for many different clients, including those clients who display the ads and those who advertise. In some cases, elaborate statistics are compiled based on tracking Web surfers.

Web beacons: Ostensibly invisible (1×1 pixels in dimension) graphics whose only purpose is to generate secondary transactions in order to set third-party cookies. If a Web beacon is placed in every page of a group of related Web sites, all those pages are effectively "linked" to the third-party server in sense that the third-party server is sent a cookie each time a given browser visits any of the sites. Large Web conglomerates (groups of "member sites") can use Web beacons to track a given browser completely as it surfs among the member sites.

EXERCISES

Don't forget the toolkit functions developed in Chapter 7! They can be downloaded from this book's Web site. Also, you may wish to use the new `one_year_from_now` toolkit function when setting persistent cookies.

1. Make a driver program to implement a "cookie sniff." A welcome page uses JavaScript and the `window.navigator.cookieEnabled` Boolean property in the Browser Object for the detection. A hidden form element, which informs the CGI program of the result, is dynamically generated using JavaScript. When the welcome page is submitted, the driver program either sets a session cookie containing a long session ID or returns a hidden form element with the ID. You need not create a state file for this driver program.

2. The `visitcounter.cgi` program from Section 8.2 can be obtained from the Web site. Extend the program with the features outlined in any or all of the following options. Each time the statistics page is printed, it should display all statistics that the program is capable of generating. You will need at least two different browsers to test this problem. Remember, simply quit the browser to kill session cookies.

   (a) Use persistent cookie(s) to store data necessary to compute statistics giving the number of different sessions a browser has done with the program and the average number of transactions per session.

   (b) Use a permanent data file on the server to enable the program to compute the number of different browsers with which a given user has loaded the program and the average number of sessions per browser. To implement this option, start with a password file that identifies users, and request the user's identity using a logon form. Thus the statistics page is password protected, but the main purpose of this step is that it gives you the user name with which to identify the data file of a particular user.

   (c) Add a checkbox to the logon form from part (b) that allows a user to set a preference to bypass the logon form in the future. Use a persistent cookie to store the preference. Include a Reset Preference link in the statistics page.

   (d) Make the program self-contained in the sense that anyone can visit the program, at which time the visitor can either log on or sign up. The act of signing up creates the permanent account file from part (b).

3. Rewrite the `admin.cgi` program of Section 7.7 using a session cookie as opposed to hiding the session ID in the Web pages.

   (a) Provide an option in the logon form that allows the administrator to choose to leave a particular browser armed with long-term logged-on state (despite the inherent security risk). Any time the administrator visits the application in the future using the same browser, the logon page is bypassed.

   (b) Also add a logout button to the protected page that the administrator can use to disarm long-term logged-on state on a given browser. Of course, if the administrator does not enable long-term logged-on state, the logout button should not appear in the protected page.

   (c) Implement a cookie sniff as outlined in Exercise 1. If the application can't use cookies, use a hidden form element to propagate the logged-on session and do not provide the extra option from part (a) in the logon form. *Hint:* Generate the form element for the extra option dynamically with JavaScript on the client if cookies are enabled.

4. Rewrite the `quiz2.cgi` program of Section 7.4 using session cookies as opposed to hiding data in the Web pages. *Note:* This exercise can be applied to any or all parts of Exercise 9 in Chapter 7, which outlines several enhancements to the `quiz2.cgi` program.

5. Rewrite the `pizza3.cgi` program of Section 7.2. In particular, do not use a state file to store data between transactions. Rather, store all state data in session cookies. In the thank-you page, write a paragraph or two on why it is now possible to implement Exercise 8(c) of Chapter 7 without using a server-side file. *Note:* This exercise can also can be applied to parts (a), (c), and (d) of Exercise 8 in Chapter 7, which outlines several enhancements to the `pizza3.cgi` program.

6. Work exercise 11 from Chapter 7 but use a persistent cookie to arm a given browser with long-term logged-on state.

    (a) Add an option to both the logon form and the signup form that says something like "Remember me next time I visit, so I don't have to log back on." If the option is enabled, subsequent visits by the user from the same browser enable a news link to go straight to a story, bypassing the logon form. If the option is not enabled, use a session cookie to propagate a logged-on session.

    (b) Implement a cookie sniff as outlined in Exercise 1. If the application can't use cookies, it should automatically resort to hiding session IDs in links to propagate a logged-on session. Also, in that case, do not provide the extra option from part (a) in the forms. *Hint:* Generate the form element for the extra option dynamically with JavaScript on the client if cookies are enabled.

7. Make a prototype news site where the user can set preferences. Start with three directories: one for each of three categories, such as sports, politics, and business. Three news stories are provided on the Web site under this exercise. You may use those stories for one category. Make very simple, one-sentence news stories to provide content for your other two categories. When the application is first visited, it displays a list of links, one list for each category (directory). Make each list by scanning a directory and creating a link for each news story file found in the directory. Clicking on a link pulls up a Web page with the corresponding news story. (You may store the news stories in HTML files or simply read plain text files into Web pages.)

    Add a link to the main page that pulls up a page that enables the user to set preferences. The preferences form should contain one checkbox for each news category, with all checkboxes initially checked. Users can then eliminate those news categories they don't want to see on the main page the next time they visit. If and only if the user has set preferences, a reset preferences link should appear in the main page. Note that there is no logon for this problem, just long-term preferences. The following features may be added.

    (a) Make the program dynamic in the sense that adding more news stories to a directory or adding another news directory automatically gives more stories or categories, respectively. Details on scanning directories are found in Section 12.6.

    (b) Add JavaScript validation that does not let the user submit the preferences form if they disable all categories.

    (c) Implement a cookie sniff as outlined in Exercise 1. If the application can't use cookies, it simply does not display the link for the preferences. *Hint:* Generate the link for the preferences dynamically with JavaScript on the client if cookies are enabled.

PROJECT THREAD

Here you will adapt the quiz application from the Chapter 7 project to use cookies, provided that the requesting browser has cookies enabled. Session cookies are used to propagate logged-on state for both users and administrators. Persistent cookies are used to provide preference settings for the administrator. Add the `one_year_from_now` toolkit function to your CGI library.

A. The logon page should perform a "cookie sniff" to determine whether cookies should be used. See Exercise 1.

B. The user part of the application changes very little. If the browser has cookies enabled, the session ID is stored in a session cookie instead of a hidden form element. This does not change the user part of the transaction diagram as shown in Chapter 7.

C. The changes to the admin part are somewhat more involved, including some relatively minor changes to the transaction diagram. If the browser has cookies enabled, the session ID is stored in a cookie instead of a hidden form element. In that case, the admin logon form should contain two preference settings: an option that enables a given browser to have long-term logged-on state (despite the security risk) and an option that disables the feature that shows cumulative statistics for the whole class (see part C(i) in the Project Thread for Chapter 7). If the browser does not have cookies enabled, these preference settings are not printed in the admin logon form. You will need to generate some HTML dynamically on the client to accomplish that.

The checkbox for the preference for showing cumulative statistics should be checked by default in the admin logon form. The checkbox for the long-term logged on state preference should not be checked by default. If the long-term logged-on state is enabled, the administrator is not required to log on on subsequent visits from the same browser. The page that lists the quiz links should have a link that allows the administrator to reset the preferences.

D. Add a new row for the updated quiz application to the table in your homework page. Make sure you preserve the version from the previous lesson and keep the link to it active. If you are assigned any other exercises from this chapter, add another row to your homework table for each exercise.

CHAPTER *9*

PERL MODULES AND E-MAIL UTILITIES

Perl was invented before the Web was born. To facilitate Perl's use in Web programming, many open-source code libraries were subsequently developed, the most popular for general Web programming being `CGI.pm`, where `pm` stands for Perl module. This chapter uses that library of external functions to demonstrate how Perl modules are used in Perl programs. With that in place, we turn to Perl's `Mail::Sendmail` module, which can be used to send e-mail messages from within Web applications.

The `CGI.pm` coverage is also geared to be a prelude to our surveys of ASP and PHP in Chapters 14 and 15, respectively. You will see in this lesson that `CGI.pm` has built-in functions to deal with tasks such as decoding query strings, dealing with incoming cookies, generating session IDs, and creating state files. You will find that you are already familiar with the theoretical concepts behind the tasks those functions perform. Indeed, we have already developed our own toolkit of functions to expose those concepts in depth. Moreover, you will find in Chapters 14 and 15 that programming environments developed expressly for Web programming have very similar built-in features, which you will already understand. When you learn the fundamental concepts, you can apply them in any environment!

9.1 PERL MODULES AND OBJECT-ORIENTED SYNTAX

Libraries of prewritten routines are available for almost any programming language to help programmers accomplish certain tasks, without having to write the code themselves. Perl is no exception. A **Perl module** is simply a chunk of prewritten code stored in a text file. Hundreds (perhaps thousands) of Perl modules are available for free on the Web. The best starting point for more information is the open-source CPAN (Comprehensive Perl Archive Network, `www.cpan.org`).

We will use several Perl modules in this book, including `CGI.pm` (for standard CGI tasks), `Mail::Sendmail` (for e-mail), `DBI` (for database connectivity), and `XML::DOM` (for parsing XML files). Note that the only module in this list that has the `.pm` extension is `CGI.pm`. When we speak of a module by name, we usually don't include the `.pm` extension, which is merely a file extension used in Perl libraries. However, it is customary to use the extension in conjunction with the "CGI" module because the term *CGI* is used in other contexts.

Loading Modules

It only takes one line with the following general syntax to load a module into a Perl program.

```
use module_name;
```

Here are some specific examples, which would load three different modules into a program.

```
use CGI;
use CGI::SecureState;
use DBI;
```

The second of these examples loads a *derived module*, with SecureState being a module derived from the CGI module. Basically this means that SecureState extends the functionality of CGI.pm. The secureState derivation deals with long session IDs.

Note that the effect of the use statement is very similar to that of the require statement (Section 5.8). We need not go into the details of the differences between use and require, but suffice it to say that the general rule of thumb is that use is for modules (which typically import objects) and require is for auxiliary helper files (which typically have less structure and import ordinary functions).

Object-Oriented Syntax

Most modules make predefined object classes available to a program. In Perl, the general syntax for instantiating the "base class" of a module is to call new on the name of the module.

```
$object = new module_name (parameters);
```

There may or may not be parameters sent to the constructor. Here $object is a scalar variable that holds a reference to the object just created. Methods of an object are called using an arrow syntax.

```
$object -> some_method (parameters)
```

Again, there may or may not be parameters sent to the method. For concrete syntax examples, the following line of code creates a base-class CGI object.

```
$cgiObject = new CGI;
```

Calling the param method of the CGI object returns the value of a text field.

```
$thevalue = $cgiObject->param("textFieldName");
```

Some methods don't return values. In the following call, the file handle of an open text file is sent to the save method to store some state data.

```
$cgiObject -> save(STATEFILE);
```

The arrow syntax is different from that of other object-oriented languages, but the concept of an object is the same. In particular, some methods might return values, whereas others might just do something.

There are some slight differences among modules. In some modules you don't create a base-class object using the new constructor but by calling a method on the name of the module.

```
$object = module_name -> method_name (parameters);
```

For example, in the next chapter we will instantiate an object to connect to a database engine as follows:

```
$dbHandle = DBI -> connect(parameters);
```

In practice, we will not have to expend much thought on the differences between modules, because the differences are minor. If you are learning to use a module, simply read the ample documentation provided on the CPAN Web site. It is worth noting that some modules don't even require the object-oriented syntax in favor of just importing stand-alone functions to call. However, we use objects for all module use in this text.

> ## NOTE
>
> Prewritten Perl modules should not be confused with ModPerl (recall Section 1.10). ModPerl is no more than a Perl interpreter compiled into the Web server software. The Perl CGI programming techniques we are developing can be implemented using ModPerl with no new considerations. It's simply a matter of the run-time strategy for execution of Perl CGI programs. The choice of using ModPerl or standard Perl, which executes on a process different from the server application, is up to the administrator of the Web server. That issue is of little concern to us here.

9.2   THE CGI.pm MODULE

The CGI.pm module is included in almost any standard Perl distribution, so there is typically no need to install it. However, if for some reason it is not part of your Perl distribution, the use line that attempts to import it will generate an error. (In fact, you can test whether your Perl interpreter has access to any module simply by attempting to use it.)

In all of the subsequent code examples you may assume that we have already imported the CGI.pm and instantiated a $cgiObject.

```
use CGI;
$cgiObject = new CGI;
```

Incoming Form Data

As part of the `new` constructor, the incoming URL-encoded data string (whether GET or POST method of submission) is automatically decoded into name = value pairs and stored in the object in some internal format. The `param` method is used to retrieve the values of submitted form elements (that is, the name = value pairs passed between client and server are sometimes called CGI parameters). The following statements store values from form elements that submit only single values:

```
$theText = $cgiObject -> param("textFieldName");
$theText = $cgiObject -> param("textAreaName");
$theChoice = $cgiObject -> param("RadioButtonGroupName");
$theChoice = $cgiObject -> param("PopUpMenuName");
```

In list context, the preceding `param` calls would return arrays with only one element, instead of returning strings. For form elements that return multiple values, this comes in very handy! Consider the following statements.

```
@choices = $cgiObject -> param("multipleMenuName");
@choices = $cgiObject -> param("checkboxGroupName");
```

In each case, the `@choices` array would contain all submitted selections. Note that in the case of the checkboxes, each would have to have the same name for this to work. If the checkboxes each have different names, one would have to loop over all of the potentially submitted checkbox names to see which `param` methods return values. That is a strategy we have employed on many occasions earlier in this text.

Finally, when `param` is called with no parameters,

```
@names = $cgiObject->param;
```

it returns a list of the names (not values) of *all* submitted form elements.

We conclude our short discussion of incoming form data using `CGI.pm` with a simple example that prints out a table of all submitted form values:

```
#!/usr/bin/perl
print "Content-type: text/html\n\n";

use CGI;
$cgiObject = new CGI;

my @names = $cgiObject -> param;
my @values = ();

print "<html><head><title>Table of form data submitted</title></head><body>\n";
print "<table border=\"1\">\n";
print "<tr><th>Name</th><th>Value</th></tr>\n";

foreach $name (@names) {
  @values=$cgiObject->param($name);
  foreach $value (@values) {
    print "<tr><td>$name</td><td>$value</td></tr>\n";
  }
}
print "</table>\n";
print "</body></html>\n";
```

If there are multiple values for a given name, the inner loop prints a name = value pair for each value. It's not evidenced in this example, so remember the point made by the following two lines of code.

```
print "SomeName's value is $cgiObject->param('someName')";  #bad
print "SomeName's value is ", $cgiObject->param('someName'); #good
```

That is, like function calls, method calls are not interpolated inside double-quoted strings.

NOTE

You can easily see that calling param works very similarly to extracting data from our %formHash. For single-value returns, it's virtually the same.

```
$choice = $formHash{"PopUpMenuName"};
```

For multiple-value returns with the same name, our %formHash contains a delimited list of values, which we split into an array.

One difference is that the CGI.pm decoding routine does not make provisions to detect when a CGI program is executed offline or to deal with HEAD requests.

Printing Form Elements

CGI.pm does have built-in methods for printing HTML form elements, but in our experience they are more cumbersome to use than simply printing form elements manually. We show one such method to make that point and to show that parameters are sent to the method as a hash, which is common in other modules we will use.

The radio_group method generates a unique-selection group of radio buttons:

```
print $cgiObject -> radio_group ( -name=>"groupName",
                                  -values=>\@values,
                                  -default=>"defaultSelectedValue",
                                  -labels=>\%hash );
```

One drawback is that the radio buttons are displayed in a fixed format,

with each button on a different line and the labels on the right. It is often desirable, however, to print several radio buttons on the same line or to right-align the buttons with labels on the left.

Aside from that, the main question is whether learning the idiosyncrasies of several such methods is worth it in the long run. The radio_group method needs an array of values (which become the hidden values behind the radio buttons) and a hash (whose keys are those values and whose values are the labels). The array and hash are sent to the method by reference.

We are not knocking using functions to automate the process of printing form elements. Indeed, different Web programming environments feature their own built-in functions for such purposes, and it pays to understand the concept. Such functions do come in especially handy for printing menus, particularly because menus are always displayed in a fixed format in terms of the labels. In that case, you typically have a hash-formatted data source, and it's easier to print a menu by sending the hash to a function than by having to iterate manually over the hash to generate the menu.

We outlined several form-element-generating toolkit functions in the Project Thread of Chapter 5. In many ways they are more limited than those of CGI.pm, but on the other hand, there is much less complexity involved using them. When preprogrammed tools feature too much "overhead," they sometimes defeat their own purpose, and programmers end up doing things manually anyway.

Tools for State Data

We have seen that an instantiated CGI object holds the collection of all name = value pairs that comes from submitted data. We can save this collection of name = value pairs to a file with the save method.

```
open (STATEFILE, ">fileName.state");
$cgiObject -> save(STATEFILE);
close (STATEFILE);
```

Of course, the file must be opened for writing. This can be a handy way simply to dump all submitted data into a file, which is a common Web programming practice, even if not all of it needs to be preserved between transactions.

However, it is still up to the programmer to create a suitable file name (usually a long session ID) and propagate the file name among several Web pages to create a session. Moreover, the CGI module does not manage the state files for you, in terms of placing an upper bound on the number of files that can be added and policing old ones.

The CGI parameters (name=value pairs) can be read back into a program (usually during a subsequent HTTP transaction) by creating a new CGI object, sending the constructor the file handle of the state file to be read.

```
open (STATEFILE, "fileName.state");
$cgiObject_from_file = new CGI(STATEFILE);
close (STATEFILE);
```

The new CGI object works just like any other, except that the name = value pairs are from a file rather than from a new HTTP transaction. Thus, the new CGI object does not contain name=value pairs from an incoming query string. The param method is used for extracting the data from the object for use in the program as previously shown.

So far we have seen enough to store all incoming name = value pairs to a state file and to get them back out again in a subsequent transaction. However, for this utility to be truly useful, we need to be able to add and delete name=value pairs manually in a CGI object before saving the information to a file so that state data can be customized.

Calling `param` in the following manner adds a `some_name=some_value` pair to the CGI object.

```
$cgiObject -> param( -name => "some_name",
                     -value => "some_value" );
```

The following syntax is used to set multiple values to a single name. (The square brackets create a reference to an array; see optional Section 5.9).

```
$cgiObject -> param( -name => "some_name",
                     -value => ["multiple", "values"] );
```

The `delete` method needs only the name to delete a name = value pair.

```
$cgiObject -> delete("some_name");
```

Note that adding and deleting name = value pairs in a CGI object is very similar in philosophy to doing so in a hash. However, hashes don't allow multiple keys. For multiple name = value pairs with the same name, the values are concatenated together as the value of the common key using a delimiting character. (That's likely to be how multiple values are represented internally in a CGI object.)

Finally, the following method deletes all name = value pairs from the CGI object.

```
$cgiObject -> delete_all();
```

One would simply overwrite a hash with the empty hash to accomplish the same thing.

NOTE

It is interesting to note that the format of CGI.pm's saved file is pretty much the same as what we decided to use for our state files in Chapter 7. That is, the name and value are delimited with an = character, and the name = value pairs are stored on separate lines. Moreover, arrays are automatically saved as delimited strings. The names and values are URL-encoded for security reasons (see Section 13.6).

It is possible to use one file to save more than one CGI object, so there is an extra line with a single = character to designate the end of the saved information for a given CGI object. We only mention these facts for curiosity reasons; it is not necessary to know how the CGI module actually stores this information, because we need to know only how to use the module's built-in functions to save and retrieve state data.

CGI::SecureState

This module is derived from CGI.pm. This means that all methods (but not constructors) of CGI.pm will also work with same effect, unless they have been overridden. We present the most useful methods provided by this module. The most significant improvements over the CGI module are that `secureState` creates long session IDs and automates operations on state files.

First load the module.

```
use CGI::SecureState;
```

Then create a new `CGI` object.

```
$cgiObject = new CGI::SecureState (-stateDir => "/home/states",
                                   -mindSet => "unforgetful",
                                   -memory => ["except", "these", "names"] );
```

Note that this constructor takes several parameters, most of which are optional:

- `-stateDir` (optional): The supplied directory is where the object will store and retrieve state files. If not supplied, the default directory is the one containing the `CGI` program.

- `-mindSet` (mandatory): This parameter takes one of the two values: `"unforgetful"` or `"forgetful"`.

  - The *unforgetful mindset* specifies that the `CGI` object will automatically save *all* name = value pairs received from the client to the state file. Moreover, the unforgetful mindset keeps the state file current in that new incoming values from the client take precedence over old ones in the state file. That is, if a name = value pair with a given name already exists in the state file, its value will be overwritten by an incoming name = value pair with that name. The `param` method is used to retrieve values from the state file.

  - The *forgetful mindset* specifies that the `CGI` object will not automatically save any name = value pairs received from the client to the state file. In this mindset, when the `param` method is used to retrieve a value, values from the state file have precedence over those from incoming client data.

- `-memory` (optional): This parameter allows the unforgetful mindset to forget some name = value pairs and the forgetful mindset to remember some. (The list is given as a reference to an array, hence the square brackets `[]`). In the unforgetful mindset, this value lists those parameters, that *should not* be added to the state file. In the forgetful mindset, this value lists parameters that *should* be added to the state file.

The issue of which values have precedence is important in practice. The unforgetful mindset is commonly used to propagate all (or most) data collected from the client effortlessly. The forgetful mindset is commonly used to prevent junk from needlessly building up in a state file, because sometimes such junk might interfere with the workings of scripts down the road during a session. Also, if state information is used for security reasons, then you would likely want the file data to have precedence. In the following example, only the username and password are propagated automatically, and new data will not automatically overwrite that in the state file.

```
$cgiObject = new CGI::SecureState (-stateDir => "/home/states",
                                   -mindSet => "forgetful",
                                   -memory => ["user", "pass"]);
```

The `SecureState` module also automatically creates the state files and session IDs based upon the existence of a special name = value pair of the form `".id=sessionID"`.

▪ If a name = value pair with name ".id" is not detected as part of the incoming data string, a new session ID is automatically created and placed into the CGI object in a name = value pair of the form ".id=sessionID". Moreover, a corresponding state file is created, and all those name = value pairs that are set to be remembered (or not forgotten) are saved to the file.

▪ If an incoming session ID is detected (in a pair with name .id), then the corresponding state file is automatically accessed by the CGI object. Thus, in a Web application with a sequence of HTTP transactions, the first transaction creates a session ID and corresponding state file. Subsequent transactions automatically read the state file into the CGI object.

Thus, regardless of the mindset, name = value pairs from the state file will continue to be propagated through subsequent transactions. Also, regardless of the mindset, those name = value pairs currently in the CGI object are available via the param method. But remember that the particular mindset determines which pairs are actually available in the CGI object, hence which ones param will access.

In the unforgetful mindset, new incoming name = value pairs are added to the CGI object (unless they are set to be forgotten) and pairs from the state file are read into the object. Also remember that in this mindset, incoming pairs have overwrite precedence over corresponding ones obtained from the state file. Note that additional name = value pairs can be manually added to the CGI object using the add method and that name = value pairs can be manually deleted from the CGI object using the delete method. At the end of the transaction, the current contents of the CGI object are automatically written to the state file.

In the forgetful mindset, only those pairs set to be remembered are placed in the CGI object along with the data read in from the state file. Of course, name = value pairs can be manually added or deleted. But remember that, in this mindset, state file data takes precedence in the CGI object over corresponding incoming data. Thus, an incoming pair with the same name as a pair read in from the state file is effectively ignored by the CGI object and hence does not go into the state file.

NOTE

The effect of this is that incoming pairs are not available in the CGI object via the param() method if a corresponding pair already exists in the state file. To alleviate that problem, one can specify short-term memory so that such incoming pairs are still accessible in the CGI object:

```
$cgiObject = new CGI::SecureState ( -stateDir => "/home/states",
                                    -mindSet => "forgetful",
                                    -memory => ["x","y"]);
                                    -shortterm =>["x"]);
```

Pairs designated for short-term memory are available in the CGI object via the user_param() method.

Think of the standard memory of the forgetful mindset as long-term memory. In this example, pairs with names x or y are remembered in the state file and are thus available via the param() method. But now, an incoming pair with name x is also available via the user_param() method. This situation is somewhat similar to keeping new incoming data separate from previously saved state data, as we did in prior lessons using %formHash and %stateHash.

Of course, in order to propagate a session over a sequence of transactions, the session ID has to be returned to the client. There are two useful methods for this task: one for links and one for hidden form elements. The following method call returns a string composed of the URL of the script with the session ID attached as a query string in the proper format (.id=sessionID).

```
$cgiObject -> state_url()
```

Similarly, the following call returns a string that is the HTML code for a hidden form element containing the session ID in proper format.

```
$cgiObject -> state_field()
```

The session ID all by itself can be retrieved with the param method using the parameter ".id".

As we have mentioned, the param method is used to retrieve name = value pairs from the CGI object in the secureState module. However, it is important to note that the param method *can not* be used to add name = pairs to the state file manually. As we mentioned previously, the add method is used to add one or more name = value pairs to the state file manually.

```
$cgiObject->add( name1 => ['value'],
                 name2 => ['value1', 'value2']);
```

The delete and delete_all methods work the same as before, but in addition they make corresponding changes to the state file. The following statement deletes the entire state file.

```
$cgiObject -> delete_session();
```

Finally, a call to the age method returns the time in days since the state file was last modified.

```
$cgiObject -> age()
```

NOTE

CGI::SecureState is an improvement over the older CGI::Persistent, with the earlier module having some major exploitable security holes. However, one limitation is that the current version of SecureState does not automatically police the state file cache. Currently (version 0.3x), it is still up to the programmer to implement that feature and others such as session timeouts when state files are used as validation certificates. Aside from the lack of cache management, secureState deals with session state for the most part in a manner conceptually similar to our session-oriented toolkit functions from Chapter 7.

Tools for Cookies

In this section we return to the CGI.pm module and assume that it has been loaded and a new $cgiObject instantiated. It is easy to retrieve the value of an incoming cookie given its name.

```
$cookieValue = $cgiObject -> cookie("cookieName");
```

To set a cookie, we first create a cookie object using the following method. Note that $cookie is a scalar reference to the created object.

```
$cookie = $cgiObject -> cookie( -name => "some_name",
                                -value =>"some_value"',
                                -expires => "+1y", # in one year.
                                -path => "/some/path",
                                -domain = ".uweb.edu",
                                -secure => 1);
```

Of course, all but the name and value fields are optional.

The header method is used to print cookie objects to output. It returns a string consisting of an HTTP header, including the Set-cookie lines. It automatically prints the Content-type line last, followed by a blank line. The header method must be told which cookie object to print.

```
print $cgiObject -> header( -cookie => $cookie );
```

We emphasize that, when you set cookies in this way, this must be the first printed output, and you must not print any other Content-type lines in your programs. To set multiple cookies, create cookie objects and send them to the header method.

```
print $cgiObject -> header( -cookie => [$cookie1, $cookie2] );
```

NOTE

Retrieving incoming cookies using CGI.pm works the same way as extracting their values from our %cookieHash. However, setting cookies with CGI.pm is perhaps more cumbersome than printing them manually. But here you do automatically get the Content-type header line and the utility for setting the expiration date.

This concludes our presentation of CGI.pm. We do mention that we have not introduced all the methods—just the most useful ones. Hopefully, you now have a conceptual feel for the types of built-in tools provided by environments such as ASP and PHP, which were made expressly for Web programming.

9.3 E-MAIL IN WEB APPLICATIONS

It is often desirable for Web applications to send e-mail messages. For example, an application may wish to send the user an e-mail that confirms a purchase, or an application may wish to send the administrator an e-mail when a problem arises. The possibilities are numerous.

No matter what client application we use to send an e-mail (Microsoft's Outlook, Netscape mail, pine on UNIX, and so forth), the client program must talk to an e-mail

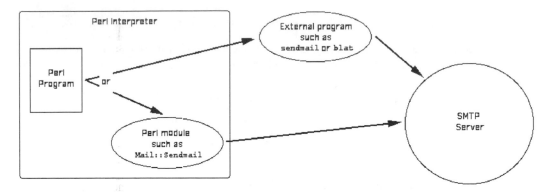

FIGURE 9.1 A Perl program can talk to an SMTP server through an imported module or via an external program.

server, which is usually an SMTP (Simple Mail Transfer Protocol) server. A good analogy is to think of the SMTP server as a post office that is responsible for physically delivering the mail; it may have to relay the mail to other post offices (more SMTP servers) along the way. An e-mail client is like the mailbox at the end of your driveway.

Similarly, a Perl program must talk to a mail server in order to send e-mail messages. In that respect, an e-mail-capable Perl program functions much like an e-mail client. The most fundamental step in configuring an e-mail client is to tell it which SMTP server it should use. This configuration, which is just the address (named or IP) of the SMTP server, is often performed when the client program is first installed. If not, the SMTP server has to be specified when the e-mail is sent. That is how it is handled in a Perl program.

When a Web application (this applies to all Web programming languages, not just Perl) wishes to send an e-mail, there are two strategies in general. Either the Web application calls an external program to send the e-mail, or the Web application itself has the capability to talk directly to an SMTP server. Figure 9.1 illustrates these two possibilities as they pertain to Perl.

We recommend using a module such as Mail::Sendmail to talk to the SMTP server. As we shall see, using Mail::Sendmail is a fairly easy task and has the advantage of being platform independent. The available mail-sending external programs vary with computer platform. However, we do present the use of an external program in the next optional section mainly because that is how many existing Perl CGI programs do it on UNIX systems through a shell command.

We first discuss the most common header fields used in e-mail transactions. They are shown in Table 9.1.

When an e-mail bounces (for example, because of an invalid To: address) when sent from your local mail client (Outlook, or whatever), it usually bounces back to the sender (From: address). However, when e-mail is sent from within a Web application, bounced (undeliverable) e-mails may not automatically be returned to the From: address. Rather, a separate *envelope sender address* may be specified. The motivation for this feature comes from a regular post office. The address on the envelope (envelope sender address) is used for returning undeliverable letters, whereas the address on the letter inside (From: address) can be different. This is often the case when multiple employees use ready-made envelopes prestamped with their company's address, for example, but different employees provide more specific return addresses in the actual letters.

Similarly, the default envelope sender address for e-mails sent from within a Web application can be the address of the server administrator, for example. That address is sent as part

TABLE 9.1   Header Fields for E-Mail

HEADER	PURPOSE

`To:`	Specifies recipient address. Real names may be included with address in one of the following formats:
	
	`John Doe <email@address>`
	`"John Doe" email@address`
	`email@address (John Doe)`
	
	Multiple e-mails should be separated by commas.

`From:`	Specifies sender address.
`Reply-To:`	Specifies address used for replying.
`Cc:`	Courtesy copy recipients.
`Bcc:`	Blind courtesy copy recipients. These addresses will not show up in the other recipients' messages.
`Subject:`	The subject of the e-mail.
`Date:`	Date of e-mail.

of the communication with the SMTP server, which is separate from the actual headers for a specific e-mail message. Some e-mail programs do use the `From:` information that you supply in the e-mail header as the envelope sender address. Others may use a default envelope sender address and require some acrobatics to reset that address. The important point here is that it is up to the particular module or external e-mail program as to how it obtains the envelope sender address. The bottom line is that if handling bounced e-mails is important in your Web application, you should test your Web application thoroughly with a few bounced e-mails.

The `Mail::Sendmail` Module

There are several Perl modules (`Mail::Sendmail`, `Mail::Mailer`, `Net::SMTP`, just to name a few) that make sending e-mail from within Perl programs uniform across platforms. These modules all have the ability to talk directly to an SMTP server. Using a module, you won't have to worry about using a UNIX shell command or some other external program such as `blat.exe` on Windows.

Currently, the module `Mail::Mailer` seems to be the most popular because it has the most features. We leave exploring that module as an exercise. We use the module `Mail::Sendmail` because it is the simplest with which to illustrate the main concepts here. Because Perl modules also evolve with time, one should always read the latest documentation and, ultimately, if sending e-mail is important for your application, you should thoroughly test the module. There are four steps to sending an e-mail using `Mail::Sendmail`:

Step 0. The `Mail::Sendmail` module must be installed on the Web server. (See Appendix D.) This needs to be done only once.

Step 1. In the Perl program, load the module.

```
use Mail::Sendmail;
```

Note the double colons. `Sendmail` is derived from the more general `Mail` module.

Step 2. Prepare a hash that stores all the parameters: the headers, the message, and an optional SMTP server. Conveniently, the `Mail::Sendmail` module uses the `From:` field as the envelope sender address.

```
%mail = (
    "To" => $toEmail,
    "From" => $fromEmail,
    "Cc" => $ccEmail,
    "Subject" => $subject,
    "message" => $message,     # This string is the entire body of the email
    "smtp"=> $smtp_server       # Specifies the SMTP server if the Web server
);                              # is not also an SMTP server
```

Step 3. Send the mail.

```
sendmail(%mail);
```

This function returns a true value if the mail was sent successfully.

For an example, we write a general-purpose signup utility. A sample execution of the program is shown in Figure 9.2. This signup page does not let the user pick a password, in favor of e-mailing the user a temporary password. Also, at that time, an account file on the server is created for the new user. Once the user has obtained the password, he or she can proceed to the logon page. The logon is then verified against the password in the account file. The main advantage this strategy offers is to ensure that the user has entered a valid e-mail address. The obvious disadvantage is that the user has to go through more motions to get a new account.

In practice, this is a very common strategy for new member signup, but there are some extra features that should be added. After the initial signup, the user should be allowed to change the password. Furthermore, the user should be encouraged (if not forced) to change the password after the initial logon. There should be a time period after which the account file is deleted, hence the temporary password expires. Thus, the account also needs to store the signup time and whether the user has ever logged on. This would allow a cleanup pro-

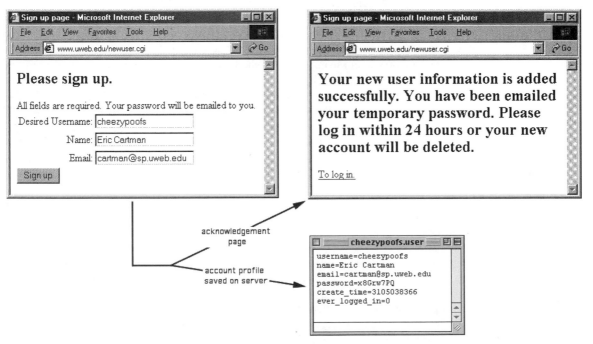

FIGURE 9.2 A sample execution of the newuser.cgi program.

gram to periodically delete new user accounts that were never activated within some allotted time period. We leave implementation of these extra features as an exercise.

The outline of the program is shown in Figure 9.3. The app logic handles only two transactions: printing the form and processing it. The `welcome_page` and `new_user` functions are listed next, followed by overviews. The `write_user_file` helper function does no more than write the contents of a hash to a file as shown in Figure 9.2. We do not show that function. Of course, it is included in the source code on this book's Web site.

```
sub welcome_page {
  my ($message) = @_;
  if(!$message){$message = "Please sign up.";} # The default message
  print <<PAGE;
<html><head><title>Sign up page</title></head><body>
  <h2>$message</h2>

  <form action="$ENV{'SCRIPT_NAME'}" method="POST">
    All fields are required. Your password will be emailed to you.
    <table>
      <tr><td align="right">Desired Username:</td>
        <td><input type="text" name="username" value="$formHash{'username'}"
          size="20"/></td>
      </tr>
      <tr><td align="right">Name:</td>
        <td><input type="text" name="name" value="$formHash{'name'}"
          size="20"/></td>
      </tr>
      <tr><td align="right">Email:</td>
        <td><input type="text" name="email" value="$formHash{'email'}"
          size="20"/></td>
      </tr>
    </table>
    <input type="hidden" name="request" value="new_user"/>
    <input type="submit" value="Sign up"/>
  </form>
</body></html>
PAGE
}
```

■ The only thing to note here is that the form is filled in with values from `%formHash`. Thus, when the application is first hit, the values will be empty, as desired. The `new_user` function imposes some constraints on the contents of the text fields. If the data is rejected, `welcome_page` is recalled. In that case, `%formHash` will fill out the text fields with the original information so that the user doesn't have to retype everything.

```
sub new_user {
  my @required_form_keys = ("username", "name", "email");
  foreach $key (@required_form_keys) {
    if($formHash{$key} eq "") {
      &welcome_page("You did not fill in the $key field.");
      exit;
    }
  }
  my $new_user = lc $formHash{"username"};
  if($new_user =~ /\W/){ ### check for nonalphanumeric characters
    &welcome_page("You may use only alphanumeric characters in the username.");
    exit;
  }
  if(-e "$userDir$new_user.user"){ # check if user name already in use
    &welcome_page("Sorry, user already exists. Please choose another username.");
    exit;
  }

  my $temp_pass = &generate_random_string(8);
```

```perl
    my %userHash = (
      "username" => $new_user,
      "password" => $temp_pass,
      "name" => $formHash{"name"},
      "email" => $formHash{"email"},
      "create_time" => time, ### Current time as an integer
      "ever_logged_in" => 0
    );
    &write_user_file($userDir, $new_user, %userHash);

    use Mail::Sendmail;
    $adminEmail = "admin\@uweb.edu"; #this should probably be a global constant
    $smtp_server = "localhost";      #this is if the local host is also an SMTP server
    my $message = "Your temporary password is $temp_pass.\n";
    my %mail = (
      "To" => $formHash{"email"},
      "From" => $adminEmail,
      "Bcc" => $adminEmail,
      "Subject" => "Your new account",
      "message" => $message,
      "smtp" => $smtp_server
    );
    sendmail(%mail) or &errorPage("Failure to send email.");

    print <<PAGE;
    <html><head><title>Sign up page</title></head><body>
      <h2>Your new user information is added successfully.
        You have been emailed your temporary password.
        Please log in within 24 hours or your new account will be deleted.</h2>
      <a href="hypotheticalloginpage.cgi">To log in.</a>
    /body></html>
PAGE
}
```

```perl
#! /usr/bin/perl
print "Content-type: text/html\n\n";


###############################################################
#    code for decoding input $datastring into %formHash      #
#       (works for GET, POST, and offline execution)         #
###############################################################

$userDir = "/home/data/users/"; # location of user files


### app logic ##################################################
if($formHash{"request"} eq "new_user") {
    &new_user;
}
else {
    &welcome_page;
}
### end app logic ##############################################


###############################################################
### Definitions of app logic functions go here.             #
### Definitions for helper functions:                       #
#     &write_user_file                                       #
### Definitions for toolkit functions used:                  #
#     &generate_random_string    (from Section 7.4)          #
#     &errorPage                 (from Section 5.7)          #
###############################################################
```

FIGURE 9.3 The outline of the `newuser.cgi` program.

- If any of the fields are left blank, return the welcome page. Note that we could easily verify this (and the next constraint) on the client with JavaScript. However, in situations like this, that's not sufficient, because someone could tamper with the HTML page and bypass the validation. That could create problems (such as a user file with no name!).
- We convert the username to all lowercase. If the username has any nonalphanumeric characters, return the welcome page. This is important, because the username will become the file name. (The syntax for pattern matching is explained in Chapter 11.)
- If the user name is already taken, return the welcome page. Because the file names are of the form `username.user`, we simply check whether a file with the user name already exists.
- Generate an eight-character password.
- Create a hash for the user profile data.
- Call the helper function to dump the hash into a new file.
- Send an e-mail to the submitted address with a message containing the temporary password. Notice that the `$adminEmail` and `$smtp_server` values need to be set appropriately. Some situations might require the address of a remote SMTP server. (These constants perhaps should be set as global variables at the beginning of the program.)
- Finally, we print the returned HTML page informing the user to expect an e-mail. Note that there is a link to a hypothetical page where the user can use the new account.

NOTE

The program as shown poses two potential security risks. First, because an account file is being created, an unscrupulous person can repeatedly hit the program and generate many bogus accounts, taking up file space on the server. Second, any time e-mail is sent out to a user-specified address, there is the potential that the program could be used as a third-party mail server for spamming. That is, an unscrupulous person who wants to send unsolicited e-mails could hit this script repeatedly with someone else's e-mail address in the query string. When designing Web applications that send automated e-mail, one should always think about security against third-party spam abuse.

Typically, an adversary would use some automated program to send out repeated HTTP requests to such a vulnerable program. A common technique to guard against automated attacks is to have a random "key" string printed in the Web page that the user has to type into the form. Such a key string would have to be stored on the server (perhaps as part of the state information) and would be used as a check. However, if the adversary knows that you are doing this, he can modify his attack program to parse the key string out of the HTML file automatically and add it to the form. One clever way to foil this attack is not to print the random string as text but to send it as an image, and preferably a somewhat distorted image that requires a human eye to read! This essentially forces human interaction (or an expensive image recognition program) and thus eliminates the possibility of an inexpensive automated attack. You undoubtedly at some point will encounter such mechanisms when signing up for services.

> Generating images corresponding to randomly generated strings on the fly requires use of specialized tools like the platform independent GD.pm Perl module (interface to GD C++ graphics library) or the UNIX/Linux GIMP (short for GNU Image Manipulation Program). Those tools are well beyond the scope of this text. The easiest "quick fix" is simply to limit the number of automated e-mails per time period. This does not prevent the server from being used for spam, but does limit the potential "damage" and provide for an opportunity to warn the server's administrator.

*9.4 E-MAIL VIA AN EXTERNAL PROGRAM

Many current Perl-CGI programs on UNIX/Linux systems simply use the sendmail shell command (not to be confused with the Perl module of the same name). In UNIX/Linux, the sendmail command usually comes with the operating system base install. There is also a port of the popular sendmail program to Windows that can be used with IIS. On Windows there is also the popular free software blat. We shall briefly discuss both of these, each time illustrating a different way of executing an external system command from within a Perl program.

The sendmail program usually takes input from the keyboard (standard input). For external programs that take standard input, we can use the Perl open command. First, locate the sendmail program, and set a variable to the external command path.

```
$mailprog = "/usr/bin/sendmail"; #typical location in UNIX
$mailprog = "/Inetpub/scripts/sendmail.exe"; #somewhere in Windows
```

By using the pipe symbol (|) with the open command,

```
open(HANDLE, "|external_program");
```

we basically execute the external program on the Web server, with standard input to the program supplied by subsequent print statements to the HANDLE. Colloquially stated, "we pipe further output on the HANDLE to the program." The pipe is closed when the Perl close statement is executed on the HANDLE. When the pipe is closed, the external program quits.

The `sendmail` program expects input to be of standard e-mail format, which means a collection of header statements followed by a blank line followed by the body of the e-mail message. (This is very similar in concept to an HTTP header.) Last, the `sendmail` program needs the option `-t` so that header information is read from the input as opposed to the command line. The following example illustrates all these points. The Perl statements are in boldface. Again, the intentional blank line after the subject line is a *must*.

```
open(MAIL "|$mailprog -t");
print MAIL <<MAIL_MESSAGE;
To: scoob@whereareyou.com
From: shagg@afraid.com
Subject: Where are you?


Get over here.
MAIL_MESSAGE
close(MAIL);
```

The `sendmail` command does not use the `From:` field as the envelope sender address. The default envelope sender address is the user that the Web server software runs under—often a "nobody" user. Usually, this is not what you want. The envelope sender address can be set to `$fromEmail` using the command line option `-f`.

```
open(MAIL "|$mailprog -t -f $fromEmail "); # Use with caution!
```

But this method must be used with caution if the value of `$fromEmail` is generated from user data! We don't want to execute some additional damaging external command mistakenly if `$fromEmail` has some clever, executable code in it. To be safe, it is best to remove any characters that should not be part of an e-mail. For example, the following line of code removes any character that's not alphanumeric, a hyphen (`-`), or a period (`.`). (Again, Chapter 11 covers patterns and substitutions.)

```
$fromEmail =~ s/[^\w\-\@\.]//g;
```

If both the `From:` address and this `-f` address are specified, then the `-f` address would usually appear (in most mail readers) as a `Reply-To:` field.

As an example, we provide a function that sends an e-mail to a system administrator. Such a function would be useful in the `get_long_id` function of Chapter 7 that was responsible for policing the state directory. If you recall, that function should send the system administrator a warning if the state directory should ever fill up, causing the site to turn away visitors. However, there should be some mechanism in place so that no further e-mails are sent once one warning is sent. Otherwise, a flood of e-mails could result.

```
sub email_sysadmin {
  my ($message) = @_; # message string parameter
  my $mailprog = "/usr/sbin/sendmail";
  my $sysadminEmail = "admin\@uweb.edu";

  open(MAIL, "|$mailprog -t");
  print MAIL <<EMAIL;
```

```
To: Sys Admin <$sysadminEmail>
From: Sys Admin <$sysadminEmail>
Subject: Message from CGI script $ENV{'SCRIPT_NAME'}


$message
------------------
This message was sent from CGI script $ENV{'SCRIPT_NAME'}
EMAIL
   close(MAIL);
}
```

We conclude the discussion of external commands by showing another way to execute an external program:

```
system(external_command);
```

For example, on Windows systems blat.exe used to be a popular program for sending e-mail. This program takes the e-mail address information in the command line, and it reads the body of the e-mail from a file. Here is an example.

```
$mailprog = "/Inetpub/scripts/blat.exe"; # location of program
$toEmail = "scoob@whereareyou.com";
$fromEmail = "shagg@afraid.com;
$subject = "Where are you?";
$message = "Get over here\n";
$messageFile = "/Inetpub/wwwroot/tmpdir/tmp1.txt";
open(TEMPFILE, ">$messageFile");
print TEMPFILE $message;
close(TEMPFILE);
$toEmail =~ s/[^\w\-\@\.]//g; #standard security precaution!
$fromEmail =~ s/[^\w\-\@\.]//g;

system("$mailprog $messageFile -t $toEmail -f $fromEmail -s $subject -q\n");
```

You may be able to deduce what the -t, -f, -s options are. The -q option is the quiet mode.

To end this section, Table 9.2 shows a comparison of sending e-mails using modules versus an external program. You can see why we recommend the module method.

TABLE 9.2 Comparison of Modules and External Commands for Sending Mail

EXTERNAL COMMANDS	MODULES
▪ Quick and easy to open a sendmail pipe on a UNIX type system. (This explains its popularity with UNIX programmers.)	▪ Requires installation of a Perl module. This is not a hassle if you can get your system administrator to do it.
▪ Code may not work if executed on a different platform (may require extensive modification).	▪ Code is platform independent (may require at most slight adjustment).
▪ Care must be taken if variables are used as part of the external command, especially if the values come from user input; one should delete all suspect characters.	▪ No external commands are executed, so this method is safer by nature.

SUMMARY OF KEY TERMS AND CONCEPTS

Perl module: Basically an external code library that is imported into a program with the `use` statement. (Not to be confused with ModPerl, which is another run-time environment for Perl programs.)

Perl objects: Perl uses an arrow (`->`) rather than the standard period (`.`) for object notation. (The period is used for string concatenation, which predates the addition of objects to Perl.) Typically, an object is instantiated from a module by calling the `new` constructor on the name of the module or by calling a method on the module's name. Once instantiated, methods available in the module for that object are called using the arrow notation.

The Perl CGI module: Usually called `CGI.pm` to avoid confusion, this module contains tools for the basic, routine tasks of Web programming. This includes decoding incoming data (including cookies), writing that data to files, and printing cookies. It also provides functions that print form elements and groups of form elements.

CGI object: The base object used in `CGI.pm`. Instantiating a `CGI` object automatically decodes incoming data and stores the name = value pairs into a hashlike format. The object provides the `param` method, which returns values when sent names.

`CGI::SecureState` module: A module derived from `CGI.pm`. A `CGI::SecureState` object inherits the same functionality as a `CGI` object. In addition, a `CGI::SecureState` object automatically creates long session IDs, creates state files with corresponding names, and reads in data from state files. In the unforgetful mindset all name = value pairs from the client are saved to the state file by default, except those specified in the memory parameter list; the opposite occurs in a forgetful mindset. In an unforgetful mindset, incoming name = value pairs have precedence in the object over corresponding ones in the state file; the reverse is true for a forgetful mindset. Also, a `CGI::SecureState` object has methods for printing (hiding) the session ID in a Web page, adding and deleting name = value pairs from the object, detecting when the state file was last modified, and erasing or deleting the state file.

Cookie object: The `cookie` method of the `CGI` object creates a cookie object, with the required cookie fields and possibly the optional ones. The `header` method simply prints an HTTP header containing a `Set-cookie` line for each cookie object sent to it.

Automated e-mail: When a Web application sends e-mail messages, it acts like a mail client in that it sends the messages to an SMTP server to start the delivery process. If the Web server (on which the Web application is running) is also running an SMTP daemon, the Web application may send e-mail messages to the `localhost` server. Otherwise it may specify the address of an external SMTP server. A Web application may have a utility in its run-time environment (in our case a Perl module) with which it can talk to SMTP servers, or it may talk to an external system program to accomplish that.

`Mail::sendmail` module: A Perl module for automated e-mail. Simply `use` the module in a program, create a hash containing the necessary header fields of an e-mail message, and send the hash to the module's `sendmail` function. The hash contains an `smtp` entry, which tells the module which SMTP server to use.

E-mail account signup: A user account signup strategy that ensures a new user provides a viable e-mail address by e-mailing a randomly generated temporary password back to the user. If used commercially, this strategy should kill a new account if the new user does not log on with the temporary password in a given time period, and it should then force the new user to change the temporary password upon initial logon. In addition, there are somewhat complicated security measures that can be put into place so that it's nearly impossible for hacker attacks to generate large numbers of spam e-mails.

General security: Any function in a Web application that generates automated e-mails and can be called directly over the Web is vulnerable to spam attacks. Often hackers seek out *third-party mail servers* with which to generate possibly large volumes of e-mail messages by using automated attack programs. Using a third-party SMTP server, they can effectively "cover their tracks." The easiest solution is to limit the number of automated e-mails per time period. This measure does not prevent the server from being used for spam, but it does limit the "damage" and provide for an opportunity to warn the server's administrator.

E-mail with external programs (optional section): A Web application can send e-mail messages to programs such as `sendmail` (UNIX/Linux shell program) and `blat.exe` (Windows program) outside of the run-time environment of the Web application. This can be done by piping output to the external program or by executing code with a `system` call. In general, this is less secure; especially the system call, because someone may enter harmful executable code instead of an e-mail address.

EXERCISES

1. Patch the `get_long_id` toolkit function of Section 7.5 so that it sends an e-mail warning the system administrator of a full state file cache. Use your own e-mail address. Make sure that only one e-mail is sent so that the administrator does not get spammed if `get_long_id` is called over and over with a full cache.

2. If you haven't already done so, write the two menu-generating functions outlined in the Chapter 6 Project Thread. Make a simple driver program to test both functions. Do some quick research on the Web and find out how to use `CGI.pm`'s menu-generating function. Add calls to it to the driver program, printing one each of the two types of menus. Add a paragraph to the output of the driver program that comments on the handiness of form-element-generating functions in general versus the learning curve necessary to use them.

3. Research the `cgi-lib` library of toolkit functions for CGI programming in Perl. The code library is currently maintained at UC Berkeley (`cgi-lib.berkeley.edu`). Determine what types of functions are available. Compare and contrast them with both our toolkit functions and `CGI.pm`. You should research further capabilities of `CGI.pm` (ones we did not cover) as well .

4. Write a function that is used to instantiate a `SecureState CGI` object (as a global variable) but also polices the state file cache if necessary. Make a driver program to test the function.

5. Make a driver program that features a form where the user can submit an e-mail address in a text field and a message in a text area. Upon submission, the message should be mailed to the address and a thank-you page returned to the browser. As discussed in the note at the end of Section 9.3, this program has an easily exploitable security hole that would allow it to be used as a third-party spam server. Implement the feature that limits the number of messages the program can send to something like three messages per five-minute period. Make the security test reusable by implementing it in a function, with a name such as `ok_to_send`, that returns a Boolean value. The function should automatically send an e-mail to the server administrator (you in this case) if the limit is reached. Also, in that case, the driver program should send a rejection page back to the user.

6. The source code for the `newuser.cgi` example of Section 9.3 can be obtained from the Web site. Add any or all of the following features:

   (a) Extend the program so that new users are forced to change their password immediately after logging on with the initial password.

(b) The user must use the temporary password within a certain time period or else it expires. An attempted logon after that time period deletes the account file and returns the signup form with a message.

(c) Add the extra security feature described in Exercise 5.

7. Make a version of the `quiz2.cgi` program of Section 7.4 that features any or all of the following:

(a) Requests an e-mail address in the welcome page. (See also Exercise 17, Chapter 3.)

(b) Uses `CGI::SecureState` for decoding submitted form data and dealing with state files.

(c) E-mails the final results to the user upon completion.

(d) Uses session cookies unless a "cookie sniff" detects that they are disabled. (See Exercise 1, Lesson 8.)

(e) Features a session timeout that gives only two minutes for each question.

(f) Uses the cache policing function outlined in Exercise 4.

8. Make a version of the `admin.cgi` program of Section 7.7 that

(a) Uses `CGI::SecureState` for all state needs.

(b) Features a session timeout that logs the administrator off after some time period.

(c) Uses the cache policing function outlined in Exercise 4.

9. Research and figure out how to send e-mail messages using the `Mail::Mailer` module, which is part of the package `MailTools`. Read the documentation at CPAN. Below are some notes we made when playing with the module. They may be of some use to you.

■ `Mail::Mailer` takes weird syntax, such as a reference to a hash for parameters and a reference to an array for multiple e-mails. (The main reason we didn't use this module in the text was not to have to explain the `{}` and `[]` syntax issues for hash and array references as covered in the optional section in Chapter 5.)

■ This module uses (among other things) the environment variable `MAILADDRESS` as the envelope sender address instead of the `From:` field. So, to set the envelope sender address, you need to set `$ENV{'MAILADDRESS'}`.

■ `Mail::Sendmail` is fast. `Mail::Mailer` seems slower sending out e-mails. (Perhaps it has too many features? Perhaps it does more machinations to be safer?)

10. For each of the following, decide what mindset and memory parameters should be used to instantiate a `SecureState CGI` object to obtain the desired features.

(a) Suppose the only data from the user that we want to save automatically is a coupon code.

(b) Suppose we wish to remember everything from the client except the name = value pairs with names `"creditCardNumber"` and `"PIN"`.

(c) Suppose we are using state files as validation certificates. Suppose the values corresponding to the names `"logonStatus"` and `"username"` keep track of the user's status. Because of this, we do not wish such values from the state file to be overwritten by values coming from client data.

(d) Suppose values corresponding to `"searchString"` and `"searchMode"` are kept as part of the state file. In contrast to part (c), here we want client data with either of these two names to overwrite the corresponding values.

11. Research and figure out how to maintain session state using the `CGI::Session` module. Read the documentation at CPAN. Here are some things to investigate.

- ▪ `CGI::Session` also uses references to hashes and references to arrays for certain (see comment in exercise 9 above).
- ▪ This module has a feature that enables you to specify when a session expires.
- ▪ This module has options to store state information in a file or in a database (see Chapter 10 for information on databases).

12. (advanced) Make the user signup strategy virtually hackproof by implementing the security feature using images as discussed in the note at the end of Section 9.3. For simplicity, use three-digit integers as the random key string. You will have to research `GD.pm` (likely easier for you to learn than GIMP and more portable) on the Web so that you can generate images on the fly. Features from Exercise 6 may also be added. *Note:* One would be tempted to generate the images on the fly using separate images for each of the digits 0–9 and placing them side by side in the Web page. Such images are readily available on the Web. However, this still has the disadvantage that someone could write an automated spam program to parse the image names out of the returned HTML file and recover the key value.

PROJECT THREAD

Here, e-mail capability is added to your application from the Chapter 8 Project Thread. In particular, a user must now enter an e-mail address at logon, and the quiz score is e-mailed to the user. The thread also features two stand-alone exercises to emphasize topics from this lesson further.

A. Add a text field for an e-mail address to the user logon form. When the quiz is submitted, the quiz score is e-mailed to the user, and the thank-you page no longer reports the score. There is no need to verify the e-mail address in any way, because entering a bogus e-mail address simply results in the user not receiving the quiz results.

B. The list of links for completed quizzes in the admin page should also contain a `mailto:` link for each user in case the administrator wants to send a personal message.

C. Do Exercise 1.

D. Add a new row for the updated quiz application to the table in your homework page. Make sure you preserve the version from the previous chapter and keep the link to it active. If you are assigned any other exercises from this chapter, add another row to your homework table for each exercise.

## CHAPTER 10

THE DATA TIER

This chapter adds another "dimension" to Web applications by exploring general concepts and specific issues concerning back-end data storage and retrieval. In particular, a three-tier Web application is driven by organized, relational data in a third, data tier. We first introduce tables and relational data. For contrast, we offer one short section on using flat text files to store relational data. But the main focus of this chapter is on using database systems and on the general concept of a three-tier Web application.

We provide a quick introduction to SQL to modify or query database tables. We explore the general notion of Web application interface to database engines, and implement such an interface using the Perl DBI module to interface with the free, open-source MySQL database system. To apply the concepts, we introduce state tables for storing intertransaction state data for Web applications and then provide an example of a completely database-driven Web application. Finally, the last sections discuss Web application database interfaces through an interesting Perl module that emulates a relational database using a structured text file, and through the popular MicrosoftAccess database system.

10.1 TABLES AND RELATIONAL DATA

So far in our examples, where data is used to generate a Web page dynamically, that data has been statically initialized at the beginning of the program in global variables. That clearly has the disadvantage that if we wish to change the data source, we have to change the program itself. Granted, the changes may not be difficult, because we were careful to place the data source centralized at the beginning of the program, but nonetheless we have to alter the program file. A second disadvantage arises if more than one program uses the same data source. In that scenario, every time we wish to update the data, we would have to update all the affected programs. Clearly a better solution is to centralize the data further outside of the programs. We will refer to this concept as *back-end data storage*.

We begin by defining some terminology important to the discussion of data—more specifically, **relational data**. Almost any course on databases begins by introducing the notion of relational data. A full exposition on that topic is well beyond our objectives here, but we do provide sufficient concepts and terminology for our goal of exploring back-end relational database support for Web applications.

Relational data is stored in tables. A simple table of data is given as Table 10.1.

The rows are called *records*. Each record in this table contains the data for one customer. The columns are called *keys*. Keys, also called *fields*, represent specific categories

TABLE 10.1 Perl Logical Operators

custID	last	first	age	purchases
12	Wiehe	Karen	40	97.25
31	O'Brien	Keiko	33	524.99
41	Lam	Lisa	35	314.15

TABLE 10.2 Table: orders

orderID	custID	stockID	date
21145	31	3123	01-12-03
21341	41	1412	01-17-03
27818	41	5001	01-21-03

of data within the records. A key that is guaranteed to be unique for each data record is called a *primary key*. In the customers table each customer would receive a unique ID, so custID would be the primary key for that table.

The real flavor of relational data comes when multiple tables are related to one another. For example, the records in a second table might contain customer orders, as shown in Table 10.2. The primary key in the orders table is orderID. Note that the two tables are related through the shared key custID. The unique record in the customers table for a given customer ID, together with the record(s) with that customer ID in the orders table, comprise all the data related to that customer.

The two actions that one would like do with tables in general are modifying and searching them. The specific modifications that one usually makes are: inserting records, deleting records, and updating existing records. We will discuss these actions in the coming sections. Searches through a table usually involve selecting records that fit a certain criteria. A simple example search might be, "Find all customers between the ages of 18 and 49." A more complex query might be, "Find the ten products most often ordered by customers between the ages of 18 and 49."

Relational data can be stored in plain text files. The easiest way is to simply put each table into a separate text file. Of course, relational data can also be stored in a relational database system—that's what they're for! But it's not really just a matter of what you prefer. There are pros and cons for each storage method.

10.2 STRUCTURED TEXT FILES

A text file is a *sequential-access* storage mechanism. That basically means the operating system records a pointer to the first memory block allocated for the file, that block contains a pointer to the next, and so forth. Thus, in terms of memory allocation, a text file is basically a linked list of storage blocks. To load a portion of the file in a given block, the operating system starts reading data into memory, block by block, starting from the first block, until it finds the desired one.

This is evidenced in how you read text files in programs—starting from the beginning and progressing through the file until you find what you need. In terms of what you see inside it, a text file is just one long string with newline characters mixed in. If stored in a text file, one of the tables in the previous section is simply flattened into one long string in memory. To recover a piece of data from the middle of the table, the string must be parsed in sequence until the age of customer 31 is found, for example. Furthermore, in order to replace the age of customer 31 with a different value, the string has to be ripped apart, the new age inserted, and then the string concatenated back together again.

Most relational databases use a *direct-access* storage mechanism for its files. That basically means that the operating system keeps a list of pointers to the various memory blocks allocated to the file. To read a given block, the operating system simply locates the correct pointer and loads only the necessary block into memory.

We don't need to think of the internal representation of data in a database as we do a big string stored in a text file. In fact, we don't directly manipulate the contents of a database as we would a text file. Rather, we issue statements in a *query language* such as **SQL** (Structured Query Language) to "talk" to the database engine and tell it what to do. Because of declarative query languages and direct access storage, the age of customer 31 can be recovered by issuing a simple SQL command that causes only the proper disk block to be loaded into memory. Better yet, the age of customer 31 can be replaced without any reading or writing of the other memory blocks used for the file.

Web applications that use a relatively small amount of data often just employ text files. Loading a few relatively small files entirely into RAM is negligible overhead for the system. In many situations, that is preferable to the full weight of a database engine and the added complexity that it brings. There is no point in using a sledgehammer to drive in an ordinary nail.

When Web applications use and collect relatively large server-side data stores, on the other hand, relational databases are the way to go, even though their use requires extra technical knowledge. You can alter and search for small chunks of data with ease. The extra system overhead caused by the database engine is far preferable to having to sift through large sequential-access files. Manipulating a sequential-access file usually requires loading the whole file into the RAM. You simply don't want to do that with huge chunks of data.

Before moving on to relational database support for Web applications, the main topic of this chapter, we give a quick look at what structured data might look like in a text file. We have had several occasions to store collections of name=value pairs into text files. The best solution was simply to store them as key=value pairs, each on a separate line in the file. That is the "hash in a file" approach, which works so well for state files, for example.

But what if a whole table of data needs to be stored in the file? The natural way to accomplish that task is to preserve the tabular structure using delimiting characters. Consider the file shown in Figure 10.1. It contains the table of customer data from the previous section. First, using the table keys (column headings), each table cell is made into a key=value pair. Second, a complete record is formed by concatenating the pairs with a delimiter. Finally, each record of the table is placed on a separate line. It is important that the delimiting characters not appear in the data. Common choices of delimiters are equal (=), colon (:), semicolon (;), comma (,), and pipe(|).

Certainly, flattening a table into a text file is not conceptually difficult. One could easily devise a more concise format, perhaps by omitting the keys that appear redundantly in each record. But finding the right strategy for reading that data back into a program, potentially modifying it, and then saving it back to the file is definitely not trivial. Typically a programmer would write some *data management functions* to automate necessary

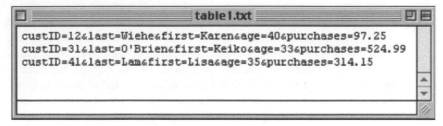

FIGURE 10.1 A table in a text file.

tasks. The data management functions we created for the "hash in a file" approach to keeping state data, namely `read_state` and `write_state`, were extremely simple—just batch reads and writes. But it would be quite cumbersome to write customized functions to handle database-like operations such as changing a table cell, adding one or more records, or deleting a record. Nonetheless, text files often are used behind Web applications in practice when storage needs are relatively uncomplicated.

> **NOTE**
>
> A supplement for this chapter on this book's Web site discusses in some detail, and offers examples of, data management functions for flat file databases. In fact, it provides the beginnings of a crude database system that utilizes flat files, one table per file.
>
> Interestingly, the text export feature of many common desktop applications (such as spreadsheets and even Microsoft's Access database software) produce flat text files in a format somewhat similar to that shown in Figure 10.1. When portability is desired, exported text files are sometimes preferable over the proprietary binary blobs in which such applications normally store data. The exported files are often referred to as CSV (comma-separated values) files, even though other delimiting characters than simply a comma may be used in practice. There is even a Perl module named `CSV` that emulates a relational database and accepts SQL queries, but the data tables are stored in flat text files! We briefly discuss that module in Section 10.9.

10.3 THE THREE-TIER MODEL FOR WEB APPLICATIONS

Most Web applications have a need for persistent long-term data. There are two general techniques for saving and retrieving data from storage: Either the programmer decides on the desired format of the structured data files, or the programmer uses an external **database system**, which in turn deals with the actual format of the data in the files. In the first scenario, the programmer writes data management functions sufficient to meet the needs of the given application. In the external-database-system scenario, the programmer issues high-level commands (namely SQL) to the database system, and it is the job of the database system to manipulate its storage files appropriately.

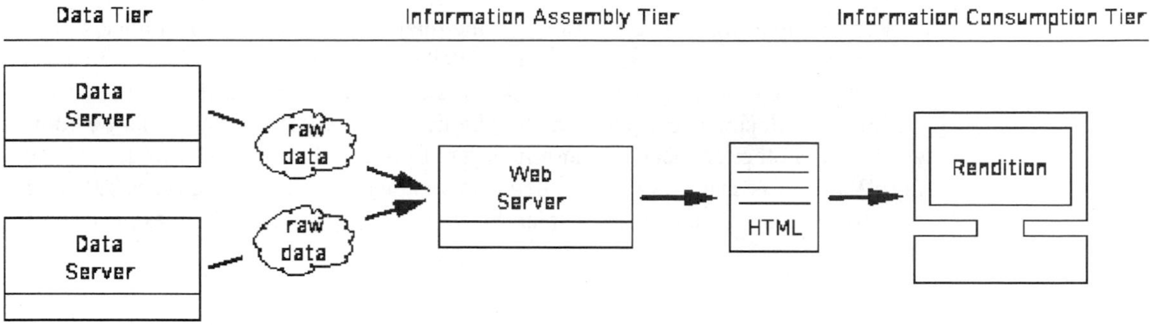

FIGURE 10.2   The three-tier model for Web applications.

Using sequential access text files for data storage is fine for small- to moderate-sized projects; text files require much less system overhead, and data access is quite fast, being handled by the system's own file utilities. On the other hand, if the data set is large and needs to be accessed by many different programs (Web or otherwise), then a heavy-duty database system is likely the better solution. You have no doubt heard of database systems such as Oracle, Access, MySQL, and mSQL. But these do require a daemon to be running in the background on top of the computer's file system.

For commercial-grade Web applications, the data management needs are often of such large scale and complexity that dedicated database servers are used. That necessity introduces the idea of a **three-tier Web application** as depicted in Figure 10.2. In such large-scale Web applications, the data management needs are often so demanding that one or more employees exist whose main job is to maintain data organization and integrity in the data tier. They are often called *data managers*. It is then the job of the Web programmers in the middle tier to write programs (ASP, PHP, Perl, or whatever) to access that data and send it to the client tier as HTML for consumer consumption. In terms of the physical computers that do the data and Web serving, this serves as a valuable division of labor so that the Web application runs smoothly, not overwhelming any one of the servers. For major commercial Web applications, entire farms of servers may be used in each tier!

In reality, the three-tier model is still conceptually valid for small Web applications in which the back-end data is stored on the same server that runs the Web server software. A program on the server accesses a data source, whether stored in flat text files or in a local relational database, and assembles the data into browser-renderable HTML pages. For that reason, Web servers are sometimes called *information servers*. Raw data is not really information in the sense that humans consume it. It is the job of the Web server (rather programs on the Web server) to transform the raw data into information. That is true whether the data source is on the Web server itself or on dedicated data servers in a full-fledged three-tier application.

NOTE

You have used caching for state data between transactions, but in a full-fledged three-tier model, caching becomes important for other reasons. In particular, when the middle tier requests data from the data tier (for a search, for example) many situations warrant caching that data in the middle tier.

For example, when a search of an online retailer turns up a list of products after searching a potentially large third-tier database it may return only the first 10 matches. When the user clicks the link for the next 10 matches, the data from the original search can be cached in the middle tier, and the third tier need not be bothered with another connection and search just to return the same data to the middle tier. We discuss this idea in more detail in Chapter 12, when we discuss database search utilities, and again in Chapter 17, when we explore the increasing role of XML in middle-tier data caching.

10.4 BACK-END DATABASE SUPPORT

Technically, the word *database* when used by itself means a collection of tables. A database is usually given a name, and the individual tables within a database also have names. For example, we can collect Tables 10.1 and 10.2 from Section 10.1 into one database named `store` as shown in Figure 10.3. This database could also contain additional tables for inventory, salespeople, and so forth.

Different database systems have different ways of storing the actual data; storage could be in text or binary form or a combination thereof. But the storage format is irrelevant to us here. We will simply issue high-level commands to the database system and let it manipulate the actual data. You might also hear the terms *database software* or *database engine*, which are synonymous with the term *database system* for most purposes.

Most sophisticated database software will have a GUI (graphical user interface) used to view and edit databases and tables. The tables can be edited by hand, and SQL commands can even be issued to query the tables, through the GUI. The screen shots in Figure 10.4 show a simple query using the GUI for MySQL. The query simply selects all columns from the `customers` table, thereby showing the whole table.

But the focus of this lesson is not to how to use a database software GUI to manipulate tables. Rather, the focus is on how to issue commands from another application, such as a Perl program, to manipulate tables within a database. For this to be possible, a database engine must be running in the background (a daemon[1]), waiting for queries. Figure 10.5 shows a comprehensive overview of database support for Web applications. The diagram applies in general, not just for Perl CGI program. In other environments (ASP, PHP, JSP), the program interpreter would simply be a module compiled into the Web server software.

The following list details the logical steps that must be performed in order for a Web application to interact with a database system. Some of these steps must be performed ahead of time, and some of them are performed during the Web program's execution.

---

[1] We have used the term *daemon* several times without explanation. It refers to a process, usually a server of some sort, that runs in the background and does not make its presence felt until called upon. It is interesting that the origins of the term actually draw upon the similarity in concept to a demon existing unnoticed in the background of a human being!

Again, we give these concepts using Perl as the application's language, but these steps apply equally well in other Web programming environments.

1. *Make sure the database software is running.* This software is often a daemon that listens for connections and queries from other programs. The daemon may be started up either manually or as part of the boot process of the server. This is true for MySQL (see Appendix G). (For a contrast to this step, see the optional sections on CSV and MSAccess.)

2. *Create a database.* Remember that a database consists of a set of one or more tables, and a database system is often responsible for several databases. A database has to be created at some point in time. There are three ways this usually happens.

   ◾ The database GUI can be used to create a new database. This is easiest if possible. Figure 10.6 shows a screenshot from MySQL.

Database: **store**

Table: **customers**

custID	last	first	age	purchases
12	Wiebe	Karen	40	97.25
31	O'Brien	Keiko	33	524.99
41	Lam	Lisa	35	314.15

Table: **orders**

orderID	custID	stockID	date
21145	31	3123	01-12-03
21341	41	1412	01-17-03
27818	41	5001	01-21-03

FIGURE 10.3   The store database.

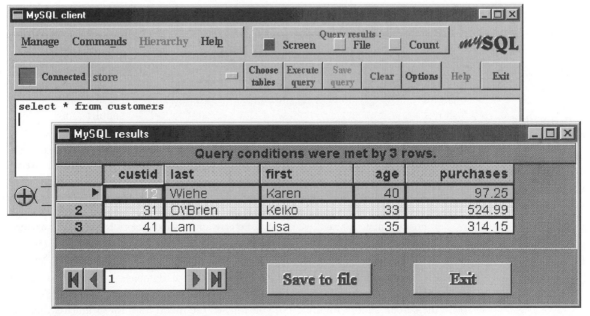

FIGURE 10.4   A query in the MySQL GUI.

① The browser issues a URL request for a `program.cgi`.

② The Web server software receives the request and retrieves the file from the file system.

③ The file is given to the Perl interpreter to be processed.

④ The Perl interpreter interfaces with external database software. This database system might reside on the Web server or on a different, third tier server. The database software interacts with the file system on its machine where its data files are stored.

⑤ The Perl interpreter gives the HTML document it forms from the data to the Web server software.

⑥ The Web server software sends the HTML document back to the client.

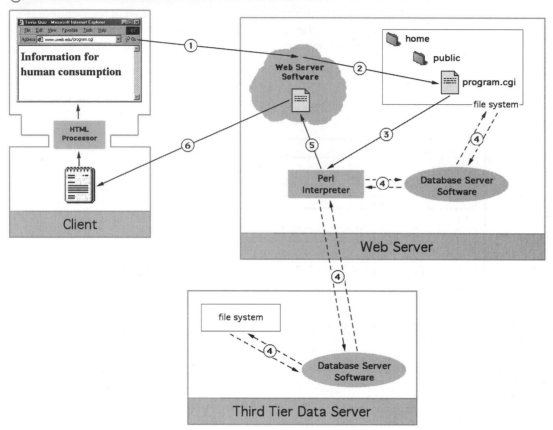

FIGURE 10.5 Database support for Web applications.

- An administrative command can be issued from within a Perl program to create a new database. Note that such an administrative command is *not* an SQL command. (We will show how to do this in Section 10.6.)

- Some database systems simply default to some specified directory. An individual database is then a subdirectory that holds all the files corresponding to the tables. Thus, to create a new database, we could just create a new subdirectory by hand. For example, for MySQL, the default directory often is `C:\mysql\data` in Windows and `/var/lib/mysql` in UNIX/Linux. However, this method does not address user/password issues.

3. *User/password permission must be given* for those database systems that require user and password validation. The easiest way to do this is to use the database GUI. In the screen shot in Figure 10.6, you can see the menu item for Grant/Revoke. Use

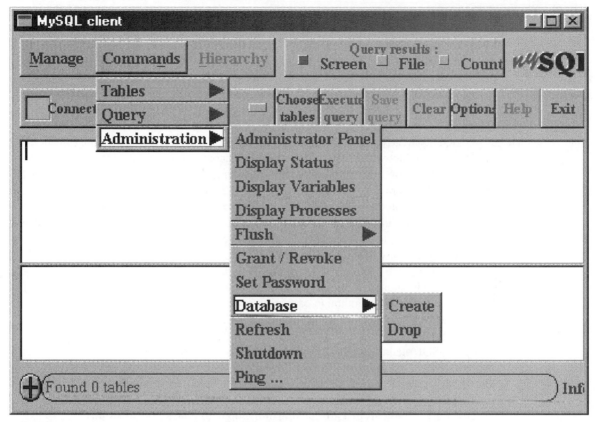

FIGURE 10.6   Creating a table using the MySQL GUI.

this option to give permissions to particular users for particular databases. Under the menu item Set Password, you can change the password for a particular user. See Appendix G for further details.

4. *Connect to the database.* Perl has a statement that connects to a specified database system and a specific database within that system. In some other Web programming languages this connection might take two steps: connecting to the database system and then selecting the database within it.

5. *Manipulate the database.* Any table within the particular database to which we are connected can then be accessed or modified. The table manipulations are accomplished by issuing SQL commands through a Perl interface.

NOTE

Steps 1, 2, and 3 are typically performed once, independently of the Web application, and often these steps are performed by someone other than the Web programmer (such as the database manager). Steps 4 and 5 are performed repeatedly by the Web application.

10.5 SQL PRIMER

The Structured Query Language (SQL) was invented by IBM in the 1970s to standardize accessing and manipulating data within a relational database system. SQL was adopted by major database systems and has evolved over the years, with the last major standardization being ANSI-SQL from 1992. This is the standard to which most major database systems adhere. Just about all database systems (Oracle, Sybase, Informix, DB2, MicrosoftAccess, MySQL, mSQL, PostgreSQL, just to name a few) accept SQL statements.

SQL itself has only statements for manipulating data within tables, including creation and destruction of tables within a specified database. Database administrative commands (not SQL commands) are responsible for the creation and destruction of databases. SQL was designed to be very easy to learn and is intuitive in many ways. Being a declarative language, it lacks features such as looping that are a staple of procedural and object-oriented programming languages. Thus, we will need a programming language such as Perl (or as you will see later in this book, PHP or ASP) to perform conditionals and loops while issuing SQL statements.

Some database systems have their own, proprietary extensions of SQL. We will, of course, use only the common SQL statements. After all, one point of being standardized is that SQL code should be portable from one database system to another. The following quick overview of SQL, although certainly not exhaustive, is sufficient to convey the main concept of SQL and to allow you to add database support to your Web applications.

We emphasize that the statements we study in this section are not Perl statements. They are SQL statements. In the next section we will learn how to issue SQL statements from within a Perl program. These SQL statements presume that we are working on *one* database to which we have already connected. Again, connecting to the database is accomplished by a Perl statement, as shown in the next section. Finally, for simplicity, we discuss only statements that are capable of manipulating one table at a time.

SQL: Creating a Table

To create a new table, use the `CREATE TABLE` command to specify the name of the table and the name of each of the columns. The data type of each column must be specified. The new table will not yet have any rows.

```
CREATE TABLE table_name
(
  Column_name_1 data_type_1 optional_column_constraint,
  Column_name_2 data_type_2 optional_column_constraint,
  .
  .
  .
)
```

Keywords in SQL are case insensitive. Some SQL programmers prefer to type SQL keywords in all caps, while others prefer all lowercase letters. We prefer using all caps so that you can easily distinguish the keywords. SQL statements are often spread over several lines so that not too many keywords appear on any one line; but this is only for readability. Some common data types are shown in Table 10.3. Note that most databases require length to be in the range 1–255. To keep the exposition simple, we will not be using any column constraints.

TABLE 10.3 Common SQL Data Types

TYPE	DESCRIPTION
CHAR (*length*)	A character string of specified length, string is right-padded with spaces and sorted with length characters (i.e., fixed-width columns)
VARCHAR (*length*)	A character string of specified length, not padded with spaces (i.e., variable-width columns)
INTEGER	Integer
REAL	Real

TABLE 10.4 Table: customers

custID	last	first	age	purchase
12	Wiehe	Karen	40	97.25
31	O'Brien	Keiko	33	524.99
41	Lam	Lisa	35	314.15

As an example, the customers table (Table 10.1) used in previous sections can be created with the following SQL statement. The table is reproduced here as Table 10.4 because we will continue to use it to explain new SQL statements.

```
CREATE TABLE customers
(
   custID VARCHAR(5),
   last VARCHAR(20),
   first VARCHAR(20),
   age INTEGER,
   purchases REAL
)
```

SQL: Inserting Records

Once a table exists, a new record can be inserted.

```
INSERT INTO customers
VALUES
   ('33', 'Doe', 'John', 30, 15.75)
```

Note that the table name is in the statement, because there may be more than one table in a database. The following useful alternative does not require adherence to the original order of the columns:

```
INSERT INTO customers
   (age, purchases, first, last, custID)
VALUES
   (30, 15.75, 'John', 'Doe', '33')
```

SQL: Quoting Data

If the data is not numeric, you should use single quotes (most systems also accept double quotes). Two single-quote characters in a row escapes the second single-quote character (most systems also accept \ ').

```
INSERT INTO customers
  (age, purchases, first, last, custID)
VALUES
  (30, 15.75, 'Miles', 'O''Brien', '33')
```

NOTE

To facilitate preparation of string data (such as escaping single quotes in the data with two single quotes), many language interfaces provide string functions that do this conversion for you.

SQL: Selecting Records and Subtables

A subtable is selected by specifying columns and rows.

```
SELECT [comma-delimited column_names or *]
  FROM table_name
  WHERE criteria
```

Either the columns are specified explicitly by name, or an asterisk (*) can be used to mean all columns. The rows are specified by giving *criteria* inside the WHERE clause. A criterion may be a numerical comparison. Applied to the customers table in Table 10.4, the following SQL statement would return a subtable that has one column and two rows.

```
SELECT custID
  FROM customers
  WHERE age > 34
```

In general, the subtable returned by a SELECT statement can be empty, consist of only one column or row, or be any other collection of columns and rows up to the whole table.

A criterion may be an exact match (numerical or string). Note that inequality is <>. Applied to the customers table (Table 10.4), the following SQL statement would return a subtable with two columns and one row.

```
SELECT last, first
  FROM customers
  WHERE custID = '12'
```

A criterion also can be a simple pattern match.

```
SELECT last
  FROM customers
  WHERE last LIKE 'La%'
```

Here the % stands for any string of zero or more characters. So this statement searches for last names that begin with the string 'La'. This is usually case insensitive but depends on the particular database system. A case-sensitive match can be specified by using the phrase `LIKE BINARY`. The negation of `LIKE` is `NOT LIKE`. (In some database systems where the match is case sensitive by default, one would use the keyword `CLIKE` instead of `LIKE` for case-insensitive matches. But `CLIKE` is not standard SQL. For example, `CLIKE` is not viable in MySQL.)

Multiple criteria can be combined into one `WHERE` clause using `AND`/`OR` logic.

```
SELECT *
  FROM customers
  WHERE age > 18 AND age < 49
```

If the `WHERE` clause is omitted, then all rows match and the whole table is returned. The order in which the rows are returned can be specified using the keywords `ORDER BY`.

```
SELECT *
FROM customers
WHERE purchases > 100
ORDER BY age ASC
```

Here the rows will be returned ordered according to the `age` column, and the keyword `ASC` specifies ascending order. The keyword `DESC` specifies descending order.

SQL: Updating Data

The following statement modifies all rows that fit the criteria, replacing their column values as specified in the list.

```
UPDATE table_name
  SET [comma-delimited list of pairs of form Column_name = value]
  WHERE criteria
```

Here are two examples.

```
UPDATE customers
  SET purchases = 0
  WHERE age < 18


UPDATE customers
  SET age = 42, purchases = purchases + 100
  WHERE custID = '12'
```

The second example also shows that the column names can be used as if they are variables inside the `SET` clause. Here purchases will be incremented by 100 in the row where the customer ID is 12.

SQL: Deleting Records

The following statement deletes all rows satisfying the criteria.

```
DELETE FROM table_name
  WHERE criteria
```

And finally, the following statement deletes the entire table.

```
DROP TABLE table_name
```

10.6   DATABASE INTERFACE IN PERL

In this section, we learn how to interface with database systems using Perl's DBI (Database Interface) module. The **DBI module** must be installed on the server in order for it to be loaded. Attempting to use it generates a fatal error if the module is not yet installed (a good way to test whether you already have the module).

```
use DBI;
```

See Appendix D on installing this Perl module (there is a chance that this module comes with your Perl installation). In addition to installing the DBI module, when you use the interface with a particular database system, you must be sure that the corresponding Perl *database driver* (DBD) is installed. Drivers for popular database systems are supported, and other drivers are added and updated frequently. We will remind you of particular drivers when we discuss particular database systems.

We use the free MySQL as the main database system in this section. MySQL will also be used as the database system in the lessons on PHP and ASP. MySQL is ideal for this text because it's free and it's representative of typical database systems. It can be easily downloaded for free from www.mysql.com. See Appendix G on its installation. To use MySQL with any Web application, you will need to start the MySQL daemon (the operating system command mysqld, see Appendix G). Important: In order to use MySQL with Perl, be sure the Perl driver DBD-mysql is installed in the Perl library. (See Appendix D.)

Figure 10.7 shows how a Perl program interacts with MySQL. The Perl program uses functions from the DBI module that prepare SQL statements.. The module then sends the SQL statements to the MySQL daemon, which accesses/modifies the appropriate data files in the file system. The MySQL daemon actually does most of the work. It is good to understand this abstractly, because other Web programming environments employ a similar strategy, even though their SQL preparatory functions might be built in.

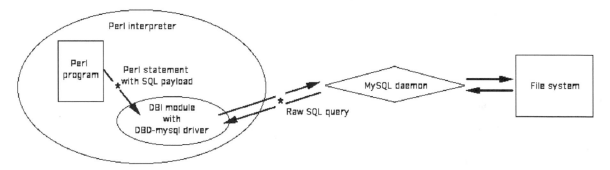

FIGURE 10.7   Conceptual overview of Perl–MySQL interface.

DBI objects

As with the modules we used in Chapter 9, DBI functions are imported through objects. Recall Section 9.1 for object syntax in Perl. There are three DBI objects that we will use for database interface:

- Database object: This is the object that holds the connection to the desired database. Usually a global variable, it works somewhat like a file handle, because it references the open database connection. For that reason, we will call this object the *database handle*.

- Query object: This object is created by calling a method of the database handle. It is through methods of this object that we are able to send SQL statements to the database system.

- Driver object: This object is seldom used. It is used only for performing administrative tasks, such as creating or destroying an entire database, which has nothing to do with SQL. (Note that we are not talking about creating or destroying tables; which is done through SQL statements.) We include this object for completeness, but will not have occasion to use it.

Connecting to the Database: The Database Handle

The following discussion assumes that we have already executed the use line to import the DBI module. In order to access a database using DBI the first step is to connect to the database by creating a handle object:

```
$dbhandle = DBI->connect(
  "DBI:driver:database=databaseName;server=serverName;port=portNumber",
  user, password);
```

When the database server is the same as the Web server, leave off the server information (name and port):

```
$dbhandle = DBI->connect("DBI:driver:databaseName", user, password);
```

That is, the default value for the server is localhost. Also, usually the driver knows what default port to use for a particular type of database system, and the port information is typically left off.

The connect method returns a false value if it fails. In that case, the errstr() method contains a descriptive error message string. So, if MySQL is running on the local server, with a database named store, and with username storeuser and password pass, the statement to create a database handle is:

```
$dbhandle = DBI->connect("DBI:mysql:store", "storeuser", "pass")
or send DBI->errstr() message somewhere such as errorPage
```

If the connection fails, we will likely print out an error page using the string returned from DBI->errstr() for diagnostic purposes.

When you no longer need the database interface, close the connection to the database server.

```
$dbhandle->disconnect();
```

Issuing SQL Statements: The Query Object

Once you have the handle to the database connection, there are two steps for sending SQL statements to the database engine. For statements that merely change a table (CREATE, INSERT, UPDATE, DELETE, DROP) those two steps are usually sufficient. However, the SQL SELECT statement returns a subtable from the database. In that case, we need a third step so that we can deal with the returned data in a Perl program.

1. *Prepare the SQL statement.*

```
$qObj = $dbhandle->prepare("SQL_statement_as_string");
```

The prepare method takes an SQL statement formatted as one long string. It returns a query object, which references the SQL statement now stored as an object in some format. In practice, the preparation is done by creating an extra Perl variable to store the SQL statement in string format, because it often takes a bit of work to concatenate the various parts of an SQL statement together into a string. We will prepare SQL statements as follows:

```
$sql = [work to put together an SQL statement];
$qObj = $dbhandle->prepare($sql) or &errorPage($dbhandle->errstr());
```

Note that the specifics of the error are sent to errorPage if preparation fails. This is very useful for debugging programs. *Warning Note:* Sometimes a bad SQL statement will crash the prepare method instead of returning a false value, thus aborting the program without any error message—a bummer.

The quote method (called on the database handle, rather than the query object) is very useful when putting SQL statements together, because it returns an SQL formatted string literal with any special characters (such as ' and %) escaped.

```
$sql = $dbhandle->quote("string");
```

This is especially useful when the string is built from uncontrolled sources such as user input. Below we build by concatenation an INSERT statement, which adds a new row based on a value from %formHash to some one-column table.

```
$sql = "INSERT INTO some_table VALUES ("
     . $dbhandle->quote($formHash{"someName"})
     . ")";
```

Note that this method returns a string that is already quoted. Also, it is possible that this method might quote a string differently for different database systems' specifications. The beauty is that you don't have to remember each database system's quoting specifications.

2. *Execute the SQL statement.*

```
$qObj->execute() or &errorPage($qObj->errstr());
```

This causes the prepared query object to send its payload (the SQL statement) to the MySQL software. Data returned by the MySQL software is stored in the query object in some format. The returned data may be about changes made to a table, such as how many rows were UPDATEd or DELETEd, or it may be a subtable of data, as returned by SELECT.

3. *Fetch the results.* This step is necessary only when you need to deal with the returned data. Sometimes we don't need to, for example when the SQL statement merely INSERTs a row in the table. However, we usually want to process the subtable of data returned by a SELECT SQL statement. Basically, we "fetch" the returned data from the query object into Perl variables.

The fetchrow_array method returns one row at a time out of the query object, with the columns split into an array:

```
@first_row = $qObj->fetchrow_array();
```

Often you need to iterate over the rows:

```
while(@row = $qObj->fetchrow_array()) {
    do something with @row;
}
```

A row can also be fetched as a hash, where the keys are the column names (table keys). Unfortunately, there is no method that does this directly. The fetchrow_hashref method returns a scalar reference to a hash. (The optional Section 5.9 has a discussion of references. However the detailed discussion there is not necessary for our purposes here.) A reference is similar to a pointer, and we merely need to dereference it as follows.

```
$rowhashref = $qObj->fetchrow_hashref();
%row = %$rowhashref; ### Note the %$ combination to dereference
```

The reference is stored in a scalar variable $rowhashref, and then dereferenced to an actual hash variable on the next line. Of course, this still fetches only one row at a time.

For SQL statements that only change the table, such as UPDATE and DELETE, you can get a count of how many rows were affected using the rows method.

```
$number_changed = $qObj->rows();
```

When $qObj contains a subtable returned from a SQL SELECT statement, the rows method works a bit differently. The query object knows only how many rows have been returned after all rows have been fetched out of the object. Presumably, the query object counts the rows as they are fetched out of the object.

Fortunately, there is a simple trick to enable you to determine quickly the number of returned rows.

```
$qObj->fetchall_arrayref();
$number_of_rows = $qObj->rows();
```

The fetchall_arrayref method returns a scalar reference to a two-dimensional array that contains the whole table, fetched out of the object. But that is not important, because we do not intend to use the array. The important thing is that now the query object knows how many rows were returned!

Note that if you want to refetch the rows, starting from the first, after the preceding code has executed, you must re-execute step 2, thereby refreshing the query object with a newly returned subtable.

> **NOTE**
>
> According to the DBI documentation, when used after executing an SQL SELECT statement, if not all the rows have been fetched from the object, the result of the rows() method might have a different meaning depending on the particular DBD driver. The result might be the number of rows fetched so far instead of the number of returned rows, or it might be −1 until all rows have been fetched. See the exercises for a more advanced way of counting the number of returned rows.

4. *Clear the query object.*

```
$qObj->finish();
```

This clears out the query object. Omitting this step is usually not fatal. We will endeavor to remember this step as a matter of good programming practice.

Creating a New Database: The Driver Object

You need to do this only if the database does not yet exist. Skip this part if you do not need to create a database from within a Perl program. Remember, there are other ways to create a database outside of a Perl program, such as with a GUI or by manually creating a subdirectory somewhere. See Section 10.4 and Appendix G for more details on using the MySQL GUI.

For most database systems, such as MySQL, you can execute an administrative function through a driver handle object. First, create the driver handle. Then execute an administrative command.

```
$driver_object = DBI->install_driver("mysql")
  or send DBI->errstr() message somewhere such as errorPage;

$driver_object->func("createdb", databaseName, host, user, password, "admin")
  or send $driver_handle->errstr() message somewhere such as errorPage;
```

The supplied user must have sufficient privileges to create the database. The admin parameter tells the driver object that the supplied user must have administrative access (likely the system's root) to create the new database. The newly created database is available by

```
$dbhandle = DBI->connect("DBI:mysql:databaseName", user, password);
```

as usual.

> **NOTE**
>
> Aside from the creation of the database, which is often done externally to the Perl program, you will notice that the only statement that is dependent upon the type of database system is the connect statement. That is, to switch from one database system to another, we need only change one line in a program! In practice, one often uses something simple such as CSV for testing, and once everything works, migrate to a heavy-duty database system.

10.7 STATE TABLES

A perfect way to put what you have just learned about SQL and database interface to good use is to explore keeping state in Web applications using a **state table**. As with other state-keeping tools we have seen (our toolkit functions and the CGI::SecureState module), the utilities that help to automate keeping state should (ideally) do all of the following:

- Generate long session IDs
- Create state records (formerly state files) identified by the long ID
- Police the state table (formerly file cache) so that it doesn't grow without bound
- Be able to read a state record (into a hash or hashlike format)
- Be able to overwrite (update) a state record
- Be able to provide session timeouts

This section develops state-keeping utilities capable of all the above features using a database table.

Whenever state information is stored on the server, there are always two crucial pieces of information that must be kept. First, there needs to be a session ID. In the state file methodology, the session ID identified the state file. Second, there needs to be a means of determining the age of the state information. In the state file methodology, the operating system kept track of the age of the file through the last-modified property.

The most straightforward strategy for implementing state tables is to keep these two pieces of information using two columns. (There are more advanced methods, such as using time stamps; but we have elected not to use such advanced methods in order to keep our SQL exposition as simple as possible.) We make a convention that the first column be named id and hold a 32-character string. The second column, named last_modified, will keep track of the last modification time by storing the integer returned by Perl's time function. The difference between the current value of the Perl time function and the stored value is the "age" of the state record. The age is in seconds because that's how the time function counts time. The rest of the columns will store values for other state data that may need to be maintained between transactions.

For example, reconsider the quiz2.cgi example from Section 7.4. The state data consists of only two integer values: one for the current question number (qnumber) and one for the current number of correct answers (correct). A state table with two different state records for that application looks like Table 10.5. This table is easily created with the following SQL statement:

```
CREATE TABLE states
(
   id CHAR(32),
   last_modified INTEGER,
   qnumber INTEGER,
   correct INTEGER

)
```

In some database systems, you may need to specify that last_modified is a LONG INTEGER.

TABLE 10.5   Table: `states`

id	last_modified	qnumber	correct
X21fFD32DSxkmdP7Vckj19nmeaAV7mpq	1022214101	3	1
C9JzoLZh998LKJtyf198GV76Y8H8kjoi	1022217571	1	0

We now write the three important toolkit functions that manage state information: namely, those for getting a session ID, saving state information, and reading state information. These functions are used in much the same way as the corresponding state file toolkit functions from Chapter 7.

The `get_long_id_db` function takes as parameters the database handle, the name of the state table, the cache limit, and the file life span. To be consistent with state file version of the function, the file life span is sent to the function in day units. The logic of the `get_long_id_db` function parallels that of the `get_long_id` function from Section 7.5. A detailed overview follows the code. The `generate_random_string` function from Chapter 7 is used to get the session ID.

```perl
sub get_long_id_db {
    my ($dbhandle, $table_name, $cache_limit, $file_life_span) = @_;

    ### count number of sessions
    my $sql = "SELECT id FROM $table_name";
    my $qObj = $dbhandle -> prepare($sql) or &errorPage("Can't prepare.");
    $qObj -> execute() or &errorPage("Can't execute " . $qObj->errstr());
    $qObj -> fetchall_arrayref();

    if($qObj->rows() >= $cache_limit) {     ### Need to police table?
        my $expiredtime = int(time - $file_life_span*24*60*60); ### in seconds ###
        $qObj -> finish();

        ### police the table
        $sql = "DELETE FROM $table_name WHERE last_modified < $expiredtime";
        $qObj = $dbhandle -> prepare($sql) or &errorPage("Can't prepare.");;
        $qObj -> execute() or &errorPage("Can't execute " . $qObj->errstr());
        $qObj -> finish();

        ### count number of sessions again
        $sql = "SELECT id FROM $table_name";
        $qObj = $dbhandle -> prepare($sql) or &errorPage("Can't prepare.");;
        $qObj -> execute() or &errorPage("Can't execute " . $qObj->errstr());
        $qObj -> fetchall_arrayref();

        if($qObj->rows() >= $cache_limit) { ### still over limit?
            # should generate e-mail message to warn administrator
            &errorPage("Site busy. Please try again later.");
        }
    }
    $qObj -> finish();

    my $id = &generate_random_string(32);
    my $currtime = time;

    ### create new state record
    $sql = "INSERT INTO $table_name (id, last_modified) values ('$id', $currtime)";
    $qObj = $dbhandle -> prepare($sql) or &errorPage("Can't prepare.");;
    $qObj -> execute() or &errorPage("Can't execute " . $qObj->errstr());

    return $id;
}
```

- Receive the parameters.
- The next three statements construct, prepare, and execute an SQL statement that returns the column of id fields. We merely wish to count the number of records in the state table and could have returned the whole table (SELECT *), but returning the subtable consisting of only the first column is more efficient.
- Fetch all of the rows so that the query object knows how many rows were returned.
- If the number of rows (that is, the number of state records) is greater than the cache limit,

  - Calculate the $expiredtime. State records that have not been modified since this point in time shall be deleted.
  - Clear the query object (before we reuse it).
  - The next three statements construct, prepare, and execute an SQL statement that deletes old state records. Then, clear the query object again.
  - Count the number of rows in the table again.
  - If the number is still greater than the cache limit, print an error page that the site is busy, which also exits the program.

- Otherwise, generate a 32-character string and insert a new state record into the table using the new ID and the current time.
- Return the ID string.

There are two things worth noting about the database version of this function. First, we never had to loop through all of the state records as we previously did with state files. That's the beauty of a declarative language like SQL: One high-level statement, and the database software loops through the table for you! Second, in the state file scenario, the write_state function created a state file if it did not already exist merely by opening it for writing. But here the get_long_id_db function creates a new state table record right after it generates the session ID.

```
sub write_state_db {
  my ($dbhandle, $table_name, $sessionID, %states) = @_;
  ### add the updated last-modified time to the front of the incoming hash of states
  my $current_time = time;
  my @updates = ("last_modified = $current_time");
  foreach $key (keys %states){
    push @updates, "$key = " . $dbhandle->quote($states{$key});
  }
  ### update the state record
  $sql = "UPDATE $table_name SET " . join(",", @updates) . " WHERE id =
    '$sessionID'";
  $qObj = $dbhandle -> prepare($sql) or &errorPage("Can't prepare.");
  $qObj -> execute() or &errorPage("Can't execute " . $qObj->errstr());
  $qObj -> finish();
}
```

The logic of the write_state_db function parallels that of the write_state function from Section 7.4. The meat of this function lies in the construction of an SQL UPDATE statement. For example, consider the state table shown in Table 10.5. Suppose we have

```
%stateHash = ("number"=>4, "correct"=>3);
```

The @updates array is first initialized to ("last_modified = 123456"), where here we made up some number for the current time. After the foreach loop, the @updates array would consist of three elements.

```
("last_modified = 123456", "number = 4", "correct = 3")
```

The join function combines these three elements into one string with commas separating the three elements. So the resulting value of $sql is a complete SQL statement string.

```
"UPDATE states SET last_modified = 123456, number = 4, correct = 3
WHERE id = sessionID"
```

The new read_state_db function is provided next. The logic of this function parallels the read_state function from Section 7.7. Recall that was the final, timeout-enabled version of the function.

```
sub read_state_db {
  my ($dbhandle, $table_name, $sessionID, $time_out,
  $time_out_function, $time_out_message) = @_;  ### $time_out is in days

  ### read the desired state record into the query object
  $sql = "SELECT * FROM $table_name WHERE ID = '$sessionID'";
  $qObj = $dbhandle -> prepare($sql) or &errorPage("Can't prepare.");
  $qObj -> execute() or &errorPage("Can't execute " . $qObj->errstr());
  my $rowhashref = $qObj->fetchrow_hashref();
  $qObj -> finish();

  if (!$rowhashref) { ### $rowhashref is an empty reference, which means no such ID...
    &errorPage("No such session.");
  }
  my %hash = %$rowhashref; ### get the actual hash containing the state record
  ### timeout test
  if (($time_out > 0) && ($hash{"last_modified"} < time - $time_out*24*60*60)){
    ### timed out...
    if($time_out_function) {
      &$time_out_function($time_out_message);
      exit;
    }
    else{
      &errorPage("Your session has timed out");
    }
  }
  ### touch the record
  $sql = "UPDATE $table_name SET last_modified = " . time . " WHERE ID =
  '$sessionID'";
  $qObj = $dbhandle -> prepare($sql) or &errorPage("Can't prepare.");
  $qObj -> execute() or &errorPage("Can't execute " . $qObj->errstr());
  $qObj -> finish();
  ### only need to return the actual state data
  delete $hash{"id"};
  delete $hash{"last_modified"};
  return %hash;
}
```

- Receive the incoming parameters. Note that the $timeout parameter and all subsequent ones are optional.
- Get the desired state record. The fetchrow_hashref method fetches the state record into the program as a hash referenced by $rowhashref.

- If the $rowhashref is empty, then there was no record that matches the ID.
- Otherwise, we recover the %hash from the reference.
- Implement the (optional) timeout feature.
- Update the last modified field of the state record (touch it). Thus, the act of reading the state record keeps it current (in case you don't overwrite it during a given session transaction).
- Finally, we delete the two hash entries for id and last_modified, because technically these are not part of the state hash. (The session ID is returned by get_long_id_db and propagated through session transactions inside %formHash or %cookieHash.)

> **NOTE**
>
> An alternative strategy in devising a state table would be to use just one third column that stored the rest of the state data as one long string of name=value pairs. Doing so would mean that the long string would manually have to be parsed into a hash, which would not take advantage of the ambient column structure of a table. Moreover, it would be necessary to URL-encode the state data to guarantee the integrity (in terms of not interfering with the delimiting characters) of the string and because of the security hole we point out in Section 13.6. Using a table column for each name=value pair of state data does not require that the data be URL-encoded.

10.8 DATABASE-DRIVEN WEB APPLICATIONS

Armed with the state table toolkit functions from the previous section, you will find that it is a simple matter to convert any program that uses state files over to using a database and a state table. For an easily understood example, we rewrite quiz2.cgi of Section 7.4.

In addition, the new version, quiz3.cgi, uses a database table to store the quiz. Thus, quiz3.cgi exclusively uses the database for its back-end data support. Both tables used by the application are contained in a database named quizdb, as shown in Figure 10.8. The quiz table is named quiz1 for scalability (in case other quizzes are added in the future).

Database: **quizdb**

Table: **quiz1**

qnumber	question	answer	choice1	choice2	choice3	choice4	choice5
1	How many hairs …	2	0	1	2	3	4
2	What planet...	Tatooine	Alderaan	Bespin	Corellia	Dantooine	Tatooine
3	What is the last...	1	1	3	5	7	9

Table: **states**

id	last_modified	number	correct
X1fFD32DSxkmdP7Vckj19nmeaAV7mpq	1022214101	3	1
C9JzoLZh998LKJtyf198GV76Y8H8kjoi	1022217571	1	0

FIGURE 10.8 The quizdb database.

Assume that the `quiz1` table in Figure 10.8 was initially created with the following SQL statement:

```
CREATE TABLE quiz1
(
  qnumber INTEGER,
  question VARCHAR(80),
  answer VARCHAR(20),
  choice1 VARCHAR(20),
  choice2 VARCHAR(20),
  choice3 VARCHAR(20),
  choice4 VARCHAR(20),
  choice5 VARCHAR(20)
)
```

Also assume that `quizdb` is in MySQL and that the user "quizuser", with password "pass", has full privileges to this database. Typically an anonymous user would have read-only privileges to the quiz table and read-write for the state table. An administrator would have full read-write privileges to the whole database.

Figure 10.9 shows the outline for the `quiz3.cgi` program. The application logic is unchanged, coming straight from the original transaction diagram in Figure 7.4 of Section 7.3. The additions are the lines that `use` the `DBI` module and connect to the `quizdb`, the global variables containing the names of the database tables, the new variable for the timeout (that's a long time given for each question!), and the new toolkit functions for state tables. Of course, the app logic functions (except `welcome_page`) and the `print_question` helper function are updated. Those are provided next, with overviews.

```
sub print_question {
  my ($sessionID, $qnumber) = @_;

  ### Get question #####
  my $sql = "SELECT question, choice1, choice2, choice3, choice4, choice5
             FROM $quiz_table_name
             WHERE qnumber = $qnumber";
  my $qObj = $dbhandle -> prepare($sql) or &errorPage("Can't prepare.");
  $qObj -> execute() or &errorPage("Can't execute " . $qObj->errstr());
  my ($question, @choices) = $qObj->fetchrow_array();
  $qObj -> finish();

  print<<QUESTION;
  <form action = "$ENV{'SCRIPT_NAME'}" method="GET">
    $qnumber. $question<br/>
QUESTION

  foreach $answer (@choices) {
    print "<input type=\"radio\" name=\"answer\" value=\"$answer\"/>$answer\n";
  }
  print<<FORM;
    <br/>
    <input type="hidden" name="id" value="$sessionID"/> ### propagate session
    <input type="hidden" name="qnumber" value="$qnumber"/>
    <input type="hidden" name="request" value="grade_question"/>
    <input type="submit" value="Submit answer"/>
  </form>
FORM
}
```

```
quiz3.cgi

#! /usr/bin/perl
print "Content-type: text/html\n\n";

#############################################################
#    code for decoding input $datastring into %formHash    #
#        (works for GET, POST, and offline execution)       #
#############################################################

### global variables ######################################
use DBI;
$dbhandle = DBI->connect("DBI:mysql:quizdb", "quizuser", "pass")
  or &errorPage("Can't connect to quizdb". DBI->errstr());
$file_life_span = 1.0/24; # in days (so is 1 hour)
$time_out = 1.0/24; # in days
$cache_limit = 300;
$state_table_name = "states";  # name of state table
$quiz_table_name = "quiz 1";   # name of quiz table
%stateHash=();
### end global variables ###################################

### app logic ##############################################
if($formHash{"request"} eq "begin_quiz"){
    &begin_quiz;
}
elsif($formHash{"request"} eq "grade_question"){
    &grade_question;
}
else{
    &welcome_page;
}
### end app logic ##########################################

#############################################################
### Definitions of app logic functions go here.            #
### Definitions for helper functions:                      #
#    &print_question                                        #
### Definitions for toolkit functions used:                #
#    &get_long_id_db              (new)                     #
#    &write_state_db              (new)                     #
#    &read_state_db               (new)                     #
#    &generate_random_string      (from Section 7.4)        #
#    &errorPage                   (from Section 5.7)        #
#############################################################
```

FIGURE 10.9 The outline of `quiz3.cgi`.

■ The logic is pretty much the same as before: Simply print a question. Note how the question is fetched out of the query object.

```
my ($question, @choices) = $qObj->fetchrow_array();
```

This call assigns `$question` the first element from the fetched row, and assigns to `@choices` the rest of the row. This is easier to work with than fetching the entire row into one array.

```
sub begin_quiz {
  my $sessionID = &get_long_id_db($dbhandle, $state_table_name, $cache_limit,
    $file_life_span);

  %stateHash = ("qnumber"=>1, "correct"=>0);
```

```
  &write_state_db($dbhandle, $state_table_name, $sessionID, %stateHash);

  print <<TOP;
<html><head><title>Trivia Quiz</title></head><body>
    Here is your first question.<br/>
TOP

  &print_question($sessionID, 1);

  print <<BOTTOM;
</body></html>
BOTTOM
}
```

■ Simple enough: `get_long_id_db` creates a state record, and the current quiz state is added to the record.

```
sub grade_question {
  my $sessionID = $formHash{"id"};
  %stateHash = &read_state_db($dbhandle, $state_table_name, $sessionID,
    $time_out);

  ### Get correct answer
  my $sql = "SELECT answer FROM $quiz_table_name WHERE qnumber =
    $stateHash{qnumber}";
  my $qObj = $dbhandle -> prepare($sql) or &errorPage("Can't prepare.");
  $qObj -> execute() or &errorPage("Can't execute " . $qObj->errstr());
  my ($correct_answer) = $qObj->fetchrow_array(); ### one-element array
  qObj -> finish();

  ### Determine total number of questions (rows in quiz1 table)
  $sql = "SELECT qnumber FROM $quiz_table_name";
  $qObj = $dbhandle -> prepare($sql) or &errorPage("Can't prepare.");
  $qObj -> execute() or &errorPage("Can't execute " . $qObj->errstr());
  $qObj -> fetchall_arrayref();
  my $number_of_questions = $qObj->rows();
  $qObj -> finish();

  if ($stateHash{"qnumber"} > $number_of_questions) {
    $sentence = "Quiz is over.";
  }
  elsif($formHash{"qnumber"} < $stateHash{"qnumber"}) { ### don't cheat!
    $sentence = "You have already answered that question.";
  }
  else {
    if($formHash{"answer"} eq $correct_answer) {
      $stateHash{"correct"}++;
      $sentence = "Your answer of $formHash{answer} is CORRECT.<br/>\n";
    }
    else {
      $sentence = "Sorry, your answer of $formHash{answer} is ".
        "INCORRECT.<br/>\n";
    }
    ### update quiz state
    $stateHash{"qnumber"}++; # The next question number.
    &write_state_db($dbhandle, $state_table_name, $sessionID, %stateHash);
  }

  print<<TOP;
<html><head><title>Trivia Quiz</title></head><body>
    $sentence
TOP
  if($stateHash{"qnumber"} > $number_of_questions) {
    print "Your final score is $stateHash{correct} correct",
      " out of $number_of_questions.\n",
```

```
       "Thank you for playing.<br/>\n",
       "<a href=\"$ENV{'SCRIPT_NAME'}?request=begin_quiz\">To play again</a>\n";
    }
    else {
      print "Your score so far is $stateHash{correct} correct out of ",
        $stateHash{qnumber}-1, ".\n",
        "Here is your next question.\n";
      &print_question($sessionID, $stateHash{"qnumber"});
    }
    print<<BOTTOM;
    </body></html>
BOTTOM

  }
```

■ First, get the correct answer to the current question and the total number of questions from the quiz table. The rest of the function is almost the same as before. Recall that two conditional clauses are needed for the main logic of the function so that `write_state_db` can't trigger the `errorPage` function (because of an invalid session ID, for example) after the function prints the top of the HTML page it generates.

*10.9 CSV: A PERL DATABASE EMULATOR

Perl has an interesting module, CSV (for "Comma-Separated Values"), which emulates a database in the following sense. There is no external database software running. The database tables are actually stored in flat structured text files, *very* much like the way we stored the table in Section 10.2. The programmer can issue SQL statements, and the CSV module will interpret those SQL statements and perform appropriate actions on the flat text files. Figure 10.10 shows the concept in general; compare it with Figure 10.7. In a sense, the CSV module plays the role of the database server.

The most important fact is that you construct query objects to issue SQL statements just as before. The only change is in how the initial connection (database handle) is created. Of course, the initial connection details are necessarily different among various database systems anyway.

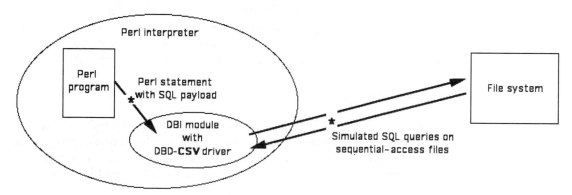

FIGURE 10.10 CSV simulates a database engine.

The main advantage of using CSV is that you do not have to deal with setting up an external database system. This avoids potential complications coming from running the database system daemon as well as the hassles of having to set up users and passwords. This might be ideal for someone who wishes to use database integration but does not have access or permission to use a true database engine. In a classroom setting, CSV can get students using database integration without the logistical issues that come with a database server. Another important use for CSV is in the development process. Indeed, one can use CSV to make sure the entire Web application is running properly. It is then a simple matter to switch over to a true database system.

To use CSV, be sure the Perl driver module `DBD-CSV` is installed. (See Appendix D on installation of Perl modules.) In CSV, a database is just a directory, and a table is stored as one structured text file within that directory. Thus you connect to a CSV database by specifying the name of a directory, which is also the name of the database.

```
$dbhandle = DBI->connect("DBI:CSV:f_dir=database_directory")
```

This call is slightly different from the syntax used for connection to a typical real database system. Be sure there is no trailing slash on the database directory name.

For example, a statement like the following would be used to connect to the quiz of the previous section using CSV for the database system.

```
$dbhandle = DBI->connect("DBI:CSV:f_dir=/home/data/quizdb")
  or send DBI->errstr() message somewhere such as errorPage;
```

After the database handle is created specifying the CSV driver, SQL statements are issued to the DBI module exactly as before. That is the whole point of the Perl `DBI` module: You select the driver, nothing else changes. Thus, the entire `quiz3.cgi` example from the previous section can be redone by changing just *one* line of code in the main part of the program. Figure 10.11 shows the quiz application modified to use CSV with the only change boldfaced. In this version, you would have to make sure that the directory `/home/data/quizdb` on the server has appropriate write permissions.

We end this short section with some advice on creating a database for CSV. Since CSV specifies databases not by name but rather by a directory, to create a new database, you merely have to create that directory manually. Just do so by normal means. If you wish to do it from within Perl, you need to execute a Perl `mkdir` (make directory) command.

```
mkdir "/home/data/database_name", 777;
```

This command gives anyone write permissions to the new directory, which is what you need if the CGI program is to be able to modify data within it at the request of anonymous users. (Normally, to give everyone only read and execute permissions for directory, you would use 755 for the permission code.) This newly created database would then be available for connections.

```
$dbhandle = DBI->connect("DBI:CSV:f_dir=/home/data/database_name")
```

```
┌─────────────────────────────────────────────────────────┐
│ □ ▓      ▒▓ quiz3(CSV).cgi ▓▒         ⊟ ▤ │
├─────────────────────────────────────────────────────┬───┤
│ #! /usr/bin/perl                                    │ ▨ │
│ print "Content-type: text/html\n\n";                │   │
│                                                      │   │
│ ##########################################################│   │
│ #    code for decoding input $datastring into %formHash    #│ ▤ │
│ #       (works for GET, POST, and offline execution)       #│   │
│ ##########################################################│   │
│                                                      │   │
│ ### global variables ####################################│   │
│ use DBI;                                             │   │
│ $dbhandle = DBI->connect("DBI:CSV:f_dir=/home/data/quizdb")│   │
│   or &errorPage("Can't connect to quizdb". DBI->errstr());│   │
│ $file_life_span = 1.0/24; # in days (so is 1 hour)  │   │
│ $time_out = 1.0/24; # in days                       │   │
│ $cache_limit = 300;                                 │   │
│ $state_table_name = "states";   # name of state table│   │
│ $quiz_table_name = "quiz 1";    # name of quiz table │   │
│ %stateHash=();                                      │ ▲ │
│ ### end global variables ############################│ ▼ │
├─────────────────────────────────────────────────┬───┴───┤
│ ▥                                                 │ ◀ ▶ ⌁ │
└─────────────────────────────────────────────────┴───────┘
```

FIGURE 10.11   Changing the driver to CSV.

NOTE

When some database systems (example, Microsoft Access) export their files for use by other applications, they are exported as CSV sequential access files! In their native format, such database files are basically just proprietary binary blobs.

NOTE

Warning: There are some advanced but standard SQL features that the CSV module does not support. These include table column constraints and aggregate functions (see exercises). All the SQL basics presented in this book are supported in CSV.

---

*10.10 PERL ODBC INTERFACE AND MS ACCESS

This section is intended for those interested in using Microsoft Access as the database system in conjunction with Microsoft's IIS or PWS.

Perl does not have a driver specifically for interfacing with Access. However, Perl does have a driver for interfacing with ODBC (Open Database Connectivity)-compliant database systems. (ODBC is a widely accepted application programming interface.) And of course, Access is ODBC-compliant.

Creating a DSN

In order for a Perl program to connect to an MS Access database, you first need to make a DSN (Data Source Name) for the particular database. Go to the Control Panel and open

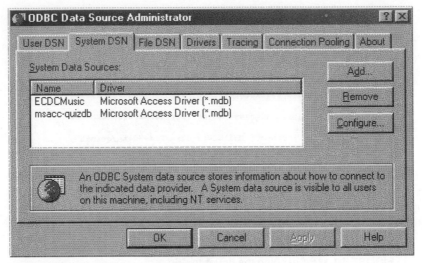

FIGURE 10.12 Available ODBC data source names.

the **ODBC Data Source** control. Be sure to select the **System DSN** tab. Here you see the list of available system DSNs. Note that `msacc-quizdb` is one such DSN in the screenshot in Figure 10.12. Then click **Add** to make a new one. As shown in Figure 10.13, you then see the a list of available drivers. Note that MS Access is one of them. In fact, you can even install a driver for MySQL to make MySQL DSNs. Then double-clicking on the **MS Access** driver selection brings up the window shown in Figure 10.14, which lets you create a DSN. Input the name, and select the database using the **Select** button.

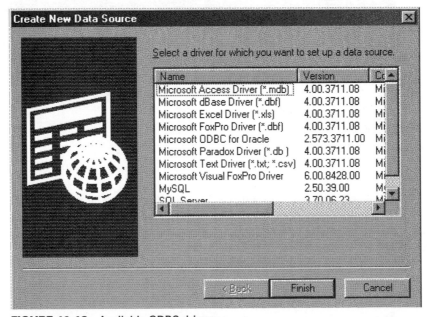

FIGURE 10.13 Available ODBC drivers.

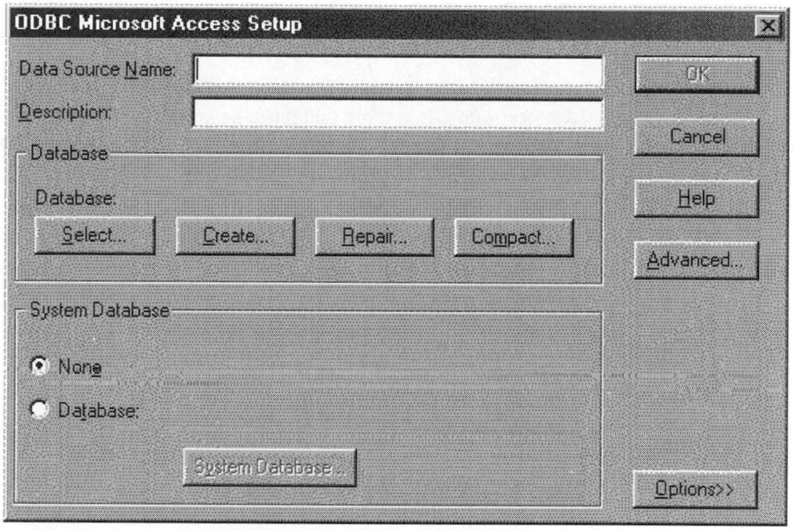

FIGURE 10.14   Creating a new DSN.

Connecting to a DSN Using the Perl DBD-ODBC Driver

Suppose that we have created the msacc-quizdb DSN associated with the MS Access database quizdb. To connect to this in Perl, you first need to make sure that the DBD-ODBC driver module is installed. Then connect to the database using its associated DSN in the following way:

```
use DBI;
$dbhandle = DBI->connect("DBI:ODBC:Data_Source_Name")
  or some error handling;
```

This example assumed that there is no password.

By making just a *one*-line change in the quiz3.cgi application of Section 10.8, we could switch to using an MS Access database with Data Source Name something like msacc-quizdb. Figure 10.15 shows in boldface the only change that would result in the *whole* program.

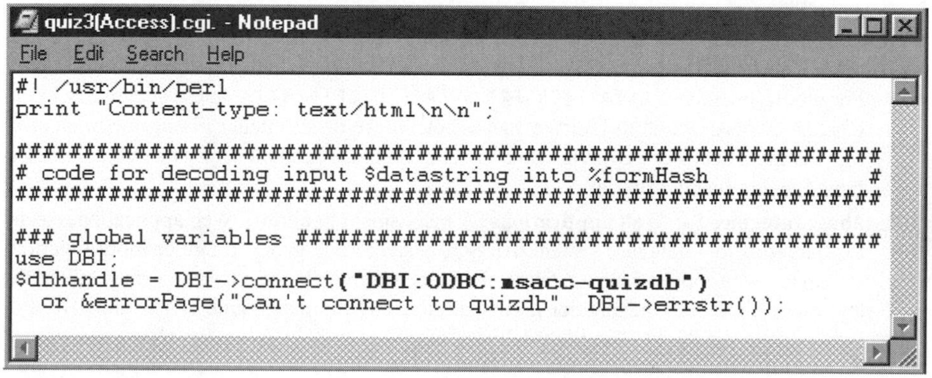

FIGURE 10.15   A Perl program using Microsoft Access for database support.

SUMMARY OF KEY TERMS AND CONCEPTS

Relational data: Data stored in tables in which the rows are called *records* and the columns are called *keys* or *fields*. In a table that has a *primary key* (a column in which no two data values are the same), each record can be retrieved from the table by its unique primary key value. Relationships are created among tables by sharing keys.

Structured text files: Text files (which are stored as sequential-access files by the file system) used for storing data tables by formatting the table records as delimited strings. Programmers can emulate database functionality by writing *data management functions* to automate actions of batch writing, batch reading, updating records, deleting records, and so forth. Because of the sequential storage, such functions involve reading the entire file into memory, ripping it apart, manipulating it, and putting it back together again.

Database storage: Most database systems use direct-access storage for its files in the underlying file system. The database system need only read into memory those disk blocks containing the data it needs. High-level SQL statements are issued to the database system, and it in turn deals with the underlying file system.

Text files versus a database: When the amount of data is small and it need not be manipulated in a complex fashion, structured text files are appropriate for Web applications. The programmer deals directly with the file system, which is fast and incurs little overhead for the system. When the amount of data is large or it needs to be manipulated in a variety of ways, a relational database is the right choice for Web applications. The added data management capabilities and high-level querying language enable robust back-end data support for Web applications.

Three-Tier Web Application: Large Web applications often use third-tier data servers, whose primary job is to run a database system. The second tier is the Web server(s), where data is assembled into information. The first tier contains the client machines, where humans consume the information. Concisely, the three tiers are data management, information assembly, and information consumption. The stratification is still conceptually valid when the third tier is a database system on, or even the file system of, the Web server machine.

Database system: (Also called a *database server* or *database engine*) features server software that listens for queries for information in a *database*: a collection of tables, possibly related to one another, which may be no more than a directory. Most database systems also feature a GUI to facilitate data management through direct access to the databases and tables.

SQL (Structured Query Language): A language used to request data from database systems. This text introduced the following SQL commands, which affect only single tables. For modifying tables: `CREATE, INSERT, UPDATE, DELETE, DROP`. These statements return either a Boolean value to indicate success or failure or an integer giving the number of records modified. For retrieving data: `SELECT`. This command returns a subtable determined by the search criteria.

Database interface for Web applications: A mechanism to allow a Web application to send SQL queries to a database system. An SQL statement is given to one or more functions within the Web application that deliver the SQL statement to the database server. In Perl the `DBI` module provides the functions, whereas other environments, such as ASP and PHP, provide built-in functions. The SQL delivery functions may also require access to different drivers for different database systems. It is up to the native Web programming environment as to how any data returned from the database is made available within a program.

DBI (DataBase Interface) module: A Perl module that provides functions to help prepare and deliver SQL statements to database servers. DBI needs specific *database drivers*, in the form of other Perl modules, in order to interface with various database systems. Returned data is stored in a *query object* within a Perl program. DBI also provides methods to "fetch" the data out of the query object into array or hash variables (or scalar references to arrays or hashes).

State table: A database table that stores data to preserve session state for a Web application between HTTP transactions. State tables can be used with the same functionality as state (text) files, where a *state record* does the job of a state file. We have supplied three toolkit functions that create session IDs, create new state records, read a given state record into a hash, update a given state record, automatically police old state records, and provide for session timeouts.

Database-driven Web application: A Web application some or all of whose data-tier support comes from a relational database. In terms of programming the application, this characteristic affects only the details of how a program interfaces with the data tier. Moreover, in terms of what we have covered so far in this text, a database-driven Web application has no major advantage over one driven by text files. But when data sources become large, the data management tools of database systems become crucial. Moreover, teaming up with SQL enables Web applications to feature robust searching capabilities, as shall be seen in subsequent chapters.

CSV (optional section; Comma-Separated Values): A Perl database emulator that accepts SQL statements but stores its tables in sequential-access files very similar to that shown in Figure 10.1. CSV is very handy for development and testing since a database system need not be installed or running. Changing one line of code can port a program to a more robust database system.

MS Access (optional section): A popular and easy to use desktop database system from Microsoft. After jumping through a few minor hoops, you can run Access to support Web applications if you wish.

EXERCISES

Note: The new toolkit functions (get_long_id_db, write_state_db, read_state_db) can be found on this book's Web site.

1. Devise a *password table* used to record user names and passwords. The record for a user should also contain an access level field (user/admin). Write two toolkit functions, similar in concept to the logon and logon_new toolkit functions from Chapter 7. Both functions should also contain an optional parameter for the access level. If the parameter is not sent to the functions, they default to user level.

   (a) Make a driver program to test the functions.

   (b) Or, adapt the admin.cgi program of Section 7.7 to use the database for all back-end data support, including a state table for logged-on state.

2. The source code for the quiz3.cgi application of Section 10.8 can be obtained from the Web site. Extend it to feature multiple quizzes. Add two extra tables to the quizdb database with quiz topics of your choice. The welcome page should contain a single-selection menu that allows the user to choose an available quiz topic. *Hints:* Assume that any table other than states in the database is a quiz. Use SQL's SHOW TABLES *database_name* statement, which returns a one-column table, to get a listing of tables in the database. Also, you will need to add another column to the state table for the quiz topic.

3. The source code for the `quiz3.cgi` application of Section 10.8 can be obtained from the Web site. Extend the program so that it uses a third table to record quiz results.

   (a) There should be one record for each quiz completed. If someone starts a quiz, but doesn't complete it no record is added. A quiz record should record fields for the answer given to each question and the final score.

   (b) Add a simple logon form to the welcome page that an administrator can use to see the table of completed quizzes. The table should be returned to the browser formatted as an HTML table.

4. Create a database and add a table similar to the `inventory` table shown in Figure 10.16, but with several more rows. Make a Web application as follows:

   (a) The application should read the table and send it to the Web browser formatted as an HTML table.

   (b) The table should show the images rather than the image file names. Find some small icons on the Web. (It doesn't really matter whether the images match the products.)

   (c) There should be three links in the page: one for each of the three columns `sID`, `stock`, and `qtySold`. Each link returns the same page, but with the table sorted according to the particular column.

   (d) Change the link for the `stock` column to a submit button and add a checkbox that goes with it. The checkbox should say something like "Show only low stock." If the button is checked, a subtable is returned to the browser containing only those products whose quantity in stock has fallen to below 10, still sorted according to the `stock` column.

5. Use the `registrar` database shown in Figure 10.16. Add a few more rows to the tables. Note in the `activeCourses` table that there is no primary key. Rather, the first two keys, when used together, are called a *composite primary key*. Together, they uniquely identify a student and course, with the more specific details being in the related tables. Make a Web application as follows:

   (a) The main page has a menu with an item for each student. A form button returns a page with that student's full data: the student record and list of courses the student is enrolled in (with description of courses and midterm grade). Organize this information with HTML table(s) and/or list(s).

   (b) The main page has another menu that lists each course section. A form button returns a complete student listing (with a whole student record and midterm grade) for that course.

   (c) The default student listing should be sorted by students' last names. Some options in the form of part (b) allow the student listing to be returned sorted by midterm grade or student ID number.

   (d) Another option in the form of part (b) can be checked, in which case only a warning list (D or below at midterm) of students is returned.

6. This exercise features applying SQL *aggregate functions* to columns. The syntax is

```
SELECT aggregate_function (column_name) FROM table_name WHERE criteria
```

This returns a one-row table in which the function is applied to all the entries in the column (fitting the criteria) and only one value is returned. The `WHERE` clause is optional, as usual. For example,

```
SELECT AVG(age) FROM customers
```

returns a one-row (and one-column) table consisting of one value, which is the average of all the values in the age column. For this exercise, create a database containing the customers table used throughout this lesson. Add a few more records, at least one of which is under the age of 18.

(a) Write an SQL statement using the AVG aggregate function to find the average of purchases of users in the 18–39 age range.

(b) Write SQL statements to find each of the following: the minimum age, maximum purchases amount, and sum of all purchases for those customers over 18.

Hint: MAX, MIN, SUM are aggregate functions that work like AVG.

(c) Write a Perl program to return an HTML table of all customer records for customers over 18. Also return the statistics collected from parts (a) and (b) somewhere in the page.

(d) Use the aggregate function COUNT to determine the number of rows in a table. This is a superior method to using a plain SELECT, fetching all the rows, and then using the rows method.

7. Create a database containing the students table shown at the end of this section. Create a CGI program that allows students to be added to the table through a Web interface.

(a) The program reads the table into an HTML table. The last row of the table is for a new student. It contains four text fields, one for each column. A submit button causes the new student to be added to the table in the text file and returns the same page but with the new student added.

(b) The program should reject the attempted addition if the new student ID matches one in the file.

(c) Include JavaScript validation so that the form can't be submitted incomplete.

(d) Do not include a text field for the student ID. Rather, generate a new student ID randomly and make sure it doesn't match an existing one.

8. Implement a Web-based remote data management program. Apply the functionality of all the SQL commands we introduced (CREATE, INSERT, UPDATE, DELETE, DROP, SELECT). Start with a database that contains a table similar to the inventory table shown in Figure 10.16.

Table: inventory

pID	desc	stock	qtySold	image
3021	ACME bird seed	12	8	seed.gif
4589	ACME rocket shoes	0	20	shoes.gif

Database: registrar

Table: courses

cID	name	number	dept	sec	enrollment
1000	Calculus I	110	Math	1	30
1001	Web Programming	312	CS	1	24
1002	Web Programming	312	CS	2	21

Table: students

sID	fname	lname	mi
3021	Steve	Luckritz	D
4589	Tim	Kouba	A

Table: activeCourses

sID	cID	midtermGrade
4589	1000	A
4589	1001	B
3021	1000	D

FIGURE 10.16 Data for selected homework exercises.

(a) (DELETE, UPDATE) The main page of the application provides an HTML table containing the data from the database table. To the left of each record is a radio button that allows a given record to be chosen for editing. To the right of each record is a checkbox that allows a record to be marked for deletion. A submit button causes those records marked for deletion to be deleted from the table. If a record is marked for editing, then a form is returned with text fields containing the data values of that record. The text fields can be modified and the record updated. (In case a record is marked for both deletion and modification, the modification takes precedence.)

(b) (INSERT) The main page also contains a form with an "insert" submit button. Clicking that brings up a form (perhaps the same "modify" form from part (a)) that allows a new record to be inserted into the table.

(c) (SELECT) The main page should also contain a form that lets the returned records be filtered. One idea is to allow complete conditions such as stock<=10 to be entered into a text field. Two text fields could even be provided with a menu in between, containing and and or options.

(d) (ADD, DROP) Add a welcome page to the application that contains a menu listing all inventory tables found in the database so that a particular one can be chosen for editing. Also provide a button that will cause the chosen inventory table to be deleted. Include an "are you sure?" alert, using JavaScript, for the delete option.

PROJECT THREAD

Here your application from the Chapter 9 Project Thread is mostly converted to database. The state data, the data for the quiz questions, and the data about the completed quizzes will be stored in database tables. The password data will not be modified, remaining in flat files.

A. Keep all state data in a state table. Of course, be sure that the logged-on states and session timeouts implemented in the Chapter 7 Project Thread still work properly.

B. Store the data for the quiz questions and correct answers in a database table. Record all data for each question in one record in the table (or use related tables appropriately). This will provide for scalability, as we will later augment the quiz database to form a test bank from which the administrator can construct customized quizzes.

C. Rather than storing completed quizzes in separate quiz files, create a database table where each record corresponds to a completed quiz. The primary key should be the user name. You may calculate the cumulative statistics for the administration page straight from this table, or you may use another table to record those. Of course, related tables may be used depending upon how you structure the data.

D. Add a new row for the updated quiz application to the table in your homework page. Make sure you preserve the version from the previous lesson and keep the link to it active. If you are assigned any other exercises from this chapter, add another row to your homework table for each exercise.

REGULAR EXPRESSIONS AND MATCHING

This chapter explores the use of regular expressions in the matching, substitution, and transliteration operators. This combination allows you to do just about anything you want to strings or text files (which are just strings replete with newline characters). Moreover, regular expressions are instrumental for constructing searching utilities for Web applications. As we shall see in the next chapter, that is true whether searching database-driven Web sites or searching through Web sites composed of stand-alone HTML files.

After exploring the fundamentals, this chapter provides an example that parses a Web server log file and generates user statistics. The second main example parses the first paragraphs out of news stories stored in text files. Following the main examples, this lesson explains our standard decoding routine, which parses incoming URL-encoded data strings. These same decoding tactics are used in pretty much the same form by environments like `CGI.pm`, PHP, and ASP.

11.1 THE BINDING AND MATCHING OPERATORS

The **match operator** has the general form

```
m/pattern/
```

and is used to test whether the pattern is found in a string. The **binding operator**, `=~`, is used to "bind" the matching operator onto a string.

```
"yesterday" =~ m/yes/
```

In this case, the pattern is simply the character sequence, `yes`. The entire expression evaluates to a Boolean value, which is true (1) in this case because `yes` is a substring of `"yesterday"`. In general, patterns can be very elaborate, as we shall see in the next section. But in this section, the examples use patterns that are sequences of characters.

Usually, the test string is stored in a scalar variable, and the Boolean expression is used in a conditional.

```
$str="yesterday";
if($str =~ m/yes/) {
  print "The pattern yes was found in $str.\n";
}
```

Rather than using conditionals in all of our examples to demonstrate binding matches onto strings, we stick to the Boolean expressions for simplicity of notation. Using $str as declared in the preceding code the first of the following expressions is true and the second is false.

```
$str =~ m/ester/
$str =~ m/Ester/
```

For the match to return true, the exact pattern must occur in the string. Thus

```
$str =~ m/yet/
```

is also false, even though the characters are found individually in the string.

There is also a negated form of the binding operator.

```
if($response !~ m/yes/){
  print "yes was not found in your response.\n";
}
```

The !~ operator returns true only if the matching action does *not* find the pattern in the string. In general, we will use the standard binding operator, =~, more often than its negated counterpart, !~.

The matching operator can be simplified syntactically. For example, the following two expressions are equivalent.

```
$str =~ m/yes/
$str =~ /yes/
```

We will use the simplified version most of the time. However, you should remember that the m signifies matching in the full syntax version. Later, we will bind operations other than matching onto strings.

In general, match binding has the following syntax (using the syntactically simplified version).

```
string_expression =~ /pattern/
```

So, matching can be bound not only onto string literals and variables, but also onto expressions that evaluate to strings. For example, the following string expression uses concatenation, and the entire Boolean expression is true.

```
$str1="wilde";
$str2="beest";
$str1.$str2 =~ /debe/
```

We conclude this section with an example that does some "platform sniffing." Refer back to Section 6.1 and the HTTP_USER_AGENT environment variable shown in Figures 6.2 and 6.3. It would be somewhat difficult to determine the user's platform using only standard string operations because of all of the extra "junk" contained in that variable. However, with

```
os.cgi

#! /usr/bin/perl
print "Content-type: text/html\n\n";

$info = $ENV{"HTTP_USER_AGENT"};

print<<TOP;
<html><head><title>Your operating system</title></head><body>
TOP

if($info =~ /Windows/){
  print "You seem to be running a Windows operating system.\n";
}
elsif($info =~ /Mac/){
  print "You seem to be running a Macintosh operating system.\n";
}
elsif($info =~ /(Unix|Linux)/){
  print "You seem to be running a Unix or Linux operating system.\n";
}
else{
  print "I cannot tell what operating system you are running.\n";
}

print<<BOTTOM;
 </body></html>
BOTTOM
```

Your operating system - Microsoft Internet Explorer

File Edit View Favorites Tools Help

Address http://www.uweb.edu/os.cgi   Go

You seem to be running a Windows operating system.

Netscape: Your operating system

Go To: http://www.uweb.edu/os.cgi   What's Related

You seem to be running a Macintosh operating system.

FIGURE 11.1 A simple platform-sniffing program.

pattern matching, the problem becomes almost trivial. Figure 11.1 shows the platform-sniffing program and two sample calls to it from different platforms. A brief outline of the program follows. In particular, we have slipped in a pattern that's more than just a sequence of characters (in the last elsif clause) in order to foreshadow the versatility of pattern matching.

■ Store the value in the environment hash for `HTTP_USER_AGENT` into `$info`.

■ Test to see if `$info` matches "Windows", "Mac", or one of "Unix" or "Linux". In the latter case (`Unix|Linux`) is a pattern that stands for either "Unix" or "Linux". So the matching operator returns true if one or the other is found. This is an example of a pattern that is more than merely a sequence of characters.

11.2 REGULAR EXPRESSIONS

A **regular expression** is a set of rules that defines a set of possible matching strings. Those rules provide for the use of escape characters, wildcards, character classes, and quantifiers, just to name a few. Many programming languages have libraries that can be used to implement regular expressions, but regular expressions are a standard feature in Perl and are particularly versatile and powerful. For simplicity, we refer to regular expressions as *patterns*.

Patterns are processed like double-quoted strings to the extent that variables are interpolated and the standard escape sequences are interpreted. Note that quotes are not used to delimit a pattern, but rather the `//` symbols. The quantifiers, qualifiers, and other special rules that build patterns come in various flavors, so this section is divided into smaller sections to help categorize various pattern-matching features.

Metacharacters

In a pattern, the following characters have special meaning:

```
[ ] ( ) { } | \ + ? . * ^ $
```

These are called **metacharacters** in the context of pattern matching. If used literally inside a pattern, their special meaning must be escaped, as demonstrated below.

```
if($sentence =~ m/\?/){
  print "Your sentence seems to be a question.\n";
}
```

Here, we just tested to see whether the sentence contained a question mark character. Usually, we won't need to test for metacharacter matches, but we will use them to add great flexibility to patterns.

Normal Characters

These include ordinary ASCII characters that are not metacharacters. That includes letters, numbers, the underscore, and a few other characters such as (@ % & = ; : ,) that are not reserved metacharacters in patterns. Normal characters need not be escaped when testing for matches. Contrast the following example with the one in the previous section, where we had to escape the metacharacter ? in order to search for it.

```
if($sentence =~ m/;/){
  print "Your sentence seems to contain an independent clause.\n";
}
```

Note that $ has to be a metacharacter since scalar variables are interpolated inside patterns. However, % and @ are normal characters in patterns (arrays and hashes are never interpolated).

Escaped Characters

A backslash followed by a nonalphanumeric character stands for that character with no other meaning. Metacharacters must be escaped in patterns. For example, * stands for one *, and \(stands for one (. The following tests whether $str contains the three-character string "(b)".

```
$str =~ /\(b\)/              true: "(b)" , "(a)(b)(c)"
                             false: "(ab)" , "( b )"
```

Here the strings following "true:" are examples of values of $str for which the expression is true, and the ones following "false:" are examples of $str values that make the expression false. We will continue to provide examples and counterexamples in this manner.

Escape Sequences That Stand for One Character

As we saw in Section 4.2, \n stands for one newline character, and \t stands for one tab character. In general, it's a bad idea to escape other alphanumeric characters, because the escape sequence might have special meaning. The following tests whether $str contains two consecutive newline characters.

```
$str =~ /\n\n/               true: "a\n\nb" , "a\n\n\n\tb"
                             false: "\na\n" , "a\n \nb"
```

Escape Sequences That Stand for a Class of Characters

Each escape character in Table 11.1 represents only one character in a pattern, but that character matches any character in the specified group. The following tests whether $str contains a four-character sequence that looks like a year in the 1900s.

```
$str =~ /19\d\d/             true: "1921" , "34192176"
                             false: "191a" , "34192-76"
```

The following tests whether $str is not the empty string or merely a sequence of whitespace characters.

```
$str =~ /\S/                 true: "x" , "()"
                             false: "" , "   " , "\n"
```

Wildcard

A period . stands for any one character, except a newline. The following tests whether $str contains a three-character substring that is c and t with anything in between, *except* a newline.

```
$str =~ /c.t/                true: "cat" , "arc&tangent"
                             false: "ct" , "cart" , "arc\ntangent"
```

TABLE 11.1 Escape Sequences That Stand for Classes of Characters

SEQUENCE	STANDS FOR
\d	Any digit (0 through 9)
\D	Any character that is not a digit
\w	Any alphanumeric character: letter, digit, underscore (w comes from "word")
\W	Any character that is *not* alphanumeric (opposite of \w)
\s	one whitespace character (blank space, tab, or newline)
\S	One nonwhitespace character (opposite of \s)

TABLE 11.2 Escape Sequences That Match Locations in Pattern

SEQUENCE	STANDS FOR
\A	Beginning of string
\Z	End of string or before a final newline character
\z	End of string
\b	Word boundary
\B	Not a word boundary (thus location between two \w type characters)

Escape Sequences That Match Locations

Each escape character in Table 11.2 does not actually represent a character in a pattern. Rather, they represent locations within patterns. The following tests whether $str begins with "T".

```
$str =~ /\AT/              true:"Tom" , "The beest"
                           false: "tom" , "AT&T"
```

The following tests whether $str begins with "The".

```
$str =~ /\AThe/            true:"Thelma" , "The beest"
                           false: "That" , "the beest"
```

The following tests whether $str contains the word "cat" but not as part of any bigger word.

```
$str =~ /\bcat\b/          true:"cat" , "my cat"
                           false: "cats" , "concatenate"
```

Note that when matching locations, the escape sequence does not "use up" a character. That is, an expression such as

```
$str =~ /ing\z/
```

tests only for the three-character string "ing" at the end of $str.

We should mention that the metacharacter ^ is equivalent to \A, and that the metacharacter $ (when not interpreted as part of a scalar variable) is equivalent to \Z.

Character Classes

Square brackets [] in a pattern define a class. The whole class matches only one character, and only if the character belongs to the class. The following tests whether $str contains a *three-character* string beginning with one of r, b, or c, and followed by at.

```
$str =~ /[rbc]at/   true: "rat" , "bat" , "cat" , "concatenate" , "battery"
                    false: "mat" , "at"
```

The escape sequences \d, \w, and \s and their opposites can be used inside a class. A hyphen (-) can be used between two characters to denote a range of characters. For example, the class

```
[\dA-F]
```

stands for one character that is either a numeric digit or one of the uppercase letters A–F. It is a concise representation of the class [0123456789ABCDEF], which matches only a single hexadecimal digit. For example, the following tests whether the string contains a two-digit hexadecimal number as formatted in query string encoding.

```
$str =~ /%[\dA-F][\dA-F]/   true: "%0A" , "data=Hi,%0A%0Dmy name is..."
                            false: "%0a" , "%3"
```

A ^ character at the beginning of a class effectively negates the class. However, a ^ character not at the beginning of a class just stands for itself as a character. For example, [^0-9] is one character that is the same as a \D character. However, [a^] is one character that matches either one of "a" or "^".

Alternatives

It was, in fact, a simple alternative that we used in the platform-sniffing example of Figure 11.1 to test for UNIX or Linux. The | character serves like an or by creating alternatives. For example, the following tests whether $str contains any of the three patterns.

```
$str =~ /cat|dog|ferret/   true: "cat" , "dog" , "ferret" , "my cat" ,
                                 "cats and dogs" , "doggedly"
                           false: "hamster" , "dodge the cart"
```

The alternatives are tested from left to right. Also, the alternatives themselves can be more complicated patterns.

Grouping and Capturing

Parentheses () are used for grouping in patterns. Grouping is particularly useful in conjunction with testing for alternatives. For example, the following tests whether $str contains one of the three alternatives, then a space, then food.

```
$str =~ /(cat|dog|ferret) food/   true: "cat food" , "dog food" , "ferret food" ,
                                        "I like cat food and dog food"
                                  false: "cats food" , "rat food" , "dogfood"
```

An important side effect of grouping alternatives is capturing. With several alternatives, it is often desirable to capture which of the alternatives caused the successful match. That is, a mere truth value indicating a match doesn't indicate which match actually occurred.

Perl provides the special, built-in variables $1, $2, $3, . . ., which can automatically capture an alternative that provides a successful match. For example, when

```
"Do you have ferret food?" =~ /(cat|dog|ferret) food/
```

is evaluated, $1 is assigned the value "ferret", because that alternative provides the match. Note that if more than one match is present, only the leftmost match is recorded, because alternatives are processed from left to right. Here,

```
"Do you have dog food or ferret food?" =~ /(cat|dog|ferret) food/
```

assigns "dog" to $1, but leaves $2 empty.

For another example, when

```
"Purina cat chow" =~ /(cat|dog|ferret) (food|chow)/
```

is evaluated, $1 is assigned the value "cat" and $2 is assigned the value "chow". Captured matches are assigned into the special variables starting from the leftmost grouping of alternatives.

To illustrate the last point further, consider the following expression, where the two groups are themselves collected into a group

```
"Purina cat chow" =~ /((cat|dog|ferret) (food|chow))/
```

In this case, $1 is assigned "cat chow", $2 is assigned "cat", and $3 is assigned "chow". The leftmost grouping symbol is for the whole group, so that group captures both matches from its constituent groups into the first special variable.

Alternatives are very useful, because they provide for a Boolean (or) capability in pattern matching. Moreover, grouping them is very useful, because you often want to know which match was found, not just that one occurred.

The disadvantage to this approach is that multiple matches that may occur within a given group are not recorded (see the "Do you have dog food or ferret food?" example above). One remedy for that is to use global matching, which is explored in Section 11.3.

Other Special Variables

Consider the following expression:

```
"I like cats and bats." =~ /[rbc]at/
```

Note that even though bat is a valid match, the expression returns true as soon as the leftmost match, cat, is detected. The match "cat" is captured into the special variable $& (match), the part before the match is stored into $` (prematch), and the part after the match is stored into $' (postmatch). So, $` contains "I like " and $' contains "s and bats".

In general, for any successful match, the original string is equivalent to the concatenation of the three special variables.

```
$` . $& . $'
```

Quantifiers

The quantifiers in Table 11.3 always follow the character that they quantify. That is, the quantified character always precedes the quantifier. If a quantifier follows a class of characters, that class is also quantified. The following tests whether $str contains at least one b character in between an a and c.

```
$str =~ /ab+c/   true: "abc", "abbc" , "abbbc" , "aabcc"
                 false: "ac" , "aBc"
```

The following tests whether $str contains a sequence of exactly three b characters in between an a and c.

```
$str =~ /ab{3}c/   true: "abbbc", "aabbbcc"
                   false: "abbc" , "abbbbc"
```

The following tests whether $str contains a sequence of at least two b characters in between an a and c.

```
$str =~ /ab{2,}c/   true: "abbc", "abbbc" , "aabbbbcc"
                    false: "abc" , "aBBc"
```

Quantifiers can be combined with special escape sequences to create some rather interesting matching possibilities. The following tests to see whether $str contains an alphanumeric word (chunk of consecutive alphanumeric characters).

```
$str =~ /\w+/   true: "beest", "1234" , "R2D2" , "x" , "##xyz##"
                false: "####" , "" , "  "
```

In the "##xyz##" example the word is xyz, and that would be stored in the match variable $&.

TABLE 11.3   Quantifiers in Perl Regular Expressions

QUANTIFIER	MEANING
+	Occurrence one or more times (consecutively)
?	Occurrence zero or one times (consecutively)
*	Occurrence zero or more times (consecutively)
{n}	Occurrence exactly n times (consecutively)
{n,}	Occurrence at least n times (consecutively)
{n,m}	Occurrence at least n and at most m times (consecutively)

The following tests to see whether $str contains one or more consecutive digits (that is, whether there is an integer inside).

```
$str =~ /\d+/   true: "1", "121 Elm. St." , "R2D2" , "##1##" , "3.14"
                false: "a" , "####" , "" , "  "
```

In the "3.14" example there are two matches, but only the leftmost match, "3", is stored into the match variable $&.

The following tests to see whether $str contains a substring that looks like a (possibly negative) integer. That is, does $str contain zero or one - characters, followed by one or more consecutive digits.

```
$str =~ /-?\d+/   true: "2", "-2" , "-3.14" , "3-21.7"
                  false: "xyx" , "x-y" , "4-x"
```

In the "3-21.7" example, the only match, "3", is stored into the match variable $&. Similarly,

```
$str =~ /\s+/   true: " ", "   " , " xyy" , "The End"
                false: "" , "xyz" , "TheEnd"
```

tests to see whether there is at least one whitespace character in $str.

Here is an example of a quantifier applied to a class of characters.

[\da-fA-F]{2}

This expression matches any two-digit hexadecimal number. That is, it matches any occurrence of two consecutive characters from the class `[0123456789abcdefABCDEF]`. The quantified pattern is equivalent to the longer pattern `[\da-fA-F][\da-fA-F]`.

Quantifiers even can be used in conjunction with grouping symbols to quantify which characters are captured. Suppose we have dates that are roughly formatted, but in the general form

month_name day_number, year

and we need to extract components of the date. The following expression tests whether $date contains (a group of one or more letters, lower- or uppercase), followed by one or more spaces, followed by (a group of one or more digits), followed by a comma and then zero or more spaces, followed by (a group of one or more digits).

```
$date =~ /([a-zA-Z]+)\s+(\d+),\s*(\d+)/
```

The previous sentence includes the parentheses that surround the groups in the pattern, because we wish to emphasize that successful group matches are captured into the special variables $1, $2, ... Since there are three groups, the month is captured into $1, the day into $2, and the year in $3. The use of quantifiers has given the expression enough flexibility to capture both of the following dates.

```
jan 1,2002
MARCH 22,  02
```

Note that, in contrast to back references (see the optional last subsection in this section), the matches in a quantified match do not have to be the same. For example,

```
/([ab])\1/
```

matches only a a or b b (or any larger string containing one of those two patterns). In contrast,

```
/([ab]){2}/
```

matches any of a a, a b, b a, or b b (or any larger string containing one of those four patterns).

Quantifiers Are Greedy By Default

By default, a quantified pattern will attempt to match as much as possible. (That is, Matching is "greedy.") For example, the following expression tests for a < character, followed by one or more of anything (wildcard), followed by a > character.

```
"<h1>Title</h1>" =~ /<.+>/
```

The quantifier's greediness passes up "<h1>", which would otherwise be a match. So the pattern matches the whole string.

If you want to match as little as possible, put an extra ? character after the quantifier. For example, if we want to find only HTML tags, we would use the pattern <.+?>, which basically says, "Test for a < character followed by one or more of anything until *the first* > character is found."

Using that idea,

```
"<h1>Title</h1>" =~ /<.+?>/
```

matches only "<h1>". Of course, that match gets stored in the special match variable $&.

This greediness applies in other situations, not just with the wildcard. For example, the following pattern (0 or more word characters followed by an x) matches the whole string.

```
"abxcdx" =~ /\w*x/;
```

The greediness passes up "abx", which would otherwise be a match. Making the quantifier stingy, \w*?x, would then match only "abx".

In summary, a ? character after a quantifier makes it nongreedy. That is different from using ? following a nonquantifier character, in which case it is itself a quantifier.

Case-Insensitive Matching

The behavior of the matching operator can be altered by using a **command modifier**, which is placed after the operator:

string_expression =~ /*pattern*/*command_modifier*

The only command modifier we use in this section is i, which specifies that the matching should be done in a case-*in*sensitive fashion. A simple example suffices to exemplify its use:

```
if($str =~ /be/i) {
  print "The string contains either be, Be, bE, or BE.";
}
```

*Back References

Back references (\1, \2, and so forth) refer to previously captured matches. \1 refers to the first captured match, \2 to the second, and so forth. They are particularly useful when looking for two or more of something. For a simple example, the following picks out the first occurrence of a character that appears twice in a row.

```
"Mississippi" =~ /(.)\1/;
```

When the grouping symbols capture any character, \1 then references that character. Thus, this pattern is two characters in a row, of which the second one has to match the first. When this two-character pattern finds the first match, the captured wildcard is stored into $1, which in this case would contain s.

The following pattern is a bit more involved. It picks out matching beginning and ending HTML tags from a string.

```
"<h1>Title</h1>" =~ /<(.+?)>(.*?)<\/\1>/
```

The name of the start tag is captured, then the back reference is used for the name of the end tag. Since there are two groups in this pattern, $1 would contain the tag name, and $2 would contain the text between the two tags.

The reason the different reference notation (\1 instead of $1) is needed is because $1 would be interpolated inside the pattern using the value of $1 from a previous match!

11.3 PATTERNS IN LIST CONTEXT

In list context a statement such as the following,

```
@array = ($str =~ /pattern/);
```

stores the list of the special ($1, $2, ...) capturing variables into the @array only if there are grouped expressions in the *pattern* to capture matches. Otherwise, if there are no grouped expressions, either (1) or () is returned into the @array depending upon whether there are successful matches or not.

For example, consider the following statement:

```
@array = ("Purina cat chow" =~ /((cat|dog|ferret) (food|chow))/);
```

This test results in the matched values being assigned to the @array as the following list.

```
("cat chow" , "cat" , "chow")
```

Just as in the scalar-context matching in the previous section, the matches are returned beginning from the leftmost grouping. Really, the only difference here is that the special capturing variables ($1, $2,...) are stored as an array.

A more common use of list context is in conjunction with the g command modifier, which indicates the matching should be done *globally*.

```
@array= ($str =~ /pattern/g);
```

When there are *no* grouped expressions in the pattern, the returned list contains all successful matches. Although global matching doesn't exploit the strength of grouped alternatives, returning all successful matches in a string is often more desirable than finding only the first match in a group of alternatives.

For example,

```
@array = ("an example" =~ /a../g);
```

results in the list ("an ","amp") being assigned to the @array. Indeed, those are all the three-character strings in "an example" that consist of an a character followed by any other two characters.

The following statement parses out all of the HTML tags and stores them as elements of the @tags array:

```
@tags = ("<h1>Title</h1>" =~ /<.+?>/g);
```

Thus, @tags contains the list ("<h1>", "</h1>"). The following statement plucks out all of the alphanumeric words from $str and stores them into the @words array:

```
@words = ($str =~ /\w+/g);
```

That is, every substring of $str matching at least one alphanumeric character is parsed out.

Suppose $document is a (perhaps long) string that contains some text document, and suppose we want to pull out all the Social Security numbers from the document. If we assume that Social Security numbers look like "123-45-6789", then a solution is

```
@soc_numbers= ($document =~ /\d{3}-\d{2}-\d{4}/g);
```

But what if the Social Security numbers are inconsistent in that some are missing the hyphens? Then a solution is

```
@soc_numbers= ($document =~ /\d{3}-?\d{2}-?\d{4}/g);
```

where only zero or more dashes need to appear in the pattern between the quantified numbers.

> **NOTE**
>
> When using a complicated pattern, especially one that involves locations or quantifiers, always thoroughly test your pattern on several revealing test strings.

We conclude this section by introducing two very useful functions that take patterns and return lists. We have actually used the `split` function on several occasions, but we can now present its general form in Table 11.4.

One use we have made for the `split` function is to split the encoded data string that is submitted from an HTML form. The `&`-delimited name=value pairs are split out of the `$datastring`.

```
@nameValuePairs = split( /&/, $datastring);
```

Now you can see that the delimiting character was actually sent to the function as a one-character pattern. Each name=value pair was also split apart around the `/=/` pattern this way.

A string with more complicated delimiting patterns can also be split:

```
$str = "23:22::455:98:::85";
@numbers = split( /:+/ , $str);
```

In this case, a delimiter is one or more colons.

We now provide an example using the `grep` function. Suppose we have an array of Web addresses stored in `@domains`, and we wish to filter out only those addresses in the ".edu" domain. One simple `grep` call does the job:

```
@edu_sites= grep (/\.edu/, @domains);
```

Only those Web addresses in `@domains` that contain ".edu" as a substring are assigned as elements of `@edu_sites`. Notice that we had to escape the period, which is a wildcard in a pattern otherwise. The `grep` function is actually much more powerful. (This is still pretty good!) We have supplied only a limited definition of the function.

TABLE 11.4 The `split` and `grep` Function

TCH	TCH
`split` (*pattern, string*)	Returns a list consisting of the fields (the substrings not used in any matches) between successful matches of the pattern against the string. Trailing empty fields are omitted.
`split` (*pattern, string, limit*)	Returns a list with at most limit number of fields.
`grep` (*pattern, list*);	Returns a list consisting of those elements in the given list that successfully matched the pattern (`grep` stands for "get regular expression pattern")

11.4   ANALYZING LOG FILES

This section introduces Web server log files and explores extracting information from them. Recall Section 6.1, where we introduced the server's environment variables and indicated that many of them are written to log files on the server. Indeed, we have used only a few of the environment variables while building Web applications.

Figure 11.2 shows a typical log file. The figure shows part of the actual `accesslog` file for `www.cknuckles.com`. You can see that a given transaction causes several lines to be written to the file. First, the "hit" for a certain page is recorded. Following that are lines containing the subsequent requests for that page's images, made by the browser as it parses the HTML file it receives.

Each line in the file contains a number of fields, and the various fields are separated by one or more spaces. Thus, the individual fields on a line can be recovered by splitting it at the spaces. The desired Perl statement is

```
@fields = split (/\s+/, $line);
```

which splits a given `$line` around one or more white spaces. So `@fields` contains all of the resulting fields. Table 11.5 shows the fields in a standard access log and exemplifies each of the fields using the first line of the file in Figure 11.2.

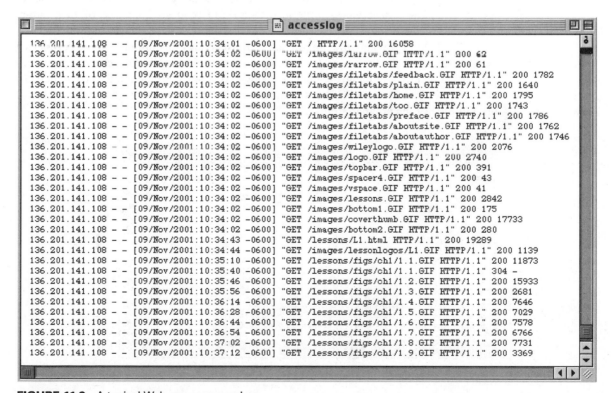

FIGURE 11.2   A typical Web server access log.

TABLE 11.5 Contents of a Line of a Standard Access Log

FIELD	FIRST LINE	MEANING
$field[0]	136.201.141.108	Address (either IP or name) of client
$field[1]	–	Not used any more
$field[2]	–	Not used any more
$field[3]	[09/Nov/2001:10:34:01	Date and time
$field[4]	-0600]	Time zone
$field[5]	"GET"	Request method
$field[6]	/	Relative part of URL (in this case the default file in the root public directory of www.cknuckles.com)
$field[7]	HTTP/1.1	"HTTP version"
$field[8]	200	Status code (success code or error code)
$field[9]	16058	Number of bytes transferred

This information commonly is used to ascertain certain facts about a particular Web site. The desired information includes the number of hits, the number of hits from unique clients, the average number of hits per day, the number of hits for certain URLs, the number of error codes returned, and so forth.

Our only example in this section counts the total number of hits and the number of unique clients who have accessed the server via HTTP requests. The heart of the program is calculating those two numbers. To count the hits, see how many lines are in the file. The main idea behind counting the unique hits is to use a hash to store the client address as a key. The associated value we assign in the hash is not relevant. When a client repeats, setting the same key will not generate a new key for the hash. So the number of unique clients will just be the number of keys in the hash. The program is shown in Figure 11.3. A brief outline of the program follows.

```
hitcount.pl

open(LOGFILE, "accesslog.txt") or print "Can't open access log";

$totalHits = 0;
%addressHash = ();

while($line = <LOGFILE>) {
  @fields = split(/\s+/, $line);
  $addressHash{$fields[0]} = 1;
  $totalHits++;
}
close(LOGFILE);

$uniqueHits = keys %addressHash;
print "The total number of hits is $totalHits\n";
print "The number of unique clients is $uniqueHits\n";
```

FIGURE 11.3 A program that analyzes the access log.

- Open the log file for reading. The path to the file could be longer. This program is intended to be run offline, so we simply print an error massage. Such a program could be executed online, but it is usually the server administrator who runs such programs.
- While there are still lines in the file (because log files are typically huge, it's better to process the file line by line rather than hogging up memory by storing the whole file into an array).
  - Split each line into the separate fields.
  - Create a new hash key to store the address. The value is irrelevant. If the hash already has a key with that address, a new hash entry is not added.
  - Add 1 to the counter that counts lines in the file.
- The keys function returns the array of keys, so storing that into a scalar results in the number of keys (unique addresses).
- Print some results.

NOTE

Examining log files is a common way of compiling demographics for a given Web site. In fact, there are numerous shareware and commercial log analysis tools that server administrators can use to extract very detailed information. For example, it might be desirable to know the average number of hits per day, the total hits in a week, or how many hits certain pages in a site get relative to others. Of course, if Web pages are generated using CGI programs, one could include a hit counter similar to the example in Section 5.7 for each page. But that records only a very limited amount of information.

That example, where a hit is counted every time a page is loaded (that is, when the CGI program is called), contrasts with the definition of a hit as used in this example. Here, the unique-visitor count is right on target, but the hit counter drastically exaggerates the count. Actually, the first 19 lines in Figure 11.2 are from one hit. The first line reflects a hit on the home page, but the next 18 lines reflect the browser requests for the 18 GIFs used in the page. (Some sites you see on the Web actually report their popularity—erroneously— in that manner.) Most good log analyzer tools take a more realistic view of hits—perhaps one hit from a given IP address per hour or day. We have provided an exercise that considers such things.

11.5   THE SUBSTITUTION AND TRANSLITERATION OPERATORS

The general form of the **substitution operator** is

$scalar_variable =~ s/pattern/replacement_string/command_modifiers;

The binding operator "binds" the substitution onto the scalar variable. Note that the s signifies the substitution operator s/// and that it effectively takes two arguments (in contrast to the match operator m//). This operator attempts to find a match for the *pattern* in the $*scalar_variable*, and if successful, replaces the match with the *replacement_string*. Thus, the scalar variable is altered if a successful match is found. In contrast, the match operator does not alter the scalar variable onto which it is bound.

For a simple example using only characters, the following attempts to replace "the" with "my".

```
$str = "the cat in the hat";
$str =~ s/the/my/;
```

This causes $str to contain "my cat in the hat". By default, only the leftmost occurrence is replaced. The g (global) command modifier can easily override the default behavior, causing the substitutions to be made globally. So

```
$str = "the cat in the hat";
$str =~ s/the/my/g;
```

causes $str to contain "my cat in my hat".

As with patterns, the replacement string is also processed as a double-quoted string. So, any variables are interpolated, and standard ASCII escape sequences may be used in the replacement string. The rules for the pattern are exactly the same as we outlined them in Section 11.2. For example,

```
$str =~ s/(cat|dog)/ferret/;
```

replaces an occurrence of cat or dog with ferret. So

```
$str = "puppy dog category";
$str =~ s/(cat|dog)/ferret/;
```

results in $str having the value "puppy ferret category". Again, only the leftmost occurrence is replaced. Using global substitution,

```
$str = "puppy dog category";
$str =~ s/(cat|dog)/ferret/g;
```

the final value of $str is "puppy ferret ferretegory". In all occurrences of cat or dog are replaced.

Substitution can also be used to replace any found matches with the empty string. For example, the following replaces all whitespace characters with the empty string.

```
$str = "h e l  l  o";
$str =~s/\s//g;
```

Of course, the result is that $str contains "hello".

The command modifiers, when used in substitution, are conceptually the same as when used in pattern matching. We have already seen that by performing global substitutions. The case-insensitive command modifier, i, can also be used to perform substitutions in which the case of characters is ignored.

Recall that the special variables $1, $2, . . . capture matches from grouped expressions. These variables can also be used to insert matches found in the pattern into the replacement string. For example, the following captures words (one or more alphanumeric characters in sequence) and adds an s onto each matched word in the replacement string.

```
$str = "puppy dog category";
$str =~s/(\w+)/$1s/g;
```

This results in $str having the value "puppys dogs categorys". In global substitutions, matches are found one at a time and replaced with the replacement string. So, for each match, $1 captures that match. If there were two grouped expressions in the pattern, then $1 and $2 would capture the matches. In general, such use of the capturing in substitutions is useful when part of what was matched needs to be left alone. (For example, two or more capturing groups are used to permute matched parts.)

This section concludes with a quick overview of the *transliteration operator*. Its general form is

$scalar_variable =~ tr/*search_characters*/*replacement_characters*/;

Note that the transliteration operator tr/// takes two arguments, like the substitution operator. It can use command modifiers, but we have no use for them here. This operator automatically makes global substitutions, replacing the search characters with the corresponding replacement characters. It does not use patterns.

Transliteration is often done using single characters. Thus

```
$str = "the cat in the hat";
$str =~ tr/a/u/;
```

results in $str containing the value "the cut in the hut": All of the a characters are transliterated into u characters.

When the transliteration operator is used with more characters, the characters are transliterated in sequence. For example,

```
$str = "the cat in the hat";
$str =~ tr/ac/ur/;
```

results in $str containing the value "the rut in the hut". All occurrences of a are replaced with u, and all occurrences of c are replaced with r. The transliterations are done in the order in which the characters are given.

Similar transliterations could be accomplished using the substitution operator and patterns. The main advantages of this operator are that most special symbols (except / and \) need not be escaped, because they are simply treated as characters, and if more than one character needs to be transliterated, then the transliteration operator accomplishes the substitutions in one line of code rather than in several lines of substitution code.

11.6 PARTIAL CONTENT RENDERING

Another practical text-file parsing example is motivated by online news sites that deliver a lot of different news stories and wish to show only the portion of each story initially. An execution of the example we present is shown in Figures 11.4 and 11.5. Both to save space and to pique a surfer's interest in a story, only the first two paragraphs (combined together) of each news story are on display in the main page. The reader can simply hit a "full story" link to read the whole story. You have no doubt encountered this online. We have fabricated the expression **partial content rendering** to describe this rendering strategy succinctly. Only a portion of a file is extracted for rendition in a browser.

This news site is built dynamically, in the sense that there is no predetermined number of news stories. Rather, the number of stories is determined by the number of files in a

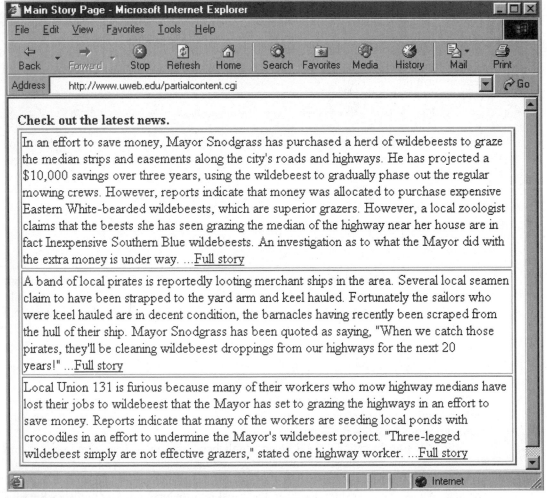

FIGURE 11.4 A news site with partial stories on the main page.

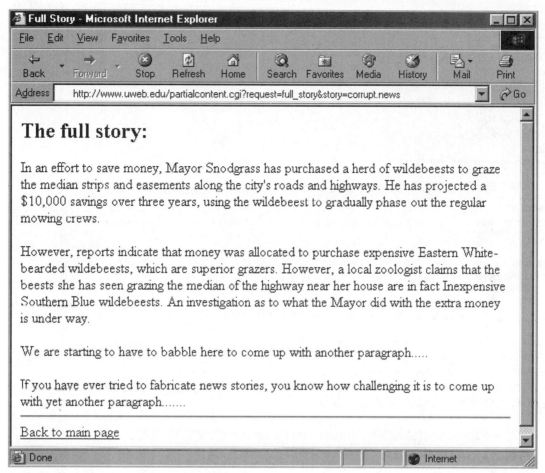

FIGURE 11.5   A full story from the news site.

directory. The news stories are stored in plain text files, as shown in Figure 11.6. Although we don't formally cover directory scanning until the next chapter, reading all the file names in a given directory is very simple.

In this case, the directory contains three story files, each with the .news extension. We have added a news story that is not yet ready and two other weird directories to make the point that we must be sure to grab only news stories out of the directory. In general, this is a factor, because some systems—UNIX/Linux in particular—automatically add . and .. directories[1] as part of the file system.

The outline of the program is provided in Figure 11.7. The app logic is typical, so we forgo a transaction diagram. One function prints the main page, and the other delivers full news stories. Near the top, a global variable is initialized with the full path to the directory containing the news stories. The two app logoc functions follow, with explanations.

---

[1]This is actually a sticky point, because many telnet and FTP clients won't even show you those directories by default, even though they are there.

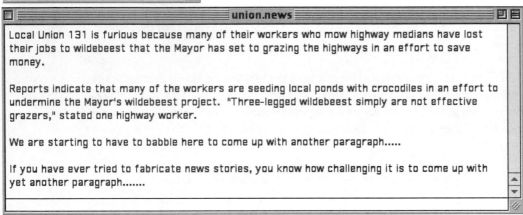

Local Union 131 is furious because many of their workers who mow highway medians have lost their jobs to wildebeest that the Mayor has set to grazing the highways in an effort to save money.

Reports indicate that many of the workers are seeding local ponds with crocodiles in an effort to undermine the Mayor's wildebeest project. "Three-legged wildebeest simply are not effective grazers," stated one highway worker.

We are starting to have to babble here to come up with another paragraph.....

If you have ever tried to fabricate news stories, you know how challenging it is to come up with yet another paragraph.......

FIGURE 11.6 A news story and the newsStories directory.

```perl
#! /usr/bin/perl
print "Content-type: text/html\n\n";

###########################################################
#    code for decoding input $datastring into %formHash   #
#       (works for GET, POST, and offline execution)      #
###########################################################

$storyDataDir = "/path/to/newsStories/";

### app logic ############################################
if($formHash{"request"} eq "full_story"){
    &full_story;
}
else{
    &main_page;
}
### end app logic ########################################

###########################################################
### Definitions of app logic functions go here.          #
### Definitions for toolkit functions used:               #
#    &errorPage          (from Section 5.7)               #
###########################################################
```

FIGURE 11.7 The outline of the news application.

```perl
sub main_page {
  print <<TOP;
<html><head><title>Main Story Page</title></head><body>
  <b>Check out the latest news.</b>
  <table border="2">
TOP

  opendir(DIRECTORYHANDLE, "$storyDataDir");
  @storyFiles = readdir(DIRECTORYHANDLE);
  closedir(DIRECTORYHANDLE);

  @storyFiles = grep (/\.news/ , @storyFiles); # only want .news files

  foreach $file (@storyFiles) {
    if(open(STORY, "$storyDataDir$file")) {
      my @wholeStory = <STORY>;
      close(STORY);
      my $story = join("", @wholeStory); # put whole story into one string

      my @paragraphs = ($story =~ /((.|\n)+?\n\s*\n)/g); ### ouch, that hurts

      print <<TABLEROW;
      <tr><td>
      $paragraphs[0]$paragraphs[2]
      ...<a href="$ENV{'SCRIPT_NAME'}?request=full_story&story=$file">Full
        story</a>
      </td></tr>
TABLEROW
    } "
  }
    print <<BOTTOM;
    </table>
  </body></html>
BOTTOM

}
```

- ▓ Print top of page.
- ▓ Read *all* files from the directory into the `@storyFiles` array.
- ▓ Grep out `.news` files only.
- ▓ For each news `$file`

    - ▓ If it opens (we don't want to send an `errorPage` here; rather we just skip the particular story if it doesn't open.)
        - ▓ Join the story into a long string.
        - ▓ Pull out array of `@paragraphs` from file. We explain this in detail next.
        - ▓ Print a table row with the first two paragraphs of the news story and link to the full story.
- ▓ Print bottom of page.

The regular expression we used to pull out the paragraphs is fairly complicated. The key is that a convention is made that paragraphs are separated by blank lines. We start with the pattern for one or more blank lines.

```
\n\s*\n   ## matches one or more consecutive blank lines
```

That is, match two newline characters with zero or more whitespace characters in between. Note that this pattern matches any number of consecutive blank lines, because quantifiers are greedy. The pattern will not stop after finding the first in a sequence of blank lines.

The following pattern matches one or more of *any character* (the only thing a wild-card (`.`) doesn't match is a newline character).

```
(.|\n)+   ## one or more of any character
```

We can then identify a paragraph with the following pattern.

```
(.|\n)+?\n\s*\n/   ## a paragraph—one or more of anything, then blank line(s)
```

There are two points to clarify. First, one would have been tempted to identify paragraphs as one or more wildcard characters (`.+`). However, that would cause us to miss paragraphs containing an inadvertent hard return (`\n`) between sentences. The second point involves the extra metacharacter (`?`) to specify nongreedy matching. This point is somewhat subtle.

For example, consider the following text file, which has four paragraphs.

```
abc

def

ghi

jkl
```

Moreover, suppose we omit the `?` from the pattern and make it greedy.

```
(.|\n)+\n\s*\n/  ## oops, doesn't stop after finding first paragraph
```

The file is just the following string.

```
"abc\ndef\n\nghi\n\njkl"
```

The greed of the quantified wildcard causes this above pattern to match as much of anything as possible followed by a blank line. Applied to the example file, the greedy pattern matches the substring

```
"abc\ndef\n\nghi\n\n"
```

which is most of the file. If there were a blank line at the end of the file, it would match the whole file!

With the nongreedy version of the pattern, on the other hand, only the first paragraph is matched, as follows:

```
"abc\n\n"
```

When the one-paragraph matching pattern is applied globally in list context to a file, it returns an array of paragraphs.

```
@paragraphs = ($story =~ /((.|\n)+?\n\s*\n)/g);
```

The outer grouping parentheses capture whole paragraphs (including any blank lines following the paragraph). The inner parentheses capture the last character in each paragraph—a by-product of needing the extra group on the inside. That is, each matched paragraph captures what we need and then some junk. Thus, the actual paragraphs are in alternating indices of @paragraphs. That is why we recovered the first two paragraphs in the main_page function from indices 0 and 2.

There are some pitfalls regarding the structure of the news files, which we did not address. A sequence of two blank lines (\n\n\n) or more at the beginning of the file will cause the first \n to be matched as the first paragraph. (That is not a problem for multiple blank lines between paragraphs, because \n\s*\n is greedy.) Moreover, if there are no blank lines after the last paragraph in the file, the last paragraph will not be matched (hence not captured). That doesn't affect this problem as long as there are three or more paragraphs in a file. But we do allow you to resolve these issues as a homework exercise. Other improvements are also left as exercises, such as allowing the storage of an arbitrary number of story files but showing only the few most recent ones, and partial content rendering of stories stored in HTML files.

```perl
sub full_story {
  my (@storyArray, $storyString);
  my $file = $formHash{"story"};

  open(STORY, "$storyDataDir$file") or &errorPage("Sorry, story not available.");
  @storyArray = <STORY>;
  close(STORY);

  $storyString = join("", @storyArray);

  $storyString =~ s/\n\s*\n/<br\/><hr\/>/g; # preserve paragraph structure into
                                            # HTML document

  print <<PAGE;
<html><head><title>Full Story</title></head><body>
  <h2>The full story:</h2>
  $storyString
  <hr/>
  <a href="$ENV{'SCRIPT_NAME'}">Back to main page</a>
</body></html>
PAGE
}
```

- Get the requested story from %formHash.
- Read the story into an array.
- Join it into a long string.
- Substitute a pair of HTML br tags for each sequence of blank lines (global substitution).
- Print the page with the story.

NOTE

Without pattern matching, one could perform line processing on the file by doing something like looping over lines and saving them until the second blank line is encountered, which (hopefully) marks the end of the second paragraph. This idea leads to the term *line processing*—processing a text file line by line. For potentially huge files (such as server log files), it is imperative to line-process so that megabytes aren't read into memory at once.

We have actually introduced whole-file processing in this example. Once a text file is stored in memory as one long string, pattern matches can easily be captured from the whole file. For example, a search engine crawler might wish to capture the HTML title element from each file, or perhaps all URLs in anchor elements. Or, as a contrasting example, global substitutions can be applied to the whole file to transform it in one fell swoop. We transformed entire news text files into HTML files by adding br tags with one line of code.

Further, line processing may be very difficult (or not feasible) in some cases. For example, HTML files are not line oriented. Structures like lists and tables span several lines, with line breaks intersperced unpredictably among the HTML tags. Or a given HTML title element might have a line break in the middle. A browser doesn't care, but a crawler does, because it has to find the whole title. Whole-file processing becomes very convenient in such cases. This was true even for our news stories, where the paragraph structure in the file was more important than the underlying line structure. But whole-file match capturing or substitution may require quite complicated patterns, as you have seen.

11.7 QUERY STRING DECODING REVEALED

We are now ready to explain how the $datastring submitted from HTML forms is decoded. As you can see in the following code (Figure 11.8), we have divided step 3 into substeps to aid in the explanation that follows the code.

■ *Step 0:* Recall that this deals with the "double line breaks" submitted from text areas. Simply search for the character pattern %0D%0A and replace it with a single newline character. Recall that 0D and 0A are the hexadecimal ASCII numbers for carriage return and line feed, respectively.

■ *Step 1:* Split the $datastring at the & characters, which delimit the name=value pairs.

```
$datastring =~s/%0D%0A/\n/g;                              #step 0
@nameValuePairs = split(/&/, $datastring);                #step 1

foreach $pair (@nameValuePairs) {
  ($name, $value) = split(/=/, $pair);                    #step 2

  $name =~tr/+/ /;                                         #step 3a
  $name =~s/%([\da-fA-F]{2})/pack("C",hex($1))/eg;         #step 3b
  $value =~tr/+/ /;                                        #step 3c
  $value =~s/%([\da-fA-F]{2})/pack("C",hex($1))/eg;        #step 3d

  $formHash{$name} = $value;                               #step 4
}
```

FIGURE 11.8 The steps used to decode the $datastring submitted from HTML forms.

- For each name=value pair resulting from the split in step 1
  - *Step 2:* Split the pair into the $name and $value parts.
  - *Step 3a:* The browser submits all spaces as + characters. So transliterate all + characters back into whitespaces in the $name. (In an ideal world, none of the names of the HTML form elements would have spaces, because those names are also used as JavaScript variables. However, the world is not always ideal, so it is a good idea to include this step.)
  - *Step 3b:* This complicated expression converts all remaining characters represented as hexadecimal numbers back into the actual characters. Recall that a browser encodes several special characters as ASCII hex numbers.

First, find all three-character strings in $name that fit the pattern

```
%[hex digit][hex digit]
```

of a hex-encoded character. The grouping captures a match into $1. The presence of the e command modifier (*e*valuate) indicates that the replacement value should be evaluated as a Perl statement rather than merely as a string. Indeed, the replacement value here is a call to the pack function. The hex function returns the integer equivalent of the ASCII hex number stored in $1. That becomes the second argument of pack. Its first argument, "C", says to convert that ASCII number into the equivalent character. (The pack function is actually a byte-level operator that converts among storage formats.) Finally, the presence of the global command modifier causes all such matches to be replaced in turn.

  - *Step3c:* Repeat step 3a for the $value. This time the step is crucial, because user data often has encoded spaces.
  - *Step3d:* Repeat Step3b for the $value.
  - *Step 4:* Store the $value into %formHash with $name as the key. Recall that a slightly more elaborate version of step 4 is necessary (see Figure 6.33) to handle multiple-selection menus, because multiple values are submitted using the same name in that case (an identity crisis). That version joins together the multiple values using a delimiting symbol. Later, those values can be recovered using the split function.

NOTE

It would be tempting to do the decoding in step 3 to the entire $datastring first,

```
$datastring =~ tr/+/ /;
$datastring =~ s/%([\da-fA-F]{2})/pack("C",hex($1))/eg;
```

and then do the splitting in steps 1 and 2 afterwards. That does eliminate the redundancy of performing these operations on both the $name and $value parts. To our astonishment, many books actually do it that way! There is a fatal flaw in that common technique.

If the user's data contains one of the characters & or =, then the name=value pairs will not be recovered properly. To see this, suppose a form has text fields for the user's name and employer, and the user enters "Tim Loga" and "AT&T". Then the data is encoded as

```
name=Tim+Loga&employer=AT%3DT
```

where the ampersand in the user's data is encoded with its hex ASCII representation %3D.

CHAPTER 11   REGULAR EXPRESSIONS AND MATCHING

Now suppose we do the decoding in step 3 first. The result is

```
name=Tim Loga&employer=AT&T
```

where the hex number is "unpacked." Now splitting the data into name=value pairs results in three would-be pairs:

```
"name=Tim Loga", "employer=AT", "T".
```

The data is now basically useless. It is imperative to leave special symbols hex-encoded until *after* the name=value pairs are recovered. (Note that you can transliterate the plusses back into spaces before splitting up the $datastring, but it's more clear to keep the actual decoding steps separate from the splitting steps.)

URL-Encoding Explained

Now that you have seen the entrails of URL-decoding, we take this opportunity to explain the URLencode function from Section 7.4. Note that the only job of this function is to encode the actual data. It would then be up to the program to form the data into larger strings, = delimited name-value for example. An explanation follows the function.

```
sub URLencode {
  my $string = $_[0];
  $string =~ s/([^\w])/"%".sprintf("%02x", ord($1))/eg;
  return $string;
}
```

■ Do a global substitution looking for characters in $string that are not alphanumeric. That is, the pattern ([^\w]) captures a match of any character in the class of nonalphanumeric characters.

A matched character is captured into $1. Encoding *all* nonalphanumeric characters is somewhat of an overkill, but is easiest to implement.

■ The substitution string contains a call to a Perl function.

```
"%".sprintf("%02x", ord($1))
```

Using the e command modifier in substution causes the replacement string first to be executed as a Perl statement.

■ The ord function returns the integer ASCII code of the character. The "%02x" format string tells the sprintf function to format the integer as a two-digit hexadecimal number (that's the effect of the x) and to include a leading zero if necessary. Then a % symbol is concatenated onto the front of the two hexadecimal digits. This is precisely URL-encoding.

Some Security Remarks

We conclude this section with some remarks about security issues related to user input. Refer back to the very simple example of Section 6.3, where the user enters a name into a text field, and a CGI program simply returns the user's name to the browser. (How much we've learned since then!) Consider what happens when the user enters HTML code into the text area, as shown in Figure 11.9. Since the CGI program simply prints the user's input back into the returned Web page, HTML code entered by the user becomes part of the HTML file.

FIGURE 11.9 A user (wise guy) enters bad input.

A solution to this problem is simply to add an extra substitution step in the decoding routine.

```
$value =~ s/[<>]//g;
```

This just looks (globally) for either of the two characters in the class [<>] and replaces them with nothing. In effect, this makes it impossible for the user to slip HTML code past the decoding routine. If the form shown in Figure 11.9 is re-submitted to a program with the extra security feature, the following results. The angle brackets have been deleted.

Now, this might seem harmless, and it is. If the user enters garbage, let garbage be returned! It would be more annoying in other programs if such user data gets stored as permanent data on the Web server or as state data, thereby affecting other Web pages. It is up to the programmer to understand the possible propagation of bad data.

The above scenario, where user-entered data disrupts the rendering of HTML code, is at worst annoying. However, when user-entered data is used within certain Perl statements, there is the potential for much more malicious harm. The Perl statements at risk are

```
open
system
'back-quote execution of a system command'
eval
```

These Perl statements are potentially capable of executing arbitrary system commands.

The point we wish to make here is that it is possible to eliminate such security threats by categorically removing all suspicious characters from %formHash values, such as

```
$value =~ s/[<>"\|'\*;`. . .]//g;   ## be gone weird characters!
```

or, for the really paranoid,

```
$value =~ s/\W//g;
```

which gets rid of all nonalphanumeric characters! Both of these blanket substitutions are not ideal solutions. It is far better to understand why we need to remove certain types of characters in certain situations. Besides, such blanket substitutions are counterproductive if we actually want to allow certain nonalphanumeric characters in user inputs. We will address all these security issues in further detail in Section 13.6.

SUMMARY OF KEY TERMS AND CONCEPTS

Regular expression: A set of rules that defines a set of matching strings. We often say *pattern* to mean a regular expression. In addition to normal characters, the rules provide for the use of escape characters, wildcards, character classes, quantifiers, and other capabilities.

Matching operator and binding operator: A pattern given inside the matching operator m/*pattern*/ is "bound" onto a string using the binding operator =~. A complete expression "*string*"=~m/*pattern*/, in Boolean context evaluates to true if the pattern matches a substring of *string*. The m may be left off the matching operator /*pattern*/. A matching operation does *not* alter the string.

Metacharacters: Characters that have special meaning within the rules for patterns. A metacharacter must be escaped to be taken literally inside a pattern.

Reserved escape sequence: In patterns, escape sequences may be reserved for ASCII characters (such as \n,\t). However, most reserved escape sequences stand for a class of characters (such as \s for any whitespace character) or a location within a pattern (such as \z for end of string location).

Character classes: A whole class of characters matches only a single character. A match occurs if any character in the class is matched. Character classes may be given by reserved escape sequences (such as \s, any whitespace character) or a programmer-defined class in square brackets (such as [aeiou] for any vowel). One metacharacter, the period, stands for the class of all characters (except \n) and is called the *wildcard*.

Or: The pipe character | works like a logical OR when placed between patterns. A programmer-defined character class (such as [aeiou]) uses juxtaposition of characters as a shortcut for OR (that is, [aeiou] is the same as a|e|i|o|u).

Capturing matches: The first matched portion of a string is automatically captured into the $& variable. The unmatched portions are automatically captured into other special variables: $` (prematch), $' (postmatch). When grouping parentheses () enclose a pattern, all matched portions of the string are captured into the special variables $1, $2, $3, … starting from the leftmost grouped pattern. Nested grouped patterns are captured starting from the leftmost outer group and progressing inward. When a quantifier needs to be applied to a subpattern of a pattern, grouping symbols may be used to define the subpattern even though there is no intention or necessity for capturing any matches.

Quantifiers: Metacharacters that specify a number of consecutive occurrences of a pattern (such as "one or more" or "exactly 2"). Quantifiers may be applied to single characters, classes of characters [], and groups of characters ().

Greedy quantifier: A quantifier will not stop at the first match it finds. For example, the pattern \d+9 (one or more digits followed by a 9) will not stop at the first match ("19") in the string "1929" but will match the whole string. A quantifier can be made nongreedy by adding an extra ? character after the quantifier character.

Patterns in list context: Assigning a global binding/match operation to an array variable assigns it the list of capturing variables ($1, $2, . . .) provided that there are patterns grouped for capturing. The grep function pulls all matched array elements out of the given array. It returns a subarray of the given array.

Substitution operator: s/*pattern*/*replacement_string*/ applied to a string using the binding operator alters the string (potentially). The replacement string is substituted for the first occurrence of the pattern in the string. The global command modifier g is often applied to cause all occurrences of the pattern to be replaced.

Command modifier: An extra command that gives instructions to the match operator and substitution operators. Examples are m/*pattern*/ig (case insensitive global matching) and s/*pattern*/*replacement*/g (global substitution).

Processing text files: Regular expressions are a powerful tool for processing text files. Potentially large text files, such as server log files, which can easily be tens of megabytes long, should be line-processed, meaning that one line at a time is read into the program. Smaller files may be read into a program as one long string and processed. This is ideal for performing global matches and substitutions on a file. In particular, line processing is not appropriate (or perhaps feasible) when lines don't define the structure of the file, as in HTML files for example.

Partial content rendering: Extracting only a portion of a file for rendition in a Web page. In most cases, line processing is not appropriate, because the file's structure is not line determined. Rather, the whole file is processed as one string.

URL-decoding/encoding: A URL-encoded string is first split apart according to the delimiters. Then global substitutions replace hex encoded characters with actual characters in the data. To URL-encode a string, first do a global substitution on the data to replace characters with hex encoded characters. The data can then be formed into a larger delimited string, even if delimiting characters appear in the data.

Security for user input: It is a good idea to remove unwanted characters from user input using a global substitution. This makes it impossible for a user to slip a Perl statement or HTML tag, for example, into your data.

EXERCISES

Pattern Practice

Parts (A) through (E) below provide some quickie questions in the capacity of a "self-test" (or simply for fun on a rainy day). A reasonable way to learn from these exercises is to use the book for reference and think them through. Merely running these in a test program defeats their purpose. The solutions are provided on this book's Web site.

A. Given that

```
$x = "A list of 12 short Computer Science homework problems"
```

which of the following are true?

(i) `$x =~ /computer/`

(ii) `$x =~ /science/i`

(iii)`$x =~ /u.*u/`

B. What is the value of `$&` (the matched substring, if any) after each of the following is applied to the original value of `$x` from part (A)?

(i) `$x =~ /\d/`

(ii) `$x =~ /\d+/`

(iii)`$x =~ /\d+\s+\w+/`

(iv)`$x =~ /s.*s/`

(v) `$x =~ /s.*?s/`

(vi)`$x =~ /\w{7}/`

(vii)`$x =~ /\w{7,}/`

C. What is the value of `$x` after each of the following is applied to the original `$x` from part (A)?

(i) `$x =~ s/[aeiou]/*/g`

(ii) `$x =~ s/(omp|em|enc)/[$1]/g`

D. What is the value of `@array` after each of the following is applied to the original value of `$x` from part (A)?

(i) `@array = ($x =~ /om?[ber]/g)`

(ii) `@array = ($x =~ /([aeiou]).*?\1/g)` *# This uses a back reference*

E. Explain in plain language what the following do.

(i) `$t =~ /\b[A-Z]+\b/`

(ii) `$t =~ /[^\s\w]/`

(iii)`$t =~ s/\d+/\#/g`

(iv)`$t =~ s/\b(.)/uc($1)/eg;` *#somewhat advanced*

Programming Exercises

1. The source code for the `partialcontent.cgi` program of Section 11.6 can be obtained from the Web site. Patch the program by fixing the potential problems discussed in the paragraph just above the definition of the `full_story` function. *Hint:* It's probably easier to "clean up" a file through substitutions rather than modifying the paragraph extraction pattern.

(a) Fix the problem caused by extra blank lines at the beginning of a news file.

(b) Fix the problem caused by no blank line at the end of a file. This fix allows the first two paragraphs to be extracted even if the story has only two paragraphs. Enable the program to detect two-paragraph stories and not print the "full story" link.

(c) Also fix the potential problem in the `full_story` function caused by initial blank lines. Such blank lines will cause `br` tags to be inserted before the story in the HTML page.

(d) Use the split function to separate `$story` into `@paragraphs` by using a suitable pattern that detects "blank lines." Note that with this method, every item in the array `@paragraphs` will be a true paragraph, so you can print the first two paragraphs by printing the first two items of the array. (Be sure to include paragraph breaks between them.)

2. The source code for the `partialcontent.cgi` program of section 11.6 can be obtained from the Web site. Use three different news categories (`.sports`, `.bus`, `.pol`, for example). You may use our stories and just dummy paragraphs for new stories you create.

(a) The main page should have three columns, one for each category, in a borderless table layout. Render only the first paragraph of each story.

(b) Have at least five stories for each category, but display only the three most recent. This feature should not rely on the last-modified property for files, because merely correcting a typo in an old news story would make it new. Rather, the story names should have embedded date/time information—for example, *id_timestamp*.`sports`, where *id* is some (short) story ID and the timestamp format is up to you. The format should be simple enough that story authors can manually assign a timestamp to the file names, and it should identify a story accurate to the minute.

(c) Store the news stories in HTML files, where the only constraint is that each paragraph must be inside a `p` container element.

3. Simulate a Web crawler by pulling relevant information out of an HTML file. Start with an HTML file and write a CGI program that simply pulls the information out of the file and returns a Web page containing the extracted information in some organized format. Pull out:

(i) The contents of the `title` element

(ii) All key words from `meta` elements

(iii) All description phrases from `meta` elements

(iv) All URLs in anchor elements

(v) All e-mail addresses in `mailto` links

(vi) Any other e-mail addresses found in the text of the page

Note: An actual crawler would function as an HTTP client and retrieve the HTML pages much as a browser would.

4. Make a program that reads in a news story from an HTML file where each paragraph is identified by a `p` container element. The objective is to read in such a file and transform it to a new HTML file with paragraphs formatted using CSS. Devise a smooth style class for paragraphs. The first sentence should be indented, the text justified (to the extent possible), and the text should be colored. Moreover, the first paragraph only should begin with a "drop cap" (the first letter of the first word is bigger). We did not cover drop caps, but a quick online search will suffice. As an added challenge, you may alternate the paragraphs colors using two colors.

5. Write the following utility functions. Make a program that tests each function on two strings. The program should return a Web page showing the test strings and the results.

(a) Given a string, the function returns an array consisting of substrings that look like e-mail addresses.

(b) Credit card numbers are composed of 16 digits. The function "cleans up" credit card numbers, which could be in a variety of formats (no spaces, delimiting characters, and so on). It returns a credit card number in the format `"xxxx xxxx xxxx xxxx"`.

(c) Add "bleeps" to text. The function should replace your favorite "four-letter" words with `****`. Start with a list of a few such words to be bleeped out. (You may use nonobjectionable words if you wish.)

(d) Write a function that takes a nicely formatted military-time string and returns a time string using AM and PM.

6. Do some research online and learn how to use a file upload form button. Such buttons allow a user to browse the local file system to choose a file to upload to the server. Make a program that requires reporters (as in the example of Section 11.7) to log on. Once logged on, they can upload newly written news stories to the server. This automates the process of updating the news Web site. However, there need to be constraints to keep the reporters in check. Before adding a news file to the actual working directory:

(a) Make sure that the uploaded file has a proper extension as outlined in Exercise 2.

(b) Make sure that the story ID does not match one already in the working directory and that the timestamp is in proper format. See Exercise 2(b).

(c) Make sure there are at least three paragraphs in the story.

7. Using the substitution operator, back references, and capturing, write a utility function that fixes doubled words in *any* string (that is, it can take the extra "the" out of strings like "The cat in the the hat"). Test the function on several strings using a driver program.

8. You will find part of a Web server's *access log* file available for download on the Web site for this exercise. Note that each entry is on a separate line, although some lines might soft-wrap depending upon the width of your editing window. Write a Perl program(s) to glean the following statistics from the log file. The final output of the program should be a Web page, but you may wish first to develop your analysis algorithm locally with a non-CGI Perl program.

(a) The note at the end of Section 11.4 indicates that the hit count used in that section's example is way too generous. One wants to eliminate all of the superfluous hits for images, but also to count return visits from a given IP address. So some middle ground between unique visitors (IP addresses) and all transactions is desirable. One solution is the notion of *day visits*—one visit per IP address per day (or 24-hour period). This eliminates superfluous hits involved with loading one page or with a typical multipage session. On the other hand, it measures return visitors reasonably accurately. Count the number of day visits in the supplied access log.

(b) Print out a list showing the number of unique visitors on each day appearing in the log file.

(c) The Web site from which the log file originates is for a book that has a Web page for each chapter. For example, the page for Lesson 1 is named `L1.html`. Print out a list showing the number of hits on each Lesson page.

(d) Count the number of HTTP HEAD transactions.

9. You will find part of a Web server's *hits log* file available for download on the Web site for this exercise. Note that each entry is on a separate line, although some lines might soft-wrap depending upon the width of your editing window. Write a perl program(s) to glean the following statistics from the log file. The final output of the program should be a Web page, but you may wish first to develop your analysis algorithm locally with a non-CGI Perl program.

(a) Print a list of the different browsers and versions that have hit the site. The entries that include parts like `compatible; MSIE 5.5` are from Internet Explorer browsers. Assume that lines without that are from Netscape browsers. (Mozilla is the open-source code base for Netscape's rendering engine.)

(b) Count the hits from each browser version. (You can make a bar graph, as mentioned in Exercise 8(b).)

(c) Peruse the file and you will see that some hits are not from Web browsers but from various Web crawlers. Print a list of the different crawlers that have hit the site and the number of visits from each.

(d) Notice that hits are recorded in a somewhat session-oriented fashion. That is, if a given browser pulls up 10 pages from the site, there are 10 entries in the log. In your analysis of parts (b) and (c), factor out the extra hits caused by sessions as best you can. That gives more accurate statistics on the different browsers that are actually visiting the site.

10. You will find part of a Web server's *referrer log* file available for download on the Web site for this exercise. A *referrer* is a link in a page that is used to hit the site. As you can see in the file, most referrers are the site's internal links. Note that each entry is on a separate line, although some lines might soft-wrap depending upon the width of your editing window. Write a Perl program(s) to glean the following statistics from the log file. The final output of the program should be a Web page, but you may wish first to develop your analysis algorithm locally with a non-CGI Perl program.

(a) Print a list of the referrers other than `cknuckles.com`. Don't print the same referrer more than once.

(b) For each of the referrers from part (a), list all the pages to which their links have targeted. Note that the paths in the file are relative to the site's root directory.

(c) Notice that some of the referrers were links clicked when search engines returned matches. List the search engine referrers separately from the non-search-engine referrers.

(d) For each of the referrers from part (c), extract and list the different queries that people typed into the search engine to generate the match.

PROJECT THREAD

This chapter's Project Thread lets your quiz application rest for a bit while you gain some experience with pattern matching. We have suggested two interesting exercises in parts C and D. However, different ones may be substituted based upon your interest or at the discretion of your instructor.

A. Add the security patch discussed near the end of Section 11.7 to your decoding routine.

B. Work the practice examples for patterns in parts (A) through (E) in the "Pattern Practice" section at the beginning of the Exercises.

C. Work Exercise 3.

D. Work Exercise 9.

E. Add a new row to your homework table for each exercise worked (not for parts A and B).

CHAPTER 12

SEARCHING IN WEB APPLICATIONS

Without search engines, finding Web pages on certain topics among the billions available would be worse than trying to find the proverbial needle in a hay stack. The data-mining operations behind commercial search engines are beyond the scope of this text, but this chapter does explore many concepts central to searching on the Web. These concepts include refining searches on database tables using regular expressions in SQL, secondary refinements within Perl programs, and caching search results. Moreover, we extend the searching ideas to sites built from collections of static HTML files, where recursion is used to construct dynamic site maps or even to search the entire site.

12.1 DATABASE SEARCHES

In this section we offer two examples that use a search form to query a very simple database. Suppose the deptstore database has only one simple table named products as shown in Table 12.1. The actual table used in the examples has many more products than are shown in the figure.

Figure 12.1 shows the search form and the HTML code for the form. When the form is submitted, a Web page displaying the results of the search is returned to the user. For this example, the search looks through the products table and returns any products that contain the user's query as a substring. For example, if the user types in "ball", any product containing "ball" as a substring is returned. From the limited list of products appearing in Table 12.1, that query would return two products.

An outline of the program, named products1.cgi, is provided in Figure 12.2. The app logic is trivial. The search_page function prints the page shown in Figure 12.1 and the search function implements the search and returns the results. Overviews of those functions follow the code. We assume that the database is in MySQL and that the MySQL daemon is running. We also assume the user "storeuser" with password "pass" has full privileges to the database deptstore. Only the second line of code in the global variables section needs to be changed if any of these assumptions change.

TABLE 12.1 Table: products

prodID	ITEM	DEPT	...
712364	archery set	sports	
146541	baseball	sports	
494654	baseball bat	sports	

463

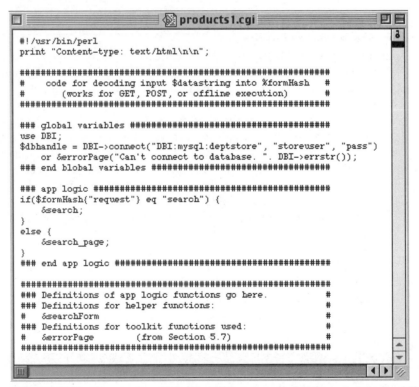

```
<form action="$ENV{'SCRIPT_NAME'}" method="GET">
  Search for
  <input type="text" name="searchstring" value="" size="15"/>
  <input type="hidden" name="request" value="search"/>
  <input type="submit" value="Search for products"/>
</form>
```

FIGURE 12.1 A search form that submits a product query.

```perl
#!/usr/bin/perl
print "Content-type: text/html\n\n";

############################################################
#    code for decoding input $datastring into %formHash   #
#       (works for GET, POST, or offline execution)        #
############################################################

### global variables ######################################
use DBI;
$dbhandle = DBI->connect("DBI:mysql:deptstore", "storeuser", "pass")
    or &errorPage("Can't connect to database. " . DBI->errstr());
### end blobal variables ##################################

### app logic #############################################
if($formHash{"request"} eq "search") {
    &search;
}
else {
    &search_page;
}
### end app logic #########################################

############################################################
### Definitions of app logic functions go here.          #
### Definitions for helper functions:                    #
#   &searchForm                                           #
### Definitions for toolkit functions used:              #
#   &errorPage        (from Section 5.7)                 #
############################################################
```

FIGURE 12.2 The program that generates and processes the search form of Figure 12.1.

```
sub search_page {
  print<<TOP;
  <html><head><title>Search our sports store</title></head><body>
TOP

&searchForm;  # no argument -> no hard-coded value for search field

print<<BOTTOM;
</body></html>
BOTTOM
}
```

■ We have used a `searchForm` helper function because we also wish to return the search form in the page with the search results. We will further explain that below. This call to `searchForm` simply prints the HTML code shown in Figure 12.1.

```
sub search {
  $searchstring = $formHash{"searchstring"};

  print<<TOP;
  <html><head><title>Results of your search</title></head><body>
    <h2>Here are the results of your search of "$searchstring":</h2>
    <ol>
TOP

  my $sql = "SELECT item FROM products WHERE item LIKE '%$searchstring%'";
  my $qObj= $dbhandle -> prepare($sql) or &errorPage("Can't prepare.");
  $qObj-> execute() or &errorPage("Can't execute " . $qObj->errstr());

  my @row;
  my @matches = ();
  while(@row = $qObj->fetchrow_array()){
    push @matches, $row[0];
  }
  $qObj-> finish();

  foreach $match (@matches) {
    print "<li>$match</li>\n";
  }
  print "</ol>\n";

  &searchForm($formHash{"searchstring"});      # hard code the search string
                                               # in the returned search form

  print<<BOTTOM;
  </body></html>
BOTTOM
}
```

■ Get the search pattern submitted by the user, which is stored in `$formHash {"searchstring"}`. (Recall the name of the text field in the HTML form.)

■ Print the top of the page, including the start tag for an ordered HTML list whose items will be the matched products.

■ The next three statements create, prepare, and execute an SQL statement. The SQL SELECT statement uses the LIKE keyword to search for `products` records containing the `$search string` as a substring of the `item` column. The `%` characters surrounding the `$searchstring` are special SQL metacharacters used for primitive patterns. We will explain this in the next section.

- Because we selected only the item column, a one-column table is returned. We fetch the returned one-column rows out of the query object one at a time, and push the value onto the array @matches.
- Finish the query object, because we are done with it.
- Print the values from @matches as individual list items and then close the HTML list.
- Return the search form with the search results.
- Print the rest of the page.

Before showing the searchForm helper function, we show a sample product search in Figure 12.3. When a search is performed using almost any commercial search engine on

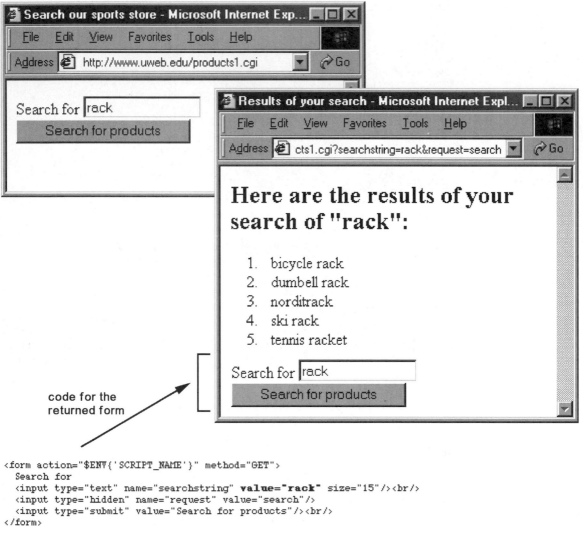

```
<form action="$ENV{'SCRIPT_NAME'}" method="GET">
  Search for
  <input type="text" name="searchstring" value="rack" size="15"/><br/>
  <input type="hidden" name="request" value="search"/>
  <input type="submit" value="Search for products"/><br/>
</form>
```

FIGURE 12.3 A sample execution of the program of the products1.cgi program.

the Web, you get more back than just a page of search results. Search engines typically return a page containing both the results of your search and the search form. Moreover, the search form returned with the results usually still contains your original data. That is advantageous, because you can readily recall your query and can easily refine your search without having to click the back button on the browser and retype things.

When we say that the previous search is *hard-coded* into the search form, we will be referring to returning the previous search criteria in the HTML code for the form, as shown in boldface in Figure 12.3. With that in mind, we provide the searchForm helper function. Note that the call to it in the original search page sent no parameter, but the call in the results page did. It is a simple matter to hard-code forms with previous contents.

```
sub searchForm {
  my ($initialstring) = @_;

  print<<FORM;
  <form action="$ENV{'SCRIPT_NAME'}" method="GET">
    Search for
    <input type="text" name="searchstring" value="$initialstring" size="15"/
><br/>
    <input type="submit" value="Search for products"/><br/>
    <input type="hidden" name="request" value="search"/>
  </form>
FORM
}
```

■ Store the incoming parameter (optional).
■ Print the search form, hard-coding the value attribute of the search field with the (possibly empty) string.

NOTE

You can see in Figure 12.3 that the search results are returned as plain text. Realistically, a list of links to various products would be returned. Clicking on a link would bring up a product description and a button that would add some quantity of the product to a shopping cart. In this example, and those to follow, we simply return text. Cluttering the examples with such details would distract from the discussion; some of those details are left as exercises. A fully functional search utility with returned links and shopping cart is presented in the next chapter.

Also note that this search utility can be included in any application that is interfaced with the deptstore database. The function that prints the search form is self-contained. One would simply have to add the search function to the app logic of the application to handle the search requests.

12.2 REFINING DATABASE SEARCHES

Notice in Figure 12.3 that results were returned in which "rack" is not the whole word but is part of a larger word. We used the LIKE keyword in the SQL statement and surrounded

TABLE 12.2 Some SQL Search Patterns

PATTERN	MATCH PROPERTIES
`'%z%'`	Matches contain a z
`'%ing'`	Matches end with "`ing`"
`'___'`	Matches any three-character word
`'_a_'`	Matches any three character word with an `a` in the middle

the search string with `%` characters to accomplish that. The goal of this section is to introduce using regular expressions to refine database searches. Indeed, one might wish to search for "rack" but not as a part of a bigger word. We begin by explaining the `LIKE` keyword used in the previous section.

`LIKE` and `RLIKE` Database Queries

Standard SQL provides for very limited pattern matching in queries through the `LIKE` keyword and two metacharacters. The underscore `_` works like a wildcard, matching one of any character. The percent `%` works like a quantified wildcard, matching one or more of any character. The SQL statement from `products1.cgi`,

```
SELECT item FROM products WHERE item LIKE '%$searchstring%'
```

returns all rows from the `products` table where the `item` column contains the `$searchstring` with any number of characters on either side. Hence, the `$searchstring` merely needs to be a substring of the item to provide a match.

Note that the `LIKE` pattern is quoted using single quotes.[1] We could do SQL searches on database tables with patterns like those in Table 12.2. However, such searching is extremely limited, compared to the full power of regular expressions.

Many database systems also offer the `RLIKE` (regular expression `LIKE`) extension to SQL. With `RLIKE`, an SQL query like the following can be issued:

```
SELECT item FROM products WHERE item RLIKE 'regular_expression'
```

The pattern can be more complicated, replete with most of Perl's regular expression metacharacters. For example, the SQL query

```
SELECT item FROM products WHERE item RLIKE '^rack$'
```

returns any table rows where the `item` column contains the word "`rack`" but not part of a bigger string.

Here we have used the metacharacters `^` and `$` for beginning and ending word boundaries, respectively. That is because MySQL `RLIKE` does not accept many of the special escape sequences (`\A`, `\Z`, `\b`, `\d`, `\w`, and so forth) that stand for locations or whole

---

[1]It is always a good idea to construct SQL statements using single quotes. Double quotes would attempt to interpolate `$` and escape characters, but those characters need to survive into the SQL statement.

classes of characters in Perl. Using RLIKE in MySQL, ∧ and $ handle the word boundary cases, and character classes easily can be constructed manually. For example, instead of \w (word character—alphanumeric character or underscore), we would use the following programmer-defined character class.

```
[a-zA-Z0-9_]
```

Except for special escape sequences, RLIKE can be used in MySQL with the other standard metacharacters: standard wildcard (.), quantifiers, classes, alternatives (|), and so forth. However, because RLIKE patterns are handled by the database engine, capturing is not an option. Indeed, SQL RLIKE queries return database subtables determined by the regular expression. Note that some database systems (such as Microsoft Access and the CSV database simulator) don't support RLIKE. We have added an optional section at the end of this lesson to discuss database searches when SQL statements don't support regular expressions.

Whole-Word Searches

We now write a second version of the products search that gives the user the opportunity to specify that only whole-word matches should be returned. This version is named products2.cgi. The refinement option is implemented using a checkbox. Figure 12.4 shows an execution of the updated products search. Note that the search form returned with the search results has been hard-coded with all of the original search criteria.

The products2.cgi program has the exact same outline as the original version in Figure 12.2. The only updates are to the searchForm function, which now includes the checkbox, and the search function, which now can handle both substring and whole-word searches. The updated functions are provided next, with overviews.

```
sub search {
  ### This function uses SQL extension RLIKE

  $searchstring = $formHash{"searchstring"};

  if($formHash{"wholeword"}) {
    $searchstring = '(^|[^a-zA-Z0-9])'.$searchstring.'($|[^a-zA-Z0-9])';
  }
  print<<TOP;
  <html><head><title>Results of your search</title></head><body>
    <h2>Here are the results of your search:</h2>
    <ol>
TOP

  my $sql = "SELECT item FROM products WHERE item RLIKE '$searchstring'";
  my $qObj= $dbhandle -> prepare($sql) or &errorPage("Can't prepare ");
  $qObj-> execute() or &errorPage("Can't execute " . $qObj->errstr());

  my @row;
  my @matches = ();
  while(@row = $qObj->fetchrow_array()){
    push @matches, $row[0];
  }
  $qObj-> finish();

  foreach $match (@matches){
    print "<li>$match</li>\n";
```

```
    }
    print "</ol>\n";

    &searchForm($formHash{"searchstring"}, $formHash{"wholeword"});

    print<<BOTTOM;
    </body></html>
BOTTOM
    }
```

■ Get the user's search string.

■ Test to see whether the `wholeword` key exists in `%formHash`. If it was checked, concatenate regular expressions that test word boundaries onto each end of the user's query. Otherwise, leave it alone. We can't use the special word boundary (`\b`) in `RLIKE` patterns, so we construct our

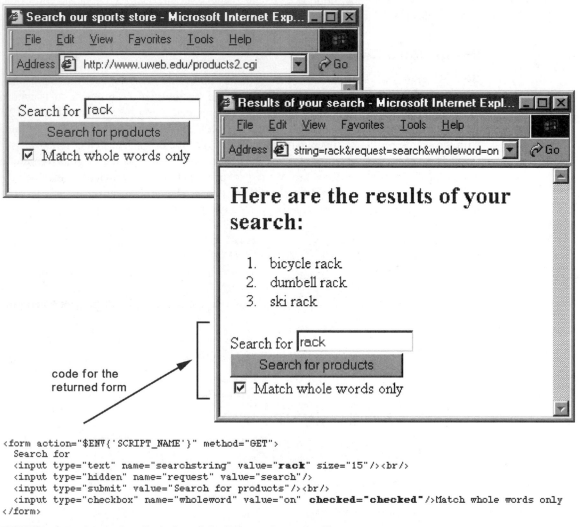

```
<form action="$ENV{'SCRIPT_NAME'}" method="GET">
  Search for
  <input type="text" name="searchstring" value="rack" size="15"/><br/>
  <input type="hidden" name="request" value="search"/>
  <input type="submit" value="Search for products"/><br/>
  <input type="checkbox" name="wholeword" value="on" checked="checked"/>Match whole words only
</form>
```

FIGURE 12.4 A sample submission of the improved search utility.

own word boundary patterns. The pattern (^|[^a-zA-Z0-9]) matches either the beginning of the string or something that is not a letter or number. (Recall that ^ inside a class negates the class.) So these word boundaries match standalone words or words with nonalphanumeric boundaries. So "rack" in "rack-o-lamb" would still be a whole-word match, for example. Similarly, ($|[^a-zA-Z0-9]) matches either the end of the string or something that is not a letter or number.

- Print the top of the page.
- The function then constructs, prepares, and executes the SQL statement as before.
- It then fetches the matches and prints a list as before.
- All of the original query data is sent to the searchForm function to be hard-coded into the returned search form.
- Finish the results page.

```
sub searchForm {
  my ($initialstring, $wholewordon) = @_;

  my $checked_or_not = "";
  if($wholewordon){
    $checked_or_not = 'checked="checked"';
  }
  print<<FORM;
<form action="$ENV{'SCRIPT_NAME'}" method="GET">
Search for
<input type="text" name="searchstring" value="$initialstring" size="15"/><br/>
<input type="submit" value="Search for products"/><br/>
<input type="checkbox" name="wholeword" value="on" $checked_or_not/> Match
    whole words only
<input type="hidden" name="request" value="search"/>
</form>
FORM
}
```

- Store the incoming parameters (optional).
- If $wholewordon is not empty, set a variable with the HTML attribute necessary to hard-code the checkbox to be checked. If the second parameter is the empty string (either because we want it that way in the default form, or the user didn't check the checkbox) the $checked_or_not variable is left empty.
- Print the HTML form, hardcoding the HTML attributes with the (possibly empty) Perl variables, which are boldfaced for emphasis.

As is almost always the case, more features could be added to this search utility. Most notably, it is geared only to take single words, rather than whole phrases. If a phrase were entered, that phrase would have to be matched character for character just as if it were a big word. Ideally, a search utility would pick words out of a phrase and test for them individually and in any order. We leave that as an exercise.

Also, we might wish to make sure that at least one character was entered into the text field to prevent empty searches (which match every product in our examples). That could be validated on the front end with JavaScript, or the CGI program could test that.

> **N O T E**
>
> The general strategy for testing whether a checkbox has been selected is to test whether (exists $formHash{checkbox_name}). In the search function just shown, we passed $formHash{checkbox_name} to the searchForm function without testing whether is was checked. Actually though, that effectively tests the checkbox for us. If the checkbox is unchecked, $formHash{checkbox_name} is treated like an uninitialized variable when passed to the function, so it is passed as the empty string in that case. Otherwise (that is if it was checked), its value (as hard-coded in the HTML code) is contained in $formHash{checkbox_name}. In this situation it was crucial to hard-code the checkbox with a value (even though we really don't care what the value is).

Further Refinement Possibilities

We now present an example execution of products2.cgi in which the user has entered a regular expression into the search form. The result is shown in Figure 12.5. Clearly this user is a Web programmer!

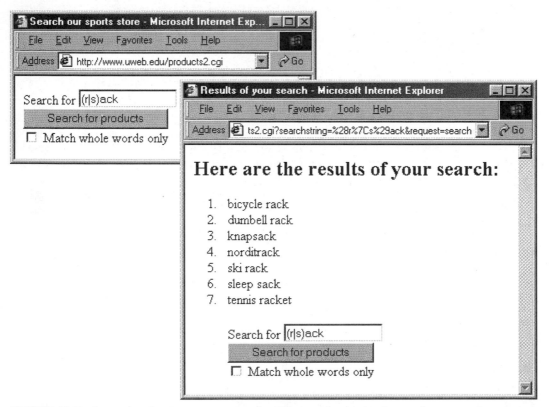

FIGURE 12.5 A search using products2.cgi, where the user has entered a regular expression.

The interesting thing is that the regular expression finds its way into the `$searchstring` variable, which then finds its way into the SQL statement, so the user has effectively refined the search. In this case, words containing either `rack` or `sack` are returned. You might be surprised to learn that all high-quality commercial search engines have mechanisms so that the user can refine searches using a combination of regular expressions and Boolean logic.

Clearly, though, people can't be expected to enter regular expressions into search forms. Furthermore, entering a regular expression would have failed in the `products1.cgi` version, because that version used only a `LIKE` pattern (try it out on the Web site).

The Google search engine implements Boolean `"and"` searches by default, in the sense that a search for "heavy metal" will prioritize results containing both of those words. You can add the special operator `"OR"` on Google (at least as of the time this was written) to perform a search roughly using an "exclusive or". That is, matches containing `"heavy"` or `"metal"`, but not both, are prioritized.

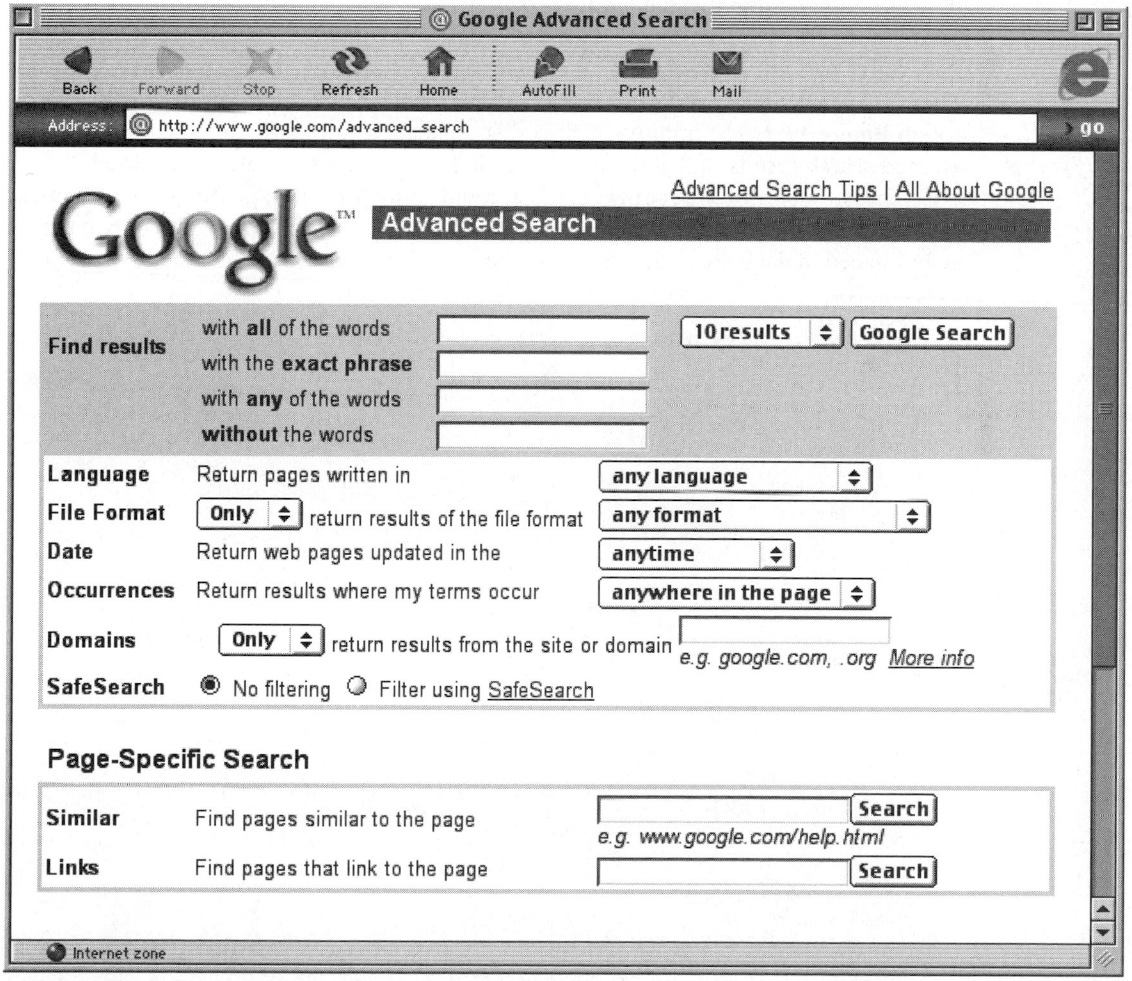

FIGURE 12.6   The Advanced Search page at Google.com.

Most search engines in the early days of the Web had special operators like (+, -, and, or) that could be typed manually between words to refine searches. Now the better ones use more elaborate search forms to let the user select a variety of options without having to know any special operators. However, many still accept special symbols that have Boolean meaning or some other meaning. Most search engines have an "advanced" search link that will pull up a page showing how to refine a search. Google's Advanced Search page is shown in Figure 12.6.

So the idea here of using a regular expression to refine a search is not novel. But, clearly, manually entered regular expressions are not the answer for users to refine searches on the front end. Several homework exercises feature the creation of options to refine searches. Those use regular expressions on the back end.

12.3 SECONDARY PROCESSING OF DATABASE SEARCHES

In this section we improve the products search example by applying a substitution operator to the records returned by the database engine. The previous version, products2.cgi, uses only pattern matching in the SQL statement. We name the new program products3.cgi. So that you can get a feel for the new version, we show a sample submission in Figure 12.7. The improvement is that a matched word is highlighted in red in the returned search results so that the user can readily see where the matches occurred.

The only part of products2.cgi that requires modification is the search function, which is provided next, followed by an overview of the modifications. The only changes are boldfaced in the body of the function. The rest of products3.cgi is exactly the same.

```perl
sub search {
  ### This function uses the SQL extension RLIKE

  $searchstring = $formHash{"searchstring"};

  if($formHash{"wholeword"}) {
    $searchstring = '(^|[^a-zA-Z0-9])'.$searchstring.'($|[^a-zA-Z0-9])';
  }
  print<<TOP;
  <html>
    <head><title>Results of your search</title>
      <style>
      <!--
        span {color:red;}
      -->
      </style>
    </head>
  <body>
  <h2>Here are the results of your search:</h2>
  <ol>
TOP

  my $sql = "SELECT item FROM products WHERE item RLIKE '$searchstring'";
  my $qObj= $dbhandle -> prepare($sql) or &errorPage("Can't prepare.");
  $qObj-> execute() or &errorPage("Can't execute " . $qObj->errstr());

  my @row;
  my @matches = ();
  while(@row = $qObj->fetchrow_array()){
    push @matches, $row[0];
  }
  $qObj-> finish();

  foreach $match (@matches){
```

```
    $match =~ s/($searchstring)/<span>$1<\/span>/ig;
    print "<li>$match</li>\n";
  }

  &searchForm($formHash{"searchstring"}, $formHash{"wholeword"});

  print<<BOTTOM;
</body></html>
BOTTOM
}
```

▤ Rather than using the deprecated HTML `font` element to change the text color of the match, we simply set a global style rule for the `span` element. We then merely need to enclose matched portions of words inside a `span` container.

▤ ... same as before

▤ For each `$match` in the `@matches` array

    ▤ Do the substitution to enclose the matched part in a `span` element. When a match is found for `$searchstring`, the matched part of the product is stored into `$1` because of the grouping parentheses. That matched part is then formatted with the HTML `span` element and substituted back into the product. Note that we had to escape the regular expression metacharacter `/` to make the closing tag `</span>`. Also note that the substitution uses both the case-insensitive and global command modifiers. We wish the substitution to occur regardless of case, and if more than one match for the user's query is found in a product, all matches should be highlighted.

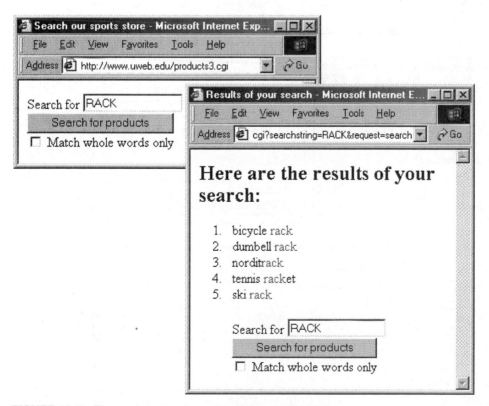

FIGURE 12.7   The `products3.cgi` version of the search utility.

12.4 LIMITING THE NUMBER OF SEARCH RESULTS

The final version of the products search example, `products4.cgi`, limits the number of returned results, as most search engines do. The user can click a link such as *next 10 results* to see more matches. A sample submission of the updated search utility is shown in Figure 12.8. We have also increased the size of the data table to include more departments. Thus the same search for "`rack`" now returns more results than before. Also note that we now print department information in the results page. (Recall the full `products` table in Table 12.1.)

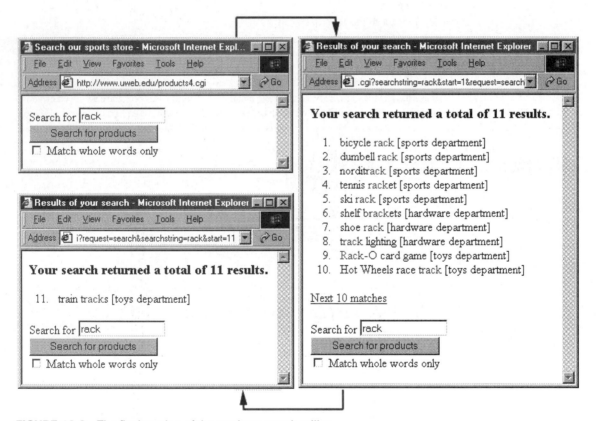

FIGURE 12.8 The final version of the products search utility.

The key to this example is keeping track of which search results should be returned to the user. When the user first submits the search form, a hidden element in the form

```
<input type="hidden" name="start" value="1"/>
```

tells the CGI program to start the list of search results at 1. That is, in fact, the only time that the form itself tells the program which results to return. When the user requests more search results, the link provided in the returned page is responsible for telling the program to return more results. For example, when the "Next 10 matches" link on the right-hand screen side of Figure 12.8 is clicked, data is manually submitted to the CGI program in the query string:

```
<a href="products4.cgi?request=search&searchstring-rack&start=11">Next 10
matches</a>
```

If there had been matches 11 through 20, then that page would have had a link that would send start=21 along with the other data. If the user were to resubmit the form from one of the returned pages, then the hidden form element would send start=1, starting the whole process all over again.

The search function contains virtually all of the changes necessary to limit the number of returned searches. That function is given next, with the additions in boldface and followed by a detailed explanation.

```
sub search {
  ### This function uses the SQL extension RLIKE

  $searchstring = $formHash{"searchstring"};

  if($formHash{"wholeword"}) {
    $searchstring = '(^|[^a-zA-Z0-9])'.$searchstring.'($|[^a-zA-Z0-9])';
  }

  my $sql = "SELECT item, department FROM products WHERE item RLIKE '$search
    string'";
  my $qObj= $dbhandle -> prepare($sql) or &errorPage("Can't prepare.");
  $qObj-> execute() or &errorPage("Can't execute " . $qObj->errstr());

  my @row;
  my @matches = ();
  my @depts = ();
  while(@row = $qObj->fetchrow_array()){
    push @matches, $row[0];
    push @depts, $row[1];
  }
  $qObj-> finish();

  my $numberOfMatches = @matches;
  print<<TOP;
  <html>
  <head>
    <title>Results of your search</title>
    <style>
    <!--
      span {color:red;}
    -->
    </style>
  </head>
  <body>
    <h3>Your search returned a total of $numberOfMatches results. </h3>
```

```
TOP

  my $resultsPerPage=10;    # default constant

  my $start = $formHash{"start"};
  my $stop = $start + $resultsPerPage - 1;

  print "<ol start=\"$start\">\n";
  for($j=$start-1; ($j<=$#matches)&&($j<=$stop-1); $j++) {
    my $match = $matches[$j];
    $match =~s/($searchstring)/<span>$1<\/span>/ig;
    print "<li>$match [$depts[$j] department]</li>\n";
  }
  print "</ol>\n";

  my $nextstart = $start + $resultsPerPage;
  if($nextstart <= $numberOfMatches){ ### any more matches in the next batch?
    print '<a href="?request=search&searchstring=',
      $formHash{"searchstring"}, "&start=$nextstart";
    if($formHash{"wholeword"} eq "on"){
      print "&wholeword=on";
    }
    print '">', "Next $resultsPerPage matches</a>\n";
  }

  &searchForm($formHash{"searchstring"}, $formHash{"wholeword"});

  print<<BOTTOM;
  </body></html>
BOTTOM
}
```

- We SELECT two columns in the SQL statement this time. The reason we execute the SQL statement before printing the top of the page in this version is that here we print the number of matches at the top of the page. We now also push the second column of returned records onto a @depts array.

- Initialize a local variable to the default number of hits returned per page. This can be changed at any time to return more or less hits per page.

- Store the $start value for the list of matches. (For example, if $formHash{"start"} contains 11, then we will generate matches 11 through 20.)

- Store the $stop value. For example, if $start contains 11, then $stop should contain 20.

- Start the ordered HTML list, including the attribute to set its starting number.

- For $j from $start-1 to $stop-1 (and of course $j has to stay less than the total number of matches; the reason is that array indices start at 0)
    - Store the product from @matches in a temporary variable so that we can highlight the matched part with red text via a substitution.
    - Print the list item containing the product and the corresponding department.

- Close the list.

- Set the starting index for the next batch of matches

- If there are matches left for the next batch
    - Hard-code the link to call the next batch of matches. At this point we have something like products4.cgi?request=search&searchstring=rack&start=11.
    - Add wholeword=on if the checkbox should be checked.
    - Print the rest of the anchor element, beginning with the closing quotes for the href attribute.

The only other modification required for `products4.cgi` is to add the extra hidden form element (which sends `start=1`) to the `searchForm` function. The new `searchForm` function is provided next. We forgo an explanation for that one.

```
sub searchForm {
  my ($initialstring, $wholewordon) = @_;

  my $checked_or_not = "";
  if($wholewordon) {
    $checked_or_not = 'checked="checked"';
  }

  print<<FORM;
  <form action="$ENV{'SCRIPT_NAME'}" method="GET">
    Search for
    <input type="text" name="searchstring" value="$initialstring" size="15"/><br/>
    <input type="submit" value="Search for products"/><br/>
    <input type="checkbox" name="wholeword" value="on" $checked_or_not/>Match
      whole words only
    <input type="hidden" name="request" value="search"/>
    <input type="hidden" name="start" value="1"/>
  </form>
FORM
}
```

NOTE

This example demonstrates preserving state through the combination of a hidden form element and data hard-coded into links. Indeed, that is how most search engines implement the feature that limits the number of returned results. Whether through the search form submission or through a link click, a `start=`*whichnumber* pair is sent to the server-side program that handles the search.

However, a limitation to our approach in this example is that the entire products search is performed again, even if the user selects a link to return more matches. That is, all of the data files are reread and researched every time. For a search utility whose database is relatively small, this approach suffices, because repetitive searches don't overly tax the Web server. But when the database is large, a search utility should implement some mechanism to store results from a given query. It is especially important to cache search results in the middle tier when the database is in a third tier. Doing so facilitates the desired division of labor in the three-tier model.

One solution is to create a temporary file to store the list of matches when the search form is submitted. When a link to return more matches is clicked, those matches are simply retrieved from the file. That way, a given search is done only once. To accomplish that goal, a unique ID must be assigned to each search, and that ID becomes the name of the cache file for that search. The ID could be returned to the client either in a cookie or hidden in the search form. This is very similar to maintaining session state as explored in Chapters 7 and 8. In fact, one can treat the list of matches as one of the state values that are to be propagated in a session. You will see how the big example in Chapter 13 does this.

Another approach is to keep one permanent cache file that collectively stores search results from all recent searches. Here all returned matches from a given search are marked with an ID and appended to the cache file. When the user requests more results from a search, the desired matches are returned from the entries in the cache matching that ID. Again, though, some mechanism must be in place to keep track of the ID numbers and to keep the size of the cache file from growing too large. Here, a new search that causes the cache to exceed, say, 5,000 entries might eliminate the oldest search in the cache. Note that this approach is better implemented with a relational database with random-access capability than with a text file, whose contents are only sequentially accessible. Thus this is like a state table. Most popular search engines employ a caching scheme similar to this using some type of random-access cache file.

12.5 SCANNING DIRECTORIES

We have referred you to this section several times, but this is the natural location to summarize directory operations, which are instrumental in whole-site searches. The contents of a directory are read using steps similar to those used for reading the contents of a file. The `opendir` function is used to open a directory, the `readdir` function to read its contents into an array, and the `closedir` function to close it.

```
opendir(DIRECTORYHANDLE, path_to_directory);
@array = readdir(DIRECTORYHANDLE);
closedir(DIRECTORYHANDLE);
```

The directory handle can be any legal identifier, just like a file handle. It is customary to use all capital letters. It is worth noting that directory handles and file handles live in different name spaces. That is, you can use the name of a directory handle as a file handle as well without confusion (to the Perl interpreter, at least).

The same concerns about directory paths also carry over. Depending on the configuration of the Web server, a complete path from the root may be required. An empty string for the path of the directory would attempt to open the "current" directory as known by the operating system, which may or may not be the directory containing the CGI program.

When giving the path to a directory, a final / is optional. That is, either

```
opendir(DIRECTORYHANDLE, /home/me/data/);
opendir(DIRECTORYHANDLE, /home/me/data);
```

will open a certain data directory. The `opendir` function returns true if successful and false otherwise, similar to the `open` function for files.

The `readdir` function returns list of the names of the files in the directory, including the names of any subdirectories that may be present. The best way to deal with the returned list is to assign it to an array variable.

For our main example on directory operations, suppose the Web site for a book has files and directories as shown in the left side of Figure 12.9. The figure shows a remote

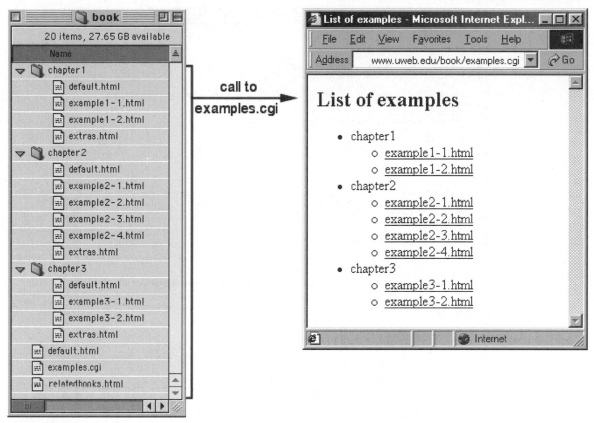

FIGURE 12.9 A CGI program that scans subdirectories for examples.

URL call to the program `examples.cgi`, which scans the book's Web site and creates the Web page you see on the right. Of course, there might be links to the examples in the other Web pages on the Web site. But here, the user can click a link provided in the main page, which calls the CGI program to generate the summary page for the examples on the fly. The idea here is that more chapter directories and examples can be added to the Web site, and the summary page for the examples will automatically reflect those additions when the CGI program is called. This example is effectively the blueprint for a *site map* utility.

The program first scans the main `book` directory, ignoring the other three files, and finding the folders for the chapters. The program then scans each chapter folder, picking out only the files for the examples. The `examples.cgi` program is shown in Figure 12.10, and an overview of the program is also shown. Note that the CGI program is sitting in the main `book` directory. (You can also see that in the browsers address field in Figure 12.9.)

- Set the path to the `book` directory and the base URL that will be used to create the links. Relative URLs (relative to the CGI program) could also be used.
- Read the main directory to get a listing of its contents (both file names and directory names).
- Make the `@chapterdirs` array, which contains only the names of the chapter directories. That is, `grep` out from the main directory's contents only the names that contain the pattern `"chapter"`.

```
examples.cgi

#! /usr/bin/perl

print "Content-type: text/html\n\n";

$mainDir = "/home/me/public_html/book/";
$mainURL = "http://www.uweb.edu/book/";

opendir(MAINDIR, $mainDir)) or &errorPage("Unable to open main directory.");
@maincontents = readdir(MAINDIR);
closedir(MAINDIR);
@chapterdirs = grep(/chapter/, @maincontents);

print <<TOP;
<html><head><title>List of examples</title></head><body>
<h2>List of examples</h2>
 <ul>
TOP

foreach $chapdir (sort @chapterdirs){
  if(opendir(DIR, "$mainDir$chapdir")){
    @files = readdir(DIR);
    closedir(DIR);

    @examples = grep(/example/, @files);

    print "<li>$chapdir<ul>"

    foreach $example (sort @examples){
      print "<li><a href=\"$mainURL$chapdir/$example\">$example</a></li>";
    }
    print "</ul></li>\n";
  }
}

print <<BOTTOM;
  </ul>
 </body></html>
BOTTOM

######################################################################
Definition of &errorPage function goes here
```

FIGURE 12.10 The CGI program whose output is shown in Figure 12.9.

- Print the top of the page, including the start tag for the main list.
- For each chapter directory, if it opens,
    - Read the @files in that directory. Note that $mainDir$chapdir evaluates to "/home/me/public_html/book/chapter1" when $chapdir contains "chapter1", for example.
    - Create the @examples array, whose elements are the file names that contain "example".
    - Print an item in the main list, and start a new inner list inside that item to hold the links for the examples.
    - For each $example file
        - Print a list item containing a link for that $example. Note that the file name of the $example is added onto the end of the base URL to create the href value.
    - Close the inner list for the examples and the outer list item for that chapter.
- Close the main list and print the rest of the page.

> **NOTE**
>
> The decoding routine is not necessary for this example, because no data from HTML forms is processed. Also, this program aborts and returns an error page to the user if the main directory fails to open, but it simply skips over a chapter directory that doesn't open successfully. Also note that we sorted the contents of each directory. Depending on the implementation of Perl, a directory listing may or may not come back sorted alphabetically.

12.6   FILE AND DIRECTORY TESTING

In performing searches over the directory tree of an entire Web site, it is desirable to be able to distinguish between files and directories. For example, as you scan a given directory, if you find a text file, you want to open it and search it. If you find another directory, you want to open it and scan its contents. Moreover, you might not want to open and search all files that are found. It is often desirable to open and search all HTML files (text files) while ignoring any binary files that may be present.

In the examples of the previous two sections, we relied solely on the file and directory names to choose only those files and directories that we wanted to search and scan, respectively. In many applications, it is better to let the system determine the nature of a file or directory rather than relying on names or perhaps file extensions. Especially when several people work on a Web site, file and directory naming conventions can become nonuniform as the Web site expands.

Table 12.3 lists some common Perl file- and directory-testing operators. The operators can be applied to both files and directories. So the argument of an operator refers to

TABLE 12.3   Operators that Test Files and Directories

OPERATOR	BEHAVIOR
-r	Returns true if argument is readable
-w	Returns true if argument is writable
-x	Returns true if argument is executable
-f	Returns true if argument is a file and not a directory
-d	Returns true if argument is a directory and not a file
-e	Returns true if argument exists
-z	Returns true if argument has zero size
-s	Returns number of bytes in file (so true if file exists and has nonzero size)
-T	Returns true if argument is a text file (as opposed to a binary file)
-M	Returns the number of days (real number) since last modification
-A	Returns the number of days since last access (the meaning of "access" may vary depending on operating system)
-C	Returns the number of days since creation (the meaning of "creation" may vary depending on operating system)

either a file or a directory. The operators -f, -d, -T are useful for scanning an entire Web site to pick out all the HTML files to search. The other operators are useful when more elaborate file diagnostics need to be performed.

These are unary operators that take a single file or directory name as the argument. The ones that return a Boolean value are typically used in conditional statements to determine what action to be taken regarding a file or directory. For example, the following might be used to test for HTML files in a given Web site.

```
$file=path/to/somefile;
if (-T $file) {
  assume the file is an HTML file and search it for the user's query
}
```

The following might be used when scanning a directory to see whether an item in the directory is an HTML file or another directory.

```
if (-d $directoryItem) {
  scan the directory to find more files
}
else {
  if (-T $directoryItem) {
  assume the file is an HTML file and search it for the user's query
  }
}
```

In another situation we might want to provide a descriptive error message if a file fails to open.

```
open(FILE, $file) or {
  if(!(-e $file)){
    print "File $file does not exist.\n";
  }
  elsif(!(-r $file)){
    print "File $file exists but is not readable.\n";
  }
  elsif(!(-T $file)){
    print "File $file is not a plain text file.\n";
  }
  else{
    print "File $file is a readable plain text file, but fails to open.\n";
  }
}
```

Going back to the observation that files and directories don't always get named consistently, we return to the example shown in Figures 12.9 and 12.10 that produced a list of links to examples. It is entirely possible that someone would put other files in the book directory that include the pattern chapter. In that case the @chapterdirs array would contain some files in addition to the chapter directories. To safeguard against that, we could test to make sure that each $chapdir is actually a directory before attempting to open it.

```
if((-d "$mainDir$chapdir") && opendir(DIR, "$mainDir$chapdir")) {
  read the examples from the directory
}
```

12.7 RECURSIVE WEB SITE SEARCHES

Web sites that are a collection of static HTML files often offer "site search" utilities. A versatile site search utility works in such a way that the utility requires no prior knowledge of the directory structure of the site. That is, the utility is not dependent on strict naming conventions for files and directories and is not limited to a preset directory tree structure. That way, the search utility still works when new Web pages and subdirectories are added to the site. The site can grow "deeper" with varying file and directory names, and the site search still works.

The best way to implement such a site search is to use a recursive function that "crawls" as deep as necessary into the site's directory tree to find and search all of the Web pages for the user's query. Before implementing such a search utility, we will talk through the logic of the recursive function, which we name recursiveSearch.

▩ sub **recursiveSearch**

   ▩ Open a directory.
   ▩ Scan its contents into a @contents array.
   ▩ **For** each $item in @contents

      ▩ **if** ($item is a directory)
         ▩ call **recursiveSearch** on $item. (This is the recursive step.)
      ▩ **else**
         ▩ $item is a file that we open and search for the user's query

To see exactly how the recursive search works, examine the Web site depicted in Figure 12.11. The Web site's root is the enclosing folder, named public. The recursive search begins by calling recursiveSearch on public. Figure 12.11 also gives the progress of the recursive search in sequential fashion. Note how the recursive function calls progress deeper into a given directory until there are no more subdirectories in that branch of the directory tree. In particular, at its "deepest" point, the recursive search progresses into dir4. The files in dir4 are searched long before those in dir6, for example, even though dir6 is only one level below the site root.

We now implement the recursiveSearch function in a scenario where an online music-related site provides a form with which users can search all of the music-related Web pages in the site. A sample submission of the search form is provided in Figure 12.12. The main page for the music store in the first window is simply a static Web page containing a search form and some links to music categories in case the user simply wishes to browse. However, the user can obtain more specific information quickly by using the site search form. From the code for the HTML form, which has been super-imposed on the Web page, you can see that no search value is hard-coded for the text field. The user has entered ozzy and clicked the submit (go) button.

The search results have been returned by a CGI program named sitesearch.cgi as shown in the second window. As we have learned to do, the search form has been returned hard-coded with the user's original data. The site (directory tree) used in the search in this example is the one shown in Figure 12.11. We simply added some text containing the word ozzy to four of the HTML files. As you can see, the search has "crawled" through the directory tree, picked out those four files, and created links pointing to them.

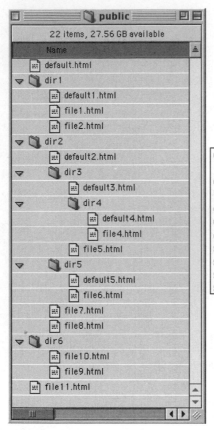

call on site root → search default → call on dir1 → search default1 → search file1 → search file2 → function call for dir1 completed → call on dir2 → search default2 → call on dir3 → search default3 → call on dir4 → search default4 → search file4 → function call for dir4 completed → search file5 → function call for dir3 completed → call on dir5 → search default4 → search file6 → function call for dir5 completed → function call for dir3 completed → search file7 → search file8 → function call for dir2 completed → call on dir6 → search file9 → search file10 → function call for dir6 completed → search file11 → function call for site root completed → end of recursive search

FIGURE 12.11   Tracing a recursive search of the entire directory tree of a Web site.

For this example, we named the Web site's root directory music, rather than public as shown in Figure 12.11. That change is evidenced in both the address fields of the browser windows and the links returned for successful matches. Also, the site-search.cgi program has been added to the site's root directory.

We do not provide the source code for the music store's home page; it's just a plain HTML file. However, the HTML code for the search form appears in the windows in Figure 12.12. The main brains behind this example are contained the sitesearch.cgi program, which is shown in Figure 12.13. An outline of the program also follows. The two functions used in the program are also provided, followed by overviews.

- Store the root directory for the site to be searched and the base URL that will be used to construct links to the matched pages.
- Store the user's search string.
- Print the top of the page.
- Call a helper function to print the form to be returned to the user hard-coded with the initial query.
- Print the code for the menu bar and the start tag for the HTML ordered list that is to display the search results.

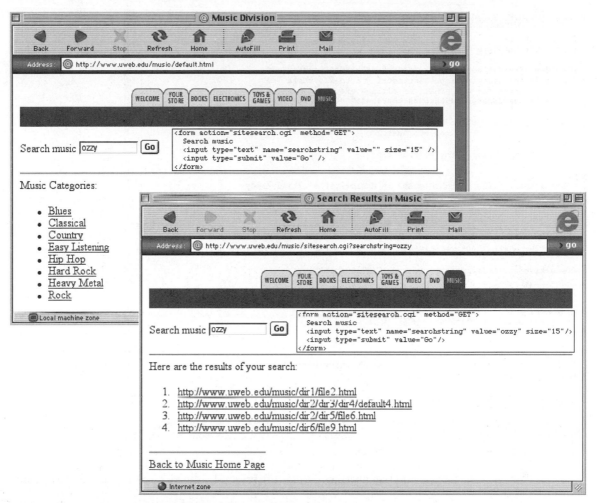

FIGURE 12.12 An implementation of a recursive site search.

▨ Call the `recursiveSearch` function, sending it the information it needs to get started. This function crawls the `music` directory tree and prints the list items containing the matches.

▨ Print the rest of the page, including the end tag for the HTML list.

```
sub searchForm {
  my $initialstring = $_[0];
  print<<FORM;
  <form action="$ENV{'SCRIPT_NAME'}" method="GET">
    Search music
    <input type="text" name="searchstring" value="$initialstring" size="15"/>
    <input type="submit" value="Go"/>
  </form>
FORM
}
```

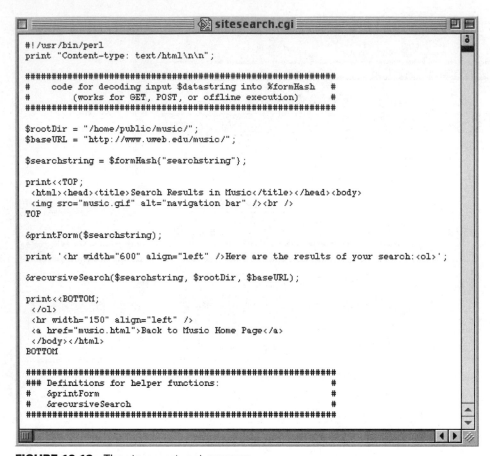

```
#!/usr/bin/perl
print "Content-type: text/html\n\n";

#############################################################
#     code for decoding input $datastring into %formHash   #
#         (works for GET, POST, or offline execution)       #
#############################################################

$rootDir = "/home/public/music/";
$baseURL = "http://www.uweb.edu/music/";

$searchstring = $formHash{"searchstring"};

print<<TOP;
 <html><head><title>Search Results in Music</title></head><body>
 <img src="music.gif" alt="navigation bar" /><br />
TOP

&printForm($searchstring);

print '<hr width="600" align="left" />Here are the results of your search:<ol>';

&recursiveSearch($searchstring, $rootDir, $baseURL);

print<<BOTTOM;
 </ol>
 <hr width="150" align="left" />
 <a href="music.html">Back to Music Home Page</a>
 </body></html>
BOTTOM

#############################################################
### Definitions for helper functions:                      #
#     &printForm                                            #
#     &recursiveSearch                                      #
#############################################################
```

FIGURE 12.13 The `sitesearch.cgi` program.

■ This function simply takes the user's query and hard-codes it as the value of the text area.

```perl
sub recursiveSearch {
  my ($searchstring, $dir, $url) = @_;

  if(opendir(DIR, $dir)) {
    my @contents = readdir(DIR);
    closedir(DIR);

    foreach $item (@contents) {
      if(-d "$dir$item") {
        if($item !~ /\A\./){ # to make sure it does not begin with a .
          recursiveSearch($searchstring, "$dir$item/", "$url$item/");
        }
      }
      else {
        if(($item =~/\.html\z/i) && open(FILE, "$dir$item")) {
          my @lines = <FILE>;
          close(FILE);
          my $wholefile = join("", @lines);

          if($wholefile =~ /$searchstring/i) {
            print "<li><a href=\"$url$item\">$url$item</a></li>";
```

```
         }# if
       }#if
     }#else
   }#foreach
 }#if
}#sub recursiveSearch
```

- Store the incoming parameters into local variables.
- If the directory opens (this function quits here and does nothing if the directory passed to it doesn't open).
  - Load the @contents of the directory
  - For each $item in the directory
    - If it's a directory (here, the diritem is the full path to the $item)
      - If it's not one of the special . or .. directories that some file systems automatically create
        - Call the recursiveSearch function on the directory. (Here diritem is now some subdirectory of $dir, and urlitem adds the path to the item onto the bas URL. In this way, the argument passed to the function "grows" as the recursion progresses deeper into the directory tree.)
    - else (it's a file)
      - If it's an HTML file and it opens
        - read all the @lines in the file
        - join the @lines of the file into one long string (it's easier to search for the user's query that way; otherwise, you would need to line-process the file)
        - If the user's query is found as a substring of the $wholefile
          - Print out a list item containing a link to the file. Again, you can see that urlfile will have been made to "grow" with successive calls to the recursive function. That is evidenced by the links in Figure 12.12.

An interesting feature of this recursive search program is that we don't quit the program and return an error page to the user if a file or directory fails to open. In such a case, that file or directory is simply skipped over. It is often the case that certain directories (or files) in a Web site are intentionally not accessible to the public for privacy or security reasons.

It is also worth noting that the recursiveSearch function can be called on any directory, not just the root of a public domain. For example, you can see in Figure 12.13 that this search was called on a music folder inside the public domain. The search then "crawled" the entire directory tree below music.

It is likely that the other departments (the other menu tabs you see in Figure 12.12) of the site would also use the same search program. In that case, the search forms in the various department pages would contain hidden fields telling the CGI program the directory on which to call the recursive search.

Better yet, the same search form could be used in the Web page for each department. The form could contain a pull-down menu that the user could use to choose which department to search or to choose to search the entire store. Indeed, that is how the site search utilities on the major commercial retail sites work. Check out Amazon.com and Buy.com, for example. (We hope those will still be in business when you read this!) A similar modification to this example is left as an exercise.

Of course other modifications could be added as well. For example, we might wish to add the whole-word option as in many of the examples of this chapter. Another feature that most online searches employ is to return the list of matches ranked according to "how well" they match the user's query.

Yet another feature you often see on the Web is to return not just a link to the matched page, but also some of the text of the page so that the user can see in what context the match for the query was made. For example, we might wish not to explore links returned for "Ozzy and Harriet" but pursue the ones for "Ozzy Ozbourne". There are several options for returning descriptions of matched Web pages. The most common are to pull out the contents of the HTML title element, some of the meta information contained in the HTML `meta` elements, or both. Several of these features that we have mentioned are also left as exercises.

NOTE

You should contrast searches that return links to Web pages, and possibly some text to elucidate the nature of the links, with searches that return matched items, such as products, from databases. The former are geared for finding Web pages, either on the Web at large or from a given site. The latter are geared for searching databases of inventories so that lists of product descriptions can be returned to the user.

NOTE

When scanning the contents of a directory, it is always best to check that the name of a file (or subdirectory) matches an expected format before using it. Sometimes the contents of a directory might include unexpected files or subdirectories of which you are unaware. For example, on some flavors of UNIX and Linux, and on Microsoft Windows, two special "subdirectories" (`.` and `..`) are automatically created as part of the file system.

Verifying that file types are as we expect is a practice to which we adhere religiously. That is evidenced in the `loadData` function, where we test for `.txt` file suffixes even though we expect only those file types to be in the data directory.

12.8 EMBEDDING WEB SEARCHES IN YOUR PAGES

There are numerous commercial search engines on the Web, as you are no doubt aware. However, it is a major undertaking to make one, particularly a good one. Here is basically how they work.

A given search engine uses an elaborate program, commonly called a *crawler* or *spider*, that systematically goes around the Web finding Web sites. Once a new site is found, the Web crawler recursively follows links in that site until all of them are explored. Typically, the spider grabs the URL of a page, the contents of the HTML `meta` elements, and the contents of the HTML `title` element. This retrieval requires only an HTTP HEAD request. But the Web crawler may grab more or less, depending on its objectives. It may even scan the contents of the Web pages recording the words that occur with the most frequency (of course, ignoring words such as *for*, *it*, and, *and*).

Typically, an entire computer(s) is dedicated to running the Web crawler. Moreover, most of them run 24 hours a day, for the most part. The gathered results are stored in elaborate databases. A large search engine might use a roomful of computers just to store the data.

When you send a query to a search engine, a CGI program (or CGI-like program) accepts the query and enacts an elaborate database search. The most popular search engines have entire server farms sitting and listening for requests. Other than use of a (huge) relational database and the elaborate algorithm that searches it, the query submission process is not much different from the examples of this chapter.

In fact, it is easy to include a form in your Web pages that can send queries to commercial search engines. The main factor is to observe what data a given search engine sends back to the server when you make a query. The following two URLs resulted from a search for `wildebeest` on `Google.com` and `Metacrawler.com`.

```
http://www.google.com/search?q=wildebeest&btnG=Google+Search

http://search.metacrawler.com/crawler?general=wildebeest&method=
    0&redirect=&rpp=20&hpe=10&region=0&timeout=0&sort=0&theme=classic
```

The pertinent information is contained in the first name=value pairs in the query strings.

```
q=wildebeest
general=wildebeest
```

Google did not send much extra data to the server, but Metacrawler sent a bunch of stuff that looks mostly like default values for search refinements.

Using only the first name=value pairs from the query strings, we constructed the Web page shown in Figure 12.14. (Ok, we did grab the logos for the search engines.) The code we created for the HTML forms is superimposed on the browser window. The bold-faced parts were deduced from the two sample URLs we showed. It is interesting that `search` and `crawler` don't appear to be names of CGI (or CGI-like) programs. They might be programs without a file extension, or they might be directories, and the actual programs that do the search are the default files in those directories. Or, perhaps, they have a specialized HTTP server that deals with the requests in its own way.

You should go to this book's Web site and pull up this page and try it for yourself. Or, find a different search engine and make your own form to send a search. It only takes a couple of minutes. Note that there is no guarantee that a given search engine will work properly if you send it only the first name=value pair. It could be that the actual query is included later in the query string or that some type of information from hidden form fields is required. However, your query is usually in the first name=value pair in the submitted data, and most search engines work when only that pair is sent.

NOTE

It's generally acceptable to embed Web searches into private pages in this way. It is customary to "cite" the search engine by providing their logo on your page. After all, that's free advertisement for the search engine.

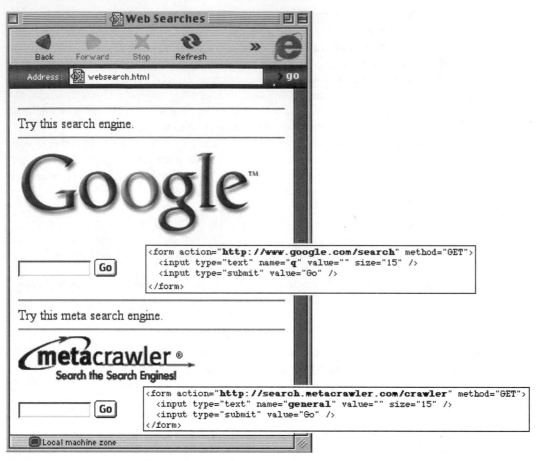

FIGURE 12.14 Two search engines manually embedded in a Web page.

It is interesting to note some of the extra stuff that is submitted to a search engine when something like a "next 10" link is clicked. We did just that for the two searches whose URLs were given previously. The following data was sent to load the next batch of search results.

```
http://www.google.com/search?q=wildebeest&hl=en&start=10&sa=N

http://mc1.metacrawler.com/
crawler?general=wildebeest&method=0&sid=107833846mc1_0_24&sno=2253&domainLimi
t=0&rpp=20&mrr=0&timeout=0&hpe=10&format=regular&power=0&tar-
get=&sort=0&refer=nav&start=20
```

You can see that both of them sent a start=*number* pair to determine which batch of results to return. Moreover, Metacrawler has sent an ID and search number, presumably to retrieve the next batch of results from a cache of recent search results. (See the note at the end of Section 12.4.)

> **NOTE**
>
> It appears that Google does not cache recent search results using ID strings. Apparently they either research for results each time or keep a cache of recent searches, where the actual query is effectively the ID for the search. If search results are cached where the cache IDs are the actual query strings, even different users can get quick results for a given search without bothering the third tier with another query. Common searches might even be cached using a prioritized scheme based on occurrence frequency.

*12.9   REGULAR EXPRESSION DATABASE SEARCHES WITHOUT RLIKE

Suppose we are using a database system (such as CSV or MS Access) that does not have regular expression capabilities. How does one do a whole-word search, as we did in products2.cgi? One technique is to use a standard SQL SELECT...LIKE statement to do a "crude search" and then use a Perl statement to refine the returned results.

In the case of matching a whole word, we first make an SQL statement that merely matches substrings. Then we perform a *secondary test* on the returned results using a Perl statement. Using regular expressions in Perl, we filter out those matches that are not whole-word matches. The general idea is that we wish to let the database system filter out as much as possible and then add a secondary filter using Perl. An alternate solution for the search function of products2.cgi follows, with an overview.

```perl
sub search {
  ### wholeword search without using RLIKE
  $searchstring = $formHash{"searchstring"};
  print<<TOP;
  <html><head><title>Results of your search</title></head><body>
    <h2>Here are the results of your search:</h2>
      <ol>
TOP

  my $sql = "SELECT item FROM products WHERE item LIKE '%$searchstring%'";
  my $qObj= $dbhandle -> prepare($sql) or &errorPage("Can't prepare ");
  $qObj-> execute() or &errorPage("Can't execute " . $qObj->errstr());

  my @row;
  my @matches = ();
  while(@row = $qObj->fetchrow_array()){
    if($formHash{"wholeword"}) {
      if($row[0] =~ /\b$searchstring\b/i){
        push @matches, $row[0];
      }
    }
    else {
    push @matches, $row[0];
    }
  }
  $qObj-> finish();

  foreach $match (@matches)
  {
    print "<li>$match</li>\n";
```

```
    }

    &searchForm($formHash{"searchstring"}, $formHash{"wholeword"});

    print<<BOTTOM;
</body></html>
BOTTOM
}
```

■ Construct, prepare, and execute the SQL using a standard SELECT...LIKE statement. No word boundary considerations are made at this time.

■ Then as the rows are fetched out of the query object, a secondary test is performed using a regular expression in Perl. A returned record is pushed onto the @matches array only if it passes the whole-word test. If the checkbox was not checked, the secondary test is bypassed.

SUMMARY OF KEY TERMS AND CONCEPTS

Search forms: Search forms should be self-contained in that a given search form can easily be added to many different pages (functions) in a Web application. It is customary to return the search form with the search results. It should be hard-coded with the original search criteria so that adjustments can easily be made.

Database searches: When a database table(s) is searched in a Web application, a list of matched records is returned. Typically each matched record would be displayed with a link or form button used to process the record further—add it to a shopping cart, for example.

Regular expressions in database searches: The SQL SELECT...LIKE statement can perform crude searches of database tables using two wildcard-like metacharacters. The SELECT...RLIKE (regular expression LIKE) extension to SQL adds the ability to query a database using the full power of regular expressions. However, the RLIKE extension may not include the special escape sequences that stand for locations and character classes.

Search refinements: Commercial search engines usually have elaborate refinement options for searches. This basically boils down to a human-friendly form with lots of refinement options, which is translated on the server into some combination of regular expressions and Boolean logic based on the submitted form.

Substitutions in search results: One example of secondary processing of returned search results is to highlight certain portions by substituting HTML tags. That is a simple matter, but it further illustrates secondary processing of results initially filtered by a database query.

Limiting returned results: It is customary to send only a few search results back to the client at a given time. Links provide means to acquire more results. The idea is simple in concept, but there are some logistics to be worked out to keep track of which results are on display and which ones a link requests.

Search result caching: When a search utility limits returned results, it should ideally cache the results from the initial search so that requesting more results does not require another database search. That can be done rather easily using state files or state tables. Some search engines seem to use the query itself as the cache ID, rather than some long session ID. That way, duplicate searches don't require a new database search.

Scanning directories: Reading all the file and directory names in a given directory into an array is nearly trivial. However, one usually wants to filter the contents in some way such as reading only files of a certain type. Also, it is a good idea to filter out all files beginning with a period, because many operating systems automatically include . and . . directories as part of the file system.

File and directory testers: Unary operators that give information about a file or directory: how old it is, whether it is a directory or a file, whether it is a text or binary file, how big it is, and so forth.

Recursive site search: A function scans a directory. When it finds another directory, it calls itself on the directory. When it finds a file, it processes it in some way. That processing might involve opening the file and searching it for some word or pattern, or it might involve processing only the file name to create a site map.

Embedding external search engines in a page: A form to query a commercial search engine can easily be constructed. You have to deduce the query string format a particular search engine uses and code your form so that it generates similar query strings.

Non-RLIKE database searches (optional section): If the database engine you use doesn't support the RLIKE SQL extension, it is really no more difficult to perform a secondary filter on the returned data records using Perl. It's really just a matter of whether the database engine or the Perl program does the filtering work.

EXERCISES

Note: The full products table, which is needed for some exercises, is available on the Web site formatted as a text file and as a MySQL file. Furthermore, all of the searching exercises can easily be fitted with a feature that returns no results (rather than the whole database table) when an empty search (only whitespace characters) is submitted.

1. Modify the products4.cgi program of Section 12.4 so that there are links [1][2], . . . (for the first five matches, second five, etc.). So, if there are a total of 17 matches, then there should be links for pages 1, 2, 3, and 4. You may still retain the "next" and "previous" links.

2. Extend the products4.cgi program of Section 12.4 so that you can refine the search according to the department. The program should automatically determine which departments are available and print a multiple-selection menu in the search form. Results are returned only from the chosen departments. If you read the department names from that column of the table, the application is vulnerable to typos in department names. The preferred solution is to create a second table, whose primary key is a department ID and another column contains the department description. The main table should then contain department IDs instead of descriptions.

3. Extend the products4.cgi program of Section 12.4 so that returned matches can be sorted alphabetically by item (the default), alphabetically by department, or numerically by price. You may choose the type of form element used to give the options.

4. Add functionality to the results returned by the products4.cgi program of Section 12.4. Add a column to the products table for items of prices. Each matched product should be returned as a row in an HTML table, which summarizes the product. Each row should have a text field for entering a quantity to purchase, and an "Add to Cart" button. Adding an item to the cart simply returns the same page (with the same group of search results). The search results page should have a "View Cart" link or button which pulls up a page that summarizes the current contents of the cart. Use anonymous state (state files or state table) for the shopping session. There is no need to include a final checkout functionality for this exercise.

5. Improve the `products4.cgi` program so that it works for phrases. So that a sequence of space-delimited words is not treated as one word, extract all stand-alone words from the search string. Do not assume that only a single space appears between each word. Then test for the words using an "or" functionality. Make sure the whole-word option still works. Add another option to the search form that says "match all words" ("and" functionality).

6. *Caching search results:* See again the notes at the end of Sections 12.4 and 12.8 (and 10.3). Set up a database table with at least 10 records, which contains some words to search for. The search form should only return three records at a time, and single-word searches are sufficient (as opposed to phrase searches). In either case below, the cache should be self-policed.

   (a) Develop a middle-tier cache for the search utility. Use long session IDs for search identification. You may use a state table or state files. This is basically just an example of anonymous state in a Web application where the state data comes from the data tier!

   (b) Make the middle-tier cache more efficient by using the query as the search ID. A search first queries the cache to see whether that search is already cached. If not, it hits the database.

7. *Ranking search results:*

   (a) Work Exercise 5 and rank the returned search results for an "or" search. Count how many of the submitted words appear in each returned record, and rank the results based upon that. This requires a substantive program logic change. The returned results can no longer be printed as they are fetched out. Rather, global arrays (or hashes) should keep track of matched records and their corresponding ranking scores. You may wish to augment the product descriptions with more words (whether meaningful or not) to help you test your ranking algorithm.

   (b) Add the "and" search option and simply sort returned records alphabetically according to product name.

8. Make a simulated Web site several directories deep. Add HTML files to the directories, with some directories having more than one file. Intersperse a few dummy files with non-HTML extensions. Write down a list of 12 words. Add these words to the HTML files, varying the number and choices of words in each file. The body of each HTML file need only contain a few such words.

   Make a CGI program whose main page has the following features. Of course, all of the following tasks should be done recursively.

   (a) A link pulls up a page with a site map, where the hierarchical directory structure of the site is reflected by nested HTML lists. Each site map link should pull up the associated file. Filter out all non-HTML files from the site map.

   (b) A search form returns a list of links to matched HTML files based on single-word matches of the words inside. The form should have an option for whole-word searches (as opposed to the default of substring matches).

   (c) Extend the search capability so that it can handle a phrase using an "and" functionality. See Exercise 5 for more details.

   (d) Extend the search capability so that it can handle a phrase using an "or" functionality. See Exercise 5 for more details.

   (e) In an "or" search, the returned results should be ranked by some algorithm. See Exercise 7 for more details.

9. Make a simulated Web site as discussed in Exercise 8. You will need to add some extra phrasing around your words for this problem. However, this problem requires fewer words for testing purposes. This problem need only use single-word searches, but any of the options from the exercise can be added.

(a) The returned list of matched files should contain added information about the match. Pull out the contents of the HTML `title` element and the description given in the `meta` description element. This information should support each link when it is found. (You will need to make sure a few of the HTML files have such elements.)

(b) Further support each link by pulling out of the HTML files up to 50 characters on both sides of the matched word.

(c) Instead of part (b), pull out up to 15 words on both sides of the matched word.

PROJECT THREAD

Here you begin a significant upgrade to the administration side of the quiz application. This upgrade will be finished in Chapter 13. The goal is to provide a test bank from which the administrator can create customized quizzes. The administrator should be able to add new questions to and delete questions from the test bank. This Chapter develops a search utility that enables the administrator to search the test bank. Before you begin, carefully read the folllowing items, and plan the new branch of the transaction diagram.

A. Develop a new database table for the pool of available questions, where each record is a quiz question. Start with the questions from your original quiz and add several more questions. The table should have a primary key to identify each question uniquely. With that done, the table containing the actual quiz questions, which you developed in Chapter 10, need contain only the keys of questions currently used for the quiz.

B. Update the the quiz application so that there is a new page after the administrator logon. It should provide an option to see the administration page (list of completed quizzes, statistics, and so forth) you have already developed and one that pulls up a new page as outlined in part C, which we will call the current quiz page.

C. The current quiz page should contain a list of the questions currently in the quiz and the correct answers. They need not be printed using menus or groups of checkboxes, for example, because the question list is only for the administrator to look at. (In Chapter 13, you will add "edit" and "delete" options for each question.) The current quiz page should also contain a search form as outlined in part D.

D. The search form should contain options to list all questions from the question pool, list only questions with single answers, or list only questions with multiple answers. There should be a text field that enables searches for questions containing a keyword. There should also be a whole-word option (not part of a bigger word) for keyword searches. A search should return a page with a list of the results and, of course, the search form hard-coded with the search criteria. As in part C, the questions (with answers) need only be formatted for human reading as opposed to being submittable questions. (In Chapter 13 you will add "edit" and "add to current quiz" options for each question.)

E. Add a new row for the updated quiz application to the table in your homework page. Make sure you preserve the version from the previous chapter and keep the link to it active. If you are assigned any other exercises from this Chapter, add another row to your homework table for each exercise.

A COMPLETE EXAMPLE AND SECURITY SUMMARY

We have learned about many facets of Web applications, but at this point, four major concepts emerge. Here are the major pieces of the puzzle we have given you:

1. Generating HTML forms dynamically from back-end data sources and processing the user data that the forms collect

2. Maintaining session state over multiple transactions, including maintaining anonymous or logged-on state

3. Using relational data in the data tier

4. Providing search capabilities

In this chapter we put these puzzle pieces together. The result is a fairly sophisticated Web application simulating an online store (e-tailer). With these four main concepts already in place, incorporating them all into one meaningful Web application chapter requires a careful design strategy. You will see that a careful plan and a systematic design process are half the battle. Also, more data is involved in larger applications, and one has to consider carefully its structure. The first two sections of this chapter address the design issues. Then the application is coded from the ground up. Next, a design for the administrative component for the application is presented. Finally, an overview of important security issues is provided.

13.1 DESIGNING THE FUNCTIONALITY OF AN ONLINE STORE

The bulk of this chapter will be focused on creating a Web application that is an online retail store. We want this application to have many of the features desired in a real-life setting. We make a decision that this store sells only music CDs. The desired features of the store are as follows:

- Users do not need an account to browse the store with a shopping cart.
- Users do need an account to check out with a purchase. At checkout time, the user is required to register an account with billing information and a credit card number. Existing users can choose to log on at the onset so that they can breeze right through checkout, or they can wait and log on at checkout.

- Users can search the store inventory. The search utility should have several refinement options (search for particular artists, albums, or songs; search for music by category). The user can have the returned results sorted by album, artist, or year.

- The search results should be returned in small groups, each with a link to return the next group.

- Users should be able to click on a link to pull up the complete details of an item.

- Users can add items to a shopping cart. They should also be able to update the purchase quantity of an item that's already in the cart and completely delete an item in the cart.

- Upon checkout, the user should get an order summary. If the user is not signed up or logged on as a user at this point, the user is required to do so.

- The user can either finalize the order or go back and make adjustments.

- When an order is finalized, the user should get a thank-you Web page and a confirmation e-mail. The store writes the order to a database table, and a confirmation e-mail is sent.

That's a lot of features. But even such a list does not adequately represent all of the transactions that the application must be capable of handling. Of course, the best way to get a handle on the complete functionality of an application is to draw a transaction diagram, complete with needed Web pages and function calls. The diagram for the store is provided in Figure 13.1. It would be unthinkable to attempt to code such an application without a solid plan in place.

Much of the transaction diagram can be developed straight from the initial plan. However, that plan does not detail all the transactions. You really have to start drawing from the top and really think about what a user should be able to do from a given page. Then more arrows and pages start to materialize. The capabilities of this application were devised by keeping in mind our previous online shopping experiences. Of course, more than one drawing was sketched before the final functionality of the application was determined. The time put into planning the exact capabilities of a Web application before starting to code it is paid back several times over before you are done.

The basic algorithm to employ when developing a large Web application is broken up into four primary steps.

- Make a plan for the basic functionality and features of the application.

- Construct a transaction diagram to refine the plan and detail the necessary printed Web pages and the transactions among them. (Then make a better diagram, because your first attempt(s) will be a jumbled mess!)

- Detail the data needs of the application. That includes any back-end data sources and any state information that is necessary. Decide on the structure of the stored data. It pays to write helper functions to write and extract data at this point. That way, your data needs are taken care of when it comes time to tackle the transaction diagram.

- Code the application, starting from the top of the transaction diagram and writing functions one at a time. At each juncture where it is possible, test the function.

We are now ready to tackle the data needs of the application in the next section.

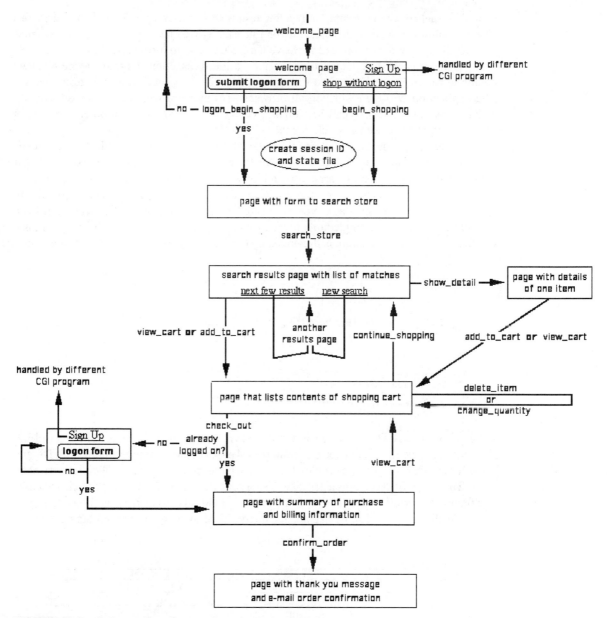

FIGURE 13.1 A transaction diagram for an online music store.

13.2 DESIGNING THE APPLICATION'S DATA TIER

One of the first decisions we make is where to store the state information. Whether the user logs on anonymously or as an existing user, state must be kept, because there are search results that need to be cached, and there is a shopping cart. (Recall from Section 12.4 that search results should be cached when returning only a few results at a time and providing links for more.) The best solution is to use either state files or a state table. We make a decision to use state files to keep all of the information, and we leave it as an exercise to use a state table.

That decision is reflected near the top of the transaction diagram. Moreover, we decide to return the session ID to the client hidden in Web pages rather than in cookies. The application will then work on all browsers. If this store were part of an advertising ring or tracking network (recall Section 8.5), where cookies are used for other purposes as well, we might have used a cookie for the session ID.

Before planning the details of the state file, it's best to begin with the data needs from the ground up. In this case, that means the product inventory. Because some of that data ends up in the shopping cart and search results, that is the first task on our agenda.

We will use a relational database named `cdstore` to store various tables containing data for the CD store, such as tables for customers, inventory, and orders. We shall store the entire inventory in a single table named `inventory`. The information about each music CD that we decide to maintain is illustrated by the following SQL `CREATE TABLE` statement:

```
CREATE TABLE inventory (
  stockID INTEGER,
  category VARCHAR(30),
  artists VARCHAR(256),
  album VARCHAR(100),
  quantity INTEGER,
  price REAL,
  label VARCHAR(30),
  songs VARCHAR(500),
  year INTEGER,
  description VARCHAR(500),
  imagefile VARCHAR(20)
)
```

For example, each CD has one row in the `inventory` table, which is depicted in Figure 13.2. For simplicity, we choose integer stock numbers. These should be unique among the CDs, and we will use the `stockID` as the primary table key. It is clear what the rest of the fields represent.

The `songs` field contains a delimited list of song names, but is only one field in the table. For flexibility, we allow the `category` and `artists` fields also to be lists, as shown in Figure 13.3. Like the `songs` field, those lists are delimited with semicolons and treated as single fields.

Table: **inventory**

stockID	category	artists	album	quantity	price	label
122	Metal	Memory Garden	Mirage	7	14.99	Metal Blade Records

— continue row —

songs	year	description	imagefile
song1;song2;song3;...	2001	Epic doom from Swedish Rockers.	coverPhoto.gif

FIGURE 13.2 The `inventory` table.

Table: **inventory**

stockID	category	artists	album
314	soundtrack;movie	Elton John;Nathan Lane	The Lion King

• • •

FIGURE 13.3 An inventory record with composite `category` and `artists` fields.

NOTE

We "flattened" some of the store's data into single records in the inventory table. A more advanced solution would be to put such data into separate tables where the primary key is the stock number and the rest of the fields are song names, for example. We would then have several tables related by the primary key. With a suitable database engine, we could then access all of the data for a given CD by the stock number without having to rip delimited strings of data apart. One concern with this solution is that the maximum number fields in the songs, category, and artists tables would need to be predetermined, because once a table is made, the number of columns is not easily extended. It is easy to extend the number of columns with most database GUIs, but not with a single SQL command.

Now we turn to the state file. Recall Section 7.8, where we discussed the general strategy for anonymous versus logged-on state. If a user logs on, we need to put the user name in the state file so that we know who is shopping when the user checks out. If the user shops anonymously, no user name will be added to the state file until the "logon for checkout" phase.

From the planning already done, we also know that we need to store search results and shopping cart data in the state file. That puts three different chunks of data in the file. Moreover, one or more of the chunks might not be in there at a given time. Of course, this is not a problem, because we are treating the state information as a hash. In fact, there will likely be additional state information we wish to save as we develop this application.

There may or may not be a state value `user=user_name`, depending upon when the user logs on. The shopping cart will be kept on one line, using only the stock numbers to identify which products are selected, but each selected product also needs an associated purchase quantity. When extracted from the state file, a shopping cart like the following results in an `&`-delimited string of cart items, stored under key `cart` in the `%stateHash`.

```
cart=742=1&412=3&125=2&...
```

This cart reflects that the user has added 1 of product number 742 and 3 of product number 412 to the cart, and so forth. For simplicity, we have decided to encode the shopping cart as one string. It is undesirable to treat each cart item as a separate state value, since it would not be predetermined how many of them there are and, hence, how many cart keys should be extracted from a state file.

For the same reason, all results returned from a product search are stored as one value in the state file. However, it is difficult at this point to determine exactly what values for a search should be maintained in the state file, because we have not yet designed the form. However, if we treat the state information as a hash in a file, it is not necessary to determine that now.

Using the state file functions from Chapter 7, we will simply extract the entire state file into a `%stateHash` when state information is required. For example, `$stateHash{"cart"}` will access the shopping cart. We can then make an addition or alteration to the cart, store the new cart back into `$stateHash{"cart"}`, and write the entire `%stateHash` back to the state file with no consideration whatsoever of what other information `%stateHash` holds.

Now we design the customer accounts. All customer accounts shall be stored in one table, named `customers`, in our database `store`. The information we shall keep on our customers is illustrated with the following SQL `CREATE TABLE` statement. The username will be the primary table key. We will also store passwords in this table. (We leave it as an exercise to use encrypted passwords.) Thus, we will have to write database versions of the `logon` toolkit function from Chapter 7.

```
CREATE TABLE customers (
    user VARCHAR(32),
    password VARCHAR(32),
    name VARCHAR(32),
    address1 VARCHAR(80),
    address2 VARCHAR(80),
    city VARCHAR(40),
    state VARCHAR(40),
    zip VARCHAR(10),
    country VARCHAR(40),
    email VARCHAR(40),
    phone VARCHAR(32),
    creditcard VARCHAR(32)
)
```

As you can see from the transaction diagram in Figure 13.1, we are going to use a separate program to deal with signing a user up. That's more on the administration side of the application, which we discuss in a later section. For our purposes in designing the application, we will just use a preconstructed user account record, such as shown in Figure 13.4.

NOTE

If you want to logon to the working version on the Web site, you will have to be Frodo Baggins (although, hopefully, you are in a better plight). His user name is `fbaggins`, as you can see from the name of his account file. His password is `hobbit`.

We are about done with the application's data needs. One consideration is the CD cover images. We can simply designate a directory for them and use them as needed. If we name the images according to the stock numbers, `234.jpg` for example, retrieving one for a given CD will pose no difficulty.

Table: **customers**

user	password	name	address1	address2	city	state
fbaggins	hobbit	Frodo Baggins	The Hill		Hobbiton	The Shire

——— continue row ———

zip	country	email	phone	creditcard
12345	Middle Earth	frodo@shire.com	123-1234	1234-1234-1234-1234

FIGURE 13.4 A user account record.

Database: **cdstore**

Table: **orders**

orderID	user	cart	orderdate	status	total	balance
413	fbaggins	742=1&412=3	7/4/2002	neworder	44.33	44.33

Table: **customers**

user	password	name	address1	
fbaggins	hobbit	Frodo Baggins	The Hill	...

Table: **inventory**

stockID	category	artists	album	quantity	
122	Metal	Memory Garden	Mirage	7	...

FIGURE 13.5 The cdstore database.

Finally, there is the store's "order to fill" table, which keeps purchase orders. We decide on something simple, as follows.

```
CREATE TABLE orders(
    orderID INTEGER,
    user VARCHAR(32),
    cart VARCHAR(100),
    orderdate VARCHAR(16),
    status VARCHAR(10),
    total REAL,
    balance REAL
)
```

In summary, we will use a database system (assume MySQL) to maintain most of the data, with the state data going into text files. The cdstore database is pictured in Figure 13.5. Assume that the user "storeuser" with password "pass" has full privileges to this database. Aside from this database, we will need a directory for the state files and one for the CD cover images.

13.3 BUILDING THE APPLICATION

With a firm strategy in place for dealing with the data required by the music store, the next order of business is to code the application. First we make a list of the toolkit functions for state file management at our disposal. Of course, our old friend errorPage is a must.

&get_long_id

&get_random_string

&read_state

&write_state

&errorPage

We will also need to write a database version of the logon function. We call it dblogon. It takes a database handle, name of the table, and user and password. The logic of the function is identical to that of the old logon function. This function should be added to the toolkit.

```
sub dblogon {
  ### It is assumed that the columns are named user and password.
  my($dbhandle, $table_name, $alleged_user, $alleged_pass) = @_;

  my $sql = "SELECT password FROM $table_name WHERE user = " .
            $dbhandle->quote($alleged_user);
  my $qObj = $dbhandle -> prepare($sql) or &errorPage("Failure to access user
  info.");
  $qObj -> execute() or &errorPage("Failure to access user/pass info.");
  my @row = $qObj->fetchrow_array(); ### one-element array
  $qObj -> finish();
  if(@row){ ### row exists implies user exists ###
    if($alleged_pass eq $row[0]) {
      return "yes";
    }
    else {
      return "Invalid password.";
    }
  }
  return "Invalid user.";
}
```

Armed with these functions, the transaction diagram, and an idea of the application's data storage needs, we start coding. After the standard intro lines and decoding routine for form data, we define the global variables.

```
$file_life_span = 1; # for state files (in days)
$cache_limit = 30;
$file_time_out = 3.0/24; # in days (3 hours)

$stateDir = "/home/store/states/";
$imageDir = "//www.uweb.edu/images/"; # used in URL for img src

%stateHash=();

$inventory_table = "inventory";
$customers_table = "customers";
$orders_table = "orders";
```

The foresight in setting the names of the tables in global variables will pay off if we ever decide to use a different table name, or more tables. We also connect to the database at the beginning of the program.

```
use DBI;
$dbhandle = DBI->connect("DBI:mysql:cdstore", "storeuser", "pass");
```

The app logic functions are apparent from the transaction diagram. Planning the functions that are needed to handle the main transactions of the application is a crucial benefit of the transaction diagram. We still have many details to iron out, but the app logic is a substantive starting point.

```
if($formHash{"request"} eq "login_begin_shopping")    {&login_begin_shopping;}
elsif($formHash{"request"} eq "begin_shopping")        {&begin_shopping;}
elsif($formHash{"request"} eq "search_store")          {&search_store;}
elsif($formHash{"request"} eq "show_detail")           {&show_detail;}
elsif($formHash{"request"} eq "add_to_cart")           {&add_to_cart;}
elsif($formHash{"request"} eq "view_cart")             {&view_cart;}
```

```
elsif($formHash{"request"} eq "continue_shopping")    {&continue_shopping;}
elsif($formHash{"request"} eq "delete_item")          {&delete_item;}
elsif($formHash{"request"} eq "change_quantity")      {&change_quantity;}
elsif($formHash{"request"} eq "check_out")            {&check_out;}
elsif($formHash{"request"} eq "logon_for_checkout")   {&logon_for_checkout;}
elsif($formHash{"request"} eq "confirm_order")        {&confirm_order;}
else                                                  {&welcome_page;}
```

We begin from the top of the transaction diagram, writing functions and testing them before moving along. In the process, the need for some more helper functions will become apparent. Those are written as needed and added to the list of those we already have at our disposal for dealing with state and logon. For organizational purposes, such a list should be kept on scratch paper.

Logging On

First, we examine the arrows outgoing from the welcome page on the transaction diagram to see what transactions the page is capable of initiating. There are three: log on, begin shopping without logon, and sign up. The first must be handled with a form, but links are sufficient for the other two. The welcome_page function follows.

```
sub welcome_page {
  my $message = $_[0]; ### takes an optional message parameter
  print <<PAGE;
<html><head><title>Music CD Store</title></head><body>
   <h2>Welcome to the Music CD Store</h2>
   $message
   <form action="$ENV{'SCRIPT_NAME'}" method="POST">
   <b>You may either log in now</b><br />
   User name: <input type="text" name="user" size="20"/><br />
   Password: <input type="password" name="pass" size="20"/><br />
   <input type="hidden" name="request" value="login_begin_shopping"/>
   <input type="submit" value="Log in"/>
   </form>
   <b>or <a href="$ENV{'SCRIPT_NAME'}?request=begin_shopping">
      begin shopping and login later</a></b>
   <hr />
   If you do not have an account with us, you may
   <a href="signup.cgi" target="_blank">sign up now</a> or sign up later.
</body>
</html>
PAGE
}
```

Since this function is called again if logon fails, it needs the optional $message parameter. The main things to note are the request values the page submits, depending upon whether the logon form or the link to begin anonymous shopping is submitted. The signup link is handled by a separate CGI program that we do not develop until Section 13.4. You can note that the link is set up to target the returned output from the signup.cgi program to a nonexistent frame name. Thus, the signup page gets displayed in a new window that pops up. (With JavaScript, we could control the size of that window.) For now, we assume the user already has an account or wishes to shop anonymously.

We now test the function by calling the main CGI program, which we name musicstore.cgi. Of course, with no request value, the welcome_page function is called. We can't do anything else with that page yet, but at least we can get it formatted nicely, as shown in Figure 13.6.

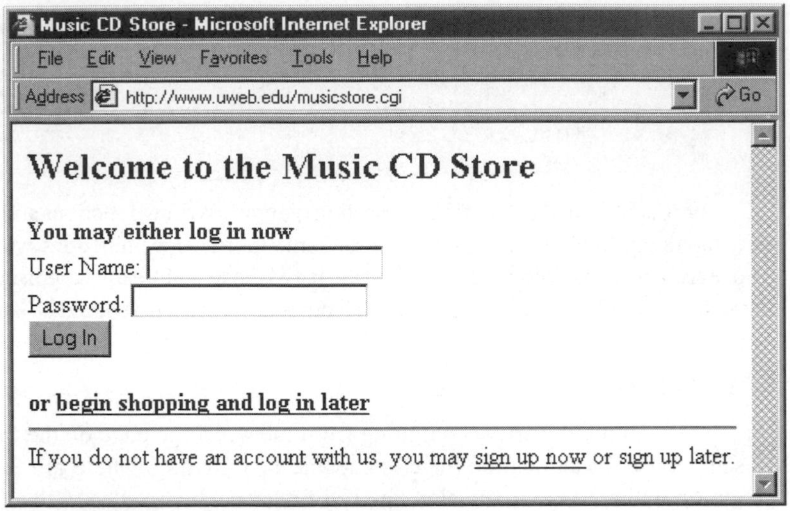

FIGURE 13.6   Calling the `welcome_page` function.

The next order of business is one of the two functions to begin the shopping spree. We write the `begin_shopping` function first because it's the most simple. The first order of business is to generate a session ID and create a state file with that name. The file is empty at this point because there is no relevant state information as of yet. The page is quite simple, and simply offers the user a form used to search the store. Since that form will also be used by the `logon_begin_shopping` function, we decide to make a helper function, `print_search_form`. Since *all* submitted forms will have to carry the `$sessionID` in a hidden element, we send that to the function.

```
sub begin_shopping {
  my $sessionID = &get_long_id($stateDir, $cache_limit, $file_life_span);
  &write_state($stateDir, $sessionID); # empty state hash

  print <<TOP;
  <html><head><title>Music Store</title></head><body>
    <h2>You will need to log in later when you check out.</h2>
    Please search our collection
TOP

  &print_search_form($sessionID);

  print<<BOTTOM;
</body></html>
BOTTOM
}
```

But we can't just charge right in to creating the `print_search_form` function. First, we need to decide what search options to provide. To that end, it is best to draw out some sample forms on scratch paper. Then, make a sample form in a text editor or HTML WYSIWYG editor. That way, you already have a good bit of the HTML code handy when it comes time to code the function that prints the form. (Such planning may not be necessary if a form is very simple.)

After some trial and error, we decide the search form similar to that in Figure 13.7 is appropriate. When a form is complicated, it also helps to have the names planned out.

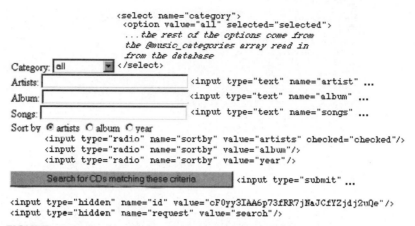

FIGURE 13.7 Design the form before making the function.

Now, everything is determined except the menu options that are created based upon the available inventory. When writing quality search utilities, it is especially important to have your hands on the form in advance. Remember from Chapter 12 that after a search, the search form should be returned to the user hard-coded with the search criteria that were submitted. That way small refinements can be made based upon the first search without the user having to remember and retype.

The hard-coding principle is especially important to remember when going from the HTML form to writing the function that prints it. When called from scratch, the function simply prints the form as shown in Figure 13.7, but when it is called after a search, it needs the previous form values in order to hard-code those into the form. Thus, the function needs to be set up to receive (optional) parameters corresponding to previously submitted form values. You can see these parameters at the top of the `print_search_form` function, which follows. An itemized overview of the function follows its code.

```perl
sub print_search_form {
  my ($sessionID, %info) = @_;
  my ($category, $artists, $album, $songs, $sortby) =
    ($info{"category"}, $info{"artists"}, $info{"album"}, $info{"songs"},
      $info{"sortby"});

  if($category eq "") {
    $category="all";
  }
  if($sortby eq "") {
    $sortby="artists";
  }
  print<<FORMTOP;
  <form action="$ENV{'SCRIPT_NAME'}" method="GET">
    Category: <select name="category">
FORMTOP

  # determine the list of categories
  my $sql = "SELECT category FROM $inventory_table";
  my $qObj = $dbhandle -> prepare($sql) or &errorPage("DB: Failure to prepare.");
  $qObj -> execute() or &errorPage("DB: Failure to execute.");

  my @row;
```

```
  my %tempHash=(); # To de-duplicate the category names
  while(@row = $qObj->fetchrow_array()){
    foreach $c (split(/;/, $row[0])){
      $tempHash{lc $c}=1;
    }
  }
  $qObj -> finish();
  my @categories = sort keys %tempHash;
  foreach $v (("all", @categories)) {
    print '<option value="', $v, '"';
    if($category eq $v) {
      print ' selected="selected"';
    }
    print ">$v</option>\n";
  }

  print <<FORMMID;
  </select><br />
  Artists:
  <input type="text" name="artists" value="$artists" size="30"/><br />
  Album:
  <input type="text" name="album" value="$album" size="30"/><br />
  Songs:
  <input type="text" name="songs" value="$songs" size="30"/><br />
  <input type="hidden" name="id" value="$sessionID"/>
  <input type="hidden" name="request" value="search_store"/>
  Sort by
FORMMID

  foreach $v (("artists", "album", "year")) {
    print '<input type="radio" name="sortby" value="', $v, '"';
    if($sortby eq $v) {
      print ' checked="checked"';
    }
    print "/>$v\n";
  }
  print<<FORMBOTTOM;
    <br /><input type="submit" value="Search for CDs matching these criteria"/>
  </form>
FORMBOTTOM
}
```

■ The previous search parameters are passed into the function in the form of a hash %info. This hash method offers easier scalability if in the future we decide to pass more parameters in.

■ If no previously selected $category is incoming, set it to the default of "all".

■ If no previously selected $sortby option is incoming, set the default sort option to "artist".

■ In order to print a pop-up menu containing an "all" blanket category, we need a list like ("all", "metal", "soundtrack" . . .) where the music categories come from only those CDs that are in stock. One would be tempted simply to use the whole column category from the inventory table. However, that could yield many duplicate values, because several CDs are likely to exist from the same music category. A nifty solution is to store the column values (after splitting at any semicolons) as keys in a $tempHash with dummy values (for example, metal =>1). That way, when another of the same music category is stored into $tempHash, a new key is not created. This has the effect of storing the union of the original column values as keys in the temporary hash. Then assigning those keys to a @categories array, we have an array of all music categories found in inventory, with no duplicates.

- For each of `"all"` and the specific `@categories` (because of the flattening effect, we just end up with a list like `("all","metal",. . .)` as desired)
  - Print an option, making it the selected menu option if it matches the incoming `$category`.
- Print the text fields, hard-coding them with the incoming values. Note that those values are empty if no previous search criteria were submitted to the function.
- Print the two hidden form elements.
- Print the three radio buttons, setting the incoming `$sortby` option to be checked.
- Print the rest of the form.

With that done, we can now test the `begin_shopping` function, which displays the search form. When the bugs are worked out, we should be able to click the "begin shopping and log in later" link shown in Figure 13.6 and get a page with a form similar to that shown in Figure 13.7. We would then look at the HTML source code returned to the browser and make sure the long session ID is hidden in the form as planned. We could also check to make sure there is an empty state file in the proper directory.

Referring back to the transaction diagram, we write the `logon_begin_shopping` function before moving on to the `search_store` function. With the `print_search_form` function already done, all we really have to deal with is the customer logon, and we already have a helper function for that.

```perl
sub login_begin_shopping {
  my $result = &dblogon(
    $dbhandle, $customers_table, $formHash{"user"}, $formHash{"pass"});
  if($result ne "yes") {
    &welcome_page("Logon failed ($result). Please try again.<br/>");
    exit;
  }

  my $sessionID = &get_long_id($stateDir, $cache_limit, $file_life_span);
  %stateHash = ("user"=>$formHash{"user"});
  &write_state($stateDir, $sessionID, %stateHash);

  print <<TOP;
<html><head><title>Music Store</title></head><body>
  <h2>You are now logged in as $stateHash{"user"}.</h2>
TOP

  print "Please search our collection.\n";
  &print_search_form($sessionID);

  print<<BOTTOM;
</body></html>
BOTTOM
}
```

- Store the `$result` of the logon attempt.
- If the user failed to log on, send the user back to the welcome page with the failure `$result` included in the message. Exit the program.
- Otherwise the user logged on successfully, so generate a session ID.
- Initialize `%stateHash` with key `user` and a value of whatever the user name is.
- This becomes a `user=`*someUserName* line in the state file that is created.
- Print the search page, giving the user a personalized message this time, and calling the helper function to print the actual form.

FIGURE 13.8 A successful logon.

We would then test this new function, bringing the application up to the point of executing the search. Using the logon feature, we now see a search page similar to that shown in Figure 13.8. Keep in mind that if the user is shopping anonymously, there is an empty state file. Otherwise, the state file contains only one line for the user name.

> **NOTE**
>
> When the search form is submitted, either after anonymous or user logon, the session ID is passed into %formHash with the transaction. To continue to track the session and identify the user's state file, *every* Web page in the application after this must resubmit the session ID to the Web server.

The Search

Now we can go on to the search_store function. Again, we have to make a plan first. For starters, we don't want to return all search results—just display the first few matches and provide links that can be used to see more matches. We saw that strategy for returning search results in Section 12.4. For simplicity we return only two search results at a time.

The plot thickens, though. At this point, we really have to examine the transaction diagram carefully to see what all the search results page should contain. There are four arrows outgoing from the results page, representing five transactions that the page should be able to initiate:

- Links to load more results (another call to search_store)
- Form for new search (another call to search_store); fortunately, we have set up the function that prints the search form to be reusable and able to hard-code the form with prior search results

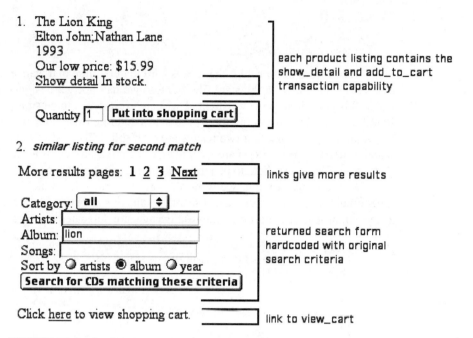

1. The Lion King
   Elton John;Nathan Lane
   1993
   Our low price: $15.99
   Show detail In stock.

   Quantity 1 [**Put into shopping cart**]

   → each product listing contains the show_detail and add_to_cart transaction capability

2. *similar listing for second match*

More results pages: 1 2 3 Next → links give more results

Category: [all ⬍]
Artists: [   ]
Album: [lion   ]
Songs: [   ]
Sort by ○ artists ● album ○ year
[**Search for CDs matching these criteria**]

→ returned search form hardcoded with original search criteria

Click here to view shopping cart. → link to view_cart

FIGURE 13.9 Design the results page before attempting to code the functions.

- A call to `show_detail` so that the user can see more details about an item before deciding to buy it
- A call to `add_to_cart` so that the user can choose the item
- A call to `view_cart` so that the user can see what's already in the cart

These five transactions need to be initiated by either links or forms. As always, it is very helpful to make a sketch of what the page might look like before starting to code the Perl functions. Figure 13.9 shows our idea of a results page that can initiate the five transactions. Each of the five transactions are marked on the diagram. A link would be sufficient for the `add_to_cart` transaction were it not for the quantity field.

This is a crucial juncture in the program. In particular, the `search_store` function has to print a lot of stuff for the five transactions. Another key point, however, is what to do with the most recent search results between transactions. If the user adds an item to the shopping cart and then returns to the results page to `continue_shopping`, it is desirable that the results of the previous search be redisplayed. Moreover, it is desirable that the user can return to the results page from anywhere in the application without "losing" the most recent search criteria and results. To accomplish that, the most recent search results are added to the state file and treated as part of the current state of the application. This also facilitates returning more search results, without having to research the product inventory. Using the search shown in Figure 13.9, the state file will contain the following lines. (Actually, it would possibly contain a user name line, and the & characters would be URL-encoded.)

```
search_results=123&345&592
start=1
artists=
```

```
album=lion
songs=
sortby=album
category=all
```

Recall from Section 13.2 that it was hard to determine in advance what lines related to a search should be in the state file, because we had not yet designed the search form. But at this point it becomes apparent: The search results are to be stored as one line in the state file, with the product numbers of matches delimited with ampersands. The start line has value 1 because the first two results are on display. The rest of the lines are the user's search criteria. Those criteria are contained in the returned search form, but keeping them in the state file allows them to be recovered during any transaction in the application.

With all this in mind, we write the `search_store` function. The main job of the function is to store the most current search results into the state file. The other tasks, such as the actual search and printing the results page, are delegated to helper functions.

```
sub search_store {
    %stateHash = &read_state($stateDir, $formHash{"id"}, $file_time_out);
    my @search_results;

    if(exists $formHash{"start"}) { # if existing start value, use previous search results
        @search_results = split(/&/, $stateHash{"search_results"});
        $stateHash{"start"} = $formHash{"start"};
    }
    else { # else do new search
        @search_results = &search_inventory;
        $stateHash{"search_results"} = join("&", @search_results);
        $stateHash{"start"} = 1;
        $stateHash{"artists"} = $formHash{"artists"};
        $stateHash{"album"} = $formHash{"album"};
        $stateHash{"songs"} = $formHash{"songs"};
        $stateHash{"category"} = $formHash{"category"};
        $stateHash{"sortby"} = $formHash{"sortby"};
    }

    &write_state($stateDir, $formHash{"id"}, %stateHash);
    &display_results_page;

}
```

- First, get the session ID that was submitted from the search form and read any state information in the corresponding state file into a global `%stateHash`. In particular, this recovers the most recent search from the state file.
- If the call to this function is the result of clicking a link to get more search results
  - Store into `%stateHash{"start"}` the start value that was submitted with the link that requested more matches. None of the other search information in `%stateHash` needs to be updated here, only which batch of results is on display.
- Else (it's a new search)
  - Store the list of `@search_results`. (We know the search itself will be gory, so we enlist a helper function `search_inventory` and deal with that later.)
  - Join the returned list of matched stock numbers into an `&`-delimited string.
  - The rest of the lines here simply record all the information about the current search into `%stateHash` so that it can be written into the state file.
- Write the updated `%stateHash` to the proper state file. Note that if we are printing more results only the `start` key is modified. Otherwise all the search data in the state file is new.

■ Call a helper function to print the actual page. It can easily obtain all the information it needs from the global %stateHash, which still contains the most current search results that were written to the file.

Because the &display_results_page function prints the actual page, we write that first, followed by the helper functions we create to handle some of its dirty work. Remember, since this function prints the results page, it has to print two kinds of forms and several links to handle the five transaction types of which the page is capable. Refer back to Figure 13.9.

```
sub display_results_page {
  my @matches = split(/&/, $stateHash{"search_results"});
  my $resultsPerPage = 2; # constant: number of results per page

print <<TOP;
  <html><head><title>Music Store</title></head><body>
    <h2>Search Results.</h2>
TOP
  &display_listing($stateHash{"start"}, $resultsPerPage, @matches);

  if( @matches > $resultsPerPage) {
    &print_search_links($stateHash{"start"}, scalar @matches, $resultsPerPage);
  }

  &print_search_form($formHash{"id"}, %stateHash);

  print "Click <a href=\"$ENV{'SCRIPT_NAME'}?request=view_cart"
      "&id=$formHash{id}\">", "here</a> to view shopping cart.<br/>\n";

  print<<BOTTOM;
</body></html>
BOTTOM
}
```

■ Receive the parameters.

■ Set the number of $resultsPerPage.

■ Call a display_listing helper function to deal with printing the list of matched products.

■ If the number of matched products exceeds the number that are to be displayed per page, call a print_search_links helper function to print the links that are used to request more matches. Otherwise, no such links are printed.

■ Print the search form, hard-coded with the original search criteria. We accomplish this by passing the hash %stateHash, which contains all the search parameters.

■ Print the link that calls the application and tells it to show the shopping cart.

The search_store function deals with updating the %stateHash and state file with the current search criteria. Its helpers do the dirty work. In turn we just delegated three tasks in the display_results_page function to helpers. The following list shows all the helper functions (and subhelpers) used by search_store to complete the results page, with helper functions indented relative to the functions they help:

```
&search_store
  &search_inventory
  &display_results_page
    &display_listing
```

```
        &getInfo
        &print_search_links
        &print_search_form
```

We continue with the helpers to print the results page. Fortunately, we have already written the `&print_search_form` function. After that we will return to the function that does the actual product search. Note that the link to trigger `view_cart` in the results page resubmits the session ID from `%formHash`. Indeed, every link or form has to resubmit that ID in order to continue the session. Refer back to Figure 13.9 to keep in mind what a product listing created by `display_listing` looks like.

```perl
sub display_listing {
  my ($start, $number, @matches) = @_;
  if(@matches <= 0) {
    print "Sorry, no matches.";
  }
  else{
    print "<ol start=\"$start\">\n";
    @matches = ("",@matches); # trick to match up index with counter
    for($k = $start; ($k < $start+$number) && ($k<=$#matches); $k++) {
      my ($album, $artists, $year, $price, $quantity) =
        &getInfo($matches[$k], "album", "artists", "year", "price", "quantity");
      print "<li>",
        "$album<br />",
        "$artists<br/>",
        "$year<br />\n",
        "Our low price: \$$price<br/>";

      print "<a href=\"$ENV{'SCRIPT_NAME'}?request=show_detail",
        "&id=$formHash{'id'}&stockID=$matches[$k]\">",
        "Show detail</a>\n";

      if($quantity > 0) {
        print <<FORM;
          In stock.
          <form action="$ENV{'SCRIPT_NAME'}" method="GET">
          Quantity <input type="text" name="qty" value="1" size="3" maxlength="3"/>
          <input type="hidden" name="stockID" value="$matches[$k]"/>
          <input type="hidden" name="id" value="$formHash{'id'}"/>
          <input type="hidden" name="request" value="add_to_cart"/>
          <input type="submit" value="Put into shopping cart"/>
        </form>
FORM
      }
      else {
        print "Out of stock. ";
      }
      print "</li>\n";
    }# end for
    print "</ol>\n";
  }# end else
}
```

■ Receive the incoming parameters.

■ If the `@matches` array is empty, the search came up empty.

■ Start the ordered list, setting `start="$start"` to determine where the list ordering begins.

■ Add an empty match onto the front of the `@matches` array so that indices align with the start numbers. That is, the first match is now `$match[1]`.

■ For `$k` from the starting number to (the starting number + the `$number` of results to display) and (while there are still matches left)

- Use a helper function &getInfo to get a list of information corresponding to the stockID. Save the elements of this list into local variables.
- Print the product information.
- Print the link to show the details of the product.
- If it's in stock
  - Print the small form that is used to add the product to the shopping cart.
- Else, it's out of stock

If you refer back to the product listing, this function is easy to understand. It is worth noting that the link to show detail and the form to add to the shopping cart both pass along the product number. That's all that is necessary to know about the product. Of course, the proper function calls and the session ID are also passed along. Here is the helper &getInfo function.

```
sub getInfo {
  my ($stockID, @columns) = @_;
  my $sql = "SELECT " . join(", ", @columns) .
            " FROM $inventory_table WHERE stockID = $stockID";
  my $qObj = $dbhandle->prepare($sql) or &errorPage("Can't prepare.");
  $qObj->execute() or &errorPage("Can't execute. " . $qObj->errstr());

  my @info = $qObj->fetchrow_array(); # We fetch only the one row
  $qObj->finish();
  return @info;
}
```

This function takes a stockID and a list of column names. It returns the list of specified column values from the row that has the specified stockID. This is a very useful helper function indeed, because we can specify the columns that we want.

After the product listing comes the links for more results. In particular, note in Figure 13.9 that the current results start number is boldfaced and not underlined as a link. Also, remember that   is the escape sequence for a blank space in HTML.

```
sub print_search_links {
  my ($start, $matches, $resultsPerPage) = @_;
  my $nextstart;
  print "More result pages: \n";

  $nextstart = $start - $resultsPerPage;
  if($nextstart >= 1) {
    print "<a href=\"$ENV{'SCRIPT_NAME'}?request=search_store",
          "&id=$formHash{'id'}&start=$nextstart\">",
          "Previous</a>  \n";
  }

  for($k = 1; $k < 1+$matches/$resultsPerPage; $k++) {
    $nextstart = ($k-1)*$resultsPerPage+1;
    if($nextstart == $start) {
      print "<b>$k</b>", "  \n";
    }
    else {
      print "<a href=\"$ENV{'SCRIPT_NAME'}?request=search_store",
            "&id=$formHash{'id'}&start=$nextstart\">",
            $k, "</a>  \n";
    }
  }

  $nextstart = $start + $resultsPerPage;
  if($nextstart <= $matches) {
    print "<a href=\"$ENV{'SCRIPT_NAME'}?request=search_store",
```

```
                    "&id=$formHash{'id'}&start=$nextstart\">",
                    "Next</a>  \n";
        }
}
```

- Receive the incoming parameters.
- Set $nextstart to be the current $start minus $resultsPerPage. This is to test whether we are far enough ahead of $start=1 that we wish to print a "previous results" link.
- If a "previous results" link is warranted,
  - Print it, setting the $nextstart value to return to the previous batch of results. (for example, if current $start is 5, $nextstart is 3)
- For $k from 1 to the number of results links to print (for example, for 11 matches, there should be 6 links, showing two at a time)
  - Set the proper $nextstart value. (for example, showing 2 results at a time, $k=1 gives $nextstart=1, $k=2 gives $nextstart=3, $k=3 gives $nextstart=5, and so forth).
  - If we're on the current $start value
    - Just print a boldface results page number, not a link.
  - Else
    - Print a link with the results page number, which passes along the $nextstart value.
- Now set $nextstart ahead of the current $start value to see whether a "next results" link is warranted.
- If a "next results" link is warranted,
  - Print it, and set the $nextstart value to move ahead to the next batch of results. (For example, if current $start is 5, $nextstart is set ahead to 7.)

This function prints a sequence of links like

Previous 1 2 **3** 4 Next

where the next and previous ones are present only if required, the current page is bold-faced rather than rendered as a link, and the $nextstart values are properly set. The main technical hurdle in the function is due to the fact that the page numbers for the links are offset from the actual $nextstart values.

OK, so the all the printing for the results page is done. That leaves the search_inventory function. Once done with that, we can test the search capability and the look of the results page.

```
sub search_inventory {
  my @matches = ();
  my $category = lc $formHash{"category"};
  my $artists = $formHash{"artists"};
  my $album = $formHash{"album"};
  my $songs = $formHash{"songs"};
  my $sortby = lc $formHash{"sortby"};

  my @where = (); # store an array of constraints
  if((lc $category ne "all") && ($category ne "")){
    push @where, "category LIKE " . $dbhandle->quote("\%$category\%");
  }
  if($artists ne "") {
    push @where, "artists LIKE " . $dbhandle->quote("\%$artists\%");
  }
  if($album ne "") {
    push @where, "album LIKE " . $dbhandle->quote("\%$album\%");
```

```
}
if($songs ne "") {
  push @where, "songs LIKE " . $dbhandle->quote("\%$songs\%");
}
my $where = join(" AND ", @where); # put constraints together
if($where ne "") { $where = " WHERE $where";}

my $sql = "SELECT stockID FROM $inventory_table $where ORDER BY $sortby ASC";
my $qObj = $dbhandle->prepare($sql) or &errorPage("can't prepare.");
$qObj->execute() or &errorPage("can't execute ".$qObj->errstr());

my $stockID;
while(($stockID) = $qObj->fetchrow_array()) {
  push @matches, $stockID;
}
$qObj->finish();

return @matches;
}
```

- Initialize a local empty `@matches` array.
- Store the search criteria submitted from the search form into some local variables. We do this because we may need to reset some of these values to default values.
- Create the `WHERE` clause that goes into an SQL `SELECT` statement. Build an array of individual conditions. Note the liberal use of the database handle method `$dbhandle->quote(...)` to quote the strings. This takes care of any special characters that might be in those strings, such as single quotes, which are possible with names, albums, and songs.
- Join the array together into one string, separated by `" AND "`.
- If this `WHERE` clause is nonempty, then we prepend the keyword `"WHERE"`.
- We then carefully construct the SQL select statement. Note the `"ORDER BY"` clause specifies the order of the returned table.
- We then go through the usual motions to execute this SQL statement. A one-column table is returned consisting of all the `stockID`s that fit the criteria. We fetch and push all these `stockID`s onto an array, and we return the array.

As you can see, building long SQL statements can be a bit tricky. The main work came in constructing the `LIKE ... AND` clause based upon the user's search criteria. After a typical search and all of the Perl variables are interpolated, the following SQL statement might result (we've added extra whitespace for readability).

```
SELECT stockID
  FROM inventory
  WHERE artists LIKE '%Elton John%' AND album LIKE '%lion%'
  ORDER BY album ASC
```

Recall that the `%` characters are SQL metacharacters that match zero or more of any character. So the search criteria are matched as substrings of fields in the `inventory` table. (We did not have to use `RLIKE` and the full power of regular expressions here.) Also, we could have used `OR` to join the `LIKE` clauses, but `AND` returns more specific results. For example, in the SQL statement just shown, the user probably doesn't want Elton John albums without the word "lion" in the title.

OK, that was a lot of function writing, but we can now test the results page. After working out numerous bugs, we get the page shown in Figure 13.10. Referring back to the

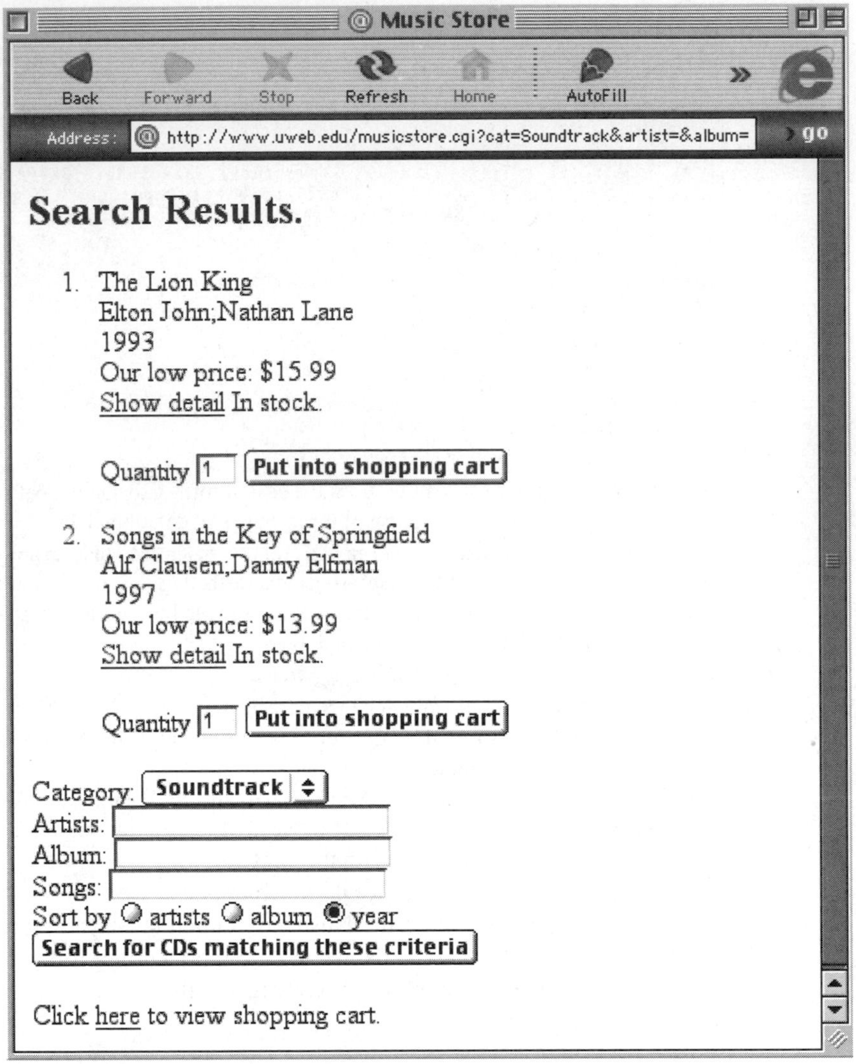

FIGURE 13.10 Testing the results page.

transaction diagram, we also see that we can test the two transactions (more results, new search) that call the search_store function again. That leaves us needing to write the functions for the three other transactions enabled by the results page.

Product Detail

Now that we have product listings returned from a search, a natural next step is to write the show_detail function so that we can see a full listing for a product. Again we sketch on scratch paper what such a listing might look like. The aesthetics are a matter of choice, but we do know from the transaction diagram that the listing should be able to handle the add_to_cart and view_cart transactions. You can see the form and link, respectively, for

Songs in the Key of Springfield
Alf Clausen;Danny Elfman
1997 Rhino
Our low price: $13.99
In stock

Songs:

1. Bad Bart
2. Lisa's Blues

Your favorite songs from the TV show.

Quantity 1 [**Put into shopping cart**]

Click here to view shopping cart.

FIGURE 13.11 Design of a product detail display.

those two transactions at the bottom of Figure 13.11. They are identical to the ones in Figure 13.10. The rest of the information in the product description comes from querying the inventory table for the record with a given stock number; this is easily done with the &getInfo helper function we have already developed.

One last thing to recall before we write the function is that the song list for a given CD is stored as one data field, where the individual songs are delimited with semicolons: song1;song2;song3; ...

```perl
sub show_detail {
  my ($album, $artists, $year, $price,
    $quantity, $songlist, $desc, $image, $label) =
  &getInfo($formHash{"stockID"}, "album", "artists", "year", "price",
    "quantity", "songs", "description", "image", "label");
  my $instock = "In stock";
  if($quantity<=0) {
    $instock = "Out of stock";
  }
  $songlist =~ s/;/<\/li>\n<li>/g;
  $songlist = "<ol><li>$songlist</li></ol>";
  print <<TOP;
<html><head><title>Music Store</title></head><body>
  <table>
    <tr>
      <td>
        <img src="$imageDir$image" height="100"/>
      </td>
      <td>
        $album<br/>
        $artists<br/>
        $year $label<br/>
        Our low price: \$$price<br/>
        $instock
      </td>
    </tr>
    <tr>
      <td colspan="2">
        Songs: $songlist
      </td>
```

```
          <tr>
          <tr>
            <td colspan="2">
               $desc
            </td>
          <tr>
       </table>
TOP
   if($quantity > 0){
     print <<FORM;
     <form action="$ENV{'SCRIPT_NAME'}" method="GET">
       Quantity <input type="text" name="qty" value="1" size="3" maxlength="3"/>
       <input type="hidden" name="stockID" value="$formHash{stockID}"/>
       <input type="hidden" name="id" value="$formHash{id}"/>
       <input type="hidden" name="request" value="add_to_cart"/>
       <input type="submit" value="Put into shopping cart"/>
     </form>
FORM
     }

   print "Click <a href=\"$ENV{'SCRIPT_NAME'}?request=view_cart",
       "&id=$formHash{id}\">", "here</a> to view shopping cart.<br/>\n";

   print<<BOTTOM;
</body></html>
BOTTOM
}
```

- Use the helper function `&getInfo` to retrieve all relevant info of the product with given `stockID`.
- Assume the product is `$instock`. If not, reverse the assumption.
- Do a global substitution on the `$songlist`, replacing each semicolon with `</li><li>`. That's a clever way to turn the delimited string into an HTML list. Note that we had to escape the `/` in the closing tag.
- Now add the "outside" tags to complete the list.
- Add the image for the CD cover.
- The next table cell contains the product's other information, including the `$instock` status we set previously.
- Put the `$songlist`, already formatted as a list, into the first table cell in the next row.
- The second cell in the second table row gets the product description.
- If the product is in stock
  - Print the form that calls `add_to_cart`.
- Print the link that calls `view_cart`.

Along with a `request` call to the proper function, the link and the form submit the session ID to continue state in the application. Also, the `add_to_cart` form submits the product ID, so the function knows what product to add. We now test the "Show detail" link as shown in Figure 13.10, hopefully getting a product description similar the original "sketch" in Figure 13.11. (OK, we are cheating. But we did make a sketch when we wrote the program!)

The Shopping Cart

We next write the `add_to_cart` function, which can be called through identical forms from either the search results page or the product listing page. Recall from Section 13.2

that the entire shopping cart is stored in the state file in the following format (actually, the value would be URL-encoded) under the key of `cart`.

```
134=1&423=2&776=1
```

The main job of the `add_to_cart` function is to read the previous cart contents from the state file, split the items apart, update the quantity of the current product being added (or add a totally new product), put the cart back together into a string, and write it back into the state file. That being done, `add_to_cart` calls a helper function to do the actual printing of the shopping cart page.

```perl
sub add_to_cart {
  %stateHash - &read_state($stateDir,$formHash{"id"}, $file_time_out);
  my $n = $formHash{"stockID"};
  my $qty = $formHash{"qty"};
  $qty = int $qty;
  if($qty < 1) {
    $qty = 1;
  }

  my %cartHash=();
  foreach $item (split(/&/, $stateHash{"cart"})) {
    my ($key, $value) = split(/=/, $item);
    $cartHash{$key} = $value;
  }
  if(exists $cartHash{$n}) {
    $cartHash{$n} = $cartHash{$n} + $qty;
  }
  else {
    $cartHash{$n} = $qty;
  }

  my @cart = ();
  foreach $key (sort keys %cartHash) {
    push @cart, "$key=$cartHash{$key}";
  }
  $stateHash{"cart"} = join("&", @cart);
  &write_state($stateDir, $formHash{"id"}, %stateHash);

  &display_cart_page($n);
}
```

- Read the proper state file into `%stateHash`.
- Get the stock number of current item, which was hidden in the submitted from.
- Get the quantity, which was submitted from the text area in the form.
- Two precaution lines: Make sure the quantity is an integer and is bigger than zero. (It would be better to do such validation on the client with JavaScript.)
- Initialize a local `%cartHash`.
- Split out the items in the cart.
- For each item in the cart
  - Split and store the `stockID=quantity` pair in `%cartHash`.
- If the product is already in the cart
  - Add the newly submitted quantity onto the previous quantity.
- Else
  - Make a new entry in the `%cartHash` for the product and quantity.

Stock#	Album	Qty	Unit price	Subtotal	To change qty	To delete
314	The Lion King by Elton John;Nathan Lane, 1993.	1	$15.99	$15.99	[1] [Change]	Delete
742	Songs in the Key of Springfield by Alf Clausen;Danny Elfman, 1997.	2	$13.99	$27.98	[2] [Change]	Delete

The total is $43.97.

[Check out]

To continue shopping.

FIGURE 13.12 Design for the shopping cart display.

- Declare a local @cart array; this will be of help turning %cartHash back into an &-delimited string of stockID=quantity pairs.
- Loop through the hash pushing the key-value pairs onto the @cart array as key=value strings.
- Join the key=value strings together into a delimited string and store them back into $stateHash{"cart"}.
- Write the %stateHash back into the proper state file. Note that only the "cart" value in the state file was modified. The other lines in the file just came along for the ride.
- Call a helper function to print the actual shopping cart.

Before printing the shopping cart page, we refer back to the transaction diagram to see what particular transactions need to be able to be initiated from the page. There are four: check_out, continue_shopping, delete_item, and change_quantity. With that in mind, we sketch what the shopping cart might look like, including a link or form for each of the transactions. The "sketch" is shown in Figure 13.12.

If you study the shopping cart, you will see links to continue shopping and delete an item, and forms to change a quantity or check out. We will have to remember to submit the session ID with each of those transactions. As an after thought, we decided to make the names of the products active as links as well. Those links simply trigger the show_detail function, sending it the stock number. It was not practical to add arrows for that on the transaction diagram, and it is quite trivial to implement with the show_detail function already at your disposal.

The only other point worthy of note is that we highlight the table row of the product that is newly updated. That way, a user who has several items in the cart can quickly find the most recently updated product. That is why we send the stock number of the current product (see the last line of the add_to_cart function). Otherwise, the stock number would not be necessary, because all of the shopping cart items are still stored in the global %stateHash created by that function.

```
sub display_cart_page {
  my $highlight_stockID=$_[0];
  print <<TOP;
<html><head><title>Music Store</title></head><body>
  <h2>Your shopping cart</h2>
  <table border=2>
    <tr>
```

```
        <th>Stock#</th>
        <th>Album</th>
        <th>Qty</th>
        <th>Unit price</th>
        <th>Subtotal</th>
        <th>To change qty</th>
        <th>To delete</th>
      </tr>
TOP

  my %cartHash=();
  my @items = split(/&/, $stateHash{"cart"});
  foreach $item (@items) {
    my ($stockID, $quantity) = split(/=/, $item);
    $cartHash{$stockID} = $quantity;
  }

  my $subtotal;
  my $total=0;
  foreach $n (sort keys %cartHash) {
    $color="";
    if($n eq $highlight_stockID) { $color='bgcolor="yellow"';}
    my ($album, $artists, $year, $price) =
      &getInfo($n, "album", "artists", "year", "price");
    $subtotal = $price*$cartHash{$n};
    $total = $total + $subtotal;
    $subtotal = sprintf "%.2f", $subtotal;
    print <<ITEM;
      <tr $color><td>$n</td>
        <td><a href=
    "$ENV{'SCRIPT_NAME'}?request=show_detail&id=$formHash{'id'}& stockID=$n">
          $album</a><br/>
          by $artists, $year.
        </td>
        <td align="right">$cartHash{$n}</td>
        <td align="right">\$$price</td>
        <td align="right">\$$subtotal</td>
        <td>
          <form action="$ENV{'SCRIPT_NAME'}" method="GET">
          <input type="text" name="qty" size="3" maxlength="3"
            value="$cartHash{$n}"/>
          <input type="hidden" name="stockID" value="$n"/>
          <input type="hidden" name="id" value="$formHash{'id'}"/>
          <input type="hidden" name="request" value="change_quantity"/>
          <input type="Submit" value="Change"/>
          </form>
        </td>
        <td><a href=
    "$ENV{'SCRIPT_NAME'}?request=delete_item&id=$formHash{'id'}& stockID=$n">
          Delete</a></td>
      </tr>
ITEM
  } # end foreach

  $total = sprintf "%.2f", $total;
  print "</table>The total is \$$total.<br/>\n";
  if($stateHash{"cart"} ne "") {
    print<<FORM;
      <form action="$ENV{'SCRIPT_NAME'}" method="GET">
        <input type="hidden" name="id" value="$formHash{'id'}"/>
        <input type="hidden" name="request" value="check_out"/>
        <input type="Submit" value="Checkout"/>
      </form>
FORM
  } # end if

  print<<BOTTOM;
```

```
<a href=
  "$ENV{'SCRIPT_NAME'}?request=continue_shopping&id=$formHash{'id'}">
  To continue shopping.</a>
</body></html>
BOTTOM
}
```

- Store the stock number of the incoming item so that its table cell can be highlighted.
- Print table header cells for each column of the shopping cart.
- Extract the individual shopping cart items back out of the `%stateHash` and store them as `$stockID` keys and `$quantity` values in `%cartHash`.
- Set up two local variables for the bill totals.
- For each `$n` (stockID) in `%cartHash`

    - If `$n` is the stock number of the newly updated one, set a color attribute to yellow.
    - Get relevant info using the `&getInfo` helper function.
    - Calculate the subtotal and running total, and format the subtotal nicely with two decimal places.
    - Print the stock number in the first table cell, the name (active as a link) and some other information in the second cell, the quantity, price, and subtotal in the next three cells, the form to change the quantity in the next cell, and the delete link in the last cell.

- Format and print the total.
- If the cart is not empty, print the form to trigger checkout.
- Print the link to `continue_shopping`.

We now go back to the search result page and attempt to add an item to it. After some debugging, trials, and errors, we get a Web page with a shopping cart that resembles the original "sketch" in Figure 13.12. The only other function that needs writing that gets called from above the shopping cart page in the transaction diagram is `view_cart`. You're going to like this one. All that it needs to do is load the current shopping cart from the state file into `%stateHash` and then call the `display_cart_page` function. This time, we send it no stock number, because there is no product being updated.

```
sub view_cart {
  %stateHash = &read_state($stateDir,$formHash{"id"}, $file_time_out);
  &display_cart_page("");  # so no item is hightlighted
}
```

We can now tie up a loose end by writing the `continue_shopping` function. Then, only functions that are called at or below the shopping cart page remain. Looking at the transaction diagram, we would be tempted to have `continue_shopping` call the `search_store` function, but recall that `search_store` merely updates the state file with the most current search results and then calls the `display_results_page` function to print the page.

So we need to bypass the `search_store` and call `display_results_page`. Recall that `display_results_page` expects no parameters. All it needs is the existence of a global `%stateHash` containing the most recent search results and criteria. Fortunately, that information is sitting in the state file.

```
sub continue_shopping {
  %stateHash = &read_state($stateDir,$formHash{"id"}, $file_time_out);
  &display_results_page;
}
```

Next, we complete the `delete_item` and `change_quantity` functions. Those are very straightforward. They simply need to get the shopping cart from the state file, alter it (delete or change an item), put the cart back in the state file, and then return the user to the shopping cart page. With that done, the battle will be over except for writing the `check_out` and `confirm_order` functions.

```
sub delete_item {
  %stateHash = &read_state($stateDir,$formHash{"id"}, $file_time_out);
  my $n = $formHash{"stockID"};
  my %cartHash=();
  foreach $item (split(/&/, $stateHash{"cart"})) {
    my ($key, $value) = split(/=/, $item);
    $cartHash{$key} = $value;
  }
  delete $cartHash{$n}; # removes the entry from the hash

  my @cart = ();
  foreach $key (sort keys %cartHash) {
    push @cart, "$key=$cartHash{$key}";
  }
  $stateHash{"cart"} = join("&", @cart);
  &write_state($stateDir, $formHash{"id"}, %stateHash);
  &display_cart_page(""); # so no item is hightlighted
}
```

- Recover the `%stateHash` from the proper state file.
- Store `$n`, the stock number of the item submitted from the link that calls this function.
- Extract the individual shopping cart items out of the `%stateHash` and store them as `stockID` keys and `quantity` values in `%cartHash`.
- Delete the item from `%cartHash`.
- Put the shopping cart string back together again and store it back into `%stateHash`.
- Call the `display_cart_page` function, setting no item to be highlighted.

```
sub change_quantity {
  %stateHash = &read_state($stateDir,$formHash{"id"}, $file_time_out);
  my $n = $formHash{"stockID"};
  my %cartHash=();
  foreach $item (split(/&/, $stateHash{"cart"})) {
    my ($key, $value) = split(/=/, $item);
    $cartHash{$key} = $value;
  }

  my $qty = $formHash{"qty"};
  $qty = int $qty;
  if($qty < 1) {
    $qty = 1;
  }
  $cartHash{$n} = $qty;

  my @cart = ();
  foreach $key (sort keys %cartHash) {
```

```
    push @cart, "$key=$cartHash{$key}";
  }
  $stateHash{"cart"} = join("&", @cart);
  &write_state($stateDir, $formHash{"id"}, %stateHash);

  &display_cart_page($n); # hightlight changed cart item
}
```

- Recover the %stateHash from the proper state file.
- Store $n, the stock number of the item to be altered, submitted from the link that calls the function.
- Extract the individual shopping cart items out of the %stateHash and store them as stockID keys and quantity values in %cartHash.
- Store the new $qty and do the simple validation.
- Replace the $qty of the item.
- Put the shopping cart string back together again and store it back into %stateHash.
- Call the display_cart_page function, this time telling it to highlight the altered item.

We first test the two cart modification functions and work out the bugs before moving on.

Checking Out

Now, it's time to check out. Again, we need to examine the transaction diagram carefully. Since the order summary page is to show the billing information, it's clear we are going to have to deal with the fact that some users are shopping anonymously. Recall that when a user logs on, all that happens is that a user=*userName* line is added to the state file. For anonymous shoppers that line is simply absent.

If that line doesn't exist, then we will call a helper function to deal with logging the anonymous user on. Otherwise, we can extract the user name from the state file, open the user's account file, and get the billing information. With that contingency thought out, we examine the arrows outgoing from the summary page to see what links or form need to be in the page to initiate transactions. There are only two: view_cart and confirm_order. So now, we sketch out a decent design for the summary page before attempting to code the function. The "sketch" is shown in Figure 13.13. We decide on a form button to complete the order and a link to go back to the shopping cart. Again, we make the product names active as links that call the show_detail function. That call does not appear on the transaction diagram but is trivial to implement.

```
sub check_out {
  %stateHash = &read_state($stateDir,$formHash{"id"}, $file_time_out);
  if($stateHash{"user"} eq "") {
    &display_logon_for_checkout;
    exit;
  }

  %userHash = &getAccountInfo($stateHash{"user"});
  print <<TOP;
<html><head><title>Music Store</title></head><body>
  <h2>Checking out...</h2>
  <table border=2>
    <tr>
```

```
            <th>Stock#</th>
            <th>Album</th>
            <th>Qty</th>
            <th>Unit price</th>
            <th>Subtotal</th>
        </tr>
TOP

    my %cartHash=();
    foreach $item (split(/&/, $stateHash{"cart"})) {
      my ($key, $value) = split(/=/, $item);
      $cartHash{$key} = $value;
    } # end foreach
    my $subtotal;
    my $total=0;
    foreach $n (sort keys %cartHash) {
      my ($album, $artists, $year, $price) =
        &getInfo($n, "album", "artists", "year", "price");
      $subtotal = $price*$cartHash{$n};
      $total = $total + $subtotal;
      $subtotal = sprintf "%.2f", $subtotal;
      print <<ITEM;
        <tr><td>$n</td>
          <td><a href=
            "$ENV{'SCRIPT_NAME'}?request=show_detail&id=$formHash{id}
            &stockID=$n">$album</a><br/> by $artists, $year.
          </td>
          <td align="right">$cartHash{$n}</td>
          <td align="right">\$$price</td>
          <td align="right">\$$subtotal</td>
        </tr>
ITEM
    } # end foreach

    $shipping = 5.00; #for simplicity
    $total = sprintf "%.2f", $total+$shipping;
    print "</table>Shipping is \$$shipping.<br />\n",
      The total is <b>\$$total</b>.\n",
      "<hr/>Please check your personal information.<table border=\"2\">\n";

    $userHash{"creditcard"} =~ s/.*(\d{4})/xxxx-xxxx-xxxx-$1/; #show only last 4 digits
    foreach $key (("name", "address1", "address2", "city", "state", "zip",
        "country", "email", "phone", "creditcard")) {
      print " <tr><td>$key</td><td>$userHash{$key}</td></tr>\n";
    }

    print <<BOTTOM;
      </table>
      We only show last 4 digits of credit card for security.
      <form action="$ENV{'SCRIPT_NAME'}" method="GET">
        <input type="hidden" name="id" value="$formHash{id}"/>
        <input type="hidden" name="request" value="confirm_order"/>
        <input type="Submit" value="Confirm purchase"/>
      </form>

      <a href=
        "$ENV{'SCRIPT_NAME'}?request=continue_shopping&id=$formHash{id}">
        To continue shopping.</a>
    </body></html>
BOTTOM
}
```

- Load the `%stateHash` from the proper state file.
- If the user is not logged on, call a helper function to deal with that. Exit the program.
- Otherwise, get the `%userHash` that has all the user's information by using a helper function `&getAccountInfo`.

Stock#	Album	Qty	Unit price	Subtotal
314	The Lion King by Elton John;Nathan Lane, 1993.	1	$15.99	$15.99
456	...And Justice For All by Metallica, 1988.	2	$14.99	$29.98

Shipping is $5.
The total is **$50.97**.

Please check your personal information.

name	Frodo Baggins
address1	The Hill
address2	
city	Hobbiton
state	The Shire
zip	12345
country	Middle Earth
email	frodo@shire.com
phone	123-1234
creditcard	xxxx-xxxx-xxxx-1234

We only show last 4 digits of credit card for security.

Confirm purchase

Back to Shopping Cart

FIGURE 13.13   Design for the confirmation page.

- Print the table headers for the item summary table.
- Load the shopping cart contents into %cartHash.
- Iterate over the shopping cart, keeping a running total for the bill, and printing product info to a table row. The info is retrieved using the helper function &getInfo. Also, turn the product names into links that call show_detail.
- Print the bill total with some shipping charges.
- Obscure all but the last four digits of the credit card number. The search string is one or more of any character followed by a group of exactly 4 digits. Due to the grouping symbols, the last four digits are captured into the special variable $1. The replacement string then uses $1 to show only those four digits.
- Iterate over the keys of %userHash, printing a table row for each piece of user data. The keys are given as a literal list so that they are iterated over in a predetermined order.
- Print the form button to buy the stuff and the link to continue shopping.

We first deal with the getAccountInfo function and then the display_logon_for_checkout function. The former is very simple. We construct a simple SQL select statement that returns the record with the specified user name. We fetch the record as a hash reference and then dereference it into a hash. (See Section 10.6.)

```
sub getAccountInfo {
  my $user =$_[0];
  my @columns = ("name", "address1", "address2", "city", "state", "zip",
  "country", "email", "phone", "creditcard");
  my $sql = "SELECT " . join(", ", @columns) .
    " FROM $customers_table WHERE user = " . $dbhandle->quote($user);
  my $qObj = $dbhandle->prepare($sql) or &errorPage("Can't prepare.");
  $qObj->execute() or &errorPage("Can't execute. " . $qObj->errstr());
  my $userHashREF = $qObj->fetchrow_hashref(); # fetch the row as a hash reference
  $qObj->finish();
  return %$userHashREF; # Dereference the hash reference
}
```

The `display_logon_for_checkout` function simply prints a standard logon form as shown in Figure 13.14. The form calls another helper function, `logon_for_checkout`, that tests the submitted user name and password. If the user fails to log on, the user is sent back to the `display_logon_for_checkout` function. You can see the "No" loop in the transaction diagram. The incoming parameter in the function, shown following, is for that potential failure message. Users are also given a link to call the CGI program that can sign them up in case they can't remember their passwords or need to sign up for the first time.

```
sub display_logon_for_checkout {
  my $message = $_[0];
  print <<PAGE;
  <html><head><title>Music CD Store</title></head><body>
    <h2>Please log in to continue checking out Store</h2>
    $message
    <form action="$ENV{'SCRIPT_NAME'}" method="GET">
      User Name: <input type="text" name="user" size="20"/><br/>
      Password: <input type="password" name="pass" size="20"/><br/>
      <input type="hidden" name="request" value="logon_for_checkout"/>
      <input type="hidden" name="id" value="$formHash{'id'}"/>
      <input type="submit" value="Log In and Check Out"/>
    </form>
    If you do not have an account with us, you may
    <a href="signup.cgi" target="_blank">sign up here.</a>.
  </body>
  </html>
PAGE
}
```

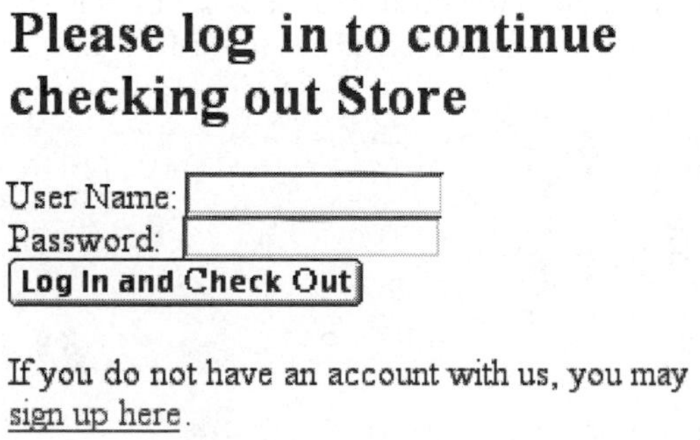

Please log in to continue checking out Store

User Name: [   ]
Password: [   ]
[Log In and Check Out]

If you do not have an account with us, you may sign up here.

FIGURE 13.14 The logon-for-checkout form.

The `logon_for_checkout` function is also quite simple, but because it calls a lot of other functions, we provide a bulleted overview rather than just talking through it.

```
sub logon_for_checkout {
  my $result = &dblogon($dbhandle, $customers_table,
    $formHash{"user"}, $formHash{"pass"});
  if($result ne "yes") {
    &display_logon_for_checkout("Logon failed ($result). Please try
      again.<br/>");
    exit;
  }
  %stateHash = &read_state($stateDir, $formHash{"id"}, $file_time_out);
  $stateHash{"user"} = $formHash{"user"};
  &write_state($stateDir, $formHash{"id"}, %stateHash);
  &check_out;
}
```

- If the call to the standard `dblogon` function does not return `"yes"`, send the user back to the logon form page with a failure message. Exit the program.
- Otherwise, the user logged on successfully, so a `user=`*userName* line needs to be added to the state file. The user name is obtained from the submitted form.
- Send the user to the `check_out` function. This time that function will find the user name in the state file, so it will give the user an order summary.

After more testing and debugging, we finally get a summary page resembling Figure 13.13. Moreover, we can go through the whole application, either anonymously or as a valid user, and make it to the summary page. We are down to the last arrow on the transaction diagram. The application is now fully functional but for the `confirm_order` function. (That is, except for the user signup program, which we present in the next section.)

When the user clicks the order confirmation button in Figure 13.13, a Web page appears, saying thank you and summarizing the purchase. The user also gets the order ID number, which can hypothetically be used in some other Web page to track their order. The application also sends an e-mail to the user as a more permanent record. Also, a record of the order is saved in the `orders` database table so that the shipping department has a record of the orders it has to fill, and hypothetically the shipping department has its own means of updating this table (such as the status and balance). We write the `confirm_order` function, but leave the e-mail part as an exercise.

Before writing the function for the final page, we decide what it should contain and how it should be formatted. Again, a sketch is in order, but this time we forgo a "sketch" and show the final page in Figure 13.15. The page is nearly identical to the summary page. One addition is that it has been stamped with the current date and the `orderID` number. One other thing the function does behind the scenes is to insert a record into the `orders` table and to send an e-mail.

```
sub confirm_order {
  %stateHash = &read_state($stateDir, $formHash{"id"}, $file_time_out);

  if($stateHash{"user"} eq "") {
    &display_logon_for_checkout;
    exit;
  }

  my $today = &currentDate;

  %userHash = &getAccountInfo($stateHash{"user"});
```

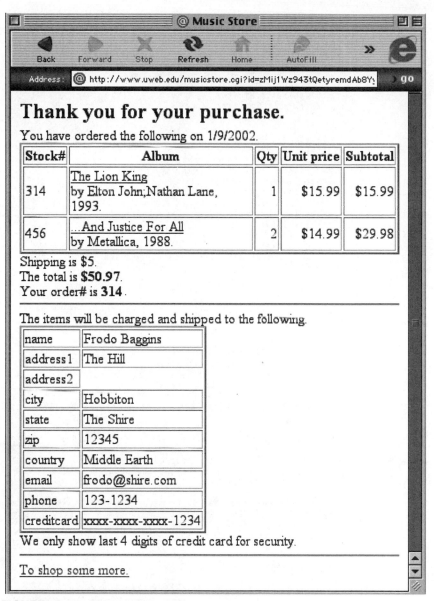

FIGURE 13.15 The user has made a purchase.

```
my %cartHash=();
my @items = split(/&/, $stateHash{"cart"});
foreach $item (@items) {
  my ($stockID, $quantity) = split(/=/, $item);
  $cartHash{$stockID} = $quantity;
}

print <<TOP;
<html><head><title>Music Store</title></head><body>
  <h2>Thank you for your purchase.</h2>
```

```perl
      You have ordered the following on $today.
      <table border=2>
        <tr>
          <th>Stock#</th>
          <th>Album</th>
          <th>Qty</th>
          <th>Unit price</th>
          <th>Subtotal</th>
        </tr>
TOP

  my $subtotal;
  my $total=0;
  foreach $n (sort keys %cartHash) {
    my ($album, $artists, $year, $price) =
      &getInfo($n, "album", "artists", "year", "price");
    $subtotal = $price*$cartHash{$n};
    $total = $total + $subtotal;
    $subtotal = sprintf "%.2f", $subtotal;
    print <<ITEM;
      <tr><td>$n</td>
      <td><a href=
      "$ENV{'SCRIPT_NAME'}?request=show_detail&id=$formHash{'id'}&stockID=$n"
        >$album</a><br/> by $artists, $year.
        </td>
        <td align="right">$cartHash{$n}</td>
        <td align="right">\$$price</td>
        <td align="right">\$$subtotal</td>
      </tr>
ITEM
  } # end foreach
  $shipping = 5.00; ### for simplicity
  $total = sprintf "%.2f", $total+$shipping;
  print "</table>Shipping is \$$shipping.<br />\n",
    "The total is <b>\$$total</b>.<br />\n";

  my $orderID = &makeOrder($stateHash{"user"}, $stateHash{"cart"}, $today,
    $total);
  $stateHash{"cart"} = "";
  &write_state($stateDir, $formHash{"id"}, %stateHash); # clear shopping cart

  print "Your order\# is <b>$orderID</b>.<br />\n",
    "<hr/>The items will be charged and shipped to the following.",
    "<table border=\"2\">\n";

  $userHash{"creditcard"} =~ s/.*(\d{4})/xxxx-xxxx-xxxx-$1/; #show only last 4 digits
  foreach $key (("name", "address1", "address2", "city", "state", "zip",
    "country", "email", "phone", "creditcard")) {
    print " <tr><td>$key</td><td>$userHash{$key}</td></tr>\n";
  }

  print <<BOTTOM;
</table>
We only show last 4 digits of credit card for security.<br/>
<hr>
<a href=
  "$ENV{'SCRIPT_NAME'}?request=continue_shopping&id=$formHash{'id'}">
  To shop some more.</a>
</body></html>
BOTTOM
  ### Send e-mail here. This is left as an exercise.
}
```

- Read in %stateHash.
- Grab today's date, delegating the work to a helper function.
- Load the %userHash from the proper user account file. The helper function &read_state was written previously.

- Load the shopping cart into %cartHash. We need that to print out the order details.
- Clear the cart from %stateHash and rewrite all the state information back into the state file in case the user wants to keep shopping during the current session.
- Print out the order and customer details in a manner nearly identical to the check_out function.
- Note that immediately after calculating the total, call a helper function, makeOrder, that saves the order information to a database table and returns the orderID. This orderID is also presented.
- Print a "To shop some more" link.

Now for the last two helper functions. The only tricky part in these otherwise straightforward functions is how the new orderID is generated. This is accomplished by selecting all the order IDs and specifying that they be ordered in a descending order. Thus, the first row would contain the maximum number. We merely add 1 to it to obtain a new order ID! (And if no order IDs exist, we start at number 100.) But you should note in the makeOrder function that the store terminates the order process if it can't record the order. You can't fill orders without record of them.

```perl
sub makeOrder {
  # This returns the new orderID.

  my($user, $cart, $today, $total)=@_;
  my $status="neworder";

  ### Get new order number ####
  my $sql = "SELECT orderID FROM $orders_table ORDER BY orderID DESC";
  my $qObj = $dbhandle->prepare($sql) or &errorPage("Can't prepare.");
  $qObj->execute() or &errorPage(
    "Error in processing order.".
    "<a href=\"$ENV{'SCRIPT_NAME'}?request=checkout".
    "&id=$formHash{id}\">Return to checkout.</a>");

  my ($orderID) = $qObj->fetchrow_array();
  $qObj->finish();
  if($orderID){
    $orderID++;  ## increment max order ID by 1.
  }
  else{
    $orderID = 100;  ### If there are no existing order IDs, we will start a new one at 100.
  }

  $sql = "INSERT into $orders_table"
    "(orderID, user, cart, orderdate, status, total, balance) "
    " VALUES "
    "($orderID, '$user', '$cart', '$today', '$status', $total, $total)";
  $qObj = $dbhandle->prepare($sql) or &errorPage(
    "Can't prepare.");
  $qObj->execute() or &errorPage(
    "Error in processing order.".
    "<a href=\"$ENV{'SCRIPT_NAME'}?request=checkout".
    "&id=$formHash{id}\">Return to checkout.</a>");
  $qObj->finish();
  return $orderID;
}

sub currentDate {
```

```
    my @timeParts=localtime;
    my ($day, $month, $year) = ($timeParts[3],$timeParts[4],$timeParts[5]);
    return ($month+1)."/".$day."/".($year+1900);
}
```

13.4 INCORPORATING AN AUXILIARY SIGNUP UTILITY

In this section we briefly discuss the auxiliary Web application that signs up new users for the CD store, as well as an issue regarding the incorporation of auxiliary programs in general. Recall in the transaction diagram in Figure 13.1 that there are two opportunities for the user to sign up. New users can do so in the welcome page, or they will be required to do so when checking out. In either case, those links featured `target="_blank"`, which directs the output of `signup.cgi`, the auxiliary program, to a new window. The pop-up window contains the signup form shown in Figure 13.16. Note in the transaction diagram that the original window will still contain a logon form.

The outline of the program is provided in Figure 13.17. The app logic is trivial. We don't show the code for the `signup_page` function; it merely prints the form shown in Figure 13.16. That form is submitted to the `new_user` function, which either prints a simple page indicating successful signup or sends the user back to the `signup_page` with an error message.

Of course, if the signup is successful, a new record for that user is added to the `customers` table in the `cdstore` database. The pop-up window is left containing a worthless thank-you page indicating successful signup. The user can then close that window and log on using the logon form in the original window. The `new_user` function is provided next, followed by an overview.

```
sub new_user {
  my @required_form_keys = ("new_user", "new_pass", "name", "address1",
    "city", "state", "zip", "country", "email", "phone", "creditcard");

  foreach $key (@required_form_keys) {
    if($formHash{$key} eq "") {
      &signup_page("You did not fill in the $key field.");
      exit;
    }
  }

  if($formHash{"new_pass"} ne $formHash{"retype_pass"}) {
    &signup_page("<b>Retyped password does not match.</b>");
    exit;
  }

  $formHash{"new_user"} =~ s/\W//g; # Delete all nonalphanumeric characters;
  $formHash{"new_user"} = lc $formHash{"new_user"};

  my $sql = "SELECT * FROM $customers_table WHERE user = ".
  "'$formHash{new_user}'";
  my $qObj = $dbhandle->prepare($sql) or &errorPage("Can't prepare.");
  $qObj->execute() or &errorPage("Can't execute. ".$qObj->errstr());

  if($qObj->fetchrow_array()){
    &signup_page("The user name $new_user is already in use;"
      " please choose another user name.");.
```

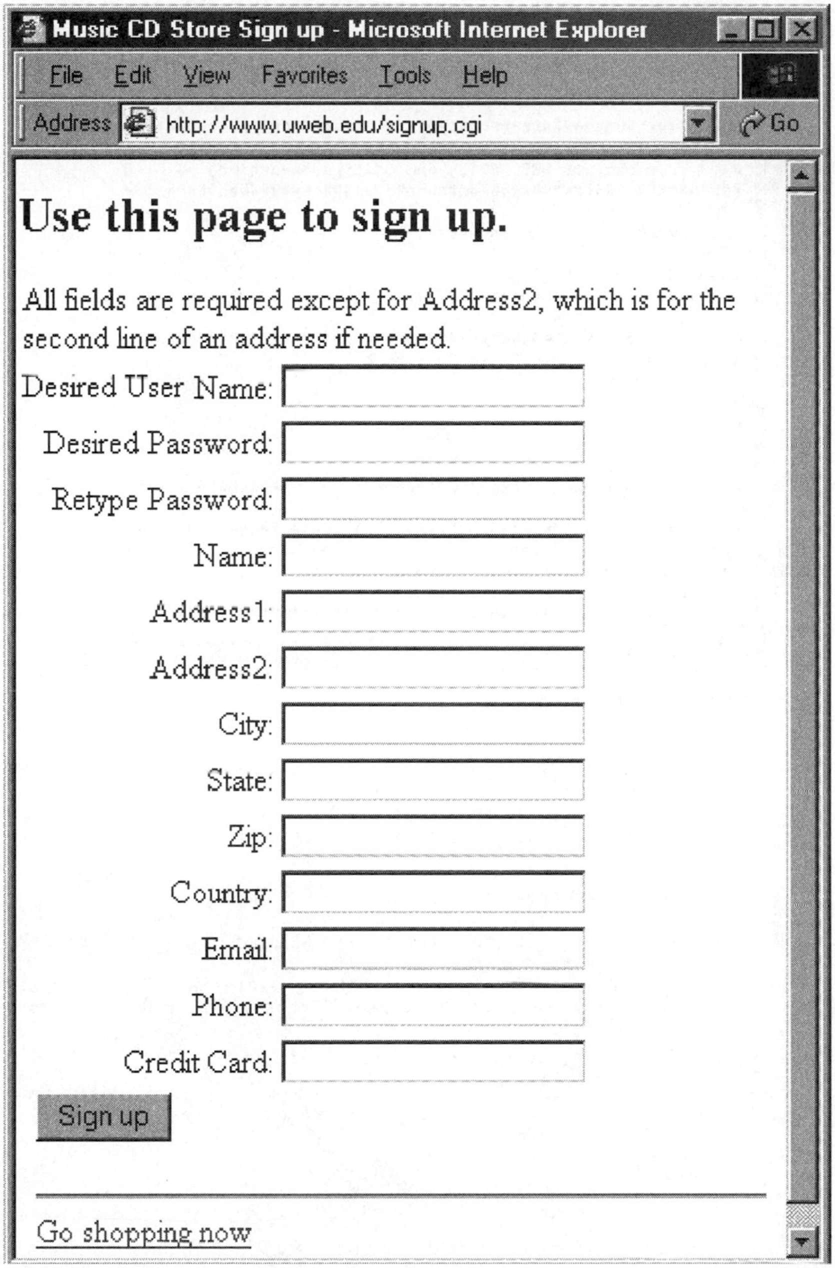

FIGURE 13.16   The signup page for `signup.cgi`.

```
    exit;
}
$qObj->finish();

my @user_info_fields = ("new_user", "new_pass", "name", "address1",
   "address2", "city",
```

```
#! /usr/bin/perl
print "Content-type: text/html\n\n";

#############################################################
#   code for decoding input $datastring into %formHash     #
#      (works for GET, POST, and offline execution)         #
#############################################################

$customers_table = "customers";

use DBI;
$dbhandle = DBI->connect("DBI:mysql:cdstore", "storeuser", "pass");

### app logic ##############################################
if($formHash{"request"} eq "new_user") {
    &new_user;
}
else {
    &signup_page;
}
### end app logic ##########################################

#############################################################
### Definitions of app logic functions go here.            #
### Definitions for toolkit functions used:                #
#      &errorPage            (from Section 5.7)             #
#############################################################
```

FIGURE 13.17 The outline of `signup.cgi`.

```
    "state", "zip", "country", "email", "phone", "creditcard");
  my @quoted_array = ();
  foreach $key (@user_info_fields) {
    push @quoted_array, $dbhandle->quote($formHash{$key});
  }

  $sql = "INSERT INTO $customers_table (user, password, name, address1,
    address2, ".
    "city, state, zip, country, email, phone, creditcard) VALUES ".
    "(". join(",", @quoted_array) . ")";
  $qObj = $dbhandle->prepare($sql) or &errorPage("Can't prepare.");
  $qObj->execute() or &errorPage("Error saving new user information.");
  $qObj->finish();

  print <<PAGE;
<html><head><title>Music CD Store Sign up</title></head><body>
  <h2>Your new user information is added successfully.</h2>
  Please return to the original window and log on.
</body></html>
PAGE
}
```

- Verify that all required fields are nonempty. Upon finding the first empty field, the user is returned to the signup page with an appropriate error message. (It would clearly be desirable to add more elaborate constraints on the user information, perhaps using JavaScript, but we leave that as an exercise.)

- Verify that the desired password matches the retyped password. If not, return the signup page with an appropriate error message.

- Delete all nonalphanumeric characters from the user name. (Allowing only alphanumeric characters in a user name can save potential headaches in the long run.)

- Check that the desired user name is not already used. This is accomplished by an SQL `SELECT` statement. If such a record already exists, the signup page is returned.
- If everything checks out, it's time to construct a new record for the `customers` table. First, the `@user_info_fields` array orders the names of the form elements in the same order as the corresponding entries in the `customers` database table.
- For each of the `@user_info_fields`

   - Push the users data, quoted in a database-friendly fashion, onto the end of the `@quoted_array`. It is crucial that the order of iteration, as determined by the `@user_info_fields` array, pushes fields onto the `@quoted_array` in the same order as fields appear in the following SQL `INSERT` statement.

- Build the SQL `INSERT` statement. The data `VALUES` are joined into a comma-delimited list as required.
- Execute the database update and print the thank-you page.

NOTE

The way in which functionality is added to a Web application through an auxiliary application such as `signup.cgi` must be carefully considered. It could have been incorporated into the app logic of the main store application, but that increases the complexity of an already complex application and makes the signup utility somewhat less reusable in other applications that may require signup.

The easiest way not to interfere with the session in the main application is to use a pop-up window for the auxiliary application, as we have done. If the auxiliary application is called into the same window as the main program, you have to be careful that the user can resume the session after signing up. So that the user doesn't have to rely on the back button to find the last page in the session before the auxiliary application was introduced, the session ID can easily be passed to the auxiliary program, with links provided to call the proper app logic function in the main program to resume the session.

13.5   INVENTORY ADMINISTRATION

You now should have a good idea of what it takes to write a relatively large Web application. In this section we provide a transaction diagram for a Web application that would allow a store administrator to edit the store inventory. The structure of the data tier is the same as that of the main store application. The transaction diagram in Figure 13.18 shows the desired functionality of the application in terms of updating, adding, and deleting records in the inventory database table.

You might be relieved to learn that we are not going to code this application. Indeed, a dozen more pages of code would not be instructive at this point. Construction of this application is left as an exercise (individual or group project). However, we do offer a brief explanation of the functions used in the transaction diagram to give you a better feel for how to approach building an application from a transaction diagram. In particular, it

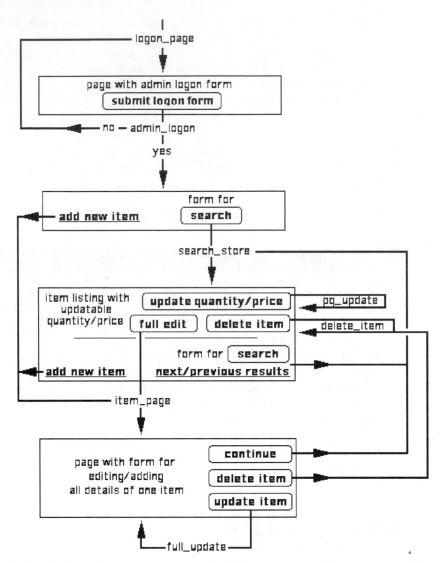

FIGURE 13.18   Transaction diagram for the inventory administration application.

pays to determine certain tasks performed by more than one app logic function and to earmark those tasks for reusable helper functions. Of course, you would begin building it from the top down, testing each function at junctures where that is possible.

- The `logon_page` and `admin_logon` functions are straightforward. The `admin_logon` function would certainly want to call a helper function to print the search form. An admin program would likely offer different search refinement options, such as searching by product numbers, by price ranges, and for items whose stock quantity is low.

- The `search_store` function should make the decision whether to initiate a new search or to retrieve previous search results from the state file. You can see that it is called from two other locations in the program. It would make use of the helper function to return the search form, hard-coded with the search criteria. It would likely also use helper functions to deal with the gory details of the actual database search and the logistics of returning partial search results.

■ The search results return only summaries of inventory items, where the only editable fields are for price and quantity. The `pq_update` function handles that quick database update and returns the search results page. Each inventory summary also has a delete button, which removes the item from inventory. It should also remove that item from the cached search results so that the item doesn't appear in the returned search results page. The `delete_item` function should be designed keeping in mind that it is also called from the page for editing full product details. The `delete_item` function may also wish to provide an extra "are you sure" confirmation step, perhaps using a JavaScript alert window.

■ The `item_page` function has to decide whether to print an empty form for adding a new item or a form allowing an item to be fully edited. Again a helper function is warranted, especially since the `full_update` function will need to print the form as well. The `item_page` function is then free to concentrate on such matters as determining new stock numbers for new products.

■ The `full_update` function should return an editable version of the newly modified (or created) item in case further changes need to be made.

> **NOTE**
>
> For security, the administration program should use a separate state file cache for validation of logged-on state. Also remember the security issues regarding logged-on state. See the following subsection on logged-on state security.

13.6 WEB APPLICATION SECURITY

We have been slightly lax about some quite subtle security issues in some of our functions, although we have already mentioned several security risks. One reason is that we did not wish to obfuscate the central concepts by adding yet more detail, of which there was already plenty. Another reason is that we feel that these subtle security issues are more easily digested if collected into one section for emphasis.

But perhaps the main reason we dedicate a full section to security issues is to emphasize that one rarely develops and deploys an application without subsequently finding the need for adding *security patches*. A security weakness might be discovered by afterthought and testing or by the less innocuous prospect of experiencing a breach of the application's integrity after it is deployed. In either case, the patch is often just a line or two of code added to a function. Indeed, if you have downloaded a security patch for an application such as Microsoft's Outlook Express mail client, the patch may have just replaced a key function with a new one where only one or two lines of code are altered. As we show in this section, most of the security issues arise from collecting user input, which is unpredictable at best.

> **NOTE**
>
> A compelling reason to understand security concerns fully is that many environments with preprogrammed tools (CGI.pm, PHP, ASP) do not necessarily address these issues for you. The lack of built-in policing for state file caches is one easily noticeable shortfall of many such tools. Regardless of your development environment, you should also be familiar with the more subtle potential risks summarized here.

The following list of subsections does not claim to be all-inclusive. Remember that sometimes even thoroughly planned countermeasures will not stop a determined adversary.

Verification of Logged-On State

When you are given a session ID by a Web application, that ID is a pointer to your session data on the server. If you tamper with the ID in the HTML source code, the next transaction will simply not find the data for the session. That may result only in the loss of data accumulated during the session. For anonymous sessions that is usually not a concern. Even if someone finds one of the exposed app logic functions used in the middle of a session, calling that function without a valid session ID just results in a meaningless Web page.

However, all exposed app logic functions behind logged-on state need protection. Our final version of the `read_state` toolkit function (Section 7.8) automatically protects app logic functions simply by the act of attempting to read a state file. If a state file matching the ID doesn't exist, the `errorPage` (or some other customized page if desired) is returned to the user. As long as a `read_state` is performed near the top of every app logic function in a logged-on session, an improper access attempt automatically "bounces" the user. You can note in the `musicstore.cgi` application that every app logic function after a session ID exists does a `read_state`. Because of that, the music store application even bounces (by `errorPage`) anonymous state if a valid session ID is not submitted. Note that the state table version, `write_state_db`, also features automatic bouncing. (These functions are like bouncers at clubs and bars. You'd better behave after you get in!)

Nevertheless, you have to remember always to validate against the state file cache. A given app logic function behind logged-on state might not require data from the state file. For example, consider the `item_page` function in the transaction diagram for the music store administration program in the previous section. That function does not need to read state data simply to print an empty form used for adding a new CD to inventory. Forgetting to do a `read_state` there, however, leaves such a function potentially exposed to calls that require no password whatsoever. Recall again Figure 7.22 in Section 7.8.

A Patch for the Decoding Routine

In Section 9.6 we discussed the possible annoyances that come from including user-collected data in a dynamically generated HTML document. One easy solution is simply to remove all angle brackets and double quotes from user input.

```
$value =~ s/[<>"]//g;
```

This removes any occurrence of each of the three characters in the class [<>"], replacing it with nothing, through a global substitution.

The appropriate place to add this patch is in the decoding routine after the user-submitted $value is decoded and before the $value is stored into %formHash. This has the effect of changing anything that might resemble HTML in the user's input (<hr width="50%">) into text (hr width=50%) that the HTML processor will not recognize as markup instruction(s). We reiterate that this eliminates a potential annoyance rather than a significant security risk.

At first, removing double quotes does not seem necessary, but that's to eliminate the potential annoyance of broken HTML code. For example, we have repeatedly returned user input (like a search query) to the user, hard-coded into HTML forms. If the user includes a double quote in the data he submits, then that data causes broken HTML code when returned to the user hard-coded into an HTML attribute.

```
value="user data with a " character inside"
```

The double quote in the user's data makes the HTML attribute in which that data is returned not well defined. That is why this patch removes double quotes as well.

Purifying File Names

As we learned in Section 9.5, the open command can also be used to execute an external command. Consider the following hypothetical situation where a file (that stores user information, for example) is identified by the user's user name, as in "fbaggins.user". Of course, when a user logs on, that particular user file name is dependent upon user input, as

```
open(INPUTFILE, "$formHash{'username'}.user"); ## risky code!!
```

Suppose the user enters data so that the value stored in $formHash{'username'} is the string ">fbaggins". The result is the Perl statement

```
open(INPUTFILE, ">fbaggins.user");
```

which, instead of attempting to open a file for reading, opens the file for writing. This could destroy someone's file by overwriting it.

Worse yet, what if a user enters data so that $formHash{'username'} contains the string "|rm *" in Unix (or "|del *" in Windows)? The resulting Perl statement is then

```
open(INPUTFILE, "|rm *.user");
```

which executes the system command rm *.user, thereby attempting to delete all files ending in .user.

For another example, what if a user enters data so that $formHash{'username'} contains the string "|anything; " in Unix. This time, the result is

```
open(INPUTFILE, "|anything; .user");
```

and since the semicolon is a command separator in Unix, this executes the shell command anything followed by the nonsensical command .user. This is why the semicolon is sometimes a threat—it is the Unix command separator.

We hope you get the feel of how an `open` command might be exploitable. Therefore, it is always a good idea to *purify* a file name or an e-mail address before using it in an `open` statement. Purify it by removing all characters that don't belong. Note that this example can be made less risky by including the "`<`" symbol for opening a file for reading, and it would also be automatically made less risky if we had a directory path in front of the file name.

> **NOTE**
>
> We have used a file name corresponding to a user name for this example, because it is easily understandable why the file name would arise from user input. However, we have used long session IDs to identify state files, putting the user name on the inside of the state file. But the same purification for file names still applies, even though the long ID is ostensibly not user-entered data. Remember that if the data is on the client, a malicious user can modify it before submitting it to the server, even if the data is not directly acquired from the user by an HTML form.

Using the `system` Statement

We briefly saw an example usage of the `system` statement in Section 9.6. *Any* time a `system` statement uses user-entered data, the data should be purified.

The `eval` Statement and Backquotes

The statement

```
eval ("some string");
```

executes the string as a Perl command, and the statement using a "backquoted" string,

```
`some string`;
```

executes the string as an operating system command. You can imagine why these two statements are risky if the string involves user-entered data. We do not use either of these types of statements in this book.

Risks in Pattern Matching

If you use user data as part of a pattern to find matches, it is conceivable that, through a clever use of metacharacters, the resulting pattern will return more results that the programmer intended. Most of the time this is not important, but sometimes it might return sensitive information. Without giving an example, we give you the bottom line. If you want control of how much a pattern should match, and user-entered data goes into the pattern, then you should remove all metacharacters (as used in pattern patching) from the user data before putting it into the pattern.

URL-Encoding for State Data

It is clear why query strings are URL encoded. Indeed, if certain delimiting characters appear in the data, then it is not possible to break the query string back down into the correct name=value pairs. But we also used URL-encoding before saving data into state files. Again in that case, an = character in the name would corrupt the name=value structure of lines in the file, as is apparent by looking at our state file format:

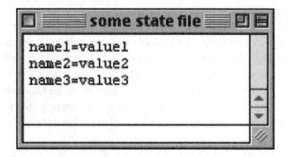

It is okay for the = character to appear as part of the value, however, because we used the split function specifying that each line be split into at most two pieces. In all of our examples, the = character was ensured not to be part of any of the names, because the names were chosen by us and hence would not affected by user input.

Then why is URL-encoding needed? This is because there is another delimiter that is even more important, namely the newline (\n). To illustrate best why we need to URL-encode the values, consider what can happen if we don't. Suppose hypothetically that the musicstore.cgi program used state file functions that did not URL-encode. Now suppose a user starts shopping anonymously, performs a search, and then modifies the query string by hand as follows.

```
musicstore.cgi?artists=%0Auser%3Dfbaggins&request=search&id= . . .
```

The relevant part is the modification of the value corresponding to the name artist. When the query string is decoded, the value of $formHash{"artist"} is then the string "\nuser=fbaggins". (Note that %0A decodes to \n and %3D decodes to =.) Thus, when the new value for artist is written to the state file, the following results because of the extra newline character:

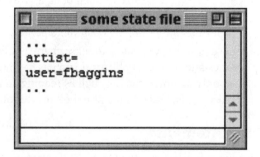

The user has magically logged on as fbaggins!

This security loophole basically allows someone to write whatever information she chooses to a new line in the state file! This is why we need to take some precautionary steps such as URL-encoding the values.

A Note on Long Session IDs

Although we generate 32-digit-long strings for session IDs, which would seem to be ridiculously hard to guess (because naively there are 62^{32} possible), there is another issue in the way we generate these long strings. In reality, if we use standard "random" methods to generate these strings, there may not actually be 62^{32} possibilities. For example, if we use a "pseudorandom" number generator, in which a "random" number is determined by the previous "random" number, then the sequence of random numbers would be determined by an initial seed. In this scenario, the number of possible 32-digit-long strings would only be the number of possible initial seeds. This would be far smaller than 62^{32}, and conceivably the ID could be vulnerable to a determined guessing attack. If this is a concern, then one should use a more sophisticated method of generating random numbers. There are prewritten Perl modules that do this.

Web Applications That Send E-mails

As was discussed in Section 9.5 in a note box, if your application sends e-mail to addresses that come from user input, then care must be taken that your Web page will not be used for sending spam (unsolicited e-mails often used for advertising). One unfortunate example was the free, easily exploitable software `formmail.pl` which was used often because it was generic and easy to configure. Here is a summary of considerations.

- If the content of the e-mail is generated entirely independently of user input, then your script cannot be used for advertising spam. However, an unscrupulous person can still use your script to send unsolicited e-mails to arbitrary addresses.

- If your script limits what addresses it will accept, then your script cannot be effectively used for sending spam to arbitrary addresses. However, those designated recipient addresses would still be vulnerable to receiving large volumes of e-mail.

Web Applications That Save *Any* Data on the Server

Applications that save data on the server are automatically vulnerable to attacks where the data saved on the server could grow in size without bound. Here are some considerations.

- One can police the size of such data, as we did in the case of state files. For applications where customers sign up, perhaps one could limit the total number of customers or the number of new customers per day.

- One can stem automated attacks where a nefarious program repeatedly sends HTTP requests to a Web application such as `signup.cgi` by forcing some sort of activity that only a human can do, such as reading an image and typing in a number it shows. This was discussed in the note box in Section 9.5.

SQL Statements

If user input is used to generate an SQL statement, then clever usage of single quotes in the user input can potentially radically alter the statement. For example, one can make an

SQL `SELECT` statement reveal more information than was intended. Or worse, suppose one uses the following SQL statement to test a logon:

```
$sql = "SELECT user FROM customers
  WHERE user = '$formHash{user}'
  AND password = '$formHash{password}'";
```

The idea here is that we execute this command and test whether any rows are returned. But what if someone enters the value

```
who cares' OR 'a'='a
```

into `$formHash{password}`? The SQL statement then evaluates to

```
$sql = "SELECT user FROM customers
  WHERE user = 'any_user'
  AND password = 'who cares'
  OR 'a'='a'";
```

This would return all records, because `'a'='a'` is always true, and hence you could log in as anyone! One way around this is to use the database handle `quote` method to escape all single quotes in user input used in SQL statements (see Section 10.5 and 10.6). So the following change patches the problem:

```
$sql = "SELECT user FROM customers WHERE user = " .
  $dbhandle->quote($formHash{"user"}) . " AND password = " .
  $dbhandle->quote($formHash{"password"});
```

The patch works, because all of the single quotes are escaped, and the `OR` is then part of the data instead of an extension to the SQL statement.

```
AND password = 'who cares'' OR ''a''=''a'
```

SUMMARY OF KEY TERMS AND CONCEPTS

Application design: First, make a list of the desired general capabilities of the application. Working from that, a detailed transaction diagram can be constructed. It usually takes several versions of a transaction diagram before the plan for the application is polished. Design of the data tier can then begin.

The data tier: If the application uses much data or the data needs to be queried, it's usually best to use a relational database and design the tables before even thinking about starting to code the application. However, ordinary text files are often the best solution for inter-transaction state data. It is best at this stage to understand the functions at your disposal for routine data-tier operations, such as state reads/writes and logon utilities. When using preprogrammed tools in environments such as `CGI.pm`, ASP, and PHP it is especially important that you understand exactly what those tools accomplish, and what they may not. Security should always be a big concern.

Coding an application: Start from the top of the transaction diagram and work your way down, testing the functions at each possible juncture. Design the Web page formats (forms, layout, and so forth) on scratch paper or in an HTML WYSIWYG editor before coding them into the application. One also should keep notes on exactly what data might be in the state file at a given time. When designing the app logic functions, careful attention should paid to tasks that will be repetitive or preformed by more than one app logic function. Such tasks as printing page components (forms, tables of search results, product listings, and the like) should be delegated to reusable helper functions. Careful study of the transaction diagram can reveal the repetitive tasks. (See Section 13.5.)

Incorporating an auxiliary application: When a Web application needs a small auxiliary utility, such as for user signup, it is sometimes best to write it separately and not include it in the app logic of the main application. The easiest way to introduce the utility without affecting the session state of the main application is to target the utility application to a pop-up window. That leaves current state of the main application preserved in the original window.

However, if an auxiliary program is introduced into the main window, it can still be programmed to return the user to the proper "state instant" in the main application. The auxiliary program needs to be passed the session ID and needs to send it back to the proper app logic function of the main application.

Security: Section 13.6 is a collection of the security issues we had encountered previously in this book, together with some new ones. They are categorized by subsection, so we don't relist them here. If you did not do so, you should carefully read that section. In particular, our discussions and toolkit functions have provided you with some security features that you may have to implement yourself if you move to another Web programming environment.

EXERCISES

Note: The exercises in this section are ideal for group exercises, where each group member writes some of the functions or adds one or more of the embellishments, as the case may be. In industry, big applications are often developed in teams. Careful coordination in matters such as information required by certain functions and how auxiliary components interface with the main application is crucial. Of course, these exercises can be used as stand-alone exercises as well.

1. Add any or all of the following modifications/augmentations to the `musicstore.cgi` application. Its source code can be obtained from the Web site.

    (a) E-mail the user an order summary upon order confirmation.

    (b) Use a state table instead of state files.

    (c) User logon expires in one hour of nonuse. Anonymous logon expires in 24 hours.

    (d) Incorporate a "forgot your password" capability into all logon forms. Add a text area to the signup utility into which the user can type a question to help them remember the password. Reject the signup attempt if the user puts the actual password in the helper question.

    (e) Limit logon attempts to three per half-hour period per IP address. Then impose a half-hour moratorium on logon attempts from any IP address that violates that limit. (See Exercise 3, in Chapter 7.)

    (f) Limit the application to 100 signups per day to protect against a runaway `customers` database table.

(g) Add the user signup e-mail verification capability (to protect against spam) to the signup utility, as discussed in Section 9.3.

(h) Add an option for users to update their billing information to all logon forms and to the order confirmation page. Use a separate program that loads into a pop-up window. Of course, logon verification is required before account information can be modified.

(i) Add client-side JavaScript validation to the user signup form.

(j) Use an SQL aggregate function to compute new `orderID` numbers in the `&makeOrder` function. That is a superior approach than what we used. (See Exercise 6 in Chapter 10)

2. Write the music store administration application as outlined in Section 13.5.

3. Any or all of the following features can be added to Exercise 2.

   (a) Use a state table instead of state files.

   (b) User logged-on state expires in one hour of nonuse.

   (c) Limit logon attempts to three per half-hour period per IP address. Then impose a half-hour moratorium on logon attempts from an IP address that violates that limit. (See Exercise 3 Section 7.11.)

   (d) Add client-side JavaScript validation to the update quantity/price fields to protect against negative numbers and typos. Add more validation to the full details form so that incomplete product listings aren't inadvertently introduced. Devise appropriate safety checks.

   (e) Deleting an item moves it to a separate `oldproducts` database table. Add an option to restore old products into the current inventory.

   (f) Use an SQL aggregate function to compute new unique `stockID` numbers based upon existing ones. (See Exercise 1(j).) Keep in mind the old numbers if you worked part (e).

4. Make a separate administration utility that can be used to mark orders as filled. Of course, it should be password protected. Start with a transaction diagram.

   (a) When an order is marked as completed, the inventory table should automatically be updated. It should also send an e-mail to the customer saying that order is shipped (randomly generate some tracking number, ostensibly to be used at a UPS or FedEx Web site).

   (b) Add features to the utility from part (a) so that a summary of all filled orders, or all nonfilled orders, can be returned to the browser. Another option "purges" the `orders` table, putting all filled orders into a `filledorders` table and returns sales statistics to the browser. Another option simply returns order history statistics from the `filledorders` table.

5. Incorporate Exercise 4 into Exercise 2. Start by redoing the transaction diagram of Figure 13.8. In particular, figure out how to organize all these options so that the administration program is as user-friendly as possible.

PROJECT THREAD

Here you complete the administration test bank for the quiz application. In particular, the table that holds the questions for the current quiz acts something like a permanent shopping cart. Questions can be added to and removed from the current quiz. Moreover, a utility is provided that allows new questions to be added to the quiz pool and existing questions to be edited. Before you begin, carefully read the following items, and plan the additions/changes to the new branch of the transaction diagram you created in Chapter 12.

A. Each question listed in the current quiz page, which you created in part C of the Chapter 12 Project Thread, should have a link or button that allows that question to be deleted from the current quiz. Each question should also have an "edit" button, which pulls up a page with a form that allows all aspects of the question to be edited. Submitting the edit question form returns the current quiz page, updated of course.

B. Each question listed in a search results page, which you created in part D of the Chapter 12 Project Thread, should have an option to add the question to the current quiz. A contingency should be in place so that the same question can't appear twice in the current quiz. Also, each question in the search results page should have an "edit question" option as discussed in part A. *Note:* You should cache the search results as we did in the CD store example in this chapter. That way, it is easy to hard-code the last search criteria into all search forms (current quiz page and search results page).

C. Both the current quiz page and the search results page should contain a link or button that pulls up a page with a form that allows a new question to be added to the pool (table) of available questions. You will need some contingency in place to ensure that new questions are assigned a unique primary key value (that is, ID number) in the table for the questions pool. *Hint:* Use a helper function to print the form, which can also be used to print the "edit question" form from parts A and B. You can decide what transactions the add/edit page should be able to initiate.

D. Add a new row for the updated quiz application to the table in your homework page. Make sure you preserve the version from the previous lesson and keep the link to it active. If you are assigned any other exercises from this chapter, add another row to your homework table for each exercise.

HTML BASICS

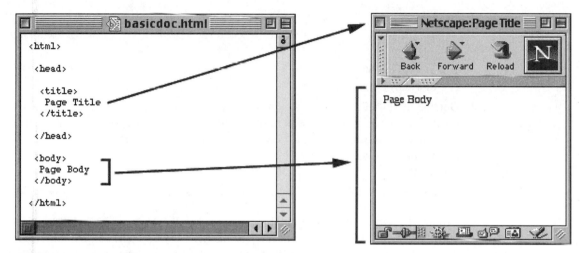

FIGURE A.1 The structure of an HTML document.

A.1 HTML LANGUAGE AND DOCUMENT STRUCTURE

Figure A.1 shows a minimal HTML document and its rendition in a browser.

A markup instruction, called a **tag**, is identified with angle brackets <>. A tag with no / (forward slash) is called a **start tag**, and a tag with a / after the first angle bracket is called an **end tag**. A matching pair, start tag and end tag, is called an **element**. Everything between the start and end tag of an element is called the **content** of the element. The `<html>...</html>` element can contain any other HTML element, subject to some constraints. The `<head>...</head>` element's contents define information about the Web page the document is to create, and the `<body>...</body>` element's contents define the actual stuff that goes into the Web page. This is shown in Figure A.1. The content of the `<title>...</title>` element is displayed at the top of the browser window, whereas the content of the `<body>...</body>` element is displayed as the Web page. For simplicity, we will not continue to refer to elements using full HTML syntax. For example, we will just say "the `title` element."

Below are some key HTML syntax rules :

■ All HTML elements should be **nested**. For example, the following elements are *not* nested:

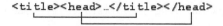

A browser builds the parse tree for the document based upon element containment. If elements are not nested, the containment hierarchy is not well defined. If you go back and examine the parse trees shown in Section 2.1, you will see that they reflect the containment relationships of the elements used there.

■ Browsers are particular about extra spaces in tags. For example,

```
< body> , < /body>, </ body>, and </body >
```

violate HTML syntax rules. However,

```
<body >
```

is permissible. When we explore HTML attributes, you will see why spaces at the end of a start tag are allowed.

■ Outside of HTML tags, browsers recognize only single spaces in an HTML document. They have to observe single spaces in text so that words don't run together. The following document structure is equivalent to the one shown in Figure A.1 as far as a browser is concerned:

```
<html><head><title>Page Title</title></head><body>Page Body</body></html>
```

Just as when you write a computer program, extra spaces, tabs, and blank lines are to make it organized and more readable for humans. Based upon containment (nesting), this HTML code generates the same parse tree as the document of Figure A.1.

The following is not really an HTML syntax rule but an issue of good practice: All HTML file names should be appended with one of the extensions .html or .htm. You can see the HTML file's name in Figure A.1 at the top of the window in which it is displayed (not in the browser window).

NOTE

Like other programming languages, HTML provides for **comments**, which the HTML processor will completely ignore. Comments are only for human benefit, allowing notes to be placed in the document. In HTML, comments can be

```
<!-- on a single line -->
<!-- or on
multiple lines -->
```

A.2 CREATING AND VIEWING A PAGE

Because every HTML document you will create while reading this book has the skeletal form shown in Figure A.1, you should create one using your favorite plain text editor. Name it something like skeleton.html. Each time you create a new page, simply make a copy of your skeleton file. That way you won't have to retype all the basic tags every time you make a new page. We recommend *Notepad* if you are using a PC and *SimpleText* if you are using a Mac. These editors come with the respective operating systems, and they create plain ASCII files. We discourage use of HTML WYSIWYG editors for your purposes in this book because they often generate sloppy HTML. Moreover, you will need to understand and be able to produce HTML code by hand as you write CGI programs that generate HTML as output. There are some plain text editors listed on the Web site that are geared more toward formatting programming code. For example, they help keep track of your levels indentation. Check those out if you wish.

A common way to view a Web page is drag the icon for the HTML file onto the icon of your favorite browser. Keep a shortcut icon for the browser handy (such as on the desktop) to load your pages quickly. Depending on your operating system, you may figure out a method you like better. For example, Microsoft's Windows typically gives HTML files an Internet Explorer icon, and double-clicking the file renders the page in IE rather than opening it in Notepad. In that case, you may wish to keep a Notepad shortcut handy on the desktop to drag a file onto for editing, or a Netscape shortcut if you like that browser better or simply wish to compare your Web pages in both browsers. Whatever the case, you should quickly be able to adapt to your environment.

When a browser displays one of your *local* HTML files, you will see a `file` **URL**, rather than an `http` URL, in the address field of the browser. By "local" we mean that the file is sitting on your hard drive rather than on a Web server somewhere. Figure A.2 shows a typical `file` URL for each of Windows and Mac.

While HTTP transactions over the Internet require an HTTP URL (`http://...`), local viewing uses the `file` **protocol**. In principle, a `file` transaction works the same way, but the browser just grabs any files necessary for the Web page off of the local hard drive. The Mac file URL in Figure A.2 shows the complete file URL structure, whereas Windows typically suppresses mention of the `file` protocol and begins the URL with the drive letter. Either way, the address field gives the absolute path to the HTML document from the local hard drive. In practice, you won't have to deal directly with `file` URLs (typing one in for example), but you should be cognizant of the fact that no Internet connection is required to view Web pages locally, and of what to expect in such cases.

FIGURE A.2   File URLs resulting from local browser renditions of `basicdoc.html`.

Understanding local `file` viewing is important because of the general strategy for developing and maintaining a Web site. Here are some tips.

- Make a folder with the same name as the public directory in your Web server account. This folder is a local version of your site's root directory and will contain a local copy of your Web site.

- Create and edit your files locally. Once you are satisfied with them, copy them onto the Web server with an FTP client.

- If you wish to update some pages in your Web site, first make the changes to the local copies. When you have tested the changes locally and are satisfied, ftp[1] them to the Web server. This way you maintain two copies of your Web site.

- It is imperative that you ftp your HTML files to the Web server as plain text, rather than some other format, such as binary.

A.3   INLINE AND BLOCK ELEMENTS

Now, let's get back to HTML. The `body` element contains all other markup elements and text that make up the Web page. In fact, you will not see any other elements that are allowed in the `head` section until Section A.7. The first category of elements we use in the body is **inline elements.** These elements (with the exception of `br`) do not cause a line break in the flow of the Web page. They are typically used "inline" within sentences or paragraphs. Table A.1 lists the inline elements we feature here, and Figure A.3 demonstrates their use.

Here are two important things to note:

- Browsers automatically wrap text around according to the width of the browser window. (You can see that by pulling up the source file for Figure A.3 on the Web site and resizing the window.) If you want a line break at a particular spot, you have to force it with a `<br />` element.

- `<br />` is an **empty element**, meaning that it has no content. All empty elements should have a space followed by a `/` before the closing bracket. This notation tells the browser that it need not wait for an end tag, which helps the browser to construct the

TABLE A.1   Inline Elements in HTML

ELEMENT	DESCRIPTION
`<b>...</b>`	Boldface text
`<big>...</big>`	Bigger text
`<i>...</i>`	Italic text
`<small>...</small>`	Smaller text
`<tt>...</tt>`	Text in a monospace (fixed-width "typewriter" or "teletypewriter") font
` `	Line break (subsequent text begins on a new line)

---

[1]For convenience, we will use lowercase "ftp" as a verb. Here, to "ftp a file to the server" means to "use an FTP client to copy the file onto the server." It's not every day you get to make up a new verb!

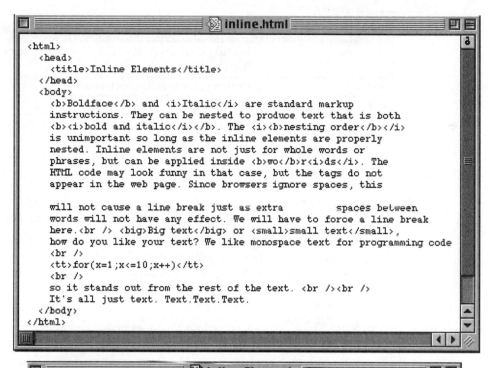

```html
<html>
  <head>
    <title>Inline Elements</title>
  </head>
  <body>
    <b>Boldface</b> and <i>Italic</i> are standard markup
    instructions. They can be nested to produce text that is both
    <b><i>bold and italic</i></b>. The <i><b>nesting order</b></i>
    is unimportant so long as the inline are properly
    nested. Inline elements are not just for whole words or
    phrases, but can be applied inside <b>wo</b>r<i>ds</i>. The
    HTML code may look funny in that case, but the tags do not
    appear in the web page. Since browsers ignore spaces, this

    will not cause a line break just as extra        spaces between
    words will not have any effect. We will have to force a line break
    here.<br /> <big>Big text</big> or <small>small text</small>,
    how do you like your text? We like monospace text for programming code
    <br />
    <tt>for(x=1;x<=10;x++)</tt>
    <br />
    so it stands out from the rest of the text. <br /><br />
    It's all just text. Text.Text.Text.
  </body>
</html>
```

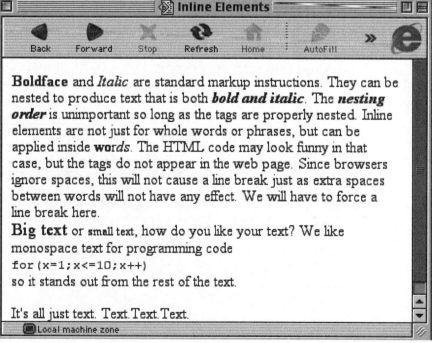

Boldface and *Italic* are standard markup instructions. They can be nested to produce text that is both ***bold and italic***. The ***nesting order*** is unimportant so long as the tags are properly nested. Inline elements are not just for whole words or phrases, but can be applied inside wor*ds*. The HTML code may look funny in that case, but the tags do not appear in the web page. Since browsers ignore spaces, this will not cause a line break just as extra spaces between words will not have any effect. We will have to force a line break here.

Big text or small text, how do you like your text? We like monospace text for programming code
`for(x=1;x<=10;x++)`
so it stands out from the rest of the text.

It's all just text. Text.Text.Text.

FIGURE A.3   A simple Web page using inline elements.

TABLE A.2 Block Elements

ELEMENT	DESCRIPTION
`<hx>...</hx>`	Headings, six levels ($x = 1, 2, 3, 4, 5, 6$), creates header blocks from largest ($x = 1$) to smallest ($x = 6$)
`<hr />`	Horizontal rule (solid horizontal division across page)
`<p>...</p>`	Paragraph
`<pre>...</pre>`	Preformatted text, typically rendered in a monospace font

parse tree efficiently. (That is, if there is no content, then terminate the branch.) Conceptually, empty markup elements are like sentences with intransitive verbs: "Cause a line break." There is no content (direct object) for the instruction to act upon. In contrast, nonempty elements are like sentences with transitive verbs: "Apply boldface to the enclosed text." Here the instruction must act upon a specific quantity.

The second category of elements we use in the `body` section are **block elements**. These elements create "block" structures in the flow of the Web page. Each block is automatically preceded and followed by a line break. Table A.2 lists the block elements we consider here, and Figure A.4 demonstrates their use.

Here are some things to note:

- Since block elements are automatically preceded and followed by line breaks, they occupy an entire "block" in the page, from the left to the right margin.

- Inline elements are used inside block elements. We used two inline elements inside the second paragraph. Block elements provide "block scope," and inline elements fine-tune text within that scope. Using block elements inside of inline elements does not make logical sense.

- The `pre` element preserves spaces. (I know, we already said that.) But the point here is to type several consecutive spaces if you need them, rather than using the Tab key. Spaces are absolute quantities, but tabs will be interpreted differently by different browsers. Also, blank lines are preserved, so don't use the `p` or `br` elements inside preformatted text. However, if you wish, you can use `b` or `i` to force fancier formatting of the monospace font.

NOTE

The best advice for the beginning Web page author (besides practicing a lot) is to forget about perfection. Pages rarely look the same in two different browsers. For an easily perceived difference, Netscape's default font size is nearly always smaller than that of Internet Explorer. You can easily see this by contrasting Figures A.3 and A.4. The former features Explorer, whereas the latter features Netscape. In practice this is no big deal. Just get your page looking pretty good, and don't worry about it.

A.4 HTML ATTRIBUTES

Elements tell the browser what to do in a minimal sense. The `hr` element makes a fine example. It just tells the browser to make a horizontal rule, but does not say how wide or

```
block.html

<html>
  <head>
    <title>Block Elements</title>
  </head>
<body>
  <h1>Heading level 1</h1>
  <h3>Heading level 3</h3>
  <h6>Heading level 6</h6>

  <p>Headers are typically rendered in boldface and cause a
  paragraph break in the page. By paragraph break, we mean a line
  break followed by a blank line. So, closing this paragraph</p>
  <p>and starting a new one is equivalent to <br /><br />
  which causes two line breaks as you can see. A <b>horizontal
  rule</b> <hr /> is a solid line and gives a vertical break in the
  page. The <tt>pre</tt> element not only gives a teletype
  (monospace) font, but preserves white spaces and blank lines. We
  have left it on the left margin so you can see that the indentions
  are preserved in the web page. As you now know,browsers ignore extra
  white spaces otherwise.</p>
<pre>
  for(x=1;x>0;x++){

    Caution, I am
    an infinite loop.

  }
</pre>
  </body>
</html>
```

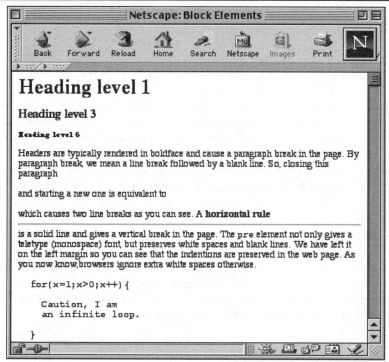

FIGURE A.4 A simple Web page using block elements.

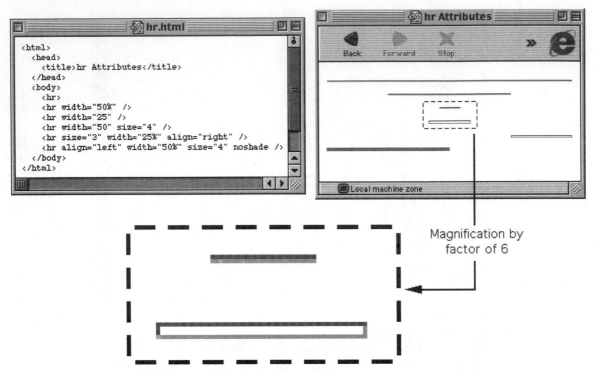

```
<html>
  <head>
    <title>hr Attributes</title>
  </head>
  <body>
    <hr>
    <hr width="50%" />
    <hr width="25" />
    <hr width="50" size="4" />
    <hr size="3" width="25%" align="right" />
    <hr align="left" width="50%" size="4" noshade />
  </body>
</html>
```

Magnification by factor of 6

FIGURE A.5 Using attributes in the hr element.

how high. In this case, a browser simply uses its *default settings*. Typically, browsers default to drawing a horizontal rule as a block 100% of the width of the browser window and two *pixels*[2] high. Figure A.5 gives an illustration for the discussion to follow.

The first hr uses the browser's default settings. Each of the other hr instances use attributes to override the default behavior. An HTML **attribute** is a *name*="*value*" pair that provides an extra instruction to tell the browser how to mark up the element. The second hr uses the width attribute to set the horizontal rule to cover 50% of the width of the browser window. The third sets it at an absolute 25-pixel width. Resizing the browser window changes the percentage setting proportionally, whereas the pixel setting remains constant. (You can see this by pulling up the source code from the Web site with your browser.) The fourth uses two attributes. Here size specifies the height of the hr to be 4 pixels. You can see that the first three horizontal rules specify no size, so the default of 2 pixels is used. The magnification of part of the diagram attests to this, and also shows how the shading effects are achieved using pixels. The last two instances use the align attribute to override the default of centering the hr in the browser window. Finally, the last instance uses the noshade attribute to override the shading effect. Contrast the noshade rule with the other rule that is also of size 4.

---

[2]Pixel stands for picture element. (We are guessing it just sounded cooler with an *x* to whoever made up the abbreviation.) These are the little colored dots that collectively make up what you see on the computer screen.

Here are some important notes regarding HTML attributes. All but the second point are evident in Figure A.5.

- Attributes must be placed in a tag, following a space, after the tag name.
- All attributes must be placed in the start tag.
- Do not put spaces on either side of the = sign.
- When multiple attributes are used in an element, the order in which they appear does not matter. Moreover, multiple attributes need only be separated from each other with single spaces.
- The quotes around the attribute value make the value well defined as a string.
- A given attribute may accept more than one value type (percentages or pixels, for example).
- Some attributes don't take values (noshade, for example). Such attributes function like true or false (on or off) Boolean quantities. Note that to be valid in XHTML syntax, the attribute would be written noshade="noshade".
- If an attribute is not specified, the browser reverts to a default setting. In many cases the default is dependent on the browser type or version.

Our choice to use hr to demonstrate attributes is based upon the fact that it uses multiple attributes that accept many of the different value types you will need to understand. Just in terms of the usefulness of hr, the foregoing discussion would be overkill. (Man, I love that hr!) With that in mind, we summarize its attributes in Table A.3 in much the same way we summarize attributes for other elements we will encounter. Here you begin to understand what a full summary for the capabilities of an HTML element entails.

We conclude this section by summarizing the two block elements we have introduced that have standard attributes (Table A.4) and by giving an example in Figure A.6 that puts some of them to good (that's a judgment call) use. What about the inline elements and other block elements? Well, they just don't have standard attributes. There is really no "fine tuning" necessary in those cases. CSS offers a better means to control font properties more explicitly.

TABLE A.3 The hr and Its Attributes

<hr /> Horizontal rule (block element)

ATTRIBUTE	POSSIBLE VALUES	DEFAULT
width	%, Pixels	100%
size (height of hr)	Pixels	2
align	left, center, right	center
noshade		Shaded markup

TABLE A.4 Block Elements with Attributes

<hx >...</hx> Headings: x = 1, 2, 3, 4, 5, 6 (block element)

ATTRIBUTE	POSSIBLE VALUES	DEFAULT
align	left, center, right	left

<p >...</p> Paragraph block element

ATTRIBUTE	POSSIBLE VALUES	DEFAULT
align	left, center, right	left

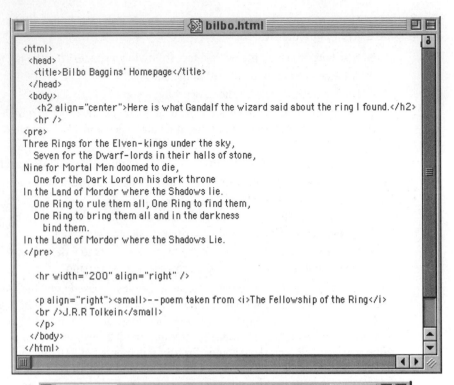

```
<html>
 <head>
  <title>Bilbo Baggins' Homepage</title>
 </head>
 <body>
  <h2 align="center">Here is what Gandalf the wizard said about the ring I found.</h2>
  <hr />
<pre>
Three Rings for the Elven-kings under the sky,
   Seven for the Dwarf-lords in their halls of stone,
Nine for Mortal Men doomed to die,
   One for the Dark Lord on his dark throne
In the Land of Mordor where the Shadows lie.
   One Ring to rule them all, One Ring to find them,
   One Ring to bring them all and in the darkness
      bind them.
In the Land of Mordor where the Shadows Lie.
</pre>

  <hr width="200" align="right" />

  <p align="right"><small>--poem taken from <i>The Fellowship of the Ring</i>
  <br />J.R.R Tolkein</small>
  </p>
 </body>
</html>
```

FIGURE A.6 Using attributes in various elements.

A.5 HYPERLINKS

Hyperlinks, or simply *links*, are created with the a (**anchor**) element, which is an inline element. Table A.5 below summarizes the attributes of the anchor element that we feature in this section.

The **hypertext reference (href)** attribute provides reference to another hypertext document. For an example, we provide the HTML code that creates a link to our Web site.

```
<a href="http://www.cknuckles.com/">go to our site</a>
```

When this element is rendered by a browser, you see only the content of the anchor element, which the browser underlines to signify that the text represents a link. When you pass the mouse over the link (but don't click it), the URL to which it points is displayed in the *status bar* at the bottom of the browser window, as shown:

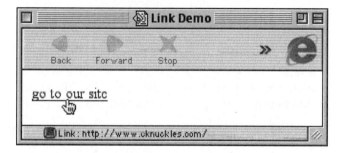

The value of the href attribute used in the example we have just given is called an **absolute URL**. This type of URL specifies absolutely the location of a resource, in this case the default file of our Web site. Of course, an absolute URL can contain more directory path information, as in

```
<a href="http://www.cknuckles.com/somepath/somefile.html">go to some
file deep in our Web site</a>
```

Recall Figure 1.7, which featured absolute URLs, although we did not call them that there.

When you create a link to another document in your own Web site, using a **relative URL** is the way to go. A relative URL specifies the file path to a document relative to the document in which the link appears. To illustrate this, we return to the example of

TABLE A.5 The Hyperlink and Its Attributes

<a >...</a> Anchor (inline element)

ATTRIBUTE	POSSIBLE VALUES	DEFAULT
href	URL (absolute or relative), URL fragment	
name	Fragment identifier	

① href="academics.html"
② href="sports/default.html"
③ href="sports/football/stats.html"
④ href="../academics.html"
⑤ href="../football/stats.html"
⑥ href="../../default.html"

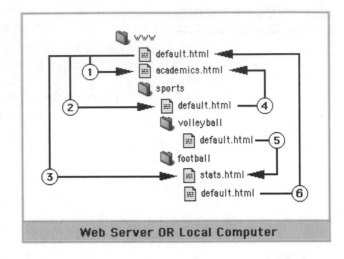

FIGURE A.7   Internal links using relative URLs.

UWEB's Web site used in Section 1.5, but this time, we create some internal links for the site using relative URLs rather than pointing to the files using absolute URLs.

Figure A.7 provides the illustration. The first three URLs in the list are for links in UWEB's home page, default.html, which is in the university's root directory. The first URL demonstrates that only the name of the file is necessary if the link points to a file in the same directory. Here the actual link would be produced by putting

```
<a href="academics.html">go to academics page</a>
```

in UWEB's home page. Similarly, the rest of the href attributes shown in Figure A.7 would be contained in similar anchor elements, but we won't write the rest of them out in full form.

As the second URL shows, targeting a file deeper in the directory structure requires a relative path. From the frame of reference of UWEB's home page where the link appears, that URL says "look inside the sports directory and grab the default file." Incidentally, the second URL is equivalent to href="sports/" because the default file is targeted. The third URL targets the stats page, two directories below UWEB's home page.

The fourth URL appears in a link in the sports home page. The construct ../ says to back up one directory. In words, the fourth URL says, "Back up outside of the current directory and find the academics page." The fifth URL is a little more involved, because the link in the volleyball home page targets a file in a folder that is "parallel" in the directory structure to the volleyball folder. Here the URL says, "Back up one directory (into the sports folder), then go into the football folder and find the stats page." Finally, the sixth URL says to back up one directory (into the sports folder), then back up one more (into the root folder) and find the default page. Note that href="../../" is equivalent.

Here are some important notes for links:

■ There should be ample description in a Web page as to where a link points. This can be accomplished through the anchor content that appears as the underlined link in the page or by the text surrounding the link. It is poor practice to leave a link's target ambiguous to the surfer.

- As your Web site gets larger, you will want to organize it with some directory structure, much as UWEB has done. It is *important* that the directory structure you create as you develop the site locally be preserved when you transfer it to the Web server. Otherwise, your links will fail. You can see that in Figure A.7. If UWEB's webmaster updates the local copy of the `sports` page but accidentally transfers it with his FTP client into the wrong folder on the Web server, the relative URLs will no longer be accurate, and the links will fail. Worse yet, if it is accidentally transferred into the root directory for example, it will overwrite UWEB's home page because both are named `default.html`. No biggie. The local copy of the Web site is still intact, and the webmaster can ftp the files over into the correct directories once the mistake has been discovered (hopefully quickly).

- Use lowercase file and directory names with no spaces between letters. File and directory names on most Web servers are *case sensitive*. That means that if the server looks for `somepage.html`, it will not find it if it's named `Somepage.html`. Even if the links with mismatched cases work in your local copy of the site, they will likely fail when the pages are HTTP requested from the Web server. When working locally, your browser and the `file` protocol are laid back about case, but HTTP Web servers are generally uptight. If you stick to lowercase names as a general rule, you will have fewer broken links in the long run.

- With the preceding point in mind, directory paths and file names of relative URLs must match letter for letter and case for case with the paths and file names within the Web site.

These bulleted notes emphasize the importance of testing your pages locally to get them right and then testing them again once you ftp them to the server. Although conceptually simple, links can be a bit tricky. Even the experienced Web programmer occasionally makes an FTP mistake or mistypes a file name. We do! But we usually catch the mistake when we test the site. How will you fare?

NOTE

You could make all of the links depicted in Figure A.7 using the absolute URLs as shown in Figure 1.7 of Section 1.5. Besides more typing, there is a major drawback to that approach. Remember, UWEB's webmaster designed the site on his personal office computer. Links with

```
href="http://www.uweb.edu/etc."
```

will obviously not work for local files. The site would not be portable. Interestingly, you can use absolute URLs with the `file` protocol. For example,

```
href="C:\www\sports\default.html"
```

would adequately link to the local copy of the sports home page, but it would be useless for HTTP requests once put on the server. Again, if internal links are not relative, the site is not portable.

A last comment on `file` URLs is important. The \ (backslash) is a Microsoft Windows directory path convention. *If you use a Windows machine, do not use \ when you write URLs.* PC browsers and servers will deal with / in a Web context. No other platform in the world (that we know of) will deal with \ in a directory path.

One of the two attributes, `href` or `name`, is mandatory in an anchor element. If you have ever clicked a link that took you to a different location in the same Web page rather than loading a different page, you have seen a *named anchor* in action. A typical situation that calls for named anchors is when a Web page is fairly long, say with several sections (such as if we put this appendix in a Web page). You would then put a list of links at the top, one pointing to each section, and a link at each section pointing back to the top. Before reading on, you should go to the Web site and play with the named-anchor demo. While the following discussion contains enough detail by itself, it would be helpful first to see in action the page upon which the example is based.

In order to set up the list of links to sections, you mark each section with a named anchor like the following:

```
<a name="section2"></a>
```

which obviously would be for Section 2. The value that the `name` attribute specifies is called a **fragment identifier**. To target the named anchor, you put the following link (`href` anchor) at the top of the page:

```
<a href="#section2">Go to Section 2</a>
```

When the "Go to Section 2" link is clicked, the named anchor is instantaneously brought to the top of the browser window. Here the URL **fragment**, `#section2`, causes the link to target the named anchor identified as `section2`. Note that the # sign is mandatory to signify that the URL is merely a fragment.

Similarly, each of the other sections is marked by a named anchor with an appropriately chosen identifier, and links at the top of the page point to them. However, for the links that point back to the top of the document, one named anchor, placed at the beginning of the `body` section,

```
<a name="top"></a>
```

suffices. The "Back to top" links then all target the one named anchor.

You can also target a named anchor with a link in a different Web page. For example, suppose you have an external table of contents in a separate Web page. If all the named anchors we just discussed are in a file named `lesson2.html`, you could then target Section 5 from the external table of contents,

```
<a href="lesson2.html#section5">Go to Section 5</a>
```

by appending the fragment onto the relative URL pointing to Lesson 2. Clicking the link causes `lesson2.html` to load into the browser, but with Section 5 at the top of the window. In this example, `lesson2.html` is in the same directory as the file with the table of contents, so the file name suffices. In general, you can append a fragment onto a relative URL with a longer directory path or an absolute URL. Note that with no content given, a named anchor is invisible in the rendered Web page. There are a couple of subtleties involved, and the demo on the Web site addresses them.

A.6   GRAPHICS

Browsers uniformly support two types of images that can be embedded in Web pages. The majority of graphics on the Web are of type **GIF (Graphics Interchange Format)**. GIF file names are appended with the `.gif` extension and the format has the following features:

- GIF supports a *color palette* of a maximum of 256 colors, but the palette can be reduced to only 2 (such as black and white), 4, 8, 16, 32, 64, or 128 colors.

- GIF is flexible. Images can have transparent backgrounds or be animated. Examples are provided on the Web site.

The other graphic type in wide use is **JPEG (Joint Photographic Experts Group).** JPEG file names are appended with the `.jpeg` or `.jpg` extension and the format has the following features:

- JPEG uses the full RGB spectrum, supporting over 16 million colors.

- JPEG uses a superior (to that of GIF) compression algorithm to create smaller file sizes.

When small graphics that only require a few colors suffice, GIF is usually used. With small color palettes, they are easier to edit. Moreover, their flexibility is ideal for creating fancy Web pages. If you see something moving in a Web page, it's likely an animated GIF. Even though GIF's compression algorithm is less sophisticated than that of JPEG, it's small color palettes tend to make small graphic files when the graphics are kept simple. Those files are typically 2K to 4K in size.

When one needs a digital likeness of a real-life photograph, JPEG is the way to go. The 16 million colors create a much sharper image, while the superior compression algorithm does a decent job of keeping the file size relatively small. For an example, pull up www.cknuckles.com/ beest.jpg and www.cknuckles.com/beest.gif in separate browser windows and compare them. You should be able to see that the GIF image gets somewhat "splotchy" in places where many of the colors were approximated with the 256-color palette. That file takes up 68K of computer memory. In contrast, the JPEG version is somewhat sharper given all the colors it uses, and JPEG compression has limited the file to 20K of computer memory.

So how do you get images to put in a Web page? If you want to put a picture of your dog (or wildebeest) on your homepage, you can upload the file to your computer from a digital camera or video recorder. Or you can use a scanner to create a digital likeness of a conventional photograph. If you want some GIFs to add some spice to your Web page, you can simply grab them from other Web pages. If you find one to your liking, you can easily acquire it:

- In Windows, right-click on the image and choose to Save Image As... from the pop-up menu.

- Using a Mac, you can simply drag the image from off the Web page onto the desktop or into a folder. Also, doing a control-click on the image provides a pop-up menu similar to that on Windows.

Of course, one should avoid acquiring copyrighted images in this manner. There are numerous free image libraries on the Web that contain virtually any GIF you might want. Links to some of these are provided on the Web site.

TABLE A.6 Image Element

`<img />` Image (inline element)

ATTRIBUTE	POSSIBLE VALUES	DEFAULT
`align`	`top,middle,bottom,left,right`	`bottom`
`alt` (alternate description)	Any text string	
`border`	Pixels	
`height`	Pixels, percent	Actual height of image
`hspace` (horizontal space)	Pixels	Browser-dependent
`src` (source; required attribute)	URL (relative or absolute)	
`vspace` (vertical space)	Pixels	Browser-dependent
`width`	Pixels, percent	Actual width of image

To mark up a graphic in a Web page, you use the `img` (image) element. It is an inline element, and it is summarized in Table A.6. In practice, marking up images is straight forward. Figure A.8 shows the source code for an HTML file that explores the `img` element, and Figure A.9 shows its rendition.

You can add functionality to an image in a Web page by making it active as a link. You simply put the `img` element as content of an `href` anchor.

```
<a href="dude/links/to/file.html"><img src="dude.gif" border="0" /></a>
```

Here are some things to note about including images in a Web page:

■ The URL value of `src` gives the location of the source file for the image. Typically, the source file is sitting somewhere in your Web site and you use a relative URL. The same rules apply that we outlined in Section A.5 for relative URLs as values of `href`.

■ When you make an image active as a link, the `href` anchor may give it a colored border, much as it underlines textual links. This is unsightly. You likely will want to suppress the border by using the `border` attribute in the image element, as we did in the image link example just above.

■ Even if you don't intend to resize an image, you should include the `height` and `width` attributes using the image's actual dimensions. That way, when the browser reads the HTML file, it knows how much space to allocate for the images. It can draw empty boxes for the images and start rendering the page before all of the images arrive. As the images arrive, it slaps them into the preallocated boxes. Otherwise, the browser would have to wait for all of the images before starting to render the page. Always using `height` and `width`, even if you don't resize an image, increases the efficiency of your pages in general. An easy way to determine the dimensions of an image is to load it into a browser by itself (not embedded in a Web page). Its height and width the should be displayed at the top of the browser window. In Windows you can right-click on the image when it is displayed by itself in Internet Explorer, and select **Properties...** from the pop-up menu.

```
┌──────────────────────────────── imagedemo.html ─────────────────────────────┐
│ <html>                                                                        │
│   <head>                                                                      │
│     <title>Image Attributes</title>                                           │
│   </head>                                                                     │
│   <body>                                                                      │
│                                                                               │
│     The top, middle, and bottom values align images inline with text. This one│
│     <img src="dude.gif" width="32" height="32" align="top" /> is top-aligned and this one│
│     <img src="dude.gif" width="32" height="32" align="middle" /> middle-aligned. Since we│
│      included no <tt>align</tt> attribute in this one                          │
│     <img src="dude.gif" width="32" height="32"> you can see that bottom is the default alignment.<br />│
│     <img src="dude.gif" width="30" height="30" align="left" /> It is often more useful to have text│
│     flow around an image, rather than putting the image inline with text.      │
│     <img src="dude.gif" width="32" height="32" align="right" hspace="10" vspace="5" />│
│     After all, that's how newspapers do it! That's precisely the effect caused by left and right│
│     alignment. It certainly does create a better effect. But, notice how the text is right up against│
│     the left aligned image. If you don't think it's cool to have text right up against the image,│
│     some <tt>hspace</tt> and <tt>vspace</tt> around the image is in order. These attributes simply│
│     add horizontal and vertical padding around the image. Please note that we're starting to have│
│     to include a substantial amount of babble here to get the text to flow all the way around the│
│     image <br> The border attribute can be used to give an image a thin       │
│     <img src="dude.gif" width="32" height="32" border="2" align="middle" /> border or a thick│
│     <img src="dude.gif" width="32" height="32" border="10" align="middle" /> border.<br />│
│     <img src="Dude.gif" width="100" height="40" align="left" alt="picture of a dude" /> The│
│     <tt>alt</tt> attribute gives a textual description of the image. This was important in the│
│     early days when computers and internet connections were slooooow, and some people would set│
│     their browsers to "text only" so they could surf faster. Now, with cable and DSL connections,│
│     pages full of images are no problem. Even with 56K phone modems, most people tolerate the│
│     extra overhead incurred by graphics. However, the importance of <tt>alt</tt> is emerging again│
│     since images are a drag on handheld internet devices. Note that we did not disable images on our│
│     browser to show the alternate description. We simply supplied a bad URL so that the browser│
│     couldn't find the image file. (When the browser asked for the image, the server software sent back│
│     a packet indicating it could not find the image file. The browser resorted to the alternative.) <br />│
│     Finally, you can resize an image                                          │
│     <img src="dude.gif" width="16" height="16" /> proportionally or           │
│     <img src="dude.gif" width="32" height="16" /> disproportionately.         │
│                                                                               │
│   </body>                                                                     │
│ </html>                                                                       │
└──────────────────────────────────────────────────────────────────────────────┘
```

FIGURE A.8 Using attributes of the image element.

▪ Recall that, whereas HTML files need to be transferred to a Web server as plain text, *it is imperative that you ftp image files to the Web server as binary data*. If you transfer them as text or a proprietary format, they probably won't show up in the Web page.

A.7 THE *body* AND *head* ELEMENTS

In this section we focus primarily on the *body* element, and include a note at the end about the *head* element. The *body* element has several attributes that set properties for the whole body of the Web page, summarized in Table A.7. Keep in mind that you put these attributes in the start tag of the *body* element that is part of the skeleton document. You don't add a new tag to the document to use these.

All but one of these attributes take values that specify colors. You can use *named colors* such as red, green, and blue. There are two problems with using named colors, however. First, many named colors have weird names ("light goldenrod yellow" or "papaya whip", for example), and browsers support somewhat different sets of named colors. Second, there are only a relatively few colors with names.

TABLE A.7 The `body` Element

`<body >...</body>` Body of Web page (block element)

ATTRIBUTE	POSSIBLE VALUES	DEFAULT
`alink` (active link)	#*hexcolor*, named color	Browser-dependent (often red)
`background` (background image)	URL (relative or absolute)	
`bgcolor` (background color)	#*hexcolor*, named color	Browser-dependent (often white or light gray)
`link` (unvisited link)	#*hexcolor*, named color	Browser-dependent (often blue)
`text`	#*hexcolor*, named color	`black (#000000)`
`vlink` (visited link)	#*hexcolor*, named color	Browser-dependent (often light purple)

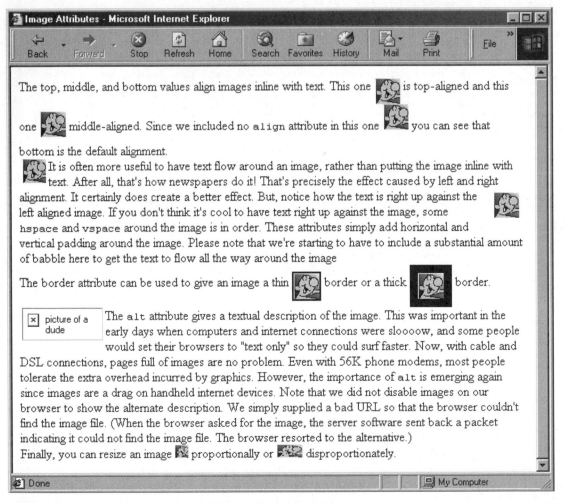

FIGURE A.9 The document of Figure A.8 rendered in a browser.

In contrast, **hexadecimal colors** (hexcolors) give you over 16 million choices (the same color spectrum used by JPEG). Hex colors have three components: one each for red, green, and blue. Thus they are sometimes called **RGB colors**. Each hex color is of the form #*RGB* where each of the three color components is a two-digit hexadecimal number. For example, #000000 is black, #FFFFFF is white, #FF0000 is red, #00FF00 is green, and #0000FF is blue. Hex colors must be preceded by a # sign. Moreover, links to some color-picking utilities are given on the Web site.

To illustrate the attributes of the body element, we stick to some simple named colors, and the few hex colors just listed.

```
<body bgcolor="red" text="white">
```

and

```
<body bgcolor="#FF0000" text="#FFFFFF">
```

are equivalent, and both produce a Web page where the entire body is colored red and the default text color is white. That's really all there is to it.

The following ensures that the Web page has a white background, while setting colors for the lines drawn under href links in the page. Text will remain the default color of black.

```
<body bgcolor="#FFFFFF" link="red" vlink="green">
```

Here, links that have yet to be visited will be underlined in red, and visited links will be underlined in green. (Browsers maintain a recent history list to keep track of such things.) Controlling link colors might seem a bit picky, but in pages with carefully chosen color schemes the blue and purple defaults for link colors can look gnarly. Setting the alink attribute is less important, because you see the link activated only the moment you click it. (If you right-click a link to get the pop-up menu, it should stay activated while the menu is open.) You can experiment with alink for yourself.

The value of the background attribute is a URL that points to an image file to be used as the background of a Web page. An image used for a background is often a GIF that provides a subtle texture for the Web page.

Such an image is *tiled* to create a solid background in much the same way as tiles are laid for a kitchen floor. If the image is cleverly made, the tiling will appear seamless, just as a kitchen floor appears to have a unified pattern even though it is a conglomerate of small tiles. Tiling is advantageous because only a small image file need be transferred to the client with the Web page. A graphic whose dimensions would actually fill up the background of the whole page would generally have much too large of a file.

If you specify both a `bgcolor` and a `background` image in the same page, the image will obscure the `bgcolor`. However, if the image has any transparent regions, the `bgcolor` will show through. You can find tons of images suitable for backgrounds in the graphic libraries we have referenced on the Web site. Some are nice and subtle, while others will make you cringe.

NOTE

Only seven elements are allowed to be placed as content of the `head` element: `base`, `link`, `meta`, `object`, `script`, `style`, and `title`. We have used the `title` element, will use the `link` and `style` elements in the section on CSS, and will use the `script` element when we utilize JavaScript. That leaves `base` and `object`, which are rarely used, and finally `meta`. The `meta` element is for information about the document: meta-information. The most common use of `meta` is for the benefit of the search engines that crawl the Web indexing pages. Some of them look for a comma-delimited list of keywords:

```
<meta name="keywords" content="key,words,that,characterize,page,..." />
```

Others look for a short description:

```
<meta name="description" content="page about wildebeest and..." />
```

Others simply read the contents of your page looking for multiple occurrences of words.

A.8 FRAMES

HTML **frames** provide a way to show more than one Web page simultaneously in the same browser window. It is best to proceed by example. Figure A.10 shows two distinct Web pages displayed in a browser window. On the right are the source files for two different Web pages. You can see that one has been stuffed into the top frame of the browser window and the other into the bottom. The source file for the page that creates the actual *frameset* is shown below the browser window. You can tell from the page title at the top of the browser that it is the page whose URL the browser called.

That document has no `body` section. Rather, the `frameset` element has taken its place. The `frameset` element has called for a frameset with two rows, the first being 75 pixels tall and the second filling up the rest of the browser window. The first `frame` element has specified that the `src` (source) for the first frame should be the file `navpage.html`, and the second `frame` element has specified `placeholder.html`. Those two pages are rendered in their respective frames in the browser window.

If you click a link in the top "navigation frame," the Web page to which that link points is loaded into the bottom "display frame", replacing the initial page contained there. (You can pull up the source for Figure A.10 on the Web site to get a feel for how it works.) You can see in the frameset document that the bottom frame was assigned a name using the `name` attribute. Each link in the top frame simply specifies `target="displayframe"` as the destination for the link. That causes the documents to be loaded into `displayframe`

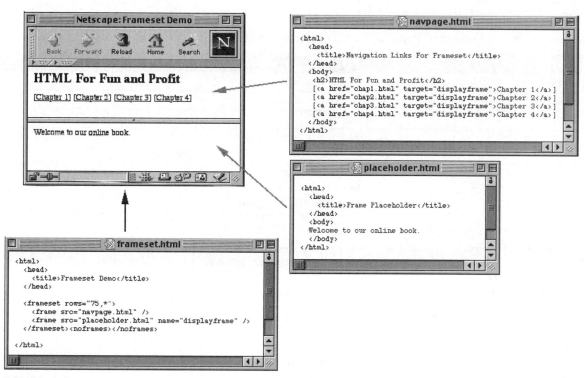

FIGURE A.10 A simple frames page.

rather than the entire browser window. Now that you have a feel for how framed pages work, we summarize the frameset and frame elements in Table A.8.

The margin, border, resizing, and scrolling attributes are self-explanatory. You would be better off experimenting with them than reading anything further we might say about them. However, the rows and cols attributes require some elaboration. We will use cols for explanation, because we used rows in Figure A.10. However, the same applies to both. It is clear that

```
<frameset cols="30%,20%,50%">
```

creates three columns of various widths relative to the size of the browser window. For fixed widths,

```
<frameset cols="200,300,*">
```

creates two columns of widths 200 and 300 pixels, respectively, while the third column would cover the rest of the browser window. The setting

```
<frameset cols="30%,*,*">
```

TABLE A.8 Elements Used in Frame Pages

`<frameset >...</frameset>` Replaces the `body` element (block element)

ATTRIBUTE	POSSIBLE VALUES	DEFAULT
`cols` (width of columns of frameset)	Pixels, percent, *	
`rows` (heights of rows of frameset)	Pixels, percent, *	
`border`	Pixels	Browser-dependent (about 5)
`bordercolor`[a]	#*hexcolor*, named color	Browser-dependent (usually some shade of gray)
`frameborder`[a]	`yes` (3-dimensional borders), `no` (plain "flat" borders)	`yes`

`<frame />` Used only inside `frameset` element

ATTRIBUTE	POSSIBLE VALUES	DEFAULT
`marginheight` (vertical padding between frame border and frame content)	Pixels	Browser-dependent (about 10)
`marginwidth` (horizontal padding between frame border and frame content)	Pixels	Browser-dependent (about 10)
`name` (background image)	Text string	
`noresize`	`noresize="noresize"`	User can resize frames in browser window by dragging borders
`scrolling` (does a frame receive its own scrollbars?)	`yes` (always, even if not needed), `no` (never, even if needed), `auto` (if needed)	`auto`
`src` (source)	URL (relative or absolute)	

[a] You can use `bordercolor` and `frameborder` in a particular `frame` element as well. In that case the border instructions from `frameset` are overridden. Browsers deal with that unpredictably, however.

would set the first column at 30 percent and divide the last two columns evenly in the remaining space. The setting

```
<frameset cols="100,*,2*">
```

would set the first column at 100 pixels, the second at one-third of the remaining space, and the third at two-thirds of the remaining space. (* says "one portion of the remaining space," and 2* says "two portions".) Finally,

```
<frameset cols="15%,2*,3*,100">
```

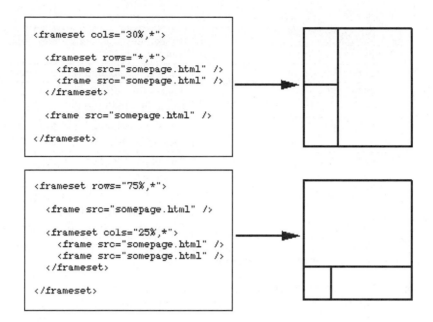

```
<frameset cols="30%,*">

  <frameset rows="*,*">
    <frame src="somepage.html" />
    <frame src="somepage.html" />
  </frameset>

  <frame src="somepage.html" />

</frameset>
```

```
<frameset rows="75%,*">

  <frame src="somepage.html" />

  <frameset cols="25%,*">
    <frame src="somepage.html" />
    <frame src="somepage.html" />
  </frameset>

</frameset>
```

FIGURE A.11   Nesting frames.

sets the first column at 15 percent of the browser window, the last column gets the last 100 pixels on the right side, the second gets two-fifths of what's left over in the middle, and the third gets three-fifths, although we can't imagine why anyone would have a practical reason to do such a thing.

To nest frames, simply use a new frameset where you would normally put a frame. The examples in Figure A.11 require only a brief explanation. The first one sets up two columns. Then the first column gets another frameset element rather than a frame. That's the two-row frameset you see in the first column. The second column gets a frame as usual.

The second example sets up a two-row frameset in which the first row gets a frame. What would be the second frame row gets a two-column frameset.

We conclude this section by further discussing the use of links in framed documents and then noting a few things about frames in general. We saw in Figure A.10 that by naming a frame, you can enable links to target that frame. If you specify no target in a link, the default is to load the Web page to which the link points into the same frame as the page containing the link. For example, in Figure A.10, if we had forgotten to specify a target in the link for Chapter 2, the Web page for Chapter 2 would get loaded into the top frame, replacing the navigation page.

With that in mind, we summarize targeting options in Table A.9. We won't enter into further discussion about targeting, because the table is self-explanatory. However, do keep in mind that the underscore is necessary for the _self, _parent, and _top special target values. You can get a hands-on feel for how targeting works by visiting the targeting demo on the Web site.

Here are some notes regarding frames.

■   Frames are ideal when a lot of information needs to be swapped in and out quickly, as in a slide show-style presentation, for example. In that case you have a "fixed"

TABLE A.9 Options for Targeting Links in Frames Pages

OPTION	RESULT
No `target` attribute supplied	Same as `"self"`
`target="`*framename*`"`	The page is loaded into the specified frame.
`target="_self"`	This is the default. The page is loaded into the frame in which the link was clicked.
`target="_parent"`	The page is loaded into the window or frame containing the parent `frameset` page.[a]
`target="_top"`	The page is loaded into the main browser window.[a]
`target="`*non-existent-framename*`"`	The page is loaded into a new window that pops up. (Misspelling a frame name usually makes for an unwanted pop-up window.)

[a] For almost any case, `_parent` and `_top` accomplish the same thing. Their difference is subtle. The target demo on the Web site explores this subtlety.

navigation bar that stays put in one frame, which swaps pages (or images) in and out of other frames. A fine example putting frames to highly functional use by can be found at

```
http://www.bnrmetal.com/
```

This site uses frames to organize a lot of information to great functionality.

- Tables provide for much more control over page layout. Indeed, nearly every major commercial site features a tabular layout. These sites usually feature a "pseudo-fixed" navigational bar. Even though the nav bar appears in the same place on several pages, it's simply part of a page template on which all the pages are based, and it gets reloaded every time.

- Besides layout deficiencies, frames have the following two disadvantages. You can't bookmark pages deep within a frames site. (Go to a band page at the site mentioned in the first item on this list, and try to bookmark it.) Also, many browsers have difficulty sending content to a printer from pages rendered within frames. That is a deterrent for many commercial sites as well.

- It is kind of cool to get a new window using the nonexistent-frame trick. However, there is a much better way to open new windows using JavaScript.

- Use your frames to load your own pages. It is generally uncool to load other people's pages into your frames. In other words, if you link to someone's page, their domain name should show in the address window. For example, you could make a page with only one frame whose source is Amazon.com. Then your domain name could effectively be for their site. (There is a way to protect pages against that.)

- There is a `noframes` element that can be used to provide alternative content for browsers or devices that can't handle frames. Just put `<noframes> <body> alternate content </body> </noframes>` right after the first `frameset` tag in your top frameset. The `body` of `noframes` provides an alternative body for the page if frames can't be used.

A.9 DEPRECATED ELEMENTS AND ATTRIBUTES

To **deprecate** means to downgrade or devalue. In the context of the W3C HTML and XHTML specifications, a deprecated element or attribute is one that has been designated potentially to be dropped from the specifications at some point in the future, although at what point in the future is not clear. The HTML elements and attributes listed in this section have been on deprecated status since the 1997 issue of the HTML 4.0 standard.

Deprecated Elements

We now summarize the most notorious deprecated elements in Tables A.10 and A.11. In particular, if you look at much HTML code currently on the Web, you will see font and center used quite a lot. We do not use these elements in this text (other than font in Section 2.1), but it pays to know which elements are deprecated and why.

With the exception of applet, all of these elements can easily be replaced using CSS. Indeed, that is why they are on deprecated status. The goal is to "keep HTML small," leaving text formatting issues for CSS. It is also worthwhile to note that, while they are not officially on deprecated status, the elements associated with HTML frames will likely be targeted for deprecation in the future. However, as noted in Section 2.5, deprecated elements, and especially frames, will not disappear from the Web for many years.

TABLE A.10   The Deprecated font Element

<font >...</font> Inline element

ATTRIBUTE	POSSIBLE VALUES	DEFAULT
color	#*hexcolor*, named color	#000000 (black)
face	Text string (font name)	Browser default font (often Times New Roman)
size	Absolute size (1, 2, 3, 4, 5, 6, 7) relative size ($\pm 1, 2, 3, \ldots$)	Browser default (typically 3)

TABLE A.11   Other Noteworthy Deprecated Elements

<basefont />	Takes the same attributes as the font element. It is usually placed at the top of the body section and sets font properties for the whole page. The font element overrides the default font properties set by basefont.
<center>...</center>	Takes no attributes and centers its contents, whether text or a block, on the page.
<applet>...</applet>	Used to embed Java applets in Web pages. Deprecated in favor of the object element, which can embed several types of multimedia objects in a page.
<u>...</u>	Causes its contents to be rendered as underlined text.

Deprecated Attributes

Stylistic properties of most HTML elements can be completely controlled using CSS. Thus, a surprising number of very common attributes are also on deprecated status. The following list gives a reasonably comprehensive overview of the deprecated HTML attributes:

- All attributes of deprecated elements such as font and applet are themselves deprecated.
- The align attribute, which is used in numerous elements such as p, hr, img, table, td, is deprecated.
- Virtually all attributes of the body element (such as background, bgcolor, link, and vlink) are deprecated.
- Most formatting and positioning attributes of the img element (border, hspace, vspace, and, of course, align) are deprecated. The src, height, and width attributes are *not* deprecated. Of course, src is necessary to specify the source file for an image. Presumably, the height and width attributes are not deprecated in favor of CSS because Web pages can be rendered more quickly when image dimensions are specified (even if the image is not to be resized) in the HTML code. See the second to last bullet note at the end of Section A.6.
- The formatting attributes of HTML lists (start, type, compact) are deprecated.
- Most table-formatting attributes (bgcolor, background, valign, align, height, width) are deprecated. However, essential table-structuring attributes such as colspan, rowspan, cellpadding, and cellspacing are *not* deprecated.

This is an alarming amount of deprecation of attributes to which we have grown accustomed as being an essential part of HTML. However, limiting the amount of *attribute-based formatting* is another part of the objective to "keep HTML small." Source-providing attributes (such as src and href) and structure-providing attributes (such as colspan and rowspan) can't easily be eliminated, but the color-providing and alignment-type attributes can be replaced by setting corresponding CSS properties.

Of course, keeping the language small by eliminating HTML attributes (and elements) means that the missing complexity is absorbed by CSS. That does serve to meet the W3C objective of keeping style formatting separate from content and structure formatting. This development is also good for the Web because it tends to result in HTML files that take up less memory. For example, if 10 table rows each have the same formatting properties, it is a waste to include 10 identical sets of attributes in each of the tr elements. Rather, one style class can be created and applied to each table row. But, on the negative side, use of CSS increases the knowledge base required of Web programmers and designers.

NOTE

We have included many deprecated attributes in this book, although we have chosen not to use the deprecated elements. The font element, for example, is quite inefficient and is becoming less frequently seen in newly created pages. Currently, use of font is considered bad stylistically from a design standpoint.

However, use of the deprecated attributes is not seeing appreciable decline, especially in images, lists, and tables. Indeed, not only do WYSIWYG HTML editors use the deprecated attributes liberally, but Web page authors are reluctant to learn CSS in great detail because they can do most of the same things with pure HTML.

A.10 LOGICAL ELEMENTS

This section introduces HTML's **logical elements**. They are used infrequently, and we include them for the sake of completeness. The most common ones are listed in Table A.12.

These are called *logical elements* because they logically describe their content to some extent. For example, `<p>`some text`</p>` makes no attempt to define the text, whereas `<address>`some text `</address>` gives you a better indication as to what the text represents. However, from a standard markup standpoint, most of them are useless. For example, these elements provide four different ways to make text italic.

That's clearly not their only purpose. They in some sense can provide some meaning to the document. For example, a particular search engine or search utility could easily pull out all of the citations in a group of Web pages to build a bibliography. Considering that Berners-Lee created HTML to mark up abstracts of physics research papers, the existence of these logical elements makes more sense. We will not use these elements in this book, and there is little point in allocating any further cerebral cortex to consideration of them unless some need arises in the future.

TABLE A.12 Logical Elements[a]

ELEMENT	DESCRIPTION	RECOMMENDED MARKUP
address	Any address	Italic
blockquote	Block of quoted material	Both margins indented
cite	Citation	Italic
dfn	Definition	Italic
em	Emphasized text	Italic
q	Inline quotation	Surround with quotation marks
strong	Stronger emphasis	Boldface
sub	Subscript	Subscript to preceding text
sup	Superscript	Superscript to preceding text

[a] These are all container elements.

APPENDIX *B*

JAVASCRIPT REFERENCE

This appendix provides a quick reference for JavaScript core objects, Browser Objects, DHTML-related objects, and reserved words. This appendix sticks to a browser-independent subset of JavaScript.

B.1 CORE OBJECTS/FUNCTIONS/LITERALS

These are shown in Tables B.1 through B.6. Where appropriate, we have used descriptive names to indicate the nature of function parameters. For example, `num` represents a number, `str` represents a string, `char` represents a single character (as in `"a"`), `expr` represents an arithmetic or string expression, and `index` represents an integer (as an array index or character index within a string). The other descriptive names used should be self-explanatory.

TABLE B.1 Array[a]

PROPERTIES	METHODS
`length` (one more than highest filled array index)	`join(char)` returns a string of all array items, separated by `char`.
	`pop()` removes the last element of the array and returns it.
	`push()` pushes all arguments onto the end of array in order, and the new length is returned.
	`reverse()` reverses the order of the array elements.
	`shift()` removes and returns the first element of the array—in contrast to `pop()`.
	`sort()` sorts the array into increasing order.

[a] May be created with the new `Array()` constructor, which takes an optional parameter to set the length of the new array.

TABLE B.2 Date[a]

METHODS
`getYear()` returns the current year, 0 is year 1900
`getMonth()` returns the month (0–11)
`getDate()` returns the day of the month (1–31)
`getDay()` returns the day of the week (0–6)
`getHours()` returns the current hours in the day (0–23)
`getMinutes()` returns the current minute (0–59)
`getSeconds()` returns the current second (0–59)
`getTime()` returns the entire date/time as a big integer
`toGMTString()` returns the human-readable entire date/time in Greenwich Mean Time
`toLocaleString()` returns the human-readable entire date/time in local time

[a] Example use: `var d = new Date(); var myTime = d.toLocaleString();`

TABLE B.3 Global Functions

`eval(str)` evaluates `str` as a JavaScript statement.
`isFinite(num)` returns `true` if `num` is not `-Infinity` or `+Infinity`.
`isNaN(exp)` returns `true` if the expression evaluates to `NaN`.
`parseFloat(str)` returns `str` as a real number (floating-point decimal).
`parseInt(str)` returns `str` as an integer, truncating any decimal places.

TABLE B.4 Special Literal Values

`undefined` (contents of an uninitialized variable)
`±Infinity` (out of bounds integer; example, division by 0)
`NaN` (value of arithmetic expression that is not representable as float or integer number)
`true/false` Boolean type literals

TABLE B.5 Math[a]

PROPERTIES[b]	METHODS
PI	`abs(num)` returns the absolute value of `num`.
E	`sqrt(num)` returns the square root of `num`.
LN2	`ceil(num)` returns the least integer greater than `num`.
LN10	`floor(num)` returns the greatest integer less than `num`.
LOG2E	`random()` returns a real number in interval (0,1).
LOG10E	`round(num)` returns `num` rounded to the nearest integer.
SQRT1_2	`pow(num,power)` returns `num` raised to `power`.
SQRT2	`exp(num)` returns the `num`th power of `E`.
	`log(num)` returns the natural logarithm of `num`.
	`max(num1,num2)` returns the greater of the two arguments.
	`min(num1,num2)` returns the smaller of the two arguments.
	`acos(num)` returns the arc cosine of `num` in radians.
	`asin(num)` returns the arc sine of `num` in radians.
	`atan(num)` returns the arc tangent of `num` in radians.
	`cos(num)` returns the cosine of `num` radians.
	`sin(num)` returns the sine of `num` radians.
	`tan(num)` returns the tangent of `num` radians.

[a] Example use: `var myEight = Math.pow(2,3);`
[b] The properties are read-only constants.

TABLE B.6 String[a]

PROPERTIES	METHODS
length	`charAt(index)` returns the character at the specified index.
	`indexOf(char)` returns index of the first occurrence of `char`, or -1 if `char` is not in the string (`char` can be a string).
	`lastIndexOf(char)` returns index of last occurrence of `char`, otherwise returns -1 (`char` can be a string).

TABLE B.6 String*ᵃ* *(Continued)*

PROPERTIES	METHODS
	match(/pattern/) returns true if pattern is found in the string (use i command modifier for case-insensitive matching).
	replace(/pattern/,str) replaces the first occurrence of pattern with the replacement str (use the g command modifier for global replacement).
	split(char) returns an array of substrings, splitting around the delimiting char.
	substr(start,length) returns a substring from start index of specified length in characters.
	toLowerCase() replaces all caps with lowercase characters.
	toUpperCase() replaces all lowercase characters with caps.

*ᵃ*Example use: var str="scooby doo"; var myScoob = str.substr(0,5); *Note:* Character indexing starts at 0.

B.2 BROWSER OBJECTS (DOM LEVEL 0)

These objects are summarized in Tables B.7 through B.18.

TABLE B.7 window (self,parent,top,opener)

PROPERTIES	METHODS
closed (Boolean)	alert(str) pops up an alert window, halting program flow.
document (see Table B.8)	clearInterval(name) clears a name=setIinterval() call.
history (see Table B.9)	clearTimeout(name) clears a name=setTimeout() call.
location (URL of current document)	close() closes the current window.
name (name set by open() method)	confirm(str) pops up a confirm window, returning true if the user clicks OK, false otherwise.
navigator (see Table B.10)	focus() brings the current window to front.
status (text in the status bar)	moveBy(changeX,changeY) moves the current window by supplied pixel values.
	moveTo(X,Y) moves the window to (X,Y) coordinates, where (0,0) is the upper left corner of the screen.
	open(URL,name,"settings") opens a new browser window.
	prompt(str,str) pops up a prompt window and returns the user's input as a string. The first parameter is the instruction, and the second is initial text.
	resizeBy(changeX,changeY) resizes the window by pixel values.
	resizeTo(width,height) sets the exact dimensions of window in pixels.
	setInterval(function,millisec) calls the function periodically at intervals of the given number of millisec.
	setTimeout(function,millisec) calls the function once after a delay of the given number of milliseconds.
EVENT HANDLERS	
onfocus, onload, onunload	

TABLE B.8 document

PROPERTIES	METHODS
alinkColor (active links)	clear() clears the document for overwriting.
bgColor (background color)	close() closes the document for writing.
fgColor (text color)	open() opens the document for writing.
forms[] (array of form objects in document order)	write(str) writes str to the document.
images[] (array of image objects in document order)	
lastModified	
linkColor (unvisited links)	
links[] (array of link objects in document order)	
vlinkColor (visited links)	
EVENT HANDLERS	
None	

TABLE B.9 history

PROPERTIES	METHODS
length (number of Web pages that have been in window)	back() is equivalent to clicking the back button on the browser.
	forward() is equivalent to clicking the forward button on the browser.
	go(num) goes forward or backward num pages in the history list.
EVENT HANDLERS	
None	

TABLE B.10 navigator

PROPERTIES
appName (example: "Microsoft Internet Explorer")
appVersion (Example: "4.0 (compatible; MSIE 6.0; Windows 98)")
cookieEnabled (Boolean)
platform (Example: "Win32")
userAgent (Example: "Mozilla/4.0 (compatible; MSIE 6.0; Windows 98)")

TABLE B.11 image

PROPERTIES
border
height
hspace
name
src
vspace
width
EVENT HANDLERS
onload

TABLE B.12   `link`

PROPERTIES
`href`
`target` (name of window or frame)
EVENT HANDLERS
`onclick, onDblClick, onmouseover, onmouseout, onmousedown, onmouseup`

TABLE B.13   `area`[a]

PROPERTIES
`href`
`target`
EVENT HANDLERS
`onclick, onmouseover, onmouseout`

[a] Image map areas basically work like link objects.

TABLE B.14   `form`

PROPERTIES	METHODS
`action` (URL of server-side program to which to submit form)	`reset()` is equivalent to clicking a `type=" reset"` input button.
`elements[]` (array of the form's elements in document order)	`submit()` equivalent to clicking a `type=" submit"` input button.
`length` (size of `elements[]` array)	
`method` (GET or POST submit method)	
`name` (object reference for form)	
`target` (name of window or frame)	
EVENT HANDLERS	
`onreset, onsubmit`	

TABLE B.15   `button, reset, submit`[a]

PROPERTIES	METHODS
`name` (object reference to button)	`click()` is equivalent to the user clicking the button.
`value` (text on button)	
EVENT HANDLERS	
`onclick, onmousedown, onmouseup`	

[a] These are all `<input type=" ... " />` elements.

TABLE B.16 `checkbox`, `radio Button`[a]

PROPERTIES	METHODS
`name` (object reference to button)	`click()` is equivalent to the user clicking the button
`value` (hidden data)	
`checked` (Boolean—is element currently checked?)	
`defaultChecked` (Boolean—is element initially checked?)	
`length` (radio buttons only—number of button in unique-selection group)	
EVENT HANDLERS	
`onclick`, `onmousedown`, `onmouseup`	

[a] These are both `<input type="..." />` elements.

TABLE B.17 `text`, `textarea`, `password`, `checkbox`, `hidden`[a]

PROPERTIES	METHODS
`name` (object reference to text element)	`blur()` removes the focus from the element.
`value` (current text in element)	`focus()` puts the focus on the element—(like putting the mouse cursor on the element).
	`select()` selects all text in the element.
EVENT HANDLERS	
`onblur`, `onchange`, `onfocus`, `onselect`, `onkeydown`, `onkeyup`, `onkeypress`	

[a] These are all `<input type="..." />` elements except for `<textarea>...</textarea>`.

TABLE B.18 `select`[a]

PROPERTIES	METHODS
`length` (of `options[]` array)[b]	`blur()` removes the focus from the menu.
`name` (object reference to whole menu)	`focus()` puts the focus on the element, like putting the mouse cursor on the menu.
`selectedIndex` (array index of currently selected option)	
`options[i].defaultSelected` (Boolean)[b]	
`options[i].selected` (Boolean—currently selected?)[b]	
`options[i].text` (the text displayed on the menu option)[b]	
`options[i].value` (the hidden data for the menu option)[b]	
EVENT HANDLERS	
`onblur`, `onchange`, `onfocus`	

[a] Single- and multiple-select menus: `<select> <option value="data1">text1</option> <option value="data2">text2</option> . . . </select>`

[b] `options[]` is the array that indexes the menu options in document order, and `options[i]` is an object reference to the menu option at index `i`.

B.3   STYLE PROPERTIES IN HTML DOM

This section, comprising Tables B.19 and B.20, primarily relates to DHTML. See Sections 16.4 and 16.5 for full reference to Core DOM objects and methods.

TABLE B.19   Every HTML Element[a]

PROPERTIES	METHODS
className (name of style class)	blur() removes the focus from the element.
id (its unique ID)	click() simulates a mouse click on the element.
style (see Table B.20)	focus() puts the focus on the element.
tagName (name of HTML tag)	
EVENT HANDLERS	
onblur, onclick, onDblClick, onfocus, onkeydown, onkeypress, onkeyup, onmousedown, onmousemove, onmouseout, onmouseover, onmouseup, onresize	

[a] These properties and methods are called on an object reference to the HTML element. Use document.getElementById(str) to return an object reference, where str is the string name of the element as set by the HTML id attribute.

TABLE B.20   style[a]

TEXT PROPERTIES
color (text color of element content)
fontSize
fontWeight ("bold","bolder")
textIndent (first line of text in element)
textShadow (cool effect)
POSITIONING ELEMENTS
left (position of the top left corner of the element relative to the left margin)
top (position of the top left corner of the element relative to the top margin)
height
width
zIndex (layer in page)
visibility ("hidden","visible")
BACKGROUNDS OF ELEMENTS
backgroundColor
backgroundImage
BORDERS OF ELEMENTS
border (border thickness around element)
borderBottom
borderLeft
borderRight
borderTop
borderColor
borderBottomColor
borderLeftColor

TABLE B.20   style[a] *(Continued)*

BORDERS OF ELEMENTS
borderRightColor
borderTopColor
padding (padding on inside of element)
paddingBottom
paddingleft
paddingRight
paddingTop

[a] These properties can be set dynamically on most HTML elements. They are most often used to control the generic span and div containers dynamically.

B.4   RESERVED WORDS IN JAVASCRIPT

Take a good look at these. These words cannot be used as variable or function names.

abstract	instanceof
boolean	int
break	interface
byte	long
case	native
catch	new
char	null
class	package
const	private
continue	protected
debugger	public
default	reset
delete	return
do	short
double	static
else	super
enum	switch
export	synchronized
extends	this
false	throw
final	throws
finally	transient
float	true
for	try
function	typeof
goto	var
if	void
implements	volatile
import	while
in	with

FILE PERMISSIONS

C.1 UNIX SYSTEMS

On UNIX systems, we can set file permissions with the command `chmod`. The general syntax of `chmod` is

```
chmod [augo] [+-] [rwx] filename(s)
```

The `+` is to turn on permission, and the `-` is to remove permission. The characters `r` (read), `w` (write), and `x` (execute) specify which permissions using various combinations. The letters `a` (all categories), `u` (owner), `g` (group), and `o` (everyone) specify whom to give or remove such permissions. Here are the common uses:

- For a file to be executable as a program, we need to give it `r` and `x` permissions. The following gives such permissions to all files in the current directory ending in `.cgi`:

```
chmod o+rx *.cgi
```

- For a specific file to be readable as a data file in a CGI program, we need to give it `r` permissions for everyone. This is usually already the default:

```
chmod o+r data.txt
```

- For a specific file to be writable as a data file in a CGI program, we need to give it `w` permission for everyone.

```
chmod o+w data.txt
```

- For a new file to be created in a directory by a Web application, it is necessary to give the *directory* `w` and `x` permissions for everyone. (That is different from you simply adding a file to the directory using your account on the server.) This is one reason why you should have the data directory separate from where your programs are.

```
chmod o+wx data_dir
```

- In any case, for a file to be executable, readable, or writable, all its parent directories must have executable permissions. (Fortunately, this is usually the default.)

```
chmod o+x *.cgi
```

- The read permission for a directory controls only whether directory listing is permitted.

To remove permissions, just change the plus to a minus, such as

```
chmod o-r sensitive_dir
```

And if you accidentally removed permissions for yourself to access something, you need to do

```
chmod u+rwx something
```

To find out what permissions are on a file, use the `ls` command with option `-l`:

```
ls -l filename
```

You will get something like

```
-rwxr-xr--  2 ownername groupname 644 Jan 01 2001 filename
```

The permissions information is in the first 10 characters. The first character is a `d` if `file-name` is actually a directory. Then, in groups of three, are the `rwx` permissions for the owner, for the group, and for everyone else. In the example shown, the permissions for everyone else are `r--`, the permissions for the owner are `rwx`, and the permissions for the group is `r-x`). This means that everyone else can read but not write and not execute. That is, the last three characters are what is relevant for Web access.

If the filename is a directory, the contents of that directory are listed. So, to get the permissions of a directory, you need to add an extra option:

```
ls -ld directoryname
```

Finally, the command

```
ls
```

lists the contents of the current directory.

C.2   WINDOWS SYSTEMS

Note that if you are using PWS on a Windows system that does not have file permissions (such as Windows 98), then file permissions are not an issue.

To change file or directory permissions, you need the following steps.

- *Right*-click on the file or folder and select **Properties**.
- In the window that appears, select the **Security** tab as shown in Figure C.1.
- Highlight **Everyone**.

The default is usually to inherit the permissions from the parent folder. If you need to change the permissions, you will usually first need to uncheck the box that specifies inheriting permissions from the parent. Here are some basic concerns.

- For a file to be executable as a program, we need to give it Read permissions. (Execute permission is not necessary, because that refers to something else.) This is usually the default.

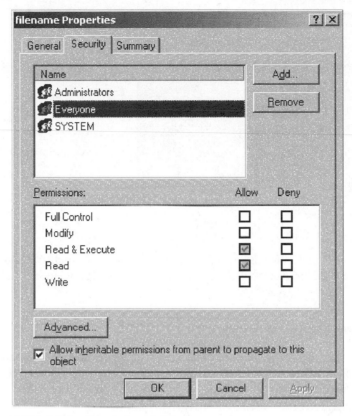

FIGURE C.1   Permissions in Windows server.

- For a file to be readable as a data file, we need to give it Read permission. This is usually the default.
- For a file to be writable as a data file, we need to give it Write permission.
- For a new file to be created in a directory, it is necessary to give the directory Write permission.

Notice that there are more options than in UNIX. In fact, there are even more options than displayed here.

C.3   USING FTP TO SET PERMISSIONS

If you are uploading your files to a server, you may often be able to change the remote files' permissions using either a menu item or a line command.

Command-Line FTP (such as on UNIX clients, or ftp.exe on Windows)

Some versions of FTP will allow the execution of a chmod command as well.

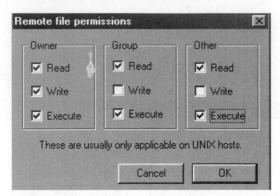

FIGURE C.2 Setting file permissions using a GUI FTP client.

Fetch 4 on Mac

You can select a file and use a menu item **Remote → Set Permissions** to change permissions (or do a Command + click on the file). You then get a window similar to that shown in Figure C.2.

WSFTP (LE) on Windows

You can right-click on a file and choose the `chmod` (or **permissions**) menu item to bring up a Change Permissions box as shown in Figure C.2. The file in the figure is set to be readable executable by everyone, which is what you need for CGI programs.

INDEX

Page numbers followed by "w" indicate subjects located on Web version of the book.